THE RISE OF
THE SPANISH EMPIRE

IN THE

OLD WORLD AND IN THE NEW

First Page of an Original Letter, Written March 3, 1575, by the Inquisitor-General (Cardinal Gaspar Quiroga) to Philip II, Respecting the Activities of the Moriscos in Aragon, with the King's Holograph Comments on the Margin. (B. M., Egerton MS. 1834, fol. 1; cf. Gayangos, *CATALOGUE*, ii, p. 228.)

Catholica M^d.

He visto esta carta y papeles y ya se entiende muy a priesa en los despachos que se han de membrar [1] algo desosegado conforme a lo acordado. Pero bien es myrar a todo y prevenirlo. El mal es que que [2] no pudiendose proveer tanto como convendria no se si es peor remover los humores destos moriscos y darles mas priesa de la que quiza ellos se tomarian. Pero lo que agora me paresce es que no| ofreciendose es [3] algun Inconveniente en ello diesedes esta tarde esa carta y papeles al [Conde de Chinchon]. . . .

[1] This seems the most probable reading, but I am by no means certain.
[2] *Sic.*
[3] *Sic.*

Oy ha llegado aqui essa carta y papeles de la Inquisicion de Aragon Por los quales podra V. M^d. mandar ver lo que los Inquisidores sienten del desasosiego de los moriscos de aquel Reyno. Y aunque podria ser que el papel que se hallo en Calatayud fuese fingido, no se deuio fingir sin causa mayormente saliendose por cosa sin duda que tienen gran cantidad de polvora y vn numero grande de armas que no es sin algun fin Y tambien es mucho de considerar la deposicion que en la Inquisicion hizo Andres de Rosales y de Alagon Alcayde de Calanda y las palabras que dixo Damian de Granada morisco *Cuerpo de Dios no fuera llegada la ora.* Y si es verdad que arman tantas fustas en Argel o galeotas, y que en la frontera de Jaca hay gente de cauallo de Vgonotes menester es que se piense en el remedio y se ponga con toda presteza Antes que nos veamos en mayor trabajo y que se acabe de creer que estos son enemigos mortales y que nos han de hazer todo el mal que pudieren y que es justo escarmentar acordandonos de lo que passo en Granada y que nunca fueran creidos los que algunos dias antes lo certificauan hasta que los moriscos saltaron en campaña. Y si tienen minadas las ciudades y puestos barriles de polvora en las [minas y les dan fuego podran degollar los cristianos sin que se puedan juntar para deffenderse]. . . . . .

Escripto esta carta
y papeles y ya se
entiende muy a

priesa en los despachos
de sembrar o que
desossado conforme
a lo acordado, pero
bien es mirar a
todo y obenirlo
el valer que y no
podiendose proveer
tando como conben
dria no se dexe por
ver no ver los humores
destos moçen dades
mas priessa dela que
juerça ellos se to no
usan, pero la v agora
me parece que que no o
ficiendose algunos
ynconbeniente en ello
diese es esta carta y que
esta carta y papeles al.

oy ha llegado aqui esa carta y
dela Inqⁿ de Aragon de los este
V.M. mandar [...] que los Inqᵉˢ [...]
desabo bieso delos moriscos de aquel
un que podria ser que el papel que se
aluⁱ que fuese fingido no se [...]
que sin causa, mayormente saber
por esa gran duda que tienen gran
de pelure y los num grandes de
ne es sin algun fin y tambien es
de consideran la depoⁿ que en la [...]
dados de Rostes y de Alagon Alca
calanda y los palabras que dixo [...]
de Granada morisco que cuerpo de
[...] llegada la ora y si es verde
tantas justas en Argel o galeotas y [...]
frontera de [...] hay gente de [...]
de [...] menester es que se pu
el remedio y se ponga con toda pro
Antes que nos veamos en mayor [...]
y que se acabe de creer que estos son
[...] mortales y que nos han de
todo el mal que pudieren y que [...]
es aumentar acordandonos de lo [...]
en Granada y que nunca ficaron
los que algunos dias antes lo a[...]
hasta que los moriscos estaran en [...]
na y se tienen minadas las [...]
y presos bariles de pelura en [...]

THE RISE OF
THE SPANISH EMPIRE

IN THE

OLD WORLD AND IN THE NEW

BY

ROGER BIGELOW MERRIMAN

VOLUME IV

PHILIP THE PRUDENT

COOPER SQUARE PUBLISHERS, INC.
New York ● 1962

Originally copyright 1918 by The Macmillan Company
Library of Congress Catalog Card No. 61-13267
Printed in the United States of America
Published by Cooper Square Publishers, Inc.
59 Fourth Ave., New York 3, N. Y.

PREFACE TO VOLUME IV

THE composition of this final volume of my "Rise of the Spanish Empire" has been spread over a period of nine years, and has suffered from constant interruptions; but I can truthfully say that I have spent much more time and labor on it than on any of its predecessors, and that it is based to a far greater extent than were they, on manuscript sources. I hope, some day, to be permitted to fortify its conclusions by the publication of a number of documents, which I have collected during the past twenty years in the archives of Spain, France, and England, and prepared for the press. The possibilities of new discoveries in this field are still infinite, and it is as inexplicable as it is unfortunate that more English and American scholars are not tempted to explore them. I trust that the appearance, during the last five years, of four different lives of Philip II (cf. *infra*, p. 75) — all in rather lighter vein — will not deter prospective readers from the perusal of the somewhat solider pages which follow. The program which I set myself to carry out when I began — more than twenty years ago — to write this book, committed me of necessity to painstaking analysis of many topics not in themselves dramatic; and I feel strongly that at the moment better service can be rendered, not only to scholars but also to the general reading public, by careful investigation of the period as a whole, than by merely concentrating on the picturesque.

A grant from the Committee on Research in the Social Sciences in Harvard University has greatly facilitated the final stages of the preparation of this volume.   My hearty thanks are also due for wise advice and criticism from many friends and colleagues both here and in Europe.   The names of all those who have assisted me are too numerous to mention here, but I would acknowledge my very special obligations to Professor Henri Hauser of the University of Paris, to Señor Antonio Ballesteros of the Universidad Central in Madrid, to Professor Conyers Read of the University of Pennsylvania, to the Reverend Robert H. Lord of St. John's Seminary, Brighton, to Professor Earl J. Hamilton of Duke University, to Professor E. D. Salmon of Amherst, and to Professors J. D. M. Ford and Chandler R. Post, and to Messrs. John M. Potter, Robert S. Chamberlain and J. Llorens of Harvard. — Mr. George W. Robinson has gone over my manuscript again and again with the most assiduous care, at the various stages of its preparation, and deserves a large share of the credit for such accuracy as it may be found to possess.   He has also prepared the genealogical table of the House of Mendoza at the end of this volume, and compiled the table of contents and the index; and I am grateful to the trustees of the William F. Milton Fund in Harvard University for a grant which made it possible for me to avail myself of his services.

My work has benefited throughout from the criticisms of the members of my immediate family, and the constant encouragement of my wife has been the inspiration which has enabled me to complete it.

R. B. M.

Cambridge, Massachusetts,
     May, 1934

CONTENTS

BOOK VII

THE SPANISH EMPIRE AT ITS GREATEST TERRITORIAL EXTENT

CHAPTER XXXI

CHAPTER XXXII

CHAPTER XXXIII

CHAPTER XXXIV

CHAPTER XXXV

BOOK VIII

THE TURN OF THE TIDE

CHAPTER XXXVI

CHAPTER XXXVII

CHAPTER XXXVIII

CHAPTER XXXIX

CHAPTER XL

FACSIMILE, MAPS, AND GENEALOGICAL TABLES

FACSIMILE

MAPS

TABLES

LIST OF ABBREVIATIONS

See the Lists of Abbreviations for Volumes I and II (Vol. I, pp. xxvi–xxviii) and III (Vol. III, pp. xxiii–xxiv), and add:

Actas de las Córtes *Actas de las Córtes de Castilla publicadas por acuerdo del Congreso de los Diputados*, i–xvii. Madrid, 1877–91.

C. de B. . . . Jerónimo Castillo de Bovadilla. *Politica para Corregidores y Señores de Vassallos.* Barcelona, 1616. 2 vols.

C. de C. . . . Luis Cabrera de Córdoba. *Felipe Segundo, Rey de España.* Madrid, 1876–77. 4 vols.

C. S. P., Foreign . Great Britain. — Public Record Office. *Calendar of State Papers, Foreign Series.* Reign of Mary, ed. W. B. Turnbull. London, 1861. Reign of Elizabeth, edd. Joseph Stevenson and others. London, 1863– 21 vols., covering the period to 1588, published to 1931.

Castries . . . . *Les sources inédites de l'histoire du Maroc de 1530 à 1845.* Edited by Henry de Castries, Première série: Dynastie Saadienne, 1530–1660. Paris, 1905–26. Archives et bibliothèques de France, 3 vols. and index. Do. des Pays-Bas, 6 vols. Do. d'Espagne, i, (to 1552). Do. d'Angleterre, i, ii (to 1625).

Correspondance de Philippe II . . *Correspondance de Philippe II sur les affaires des Pays-Bas (1558–77).* Edited by L. P. Gachard. Brussels, 1848–79. 5 vols.

Forneron . . . Henri Forneron. *Histoire de Philippe II.* Paris, 1881–82. 4 vols.

Froude . . . . J. A. Froude. *History of England from the Fall of Wolsey to the Death of Elizabeth.* London, 1856–70. 12 vols.

Lavisse . . . . Ernest Lavisse. *Histoire de France depuis les origines jusqu'à la Révolution.* Paris, 1900–11. 9 vols. The age of Philip II is covered by tom. vi, pt. 1, "La Réforme et la Ligue — L'Édit de Nantes (1559–1598)," by J. H. Mariéjol (Paris, 1911).

Pastor . . . . Ludwig, Freiherr von Pastor. *The History of the Popes from the Close of the Middle Ages.* English translation edited by R. F. Kerr. Vols. xiv–xxiv (London, 1924–33) deal with the period 1555–1605.

Pirenne . . . . Henri Pirenne. *Histoire de Belgique.* Vols. i–vii. Brussels, 1900–32.

S. I. . . . . . Julián Suárez Inclán. *Guerra de Anexión en Portugal durante el Reinado de Felipe II.* Madrid, 1897–98. 2 vols.

BOOK VII

THE SPANISH EMPIRE AT ITS GREATEST TERRITORIAL EXTENT

CHAPTER XXXI

A SPANISH SOVEREIGN, CHAMPION OF THE CHURCH

THE transition in Spanish history from Charles V to
Philip II forms the antithesis to that from the Catholic Kings
to the Emperor. In 1516 the destinies of the Spanish
Empire had passed from native to alien hands; Spanish
interests had been suddenly subordinated to those of the
house of Hapsburg. Forty years later the reaction is complete; a process whose beginnings we have already noted in
the Emperor's closing years has now attained its final stage;
the outlook of the Spanish monarchy is once more thoroughly Hispanicized. The second of these transitions was
more gradual than the first, but when it was completed it
was much more permanent and far-reaching. Philip the
Prudent will go down in history, both within the Iberian
peninsula and without it, as the typical Spanish sovereign
of all time.

There can be no doubt that the heart's desire of the new
king, when on January 16, 1556, the huge burden of governing the Spanish Empire had at last fully devolved upon his
shoulders, was to make peace with his enemies and get home
to Spain. The first sixteen years of his life had been spent
wholly in the Iberian peninsula, and had satisfied him of its
immeasurable superiority to every other part of the world.
His many disagreeable experiences during the ensuing
Wanderjahre had but served to emphasize this conviction,
and to implant in him a deep aversion to everything north

3

of the Pyrenees. His political education, the precepts and
example of his imperial father, were but added arguments in
support of the same conclusion. Charles had preached
peace and defensiveness to him with increasing fervor in his
later years. He had also publicly confessed at the last, by
his abdication and the division of his inheritance, that his
own life had stood for an unrealizable ideal, that the great
task he had undertaken entailed an impossible amount of
travelling, and that a single sovereign could not continue to
rule both the northern and the southern halves of the Hapsburg inheritance. And if it had been impossible to combine them under the Emperor, it was certainly even more
so now, because, to the vast number of preëxistent incom-
patibilities, there had recently been superadded that of
religion. On October 3, 1555, only twenty-two days before
Charles's abdication of the rule of the Low Countries, there
was signed the peace of Augsburg, giving Lutheranism, under
certain restrictions, legal right to coëxistence with Catholicism in the Empire. Heresy, in other words, had at last
been formally recognized, in a fashion which Philip could
neither tolerate nor comprehend. Unswerving zeal for unity
of the faith was the lesson from his Spanish education that
he had taken most deeply to heart; it must have seemed
to him almost the result of divine intervention that he
should have been relieved of the responsibility of ruling
Germans at the very moment of their adoption of a *modus
vivendi* so abhorrent to him. From every point of view —
personal, political, and religious — he deeply longed to
return to his native land.

At first there seemed good prospect that he would soon
be able to satisfy this desire. An honorable peace with his
French foes was the indispensable preliminary to his departure, and that was furnished him, apparently at least, by the

truce of Vaucelles, on February 5, 1556, just twenty days
after he had become the official ruler of Spain and of the
Spanish dominions. In the three other possible centres of
disturbance for him, outside the Iberian peninsula, the
situation, during the first half of this same year, 1556, while
not entirely satisfactory, might well have been far worse.
In England there was little open indication of disloyalty to
the Spanish alliance. The conspiracy of Sir Henry Dudley
was easily detected and foiled, and the government seemed
principally occupied with the burning of the Protestant
martyrs. In the Low Countries, destined to become a few
years later the worst sore spot of all, the discontent for the
time being was also latent. Philip had been amply warned
against the dangers of any rapid Hispanicization of the
administration there. For the present he seemed chiefly
bent on preserving intact all the measures and policies of
his beloved father, and his appointment to the governor-
generalship of Emanuel Philibert of Savoy, though really
dictated by considerations of foreign policy and the military
ability of the nominee, was taken by the Netherlanders as a
pledge of respect for their liberties.[1] In Italy, indeed,
Paul IV had virtually declared war; but he seemed — at
least until July — to be quite incapable of waging it. The
truce of Vaucelles had deprived him of French support; the
cardinals, though they dared not openly oppose, silently
disapproved;[2] and meantime the Duke of Alva, now viceroy
of Naples, was getting his *tercios* into an admirable state of
readiness. In midsummer, 1556, it really looked as if Philip
would soon get home to his beloved Spain; indeed, there
seemed an even chance that he would get home without a
fight.

[1] Pirenne, iii, pp. 365 f., and notes
there. Cf. also Forneron, i, pp. 86 f.,
and Lucien Romier, *Les origines poli-*
tiques des Guerres de Religion, ii, pp.
179 f.
[2] Pastor, xiv, pp. 114–118.

But six months later the situation had entirely changed. So complicated were the cross currents, so self-contradictory the combinations of international politics, during these critical years when Charles was giving way to Philip, that it was impossible to foretell from day to day whether it was to be friendship or enmity, peace or war. The decision was likely to remain with the most strong-minded of the powers concerned, and in 1556 there can be no question that that distinction belonged to the octogenarian pontiff. For the moment, at least, his hatred of the house of Hapsburg took the precedence of his devotion to the church; blind to the disastrous effect on Catholicism, not only in the Hapsburg lands on the continent, but also in England, of a war between the see of Rome and the king of Spain, he offered such provocation to the representatives of his enemy in the summer months of 1556 that in September the Duke of Alva invaded the Patrimonium Petri from Naples with an army of 12,000 men.[1] The papal levies were quite unable to resist him. Though he waged war with the utmost scrupulousness,[2] as befitted a Spaniard who was attacking the States of the Church, his advance on Rome was methodical and rapid, and the 18th of November saw the Spaniards established in Ostia, where their leader offered an armistice to the Pope. But the lion-hearted Paul was not yet prepared to surrender; he still cherished the hope that he would be rescued at the last moment by France.[3] Everything, in fact, depended on whether or not Henry II could

[1] Pastor, xiv, pp. 130–137.

[2] When Philip sent Alva against Paul, he wrote to him that the sole fruit which he desired of his victory was that it should be the means of causing the Pope to admit him to his grace; and the Duke wrote to the pontiff, "I do not wage war on Paul IV as the vicar of Christ, but as the sworn enemy of the Catholic King, and I shall employ the most rigorous means to force him to make himself worthy of the title of Holiness which is given him by the faithful." Duque de Berwick y de Alba, *Contribución al estudio de la persona de Don Fernando Álvarez de Toledo, III Duque de Alba* (Madrid, 1919), pp. 57, 70 f.

[3] Pastor, xiv, pp. 147–150.

be induced to break the truce of Vaucelles. Such a breach had seemed inevitable to the Argus-eyed Simon Renard in London as early as May, 1556, only three months after the truce had been signed, and the events of the following autumn proved the accuracy of his foresight. The urgency of Carlo Caraffa and of the cardinal of Lorraine prevailed over the more cautious policy of Anne de Montmorency. In the end of December the Duke of Guise was permitted to cross the Alps with an army of 13,000 men to go to the rescue of the Pope; in the first week of January the Admiral Gaspard de Coligny made an ineffectual attempt to surprise Douai. A state of war between France and the Hapsburgs had existed in fact, both in the Low Countries and in Italy, for more than a month before Henry II actually declared it, on the last day of January, 1557.[1]

Though deeply discouraged by his failure to preserve peace, Philip entered the ensuing struggle with the better courage because it had not been of his seeking; he could honestly say that he was waging a defensive war of the type which his father had approved. Moreover the fact that he had not been the aggressor did not prevent him from acting vigorously when the crisis came; himself proverbially incapable of taking the initiative, he at least on this occasion permitted his representatives to seize it for him. During the first nine months of the year 1557 the course of the conflict was wholly favorable to Spain.

There was throughout the closest interdependence between the events in both theatres of the war, widely separated though they were. The Spaniards planned to force the fighting on the northeastern frontier of France, so as to win a decisive victory there before the Duke of Guise could get

---

[1] Romier, ii, p. 178; Francis Decrue, *Anne de Montmorency sous Henri II, François II, et Charles IX*, pp. 186–197.

back from Italy; the French strategy was to rest on the
defensive in Artois and Picardy in order to enable Guise not
only to rescue the Pope, but also to rehabilitate all possible
anti-Spanish combinations among the lesser Italian states.[1]
The fact that the French leader was given so many different
things to do was probably the chief reason for his initial ill
success; it led to sharp differences of opinion among the
leaders of the Franco-papal forces, and prevented them from
concentrating in any one direction. When the Duke finally
reached Rome (March 2, 1557), he found the pontiff most
anxious to resume the offensive against the Spaniards.
Paul had been greatly encouraged by the recent recapture of
Ostia through the efforts of his generalissimo, Pietro Strozzi;
he had visions of driving "this mixture of Jews, Marrani,
and Lutherans" — such was his characterization of Alva's
army — not only out of Naples but out of the rest of Italy as
well. But his French and Italian allies did not share his
aggressiveness. In May the French king commanded Guise
to turn his attention to Lombardy and Tuscany; not till
two months later was he persuaded to countermand his
order, and allow the army to remain in the States of the
Church. And then, just as everything was at last in readiness for a vigorous offensive against the Duke of Alva, there
arrived the stunning news of the great defeat which the
French had sustained at St. Quentin in the North, followed
the next day by an urgent message from Henry II recalling
Guise and his troops for the defence of Paris. This, of
course, meant the ruin of Paul's hopes of chastising the
Spaniards; the only question now was whether he could save
Rome from a repetition of the great sack which had so horrified all Europe just thirty years before. But fortunately
the Duke of Alva was not minded to follow the example

[1] Romier, ii, p. 178.

of the leaders of the imperial armies in 1527. He was himself far too scrupulous a Catholic. He knew, moreover, that his master wanted peace, and the papal defences were not entirely negligible. On August 25, he advanced to the outskirts of Rome as if to demonstrate the fact that the game was in his own hands, and just two weeks later the Pope admitted it, by sending out to him three cardinals to discuss terms of peace. On September 12, a treaty was arranged, whereby Alva was to make solemn submission to the Holy See in the name of his sovereign, to restore to the Patrimonium Petri all cities and territories which he had captured in the preceding months, and to receive in return the Pope's forgiveness and his promise thenceforth to remain neutral in the war between Spain and France. The moderation of the Spanish leader had been well rewarded. He had restored the *status quo ante bellum* in Italy, which was all that Philip could have asked for. Henceforth Paul IV was to devote himself exclusively to his spiritual duties, and ceased to breed trouble for Spain and the house of Hapsburg.[1]

Meantime in the North the struggle had begun more successfully still. In the spring a large army was assembled at Brussels under the leadership of the duke of Savoy. Its ultimate object was to strike directly at Paris, and on March 18 Philip crossed over from Calais to Dover, in order to enlist the support of his wife.[2] From the standpoint of Englishmen his visit was entirely disastrous. To all the old difficulties of 1554–55 was now added the fact that Philip's hostility to the Pope made it impossible for him whole-heartedly to support the great work of reconciliation

---

[1] Pietro Nores, "Storia della guerra di Paolo IV contro gli Spagnuoli," in *Archivio storico Italiano*, serie i, xii (1847), pp. 1–299; Romier, ii, pp. 167–194; Pastor, xiv, pp. 152–174.

[2] Jean de Vandenesse, "Journal des voyages de Philippe II," in *Collection des voyages des souverains des Pays-Bas*, edd. L. P. Gachard and Charles Piot, iv (1882), p. 24.

on which Mary's heart was set ; never before had it been so obvious that he proposed to utilize the resources of the island kingdom simply and solely in the interests of Spain. But the queen's loyalty to him never faltered. Her hopes of the heir whose advent would solve so many puzzling questions were renewed once more ;[1] with that happy prospect before her, there was no sacrifice she was not prepared to make. In June she sent a herald to Henry II to carry him the English declaration of war on France; before July 6, when Philip left her for the last time, she had sold crown property to the annual value of over 10,000 pounds for the support of his campaign, and had raised upwards of 5000 troops for the service of Emanuel Philibert.[2] By the beginning of August everything was in readiness, and an army of over 50,000 men was launched at St. Quentin on the Somme. The fortifications of the place were almost in ruins. Coligny, who was in command, had a mere handful of soldiers ; on learning of the approach of the Spanish army he sent word to his uncle Anne de Montmorency, who was at La Fère with about 18,000 troops, that unless he was speedily reënforced he could only hold out a few days. Montmorency came to his rescue on the morning of August 10, but his tactics were so faulty that he suffered a crushing disaster outside the walls of the town. Over 3000 of his men were killed ; 7000 were captured, among them the constable himself ; the rest only saved themselves by ignominious flight.[3]

It was a notable defeat for France and a glorious victory for Spain : the most glorious, perhaps, ever won by the armies of the Prudent King over any of his Christian foes. But so incapable was Philip of utilizing his opportunity that

[1] C. S. P., Venetian, vi, nos. 1142, 1146.

[2] C. S. P., Venetian, vi, nos. 886, 891.

[3] D. I. E., ix, pp. 486–495; Forneron, i, pp. 86–93; Decrue, op. cit., pp. 203–206; Romier, ii, pp. 178–187, and references there.

the battle remained almost barren of advantage to the Spaniards. Indeed, it may justly be said of it, as of Malplaquet a century and a half later, that its chief importance was that it marked the turn of the tide against the would-be invaders of France. When the news of it reached the Emperor at Yuste, he eagerly demanded whether his son had clinched his victory by marching on Paris, and was deeply cast down when word came that he had failed to do so. Philip, indeed, had not even been present at the battle. He was writing letters at the time, a few miles distant, at Cambray;[1] and on reaching the scene of the victory that had been won for him, he gave orders to besiege and capture St. Quentin before entering any farther into the enemy's territory. But the town was heroically defended by Coligny with 700 men; every day that Philip could be made to waste before its walls would bring nearer the winter season and the return of the Duke of Guise. Not till August 27 was it finally taken and subjected to an unusually horrible sack;[2] by the time that Philip's troops had recovered from their orgies, the autumn rains had already begun, and further advance was regretfully abandoned. The most that Philip could do was to take Le Catelet, Ham, and Chauny, and retire to Brussels to put his army into winter quarters. Shortly afterwards came the counterstroke, not indeed against Philip and the Spaniards, but against his English allies, the subjects of his sorrowful queen. When the Duke of Guise got back from Italy he found to his intense relief that Paris was safe. Discerning that what France needed above all things was a restoration of her morale, he determined to effect it by the capture of Calais. Concealing his real object with masterly cunning, he arrived before the

---

[1] *Papiers d'état du Cardinal de Granvelle*, v, pp. 120–122.
[2] *D. I. E.*, ix, pp. 495–522.

town on January 2, 1558 ; eighteen days later he had taken it, together with its various outposts, before Philip had been able to send a man to its defence.[1] The last remnant of the conquests of the Hundred Years' War had been torn from the grasp of England as the result of her sacrifice in the interests of a foreign power ; the queen and the nation were cast into the depths of despair.[2] It was a final and overwhelming demonstration of the error of the Spanish alliance.

The remaining operations of the war were unimportant. The strategy of both sides aimed at avoiding decisive battles. Philip's financial resources were completely exhausted ; the majority of Frenchmen were obviously war-weary ; peace in the near future was the inevitable conclusion. Conferences were opened in October, 1558, at the abbey of Cercamp in Cambrésis, the principal Spanish representatives being the Duke of Alva, the prince of Orange, Ruy Gómez da Silva, and Granvelle.[3] It is unnecessary to enter into the details of the ensuing negotiations, which were interrupted several times between the end of November, 1558, and the beginning of March, 1559, on account of the death of Mary Tudor and the proposal of Philip to marry her successor Elizabeth. So many and so weighty were the issues that hung on the acceptance or failure of that proposal that nothing else could be definitely determined until the question was permanently settled in the negative. Finally on April 2 and 3, 1559, the different articles of the treaty were signed in the little village of Cateau-Cambrésis. In the North, France kept Calais, and there were mutual restorations of conquests between the belligerents on France's eastern frontier. All the territories of which the duke of Savoy had been despoiled by Francis I in 1536 were duly returned to

---

[1] D. I. E., ii, pp. 514–518 ; Romier, ii, pp. 215–217.

[2] Froude, vi, pp. 488–507.

[3] Papiers d'état du Cardinal de Granvelle, v, pp. 207–584 ; Decrue, op. cit., p. 216.

him,[1] and the settlement of the outstanding questions in Italy was such as connoted the abandonment by France of further schemes of aggrandizement in the peninsula. As was suitable at the close of a long dynastic war, the treaty ended with a marriage. Since Philip had been unable to win the hand of Elizabeth of England, he was given, in her stead, Elizabeth of Valois, the eldest daughter of the king of France.[2] The proxy marriage was celebrated in Paris on the 22d of the following June, the bridegroom being represented by the Duke of Alva. In January, 1560, the new queen arrived in Spain.[3]

The treaty of Cateau-Cambrésis put an end to that long series of wars between the French and the Spaniards which began with the raid of Charles VIII on Naples in 1494. Though the prize for which the contestants were striving was originally Italy, the struggle later ramified in such fashion as to affect most of the rest of Western Europe, so that the peace which concluded it was of universal significance; it was, in fact, the international settlement to which men perpetually referred back, as establishing the normal state of the relations of the European powers, down to the treaties of Westphalia in 1648. In France it was generally regarded by contemporaries as disastrous, as "a great misfortune to the king and to his whole kingdom," [4] and though some subsequent historians have judged it more leniently, the most recent authority confirms the earlier verdict. He censures Henry II for having granted such favorable terms

---

[1] A separate secret convention, signed on March 25 at Grünendal near Brussels between the representatives of Philip and of Emanuel Philibert, virtually converted the neutrality of the duke of Savoy into obedient alliance with the king of Spain. Cf. Arturo Segre and Pietro Egidi, *Emanuele Filiberto* (Turin, 1928, 2 vols.), i, pp. 164–166.

[2] Born April 2, 1545, she was three months older than Don Carlos.

[3] The standard account of the peace is that of Baron Alphonse de Ruble, *Le traité de Cateau-Cambrésis* (Paris, 1889). Cf. also Decrue, pp. 227–230, and Romier, ii, pp. 345–347.

[4] Decrue, *Anne de Montmorency sous Henri II*, p. 228.

to an adversary so exhausted that he could not have continued to fight, and finds the explanation of the French king's error in his zeal for the extirpation of heresy.   If this estimate be just, the treaty must, *ipso facto*, be regarded as a notable victory for Philip II.   In Italy, the original cause and theatre of the strife, there can be no question that Spain had come out on top.   Her power was now securely established both in the north and the south of the peninsula, and the concessions of France at Cateau-Cambrésis enabled her to control the destinies of most of the intervening states. But in Northern Europe there is a different tale to tell.   The settlement of France with England, her reconquest of Calais, and her military occupation of Metz, Toul, and Verdun could not fail to be ultimately prejudicial to the maintenance of the Spanish power in the Low Countries and everything which that implied.[1]   The Netherlands, during Philip's reign, were to be the focal point of international affairs.   If the termination of the great dynastic struggle in 1559 was of baleful portent for France in Italy, and delivered her over at home to the miseries of religious war, it was also, as things ultimately worked out, of ominous significance for Spain. It weakened her hold in a region where her power should never have been established, and it was a factor in forcing her into a struggle to maintain it, which lost her not only the Netherlands but also the sovereignty of the seas.

---

[1] Romier (ii, p. 346) points out that France got possession of Calais before the peace of Cateau-Cambrésis, and that the treaty, instead of legally confirming her possession of the town, actually rendered it provisional; furthermore, that the peace did not expressly give to France the three Lotharingian bishoprics, which therefore remained militarily occupied, as they had been since 1552, but not officially conquered.   This seems somewhat captious.   France certainly did not expect that the provisions of the peace would so work out as to require the recession of Calais; while her occupation of the three bishoprics was safeguarded by the express inclusion in the treaty of their bishops and chapters in the list of her allies.   Dumont, *Corps universel diplomatique*, v, 1 (1728), p. 40.

All this, however, was an affair of the future; for the present there could be no doubt that Philip had emerged victorious. He had got the peace for which his whole soul longed, and the opportunity which it offered him to return to his beloved Spain; he had got it, moreover, on ostensibly triumphant terms. "During the spring of 1559" his court at "Brussels was the political capital of Catholic Europe." [1] Thither flocked the political representatives of the petty Italian states to pay grateful homage to their protector and master, "the greatest monarch," so the Florentine ambassador described him, "that Italy has known since the day of the Romans." Thither also came the princes of France to congratulate their conqueror on the victories that he had won; they begged him to come to Paris for his wedding, and were visibly cast down when he refused; "The custom of the kings of Spain," he haughtily replied, "is not to go and fetch their brides, but to have them brought to them in their own country and their own house." [2] Philip, indeed, was wholly bent on getting home; and the sole reason why he delayed his departure was to give himself time to make arrangements in the North which would relieve him of the necessity of ever leaving home again. In view of the role that he was to play in the immediately ensuing years, it is worth remarking that for the moment he seemed more preoccupied with political than with religious cares. His quondam rival, Henry II of France, was apparently far more anxious to extirpate heresy than he. Philip refused to collaborate in an expedition against the Calvinists of Geneva, which the Most Christian King was desirous to undertake. [3] He was also totally unwilling to take any measures for the subversion of English or Scottish Protestantism; indeed, for

[1] Romier, ii, p. 348.
[2] Romier, ii, pp. 349–353, and references there; Vandenesse, "Journal des voyages de Philippe II," *loc. cit.*, pp. 66–73.
[3] Romier, ii, p. 359.

the time being, he appeared to regard the British heretics
rather as a chief bulwark for the defence of the island kingdoms against the designs of the Valois and the Guises.[1]
When, on July 9, the lance-thrust of Montgomery put a
sudden end to the life of the king of France, Philip's fears
in regard to these matters were naturally much relieved.
If France and Scotland were to be brought closer than ever
through the fact that their respective sovereigns were now
husband and wife,[2] the youth and weakness of the new
Valois monarch gave adequate assurance that Spanish interests in Northern Europe were at least temporarily safe; and
Philip prepared to depart. His date of sailing, fixed originally for August 18, was delayed till the twenty-third because
of the advice of his astrologer, Nostradamus, who "with his
threats of tempests and shipwrecks . . . did put the sailors
in great fear"; on September 8 he landed at Laredo.[3]

If Philip before his departure from the Netherlands had
devoted himself rather to the regulation of political than of
religious affairs, his return to the peninsula gave the signal
for the emphasis to be reversed. His journey to Spain is,
in fact, the real dividing line, as far as he was concerned,
between the era of the Hapsburg-Valois wars and that of
the Counter-Reformation. During the next twenty years,
at least, his principal interest was to be the advancement of
the faith. Now that he had got home he could follow undisturbed the path that was indicated to him by the traditions of his native land. Arrangements had been made
there, even before his arrival, for a public demonstration of
his detestation of infidelity and heresy, and of his solemn

[1] Romier, ii, p. 359, and Forneron, i,
pp. 122 f., and references there.

[2] Francis II and Mary queen of Scots
had been married on April 24, 1558.

[3] Forneron, i, p. 128, and references
there; Vandenesse, loc. cit., p. 73; cf.

Carl Bratli, *Philippe II*, p. 104, who
asserts that Philip was far in advance
of his age in freedom from superstition
and in despising the prophecies of
astrologers; unfortunately he cites no
contemporary evidence for his view.

determination to extirpate them, and this demonstration took the form of a most imposing auto-da-fé. It was held, directly in front of the great church of St. Francis, at Valladolid, on Sunday, October 8, 1559. At six o'clock in the morning the officials of the Inquisition took their places on a magnificent dais at one end of the square. Close by was the royal gallery, occupied by the king, the Prince of Asturias, a number of privileged grandees, and the ambassadors of foreign powers; directly opposite was the scaffold. Then the bells began to toll, and the sad procession of guards, clerics, familiars, and convicts — the latter all duly attired in *corozas* and *sanbenitos* — filed slowly out of the gates of the Inquisition prison and into the great square. Spectators to the number of 200,000 are said to have followed. The ceremonies began with the "sermon of the faith," which was preached on this occasion by Doctor Juan Manuel. Then Hernando de Valdés, the inquisitor-general, rose and faced the king, who also rose and bared his sword as a sign that he would champion the cause of the Holy Office; whereupon Valdés addressed to him the following solemn demand: "Since the apostolic decrees and the sacred canons have ordained that sovereigns must swear to favor the Holy Catholic Faith and the Christian religion, does your Majesty swear by the Holy Cross to give all necessary support to the Holy Office of the Inquisition and its ministers, against heretics and apostates and against those who help and favor them, and against all who directly or indirectly shall hinder the activities of the Holy Office; and to force all your Majesty's subjects and the inhabitants of your Majesty's realms to give obedience to the constitutions and decrees which are published for the defence of the Holy Catholic Faith against heretics and against all who believe, receive, or support them?" The king replied, "I swear it." Then followed the interminable reading of the sentences of the condemned, the separation of those to be 'reconciled' from those to be 'relaxed' to the secular arm, and the subsequent subdivision of those in the latter category into a larger group who elected by confession at the last moment to purchase the privilege of the milder form of death by the garrote, and a small minority — only two on this occasion — who preferred to undergo all the horrors of the *quemadero*. One of these was a Florentine noble, Carlo de Sesa, a godson of Charles V, who had once stood high in the imperial favor. As he passed by the king, he haughtily demanded of him how he could suffer such things to be. And Philip replied, "If my son were as evil as you are, I myself would fetch the wood wherewith to burn him." [1]

So Spain at last got back her king. The wish, so often expressed by the Cortes of Charles V, that the Spanish monarch would stop his travelling, had now been fulfilled with the advent of his son. In all the thirty-nine years of life that remained to him Philip never once set foot outside the peninsula; and his constant presence there during so long a period, and in such a monarchical age, made its administration the faithful mirror of his own policy and ideals. Seldom in history has it been given to any sovereign to stamp the impress of his personality so deeply upon the lives of his subjects. If one would learn the destinies of the vast dominions over which he bore sway, one must begin with a careful study of his character and men-

---

[1] There is an excellent manuscript account of this auto-da-fé in B. M., Egerton Ms. 2058, fols. 21–33 (cf. Gayangos, *Catalogue of the Manuscripts in the Spanish Language in the British Museum*, ii, p. 225); it describes Sesa as a "hereje pertinax, . . . que no bastaron frayles ni personas religiosas ni muchos letrados a convertirle." Cf. also C. de C., i, pp. 275 f.; Prescott, *Philip the Second*, i, pp. 426–436; Gachard, *Don Carlos et Philippe II*, pp. 46–49; Forneron, i, pp. 176–179.

tality; and these in turn cannot be adequately understood without remembering the Spanish origin and background out of which they were evolved. If Spain and the Spanish Empire were represented in Philip, so Philip was a typical product of Spain and the Spanish Empire.

His ancestry, of course, was predominantly Iberian. His father was half Spanish, his mother half Spanish and half Portuguese; and she doubtless impressed him in his boyhood years with the idea that it was Portugal's destiny to be ultimately reunited with Spain, the idea which her own marriage with the Emperor had represented, and which Philip was subsequently, if only temporarily, to carry out. The influence of the Empress was also a potent cause of Philip's proverbial respect for the clergy. She was very devout and spent many hours in prayer;[1] from his infancy the prince was surrounded by clerics and subjected to ecclesiastical influences. The other two chief things that stand out, as one reads the story of his early years, are the joylessness of his life and the deficiencies of his linguistic equipment. He was never allowed to have a playmate worthy of the name; the Portuguese Ruy Gómez da Silva, who afterwards became his chief councillor, was perhaps the nearest to it, but Ruy Gómez was Philip's senior by no less than five years.[2] The Empress insisted that the prince be treated with the respect due to "the son of the greatest emperor that the Christian world had ever seen";[3] his every movement was regulated by an etiquette so strict that it was scarcely possible for him to laugh. Everything combined to make him cold and reserved, to train him to conceal his real feelings, to enhance the characteristics of gravity

[1] Cf. J. Vales Failde, *La Emperatriz Isabel* (Madrid, 1917).
[2] Bratli, p. 74.
[3] Michele Soriano (1559) in *Relazioni degli Ambasciatori Veneti al Senato*, ed. Eugenio Albèri, serie i, iii, p. 378.

and melancholy which he had inherited from his father.[1] The latter, though absent from Spain during the greater part of his son's early life, had given much thought to the question of the prince's studies, and had provided him with the best tutors that could be had. Philip made good progress in science and in art; he read much history, and gave promise at an early age of possessing unusually sound political judgment.[2] But for languages he showed even less aptitude than the Emperor; indeed it was well said of him that from his childhood days he preferred to communicate by writing rather than by word of mouth. Even in his native Castilian he always spoke slowly, though with great precision, and he seemed to have much difficulty in choosing his words.[3] He could write and speak his Latin reasonably well. He could understand a little French and Italian, and speak a little French; but to converse readily in these or any other foreign tongues was utterly beyond him.[4] Small wonder that he was so uncosmopolitan. He had no means of free communication with any one beyond the Pyrenees.

Numerous contemporaneous accounts of his physical traits have come down to us; those of the Venetian ambassadors are on the whole the most valuable, though we have Spanish, French, and English testimony besides. Philip was of less than medium stature, but finely proportioned, and of a carriage "so straight and upright as he loseth no inch in height"; the grace and dignity of his presence were further enhanced by the care, restraint, and elegance with

[1] C. de C., lib. i, cap. i; Prescott, i, p. 32, and references there; Florentine "Relazione di Spagna" (1591?), probably by Cammillo Guidi Volterrano, in Bratli, p. 212.

[2] Federico Badoero (1557) in Albèri, Relazioni, serie i, iii, p. 236.

[3] "Il re quasi mai non parla con i suoi della camera." Leonardo Donato (1573) in Albèri, serie i, vi, p. 463.

[4] Federico Badoero, loc. cit.; Prescott, i, pp. 30 f.; Bratli, pp. 73 f.

which he dressed.[1] His eyes were blue and his hair and beard light, so that he seemed at first sight to be rather a Fleming than a Spaniard. His large protruding under-jaw and lip, though considerably less prominent than those of his father, were yet sufficiently noticeable to betray the Hapsburg ancestry.[2] In early manhood he wore his beard "short and pointed, after the Spanish fashion";[3] later in life he permitted it to increase in length and breadth until it approached the style customary in the Netherlands.[4] The pallor of his complexion was also remarked on by all observers, and most of them drew the proper conclusion, namely, that it indicated a weak stomach and lack of exercise. Reddened eyes were a penalty of his excessive devotion to the written word both day and night.[5] He ate slowly, sparingly, and usually alone, restricting himself to meats and the "most nutritious foods"; almost all the accounts of him emphasize his avoidance of fruits and of fish.[6] He also suffered from asthma, stone, and gout;[7] and though his doctors recommended him to go hunting and get out into the open air "as the best means of strengthening his body and distracting his mind from melancholy reflec-

[1] John Elder (1555) in Joseph Ames, *Typographical Antiquities*, ed. T. F. Dibdin (London, 1810–19, 4 vols.), iii, p. 526; Giovanni Micheli (1557) in Albèri, *Relazioni*, serie i, ii, p. 333; Michele Soriano (1559), *ibid.*, iii, pp. 378 f.; Marcantonio da Mula (1559), *ibid.*, p. 394; Philippe de Caverel (1582) in *Relations des ambassadeurs Vénitiens sur Charles-Quint et Philippe II*, ed. L. P. Gachard (Brussels, 1855), p. lxx; Camillo Borghese, later Pope Paul V (1594), "Diario," in A. Morel-Fatio, *L'Espagne au XVIe et au XVIIe siècle* (Heilbronn, 1878), p. 175.

[2] Micheli (1557), *loc. cit.*; Federico Badoero (1557) in Albèri, serie i, iii, p. 233; Giovanni Soranzo (1565), *ibid.*, v, p. 112.

[3] Federico Badoero (1557), *loc. cit.*

[4] Philippe de Caverel (1582), *loc. cit.*, p. lxxi.

[5] Philippe de Caverel (1582), *loc. cit.*, p. lxx.

[6] Federico Badoero (1557), *loc. cit.*, iii, pp. 233 f.; Soriano (1559), *ibid.*, p. 379; Paolo Tiepolo (1563) in Albèri, serie i, v, pp. 61 f.; Soranzo (1565), *ibid.*, p. 112; Borghese (1594), *loc. cit.*, p. 190. Philip apparently got leave from the Pope to transgress, save on Good Friday, the rules for fasting prescribed by the church. Cf. Soranzo, *loc. cit.*, and Sigismondo Cavalli (1570) in Albèri, serie i, v, p. 183.

[7] Cavalli, *loc. cit.*; Gioan Francesco Morosini (1581), *ibid.*, p. 322.

tions,"[1] he paid little or no attention to them; apparently,
too, he was haunted by the fear lest he should die as the
result of an accident, and kept constantly before his mind
the experience of the king of France.[2] He was totally deficient in that capacity for sudden and almost superhuman
physical exertion which, in the case of some of Spain's greatest empire builders, alternated so strikingly with long periods of doing nothing at all; "Ohne Hast, aber ohne Rast"
is an accurate description of him, if one remembers that his
activities were not those of the body, but of the mind. He
was ever a great sleeper, and the tendency increased with
advancing years. In the later part of his life he seldom rose
before half past nine, and always took a long nap after his
mid-day meal; sometimes, it is true, he would work till
midnight, but more often he retired early in the evening to
read for a couple of hours before he closed his eyes; indeed
it was well said of him when he was an old man that his only
recreation was repose.[3] The effect of these habits on his
policy and methods of government was foreseen with striking clarity by the Venetian ambassador in 1559. "From
them it results," so remarks the report, "that though he is
at the age of youthful appetites and insatiable desire to rule,
nevertheless all the actions of his Majesty are invariably
directed, not to the aggrandizement of his kingdoms by war,
but rather to their conservation through peace."[4] The
counsels of the Emperor to avoid aggressive action and rest
on the defensive had certainly been heard by willing ears.
What his father had acquired with the sword, Philip pro-

---

[1] Federico Badoero (1557), *loc. cit.*,
iii, p. 233.
[2] Mula (1559), *loc. cit.*, iii, p.
394.
[3] Morosini (1581), *loc. cit.*, v, p. 322;
Martin Philippson, *Ein Ministerium
unter Philipp II.: Kardinal Granvella*

am spanischen Hof, p. 44. Cf. Donato
(1573), *loc. cit.*, vi, p. 463: "Legge con
una candela appresso il letto alcune
ore innanzi che dorma."
[4] Soriano (1559), *loc. cit.*, iii, p.
379.

posed to preserve with the pen.[1]   From first to last he was
the 'Prudent King.'[2]

Reading and writing occupied the major portion of
Philip's day; indeed he not seldom continued to read and
to write while taking a drive in his carriage.[3]   We have
already alluded to his preference for written over oral communications; add to this his firm determination to keep in
touch with everything that was going on,[4] even in the re-
motest corner of his vast dominions, and his own persistent
unwillingness to leave the centre of Castile, and it furnishes
the key to his methods of government.   He had the highest
possible sense of his royal prerogatives and duties; he had
taken deeply to heart his father's injunction to direct everything himself, and never to give his full confidence even to
the most faithful of his ministers, and the natural result
was that his time was completely occupied with receiving
and answering reports and letters.   Most of these were concerned with immediate affairs of state, and their number
mounted so fast that in 1566 Philip took the first measures
for their conservation in the ancient castle of Simancas,
which soon became a national archive.[5]   Others — like
the famous *Relaciones Topográficas*[6] — were elaborate an-
swers to royal requests for information in regard to existing
conditions from all the cities of the realm.   "They are sent
to him," writes the Venetian ambassador Morosini, "from
all sorts and conditions of men and treat of every sort and

[1] Francesco Vendramino (1595) in
Albèri, serie i, v, p. 446; cf. Donato
(1573), *loc. cit.*, vi, p. 463: ". . . è più
pronto nello scrivere che qualsivoglia
segretario. . . .   Il nunzio diceva che
finalmente bisognava negoziar con il
re per biglietti, cioè con polizze, tanto
si fa grande il suo ritiramento."
[2] Bratli, p. 225, and reference there.
[3] Lorenzo Priuli (1576) in Albèri, serie
i, v, p. 257.
[4] "Vede tutti i fatti suoi e sa tutto.

. . . Dicono i suoi ministri che la sua
intelligenza è tanta, che non è cosa che
non sappia e che non veda." Donato
(1573), *loc. cit.*, vi, pp. 463 f.
[5] "Considerando la importancia de
que son papeles, como quien por medio
dellos meneaba el mundo desde su
Real asiento." C. de C., i, p. 504.
[6] A list of these, most of which still
remain in manuscript, may be found
on pp. 614–617 of vol. vi of the *Memorias* of the R. A. H.

kind of subject, both great and small, in such fashion that
it may be said that the number of them is infinite; indeed,
having so many subjects and trusting no one,[1] and insisting
that everything pass under his own hand and eye, he is so
perpetually preoccupied with this business, with so great
labor and toil, that I have heard many people say that they
would not for the world be the ruler of so many states as is
his Majesty, if it meant living the kind of life he lives."[2]
Reports, reports, and ever more reports; Philip was literally
submerged with them in his later years, and moreover he
did not stop at reading them; he annotated them, as he went
along, with comments on matters as absurdly trifling as the
spelling and style of the men who had written them — all
in that strange, sprawling hand of his, one of the most
illegible hands of an age more than usually replete with
chirographical difficulties.[3]   A story of somewhat uncertain
origin which has come down to us, in regard to the results
of a night's work of this sort, is perhaps worth quoting in

[1] Donato (1573), loc. cit., vi, p. 464:
"Il re, per detto comune, è assai sospet-
toso; e dicono i suoi proprj servitori:
De la risa al cuchillo del rey no ay dos
dedos." Cf. Morosini (1581), loc. cit.,
v, p. 324. The story of Antonio Pérez
and other episodes illustrate this
proverb of Philip's court, which is
echoed, e.g., by Cabrera de Córdoba,
i, p. 562 (of Philip's treatment of Don
Carlos), "unos le llamaban prudente,
otros severo, porque su risa y cuchillo
eran confines," and by Antonio Pérez,
Relaciones (Paris, 1598), p. 20. Bratli's
discussion (pp. 232 f.) is nugatory;
he betrays no knowledge of the passages
in Donato and Morosini and accordingly overlooks the proverbial character
of the saying. Cf. also Zane (1584),
loc. cit., v, p. 356.

[2] Morosini (1581), loc. cit., v, p. 322.
Cf. Donato (1573), loc. cit., vi, p. 464:
"Travaglia con tanta assiduità, senza
prendersi ricreazione, che non è official
alcuno nel mondo, per assiduo che sia,

il qual stia tanto nell'officio suo come
S. M. Così dicono i suoi ministri, e
pare che sia vero." See also Ranke,
Die Osmanen und die spanische Monarchie, 3d ed., p. 148: "So war er der
allerthätigste Geschäftsmann von der
Welt."

[3] Donato (1573), loc. cit., p. 464: "I
suoi segretarj gli scrivono lasciando
tanto di margine quanto è lo spazio
dove scrivono, acciocchè il re, secondo
il suo costume, possa capo per capo
rispondere quanto gli piace." Cf. also
Correspondance de Philippe II, ed.
L. P. Gachard, i, pp. xlvii–lii; G. Kurth,
"Comment Philippe II travaillait,"
in Mélanges Paul Fredericq (Brussels,
1904), pp. 289–293; Bratli, p. 207;
Baltasar Porreño, Dichos y Hechos del
Señor Rey Don Felipe Segundo (Seville,
1639). If the king desired to call
special attention to any passage, he
would usually jot down the word Ojo in
the margin.

this connection; it is primarily a proof of Philip's unlimited patience and self-control, but it also reveals his great kindness to his servants, an excellent test of a gentleman. Apparently the king had sat up unusually late, covering sheet after sheet with handwriting and annotations; when at last he had finished, he called his attendant to throw sand over the papers in order to dry the ink. The attendant, however, was so confused and appalled by the responsibility placed on his shoulders that instead of the sand box, he took up the ink pot and emptied its contents over his Majesty's labors; but Philip forbore to reproach him. "*This* is the sand, *that* is the ink," was his only comment on the damage that had been done.[1]

If we can visualize Philip niggling over these innumerable reports, we are furnished with the explanation of much else besides. He possessed a tenacious memory,[2] and was resolved to superintend everything himself; "bien es myrar á todo" is a phrase frequently found in his writings.[3] But he was curiously unable to separate the essentials from the details, or to persuade himself ever to delegate the latter to subordinates;[4] he was like the historian who has vastly more material than he can possibly hope to handle. And the obvious result was that under his rule the administration of the Spanish Empire became more notorious than ever

---

[1] This tale seems to be derived from Baltasar Porreño, "the most Iberian Parson Weems of the Prudent King," *Dichos y Hechos* (Seville, 1639), fol. 144; cf. also Prescott, iii, pp. 411 f. It is worth noting, as an evidence of the way in which stories of that kind were passed around in those days, that it appears in a brief paragraph appended, with other notes on miscellaneous subjects, to the second volume of John More's manuscript journal of the House of Commons, February–April, 1641; B. M., Harleian Ms. 476, fol. 455 (bottom).

[2] Matteo Zane (1584), *loc. cit.*, v, p. 361.

[3] "It is well to consider everything." Cf., e.g., B. M., Egerton Ms. 1834. "Non s'espedisce alcuna sorte di negozio, sia di grazia o di giustizia, grande o picciolo, che non passi per mano sua." Morosini (1581), *loc. cit.*, v, pp. 322 f.

[4] "Pare che il re si occupi in molte minuzie che levano il tempo per le cose maggiori." Donato (1573), *loc. cit.*, vi, p. 463.

for its slowness.[1] It had been bad enough under the
Emperor, but it was to be infinitely worse under his son.
So poor were the means of communication in those days, so
vast and so widely scattered were the dominions over which
Philip ruled, that the only possible method of governing
them successfully was to invest the king's local representatives with a large measure of independence. But this was
just what Philip could never bring himself to do; and he
was the more convinced that his own way was the only right
one because it tallied so closely with the precepts of his
imperial father. It was centralization carried to the breaking point, pushed so far that it paralyzed efficiency. While
Philip was deciding how the sailors on the Armada could best
be kept from swearing, Sir Francis Drake raided the Spanish
coast. His viceroys and ambassadors, who were constantly
kept waiting for orders, and for subsidies to enable them to
carry them out, frequently expressed the hope that death
would come to them by way of Spain, for thus they would
be certain to live to a ripe old age.[2] Prescott [3] prints part
of a letter addressed to Philip by Luis Manrique, the grand
almoner, telling him in vigorous terms of the discontent
of his subjects because of his manner of doing business,
"sitting forever over your papers, from your desire, as they
intimate, to seclude yourself from the world, and from a
want of confidence in your ministers. Hence such interminable delays as fill the soul of every suitor with despair. . . .
God did not send your Majesty and all the other kings, his
viceroys on earth, to waste their time in reading or writing,
nor yet in meditation and prayer." The Cortes also point-

---

[1] "Non si tien conto del tempo, che
un negotio, benchè facile, vuole gl' anni
in terminarlo." Camillo Borghese
(1594), loc. cit., p. 192. Cf. Prescott,
iii, pp. 419–421.

[2] As, for instance, Bernardino de
Mendoza at Paris in 1590; cf. C. S. P.,
Spanish, 1587–1603, p. 579. This
aphorism became a byword among
Philip's foreign representatives.

[3] Philip the Second, iii, pp. 420 f.

edly advised him to relieve himself of the details of administration and intrust them to the councils and tribunals to
which they belonged, so that business might be transacted
more speedily and his time be free for weighty affairs
of state and war.[1] And the tragedy of it all was that
these disastrous mistakes were really brought about
chiefly as a result of one of Philip's finest qualities, his
exalted idea of the duties of kingship. Certainly his
worst enemies cannot justly accuse him of being a *roi
fainéant.*

Two other outstanding virtues of Philip call for special
comment; they were both of them salient characteristics
of his great-grandmother, Isabella the Catholic, and in both
he showed notable improvement over the ways of his father.
The first was his love of justice and determination to see
it done throughout his dominions. "Justice is his favorite
interest," writes the Venetian ambassador in 1563; "and
in so far as its administration concerns him, he does his duty
well." [2] "He is by nature the justest of rulers," writes
another in 1584, "and his justice extends so far that were it
not regulated by the greatest prudence and experience in the
affairs of the world, it would pass into severity." [3] The
good old custom of the Catholic Kings — that of hearing
the pleas of their subjects on Fridays — had by this time
fallen into desuetude, and Philip made no effort to revive
it; in this matter at least — and it would seem to be the
exception that proves the rule — the king consented to
delegate to others; and it should be added that the judges
whom he selected were famed for their probity and com-

---

[1] *Actas de las Córtes*, xi, p. 501 (1588–90, pet. 1).

[2] Tiepolo, *loc. cit.*, v, pp. 62 f.

[3] Zane, *loc. cit.*, v, pp. 360 f. Cf. Agostino Nani (1598), *loc. cit.*, v, p. 488: "era religioso, giusto, parco, e pacifico.

Ma la prima qualità si convertiva in ragion di stato, la seconda in severità crudele, la terza in avarizia, la quarta in voler esser arbitro della cristianità." Cf. also Bratli, pp. 105, 223.

petence.[1] Nevertheless, Philip was by no means entirely
inaccessible, much as he loved solitude and detested the
fatigue of audiences.[2] We are assured that on the way
to and from divine service, "he accepted all the supplica-
tions that were handed to him, and that if any one desired
to speak with him, he stopped courteously to listen;" but
Philip never showed, either by expression or gesture, how he
proposed to deal with such requests;[3] they were all distributed to the officials whom they respectively concerned, to
be acted upon favorably or the reverse as the case might be;
if favorably the signature of the king was necessary before
final action could be taken.[4]

The other matter by which Philip earned the gratitude
and respect of his subjects was his gradual restoration of the
pristine simplicity of the royal court and household. It
will be remembered that in the days of Charles V there had
been constant complaints of the luxurious 'Burgundian'
fashions of the imperial establishment, and demands for a
return to the ancient customs of Castile;[5] and at the beginning of Philip's reign there was no evidence of improvement. When he got back from the Netherlands his
establishment was fully as magnificent as ever it had been
in the days of his father; it numbered no less than 1500
persons, of whom nine-tenths were Spaniards, and the rest
Flemings, Burgundians, Englishmen, Italians, and Germans; there are, moreover, countless testimonies to the
excessive liberality of his grants and pensions, especially to

[1] See, however, Morosini (1581), loc. cit., v, p. 293; Florentine "Relazione di Spagna" (1591?) in Bratli, p. 208.

[2] Cavalli (1570), loc. cit., v, p. 183; Alberto Badoero (1578) in Albèri, serie i, v, p. 275.

[3] Donato (1573) reported, in regard to Philip's facial immobility and control, that "il re è tale, che quando bene

avesse un gatto nelle brache, non si moverebbe nè dimostrerebbe alterazione alcuna." Loc. cit., vi, p. 464.

[4] Mula (1559), loc. cit., iii, p. 395; Soranzo (1565), loc. cit., v, p. 113; Tommaso Contarini (1593) in Albèri, serie i, v, p. 422; Philippson, Kardinal Granvella, p. 44.

[5] Cf. ante, Vol. III, p. 177.

Spaniards.[1] But Philip himself was by nature frugal; the lavish cost of his household at the beginning of his reign represents rather the system which he had inherited from his father than what he would have chosen for himself; and as the years went on, with his resources growing gradually smaller and smaller, with Spanish influence increasing and Burgundian growing correspondingly less, and with his own fondness for solitude becoming steadily more marked,[2] his natural frugality began to assert itself. In the middle of his reign we have numerous evidences that the expenses of the royal household diminished year by year;[3] at Madrid only barely enough pomp and circumstance were maintained to suffice for the preservation of the dignity of a king.[4] And at the end, we find Philip living and dying in a little cell in the Escorial, only twelve feet square, unadorned and austere; it has been well said that the humblest monk of San Lorenzo "had a better room and better furnished than did the king of Spain."[5] And the contrast, striking as it is with the ways of his father, is even more obvious with those of his son. The gorgeousness of the courts of Philip III and Philip IV was a prominent part of that great game of bluff behind which the internal rottenness of seventeenth-century Spain was concealed from the observation of foreigners;

[1] Federico Badoero (1557), loc. cit., iii, pp. 234, 236; Prescott, iii, pp. 417 f., and references there.

[2] Marcantonio da Mula (1559), loc. cit., iii, p. 395.

[3] A detailed account of these expenses, as they stood in the year 1577, may be found in B. M., Cotton Ms. Vesp. C. VI, fols. 37 ff. Cf. also Donato (1573), loc. cit., vi, p. 463: "Il re coll' esempio suo ha introdotto molta modestia nella corte." Something may perhaps be ascribed to the influence of the king's confessor, the bishop of Cuenca. Brantôme, Oeuvres, ii (Paris, 1866), p. 90, speaks of Philip's sparingness as

compared to his father's profusion: "espargne fort pour employer tout à la guerre et au maintien de sa grandeur et estat, fors le superbe bastiment de l'Escurial."

[4] Donato (1573), loc. cit., vi; pp. 384 f.

[5] Jerónimo Montes, "El Carácter de Felipe II," in Ciudad de Dios, xlvii (1898), pp. 73 f. Philip also desired to maintain a certain standard of morality in his court. B. M., Add. Ms. 28,361, fols. 150–173 (cf. Gayangos, iii, pp. 84, 86 f.), shows that he was much disturbed by the prevalence of unnatural vice at the royal court in the spring of 1588. Cf. C. de C., iii, pp. 205 f.

but the Prudent King's mode of living at the end of his days was an accurate mirror of existing national conditions. There can be no doubt that his subjects respected and admired him for it. If he had impoverished them, he had not done it for his own advantage.

Yet it would be a grave error to think of Philip as being naturally dead to all the pleasanter sides of life, and an even graver one to conceive of him as deficient in affection or incapable of friendship. The joylessness of his early years, to which we have already alluded, was but the inevitable consequence of the way in which he had been brought up; that he so loved to be alone during his later life was chiefly the result of circumstances and of a long series of family bereavements. Though he detested physical exercise of every sort, he got recreation in other ways. To the end of his life he took much pleasure in the jokes of professional buffoons — a peculiarly Spanish trait; [1] we also get a glimpse of him playing piquet after dinner.[2] Still more notable were his knowledge and enthusiasm for art. He loved music and could play the guitar; [3] he was a patron of artists and a real connoisseur of painting and tapestry, sculpture, and architecture; [4] we shall return to this phase of his activities in more detail in connection with the building of the Escorial. And there can be no doubt that in his earlier years he had various mistresses. The Venetian ambassadors and others frequently advert to his incontinence,[5] but save for his liai-

---

[1] Federico Badoero (1557), *loc. cit.*, iii, p. 237; Zane (1584), *loc. cit.*, v, p. 361; Bratli, pp. 116, 197 f.

[2] "Relazione di Spagna" (1591?) in Bratli, p. 204.

[3] Luis Villalba, "Felipe II, Tañedor de Vihuela," in *Ciudad de Dios*, xciv (1913), pp. 442–457.

[4] José Fernández Montaña, *Felipe II en relación con Artes y Artistas, con Ciencias y Sabios* (Madrid, 1912); Juan

Mateos, "Felipe II y la Cultura Española," in *Ciudad de Dios*, xlvii (1898), pp. 86–137.

[5] Federico Badoero (1557), *loc. cit.*, iii, p. 234; Tiepolo (1563), *loc. cit.*, v, p. 63; Soranzo (1565), *loc. cit.*, v, pp. 114 f.; Pascual de Gayangos in the preface to his edition of Andrés Muñoz, *Viaje de Felipe Segundo á Inglaterra* (Madrid, 1877), p. xxviii; Forneron, i, p. 9.

son with the Princess of Eboli, about which there are so many divergent opinions,[1] his amours do not seem to have had the slightest influence on his policy or methods of government; *si non caste, saltem caute.*[2] But it was not, after all, in the company of his mistresses that Philip found his principal relaxation from the cares of state; indeed his ill health gives good reason for believing that he was rather less than more amorous than the average man.[3] It was in the bosom of his own family that the king hoped to find the affection and companionship for which he hungered, and it was perhaps the deepest tragedy of his whole life that that hope, save for a few brief intervals, was destined to be disappointed.

His mother had died when he was but twelve years old; his first wife, Maria of Portugal, when he was eighteen, in bearing him the Infante Don Carlos. He wedded Mary Tudor at twenty-seven, but of the four years and four months during which he was married to her he passed less than one-third in England with the queen; the union had been dictated solely by political expediency; no child was born of it, and it was profoundly distasteful to Philip. Until the time of his return to Spain in 1559 he had scarcely tasted of the joys of a happy family life. Thereafter followed the brightest period of his whole existence. His third spouse, Elizabeth of Valois, reached Spain in the following January; her advent was the occasion of festivals and rejoicing, for it was regarded as the sign and seal of permanent reconciliation with France, and the new queen was popularly known as the *Reina de la paz.*[4] Soon after her arrival she was stricken with small pox; it was a light case,

---

[1] See below, Chapter XXXV.
[2] Forneron, i, p. 10; Bratli, pp. 114 f.

[3] Florentine "Relazione di Spagna" (1591?) in Bratli, p. 212.
[4] Forneron, i, pp. 220 f., and references there; Bratli, pp. 115 f.

and she soon recovered, but it is interesting to read of the
worries of her mother Catharine de' Medici, lest the disease
should so disfigure her that she would lose her influence on
her husband and imperil the safety of the Franco-Spanish understanding.[1] Much depended indeed on whether or not the
new queen should bear a child, and that question was not
answered in the affirmative till six years after her arrival.
On August 12, 1566, she was delivered of a daughter; the
birth of the child was believed by the queen to have been due
to the beneficent influence of the Spanish Saint Eugenius,
whose remains the king, after interminable correspondence,
had recently succeeded in having transferred to Toledo
from their former resting place at St. Denis,[2] and the
Infanta was accordingly named Isabella Clara Eugenia.
This daughter and her younger sister Catharine, born
October 9, 1567, were the joy of their father's heart; and his
affection for them increased with the death, on October 3,
1568, of their mother, who was mourned by the Spaniards
as "the best queen that they had ever had or could have."[3]
That year, 1568, which also witnessed the death of Don
Carlos, was unquestionably one of the saddest in Philip's
whole life. But the necessity for a male heir took the precedence over everything else; in November, 1570,[4] Philip
married his fourth and last wife, Anne of Austria, the daughter of his cousin, the Emperor Maximilian II. She bore
him four sons and one daughter, and died October 25, 1580,
but of her children only one, who was to succeed his father
as Philip III, lived to be more than eight years old. The

[1] Forneron, i, pp. 222–224, and
references there.

[2] On this curious affair, which occupies
a large place in the correspondence
between the French and Spanish courts
between 1563 and 1566, cf. Forneron, i, pp. 334–336, and references
there.

[3] Fourquevaux, Dépêches, ed. Douais,
iii, p. 107 (October 3, 1568); Marquis
Du Prat, Élisabeth de Valois (Paris,
1859), p. 365.

[4] Forneron, ii, p. 400, note 7.

Escorial was scarcely finished before it was filled with coffins. Philip had laid no less than seventeen members of his own family to rest there before he had completed his sixtieth year.[1]

This terrible series of family bereavements is an element too often forgotten by those who have attempted to portray the life and character of Philip II. One chief reason why it has been so much neglected is doubtless the king's own extraordinary self-control. It was one of his fundamental principles that a sovereign should never, under any circumstances, exhibit his inmost feelings. "He is an adept at concealing his affections," writes Morosini in 1581.[2] "No display of sorrow," was his order at the time of the death of the Infante Don Ferdinand, in October, 1578; "nothing but processions and public prayer, returning thanks to God and humbly supplicating that he mitigate his wrath."[3] Certainly it would be unfair to judge Philip by externals. But there has fortunately been preserved to us one glimpse of the man, as he really was in the bosom of his own family, one rift in the clouds of his impenetrable reserve; and that is a series of letters exchanged between him and his daughters Isabella and Catharine when he was absent on the campaign for the annexation of Portugal. These letters were discovered by Gachard in the archives of Turin, and published by him at Paris in 1884;[4] they prove, beyond the possibility of doubt, that whatever the crimes and barbarities of which Philip may have been guilty in his capacity of Spanish monarch, he was a most loving and tender father, who longed, in his self-imposed isolation, for the sympathy and love which only a family can afford. Their contents

---

[1] *D. I. E.*, vii, p. 410.
[2] *Loc. cit.*, v, p. 324.
[3] Herrera, *Historia General del Mundo*, ii ,p. 109.

[4] *Lettres de Philippe II à ses filles les Infantes Isabelle et Catherine écrites pendant son voyage en Portugal (1581–1583)*.

are well known and need not be repeated here : the evidences
of his solicitude for his daughters' spiritual and physical
welfare, his interest in the most intimate details of their
daily life, his desire to know if they had begun to make use
of the new Gregorian calendar, which went into effect during
the period of the correspondence, his descriptions of the
storms, the birds, the flowers, and of the local customs of
his new kingdom, of everything, in fact, that would interest and amuse them.   These letters also afford additional
evidence of the king's friendly relations with his servants;
his kindly tolerance of the cranky eccentricities of Mada-
lena, the old nurse of the Infantas, forms the most amazing
contrast to the cold, stern lord of the Spanish Empire, as
portrayed by his official visitors.   And yet it was the real
man that these letters reveal — the man whom Philip was
irrevocably determined that the outer world should never
know.[1]

It is not impossible that this contrast between the real
and the official Philip, coupled with his firm resolve that
the feelings of the former should never interfere with the
duties of the latter, may point the way to the most reasonable solution of the mysteries that still surround the life and
death of the son of his first marriage, the Infante Don Carlos, born July 8, 1545.   For over three centuries and a half
it has been a favorite theme of historians, novelists, and play-
wrights.   All sorts of different theories have been offered in
the explanation of it, but none of them has as yet been
accorded any general acceptance.[2]   The legend which forms

[1] Cf. H. C. Lea, "Ethical Values
in History," in *American Historical
Review*, ix (1904), pp. 233–246, particularly pp. 242 f.; and John Mase-
field, *Philip the King* (London, 1914).
[2] The works of the most important
writers on the subject have been carefully analyzed on pp. 1–12 of Felix
Rachfahl's *Don Carlos, Kritische Unter-
suchungen* (Freiburg i. B., 1921), and
it does not seem worth while to enumerate them here.   But it is only fair to
point out that modern research, which
down to 1914 had on the whole shown
a trend increasingly favorable to Philip,
has recently, owing to the contributions

the basis of Schiller's famous tragedy, namely, that the Infante was sacrificed because of his love for his step-mother, Elizabeth of Valois, is devoid of any solid historical foundation;[1] the tales that the sources of the trouble were his fondness for the Protestants, intrigues in the Netherlands, or deep-laid conspiracies against the royal authority in Spain, seem also, on the whole, to be unworthy of credence. On the other hand it would appear reasonably certain, despite the arguments of a recent authority to the contrary,[2] that Don Carlos, from his earliest years, showed himself physically and mentally quite unfit for the vast responsibilities that would devolve upon him should he ever be permitted to succeed his father as the ruler of the Spanish Empire. His excesses in eating and in drinking, his passion for swallowing things and making others swallow them, his whimsical cruelties all tell the same tale; his picture by Sánchez Coello confirms it, as do the reports of the different ambassadors at the court of Madrid.[3] These bad symptoms, sufficiently alarming during his boyhood, became rapidly worse when, at the age of sixteen, he "fell down a pair of stairs, broke his head and had two fits of an ague."[4] It seems probable that his life was only saved on this occasion through the efforts of the learned Vesalius, who performed the operation of trepanning;[5] and the measure of

of Anton Ohroust, in the *Mitteilungen* of the Institut für österreichische Geschichtsforschung, xxxv (1914), pp. 484–494, and of Viktor Bibl, *Der Tod des Don Carlos* (Vienna, 1918), taken a turn in the other direction. Rachfahl's monograph is essentially a critique and correction of that of Bibl; it adduces no fresh evidence.

[1] See the careful study by F. W. C. Lieder, "The Don Carlos Theme," in *Harvard Studies and Notes in Philology and Literature*, xii (1930), pp. 1–73.

[2] Bibl, *op. cit.*

[3] Tiepolo (1567), *loc. cit.*, v, pp. 148 f.;

Forneron, ii, pp. 108–116, and references there. The possibility that Don Carlos was sexually impotent is not to be excluded.

[4] Further details of this accident may be found in a letter of Sir Thomas Chaloner to Queen Elizabeth, written from Madrid on May 11: cf. *C. S. P.*, *Foreign*, 1562, no. 46, especially paragraphs 3, 8, 9.

[5] *C. S. P.*, *Foreign*, 1562, nos. 46, 171, and Joaquín Olmedilla y Puig, *Andrés Vesalio* (Madrid, 1913), pp. 9–15.

Philip's superstition and ignorance is revealed by the fact that he insisted on attributing his son's survival to the miraculous healing powers of the corpse of the cook of a Franciscan convent, long since dead, which was placed in bed beside the fever-stricken body of the Infante.[1] In any case the evidences that Don Carlos would make an absolutely unendurable sovereign multiplied apace after his recovery from this accident. When his father, in the hope that the possession of authority might rouse him to some sense of his duties and responsibilities, tried the experiment of placing him in the Council of State, the Infante upset everything. He insulted and even assaulted his fellow councillors as no sane man would have done, and seemed to take a malicious pleasure in revealing the most important state secrets with which he had been intrusted. Irritated by the strictness of the surveillance to which he was subjected, he laid plans to flee to Italy or Germany and make trouble for his father abroad.[2] Whether he had thoughts of murdering Philip seems much more doubtful.[3] The difficulty, in this case, is not the lack of evidence, for there is an abundance of it, but rather to know how much to believe.

How to deal with the situation was a truly terrible problem — one of the most agonizing with which a royal father has ever been confronted ; but early in the year 1568, Philip came to a decision. He was convinced that a strong monarchy was essential to the welfare of Spain. The experience of his predecessors had inspired him with a deep dread of

---

[1] Forneron, ii, p. 107. Two contemporary accounts of the case, by official doctors of the crown, have come down to us; they are to be found in D. I. E., xv, pp. 553–574, and xviii, pp. 537–563. It is perhaps needless to add that neither of them shows any confidence either in the methods of Vesalius, or in the efficacy of the corpse.

[2] Fourquevaux, Dépêches, ed. Douais, i, p. 321; Forneron, ii, p. 119; Rachfahl, op. cit., pp. 94–96.

[3] We possess, it is true, contemporary documents to show that he did; but whether they can safely be given credence is another question. Rachfahl, p. 109.

the grandees, who had always seized the government when the kingship was weak; only a century before, under Henry the Impotent, there had been a striking demonstration of it, and Philip knew his Spanish history. Don Carlos promised to be far worse than Henry the Impotent had ever been; was it not obvious, then, that Philip's duty to the state, of which he had the very highest conception, demanded that he should spare his realms from the perils of the rule of a madman? To imagine that he could answer this question in the affirmative without a pang is to ignore the evidence we have already adduced to prove that Philip had an intense family feeling and a deep affection for his own offspring; moreover there were some risks in setting the Infante aside, for the king, in that moment, had no other son. It must have been a heart-rending decision to make, but finally, on the night of January 18, 1568, Philip summoned to his palace at Madrid Ruy Gómez, Luis de Quijada, and the Prior Antonio, and, "speaking as no man had ever spoken before," apprised them of the resolution he had taken. Then, with his helmet on his head and his sword in his hand, he led the way silently along the dark corridors of the palace to the apartments of the Infante. Everything had been carefully arranged beforehand. The bolts had been removed, and the door was opened without the least difficulty; before Don Carlos had waked up, the loaded pistols which he always kept by his bedside were taken away. The brief agonized queries of the Infante as to the meaning of it all were answered coldly and noncommittally by the king. The doors and windows were swiftly nailed up, Philip superintending the whole process with the utmost care. When all was finished he committed his son to the guard of the Duke of Feria, commanded that no one should be permitted to speak to him or bring him letters, and went

out without speaking a word to the Infante.[1]   He was never
to see him again.

Six months later, on July 24, the world learned that Don
Carlos was no longer living, and stories were circulated for
more than a century afterwards to the effect that the king
had given orders that in one way or another he should be
put to death.[2] Some maintained that he was beheaded,
and two of the various post-mortem examinations of the
body (the last in 1812) [3] appear to support this conclusion;
but the evidences to the contrary are stronger and more
reliable. The reports that he was strangled by slaves or
suffocated in bed are totally lacking in solid historical
foundation; while the tale that he was poisoned rests principally on the testimony of Antonio Pérez, who, at the time
that he wrote his account, was bent on vilifying the name
of Philip II. No one of the countless stories of the Infante's
being made away with at the royal command can be definitely substantiated; that being the case, the king should be
given the benefit of the doubt, if any continues to exist.[4]
Perhaps the best of all reasons for believing Philip to be
innocent of the crime with which, before the days of critical
historical scholarship, he was so often charged, is that it was
unnecessary to the attainment of his ends; for he must have
foreseen that Don Carlos's physical excesses in solitary
confinement would be ultimately certain to cause his death.
Philip's object was to remove his son from the possibility of
any active participation in the life of the world, and he
effected that end by imprisoning him. That the Infante's
death, six months after his arrest, relieved the king from a
most painful and embarrassing predicament is indubitable,

---

[1] Such is the story in the contemporary letters and relations. On its
validity, cf. Rachfahl, *op. cit.*, p. 108.
[2] Rachfahl, pp. 157–160.
[3] Chroust, *loc. cit.*, p. 490.

[4] Cf. Ballesteros, *Historia de España*,
iv, 1, p. 126: "Hoy nadie acusa seria-
mente a Felipe II de haber ordenado la
muerte de su hijo."

but there is no adequate ground for believing that Philip was guilty of accelerating it.[1]

The most recent authority on this tragic affair [2] regards it simply as "a matter between father and son." He rejects the hypotheses of treasonable or heretical conspiracies on the part of the Infante, but fully admits his unfitness to rule; on the other hand he is very harsh in his verdict on the king. Philip's refusal to visit his son during his imprisonment seems to him utterly heartless. He cannot understand why the king failed to reward the improvement in Don Carlos's disposition toward him, which apparently took place after the Infante had been permitted to receive the communion at Eastertide, with any relaxation of the rigor of his confinement; he even blames Philip for his unwillingness to take part in the prince's funeral, which the king watched, with his accustomed calmness, from a window in the palace.[3] But these strictures seem to reveal a very imperfect comprehension of the true character of Philip II. If the king was notoriously slow in making up his mind, he was equally firm in adhering to a course of action, once he had embarked upon it; to reverse the line of conduct which it had cost him such sorrow to adopt was unthinkable. Moreover, is not Philip's refusal to visit his son in his prison

[1] The official story of the Infante's death, as furnished by Philip to his *corregidores*, may be found in B. M., Add. Ms. 8219, fol. 216; his letter to the Pope of July 28, 1568 (Archivo de la Chancillería de Valladolid, Reales Cédulas y Pragmáticas, legajo 3), contains many of the same phrases. Cf. also R. A. H., Mss., est. 21, gr. 3ª, no. 36, and B. M., Add. Ms. 8219, fol. 215 b. B. M., Ms. Sloane 2802, which is a "Breue Compendio . . . de la vida . . . de Phelipe Segundo . . . compuesto in frances por Pierres de Prette, coronista del Rey de Francia, y traduzido en español," contains (fol. 18) the following significant sentence: "El Rey de España quisso mas perder la Prenda mas cara que tenia en esta vida que ver alborotado sus estados, cossa nunca oyda que un Principe preferia la Republica á la vida de un hijo de tanta edad y unico." I have not been able to identify Pierres de Prette.

[2] Rachfahl, *op. cit.*

[3] It is perhaps worth noting, in this connection, that the king also witnessed the baptism (August 25, 1566) of his daughter Isabella Clara Eugenia from a secret window. Don Carlos acted as godfather on this occasion. Cf. *Lettres de Philippe II à ses filles*, ed. Gachard, p. 21.

and to participate in his funeral quite as explainable on the hypothesis that he could not stand the strain upon his own affections as on that of heartless cruelty? We have seen that it was a cardinal principle of the Prudent King never to reveal his inmost feelings. How can we be sure that his heart was not filled with mortal anguish all the time — an anguish which he dreaded every moment to find himself unable to control?

The parallel between Philip II of Spain and his great-grandson, Louis XIV of France, has been often drawn by historians. It was first attempted over two centuries ago by the French Protestant, Jean Jacques Quesnot de la Chesnée,[1] who held strong views on the dangers of universal monarchy. He shows how the liberties of Europe had been threatened, first by the house of Austria, "which attained its preponderance through the two most unstable things in the world, namely, women and the sea,"[2] and then by the Bourbons under the *Roi Soleil*; he points out that "whenever a Holofernes has threatened to seize the sovereignty of the world," a "Judith has been supplied by England,"[3] in the persons of Queen Elizabeth and Queen Anne, to curb his insatiable ambitions. He compares the political and economic results of the expulsion of the Moriscos with those of the revocation of the Edict of Nantes;[4] he is convinced that both Philip and Louis were led astray by evil

---

[1] This book, of which, as far as I know, there is no copy in the United States, was published at Cologne in 1709; its full title is "Le Parallèle de Philippe II. et de Louis XIV.," and the author describes himself as "I. I. Q."; apparently he did not care to have his full name known. He had fled from France on the Revocation of the Edict of Nantes, and established a lace factory in Berlin, but subsequently moved on to Denmark. Returning to France in 1688 to claim an inheritance, he was cast into prison, but after a few months he was released, at the urgent request of the Danish ambassador, and went back to his adopted country. Cf. E. and E. Haag, *La France Protestante*, viii (1858), pp. 339 f.

[2] P. 11.

[3] P. 13.

[4] Pp. 129 f.

counsellors, and envies the kings of China, "who have ministers of incorruptible probity." He stoutly maintains that
"all men are by nature equal," that "Princes derive their
authority from the consent of those they govern," and that
"those who do not regard their subjects as their sovereigns
are no better than tyrants." He violently assails the theories
of absolutism and of monarchy by right divine, on which the
governments of the Prudent King and of his great-grandson
were both built up.[1] But there are other points of resemblance than these. Quesnot was primarily a political theorist
of Anglophile ideas, and he used the similarities between
Philip and Louis in order to point a moral. Had he been
an historian, desirous of describing what actually existed,
he would have found that there was even more to his
'Parallèle' than he had thought. Both monarchs had the
same high conception of their kingly duties and prerogatives, both the same haughtiness and reserve, both the same
willingness to work constantly and hard for what they conceived to be the welfare of their subjects and the glory of
their kingdoms. Both were unwilling to give full confidence
to any of their ministers; both were methodical rather than
brilliant in their conduct of affairs; there is the same dead-
weight impression about both of their reigns. Both of them,
finally, built themselves residences in the country, not far
from their respective capitals. But the nature of these residences, and the motives that led to their erection, were
widely divergent. Louis hated Paris, which had been full
of disagreeable associations for him since the days of the
Fronde in the period of his minority; he therefore constructed for himself, at enormous expense, a luxurious
palace in the forest of Versailles, and permanently transferred thither both his court and his government on May 6,

[1] Pp. 233–235.

1682; there they were to remain till the time of the French Revolution. Philip, on the contrary, was fond of Madrid; in fact he made it, for the first time, the capital of Spain, and formally established his court there in the spring of 1561;[1] but his desire to find repose from his regular duties, his love for clerics and fondness for religious contemplation, combined with certain special episodes of his own early career to bring into existence on the spurs of the Guadarramas a dwelling which bears no resemblance whatever to the palace at Versailles, the famous monument known as the Escorial.[2]

The word 'monument' has been purposely used to characterize it, because it emphasizes the fact, which is too often forgotten, that the Escorial was in a large measure designed as a mausoleum for the remains of Charles V, who had directed in his will that his bones should remain at Yuste until his son should have provided them with a permanent resting place. The story, often denied and as often reasserted, that the building owes its origin to a vow made by

[1] Cf. José Amador de los Rios and Juan de Dios de la Rada y Delgado, *Historia de la Villa y Corte de Madrid* (Madrid, 1861–64, 4 vols.), ii, p. 450, and Ramón de Mesonero Romanos, *El Antiguo Madrid* (Madrid, 1861), pp. xxiv ff. The latter describes the chief reason for the move as "la política . . . de crear una capital nueva, única, y general á todo el reino, agena á las tradiciones, simpatías, ó antipatías históricas de las anteriores, y que pudiera ser igualmente aceptable á castellanos y aragoneses, andaluces y gallegos, catalanes y vascongados, estremeños y valencianos." Amador de los Rios, ii, p. 450, n. 4, cites, without specific page reference, "el analista Leon Pinelo con referencia al mismo año 1561" as follows: "El Rey don Phelipe Segundo, haviendo elexido esta Villa [de Madrid] para la residenzia de su corte, la trujó á ella desde Toledo

este año: del dia en que entró el sello Real, que es la insignia formal de la corte, no consta; sólo se halla que á 22 de Febrero estava en Consejo en Toledo, y que á 19 de Julio despachava en Madrid . . . aunque don Francisco de Herrera Maldonado pone esta entrada de la corte el año de 60, y el licenciado Gerónimo de Quintana, no sé con qué fundamento, el año de 63."

[2] José de Sigüenza, *Historia del Monasterio del Escorial* (Madrid, 1881); *D. I. E.*, xxviii, pp. 564–567; "Memorias de Fray Juan de San Gerónimo" in *D. I. E.*, vii, pp. 5–442; Prescott, iii, pp. 448–470. The name is most probably derived from the *scoriae*, or dross, of the neighboring iron mines; another view traces it to *Aesculetum*, a place of scrub oaks, these being, according to the guide book, "the weed of the locality."

Philip at the battle of St. Quentin, does not seem likely to be true, at least in the form in which it is usually told, for the reason that Philip was not present at the fray : [1] we may, however, well believe that the fact that that great victory had been won on St. Lawrence's day, together with the tradition that the saint was born in Spain, was of decisive influence in determining the form which the structure permanently took. Finally, there can be little doubt that the retirement of the Emperor, after his abdication, to Yuste, strengthened Philip in his natural inclination to build himself a residence in combination with a monastery and church. Whichever of these various motives is to be regarded as dominant, we can be pretty certain that when Philip came back to Spain in 1559 the plan of the building had already taken shape in his mind. Soon after the royal capital had been established at Madrid, a site was selected some twenty miles to the northwest. The first stone of the great edifice, styled by the Spaniards the 'eighth wonder of the world,' was laid on April 22, 1563,[2] the last on September 13, 1584.[3]

To describe the Escorial is wellnigh impossible : if it is to be understood or appreciated it must be seen. Yet it is essential to try to give some idea of it, for it sums up the Spanish Empire in the period of Philip II more perfectly than any book can possibly hope to do. Its plan is that of a gridiron, in commemoration of the instrument on which St. Lawrence was tortured to death ; the church, the courtyard, and the cells of the monks form the lines of the bars ; the royal apartments, the handle. The main rectangle is

---

[1] Cf. *ante*, p. 11. Louis Bertrand, however, *in Revue des deux mondes*, septième période, xlviii (1928), pp. 528 f., accepts the tale.

[2] *D. I. E.*, vii, pp. 7–23 ; Prescott, iii, pp. 449–453. The volume of manuscripts in the British Museum designated as Add. Ms. 28,355 (cf. Gayangos, iii, pp. 24–32) deals almost exclusively with the founding of the Escorial.

[3] *D. I. E.*, vii, p. 393.

of gigantic proportions, 675 feet long by 530 feet wide, and it took twenty-one years to complete it;[1] its style, though unique, is distinctly reminiscent of that of the Italian school of the second half of the sixteenth century, as illustrated by the Gesù at Rome and the Granvelle palace at Besançon.[2] Its material was the gray stone obtained from the quarries near by;[3] perhaps the most remarkable feature of it, as one views it from a distance, is the way in which it fits into the surrounding landscape, the sombre colors of the lonely hills, the wild inhospitality of the frowning crags. Philip superintended the planning of it with that meticulous care for which his name has become a byword, and his ideas were faithfully carried out by its principal designer, Juan Bautista Castillo de Toledo, and also by his successor, Juan de Herrera, who completed the work. The king constantly visited it while it was in the process of construction, and urged on the workmen with an energy such as he seldom displayed in anything else.[4] He shared with the ascetic Hieronymite monks whom he had determined to establish there the rude habitation in which they were temporarily installed; he watched the rising of the great walls for hours on end from the *Silla del Rey*, a rocky nook on one of the mountain spurs a mile and a half distant from the edifice itself. The whole scene is an epitome of the sterner and lonelier aspects of his character. Philip can be studied in that landscape perhaps even better than in the books and manuscripts of the great monastic library.

But if the prevailing impression of the Escorial as seen from without is one of sombre simplicity and gloom, the gorgeous-

[1] Apparently, however, the burial vault was not finished till the reign of Philip IV; cf. Baedeker, *Spain and Portugal*, 4th ed. (Leipsic, 1913), pp. 108 f.

[2] Cf. Arthur Byne and Mildred Stapley, *Spanish Architecture of the Six-teenth Century*, pp. 409–427.

[3] The name of the stone is *berroqueña*; it resembles granite, but is not quite so hard.

[4] Bertrand, *loc. cit.*, p. 547; *con toda furia* was the phrase used by the annalists of the convent.

ness of its interior furnishes a most notable contrast. There is no trace of this, indeed, in the royal apartments, which accurately reflect the asceticism of their inmate; but the church, the galleries, the library, and its collections remain as a permanent memorial to Philip as a patron of art. The king wished the Escorial to contain samples of the best products of all his dominions. Jasper was fetched from Burgo de Osma, and marble from the quarries of the Sierra Nevada. The iron work was principally contributed by Toledo, which had been renowned, since the days of the Goths, for its preëminence in that art. Milan furnished fine specimens of its workmanship in silver, gold, and precious stones, the Low Countries their most exquisite tapestries; and the colonies in the New World sent their curiously tinted woods.[1] Philip's determination to get the best paintings is more notable still. Like his father before him, he was a great patron of Titian and Tintoretto, who are both splendidly represented in Madrid, though much less adequately at the Escorial; another of his early favorites was the Fleming Antonio Mor, who first came to Spain in 1552 and enjoyed Philip's special good will for a number of years, only to lose it in a trice by committing the unpardonable error of presuming too far on the royal good-nature. The Cretan Domínico Teotocópuli, better known as El Greco, crossed over to Spain in the middle seventies; though the altar piece which he was commanded to paint for the Escorial failed to please, he lived on at Toledo till his death in 1614, doing work whose true greatness has only been appreciated in very recent years.[2] More satisfactory to the royal taste was the Italian Federigo Zuccaro, who was summoned to Spain about 1585 for the special purpose of

---

[1] Lafuente, xiv, pp. 426 f.
[2] The recent literature on El Greco is enormous. See, e.g., A. L. Mayer, *Dominico Theotocopuli El Greco* (Munich, 1926).

decorating the Escorial, and who brought the two Carducci brothers with him when he came. But this long list of foreigners must not lead one to suppose that Philip had no faith in Spanish talent; quite the contrary, he was firmly convinced that in painting, as in everything else, it was the destiny of his native land to emerge supreme, and his faith was gloriously rewarded in the age of his grandson. In his own day he showed special favor, particularly when it came to the painting of portraits, to the Spanish-born Portuguese Alonso Sánchez Coello (1531–90) and to his pupil, Juan Pantoja de la Cruz (1551–1609). These two, and, in the early years, Antonio Mor, painted pictures of almost every member of the royal family, as well as of the prominent courtiers, secretaries, and generals of the day. It is worth noting that Sánchez Coello got only fifteen ducats apiece for his portraits executed from life, and twelve for copies; for determined though he was that nothing should be lacking for the decoration of the Escorial, Philip was constantly anxious to save expense. Raphael's famous 'Lo Spasimo di Sicilia' was obtained without cost to the king by a really scandalous piece of corruption; and Arias Montano, his representative in the Netherlands, drove the hardest of bargains in the purchase of books and of manuscripts.[1]

No part of the Escorial was more precious to the king than its library. His fondness for reading was one of his most prominent characteristics; he was also a real connoisseur of rare books and precious manuscripts. He gave constant employment to Fray Andrés de León, one of the greatest masters of the art of illumination then living; he

[1] On all this see Juan Mateos, "Felipe II y la Cultura Española en el Siglo XVI," in *Ciudad de Dios*, xlvii (1898), pp. 86–137; *D. I. E.*, xli, p. 137; lv, pp. 344–355, 450–457; Forneron, ii, pp. 134–139; and especially Julián Zarco Cuevas, *Pintores Españoles en San Lorenzo el Real de el Escorial* (Madrid, 1931), and *Pintores Italianos en . . . el Escorial* (Madrid, 1932), publications of the Instituto de Valencia de Don Juan.

spared no pains to furnish the monks of the Escorial with the most magnificent copies of the liturgy and the Scriptures.[1] Into the library itself there poured a steadily increasing stream of volumes and codices, both ancient and modern, in manuscript and type, some donated from the royal collections, but most of them acquired through the Argus-eyed agents whom Philip employed all over Europe.[2] The treasures in the Greek and Oriental languages were probably the most precious of all; indeed a complete history of the library of the Escorial would be practically that of the renaissance of classical literature in Spain.[3] The richness of the decorations rivalled that of the content of the collections, and is described in glowing terms by the first librarian, José de Sigüenza;[4] and the books, which are placed on the shelves with the backs inward, and the titles stamped on the edges of the pages, furnish the walls of the rooms in which they are stored with a mellow background of old gold.

But it was not merely books and manuscripts that Philip was determined to gather in. He was also resolved that the Escorial should be a great repository of precious relics and bones of the saints. His zeal for amassing these was well known all over Europe; one of the surest ways to win his favor was to send a gift to his collections. In them were to be found the remains of St. Justus and of St. Pastor, an arm of St. Lawrence for whom the monastery was named, "a head of St. Undelina who was queen of Sicily and suffered martyrdom together with the 11,000 virgins, and another head of one of the 11,000 virgins, and another head of one of the companions of St. Maurice the martyr, and

[1] José de Sigüenza, *Historia del Escorial* (1881), pp. 403–406.

[2] *Ibid.*, pp. 399–408.

[3] J. Mateos in *Ciudad de Dios*, xlvii, pp. 109–111; Charles Graux, *Essai sur les origines des fonds grecs de l'Escurial* (Paris, 1880); also B. M., Add. Ms. 28,-355, fols. 271–273 (cf. Gayangos, iii, p. 29).

[4] Sigüenza, pp. 388–399.

another head of one of the companions of St. Gereon the martyr, and a bone of the same St. Gereon, and another bone of one of the Holy Maccabees; and two bones together of the blessed apostles St. Philip and St. James, and another bone of the blessed apostle St. Bartholomew." [1] Such an assemblage of pious relics "out of those good old centuries when there was so much faith and so little money" [2] not unnaturally produced the most gratifying results in the shape of miracles, and miraculous visions by the Hieronymite monks. 'At four o'clock in the morning of the day after the delivery of the remains of St. Justus and St. Pastor, the prior was awakened by two young people who urged him to say mass. He made haste to obey and to run to the altar, for the holy friar fully understood that those two young people were indeed St. Justus and St. Pastor.' [3]

This brief description will at least have served to make it clear that Versailles and the Escorial are quite as incomparable as are the motives of the two monarchs that led to their construction. Versailles symbolizes the splendor of the age of Louis XIV; it became the centre of French society and the seat of the French government. The Escorial was a place of retirement for Philip II. He brought his court there, it is true, for a brief period during the summer, and is said to have been able to accomplish four times as much work there as in Madrid; but it never became the capital of Spain. The real reason why the Spanish monarch was so deeply attached to it was that it gave him a chance to live in the atmosphere of a monastery and contemplate the glory of

---

[1] *D. I. E.*, vii, pp. 54–59; also Richard Twiss, *Travels through Portugal and Spain in 1772 and 1773* (London, 1775), pp. 104–108.

[2] Sigüenza, *op. cit.*, p. 197.

[3] *D. I. E.*, vii, p. 54. Cf. also B. M., Add. Ms. 28,355, fols. 304–326 (Gayangos, iii, p. 30); C. de C., ii, p. 214; iii, p. 199.

God.[1] In order to complete the picture of Philip which we have drawn, it remains to say something of the nature of his religious life.

Castilian tradition for eight centuries past furnished the background for it. Philip was a typical product of a country whose national existence and imperial expansion had been inseparably bound up with the advance of the Christian faith, whose greatest victories had been won hand in hand with the church. No sooner had Spain driven the infidel from her dominions than she began to carry the Cross to the inhabitants of the New World, and to make herself the bulwark of Roman Catholicism against the forces of the Reformation. The natural consequence of this historical development was that she had come to regard her welfare as necessarily identical with that of the ancient faith and even with that of Almighty God; and this conviction was personified in Philip the Prudent. But that was by no means all. The conditions which obtained, both within the peninsula and without it, at the time of the king's return there in 1559, were such as must intensify all his inherited zeal for the Roman Catholic cause. As Charles V got his opportunity in the Hapsburg-Valois wars, so Philip was given his by the era of the Counter-Reformation.

The blows that had been struck during the previous forty years by the Protestants in their different branches against the authority and supremacy of the Roman church had been sufficient to convince its leaders that they constituted the most serious threat that it had ever been called upon to face. On all hands there went up a cry, spontaneous and enthusiastic, for the revival of the morals, discipline, and zeal of the Catholic clergy and laity. The movement it

[1] Cf. Bertrand in *Revue des deux mondes, loc. cit.*, p. 545. On the routine of Philip's everyday life at the Escorial, see Forneron, iii, p. 264, and references there.

elicited gathered headway with miraculous speed; it was led by devoted priests and bishops, theologians and scholars, saints and mystics, who, though widely scattered over the face of Western Europe, were united by the inspiration of service in a common cause. Spain contributed more than her share to this galaxy of splendid figures. We have no space to enumerate them all, but must restrict ourselves instead to a few words about the greatest of them, the noble Santa Teresa of Avila.

She was forty-seven years of age when first it was revealed to her that her mission in life was to effect a permanent reform of the life of the Spanish clergy. It was indeed a stupendous task. The position of the clerical estate had become so unassailable, and its authority so unquestioned, that its members had come to neglect their spiritual functions; many of them were notoriously corrupt, and the multitude of the hangers-on who participated in their privileges and immunities was a public scandal. But Teresa was nothing daunted; in the year 1562 she founded the order of the barefoot Carmelites in the convent of San José, to serve as a model of her conception of what monastic life should be. The rigor of the discipline to which she subjected her followers almost passes belief; her own deepest grief, so she once confessed, was the necessity of eating, especially when it meant the interruption of her prayers; when she died in 1582, at the age of sixty-seven, she left a reputation so spotless that forty years afterwards she was canonized. She was not wholly successful in effecting the reforms to which she had dedicated her life; the evils against which she fought were too firmly intrenched, and her own ideals were so exalted as to be practically unattainable. But it is certain that the veneration which her own career evoked among the Spaniards tended to emphasize their already strong tendency towards the mystical and emotional phases of religious observance, possibly even somewhat to the detriment of their zeal for the rectification of abuses and other practical demonstrations of their loyalty to the faith.[1]

Philip himself was profoundly influenced by all these things. There seems to be some reason for believing that he received Santa Teresa at the Escorial either in December, 1577, or in May, 1578 ;[2] even if he did not, it is certain that the training that he had received in his early years rendered him particularly susceptible to the examples and precepts of such a person as she, and that his religious life, particularly at the close, was marked by the intensity of its devotional manifestations. This was evident not only in the frequency of his attendance at mass, in the strictness of his observance of ecclesiastical ceremonies, and in the fervor of his prayers ; it was discernible also in his musical and artistic predilections, and he could give it fullest play when living with the monks in the gloomy solitudes of the Escorial. In it he found his only consolation for the defeats and bereavements of his later years ; by it he persuaded himself that however patent the ruin and decay which were going on around him, his cause was the cause of God and must, therefore, triumph in the end.[3] But it was not only in his own dominions and by seconding the efforts of such enthusiasts as Teresa of Ávila that he proposed to play his part ; he was also convinced that it was his most sacred duty to champion and protect the cause of Catholicism all over the face of the

[1] See Santa Teresa, *Obras*, ed. Vicente de la Fuente (Madrid, 1881, 6 vols.), particularly her autobiographical *Vida* (i, pp. 1–271). The best known modern life is that by Louis Bertrand (Paris, 1927) ; Rodolphe Hoornaert's *Sainte Térèse écrivain* (Paris, 1922) has a good bibliography.

[2] It seems probable, however, that the letter published in the *Boletín* of the R. A. H., lxvi (1915), pp. 439–442, in which Teresa describes her interview with the king, is apocryphal. Cf. Bertrand, *Sainte Thérèse*, pp. 379 f.

[3] On the decay of the Escorial and the dispersal of its treasures, see Prescott, iii, pp. 468 f.

globe. And by the time that he got back to Spain in 1559, the reform movement within the church had progressed so far and become organized to such an extent as to give him precisely the opportunity he desired.

Clearly, unless the Protestants should voluntarily come back within the fold, that reform movement was ultimately bound to mean religious war; its connotations were essentially militant. In the Emperor's day the political and dynastic issues had predominated — witness Charles's constant postponement of the war against the Lutherans, and the French king's alliance with the Turk; Europe had been divided on the basis of Hapsburg against Valois rather than on that of Catholicism against Protestantism. But now that was no longer the case. The Catholic church bade fair to be reëstablished on a firmer foundation. Long steps had been taken toward the elimination of those abuses which had given point and justification to the complaints of the Protestants. Rome felt she had a right to reclaim their allegiance, and if it was refused, to compel it. More and more did she convince men that her cause was more worth fighting for than the worldly ambitions of rival sovereigns, that earthly triumphs were as nothing compared to salvation in the world to come. And what rendered the impending religious conflict even more bitter and more certain was the fact that almost at the very moment that the church of Rome had purged itself for the fray, the hegemony of the Protestants passed from the Lutherans to the Calvinists, and therewith from passive to aggressive hands. The Saxon reformer had always maintained that "the word of God would take care of itself"; the Genevan was equally convinced that it needed vigorous human effort to support it, and he preached the duty of fighting for its active advancement as ardently as the Catholic leaders sounded the call to arms on the other side.   Under the circumstances religious war, on a scale hitherto unprecedented, was inevitable. Dynastic and national lines of cleavage were bound to fall into abeyance ; and Europe for some time to come would be divided, irrespective of political allegiances, into Catholic and Protestant camps.   It is also interesting to observe that at the same moment and in some measure for the same reasons that the issues which disrupted Europe changed from a predominantly political to a predominantly religious character, the scene of the conflict shifted too.   In the days of Charles V and Martin Luther, the centres of interest were in Germany and Italy ; henceforth, they were to move westward to the Low Countries, to France, and to England.

But we must not wander too far afield.   Our interest lies solely in those phases of the European situation which vitally affected Philip II and the Spanish Empire ; it is, therefore, on the Roman Catholic side of the drama that we must focus our attention.   Obviously the success of the Counter-Reformation would depend, in large measure, on the effectiveness of its organization.   It had got started, indeed, on a great wave of spiritual enthusiasm ; it had been borne forward on the shoulders of devoted men and women who had dedicated their lives to the task ; but their efforts might well have proved unavailing, particularly in the impending struggle against heresy, without a correlation of its energies and a marshalling of its hosts.   Clerical leadership was furnished by what a Protestant historian has characterized as the 'rechristianized' papacy.   Certainly popes like Pius IV, Pius V, Gregory XIII, and Sixtus V, whose joint pontificates cover the years 1559 to 1590, were men who would put their ecclesiastical duties first of all, and not sacrifice them, as had some of their predecessors in the Emperor's day, to the patronage of scholars and artists, and to the aggrandizement of their relatives and bastards. Even Paul IV deserves a place in the roll of these reforming Popes. Certainly his zeal for the church was unbounded, though the effectiveness of his efforts on its behalf was impaired by his undying hatred of the house of Hapsburg; his pontificate forms a fit transition from the age of the Emperor to that of his son. And at the same time that reinvigorated Catholicism had once more got a leader worthy of the name, it was supplied with a militant platform by the decrees of the Council of Trent. That assembly, during whose earlier sessions there had been some faint hope of compromise with Protestantism, was summoned for its final and decisive meeting on January 18, 1562; and it promptly proceeded to render irreparable the breach between the two faiths. All the doctrines and principles to which no Protestant could possibly subscribe, transubstantiation, the necessity of good works for justification, clerical celibacy, and the rest, were unequivocally sanctioned and upheld; all the heretical ones were equally unequivocally condemned. No loyal Catholic could henceforth have any doubts about the tenets he was expected to maintain.

There still remained the important question of the instruments of which the 'rechristianized' papacy could avail itself in order to carry the Tridentine decrees into effect. A number of primarily ecclesiastical ones were already to hand. Some of the mediaeval religious orders, such as the Franciscans and the Carmelites, had already been thoroughly reformed and placed at the service of the church of Rome; other new ones, like the Theatines and the Jesuits, had recently sprung into being and were animated by the same purpose. The Roman Inquisition had been reorganized for the great conflict on lines reminiscent of the sister institution in Spain, and the first *Index Librorum Prohibitorum* was drawn up in 1557.[1] But all these, efficient though they indubitably were, would avail but little by themselves, without the support of the lay powers. It still remained for the religious leaders of the Counter-Reformation to find some great sovereign who would marshal his armies in the interests of the church, extirpate heresy in Western Europe, repel the infidel in the Mediterranean and in the Danube valley, and carry the Cross to the heathen. Rome found such a champion in Philip the Prudent, to the lasting misfortune of both.

Of course it was evident from the outset that it must be he. In the first place there was the conclusive negative argument that there was no other possible candidate for the place. Ferdinand, in the Empire, was too weak and too lukewarm; the last scions of the house of Valois were unworthy; the king of Poland was not to be thought of, and Elizabeth of England had gone over to the foe. There were also positive reasons in abundance. The Spanish Empire had been the product of a great crusade; the peninsula was the only portion of Western Europe that was virtually untainted by heresy, and Charles V had taken stern measures against the Protestants in the Low Countries. The Spanish monarch was also master of the New World. If the Western Hemisphere was to be preserved for Rome, his coöperation was absolutely essential. Finally, there was the decisive factor of Philip's own personality. Of his zeal for the faith there could not be the least possible doubt; his character, his training, and the precepts of his father combined to make that certain. He ardently longed for the great task that awaited him. He instinctively felt that he was the man of the hour, specially fitted and summoned by Divine Providence to win the great battle for which Rome was girding her loins.

[1] Pastor, xiv, pp. 276–282.

Yet the situation was not, after all, quite so simple as at first sight it would appear. Ardent though he was in his loyalty to the church, Philip was not the man to give without getting something in return. Abundantly conscious of the importance of his own support, he would be tempted to ask, as the reward of it, for favors of a nature that the papacy might be unwilling to grant. There could be little doubt as to what those favors would be, namely, such a share in the control of the policy of the Holy See as would ultimately make Madrid and the Escorial, rather than Rome, the real centre of Catholic authority. In other words, if the battle was to be won, and won with Spain's support, the church of the future was to conform to Spanish interests and principles; that was Philip's idea of his share in the spoils. It was not difficult to foresee the vast implications of this demand. Religiously they foreshadowed a Pope in Spanish leading-strings, but politically their import was wider still. We have already seen that Philip had openly renounced all schemes of further territorial aggrandizement at the expense of the Valois and his other Christian foes. Following his father's advice, he had proclaimed his intention of remaining henceforth politically on the defensive; he had retired to Spain after the treaty of Cateau-Cambrésis, ostensibly to busy himself with internal problems. But now, as the lay leader of the militant forces of Catholicism, he was reëntering the international arena by another door. If his conception of his relation to the church should prevail, the power of Spain would inevitably be increased by every victory that he won for Rome; under cover of advancing the faith, he would be adding to the already intolerable preponderance of his native land.[1] It is doubtful if this conception had taken

[1] Cf. here *Correspondencia Inédita de Guillén de San Clemente, Embajador en Alemania, sobre la intervención de España en Polonia y Hungría, 1581–1608*, ed. the Marquis of Ayerbe (Saragossa, 1892).

definite shape in his mind at the time of his return to the peninsula in 1559; but as the century wore on, and the political lines of cleavage began gradually to reassert themselves, it became increasingly obvious whither he was tending. Perhaps the earliest of all the powers to appreciate the true state of affairs was the papacy itself, the head of the church whose lay champion he had become. On the closeness of the coöperation of the two allies in the great cause much depended, far more, in fact, than could have been evident to contemporaries during the early years of Philip's reign. It is high time, therefore, that we should give some attention to the story of the relations of the Prudent King to the successive occupants of the Holy See during the forty-two years in which he wore the crowns of the Iberian realms.[1]

The age-long tradition of Spanish loyalty to the church must not blind us to the fact that the more recent history of the relations between Spain and the papacy had not been entirely happy. Europe had not forgotten the terrible sack of Rome in the days of Clement VII. Charles V had openly quarrelled with Paul III. The war between Paul IV and Philip was still fresh in men's minds. With the advent of the Medici Pius IV in 1559,[2] there was indeed much reason to expect a marked change for the better. Political complications, the chief cause of the Emperor's quarrels with the different pontiffs of his day, had been at least temporarily ended by the treaty of Cateau-Cambrésis. Philip was back in Spain, apparently using all his influence to secure the

---

[1] Cf. Martin Philippson, "Philipp II. von Spanien und das Papstthum," in *Historische Zeitschrift*, xxxix (1878), pp. 269–315, 419–457. The important volume *Los Despachos de la Diplomacia Pontificia en España*, tom. i (no more published), by Ricardo de Hinojosa (Madrid, 1896), extends to 1605 and is devoted chiefly to the reign of Philip II.

[2] On the conclave that elected him and Philip's attitude thereto, cf. Ricardo de Hinojosa, *Felipe II y el Cónclave de 1559* (Madrid, 1889); Paul Herre, *Papsttum und Papstwahl im Zeitalter Philipps II.*, pp. 33–64; Pastor, xv, pp. 1–65; Ludwig Riess, *Die Politik Pauls IV. und seiner Nepoten* (Berlin, 1909), pp. 379–398.

prompt election of a good Pope, and Pius was far gentler and more complaisant than his predecessor. But all these favorable circumstances were insufficient to prevent clashes between Philip's *Caesaropapismus* and the determination of Pius to maintain the dignity of the Holy See. Trouble arose in the first place over the status of the Spanish Inquisition, whose autonomy and 'supereminence' Philip regarded as the brightest jewels of his crown. The story of the king's persecution of Bartolomé Carranza, archbishop of Toledo, who was unjustly suspected of Protestant leanings, and the papacy's interference therein is the most obvious case in point; it will be narrated more fully in a subsequent chapter.[1] For the present it will suffice to remark that there is no reason to think that the Prudent King cherished any personal antagonism to the archbishop; it was simply a case of asserting the authority of his own favorite tribunal as against that of Rome, and possibly also of getting a chance to seize for the crown the archiepiscopal revenues during the vacancy of the see.

Whether financial considerations had any bearing on the Carranza case, it is certain that they were a constant source of friction between Philip and his papal contemporaries. In 1556, the distinguished theologian Melchior Cano boldly advised the king to reform the administration of the Spanish church in such fashion that it should be able to enjoy its own revenues instead of having them drained away to Rome; as things stood, he maintained, Spain had to go on her knees to the papacy in order to get the clerical subsidy, which was paid her in funds that were really her own.[2] As far as

---

[1] *Infra*, pp. 480 f.
[2] On Cano cf. Fermín Caballero, *Conquenses Ilustres*, ii (Madrid, 1871), pp. 289 f., and J. M. Guardia's edition of the *Arte de Gobernar* sometimes ascribed to Antonio Pérez (Paris,

1867), pp. 331–396; Cano's "Parecer . . . en lo tocante al estado en que se hallan las cossas de la Iglessia" (1. Nov. 1556) is to be found in Caballero, ii, pp. 508–523. At present, so Cano insists, "aunque estemos agraviados

this Philip did not venture to go ; on the other hand he made it plain at the outset that he did not propose to fight the infidel unless he was adequately reimbursed. Not only did he demand the continuance of the *cruzada*, but also an extraordinary subsidy [1] to reimburse him for the special efforts that he was to be called upon to make. Pastor calculates that he derived no less than 1,970,000 gold ducats a year from clerical subventions sanctioned by the Pope.[2] But the 'special efforts' for which these revenues were demanded often failed to equal the papal expectations. At Rome Philip was regarded as almost criminally slack in sending aid to the Knights of Malta in 1565 ; [3] and after the campaign of Lepanto and the loss of Tunis, when the Spanish monarch refused to make any further efforts to recover Algiers and even began negotiating with the Sultan for peace, Gregory XIII put a stop to the extraordinary subsidy for a period of two years.[4] Philip's attitude toward the Council of Trent was another fertile source of trouble. At the outset he no doubt agreed with his ambassador at Rome, Francisco de Vargas, who could see nothing in it but a reunion of heretics and Gallicans 'in which the devil was working and plotting,' [5] and he kept the closest watch, through Vargas and his satellites, on the doings of all its members. Not until the Spanish bishops had fully gained the upper hand there were his suspicions allayed, and he

y damnificados, con nuestros propios dineros nos pagan, sin que nada les cueste," whereas "no dependiendo en lo temporal de la providencia de Roma, Roma dependiera de la nuestra; y les podriamos dan el agua y el pan por pesso y medida sin gastar hacienda, sin peligrar conciencia, ganando mucho crédito, con hacer de los mas enemigos que allá tenemos, los mejores y mas ciertos ministros de nuestra voluntad y pretensiones."

[1] This began in 1561, and was after-wards supplemented by an additional grant called the *excusado*. Donato (1573) in Albèri, *Relazioni*, serie i, vi, pp. 379–383, and *infra*, pp. 442 f.

[2] Pastor, xvi, p. 361. According to B. M., Cotton Ms. Vespasian O. VI, fol. 86, the *cruzada* amounted to 600,000 ducats a year, the *subsidio* to 350,000, and the *excusado* to 293,000: total, 1,243,000 ducats.

[3] Pastor, xvi, pp. 367 f.

[4] Pastor, xix, pp. 347–368.

[5] *D. I. E.*, ix, p. 291, October 7, 1562.

deeply resented every effort of Pius to guide its deliberations. Small wonder if the gentle Medici took alarm at such tremendous pretensions. "You in Spain," he once burst out, "want to be popes and submit everything to the king;" but "if the king wants to be king in Spain, I want to be Pope at Rome." [1]

It was evident that the difficulties which had begun under Pius IV would sensibly increase when, in January, 1566, that peace-loving pontiff was succeeded by the much abler and more vigorous Pius V.[2] He had been elected with the full approval of the Spanish monarch, who, as usual, professed himself to be chiefly desirous of a 'good Pope for Christendom,' [3] but the contest which had begun under his predecessor was to ramify and intensify under him. The new pontiff was not content to rest on the defensive; he proposed to take active measures for the rehabilitation of ecclesiastical authority. Most of these measures had a special bearing on the situation in the Spanish dominions in Italy. Especially noteworthy were his efforts to undermine the so-called *Monarchia Sicula*, or claim of the secular rulers of Sicily to exercise there all the rights of a legate of the Holy See; the resources of some of the most notable historical scholarship of the period were brought to bear to prove that the crucial words in the bull of Pope Urban II (July 5, 1098) to Count Roger I of Sicily, on which this claim was based, were in all probability forged, and thus to restrict the pretensions of the Spanish king in the island.[4] Three years earlier, by republishing the ancient bull *In coena Domini* in a skilfully altered form, he took further steps to emancipate

---

[1] Pastor, xvi, pp. 363–366, 372; Döllinger, *Beiträge*, i, pp. 640 f.

[2] On this period cf. *Correspondencia Diplomática entre España y la Santa Sede durante el Pontificado de Pio V*, ed. Luciano Serrano (Madrid, 1914, 4 vols.).

[3] On the conclave see Herre, *op. cit.*, pp. 103–131; Pastor, xvii, pp. 1–45.

[4] Cf. *ante*, Vol. I, p. 515; Pastor, xviii, pp. 35–42.

ecclesiastical authority all over the world, particularly in financial matters, from secular control. This naturally affected all the dominions of the Spanish Empire, but it was specially aimed at the kingdom of Naples, where the papal pretensions were greater than anywhere else.[1] In Milan there were a whole series of clashes between the ecclesiastical authorities and the representatives of the king of Spain, the case of the former finding a strong champion in the archbishop, Carlo Borromeo, the nephew of Pius IV.[2] Yet Philip succeeded in maintaining his position. Both in the north and in the south of the peninsula, his authority was more unquestioned and the rivalry of the papacy less menacing at the end of the reign than at the beginning; and an Italian proverb, current at the time, declares that while "in Sicily the Spaniards nibble, in Naples they eat, and in Lombardy they devour."[3] Most of the older causes of friction inherited from the previous pontificates also continued under Pius V. The affair of Carranza reached its acutest stage during this period; there were interminable difficulties about clerical subsidies; Castagna, the papal nuncio in Spain, wrote back to Rome that he found the authority of the Pope there diminishing on every hand.[4] Yet the period of Pius V ended without an open breach. The pontiff praised Philip's conduct in the matter of Don Carlos;[5] above all, the king and the Pope were drawn together again in 1571 by their common interest in the campaign of Lepanto. The outstanding fact still remained that, despite perpetual quarrels, they were mutually indispensable.

Under Gregory XIII (May, 1572–April, 1585), the

---

[1] Cf. *ante*, Vol. I, pp. 524 f.
[2] Cf. below, pp. 474 f., and Pastor, xviii, pp. 16–26.
[3] Cf. below, p. 472; Pietro Orsi in

E. Lavisse and A. Rambaud, *Histoire générale*, v, p. 700.
[4] Pastor, xviii, p. 9.
[5] *Ibid.*, p. 45.

situation went from bad to worse; and during the years 1579–81, matters came nearer to a formal break than they had been since the time of Paul IV.[1] Political difficulties were in large measure responsible; as Gregory complained of Philip's slackness in fighting the infidel, so Philip insisted that Gregory's unwillingness to proceed vigorously against the heretics in the Netherlands was due to his desire to see the Low Countries lost to Spain.[2] The Pope's attitude on the annexation of Portugal was also displeasing to the Spanish king. It was evident that Gregory dreaded the extension of Spanish power which would inevitably result from it, and for some time he strove to remain neutral between the different claimants; indeed his final recognition of Philip as lawful Portuguese monarch was largely due to the fact that the latter, who, on this occasion, for once in his life was on time, was able to present him with the accomplished fact before he had had a chance to lay plans for anything else.[3] These matters will be taken up more fully in another connection; for the present we must confine ourselves to topics ecclesiastical, and point out that under the new Pope another source of friction with the Spanish monarch came prominently to the fore in the widely divergent attitudes of the two powers in regard to the Society of Jesus. Some of the previous pontiffs had taken a rather negative attitude in regard to the Jesuits, but Gregory supported them heart and soul; he showered privilege after privilege upon them; indeed, the order was generally admitted to be his favorite.[4] Under the generalship of Claudius Aquaviva (elected February 7, 1581), it had entered upon one of the really great periods of its career; it gave countless proofs of its growing influence and power; it won notable victories over many of its

---

[1] Pastor, xix, pp. 362 f.
[2] Ibid., p. 364.
[3] Ibid., pp. 357–361.
[4] Ibid., p. 234.

bitterest enemies. Among these enemies, not the least considerable was Philip the Prudent. It may seem strange that an order which had such a distinctly Spanish origin [1] should have found itself opposed by the lord of the Spanish Empire; the explanation lies in the king's dread lest the Society, like his counsellors and generals, might become so powerful as to get beyond his control.[2] So useful had the Jesuits proved themselves in advancing the cause of Catholicism all over the world, that it is doubtful if Philip would have ventured to proceed directly against them, had not the way been prepared for him by other foes of the Society. It so happened, however, that, some years before his accession, they had aroused the lasting jealousy of the Dominicans, who always regarded themselves as the preëminently Spanish order; in 1549 they had been bitterly attacked as precursors of Antichrist by Melchior Cano; the archbishops of Toledo and Saragossa were also openly hostile.[3] In the early part of Philip's reign the quarrel slumbered, though the new king's ardent support of the Inquisition, in which Dominican influence had always been very strong,[4] made it evident that an open breach could not be long delayed; not until the year 1580 did the Spanish monarch get the opportunity which he so ardently desired. At that time a few malcontents within the order started a movement for the

[1] For the detailed history of the Spanish Jesuits, see Antonio Astrain, *Historia de la Compañía de Jesús en la Asistencia de España* (Madrid, 1902–25, 7 vols.).

[2] Philip was generally hostile to all new religious orders, particularly to those of foreign origin. It is said that when certain Italian monks crossed over to Spain to obtain his license to establish a branch of their brotherhood within his realms, he replied: "Padres mios, vayanse con Dios, que yo en España quiero que haya mucha religion y pocas religiones." Bib. Nac. Madrid,

Ms. 5972, "Discorso Político intorno al Governo di Napoli di Incognito Autor."

[3] Joseph Brucker, *La Compagnie de Jésus* (Paris, 1919), pp. 119–125.

[4] Cf. Lea, *Inquisition of Spain*, ii, pp. 30–37. T. J. Campbell, *The Jesuits* (New York, 1921), p. 202, says that the king frequently expressed a wish to have a Jesuit in one or another of the important offices of the Inquisition, in order, it was suspected, that by that means he might "lay hold of the machinery of the Society and control it."

purpose of diminishing the authority of the general at Rome, so as to render the different provinces of the Society more independent of his control. The plea for this change was that in no other way could the Spanish Jesuits remain free from the contamination of heresy ; the effect of it, of course, would be to give Philip just the opportunity to control them for which he longed, and which he could not possibly acquire as long as they were ruled from outside the realm ; he therefore supported the malcontents in every possible way, while the Pope, for the same reason, did his utmost to put them down. During Gregory's pontificate, Philip accomplished nothing. When in 1587 he applied to Sixtus V for a revision of the constitution of the order, he found that the new pontiff, though far less well disposed to the Jesuits than his predecessor, had no intention of changing its rules in accordance with the interests of Spain, but rather cherished schemes of modifying them to suit his own views.[1] From that time on the quarrel continued, with fluctuations according to the attitude of the successive Popes toward the order, till the end of the reign and beyond ; but Philip's enmity to it never ceased till the end of his days.[2]

Under Sixtus V, and finally under Clement VIII, the ecclesiastical phases of the quarrel between the see of Rome and the Spanish monarch were again largely obscured by the political. Sixtus, who had been elected against the will of Philip, was a fiery, impetuous soul, not unlike Julius II — just the sort of a person that could not possibly understand or coöperate with the slow-moving Spanish king ;[3] and the haughty Spanish representatives at the Vatican, the Count

[1] Such a modification was foreshadowed by an order, drawn up by papal command in the last days of the pontificate of Sixtus V, requiring the society to drop the name of Jesus from its title; but the death of Sixtus was followed by a reversal of his policy, and Gregory XIV by the bull *Ecclesiae Catholicae* (June 23, 1591) confirmed the society in its name and privileges. Cf. Brucker, *op. cit.*, pp. 194–196.

[2] On all this cf. Brucker, pp. 193–200.

[3] Pastor, xxi, pp. 362–373.

of Olivares and the Duke of Sessa, grew more and more
unpopular there as the years went by.   The Pope's relations
with the non-Spanish Italian states, particularly his intimacy
with Venice, were also highly displeasing to Philip II, and
the refusal of Sixtus in 1589 to contribute to the sending of a
second Armada against England was an even greater source
of complaint.   But it was with regard to the situation in
France that the most serious divergence occurred.   The
death of Catharine de' Medici and the assassination of
Henry III in 1589 eliminated the middle party in the civil
wars there; Henry of Navarre and the League were left to
fight it out for the mastery and the throne of the realm.
Philip, who had many other grounds besides religious ones
for detesting the Bourbon claimant, ardently supported the
cause of the League, for its triumph would enable him to
keep France in leading-strings and prevent her from becoming a rival of Spain.   The papacy, on the other hand, desired
a France loyally Catholic indeed, but independent and
strong, to use as a counter-weight to the preponderance of
Spain.   The all-important question, then, was whether Henry
of Navarre could be induced to abandon the religion of his
fathers and accept the Roman faith.[1]   For four long years,
covering the last twelve months of Sixtus, the three brief
pontificates that followed, and the first year and a half of
Clement VIII, that question remained undecided; when
finally, in July, 1593, it was answered in the affirmative, not
only did Philip lose all hope of controlling the destinies of
France, but also a large measure of his influence with the
see of Rome.   He was no longer indispensable to it, for there
was at last a possible alternative to his support.[2]   Yet it was
thoroughly characteristic of him that he refused, to the very
last, to abate one jot or one tittle of his earlier pretensions,

[1] Pastor, xxi, pp. 273 f., 358–364.   [2] Pastor, xxiii, p. 202.

but heroically brazened it out to the bitter end, and so successfully, moreover, that despite the altered situation, Clement VIII continued to the very end of his life to show marked reluctance to adopt any measures that might tend to bring about a breach with Spain. Filippo Sega, the papal nuncio at Madrid during the pontificate of Gregory XIII, summed up the story of the whole period admirably when he compared Philip and the Pope to two merchants, each of whom was firmly convinced that the other had wronged him in countless different ways, but who nevertheless could not afford to stop doing business with one another.[1]

One final phase of the relations of Philip to the papacy remains to be mentioned : namely, the attitude and conduct of the Spanish king and his representatives at Rome with regard to the different conclaves. It has been made the subject of a most painstaking investigation by a competent German scholar ;[2] and his general conclusion furnishes a significant confirmation of the tendency, noticed in the immediately preceding pages, of political issues to regain, in the last two decades of the century, that predominance over religious ones which they had enjoyed in the time of Charles V, but had temporarily lost during the first part of the rule of his son. Down to, and including, the election of Sixtus V, Philip had really interfered comparatively little with the choice of the successive pontiffs for the purpose of advancing the interests of Spain. The most that he did was occasionally to insist on the exclusion from candidacy of persons whom he knew to be avowedly hostile to his own political ends ;[3] his chief interest seemed to be — as he was never tired of reiterating — the 'choice of a good Pope for

---

[1] Pastor, xix, pp. 366 f., and references there.

[2] Paul Herre, *Papsttum und Papstwahl im Zeitalter Philipps II.* (Leipzig, 1907).

[3] Cf. Herre, pp. 96 f., 313, 318 f., for instances of this; also Florentine "Relazione di Spagna" (1591?) in Bratli, p. 211.

Christendom.' [1] But during the pontificate of Sixtus there
was a great change. The close bond between Spain and the
papacy, which had made possible the Counter-Reformation,
had done its work; the old political lines of cleavage were
struggling to regain the mastery; indeed, the Pope's own
attitude towards the various projects of the Spanish king
was a powerful factor in bringing this to pass.[2] When
Philip realized the new state of affairs, his policy towards the
succeeding conclaves altered accordingly. More vigorous
measures were clearly necessary in order to keep the papacy
in line with the interests of Spain; and the obvious method
of accomplishing this end was to take a more positive attitude with regard to the papal elections. In the four conclaves which succeeded one another with such extraordinary
rapidity in the eighteen months following the death of
Sixtus V, the Spanish monarch came boldly forward and
indicated the names of the candidates whom he wished to
have chosen; the policy of merely excluding undesirables
was thus exchanged for the much more far-reaching one of
putting through the election of favorites. "The least we
can demand at this time," so wrote Philip to his representative at Rome in November, 1591, "is that the victorious
candidate should coöperate with me." [3]

For the time being the new policy seemed outwardly to
attain its end. Despite the defeat of the Armada and the
ensuing reverses in the Low Countries and in France, Philip
was still both respected and dreaded at Rome; and the four
successors of Sixtus V were all, at least at the time of their
respective elections, among the candidates recognized as
'agreeable' to the representatives of the Spanish king.[4] Yet
one of Philip's keenest henchmen at Rome, Francisco de

[1] Herre, p. 603, note 3.
[2] Herre, pp. 363 f.
[3] Herre, p. 603, and references there.
[4] See Herre, pp. 442-444, 453, 532,
541-543, 588 f., 624 f., for details.

Peña, auditor of the Rota, was not without his apprehensions in regard to the ultimate effects of the new attitude that had been assumed. Very serious consequences, he insisted, might result from the naming of persons whom his Majesty wished to have made Pope; "certainly it is not good policy to do so openly; it would be far less dangerous to rest content with the exclusion of undesirables. The latter gains us merely the ill will of a certain number, who feel that they have been wronged; the former makes us hated by the entire Sacred College; for there is not a single cardinal who does not daily conceive of the possibility that through some particular merit, capacity, or means, he may himself be chosen Pope." [1]   But if Philip shared the auditor's fears, he could not be induced to alter his policy.   While all the world was changing around him, he remained at heart the same; he continued to cherish his original ideal of a universally triumphant Roman Catholic church which should be guided and controlled from Spain.   The more dominant attitude towards the see of Rome, which circumstances had compelled him to adopt after the death of Sixtus V, turned out ultimately to be a powerful factor in forcing the two powers apart; it had results, in other words, precisely opposite to those which he had intended.   The era which made Philip, and which he in turn contributed so much to make, was the era of the Counter-Reformation at its height, the era in which he began his reign.   When Europe began to regulate its life along other lines, he was never quite able to accommodate himself to the change, and Spain and the Spanish Empire paid the penalty for his failure.

[1] See Herre, p. 541.

NOTE ON THE GENERAL AUTHORITIES
ON THE REIGN OF PHILIP II

Guides to the Archives and Indices to Manuscript Collections. —
In view of the fact that the field covered by this volume is so enormous,
and the material on it so much more abundant than that for the period
of Charles V, it seems worth while to give the names of the principal
printed indices and analyses of the more important collections of
manuscripts for the benefit of those who desire to pursue researches
into any one of the different phases of the story. It is the more
important to do this because so many admirable catalogues and indices
have appeared in the last ten years.

Of the older ones, the earliest is the list of manuscripts relating to
Philip in the Biblioteca Nacional at Madrid which is to be found on
pp. 50 f. of the appendix to vol. ii of Bartolomé José Gallardo's *Ensayo
de una Biblioteca Española* (Madrid, 1863–89, 4 vols.) ; but it is most
inaccurate and incomplete ; and there are also some manuscripts listed
in Gallardo which are not to be found in the Biblioteca Nacional today.
Next, and far more valuable, though also often inaccurate, is the
*Catalogue of the Manuscripts in the Spanish Language in the British
Museum* by Pascual de Gayangos (London, 1875–93, 4 vols.). The
most of the material on Philip II is listed on pages 653–824 of vol. ii
and 1–194 of vol. iii ; but much more is to be found in other parts of
the catalogue under other headings. The collection is enormous and
has been relatively little used. Corresponding to this is the *Catalogue
des manuscrits espagnols et des manuscrits portugais* in the Bibliothèque
Nationale at Paris by Alfred Morel-Fatio (Paris, 1892).

More recently we have a *Catálogo de los Manuscritos Castellanos de
la Real Biblioteca del Escorial* by Julián Zarco Cuevas (Madrid, 1924–
29, 3 vols.) ; curiously enough this collection is rather disappointing
for the student of Philip II ; it is far richer on Charles V. Finally we
have a whole series of indices and analyses of manuscript collections
in Spain and elsewhere by Julián Paz, the chief of the Department of
Manuscripts in the Biblioteca Nacional at Madrid. Of these the first
five are all officially labelled *Archivo General de Simancas*, and have for
their titles *Diversos de Castilla* (Madrid, 1904) ; *Capitulaciones con la
Casa de Austria y Papeles de las Negociaciones de Alemania* (Vienna,
1913) ; *Documentos de las Negociaciones de Flandes, Holanda, y
Bruselas* (Paris, 1915) ; *Capitulaciones con Francia y Negociaciones
Diplomáticas de los Embajadores de España en aquella Corte*, i, 1265–
1714 (Madrid, 1914) ; and *Patronato Real* (Madrid, 1912) ; but it
should be carefully noted that the fourth of these volumes is really a

catalogue of the manuscripts from Simancas in the Archives Nationales at Paris, whither they were carried off by Napoleon at the time of the Peninsular War. Valuable also is the " Inventaire de la Collection Tiran " in the Archives Nationales, by G. Daumet, in *B. H.*, xix (1917), pp. 189–199; xx (1918), pp. 36–42, 233–248; xxi (1919), pp. 218–230, 282–295. Paz has also published a *Catálogo de Documentos Españoles existentes en el Archivo del Ministerio de Negocios Extranjeros de París* (Madrid, 1932; cf. especially pp. 80–155 for the period of Philip II) and a *Catálogo de Manuscritos de América existentes en la Biblioteca Nacional* (Madrid, 1933). In 1930–31, moreover, he put forth an admirable two-volume *Catálogo de la Colección de Documentos Inéditos para la Historia de España*. It is an indispensable guide to the 112 volumes in question, and is far more useful than the less exhaustive analysis of the *D. I. E.* by R. Foulché-Delbosc and R. Barrau-Dihigo on pp. 113–179 of vol. ii of the *Manuel de l' Hispanisant* (New York, 1925). These catalogues of Paz leave something to be desired. He often ignores the work on Spain and Spanish bibliography that is being accomplished beyond the Pyrenees; there is no evidence, for instance, that he knew of the analysis of Foulché-Delbosc and Barrau-Dihigo at the time that he published his catalogue of the *D. I. E.* His indices, too, are often faulty, no distinction being made between different men of the same name. But it is all so much better than anything of the sort that has gone before that one is not disposed to complain.

Naturally these indices contain material on other reigns as well as on that of Philip II; but the Prudent King occupies a prominent place in them all. There also remain many important manuscript collections, like those of the R. A. H., of which no printed catalogue has yet appeared. But the way of the historical student in Spain is far smoother than it was ten years ago, and it is sure to become smoother still in the near future. It is a pleasure to add that the Spanish librarians and archivists put themselves generously and courteously at the disposal of those who visit their collections or write for information about them, and do their utmost to facilitate their investigations in every way.

Bibliographies. — An enlarged and improved edition of Benito Sánchez Alonso's *Fuentes de la Historia Española* has appeared (1927, 2 vols.) since the publication of the third volume of this work, and the pages on the period of Philip II are particularly good. Pages 17–55 and 239–284 of the revised French translation (Paris, 1912) of Carl Bratli's *Philippe II, roi d' Espagne*, first published in Danish at Copenhagen three years before, are exclusively devoted to the historical literature of the reign of the Prudent King. This author spent many years of laborious research in Spanish and foreign archives collecting material for a fresh picture which should refute the various calumnies and misconceptions of which, in his opinion, the king had so long been the victim, particularly among Protestant historians; his attitude throughout is frankly favorable to Philip. Bratli's book is not, strictly speaking, a history of the reign, but rather a portrait of the king and a summary of his life's work; but he gives full references for his facts, and publishes a number of valuable documents in his appendix. Pages 17–55 comprise an essay on the historical literature relating to Philip, both in Spain and abroad; pages 239–284, an alphabetical list of the principal authorities. The book is the work of an amateur, rather than of a professional historian; it is not for a moment to be compared with A. Morel-Fatio's *Historiographie de Charles-Quint*. There are many careless mistakes; the author is primarily interested in Philip's rule in Spain, and therefore neglects, both in the text and in the bibliography, the progress and literature of foreign affairs; worst of all, one feels throughout that he is more interested in fortifying his own conception of the Prudent King than in characterizing impartially the different authorities on the reign and letting the reader draw his own conclusions. With these reservations, however, the book may be used to great advantage. It contains much that is available nowhere else, and the hostile tendencies which it seeks to refute are still so prevalent, particularly in England, Holland, and America, that there is a certain advantage in having the emphasis placed on the other side.

Sources and Contemporary Works. — The *Colección de Documentos Inéditos* is particularly valuable for the reign of the Prudent King. Many of its volumes are filled with original material for the study of his reign; it is also worth noting that a considerable number of the most important documents, which are given in sometimes abbreviated English translation in the *Calendar of State Papers, Spanish*, are to be found there in full in the original. That *Calendar*, however, for the years 1558–1603, ed. M. A. S. Hume (London, 1892–99, 4 vols.), is also indispensable, not only for Anglo-Spanish relations, but also for other phases of Spain's foreign affairs; as are likewise volumes vi–ix of the *Calendar of State Papers, Venetian*, edd. Rawdon Brown, G. C. Bentinck, and H. F. Brown for the years 1555–1603 (London, 1875–97), and the first series, in six volumes, of the *Relazioni degli Ambasciatori Veneti al Senato durante il secolo decimosesto*, ed. Eugenio Albèri (Florence, 1839–62). The most valuable volumes in the great *Collection de documents inédits sur l'histoire de la France* for the reign of

Philip are the *Papiers d'état du Cardinal de Granvelle*, ed. Charles Weiss (Paris, 1841–52, 9 vols.). For internal affairs the first seventeen volumes of the *Actas de las Córtes de Castilla publicadas por acuerdo del Congreso de los Diputados* (Madrid, 1877–91) are the most important source of all, though it is not so easy to find one's way about in them as it is in the five volumes of the preceding set, which close with the death of the Emperor; and one sadly misses the learned introduction of Manuel Colmeiro. The *Nueva Recopilación* was first published in this reign (*infra*, pp. 427, 455) and is particularly useful for the period.

At the head of the list of contemporary authorities on Philip's reign stands the monumental work of Luis Cabrera de Córdoba (1559–1623), *Felipe Segundo, Rey de España*, of which the first part only (to 1583) was published at Madrid in 1619; the complete edition, in four volumes, appeared in 1876–77. The author's father and grandfather had been noted soldiers; he himself was employed on different missions by the Prudent King, in Naples, in Flanders, and elsewhere, but returned to the royal service in Madrid before the end of the reign; during these years he took copious notes for the composing of his history, " which could not have been accomplished without them." In view of the fact that Philip would never allow his life to be written (*C. S. P., Venetian*, ix, no. 737), it seems natural to suppose that Cabrera de Córdoba did not actually begin the composition of his work till the next reign, but it deserves, nevertheless, to be treated as a contemporary authority. It is chiefly a very detailed narrative history of the reign, with the main emphasis on foreign affairs and military campaigns, but the constitutional, economic, and social sides of the story are not wholly neglected, and there are occasional glimpses of the progress of the Spanish régime in the New World; the standpoint throughout is of course highly favorable to the Prudent King. Like the vast majority of the historians of his day and generation, Cabrera was a constant plagiarist; indeed the second half of his work has been described as little more than a compilation of the writings of others; Herrera (cf. *infra*) is perhaps the one from whom he took the most. But the thing that distinguishes the plagiarism of Cabrera from that of the mass of his contemporaries is that he was not ashamed to steal a passage or phrase from another writer and utilize it for a totally different purpose from that for which it had been orginally composed; he takes, for instance, the very words which Diego Hurtado de Mendoza in his *Guerra de Granada* uses to characterize the men of Seville who volunteered for the war against the Moriscos in 1570 (cf. *B. A. E., Historiadores de Sucesos Particulares*, i, p. 114, col. 1, lines 13–34), and applies them to the Sevillans who were recruited by the Marquis of Santa Cruz for the second expedition against the Azores in 1583 (cf. C. de C., iii, p. 16, lines 2–17). Despite these defects, however, his book is indispensable, and any serious historian of the reign must have it constantly by his side. The only other contemporary works of a general nature on Philip and his period which it seems worth while to mention here are the brief Latin biography by the learned Juan Ginés de Sepúlveda, which only goes to 1564, and was first published at Madrid in 1780, in the third volume of the collected edition of the author's works put forth by the R. A. H.; the *Historia General del Mundo del Tiempo del Rey Felipe II. el Prudente* by Antonio de Herrera y Tordesillas, better known as the ' Coronista de las Indias ' (best edition, Madrid, 1601–12, 3 vols.); and the *Historiae sui Temporis* (1543–1607) by the Frenchman J. A. de Thou (best edition, London, 1733, 7 vols.). The works of Cabrera de Córdoba and of Herrera served as the basis for the formation of the Spanish conception of the Prudent King, which, fortified by Baltasar Porreño's more popular *Dichos y Hechos del Rey Philipe Segundo* (first ed. at Cuenca, 1621, latest at Valladolid, 1863), endured unchanged for over two centuries to come. That of de Thou, reënforced by such partisan accounts as the *Relaciones* of Antonio Pérez and the tales of Brantôme, laid the foundation for the hostile and distorted estimates of him which were perpetuated during the same period outside the peninsula.

Later Works. — It is no wonder that the latter of these views became overwhelmingly prevalent during the seventeenth and eighteenth centuries, so prevalent, in fact, that it has not been entirely abandoned even today. In Spain Porreño's work had no successor for over two hundred years, either in history, drama, or fiction. In other countries, however, Philip steadily continued to be presented in a most unfavorable light, in histories, such as the prejudiced and inaccurate *History of the Reign of Philip the Second* by Robert Watson, first published in London in 1777; in historical novels, such as the *Don Carlos* of César Vischard de Saint-Réal, which first appeared in Amsterdam in 1672; and above all in dramas like the *Don Carlos* of Thomas Otway (London, 1676) and the still more famous play of the same name by Friedrich von Schiller (1787); it was chiefly indeed by historically inaccurate dramatizations of the tragic story of Philip's relations with his son that the popular hostile conception of the Prudent King was kept before the public eye. Practically the only writer in all this period who had a good word to say for him was the Italian Protestant, Gregorio Leti, whose *Vita del Catolico Re Filippo II* appeared in 1679; but as Leti wrote primarily to amuse, and was not ashamed to invent stories out of whole cloth when he could not find what he wanted in the authorities, his work was never taken seriously by historians. It thus came about that when history began to be scientifically studied and rewritten in the middle decades of the nineteenth century, an enormous amount of revision of the older verdicts was inevitable.

The Spanish share in that process of revision has been rather that of rendering accessible fresh material than of examining and sifting it and utilizing it in the composition of scientific historical works. The Spanish archives were thrown open for the first time in 1844; the publication of the *Colección de Documentos Inéditos* was forthwith begun, and the activities of the Real Academia de la Historia took on a new lease of life. Notable histories covering wider fields, such as Cesáreo Fernández Duro's *Armada Española*, in which many of the misconceptions of Philip have been corrected, have also appeared; and likewise a number of excellent monographs of a more special nature, such as the Marquis of Pidal's *Historia de las Alteraciones de Aragon en el Reinado de Felipe II* (Madrid, 1862–63) and Julián Suárez Inclán's *Guerra de Anexión en Portugal*, which will be described more fully in the subsequent bibliographical notes. But for the most part the saner verdicts on Philip II which have begun to prevail in recent years are the fruit of the investigations of historians from beyond the Pyrenees.

It took some time for the older prejudices to be forgotten; W. H. Prescott's *History of the Reign of Philip the Second* (Boston, 1855–58, 3 vols.), is a case in point. One cannot help feeling that it was almost a pity that he undertook this work. It seems clear that he failed to gauge the enormous amount of the available material, for he barely succeeded in carrying his story to the middle of the reign; it breaks off in some of its phases at 1568, and in others at 1581. His eyesight, moreover, was failing at the time, and he had to rely, far more than in any of his earlier books, on the labors and investigations of others. No one can question his perfect historical honesty, or his desire to be absolutely fair; but the difficulties we have already enumerated, coupled with his inherited training and predilections, made it impossible that he should produce, in this his final effort, anything comparable with his previous masterpieces. In Europe the tide began to turn at an even earlier date. In a sense it may be truthfully said that the first really accurate modern portrait of the Prudent King was drawn by Leopold von Ranke in his *Die Osmanen und die spanische Monarchie im sechszehnten und siebzehnten Jahrhundert*, first published at Hamburg in 1827. That portrait was chiefly based on the *Rela-*

zioni of the Venetian ambassadors which Ranke's efforts had just brought to light; and it started subsequent investigators on the right road. Reinhold Baumstark's *Philipp II. König von Spanien* (Freiburg i. B., 1875), Martin Philippson's " König Philipp II. von Spanien " in *Der neue Plutarch*, iii (Leipzig, 1876), pp. 1–116, and M. A. S. Hume's very readable *Philip II. of Spain* (London, 1897) are typical, each in its different way, of the sort of monograph that has begun to be produced by those who have had the opportunity to examine the new material recently made available, and have been trained in modern methods of scientific historical research. The largest and most ambitious work which has appeared on the Prudent King in the period under review is Henri Forneron's *Histoire de Philippe II*, which was published in four volumes at Paris in 1881–82. The author was exceedingly inaccurate in details (cf., e.g., Suárez Inclán, *Guerra de Anexión en Portugal*, i, p. xvii, and ii, pp. 157 f.) ; it is not a difficult task for any one who knows the period to go through his book and find petty mistakes on almost every page. Forneron also was overfond of dramatic effect and dearly loved a good story ; his outspoken admiration of Brantôme is thoroughly characteristic of him. On the other hand, he spared no efforts to get at the sources ; he cites his authorities — though often incorrectly — for every important statement that he makes, and an unusually large proportion of those authorities are original manuscripts ; the broad outlines of his picture, moreover, are essentially correct. The book is at once profoundly irritating and wellnigh indispensable. None of its statements can be accepted without careful verification ; on the other hand, the task of the historian of Philip II would be far harder if he did not have it beside him.

There have also appeared, in the course of the past fifty years, several over-favorable estimates of the character of the king, such as José Fernández Montaña's *Nueva Luz y Juicio-Verdadero sobre Felipe II* (2ª ed., Madrid, 1891), his *Más Luz de Verdad Histórica sobre Felipe II el Prudente* (Madrid, 1892), and Fidel Pérez Mínguez's *Psicología de Felipe II* (Madrid, 1925) ; but these are scarcely to be regarded as serious historical works. The same may in general be said of the four most recent books on the Prudent King: Jean Cassou, *La vie de Philippe II* (7e éd., Paris, 1929), Reinhold Schneider, *Philipp II, oder Religion und Macht* (Leipzig, 1931), David Loth, *Philip II of Spain* (New York, 1932), and J. H. Mariéjol, *Philip II, the First Modern King* (New York, 1933). The last named is the work of a recognized master in the field ; but unfortunately it is little more than a translated expansion of the author's excellent article " L'Oeuvre de

Philippe II," which first appeared in vol. v, pp. 49–107, of Lavisse and Rambaud's *Histoire générale* in the year 1895.

BIBLIOGRAPHICAL NOTE TO CHAPTER XXXI

See notes at the end of Chapters XXVI, *ante*, and XXXIV and XXXVI, *infra*, and add :

Sources. — The *Relazioni degli ambasciatori Veneti durante il secolo decimosesto*, ed. Eugenio Albèri, serie i, vols. ii, iii, v, and vi ; the *Relations des ambassadeurs Vénitiens sur Charles-Quint et Philippe II*, ed. L. P. Gachard (Brussels, 1855) ; and the *D. I. E.*, especially vols. ii, vii, ix, xv, and xviii, all contain precious material for the topics covered in this chapter. The "Journal des voyages de Philippe II de 1551 à 1560" by Jean de Vandenesse, edd. Gachard and Piot in vol. iv of the *Collection des voyages des souverains des Pays-Bas* (Brussels, 1882), is also useful ; and the *Lettres de Philippe II à ses filles les Infantes Isabelle et Catherine écrites pendant son voyage en Portugal (1581–1583)*, ed. L. P. Gachard (Paris, 1884), shed a flood of light on the true character of the king. *Los Despachos de la Diplomacia Pontificia en España*, i (no more published), by Ricardo de Hinojosa (Madrid, 1896), the *Correspondencia Inédita de Guillén de San Clemente, Embajador en Alemania*, ed. the Marquis of Ayerbe (Saragossa, 1892), and the *Correspondencia Diplomática entre España y la Santa Sede durante el Pontificado de Pio V*, ed. Luciano Serrano (Madrid, 1914, 4 vols.), will be found indispensable by those who desire to follow the details of the negotiations of Philip with the see of Rome. The *Historia del Monasterio del Escorial* by José de Sigüenza (1544–1606) (best edition, Madrid, 1881) is still the standard authority on the subject with which it deals.

Later Works. — The English translation by R. F. Kerr of Ludwig von Pastor's *History of the Popes* has now reached the seventeenth century in twenty-four volumes and is an invaluable guide to the whole period of Philip's reign ; vols. iii and iv of Henri Pirenne's *Histoire de Belgique* and H. C. Lea's *History of the Inquisition of Spain* (New York, 1906–07, 4 vols.) are also exceedingly useful. The standard biographies of the Prudent King are discussed in the preceding "Note on the General Authorities" ; and volumes xlvii and xciv of the *Ciudad de Dios* contain additional information in regard to the king's character and personality. The footnotes to pp. 34–39, *supra*, give adequate indications of the literature in regard to Don Carlos. Paul Herre's *Papsttum und Papstwahl im Zeitalter Philipps II*. (Leipzig, 1907) and Ludwig Riess's *Die Politik Pauls IV. und seiner Nepoten*

(Berlin, 1909) are useful monographs on the subjects with which they deal. Louis Bertrand's *Sainte Thérèse* (Paris, 1927) and Joseph Brucker's *La Compagnie de Jésus* (Paris, 1919) are also valuable; and everything from the pen of Julián Zarco Cuevas in regard to the Escorial and its contents may be accepted as authoritative. Numerous other monographs of too special a nature to be inserted here will be found in the footnotes to the preceding pages.

CHAPTER XXXII

THE LAST OF THE CRUSADES

BEFORE Philip could undertake the great task of marshalling the hosts of regenerate Catholicism against the infidel and the Protestant outside the limits of the Iberian peninsula, it was essential to make certain that Spain itself was as nearly as possible untainted by any suspicion of heresy or unbelief. One of the principal reasons why he had been so anxious to get home was that he might give personal supervision to such work as should prove necessary to the accomplishment of this end; and the history of the early years of his reign is largely the record of his efforts to attain it.

As far as Protestantism was concerned, the task was comparatively simple. So far removed was Spain from the centres of the Reformation, and so powerful and all-pervading was the machinery of the Inquisition, that the doctrines of Luther and Calvin never really got a chance to establish themselves there. It used, indeed, to be thought that the Spanish Protestants were so numerous and well organized that considerable efforts were necessary to suppress them; but thirty years ago, it was conclusively proved that this was a gross exaggeration, that the number of native Spanish Protestants tried by the Inquisition, exclusive of the congregations of Valladolid and Seville, was probably not over four hundred in all, and that of those who preferred death in the flames to recantation there were perhaps hardly more than a score, though a much larger number perished by the garrote.[1] The greater part of the work of extirpating them, moreover, was finished at the very beginning of the reign. In 1557, while Philip was still in the Netherlands, two small Protestant conventicles were discovered, one at Valladolid and one at Seville; it would also appear that many of the heretics in the latter city were of Jewish origin, and thus had a tradition of nonconformity behind them. The Holy Office made haste to pounce on them. It had been in a somewhat decadent condition during the latter years of the reign of Charles V, for lack — the metaphor is particularly apt — of fuel to feed the flames, and it now eagerly seized upon the opportunity for renewed activity, exaggerating the peril and posing as the saviour of society in averting it. Indeed, it is largely through the rumors and reports which it circulated that contemporary and modern historians were misled into thinking that the danger was much greater than was actually the case. Most of the suspects were disposed of in two autos-da-fé at Valladolid, on May 21 and October 8, 1559; the latter was considerably the more important, and Philip, as we have already seen, graced the occasion with his presence.[2] After this, the process of extirpation continued in much less wholesale fashion, and the culprits were increasingly few. After the middle seventies they were mostly foreigners, who naturally claimed immunity from the jurisdiction of the Holy Office, and the problems which arose in connection with their cases played their part in the formation of the then nascent science of international law. One of the most bitterly contested points was whether or not the ambassador of the queen of England should be permitted to have the Anglican service performed in his own house. Dr. John

[1] E. Schäfer, *Beiträge zur Geschichte des spanischen Protestantismus*, i, pp. 208–232.

[2] Schäfer, *op. cit.*, iii, *passim*; and Lea, *The Inquisition of Spain*, iii, pp. 437–442.

Man, who was sent to Madrid in the spring of 1566, insisted on this privilege, and apparently was given reason to believe that it would be accorded to him; but the king was obdurate, and required him to 'sequester himself' from the capital at the little village of Barajas, where it was impossible for him to perform the duties of his office. Man forthwith demanded his recall, which was immediately granted him; and it is significant of the intensity of Philip's dread of Protestant contamination that he would not even permit the envoy to return to Madrid to make provision for his journey.[1]

But Protestantism in the full sense of the word was not the only form of heresy against which Philip waged relentless war. The slightest deviation from the laws of the church, as upheld by the lay and ecclesiastical authorities of Spain, was almost certain to be detected and mercilessly punished. It might be failure to observe a fast, or to conform to the established rules of the service of the church of Rome; it might be the possession of forbidden books, or any one of a multitude of other derelictions; the agents of the Inquisition were sure to be on the watch and to receive Philip's enthusiastic support in their demands for investigation and judgment. The Holy Office was also much concerned in this period with the suppression of another form of heresy, that of the *Alumbrados* or Illuminati, which, though its origin is usually associated with the Bavarian Adam Weishaupt in 1776, really arose for the first time nearly three centuries earlier, in the Spain of the Catholic Kings. As it appeared in the Iberian peninsula it was essentially a form of mysticism, whose adherents recognized the supremacy of the internal light, and consequently regarded themselves as released from the obligation of obedience to the

---

[1] Forneron, i, pp. 190 f.; *C. S. P., Foreign*, 1566–68, nos. 2087, 2098, 2109, 2112, 2127, 2139, 2227, 2297, 2360.

regular ecclesiastical authorities. It often vented itself in hallucinations and in sexual aberrations, and was utterly abhorrent to the officials of the *Suprema*. There had been processes against the *Alumbrados* in the Emperor's reign; on the other hand, the edict formally declaring their faith to be heresy was not published till the time of Philip IV; but it was under Philip II that the problem of extirpating them was first seriously and systematically taken up, so that thenceforth the ultimate issue could not reasonably be in doubt.[1]

It was indeed the heyday of the Holy Office. Never had its supereminence been so far-reaching and complete. For the king it was not only the emblem and instrument of his own conception of the purity of the faith, but also of the dominance of that conception throughout the Roman Catholic world. He kept full control of it in his own hands.[2] He appointed and dismissed the inquisitors at will; he kept them all under the closest surveillance; he gave them definite orders for the discharge of their functions. In the dread and impenetrable secrecy which shrouded all its operations, it seemed to be the very mirror of himself. He used it not only to keep his own subjects, both lay and ecclesiastical, in strict conformity to the lines he laid down, but also to fortify his own position with regard to the see of Rome.[3] It made trouble for the Spanish poet, Fray Luis de León, the glory of the order of the Augustinian Friars, and even attempted to do the same for Santa Teresa; that her persecution did not proceed further than certain rather humiliating inter-

---

[1] Marcelino Menéndez y Pelayo, *Historia de los Heterodoxos Españoles*, ii, pp. 521–585 (2d ed., v, pp. 205–280); Lea, *Inquisition of Spain*, iv, pp. 1–94; J. Melgares Marín, *Procedimientos de la Inquisicion*, ii, pp. 5–159; J. A. Llorente, *Histoire de l'Inquisition d'Espagne*, iii, pp. 102 ff.

[2] On the supposed subjection of Philip to the Inquisition, cf., e.g., C. S. P., *Foreign*, 1566–68, no. 2109.

[3] Lea, *Inquisition of Spain*, ii, pp. 129–131.

rogations was less due to the attitude of the king, to whom
she applied for protection, than to her own high character
and saintly presence, and to the support of the Society of
Jesus.[1] The hostility of the Inquisition to the members of
that order, though latent, was absolutely consistent throughout the reign, and had the widest ramifications. The Jesuits
upheld the authority of the Holy See almost as vigorously
as did the Inquisition the supremacy of the king; and the
struggle between the two institutions, from the time of the
accusation of Carranza to the very end of the reign, is a useful barometer of the mutual jealousies between Rome and
Spain.[2] The tale of Philip's repeated efforts and ultimate
failure to introduce the Holy Office into the Spanish possessions in Naples and Milan forms another significant chapter
of the same story. Its establishment was, for him, an insepa-
rable adjunct and *sine qua non* of the solidification of his own
authority in his Italian dominions; but the intensity of the
local detestation of it, and the hostility of the Council of
Trent and of the successive Popes, were finally successful in
keeping it out.[3] But it would be a great mistake to think
of the power and influence of the Holy Office as restricted
solely to Spain and her relations to the see of Rome. It was
also of profound importance in Philip's political dealings with
the other realms of Western Europe; for church and state
were, in his eyes at least, so closely fused that it was impossible to interfere in the one without affecting the other as
well. We have already alluded to the trouble that arose
with Elizabeth of England over the question of a Protestant
service at the house of her ambassador. It is also worth
noting that in 1578, when the Spanish customs officials
showed themselves incapable of preventing the exportation

---

[1] Lea, *Inquisition of Spain*, ii, p. 520;
iv, pp. 16 ff., 149 ff.

[2] Lea, *op. cit.*, ii, pp. 33–36.

[3] Lea, *The Inquisition in the Spanish
Dependencies*, pp. 86 ff., 125 ff.

of horses to France, the king, on the pretence that these animals were intended for the forces of the Huguenots, handed the whole matter over to the jurisdiction of the Holy Office, with the result that a Saragossan horse dealer, who had broken the regulations, was punished with two hundred lashes, a fine of a hundred ducats, and five years in the galleys.[1] There were countless other instances of Philip's utilization of the Inquisition for his political ends; the most significant of them all will be discussed in a later chapter in connection with the 'troubles' of the kingdom of Aragon. But enough has already been said to indicate how all-pervasive was its power and how completely it fulfilled the ideas of the King.

Philip's firm resolve to make himself the unquestioned leader of the forces of militant Catholicism, his determination to extirpate Protestantism, and the measures which he adopted to attain these ends, were thus potent factors in shaping the course of Spain's relations to the other states of Western Europe. But there was another very serious matter — as essentially and traditionally a *cosa de España* as Philip's attitude towards heresy was international in its implications — which demanded his attention before he could embark on any crusade. This was the treatment by the Spanish government of the remnants of the Moorish population of the peninsula, which had been suffered to remain, under increasingly rigid restrictions, since the conquest of Granada by the Catholic Kings.

One result of the Germanía of Valencia, as has already been indicated in the preceding volume, was to extend in 1525 to the realms of the crown of Aragon the edict in regard to the Moriscos which had been in operation in Castile since

[1] Llorente, *op. cit.*, ii, pp. 394 f. Cf. *infra*, p. 582.

1502;[1] for thirty-one years before Philip succeeded his father all the Moorish inhabitants of Spain had, in theory at least, accepted the Christian faith. But there had naturally arisen grave doubts as to the genuineness of this enforced conversion. Under the Emperor, who was so much of the time absent from Spain, the policy adopted in regard to the Moriscos had been chiefly remarkable for its fluctuations. It must have been obvious that a certain amount of instruction in the tenets of the faith they were now compelled by law to adopt would be the indispensable preliminary to their loyal acceptance of it; but the efforts in this direction were spasmodic, untactful, and constantly beset with almost insurmountable linguistic difficulties; and the Inquisition, to put it mildly, was not helpful. Another method, to which the Holy Office was likewise uncordial, was to facilitate intercourse between the Moriscos and Old Christians in every possible way. The walls which marked off the *barrios,* or Moorish quarters, in the different cities were occasionally pulled down; there were a few edicts to the effect that Old and New Christians should occupy alternate houses; and marriage between the two races was sometimes encouraged by providing that the dowry which a Morisco bride should bring to her Christian husband should never be subject to confiscation. But the tradition of intolerance and persecution was a potent influence against the permanent adoption of any of these wise policies. The wealth of the Moriscos, which was great, and was probably supposed to be even greater than it was, made a constant temptation to subject them to penalties which would involve confiscation; nowhere is the avarice of the officials of the Holy Office revealed in a more odious light than in its grasping after the property of relapsed *con-*

[1] Cf. *ante,* Vol. III, pp. 128–131.

versos. The ability of the Moriscos to pay, moreover, often resulted in flagrant disregard of the government's solemn promises that, upon their conversion, they should in all respects be treated like Christians, and regarded as entitled to the possession of Christian privileges. It suited the purpose of their quondam masters, especially on the great Valencian estates, to retain them in semi-serfdom and not to set them free; it has been well said of them that they virtually remained *taillables et corvéables à merci.*[1] And those who knew the character and ideals of Philip the Prudent must have realized that when he succeeded his father and returned to Spain, it was the less enlightened side of the government's Morisco policy that was ultimately bound to prevail. One thing, in any case, was absolutely certain; there would be no toleration of the slightest indication of a relapse to the religion or customs of Islam.

Yet it would be unfair to the new monarch to assume that he at once gave full adherence to a policy of persecution, without making any efforts to attain his ends by gentler means. While he was still in Flanders, he had been approached by envoys of the Moriscos, and though nothing definite came of it at the time, it is evident that he realized that there were two sides to the case.[2] In 1564, we have a record that he strove to mitigate the severity of the Inquisition against the Moriscos of Valencia, where it had recently been particularly active, owing, apparently, to letters which it had received from Paul IV.[3] In the same year he also made an effort to improve and extend the instruction vouchsafed to the *conversos*; he even ordered that those who were intrusted with it should possess, whenever possible, the obvious qualification of knowing Arabic. One of his arch-

---

[1] Lea, *The Moriscos of Spain*, pp. 82–212, *passim.*
[2] *Ibid.*, pp. 222 f.
[3] *Ibid.*, pp. 102 f.; Danvila y Collado, *Expulsión de los Moriscos*, pp. 160–172.

bishops sanctioned the profanation of having the catechism printed in that language;[1] but unfortunately the vast majority of Philip's henchmen, and particularly the officials of the Holy Office, were far less anxious to make the most of their master's fleeting enthusiasm for a more liberal policy, and the experiment did not yield the fruits that were expected of it. In the year 1566, more sinister forces were brought into play. Diego de Espinosa, who, though Philip once declared him to have been the best minister he ever had, was in reality the king's evil genius, had been recently rising into prominence.[2] He had just been made president of the Council of Castile, and was shortly to become inquisitor-general; and he and his agent, Pedro Deza, prevailed on Philip to permit the full reënactment for the Moriscos of Granada of a series of restrictions, generally known as the Edict of 1526, which a similar set of influences had extracted from the Emperor, but which, in the succeeding years, had been suffered to fall into desuetude. This edict was one of the most vexatious and unwise in the whole history of Spanish legislation. It forbade the use of Arabic, and required the education of all Moriscos in Castilian. Moorish names, dress, and ornaments were subjected to the ban; Moorish baths were strictly prohibited; and disarmament was to be strictly enforced. All births were to be attended by Christian midwives, so as to make sure that no Moorish ceremonies were secretly performed; and all the doors of the houses of Moriscos were to be kept wide open on feast days, fast days, and special occasions, so that any one could look in and satisfy himself as to the conditions inside.[3] And the reënactment of the edict, at this particular time and under

[1] Lea, *Moriscos*, p. 149; Danvila y Collado, p. 169.

[2] Lea, *Moriscos*, p. 226.

[3] *Nueva Recopilación*, lib. viii, tit. ii, leyes 13, 15, 17; Luis del Mármol Carvajal, *Rebelion y Castigo de los Moriscos del Reino de Granada*, in *B. A. E.*, Historiadores de Sucesos Particulares, i, p. 158; Lea, *Moriscos*, pp. 215 f.

these circumstances, was vastly more irritating to the Moriscos than the original had been to their ancestors. There was no excuse for it, as there possibly may have been before, in the state of Spanish foreign affairs. Its long period of suspension, though largely the result of a bribe which the Emperor, unlike his son, had been unscrupulous enough to accept, had naturally given its victims the notion that the Spanish government was not really in earnest in its policy of persecution; and it came as a great shock to them to learn that they were wrong. Finally, the reënactment, in itself, was far harsher than its original; though it aimed at the same end, its methods were much more severe. The Moriscos were now flatly ordered to learn Castilian within three years, though no provision whatsoever was made for their instruction. All contracts in Arabic were pronounced invalid. Not only were the Moorish baths no longer to be used; they were to be formally destroyed — both the public and private ones. The government, in fact, seemed bent on blotting out every trace of the existence of the ancient Moorish civilization.[1]

If the edict itself was inspired by principles which contradicted all the dictates of humanity and statesmanship, the way in which it was published showed an equally criminal lack of foresight. Iñigo López de Mendoza, Count of Tendilla and third Marquis of Mondéjar, was captain-general at Granada at the time. He had the benefit of a long family tradition, besides thirty years' personal experience in that high office, and was generally respected and trusted by Morisco and Christian alike. It would, therefore, have seemed indispensable to consult him in regard to the violent change of policy that was proposed.[2] This, however, was

[1] Mármol Carvajal, loc. cit., pp. 161 f.;   [2] Lea, Moriscos, p. 219, note 2.
Lea, Moriscos, p. 229.

not done, although he was actually at the court at the time; indeed, the first intimation of it that he received was an order to go back to his post, and be ready when the edict should be published. He not unnaturally remonstrated at being treated in such fashion; he vigorously represented the probability of a Morisco rising, and the inadequacy of the garrison, munitions, and state of defences at Granada, and he was heartily supported by the Consejo de Guerra. But the government chose to pay no attention to his advice. It was the priests, and not the soldiers, that for the moment held the upper hand, and Mondéjar was commanded to stop complaining and mind his own affairs. He had every right to be bitter about it. It had already become, as he plainly foresaw, and as Cabrera de Córdoba afterwards wrote, a case not for friars' caps but for steel helmets.[1]

It was on January 1, 1567, the seventy-fifth anniversary of the capture of Granada, that the new edict was formally published with appropriate ceremonies; and as an earnest of the government's intention rigorously to enforce it, the destruction of the Morisco baths was immediately begun.[2] That the answering insurrection was postponed for nearly two years was due, in the main, to the fact that it had been arranged that some of the more vexatious provisions of the edict should not go into immediate operation; and, to a lesser extent, to the representations which even Espinosa's minions at Granada were now induced to make to the government, in regard to the evident danger of the policy they had been commanded to carry out. But the postponement only served to make the outbreak the more serious when it occurred; for the Moriscos had had time to muster their

---

[1] Bleda, *Coronica de los Moros de España*, pp. 658 f.; C. de C., i, pp. 552 ff.; Memorial of the Marquis of Mondéjar in Morel-Fatio, *L'Espagne au XVIe et au XVIIe siècle*, pp. 17 f.; Mármol Carvajal, *loc. cit.*, p. 167; Lea, *Moriscos*, pp. 227 f.

[2] Mármol Carvajal, *loc. cit.*, pp. 166 ff.; Lea, *Moriscos*, pp. 230 f.

own resources, as well as to become acquainted with the weaknesses of their oppressors. Their fighting blood grew hotter as the different provisions of the edict were successively enforced; and the failure of their various deputations to procure its relaxation served to drive them to despair. They began secretly to accumulate munitions and stores, and to prepare strong places in the sierras to which they could retire.[1] They sent messages to ask for aid from their coreligionists in North Africa;[2] and some of them dressed themselves after the Turkish fashion, in order to make the Spaniards believe that they were receiving aid from Constantinople.[3] They encouraged each other by reciting ancient prophecies of the reconquest of Spain by Islam;[4] and they found a leader in one Aben Humeya, who had already made a name for himself by shedding Christian blood, and who boasted descent from the Omayyads.[5] Appreciating the obvious advantages of striking their first blow on the day of a Christian festival, when their oppressors would be off their guard, they planned their initial rising for Holy Thursday (April 15), 1568; but the Spaniards on this occasion were better prepared than they had supposed, and the rebels were obliged to abandon the attempt.[6] At Christmas time, however, they struck again, this time with better results. Excess of caution at the critical moment prevented them, indeed, from capturing the Christian garrison of the Albaycin, or Moorish quarter of the town, which at the time numbered only twenty-three men; but in all the

[1] Bleda, *Coronica*, pp. 660–666; Mármol Carvajal, *loc. cit.*, pp. 181 ff.

[2] Castries, *France*, i, pp. 286–289; Antonio Tiepolo (1567) in Albèri, *Relazioni*, serie i, v, p. 145; Mármol Carvajal, *loc. cit.*, p. 179; Memorial of the Marquis of Mondéjar in Morel-Fatio, *L'Espagne au XVI⁰ et au XVII⁰ siècle*, p. 19; Bleda, *Coronica*, pp. 674 f.

[3] Castries, *France*, i, p. 294.

[4] Lea, *Moriscos*, pp. 234, 434–437.

[5] C. de C., i, pp. 595 ff.; Hurtado de Mendoza in *B. A. E.*, Historiadores de Sucesos Particulares, i, pp. 74, 102; José Palanco Romero, *Aben-Humeya en la Historia y en la Leyenda* (Granada, 1915).

[6] Lea, *Moriscos*, pp. 234 f., and references there.

country about Granada the Moriscos rose in arms, robbing, spoiling, and desecrating churches, and torturing and murdering their Christian foes.[1]

Having brought on, by its intolerance and ineptitude, the very uprising which the wiser heads had foreseen, the government turned to Mondéjar to put it down. So violent were the jealousies between the different factions at Granada that he was given practically no support; indeed, it would appear that Deza actually put obstacles in his path.[2] But Mondéjar was equal to the occasion. The Andalusian cities were called on to send in their contingents, and on January 3, 1569, he was able to set forth from Granada with a force of about 2000 men.[3] The critical point was the bridge over the deep gorge of Tablate, which commanded the approach to the sierras. Though the Moors had so dismantled the bridge that only a single soldier could cross it at a time, Mondéjar managed to drive away the force that guarded its further end, and so possess himself of the key to the country beyond.[4] From that moment the first phase of the rebellion was over. Mondéjar was relentless in following up the advantage that he had gained. Town after town surrendered at discretion. By the beginning of February the revolt was practically put down.[5] In case of useless resistance the victor was very stern, and there is at least one instance of his commanding a general massacre;[6] but when submission, as was usually the case, was absolute and complete, he promised the vanquished that they should not be permitted to suffer harm. His sole object, so he

[1] Mármol Carvajal, loc. cit., pp. 183 ff.; Mondéjar in Morel-Fatio, op. cit., pp. 19 ff.

[2] Lea, Moriscos, p. 238, and references there.

[3] C. de C., i, p. 649; Mármol Carvajal, loc. cit., pp. 219 ff.

[4] Ibid., pp. 226 f.; Mondéjar in Morel-Fatio, pp. 24 ff.; Bleda, Coronica, pp. 682 ff.

[5] Letter of the Marquis de los Vélez in R. H., xxxi, pp. 507–509.

[6] Lea, Moriscos, pp. 242 f.

repeatedly assured them, was to bring about a permanent pacification of the land. Such a plan, however, did not suit the views of the vast majority of the soldiers who composed his forces; their main object was to gorge themselves with booty. Nowhere in the annals of sixteenth-century warfare is there a blacker record in this respect; "There were even men who stole cats, caldrons, turnspits, kneading troughs, reels, cow bells, and other worthless things, all simply because they would not give up the right to plunder. I mention no names," adds the soldier who wrote the account, "for in this campaign we were all thieves together, and myself the first of them." [1] With all his efforts, Mondéjar found it impossible to restrain these outrages; this, in turn, convinced the Moriscos that he had no intention of observing the fair promises he had made them, and consequently encouraged them to continue their revolt. A few weeks after he had reported to Philip that the rebellion was at an end, the evidences began to multiply that it was about to burst forth afresh. Aben Humeya, who just previously had been a fugitive in hiding, was now reported to have an army of at least 4000 men. [2]

But if the weary work of suppression was to be done all over again, the government was resolved that it should not be done by Mondéjar. Deza's hatred of him had been increased by the success of his campaign, and by the high regard in which he was held by Christian and Moslem alike; and he assured Philip and Espinosa that things would never go the way they wished until the Marquis was removed. Deza's representations, fortified by the soldiers' complaints of the way in which it had been attempted to put a term to their pillagings, finally produced the desired effect; in

[1] Mármol Carvajal, as cited in Forneron, ii, p. 163; cf. also Hurtado de Mendoza in B. A. E., Historiadores de Sucesos Particulares, i, p. 106.
[2] Lea, Moriscos, p. 246.

March, Mondéjar was ordered to relinquish the supreme command to the king's half-brother, Don John of Austria, the bastard of Charles V and Barbara Blomberg.[1] This prince, who was born at Ratisbon on February 24, 1547,[2] had been kept in concealment during the Emperor's day, and even Philip did not learn of his existence until after his father's death. The news may very likely have been unwelcome, but the king determined to make the best of it. He gave his newly discovered kinsman the name by which he was afterwards to be known,[3] and commanded that he be furnished with a large household and many servants. There was, perhaps, a certain measure of sound policy in placing this royal bastard in a position far above the grandees, so as to accentuate the vast difference that separated them from the throne. Don John was certainly, in all outward respects, a most agreeable contrast to Philip. Good-looking, affable, and courteous, without any of that air of suspicion and taciturnity which no one could help remarking about the king, he seemed to contemporaries as one intrusted with a divine mission, prepared, nay, almost predestined to play a hero's part.[4] The task of putting down the insurrection at Granada was to be his first public appearance, so to speak, and Philip was determined that he should be equipped for it in such fashion as would secure complete success. He was given many times more troops than Mondéjar had been able to command (a whole *tercio* was brought

[1] Hurtado de Mendoza and Mármol Carvajal in *B. A. E.*, Historiadores de Sucesos Particulares, i, pp. 86, 250, 253; Mondéjar in Morel-Fatio, p. 49. The little Spanish monograph, *Bárbara de Blomberg*, by Nicolás Acero y Abad (Logroño, 1901), has been completely superseded by Paul Herre's *Barbara Blomberg* (Leipzig, 1909).

[2] The date may be regarded as having been definitely established by Stirling-Maxwell, *Don John of Austria*, i,

pp. 1–3; though most of the older authorities, and some even of the more recent ones, give it as February 24, 1545. Cf. P. O. von Törne, *Don Juan d'Autriche*, i, pp. 189 f., note.

[3] It would appear that Don John was originally called Gerónimo; cf. Forneron, ii, pp. 168 f., and references there.

[4] Cf. *D. I. E.*, xxviii, pp. 8–12, 60 f., 72–87, 92 f.; Stirling-Maxwell, *Don John of Austria*, i, pp. 146 ff.; Pirenne, iv, pp. 83 f.

over from Naples for the purpose) ; a detachment of Spanish galleys cruised up and down the coast so as to prevent all possibility of aid from without ; and Don John had a war council of experienced captains.[1]   But there was also a whole series of restraints and inhibitions, such as was inevitable in any enterprise in which Philip was concerned.   Don John's youthful pride was galled by being commanded to remain at Granada to issue orders, and on no account to take a personal part in the campaign ; his war council was rent with conflicting opinions ; everything had to be referred to Madrid.   Nine whole months went by with practically nothing done, save to encourage the Moors to continue their new resistance.   Many of those places which, in the spring, had unconditionally submitted to Mondéjar now renounced their allegiance and made common cause with the rebels, whose forays reached right up to the gates of Granada.   The town was virtually isolated in the midst of a hostile land.[2]

Finally, on October 19, 1569, Philip issued an edict proclaiming a war of fire and blood — hitherto it had been only the suppression of a revolt — against the Moors of Granada, giving the soldiers leave to plunder at will and keep all they could get, and considerably increasing their pay.[3]   At the same time he yielded to the entreaties of Don John, and gave him leave to take the field in person.   On January 19, the prince was able to sit down before the stronghold of Galera with an army of at least 12,000 men.   Despite the fact that the garrison was scarcely one-fourth as large as the besieging force and pitifully lacking in arms and munitions, it was over

---

[1] A set of instructions from the Duke of Alva to Don John on the conduct of the war against the infidels both on land and sea is to be found in the R. A. H., est. 27, gr. 3a, E, no. 80 ff., 30 ff.   See *D. I. E.*, iii, pp. 273–283. Cf. also *D. I. E.*, xxviii, pp. 5–19;

Hurtado de Mendoza and Mármol Carvajal in *B. A. E.*, Historiadores de Sucesos Particulares, i, pp. 89–91, 251 f.

[2] Lea, *Moriscos*, pp. 248 f., and references there.

[3] Hurtado de Mendoza and Mármol Carvajal, *loc. cit.*, pp. 107, 292.

three weeks before the place could be captured; one of the Spanish assaults was disastrously repulsed; Don John himself was wounded, and the Moors got the better of such hand-to-hand fighting as occurred.[1] When Galera was taken, all the survivors were put to the sword without distinction of age or sex; and the ensuing orgies so demoralized the victors that, at the next stronghold which they attacked, they were speedily put to flight by the sorties of a handful of their foes; "I would never have believed," wrote Don John to the king, "that such a panic as I have witnessed could possibly have taken place."[2] It is needless to follow the campaign in detail. There were a few bright spots in it, particularly the duels of certain doughty champions reminiscent of the heroic days of the wars of the Catholic Kings:[3] but for the most part it was the sort of struggle that it is not pleasant to dwell upon. Despite all their bungling and barbarity the Spaniards were not to be denied. The overwhelming preponderance of their numbers and resources finally decided the day, and though the last embers of resistance were not stamped out till the first weeks of 1571, when the Moorish leader, Aben Aboo, successor to Aben Humeya, was treacherously murdered by an outlaw in Spanish pay,[4] the end was plainly inevitable at least a year before. It had become evident to the more intelligent of the Moriscos that they must accept whatever terms the victors should please to impose.[5]

There could be little question what the nature of those terms would be. In the eyes of the government the con-

---

[1] C. de C., ii, pp. 42 ff.; Mármol Carvajal, loc. cit., pp. 313 f.; Forneron, ii, pp. 183 ff., and references there; F. Cáceres Pla, "Asalto de la villa de Galera," in Sociedad Española de Excursiones, Boletín, xvi (1908), pp. 63–67.

[2] D. I. E., xxviii, pp. 49 f.

[3] Forneron, ii, p. 186.

[4] Cf. M. H. E., iii, pp. 35–37. Aben Humeya had been assassinated by two of his own followers in October, 1569. Castries, France, i, pp. 291, note 4, 294.

[5] Lea, Moriscos, p. 256; Forneron, ii, p. 189.

centration of so large a portion of the Morisco population of
the peninsula in the neighborhood of Granada was the fundamental cause of all the difficulties of the past. The
Moriscos were, therefore, to be deported inland and arbitrarily distributed throughout the country. Orders for the
execution of this measure were issued to Don John as early
as February, 1570, long before the successful termination of
his campaign. The peaceable Moriscos of each place that he
conquered were successively to be collected and sent inland,
in batches, under guard. They were allowed to take with
them their women and children, to carry with them such
movables as they could, and to sell the rest; but it is difficult
to believe that they ever got fair prices, and there is abundant
evidence that they were often robbed.[1] The Venetian envoy,
Donato, writing in 1573, calculates that the king got an
annual revenue of 125,000 crowns from the dues on their
confiscated lands and from their goods which had fallen to
the crown since their rebellion.[2] On October 6, 1572, an
elaborate *pragmática* was drawn up, regulating the conditions
under which they were to be permitted to live.[3] They were
to be kept under the perpetual surveillance of a series of
different functionaries, who were encouraged to spy upon
them in every way. They were forbidden to change the
residences that had been assigned to them without a royal
license, or to return to within ten leagues of the kingdom of
Granada under pain of death; all the restrictions of the
detestable edict of 1566 were declared to be fully in force.
That the Moriscos were unwelcome guests in the communities where they were quartered is evident from all the contemporary records; and the archives of the Inquisition

[1] Hurtado de Mendoza and Mármol
Carvajal, *loc. cit.*, pp. 116–120, 342–
363, *passim*.
[2] Leonardo Donato in C. de C., iv,
p. 421 (last line), also in Albèri, *Relazioni*, serie i, vi, p. 378.
[3] *Nueva Recopilación*, lib. viii, tit. ii,
ley 22.

furnish ample proof that their enforced conversion to Christianity was but nominal. But perhaps the most remarkable feature of the whole affair was the success with which the exiles, in spite of all limitations and persecutions, found means to make good livings. In 1582 an official report declared that their numbers were fast increasing, because they were not "wasted by war or religion," and that they were so industrious that, though they came to Castile ten years before without a scrap of land, they were becoming well-to-do, and even rich; and that there was good prospect that in twenty years more the natives would become their servants.[1]

It must have been pretty obvious by the death of Philip II what the end was to be, though the final act of the tragedy was to be reserved till the reign of his son. Dispersion and persecution were not enough; Spain would never be satisfied short of absolute expulsion. Dread of religious contamination was the fundamental cause; but it is also worth noting that the government welcomed every other kind of complaint, whether political, social, or economic, that was addressed to it, for all contributed to exculpate the final action. It was in 1609 that the blow at last fell. By a series of edicts all the Moriscos in the different Spanish kingdoms were forced to depart from the peninsula, by routes or from ports that were designated to them in advance. No adequate time or opportunity was given them in which to dispose of such property as they could not carry with them; sales at forced prices and robberies were the order of the day.[2] Yet there was surprisingly little resistance. Despite the deep sorrow that it must have

[1] F. Janer, *Condicion Social de los Moriscos*, pp. 254–272; Lea, *Moriscos*, pp. 265–270. Cf. *Actas de las Córtes*, xi, pp. 542 f., and p. 431, *infra*.

[2] Lea, *Moriscos*, pp. 320 ff.; Janer, *op. cit.*, pp. 297 ff.

caused them to abandon their last hold on a land where
their ancestors had reigned supreme, the majority of the
Moriscos were by this time so thoroughly convinced of
the horror of all things Christian that they seemed, for
the most part, to be glad to go, and even competed for the
first places on the transports that had been provided.[1]
Most of them sought the Barbary coasts; but there were
also a considerable number who made their way into France,
where they found themselves far less welcome than they
had been given reason to expect, and whence most of them
ultimately embarked for North Africa.[2]　A trifling number
attempted to remain hidden in Spain, and had to be hunted
down in the succeeding years by commissioners specially
appointed for the purpose; and some of the exiles were so
ill treated in Barbary, that they elected to return to Spain
and be consigned to the galleys.[3]　A fair estimate of the
total number of those deported would be probably not far
from half a million — about one-sixteenth, that is, of the
population of Spain.[4]　That such a small proportion of the
inhabitants of the peninsula should have been regarded
by the government as constituting a serious menace, furnishes a final and conclusive proof of the intensity of the
passion that animated Spain's rulers for sacrificing everything on the altar of unity of the faith.

The government's treatment of the Moriscos, and the
rebellion which it evoked, belong primarily, as we have
already remarked, with the internal history of Philip's
reign; but it would be an error to assume that they were
entirely without effect on the course of Spain's foreign
affairs.　For the dream of a reconquest of the Iberian
peninsula by Islam had never wholly lost its place in the

---

[1] Lea, *Moriscos*, pp. 327 ff.
[2] *Ibid.*, pp. 340 ff.
[3] *Ibid.*, pp. 363 ff., and references there.
[4] *Ibid.*, p. 359, and references there.

visions of the Moslem prophets, nor had it ceased to be
contemplated as a possibility by the Christians;[1] and the
rising of 1568 certainly furnished a better opportunity for
the realization of it than had ever been presented since
the days of the Catholic Kings.   That more advantage was
not taken of it is one of the most curious facts in the history of the period.   The coasts of Andalusia were virtually
unguarded,[2] and there was considerable correspondence between the Morisco leaders and the Moorish kings of North
Africa; the rebels even circulated stories that these sovereigns had landed in Spain with overwhelming forces, in
order to encourage one another to persist in their uprising.[3]
But beyond the sending of messages and the spreading of
false reports, the North African monarchs did little to avail
themselves of a really golden opportunity, and the same was
the case with the Turks farther eastward.   Writing in 1573,
the Venetian envoy, Donato, declares that if the Sultan,
instead of breaking with the signory, had sent a few galleys
and troops to the south coasts of Spain at the time of the
insurrection, he could have kindled a flame which would not
even then have died out; and that he had heard on the best
authority that it had often been feared in the Council of
Castile that the Granadan rising might be the means of
encouraging the Huguenots to pour across the Pyrenees.[4]
The Franco-Turkish alliance, which had been such a thorn
in the side of the Emperor Charles V, was no longer, indeed,
in full working order; but there was considerable fear of
its resuscitation, and that fear continued to persist after
the suppression of the Granadan insurrection.   A plot,
real or pretended, for an attack on Mers-el-Kebir by the

[1] Cf. Peter Martyr d'Anghiera, *Opus
Epistolarum*, no. 499 (1512).
[2] Cf. Antonio Tiepolo (1567) in
Albèri, *Relazioni*, serie i, v, p. 145.

[3] Lea, *Moriscos*, pp. 236, 237, 279,
and references there.
[4] In Albèri, *Relazioni*, serie i, vi, p.
409.

rulers of Tlemcen and Algiers, to be aided by a rising of the
Valencian Moriscos, by a possible invasion of Spain from
France, and even by promises of support from Constantinople, was unearthed in 1573 and again in 1577.[1] Another similar plan was said to be afoot in 1583, and incriminating correspondence was reported to have been intercepted ; and the danger apparently recurred again in later
years.[2] All these episodes, however, were little more than
aftermaths. The great chance had passed in 1570, before
Philip's foreign enemies could combine to utilize it, and it
never was to present itself in such favorable form again.[3]
But the fact that the Spanish government took the peril so
seriously shows that the Granadan revolt had the possibility
of the widest ramifications, and it will thus serve as a connecting link between the events we have already described
and the great naval campaign against the Turks on the
Mediterranean, to which we devote the remainder of the
present chapter.

However much the advice of the Emperor and Philip's
own inclinations may have dictated a policy of peace with
Christian sovereigns during the first part of the new reign,
there were abundant reasons why the Prudent King should
adopt a more aggressive attitude in his relations with the
infidel. In the first place, over and above the age-long
tradition of the Spanish monarchy, Philip's conception of
himself as the true head of Christendom demanded some
striking demonstration of his worthiness to champion the
cause of the Cross. In the second, the opportunity was
unusually favorable. The peace of Cateau-Cambrésis,
in addition to ending the strife with France which had

[1] Lea, *Moriscos*, pp. 281 f.
[2] *Ibid.*, pp. 279, 283–285.

[3] Forneron, ii, pp. 158 f., and references there.

absorbed such a large proportion of Spain's energy during
the preceding reign, had naturally served to loosen the
bonds of the Franco-Turkish alliance.[1] The infidel was
unsupported in the Western Mediterranean, as he had not
been since 1535; furthermore, his own attention was now
constantly distracted by revolts at home and by the pressure
of his wars with the Shah of Persia.[2] And lastly, there
were a long series of defeats and affronts which called
aloud for revenge. We have already alluded to the tragic
tale of reverses in North Africa which had saddened the
last years of the Emperor's reign;[3] but that was by no means
all. Never had the ravages of the infidel corsairs, of whom
by far the most terrible was the ubiquitous Dragut, attained
such shocking proportions. Not only did they harry the
Mediterranean shores of Spain, swooping down like vultures
on commercial vessels and fishermen, seizing their cargoes,
and sending their crews away to terms of dreadful servitude
in the Orient; they now also ventured out into the broad
Atlantic, and played havoc with the Indian galleons outside
Cadiz and Seville.[4] Even worse than the lot of Spain was
that of the Italian states; and of these it was the Spanish
realms of Sicily and Naples that suffered most of all. Defenceless towns and villages were sacked, and their inhabitants carried off to slavery, never to be seen again in Western
Europe, save in the exceptional cases where a chance victory
over an isolated Turkish galley served to deliver individuals
from the rowers' benches.[5] It has been well said that one

[1] The comments of the Sultan on the
peace, as communicated to the representative of Henry II at Constantinople,
may be found in Charrière, *Négociations*, ii, pp. 586 ff.

[2] Charles Monchicourt, *L'expédition
espagnole de 1560 contre l'île de Djerba*,
p. 86.

[3] *Ante*, Vol. III, pp. 335–346.

[4] On June 24, 1562, Sir Thomas
Chaloner, the English ambassador to
Spain, wrote home to Queen Elizabeth
that "the Moors have spoilt many
merchant ships about Seville and
Cadiz, and amongst them three English
ships, with a booty of more than
100,000 ducats." *C. S. P., Foreign,*
1562, no. 248.

[5] Charrière, *Négociations*, ii, pp. 508–
523; Bosio, *Istoria*, iii, pp. 397–399;

of the chief reasons why the Turks were so dangerous to
Europe was because they were so successful in employing
Europeans against her. Every one of their recent victories
may be regarded, in other words, as possessing a double
significance; not only did it strengthen them and weaken
their foes; it almost invariably furnished them with the
material for repeating it.[1]

Clearly then, at the time of the return of Philip II to the
peninsula, there were both ample justification and an
exceptional opportunity for Spain to launch a vigorous
attack against her traditional foe. If the Prudent King had
come boldly forward and himself assumed the leadership
of the different forces that demanded that a campaign be
forthwith begun, it would probably have taken the form
of another assault on Algiers, one of the recognized centres
of the Turkish power in North Africa, or at least on some
one of the infidel ports on the western part of the North
African coast, where a victory would have chiefly redounded
to the benefit of Spain.[2] But Philip, as usual, failed to seize
the initiative, with the result that the early stages of a
game which really mattered more to the Spaniards than to
any one else were chiefly played by others, and in regions
comparatively remote. It was Jean de La Valette, grand-
master at Malta, and Juan de la Cerda, Duke of Medina
Celi and viceroy of Sicily, who planned the blow and decided
where it should be planted; and it was consequently the
Central and not the Western Mediterranean that became
the scene of action. The grand-master longed to recover

P. de Salazar, *Guerra de Africa*, fols.
i–iiii.
[1] Forneron, i, p. 353. It might
perhaps be argued that this statement
holds equally true of the employment
of Turkish captives by the Christians;
but as the Turks had won the large
majority of the recent encounters, the
principle applied, for the time being
at least, in a manner wholly favorable
to them.
[2] Mercier, *Histoire de l'Afrique septentrionale*, iii, p. 98.

Tripoli, whence the Knights had been expelled in 1551.[1] The viceroy had had an unusual number of pirate raids to avenge; he adopted the grand-master's proposals with an enthusiasm to which his criminal dilatoriness in action forms a shocking contrast, and was duly appointed general-in-chief. He also got the approval of Philip — but not much more. Despite the urgency of the viceroy, the Prudent King gave him little active support; he did not wish to imperil his ships in an enterprise so remote; he proposed to participate in the expedition to just such an extent as would enable him to claim some credit and derive some advantage if it should succeed, but not enough to run grave risks in case of defeat.[2] The composition of the expeditionary forces is highly significant. The fleet, of fifty-four ships of war and thirty-six transports, was exclusively composed of Italian vessels,[3] and was commanded by Gian Andrea Doria, twenty-one years old, the grand-nephew and successor of the Emperor's great admiral; the Spanish naval leader, Juan de Mendoza, who was at Naples with a number of Spanish galleys at the time the fleet was being collected, entirely refused to coöperate, and it is difficult to resist the conclusion that his refusal was dictated by the king. The army which the fleet carried, between 11,000 and 12,000 strong, was only a little more than half composed of Spanish troops, and all of these were taken from the *tercios* of Lombardy, Naples, and Sicily; their general-in-chief, Álvaro de Sande, was a Spaniard commanding at Naples; the expedition was in no sense truly Iberian, either in its origin, composition, or

---

[1] Cf. *ante*, Vol. III, p. 343.

[2] U. Foglietta, *De Sacro Foedere*, etc., pp. 206–224. It is worth noting that the Cortes were apparently more enthusiastic for the enterprise than the king. *Cortes*, v, pp. 857 f.; *infra*, pp. 430 f.

[3] It is but fair to add that of these, four were furnished by Sicily and five by Naples. Cf. Monchicourt, pp. 87 f.

purpose.[1] And it is reasonable to suppose that Philip's failure
to take a more active interest in it was chiefly responsible for
the long delays and lack of coöperation which characterized
the enterprise from the very start. By no means all the contingents reached Messina, the original rendezvous, at the
appointed time. There was a month's wait at Syracuse
to permit the laggards to join. Not till February 10, 1560,
did the expedition finally set sail from Malta.[2]

These delays were of evil augury for the success of the
enterprise, and the events of the ensuing weeks made its
failure inevitable. Lack of drinking water compelled the
fleet to touch at Rocchetta, on the east coast of the island
of Gerba, on the way; though it replenished its stock at the
cost of a trifling encounter with the inhabitants, it gained
no information in regard to the plans or resources of Dragut,
who commanded at Tripoli.[3] Failure to inquire about the
enemy's position and plans was, throughout, one of the
worst mistakes of the crusaders. Their next landing was
effected on the North African coast at a point some seventy-
five miles to the west of their ultimate objective; but the
place was unhealthy, the water bad, and Dragut, who knew
every inch of the country, within disagreeable proximity;
and so, after interminable disputes as to the proper course
to take, it was decided to return to Gerba, where they felt
they could be safe and prepare at leisure; on March 7,
accordingly, the expedition finally disembarked at the
northwest corner of the island.[4] The inhabitants at first
made no effort to prevent them. They belonged to a

[1] For details, cf. Monchicourt, *op.
cit.*, pp. 87–94. It is worth noting,
however, that the number of troops sent
on this expedition was as large as that
used in the attack on El Mehedia in
1550 (cf. *ante*, Vol. III, p. 342), and
had only been exceeded, in all the
various Spanish enterprises against

the infidel since the fall of Granada
in 1492, by those employed in the
battle of Prevesa in 1538, and against
Algiers in 1541.

[2] Mercier, iii, p. 98; Monchicourt,
p. 87.

[3] Monchicourt, pp. 98 ff.

[4] Monchicourt, p. 101.

different tribe (Sof) from the men of Rocchetta, whose resistance three weeks before had been inspired by Dragut ; [1] they professed the deepest hatred of the pirate, and permitted the Christians to occupy the castle of Gerba without making any serious difficulty. But when they saw signs that the new comers intended to establish themselves permanently, their suspicions were aroused. Their original hope, that the Christians would rid them of Dragut and then depart, now seemed illusory. Before long they began to make overtures to their neighbors to the southeastward for a joint assault upon the crusaders, to be delivered at the first favorable opportunity.[2]

While the evidences that the Spaniards proposed to remain at Gerba were converting its inhabitants from potential allies into formidable foes, the ubiquitous Dragut made active preparations to expel them. The excellence of his information in regard to the movements of his Christian enemies stands out in sharp contrast to their ignorance of his ; and the hesitation of the crusaders had given him a chance not only to repair the defences of Tripoli, but also to send for naval aid to Constantinople. On May 10, while the viceroy was in the midst of his leisurely arrangements, a galley arrived from Malta with the stunning news that a Turkish fleet of eighty-five sail, under the dreaded Piali Pasha, had been sighted off Gozzo and was making straight for Gerba.[3] A scene of terrible confusion ensued. Doria wished to take flight at once and save his galleys.

---

[1] The pirate was actually present at Rocchetta at the time the Christians touched there, though they were not aware of it at the time; cf. Monchicourt, p. 98.

[2] F. Cirni, *Successi*, pp. 74 ff.; Alfonso de Ulloa, *Historia dell' Impresa di Tripoli*, fols. 11 ff.; cf. Fernández Duro, "Desastre de los Gelves," in his *Estudios del Reinado de Felipe II*,

pp. 1–63, and the two contemporary *relaciones* which follow on pp. 67–244; Monchicourt, pp. 101 f.

[3] Monchicourt, p. 109. It is worth noting that Piali Pasha and Aluch Ali were both Italian born; and Brantôme asserts that the latter was once a monk. Cf. Forneron, i, pp. 355, 364, and Charrière, *Négociations dans le Levant*, ii, pp. 610–613, note.

The viceroy, whose sense of honor was far higher than his military skill, insisted that it would be an outrage to abandon his men, who were too scattered and too distant to make it possible to embark them all.   The point was finally settled in Doria's favor;[1] there was a wild scramble for the ships, and a certain number finally managed to get on board. On the morning of May 11, the admiral gave the order to put to sea; but before even his best ships could gain the open water, the Turkish fleet appeared on the northern horizon, bearing down on them before a favorable breeze. A panic seized the Christian forces, who were so anxious to escape as to be totally unable to fight, and the result was a foregone conclusion.   The Turkish admiral, almost without striking a blow, captured twenty-seven Christian galleys and one galliot, and killed or took prisoners some 5000 men.   Doria and the viceroy succeeded in effecting their escape, but Alvaro de Sande and about 6000 soldiers were left, without adequate supplies, in the castle of Gerba, virtually sentenced to death or capture before succor from Europe could possibly arrive.   The news of the disaster came as an awful shock to Spain, to the Italian states, and to the Knights of Malta, and perhaps most of all to old Andrea Doria, the admiral of Charles V; indeed, it is reasonable to suppose that it hastened his death, which occurred on Monday, the 25th of the following November, at the age of five days less than ninety-four years.[2]

There were many brave resolves, both in Italy and in Spain, that help should be forthwith dispatched to Álvaro

---

[1] "Une belle fuite valait mieux qu'un brave combat." Cf. Monchicourt, pp. 109–114, and references there, especially to F. Cirni, *Successi*, pp. 81 ff.

[2] Monchicourt, p. 114.   C. Sigonius, *De Vita et Rebus gestis Andreae Doriae*, lib. ii, cap. xliii, makes him just one year younger at the time of his death; but Lorenzo Capelloni, *Vita del Prencipe Andrea Doria*, p. 185, E. Petit, *André Doria*, p. 353, and Fernández Duro, *Armada Española*, ii, p. 43, note 3, give his age as I have given it in the text.

de Sande and his men who had been left behind ; but there were, as usual, interminable delays when it came to the point of execution.[1] Philip showed energy in forwarding the necessary preparations, but refused to let the expedition set sail. It seems evident that, for the time being, he favored a dispersal of Spain's naval resources rather than their concentration as a united fleet, and that his worries over the maintenance of the Spanish hold on Tunis prevented him from giving his undivided attention to the problem of the moment. Meantime, Piali Pasha summoned Dragut out of Tripoli to aid him in the capture of the fortress of Gerba, which he planned, not to assault, but to surround and starve out, rightly judging that its scanty supplies and lack of water would compel it to capitulate before reënforcements could arrive.[2] On May 26, he sat down before it, with some 8000 men and about twenty pieces of artillery, and occupied the next five days in cutting off all possibility of access by the garrison to the various wells in the neighborhood.[3] Don Álvaro, who had failed to seize several excellent opportunities for a vigorous attack before the investment was completed, tried sorties, too late, on June 2 and on July 28. The first, which had some chance of success, was inadequately supported and finally driven back ; while the second, which was attempted after the troops had lost their morale, had no other result than the capture of Don Álvaro. On July 31, the castle surrendered. All of its 6000 defenders who were not already dead were taken prisoners.[4] The fortifications were razed to the ground. The victors returned in triumph to Tripoli, where Dragut was now established beyond possibility of overthrow ; and Piali Pasha, after ravaging the eastern shores of Sicily,

---

[1] Monchicourt, pp. 124 f.
[2] *Ibid.*, pp. 120 f., 225 f., 241 f.
[3] *Ibid.*, p. 126.

[4] The Christian losses, soldiers and sailors, did not fall short of 15,000; cf. Monchicourt, p. 135.

got back safely in the end of September to Constantinople, to receive the plaudits of the multitude and the thanks of Suleiman the Magnificent.[1]

This reverse was by far the most serious that had been suffered in North Africa since the defeat of Charles V before Algiers. The object of the expedition had been to regain, through the reëstablishment of the Knights of St. John at Tripoli, the control of the central part of the Mediterranean for the Christians; and its failure naturally encouraged their enemies to believe that it would be possible completely to expel them from it. In the following year Dragut asked the Sultan to grant him an army to recapture La Goletta from the Spaniards; the idea, in other words, which bore fruit in 1574, was first conceived just after the Gerba campaign.[2] Moreover, the Turkish attack which was to be delivered against Malta in 1565 should be logically considered as the counterthrust to the Christian attempt on Tripoli in 1560; since the Knights had so signally failed to win back their African home, was it not reasonable to suppose that it would be possible to oust them from their stronghold on the island?[3] But most important of all for the student of the Spanish Empire was the effect of the disaster at Gerba on the situation farther west. Philip's slackness in supporting the expedition against Tripoli is to be chiefly explained, as we have already remarked, by his conviction that the blow was to be planted in a region so remote as to be of comparatively little consequence to the maintenance of Spanish power in North Africa; now he was to learn that the encouragement [4] which his enemies

[1] Monchicourt, p. 134; also Fernández Duro, "Desastre de los Gelves," in his *Estudios Históricos del Reinado de Felipe II*, pp. 50 f.; A. de Ulloa, *op. cit.*, fols. 34 ff.

[2] Monchicourt, p. 136.

[3] *Ibid.*, p. 135; Bosio, *Istoria*, iii, p. 441.

[4] The authorities at Constantinople, however, were much more inclined to caution than was Dragut. Cf. Charrière, *Négociations*, ii, pp. 616 f.

had derived from their victory was to carry the contest to his very doors. In the spring of 1561 the Turkish fleet suddenly appeared before Soller in Majorca and proceeded to attack it. The inhabitants, fortunately, were both brave and resourceful, and the assault was repulsed on May 11; but the expedition was of sufficient magnitude to show that the enemy meant to force the fighting.[1] Vague rumors also poured in of an infidel attack to be launched against Oran, the most important Spanish stronghold still remaining on the Mauretanian coast; everything pointed to the necessity of more vigorous action on the part of the Prudent King.[2] The next chapter of the story was to be staged in the western basin of the Mediterranean, on the Barbary coasts, with the infidels at the outset taking the role of aggressors, and Spanish soldiers and sailors resisting them; but the ultimate result of it was to restore the prestige of the Christian arms.

In the beginning, the weather took a hand in the game and played it, as was usually the case in these Mediterranean wars,[3] in a manner adverse to the interests of Spain. In response to the petition of the Cortes of Toledo of 1559, Philip had taken measures to enlarge his navy;[4] he ordered a number of new galleys to be built, and sent for others from Genoa to guard the coasts of Spain; in October, 1562, a large squadron was collected off Malaga, ready at need to defend either Valencia or Oran. Fearing the east winds which raged at that season, the Spanish admiral, Juan de Mendoza, who had been brought up on shipboard by the side of his famous father, Bernardino, sought refuge forty

[1] J. M. Bover, *Historia de la Espugnacion de Sóller* (Palma, 1856), *passim*.

[2] Mercier, iii, pp. 99 f.; Fernández Duro, *Armada Española*, ii, pp. 44–46. The Moors at Algiers and Tlemcen were also reported to be in close touch with the Moriscos of Valencia. C. de C. i, pp. 356 f.

[3] Cf. *ante*, Vol. III, pp. 293 f., 326, 338 f.

[4] *Cortes*, v, pp. 836, 857 f.

miles eastward in the anchorage of La Herradura, which was admirably adapted for protection against the Levanters; but no sooner had he arrived than the storm shifted to the south, whence it soon began to blow with the violence of a tempest. A good defence against the east winds, La Herradura was worse than useless against such a gale as this. Some of the galleys began to drag their anchors. Others cut their cables and were dashed in pieces on the rocks, and most of those that were able to hold their moorings were sunk. No less than twenty-five of the twenty-eight vessels that composed the squadron were lost, together with at least 4000 lives, among them that of Juan de Mendoza, who assuredly deserved a better fate.[1]

The news of this disaster, which was promptly reported at Constantinople, naturally caused the Sultan to hasten the plans, which he had been maturing since the disaster at Gerba, for an attack against Oran. The execution of this project was intrusted to Hassan, the son of Kheireddin Barbarossa, who was now Suleiman's representative at Algiers; he had a small fleet[2] at his disposal to carry his cannon and supplies, and an army of over 25,000 men. In April, 1563, he arrived before Oran, and at once made preparations for a vigorous attack. The place was defended by Alonso de Córdova y Velasco, son and heir of the Count of Alcaudete who had been slain there in 1558, and the neighboring fortress of Mers-el-Kebir, which was the key to it, by his younger brother, Martín;[3] the combined garrisons cannot have numbered much more than 1000 men.[4]

---

[1] D. I. E., l, pp. 285-287 (the date of this letter is wrongly given in the heading as 1572 instead of 1562); Fernández Duro, ii, pp. 46-49.

[2] It is a significant fact that among the ships were three French caravels. C. de C., i, p. 361; Mercier, iii, p. 101.

Fernández Duro, ii, p. 49, speaks of the depredations of cosarios franceses.

[3] Pedro de Salazar, Hispania Victrix, fol. 73.

[4] This is only a guess. But there were only 470 left in Mers-el-Kebir after the repulse of the first assaults, and as it

To maintain themselves indefinitely was clearly impossible; everything really depended on whether or not they could hold out until the arrival of help from Spain. During late April and early May, they delayed the besiegers before two subsidiary outside forts; not until May 8 were they driven back into Mers-el-Kebir. There for a month more they continued to defend themselves; they repulsed one assault after another, and refused to haul down their flag. Reports occasionally reached them that the Spanish fleet was on its way, and finally, in the middle of June,[1] their endurance was rewarded. By superhuman efforts Philip had collected thirty-four galleys, some of them from the Italian states,[2] and the rest brand new, off the dockyards of Barcelona, and despatched them, under Francisco de Mendoza,[3] to the relief of his hard-pressed subjects.[4] They reached Oran in the nick of time.[5] Hassan had learned that their coming was imminent, and was preparing to launch the decisive blow which should forestall them; but Mendoza arrived just at the very moment that the attack was beginning, and threw the besiegers into confusion. Twenty of their ships succeeded in escaping to the eastward, but five others were captured, and also four large French vessels which formed a part of the infidel fleet.[6] Hassan's land forces, it is needless to add, made haste to raise the siege and seek safety in flight; they left behind them a large quantity of munitions and supplies, and also sixteen pieces of artillery.[7] Altogether, the defence of Mers-el-Kebir was

---

was strategically more important than Oran, it does not seem probable that the latter had any more.

[1] Mercier, iii, p. 102, says June 7; Fernández Duro, ii, p. 51, makes it the 16th.

[2] Cf. *D. I. E.*, xxiii, p. 165.

[3] Son of the old viceroy of Mexico and Peru, and commonly known as *el Indio*.

Cf. Morel-Fatio, *L'Espagne au XVI* *et au XVII* siècle, p. 62.

[4] Fernández Duro, ii, p. 52.

[5] Cf. *M. H. E.*, xi, p. 42.

[6] Mercier, iii, p. 102; Fernández Duro, ii, p. 53.

[7] In addition to the standard accounts, such as those in C. de C., i, pp. 359–370, U. Foglietta, *De Sacro*

the most successful operation which the Spaniards had conducted on the shores of North Africa since the capture of Tunis twenty-eight years before. Both the Alcaudetes were worthily rewarded : the elder by the viceroyalty of the kingdom of Navarre, the younger by a grant of 6000 ducats.[1]

If full advantage was to be reaped from the victory before Oran, it was indispensable to follow it up with a vigorous counter-offensive. There could be little doubt where Philip would elect to strike the blow. The disaster at Gerba had but strengthened his aversion to operations in the Central Mediterranean ; Algiers was still too strong ; but there was another pirates' nest farther westward, two-thirds of the way from Oran to Tangiers, which had been in Spanish hands from 1508 to 1522,[2] and which he was eager to recover from its infidel possessors. This was the town of Vélez de la Gomera, commonly known at the time as the Peñon de Vélez from the rocky islet which guarded the approach to it from the sea. Soon after the victorious fleet had got back from Oran, orders were received from the king to attack it. As Mendoza, who had captained the galleys on the previous expedition, was suffering from a fever at the time, the command devolved on Sancho de Leyva, who, captured at Gerba, but subsequently released, was now general of the galleys of Naples.[3] On July 23, 1563, he put to sea with some fifty ships in the hope of surprising the Peñon by night, but the defenders were keenly on the watch, and at daybreak de Leyva retired. His next move

Foedere, pp. 225 ff., and Fernández Duro, ii, pp. 51 ff., cf. an anonymous account by an eyewitness, which is published by J. M. Sánchez in the *Archivo de Investigaciones Históricas*, 1911, ii, pp. 206–235.

[1] C. de C., i, p. 384.

[2] Cf. *ante*, Vol. II, pp. 248 f. ; III, p. 294.

[3] He was the nephew of Antonio de Leyva, the defender of Pavia ; though socially prominent, his military and naval reputation was not high. Fernández Duro, ii, pp. 55 f.

was to disembark his troops, to the number of some four or five thousand, at a point six miles distant from the fortress, in the hope that a land attack would make him master of the town, but this enterprise failed even more signally than the first. The infidels knew every inch of the ground and used their knowledge well; at one moment de Leyva was in terror lest he should be surrounded and cut off. Turkish galleys, moreover, soon appeared on the horizon and eluded all the efforts of the Christians to capture them. A council of war was finally held, and despite the vigorous protests of Álvaro de Bazán, who insisted that the Peñon should and must be taken, de Leyva abandoned the enterprise. On August 2 the expedition returned to Malaga, after having suffered some damage from a storm.[1]

The effect of this miserable fiasco was in turn to encourage the infidels, who not only seized the opportunity to strengthen the Peñon and raid the Spanish coasts, but even carried their depredations to the Canaries.[2] Rumors also came in of the preparation of a huge fleet at Constantinople for operations on an unprecedented scale in the following spring. Other maritime rivals of Spain likewise took heart. Eight English vessels which were lying off Gibraltar attacked a French ship which came up and anchored near them; they were finally captured by Álvaro de Bazán, and long correspondence ensued before the prisoners were released, but the boldness of the attempt was highly significant.[3] It was obvious that strong measures must be taken for a fresh rehabilitation of Spain's prestige, and that the first of them would be to find a leader more capable than de Leyva; as

[1] C. de C., i, pp. 394–396, who gives the date as August 6; Fernández Duro, ii, pp. 56–58; A. de Ulloa, op. cit., fols. 50 ff.
[2] Fernández Duro, ii, p. 59.
[3] On this singular affair cf. Froude, viii, pp. 443–446; Fernández Duro, ii, p. 60, note; C. S. P., Foreign, 1563, nos. 1424, 1465, 1483, 1488, 1 8, 5, 1525, 1526, 1541, 2, 1561. England was, of course, intervening at this time in the first Civil War in France.

Mendoza, in the meantime, had died as a result of his illness, the choice finally fell on García de Toledo, a cousin of the Duke of Alva and the son of the viceroy of Naples, who had seen service on the sea for a full quarter of a century before.[1] He was not in all respects an attractive personality, but he had proved, during his tenure of the viceroyalty of Catalonia, that he possessed great talent as an organizer. It was characteristic both of his own abilities and of those of his subordinates, that, just as the expedition which he headed was about to start, he discovered that all the gunpowder had been left behind.[2] His mission, of course, was to renew the attack on the Peñon ; Philip's persistence would not tolerate the abandonment of the enterprise, and every effort was made to insure its success. The whole winter of 1563–64 was spent in preparation. Galleys were contributed by Portugal, by Savoy, by the Knights of Malta, and by the Italian states. When Don García set sail from Malaga on August 29, 1564, he had a fleet of at least 150 ships, in addition to the transports, and land forces of over 16,000 men.[3] The prompt success of this second expedition more than atoned for the failure of the first. The defenders of Vélez were terrified and amazed when they saw Toledo's imposing armament appearing over the horizon.[4] Most of them gathered up their belongings and fled to the interior, so that the Christians were able to land and possess themselves of the ancient castle of Alcalá and then of Vélez itself, almost without striking a blow. The Peñon gave promise of more serious resistance ; a few companies of Turks shut

[1] He was given the title of captain-general of the Mediterranean, which had previously been held by Andrea Doria. Cf. Fernández Duro, ii, pp. 59–61.

[2] D. I. E., xxvii, pp. 448 ff. ; Forneron, i, p. 372.

[3] Fernández Duro, ii, pp. 67 f. Philip went off to Monzon to get funds from the Cortes of the realms of the crown of Aragon, convoked there in October, 1563. C. de C., i, pp. 396 f.

[4] D. I. E., xxvii, pp. 398 ff.

themselves up within its walls with the obvious intention of holding out until the last. But Toledo set up his heaviest batteries in a favorable position on the shore, and speedily opened a breach in the walls; shortly afterwards the defenders began to make their escape, and when the Spanish leader entered the place on September 8, he found it practically deserted. He installed a strong garrison under Álvaro de Bazán, with instructions to repair and improve the defences, and got back to Malaga by the middle of the month; he had captured, with the loss of only thirty men, a place which was certainly one of the most dangerous of pirate nests, and which many contemporaries had regarded as impregnable.[1] In the following spring, the good work was continued by Álvaro de Bazán, who sank several transports, laden with stones, in the mouth of the River Tetuan (now the Oued-Martine), thus temporarily immobilizing a dozen infidel vessels which lay at anchor farther up the stream, and preventing its utilization as a corsairs' refuge for many months to come.[2]

In the Western Mediterranean, then, the tide had apparently turned. Philip had shown vigor and persistence in his efforts to maintain control of the waters near his own shores; he had scored two considerable victories on the coasts of North Africa; the memory of the defeats of his father's closing years and of the disaster at Gerba had been at least partially wiped out. But the next trial of strength was to come farther eastward, in a region for whose safety the Spanish monarch was far less solicitous; he was afraid of dissipating his energies, and failed to envisage the

---

[1] Charrière, *Négociations*, ii, pp. 749–753; Castries, France, i, pp. 246–269; *D. I. E.*, xiv, pp. 505–537; xxvii, pp. 398–574; xxviii, pp. 569–572; C. de C., i, pp. 403 ff.; Fernández Duro, ii, pp. 65–71.

[2] Fernández Duro, ii, p. 74, and references there.

Mediterranean as a single whole. The issue of the new conflict was to be favorable to the Christian arms; but only a very small part of the credit for it can be given to the too Prudent King. The only real hero of the ensuing campaign, at least as far as Spain's participation in it was concerned, was García de Toledo, now promoted, as a reward for his success against the Peñon de Vélez, to the difficult office of viceroy of Sicily.

Rumors of a great naval expedition that was being prepared at Constantinople became increasingly definite and alarming in the early months of 1565; and it was an open secret that its objective was to be the island of Malta.[1] It was the sole remaining stronghold of the Knights of St. John of Jerusalem, whom Suleiman had already expelled from Rhodes and from Tripoli. Its capture would be the culmination of his achievements in the Mediterranean; it would open for him a road to Sicily and Naples and perhaps into the western basin of the inland sea. The Sultan collected a fleet of 200 sail, of which 130 were galleys fit for combat; they carried ample supplies of artillery and munitions and land forces to the number of 30,000 men. The latter were commanded by Mustapha, a veteran of the Danube wars, and the fleet by Piali Pasha; and most of the more famous of the Turkish corsairs, among them Dragut, and Hassan of Algiers, joined in with their special contingents. On May 18 a cannon-shot from the castle of St. Elmo announced the arrival of this formidable armament, a full month before the Christians had expected it, in the waters surrounding the island fortress of the Knights.[2]

The grand-master, Jean de La Valette, had realized for many months the peril of his position and had been making

[1] F. de Salles, *Annales de l'Ordre de Malte*, p. 124.
[2] Pedro de Salazar, *Hispania Victrix*, fols. 157–159; C. Sanminiatelli Zabarella, *Assedio di Malta*, p. 170.

superhuman efforts to get ready to avert it. He strengthened
his defences, he besought the aid of the European powers,[1]
he recalled his absent knights, he mustered his auxiliaries,
and armed the inhabitants of the island. In all he disposed
of some 8500 men,[2] of whom possibly 700 were members of
the Order; but unfortunately St. Elmo, the key to the entire
position, against which it was obvious that the enemy would
launch his first attack, was only able to contain 600. Failing
help from outside, that fortress was doomed; and virtually
the sole possible source of such outside help was García de
Toledo, the new viceroy of Sicily.

Toledo had shown feverish energy from the moment of
his arrival in his new domain. He saw the coming danger
quite as clearly as the grand-master; not only did he muster
all the military and naval resources of his own realm, he also
visited both Naples and La Goletta, in order personally to
assure himself that they were in an adequate state of defence.
La Valette began to correspond with him at once; a few
weeks before the Turks arrived he sent for him to come to
Malta to inspect the fortifications, which Toledo found in a
satisfactory state, though inadequately provided with soldiers to man them.[3] The viceroy himself did everything he
possibly could; he loaned the grand-master several companies of his Spanish regiments; he shipped him grain and
money, and did his utmost to persuade the king to do still
more. But Philip, with the disaster of Gerba still fresh in his
mind, could not be brought to see the importance of a peril
so far to the eastward; the most that Toledo could induce
him to do was to order the assembling of 4000 men in Corsica,
and to command the viceroy of Naples to send troops into

---

[1] Fernández Duro, ii, p. 79; F. de
Salles, *Annales*, p. 124.
[2] Jurien de la Gravière, *Chevaliers
de Malte*, i, p. 162.

[3] *D. I. E.*, xxix, p. 314; Sanminiatelli
Zabarella, *Assedio di Malta*, pp. 127
ff.

Sicily; food and money were all that Philip would permit to be despatched direct to Malta from Spain.[1] It will readily be believed that the Turks made the most of these delays. On May 19, they began to land their troops, without any opposition on the part of the grand-master;[2] and after a dispute of four days' duration as to whether to start in with an attack on Il Burgo, the principal fortress of the island, or on the outer castle of St. Elmo, they decided in favor of the latter; on the 24th they opened their trenches within 600 yards of their objective.[3] Thereupon there ensued a furious bombardment both by land and sea. It lasted for no less than twenty-three days, and under cover of it the besiegers were able to advance their parallels of approach so close to St. Elmo that on June 16 they could launch their first assault. Every day La Valette reënforced the little garrison in the confident expectation that succor would soon arrive; he redoubled his demands for help in his extremity, but all without avail. The heroism of the besieged was beyond all praise. They slew some 6000 of their assailants, among them Dragut, and wounded Piali Pasha; but it was impossible permanently to resist the overwhelming superiority of the Turkish forces. On June 23, the walls were so badly breached that the enemy was able to enter the castle, where they found only nine of the defenders alive.[4] And having taken St. Elmo, they at once made their preparations to attack Il Burgo and the other forts.

García de Toledo in Sicily was at his wits' end. On May 31, while the cannonade was at its hottest, he wrote another despairing letter to Philip, beseeching him to act vigorously and without delay. "If Malta is not succored,"

[1] *D. I. E.*, xxix, pp. 53–68.

[2] Pedro de Salazar, *Hispania Victrix*, fol. 159.

[3] Fernández Duro, ii, pp. 77 f.; Gentile and Achélis, *Deux veritables discours*, ed. H. Pernot (Paris, 1910), pp. 12 ff.

[4] *D. I. E.*, xxix, pp. 413–419; Defontin-Maxange, *Eudj'Ali*, pp. 89–92.

he declared, "I hold it to be lost." [1] He even suggested that if Philip feared the loss of his Spanish galleys, he might borrow those of France, not knowing that Catharine de' Medici at that very moment was sending a special emissary to Constantinople to assure the Porte of her friendship.[2] But the king of Spain still hesitated. He continued to prepare, but would not give the word to start. Even the news of the fall of St. Elmo did not avail to persuade him to risk his precious navy in a sea fight; the most he would do was to sanction the landing of troops, "provided it could be accomplished without evident peril of the loss of the galleys." [3] A month earlier Don García had demonstrated that the thing could be done. Taking full advantage of every atom of autonomy that Philip had permitted him, he had managed, after two failures, to introduce, on June 29, a reënforcement of some 600 soldiers, mostly Spanish, into Il Burgo, where the grand-master was so overjoyed at their arrival that he rushed amongst them in tears and embraced them.[4] But this, after all, was but a handful; moreover, the numbers of the garrison dwindled rapidly under the pressure of the Turkish assaults. Every day the blockade became stricter and stricter; even the best of the grand-master's divers found it almost impossible to get through with his desperate appeals. Every letter that Toledo received from Malta seemed certain to be the last; a note from the governor, Pedro de Amezqueta, dated August 22, contained the significant message: "Four hundred men still alive . . . don't lose an hour." [5]

Had there been other causes of delay than the hesitations

---

[1] *D. I. E.*, xxix, pp. 171–173; Fernández Duro, ii, pp. 416–419.
[2] Charrière, *Négociations*, ii, pp. 791 ff.
[3] *D. I. E.*, xxix, pp. 184–318, *passim*; Fernández Duro, ii, pp. 82 f.

[4] *D. I. E.*, xxix, p. 276; Fernández Duro, ii, pp. 84 f.
[5] *D. I. E.*, xxix, pp. 466–468; Sanminiatelli Zabarella, pp. 468–553; Gentile and Achélis, ed. Pernot, pp. 51 ff.

of the king, Malta must assuredly have fallen. But fortunately when, about August 20, Philip's consent to a landing
operation had at last been received, all the men and material were ready for the enterprise. This was chiefly due to the
energy of García de Toledo; but a share of the credit also
belongs to Álvaro de Bazán, who was at that moment in
command of the galleys of Seville and charged with the
defence of Gibraltar. In May he had been ordered to take
reënforcements from Malaga to Oran;[1] subsequently he got
leave to pass on to Cartagena, Barcelona, and Genoa, where
he added to his fleet and picked up the *tercio* of Lombardy,
which Philip had at last allowed to be sent to Sicily. At
Civitavecchia he was further reënforced by a detachment
of papal galleys, and at Naples he took on more troops.
Finally, in early August, after his forces had joined Toledo's,
there was united at Messina an armament of some ninety
galleys, forty transports, and over 11,000 men.[2] All that
was now lacking was the consent of the king, which finally
arrived after a delay of three more weeks; it only sanctioned, as we have already seen, the landing of soldiers for a
battle on the shore; to imperil the Spanish fleet against the
obviously superior forces of the Turks was still to Philip's
cautious nature unthinkable. This inhibition, however, had
been foreseen. During the weeks of waiting for the royal
missive, the various leaders of the Christian armament had
been discussing the best methods of carrying out the only
operation to which Philip would consent, and they finally
agreed on the adoption of a scheme suggested by Álvaro de
Bazán. This was, in brief, to choose the best sixty of the
Christian galleys, place 150 soldiers on each, and make a
dash for the shore of Malta at a point some distance from the
fortress, trusting that the main body of the Turkish fleet

---

[1] Salazar, *Hispania Victrix*, fol. 157.   [2] Fernández Duro, ii, pp. 88 ff.

would be so occupied with the bombardment, and the rest of it so widely dispersed, that a naval action could either be avoided, or if it occurred, would be fought against so small a detachment of the enemy's vessels that there would be no doubt that the Christians would be able to account for them.[1]

The weather was at its very worst when the time came to put this plan into effect. The ships left Messina on August 26 in a "tempest the like of which few sailors had ever seen before"; it continued to rage for the next two weeks, and the fleet was cruelly buffeted about; its first attempt to make a landing was unsuccessful, and it had to return to Sicily for fresh water and supplies.[2] Finally, however, on September 7, Toledo was able to report to the king that 9600 men had been safely set ashore on the island of Malta without the loss of a single oar; on his return for reënforcements, moreover, the viceroy passed contemptuously within sight of the main body of the Turkish fleet, firing a salute as he sailed by as a tribute to the besieged, and a confirmation of the great news that the longed for succor had at last arrived. The infidels were dismayed when they realized what had happened. If the little band of the original defenders had been able to detain them for so long, what could they hope to accomplish against a large force of the dreaded Spanish infantry, whose superiority to all other soldiers of the period was quite as fully recognized in the East as in the West? For a moment Piali Pasha had a thought of attacking the Christian fleet, but he abandoned it when he reflected that the loss of the support of his galleys would expose the Turkish land forces to inevitable destruction; one final attack on the relieving forces was attempted and

[1] Fernández Duro, ii, pp. 91–95; Altolaguirre y Duvale, *Álvaro de* *Bazán*, pp. 35 ff., and references there; Sanminiatelli Zabarella, pp. 557 ff.
[2] Fernández Duro, ii, p. 94.

repulsed,[1] and on the following day the infidels began to retire. On September 12, the last of their sails had disappeared over the horizon: Hassan toward Algiers, Piali Pasha and the rest to the eastward. The second lot of reënforcements which the viceroy was bringing over from Sicily reached Malta at the very moment of the departure of the Turks, and was not even landed, and Toledo spent the rest of the month in removing from Malta the now unnecessary original detachment, and in pursuing the enemy to the coasts of Greece.[2]

It was a glorious deliverance, and was fittingly celebrated both in Spain and in Rome. Coupled with the death of Suleiman the Magnificent, which occurred in the following year, it marked the passing of the climax of the Turkish peril, both on sea and on land. But though the credit for it, as we have already remarked, belongs largely to García de Toledo, and in a lesser degree to Álvaro de Bazán, Spain as a whole got little or nothing of the glory, because of the hesitations of her king. Indeed, it is scarcely too much to say that she lost rather than gained in reputation from the whole affair. It had been the first occasion since his return to the peninsula in which Philip had been concerned in an enterprise which interested the whole of Europe. He was, for a moment, the cynosure of all eyes, and men satisfied themselves for the first time of his slowness and vacillation. "The King has lost a great deal of reputation by not succoring Malta," reported the English special agent at Madrid on September 3, 1565,[3] and there is every reason to think

---

[1] Pedro de Salazar, *Hispania Victrix*, fols. 258–261.

[2] F. Balbi de Correggio, *Verdadera Relacion*, pp. 105 ff.; J. Bosio, *Istoria*, iii, pp. 690–703; Fernández Duro, ii, pp. 94–97; Sanminiatelli Zabarella, pp. 577–603. Balbi de Correggio (fol. 121) gives the Turkish losses as "treynta y cinco mil hombres, y entre ellos Dargut, y otros muy muchos señalados."

[3] *C. S. P.*, *Foreign*, 1564–65, no. 1455. The succors, of course, had by this time arrived, but the fact was not yet known in Spain. Cf. also Pastor, xvi, pp. 369 f.

that other foreign envoys sent similar opinions to their governments. In some respects the verdicts were probably harsher than Philip really deserved; the fact of the matter was that he had never been quite whole-hearted in his desire to have Malta saved. The enterprise lay beyond the Spanish horizon, at least as he conceived of it, and his interests, at that period of his rule, were strictly limited to Spain. He was intent on the preservation of the safety of his own shores and of his control of the adjacent seas. And he could never quite forget that the large majority of the Knights were Frenchmen and commanded by a French grand-master; why, then, should he bestir himself to give aid to subjects of a state, which, though friendly at the moment, had a long anti-Spanish and pro-Turkish tradition behind it, and might subsequently revert to its former hostile attitude?[1] He had certainly shown himself considerably more energetic when it was a question of purely Spanish enterprise, such as, for instance, the defence of Oran. Yet, even allowing for all this, there can be little doubt that Philip's conduct in connection with the relief of Malta had an adverse effect on his position in Western Europe. It showed his fellow sovereigns that he was not to be the factor of ubiquitous and universal importance which his father had been before him; it confirmed many disagreeable suspicions in regard to his fitness to champion the interests of the faith. And if Philip's hesitations diminished his prestige, and increased the jealousy and distrust of his neighbors, they may also have begun to reveal, at least to the keener minds, the methods whereby it would ultimately be possible to defeat him.

The years immediately succeeding the attack on Malta saw a temporary lull in the activities of the Turks in the

[1] Forneron, i, p. 383, and references there, especially *D. I. E.*, xxix, p. 545, and xxx, pp. 12 f.

Mediterranean. It was expected that Suleiman would seek vengeance for his defeat in 1566, and Philip ordered the construction of eighty galleys to meet the threatened peril;[1] but the Sultan's anger vented itself principally in a last campaign against Hungary, in which he met his death; and Piali Pasha, who had begun to ravage the coasts of Apulia, was prompt to retire when García de Toledo's fleet drew near. But this same year 1566, though in itself comparatively quiet, witnessed the advent on the scene of a new personality, the incarnation of the crusading ardor of the Counter-Reformation, who was to arouse and unite the Christians for a holy war against the infidel with an enthusiasm which they had rarely shown before, and to carry the combat into the waters of the foe. Eight months before Suleiman the Magnificent gave way to Selim the Sot, the papal tiara had passed from Pius IV to the far abler and more energetic Pius V.

From the moment of his accession the new pontiff was inspired with the idea of the creation of a Holy League: not the sort of Holy League which the sixteenth century had already occasionally produced, in which religious pretexts were put forward to cover the most selfish of political ambitions, but a genuine alliance for the purpose announced, the defeat and humiliation of the infidel Turk.[2] The death of Suleiman, with the prospect which it opened of plots and revolts before the recognition of his successor, seemed to furnish an unusual opportunity for decisive action, and the depredations of Piali Pasha, to justify it. In the winter of 1566–67 the Pope sent messages to all the Catholic powers of Western Europe to urge them to take arms and unite for a

[1] Fernández Duro, ii, p. 101.

[2] Pastor, xviii, pp. 353 ff. Luciano Serrano, *La Liga de Lepanto* (Madrid, 1918–19), i, pp. 1–27, gives an admirable account of the principal authorities, contemporary and modern, on the League.

crusade.[1] From France, as was to be expected in view of her
recent policy, he obtained nothing, and he was also quite
unable to move the Emperor Maximilian II ; before long it
became obvious that the sole possible sources of help were
Venice and Spain. But the tradition of Venice was to maintain peace with the Turk, particularly for commercial purposes ; furthermore, she feared that a war would mean the
loss of her colonial possessions in the Levant, and especially
of the island of Cyprus, which she had held since 1489 ; she
therefore refused, for the time being, to consider the papal
proposals.[2] Philip also, at first, held aloof, though for somewhat different reasons.[3] He had great respect for the character of the new pontiff ; moreover, it seems probable that
the narrow escape of Malta had given him some inkling of
the fact that the Mediterranean situation must be considered as a whole, and that the western basin could not be
really safe as long as the infidel was in control of the
eastern. The principal consideration which caused him
to hold back was the threatening state of affairs in the
Netherlands, where rebellion was plainly beginning to raise
its head. Dissipation of his forces in a crusade against the
Turks would be certain to increase his difficulties in that
quarter ; it might even conceivably encourage the Protestant
states of the Empire to move against him.[4] Like his father
before him, Philip was beginning to discover that the size
and extent of his scattered dominions exposed him to peril
from many different directions at once.

Pius, however, was not discouraged ; despite his first

[1] Serrano, *op. cit.*, i, pp. 34 f.
[2] Pastor, xviii, p. 356 ; Serrano, i,
p. 37 ; cf. also the contemporary *Guerra
di Cipro*, by Paolo Paruta (Siena,
1827), pp. 5 ff.
[3] The letter of Pius V to Philip, urging him to make war on the Turks, was,
of course, written in 1568, and not in
1598 as the *Semanario Erudito*, viii,
pp. 238–244, and Sánchez Alonso,
no. 6720, have it.
[4] Serrano, i, pp. 36 f. ; Pastor, xviii,
pp. 356 f. ; P. Herre, *Europäische
Politik im cyprischen Krieg*, pp.
37–43.

rebuff, he refused to abandon his crusading projects, and in 1570 his persistence was rewarded. The primary cause of the change in his fortunes was the rashness and stupidity of the new Sultan, which drove the Venetians, who really desired to keep the peace, into the reluctant necessity of declaring war. The island of Cyprus was the chief bone of contention. It lay "in the vitals of the Turkish Empire" ; [1] in Venetian hands it imperilled the infidel control of the eastern basin of the Mediterranean ; it menaced the coasts of Syria and Palestine, and was a bar to maritime communication between Constantinople and Egypt.[2] The Sultan, moreover, was firmly convinced that he would never have a better opportunity to wrest it from Venice; a bad harvest in 1569 had deprived her of supplies, and the explosion of a powder magazine was reported to have destroyed a large number of her galleys. In March, 1570, accordingly, an ambassador from Selim appeared in Venice with a curt demand for the cession and evacuation of the island. There was still a strong faction in the councils of the republic, to be heard from again and again in the succeeding years, which held that peace with the infidel must at all costs be preserved ; but the Turkish demand was so uncompromising and so insolent that the majority felt that compliance was impossible. Selim's envoy was accordingly sent back to his master without even being permitted to make formal statement of his errand, and war was therewith practically declared between Venice and the Porte. No one realized better than the republic that she was incapable of waging it alone. The only possible course was to apply to the Pope

[1] Serrano, i, p. 42, note 1.

[2] *Ibid.*, pp. 37–41; Pastor, xviii, pp. 361 f.; Stirling-Maxwell, *Don John of Austria,* i, pp. 303–305. The possibilities of Cyprus as a haven for Christian corsairs at this time were well brought out by the exploit of three galleys of the Knights of St. John, which, issuing from one of its harbors, captured two Moslem treasure-ships en route from Alexandria to the Porte.

and through him to the other Catholic powers of Western
Europe for the formation of the very Holy League in which
three years before Venice had refused to participate.   Her
own crusading ardor was no whit stronger than it had been
then, but she was only too glad to utilize that of others,
provided it could avail for the preservation of her colonial
empire.[1]

The Pope had no illusions about the attitude and objects
of the republic.   He knew that her motives were exclusively
selfish, and that the welfare of Christendom did not appeal
to her at all ; but the chance was too good to lose.   He also
realized that nothing of importance could really be accomplished unless he secured the coöperation of Spain.   France
and the Empire were clearly of no avail ; his own military
and naval resources were scanty ;   the independent Italian
states would only follow a Spanish lead.   To Philip, accordingly, Pius once more applied, and sent over to Spain in the
spring of 1570 a Malagan cleric, Luis de Torres, who had
resided for years at the papal court, to ask for the support
of the Prudent King.   The envoy had his first interview
with the Spanish monarch at Cordova in April.[2]   Fortunately for the success of the Pope's proposals, the situation
in Spain, as well as in Venice, had altered in such fashion
as to make them much more acceptable on the present
occasion than they had been three years before.[3]   The rebels
in the Low Countries, now confronted by the terrible Alva,
were far less of a menace than they had been in 1567.   The
infidel corsair, Aluch Ali, had recently captured the city of
Tunis, and expelled the local Hafside ruler, who was still,

[1] Serrano, i, pp. 41–46; Pastor, xviii,
pp. 362–371.

[2] The correspondence of Torres has
recently been published, with an excellent introduction, by A. Dragonetti
de Torres, under the title of La Lega di
*Lepanto nel carteggio diplomatico inedito
di Luys de Torres* (Turin, 1931) ; see
particularly pp. 97–115, and see also
Pastor, xviii, pp. 369–372 ; Serrano,
i, pp. 50–52 ; Herre, *op. cit.*, pp. 84–111.

[3] Serrano, i, pp. 54–63.

in theory at least, a vassal of the Prudent King; a subsequent assault on La Goletta had been repulsed, but it had at least served as a reminder that Spain was still menaced by a Turkish peril.[1] The high character and reputation of Pope Pius himself doubtless counted for something. But the consideration which unquestionably had the greatest weight of all was the fact that the Morisco rebellion in Granada, if not yet completely suppressed, was doomed to inevitable failure; its back had by this time been thoroughly broken. That revolt and the manner of its suppression had done much to undermine the prestige of the Prudent King. That it should have been permitted to occur at all was an evidence that he was not master in his own dominions; that such overwhelming force and such cruelty had been necessary to put it down, had but strengthened the bad impression at the different courts of Western Europe.[2] The Spanish *tercios* which had been called on to do the bloody work longed to win back their good name in a war that concerned all Christendom; their leader, Don John of Austria, was the most insistent of all. Finally, there had been just enough danger that the rebellion might be aided by infidel coöperation from without to make adherence to the League which the papacy was proposing the logical sequel to what had already been accomplished at home. And whatever remaining doubts the king may have entertained, on the ground of the perennial emptiness of his exchequer, were cleared up by the papal offers, conveyed through Luis de Torres, of wellnigh unlimited concessions in the matter of clerical subsidies.[3]

By the middle of May, then, in the year 1570, Philip had

---

[1] Defontin-Maxange, *Eudj' Ali*, pp. 121 ff.; Fernández Duro, ii, pp. 117 f.; Mercier, iii, pp. 106–108.

[2] Serrano, i, pp. 56 f.

[3] Serrano, i, pp. 58 f.; Pastor, xviii, pp. 372, 386, 390; Dragonetti de Torres, pp. 144–163; cf. also below, p. 131.

determined to join the League; but it is scarcely too much
to say that the Venetians deplored rather than welcomed
the news that he had decided to become their ally. Much as
they feared the Turk, they dreaded yet more lest they
should become the cat's-paw of Spain; and they were
determined that the League should be constituted in such
fashion as to prevent its being directed in Spanish interests.[1]
From the outset the republic desired a merely temporary
agreement, from which she could withdraw when it suited
her own convenience; she would have nothing to do with
the more permanent and binding treaties which were advocated by Philip and the Pope. She also proposed to keep
the control of the naval campaign as far as possible out of
Spanish hands, by the creation of a pontifical fleet to which
all the allies should contribute their contingents, and which
was to be commanded by the papal general, Marcantonio
Colonna; this appointment had the additional advantage
in Venetian eyes that it was certain to be resented by Gian
Andrea Doria, who had been placed in command of the
galleys of Spain.[2] Philip could not be blind to the meaning
of these arrangements, and was naturally slow to acquiesce
in them. The different contingents took a long time to
mobilize and longer still to combine; not till the last day
of August did they unite off the shores of Crete.[3] The
Venetians wished to rescue Cyprus, which was already
besieged by the Turks, but Doria and Colonna did not
believe that this would be feasible; and in the midst of
the ensuing discussions there arrived, on September 21, the
stunning news that the Turks, twelve days before, had
captured Nicosia, and therewith become masters of all of

[1] Serrano, i, pp. 67 ff.; Pastor, xviii,
pp. 379 ff.
[2] Serrano, i, p. 71; Paruta, Guerra di
Cipro, pp. 68 ff.; Manfroni, Marina
Italiana, pp. 447 f., 458 f.
[3] Serrano, i, p. 78.

Cyprus save Famagosta.[1] This disaster and the advent of the autumn winds put an end to all projects for a vigorous offensive during the remainder of the year. Plans were proposed for various minor operations, all of which were abandoned after mutual recriminations between the allied leaders; and the upshot of the matter was the ignominious retirement of Doria to Sicily and of Colonna to Rome. Had the Christians acted vigorously and unitedly in the early summer, before the Turks had got a foothold in Cyprus, they could almost certainly have prevented its loss. As things fell out, their sole achievement was the tardy reënforcement by the Venetian leader, Zanne, of the garrison of Famagosta with a force of 1500 men; and on his return from it he lost thirteen vessels in a storm.[2]

The unhappy issue of the campaign of 1570 proved that larger forces and better organization were imperative if anything was to be really accomplished in the ensuing year. The terms of the League had not yet been settled, though plenipotentiaries for the arrangement of them had met at Rome in June.[3] By this time it also became evident that Philip was determined to enter upon the undertaking with all his might. Whether it was that he had caught the spark of the Pope's crusading ardor, or because of the unusually favorable state of Spain's foreign and domestic affairs, it is hard to say; in any case he seemed more anxious to fight than he had ever been before. But if Philip was resolved to give whole-hearted support to the League, and was prepared to shoulder the principal burden of the work that it was to be called upon to do, he was equally determined to have the principal voice in the control of it, and to have its constitution so drawn up that Spain should derive

---

[1] Stirling-Maxwell, *op. cit.*, i, p. 321.
[2] *Ibid.*, p. 324.

[3] Serrano, i, pp. 85 ff.; Pastor, xviii, pp. 382 ff.

due benefit from its activities. The representatives whom he sent from Madrid were given ample instructions to this effect, and at Rome they were powerfully aided by the efforts of Cardinal Granvelle, who was accused of being more Spanish than the Spaniards themselves.[1] As the principal means of attaining their end, they insisted that the chief command of the forces of the allies should be conferred on Philip's half-brother, Don John of Austria, who had been fighting the infidel in Granada for nearly two years past. Don John himself had applied for the position on November 19, 1570,[2] and though the appointment elicited some objections from the other allies, it was thenceforth recognized as inevitable. He was at that time nearly twenty-four years old, in the fresh vigor of his early manhood, graceful, gallant, courteous, and well fitted by his inheritance and by his personal attractions to arouse men's enthusiasm. There is no reason to believe that he possessed any great knowledge of naval affairs, despite the fact that since the spring of 1568 he had been commander-in-chief of the fleets of Spain; in matters of strategy he had to be guided by the counsels of older seamen like Gian Andrea Doria and Álvaro de Bazán.[3] But such an arrangement was not uncommon at the time; and it seemed particularly desirable on the present occasion, when charm and personality were so obviously indispensable for the holding together of mutually distrustful allies. And it was not solely in the matter of the command that Spain manifested her resolve that the operations of the League should redound to her own advantage. She insisted that its objects should be both offensive and defensive, and, as a guarantee against

[1] Serrano, i, p. 94.
[2] D. I. E., xxviii, pp. 143, 146 f.
[3] Stirling-Maxwell, i, pp. 81–84; Altolaguirre y Duvale, *Álvaro de* *Bazán,* pp. 51 ff.; Fernández Duro in *Boletín* of the R. A. H., xii, pp. 192 ff. Cf. also *ante,* p. 93, note 1.

desertion by her colleagues,[1] that it should last for at least twelve years. She also demanded that Algiers, Tunis, and Tripoli should be included in the sphere of its activities as well as the territories of the Eastern Mediterranean, and succeeded, with some reservations, in carrying her point.[2] The question of relative costs made less trouble than usual in such cases. Spain was quite ready to pay for the preponderant position which she had elected to assume, and promised not only to meet half the total expense on her own account, but also to be responsible for such portion of the share allotted to the see of Rome as the papal exchequer might be unable to contribute. It was, after all, but the retort courteous for the financial concessions of Pius, of which Philip had taken special pains to make doubly sure beforehand.[3]

The Holy League was solemnly concluded on May 26, and on the following day it was published to the world in the basilica of St. Peter.[4] In view of the history of previous Holy Leagues it did not seem superfluous to proclaim at the outset that it was formed "for the destruction and ruin of the Turk," including his subject states of "Algiers, Tunis, and Tripoli of Barbary"; and that there was to be no limit to the period of its duration. Spain was to furnish one-half of the funds, troops, ships, and munitions of war, Venice one-third, and the Pope one-sixth.[5] Don John was

[1] That her fears of such desertion, at least on the part of the Venetians, were by no means groundless, is proved by the fact that in January-February, 1571, Venice entertained a proposal for a separate peace with the Porte. It was just at the time that the plenipotentiaries at Rome were having the greatest difficulty in reaching an agreement, and their sessions were suspended for more than a month. For details cf. Serrano, i, pp. 95 f.

[2] Serrano, i, pp. 88 f.

[3] Cf. *ante*, p. 127; Serrano, i, pp. 89–90; Pastor, xviii, pp. 385 ff.

[4] C. de C., ii, pp. 86–92; Paruta, *Historia Vinetiana* (Venice, 1605), ii, pp. 162 f.; Pastor, xviii, p. 405. The treaty is printed in Dumont, *Corps universel diplomatique*, v, 1 (1728), pp. 203–205.

[5] Serrano, i, pp. 87, 97 ff.; Stirling-Maxwell, i, pp. 340 ff. As a matter of fact Venice contributed a few more than her share of the galleys, and fell somewhat short of her assigned propor-

invested with all the powers of commander-in-chief, and in
his absence Marcantonio Colonna was to fill his place,
but the authority of the generalissimo was limited by the
provision that he was not to be permitted to take any
decisive action without the consent of the general of each
of the forces of the allies; this stipulation originated with
the Venetians, who thus hoped to prevent the Spaniards
from directing the League to suit themselves. It was
recognized that the chief interests of Venice lay in the
Adriatic and in the Levant, and those of Philip in North
Africa; and it was provided that in years when no common
enterprise should be undertaken each of the two powers
should have the right to engage in ventures of its own, and
to call upon its ally for support and assistance, save when
the territories of that ally were themselves actually in
danger from the Turk. The Emperor and the kings of
France and Portugal were invited to join the League, under
conditions to be agreed upon; but no one can have been
surprised at their determination to hold aloof. In France
the belief was openly expressed that the differences between
Spain and Venice were too deep-rooted to make it possible
for them to accomplish anything in alliance;[1] nay more,
such was France's jealousy of the power of the Spanish
king that her government actually tried to thwart the
purposes of the League by offering every facility to the
Venetians for a separate peace with the Porte. Still less
welcome was the news in England, in the Netherlands, and
in the Protestant states of the Empire, all of which felt
themselves menaced directly or indirectly by the power of
the king of Spain. In their eyes the League could not fail

tion of troops and supplies; Spain
furnished these, and was permitted, in
turn, to fall as much short of her
complement of ships as Venice had
exceeded hers. Any deficiency in the
Pope's contingent was to be made up
by Spain and Venice in due proportion.

[1] Serrano, i, pp. 99–101.

to be a fresh means of enhancing the already dangerous preponderance of the 'Demon of the South.' [1]

News of the conclusion of the League reached Madrid on June 6; that very day Don John left for Barcelona on the way to Messina, the appointed rendezvous of the allied fleets.[2] He was himself in a fever of impatience to reach the scene of action. If there was to be a real campaign before the coming of the autumn winds, there was not a moment to be lost. It was indispensable, moreover, to reassure the Venetians, who were clamoring for the rescue of Cyprus before Famagosta should fall, and who suspected the Spaniards of trying to delay matters in order to divert the expedition to North Africa.[3] But despite the fact that all the leaders professed to be in such haste, it was not until September 2 that the entire armament could be united at the appointed place. The Spanish galleys had been scattered up and down the coasts and in the harbors of the Balearics, and it took a long time to collect and repair them. Though Venice had been so anxious for the Spaniards to make haste, her own preparations were the most tardy of all; and it was typical of her jealous and distrustful attitude that the last of all the allied squadrons to reach Messina was a detachment of sixty ships of the republic which had wintered at Crete.[4] At the council of war, which was held immediately afterwards to determine the course of the ensuing campaign, the Venetians soon learned that Don John was fully as anxious as they were themselves that a vigorous blow be immediately struck; and as the news of the fall of Famagosta, on August 1, and the dastardly massacre of its defenders in the ensuing weeks, made it evident that an operation against Cyprus was no longer to

[1] Serrano, i, pp. 100 f.
[2] Serrano, i, p. 103.
[3] Serrano, i, p. 102.

[4] Paruta, *Historia Vinetiana* (1605), ii, p. 199; Serrano, i, p. 112.

be thought of, it was resolved to seek out the infidel fleet
and give it battle wheresoever it should be found.[1] It was
a daring decision : one which the Emperor at the height of
his power had never been able to bring himself to make, and
one which the sages of the time universally condemned as
utterly contrary to the dictates of common sense.[2] The
enemy was known to be more numerous, both in ships and
in men, and his janizaries were still the terror of much of
Western Europe. A Christian defeat in eastern waters,
where there would be practically no chance of escape for
surviving galleys, would give the Turks unquestioned
mastery of the Mediterranean. Spain in many ways was
taking a much greater risk than the Venetians ; she had
far less to gain and infinitely more to lose. For the republic,
immediate and drastic action was imperative ; without it,
she would be deprived of all her colonies in the Levant.
For Spain, on the other hand, the status quo was at least
tolerable. With her navy at its existing strength, the Turks
might venture to raid the Western Mediterranean, but
could scarcely hope to control it. If, on the other hand,
all her galleys should be lost, her hold on North Africa
would infallibly be broken, and the enemy permanently
established within striking distance of her own coasts.
When we join with these considerations the caution and
hesitancy which usually characterized Philip II, and the
difficulties born of the distrust between the allies, we shall
be the better able to appreciate the meaning of the leadership of Don John. He seemed to personify the crusading
ardor of the Pope. His inspiring presence swept men off
their feet, and made them temporarily forget their own

[1] Serrano, i, p. 118.
[2] Cf. the contemporary *Relacion de la
Guerra de Cipre y Suceso de la batalla
naval de Lepanto*, by Fernando de
Herrera, originally published at Seville
in 1572, and reprinted in *D. I. E.*, xxi,
pp. 242–382, especially chapter xxi
(pp. 331–334).

selfish aims in an overwhelming enthusiasm for the common cause. He seemed the incarnation of the spirit of 1095. Never had the Counter-Reformation given evidence so dramatic of the power of its creed.[1]

When finally assembled in the port of Messina, the entire Christian fleet numbered six heavy galleasses, floating forts carrying 44 cannon apiece, which were contributed by the Venetians; 208 galleys, of which the republic furnished 106, Spain 90, and the papacy 12; and about 100 smaller vessels and transports, of which three-quarters were either Spanish or in Spanish pay; and there were in all some 50,000 sailors and rowers on board. The fleet carried about 31,000 soldiers, of whom 19,000 were either Spaniards, or Italians and Germans enlisted in the Spanish *tercios*, 2000 volunteers, fitted and equipped at their own cost but credited to Spain, 8000 Venetians, and 2000 troops furnished by the Pope. The Venetians galleys were by no means the equal of the Spanish ones,[2] and the surplus number of them in excess of the proportion that had been allotted to the republic was further compensated by a corresponding surplus of the troops and equipment that were furnished by Spain. This arrangement, which had been tentatively agreed upon at the time of the formation of the League, was clearly to the advantage of all concerned, and was a tribute to the recognized superiority of the Spanish veterans. The forthcoming action, as had been plainly foreseen, was to be a contest at close range, of ramming and boarding, between vessels which relied chiefly for their propulsion on oars: a transference, one

[1] Costiol, *Chronica*, lib. ii, cap. xiii; Stirling-Maxwell, i, pp. 380–383, 406 f.
[2] On the galley of Don John cf. G. de Artíñano y de Galdácano, *Arquitectura Naval Española*, p. 47; and the contemporary *Descripcion de la Galera Real del Sermo. Sr. D. Juan de Austria* by Juan de Malara (1527–71), published by the Sociedad de Bibliófilos Andaluces (Seville, 1876).

might almost say, to the decks of ships, of a land battle of the type in which the Spaniards excelled. Sailing ability and skill at long-range cannonading would consequently count for comparatively little, and the troops which the galleys transported would be quite as important as the galleys themselves.[1]

On September 16 the great fleet streamed out of the port of Messina and headed across the Ionian Sea for Corfu, each galley being separately blessed by the papal nuncio as it passed.[2] Once at sea, it assumed the formation which it was to retain, with a few trifling changes, when it encountered the foe. There was a vanguard of eight swift galleys under Juan de Cardona; behind it, in the centre, a squadron of sixty-six galleys under Don John; on the left, the main body of the Venetians, to the number of fifty-four, under Agostino Barbarigo;[3] on the right, another detachment of equal size under Gian Andrea Doria; in the rear, a reserve of thirty-one, under Álvaro de Bazán.[4] On September 27, the Christians arrived at Corfu, where they

[1] All the accounts, both contemporary and modern, of the Christian armament differ slightly from one another in regard to the numbers of the men and the ships; the discrepancies, however, are not large, and the figure of 208 for the sum total of the galleys seems to be accepted by practically all, except Normann-Friedenfels (p. 23), who makes it 209. I have relied chiefly on Fernández Duro, ii, pp. 137 f., and Serrano, i, pp. 97, 119 f., and the contemporary authorities cited by them.

[2] Costiol, *Chronica*, lib. ii, cap. xiii; Fernández Duro, ii, pp. 138 f.

[3] At the time of leaving Messina, the Venetians were commanded by Sebastian Veniero; but he was replaced by Barbarigo in the harbor of Corfu as the outcome of an incident too significant to be omitted. When a small detachment of troops which Don John had lent to Veniero became insubordinate, the Venetian leader hanged the captain and three others, despite their plea that he had no jurisdiction in their case. Don John not unnaturally was highly incensed at what he regarded as an affront to his honor, and for a time there was good prospect that the Spaniards would fire into their allies; but it was finally arranged, through the mediation of Colonna, that Veniero should be punished by the loss of his command and of his seat in the war council. Serrano, i, pp. 121 f.

[4] The galleys were scattered, generally without reference to the power that furnished them, among the different detachments of the fleet, but it is worth noting that there were no Spaniards and only three Neapolitans in the left wing, where the Venetians were in preponderance. The six Venetian galleasses were distributed, two apiece, among the three main squadrons of the allied fleet.

received the first news of their foe. The Turks had been plundering Corfu shortly before; from prisoners exchanged at their departure it was learned that the enemy had a fleet fully equal to that of the Christians, that its chiefs were in two minds whether or not to offer battle, and that when last seen, it was steering for the Gulf of Lepanto.[1] Whether the forces of the infidel had remained united, or had subsequently split into two detachments, it was impossible definitely to determine; but in any case Don John was resolved to pursue them, and he soon succeeded in persuading the war council to agree.

The Turkish fleet was, in fact, all collected at the time in the inner harbor of the Gulf of Lepanto, doubly secure in the protection of the fortresses that guarded its narrow mouth. The contemporary estimates vary widely in regard to its size. It seems probable that the total number of its ships was approximately equal to that of the Christians, but that a larger proportion — perhaps as many as 230 — were galleys. There is also reason to believe that it carried a somewhat larger number of troops.[2] It was now commanded by Ali Pasha, substituted for Piali at the order of Selim, who had been displeased at the manner in which the latter had permitted aid to be brought to the garrison of Famagosta in the preceding year.[3] Ali Pasha was young, vigorous, anxious to distinguish himself, and probably somewhat over-confident as a result of his recent promotion;

The title of Marquis of Santa Cruz had been conferred upon Álvaro de Bazán by a royal *cédula* of October 9, 1569. Altolaguirre y Duvale, *Don Álvaro de Bazán*, p. 49.

[1] Stirling-Maxwell, i, pp. 390 f.

[2] Costiol, *Chronica*, lib. ii, cap. xv; Fernández Duro, ii, p. 152; Serrano, i, p. 130, and references there. Normann-Friedenfels (p. 29) says the Turkish fleet was originally composed of 170 large galleys and 200 smaller vessels, but gives no reference for his statement. The contemporary *Relacion Española*, printed at Rome, puts the total of Turkish soldiers, sailors, and rowers as high as 130,000.

[3] Cf. *ante*, p. 129; and Fernández Duro, ii, p. 133.

he also believed the Christian forces to be considerably
smaller than they actually were, and wished to sally forth
and give battle in the open.   But many voices in the Turkish
war council were raised against this plan as too audacious :
among them those of Pertau Pasha, the general of the
Turkish infantry, and of Aluch Ali, the viceroy of Algiers,
a renegade Calabrian fisherman who had become a Moslem,
and had crowded a multitude of adventures into the fifty-two
years of his existence ; he was to be a thorn in the side of
the Christians for many years to come.[1]   These men, who
could scarcely be accused of timidity, had their own information in regard to the Christian fleet, and stoutly maintained that Ali Pasha underestimated both its quality
and its size.   They knew that their own crews were largely
composed of Christian captives, who would naturally desert
them at the first favorable opportunity.[2]   They therefore
favored a policy of avoiding decisive action, and of awaiting
their enemies under the protection of the fortress of Lepanto,
where they would have every advantage, and a safe place
of retreat ; they were confident, moreover, that the coming
of the autumn winds would soon oblige the Christians to
disperse.   But Ali Pasha rejected these opinions as derogatory to the honor of the Turkish Empire.   He pointed out
that there were many other fortresses to the south of Lepanto
to which his fleet could retire in case of need ; and his views
were confirmed at the last moment by a peremptory order
from the Sultan, commanding him to go forth at once and
seek the foe.   On October 6, accordingly, he weighed anchor
and moved slowly west out of the inner harbor of Lepanto,
in the direction of Cephalonia ; one hour after daybreak, on
the morning of the 7th, he sighted the Christian armament

[1] Stirling-Maxwell, i, pp. 397 f.;   [2] Serrano, i, pp. 125 f.
Forneron, ii, p. 207, and references
there.

in battle array, moving slowly down out of the northwest.[1] The moment which both commanders so ardently desired had at last arrived. A decisive battle was inevitable.

That battle, however, did not begin till eleven o'clock in the morning; no less than four hours were spent by both combatants in arranging their respective fleets for the oncoming encounter. The Turks exchanged the crescent formation in which they had issued forth from the inner harbor for a linear one, with a centre and two wings, closely resembling that of their foes. Since it would clearly be the object of the Christians to keep them penned up in the narrow waters of the gulf, where the superior number of their galleys would be of no avail, it would be necessary for them, in order to defeat this aim, to get around their enemy's flanks, and the sole way to do this was to advance the two ends of their line. The Christians, on their side, brought forward their six heavy galleasses and placed them, two in front of each of the three divisions of their fleet, to serve as a sort of vanguard; with the great cannon of these floating castles they could hope to disable the enemy's best ships before they came within range of the main body of the Christian armament, and thus break the force of the infidel attack. Don John also gave orders for the removal of all the *espolones*, or high wooden structures which were built over the prows of the Christian galleys to facilitate the operations of ramming and boarding; he thereby rendered his ships more difficult for the enemy to hit, and at the same time made possible the more effective working of his own guns. The wisdom of this proceeding was made evident in the approaching battle; while a large proportion of the enemy's missiles passed harmlessly over the heads of the

---

[1] Stirling-Maxwell, i, p. 402; Serrano, i, pp. 126–128; Forneron, ii, p. 200, and references there.

Christians, their own discharges usually found the Turkish vessels at the waterline.[1]

The spectacle presented by the two fleets as they approached one another is described in glowing terms in all the contemporary accounts. The day was a Sunday; a gentle westerly breeze was blowing, and the Christians advanced before it with their sails unfurled; and "it was a sight of marvellous beauty to see the sea covered with so many galleys with their banners and standards of different colors, in all their magnificence."[2] When everything was ready, Don John, clad in shining armor, transferred himself to a fast galley and ran along in front of the Christian line, exhorting and encouraging each of the different contingents in the words best suited to arouse its fighting ardor; and such was the enthusiasm which his eloquence inspired that even the Venetians forgot their distrusts and grievances.[3] As the Turks drew near, they rent the air with taunting shouts and screams; they blew their trumpets, clashed their cymbals, and shot off their musketry to frighten the foe; the Christians, on the contrary, preserved complete silence. At the last moment, however, a signal gun was fired, and a crucifix was raised aloft on every vessel in the line. Don John, standing in a prominent place on the prow of his flagship, knelt to adore the sacred symbol, and his example was followed by every soldier and sailor in the fleet. The decks were bright with the gleaming arms of kneeling men, while friars, erect and conspicuous in their robes of black and brown, promised absolution to all who should loyally fight the battle of the Cross. Never before, in the whole course of the sixteenth century, had there been so striking

---

[1] Costiol, *Chronica*, lib. ii, cap. xvi; Stirling-Maxwell, i, pp. 404–406; Manfroni, *Storia della Marina Italiana*, pp. 487 ff.; Serrano, i, pp. 129–131;

Normann-Friedenfels, pp. 36 ff.
[2] *D. I. E.*, xxi, p. 348.
[3] Stirling-Maxwell, i, p. 407.

a demonstration of the power of religious enthusiasm as a motive force in a fight.[1]

On the Christian left, where the Venetians were stationed, the combat began with the utmost fury. The two galleasses in advance of the main line did yeoman service with their artillery in breaking the force of the initial Turkish attack; but most of the infidel ships finally got past them, and sought safety from their fire by laying themselves alongside the Christian galleys.[2] Some few of the Turkish vessels contrived to get around the Christian flank, despite all the efforts of Barbarigo to prevent it, so that for a time the Venetians found themselves between two fires. There were murderous discharges of cannon, musketry, and arrows, and Barbarigo received a wound in the eye which three days later proved mortal; no quarter was asked or given, and the slaughter was very great. But fortune finally declared itself for the Venetians, who were as much encouraged as their adversaries were disheartened by the course that the conflict was taking in the centre. By the middle of the afternoon large numbers of the enemy's galleys had been either captured or sunk. A few ran ashore, and their crews sought safety by jumping overboard and swimming for land, where they were pursued and mostly slain by their relentless foes.[3]

It was principally on the result of the combat in the centre that the fate of the entire engagement depended; and as soon as the hostile fleets had closed for the encounter, it became evident that each of the rival commanders was making directly for the flagship of his foe. Within half an hour of the opening of the fight the two galleys had

[1] Stirling-Maxwell, i, p. 408; Fernández Duro, ii, p. 156; Normann-Friedenfels, pp. 38 f.
[2] Costiol, lib. ii, cap. xviii; Serrano, i, p. 134.
[3] Paruta, *Historia Vinetiana*, ii, pp. 215 ff.; Stirling-Maxwell, i, pp. 412 f.; Manfroni, *Storia della Marina Italiana*, pp. 490 ff.; Normann-Friedenfels, pp. 55 f.

grappled one another, and the soldiers that they carried were engaged in a desperate hand-to-hand conflict — the pick of Selim's janizaries against the flower of the *tercio* of Don Lope de Figueroa. Both of the rival flagships were supported by their best galleys, from which reënforcements swarmed forward on ladders as fast as they were needed; and for two long hours the issue remained in doubt. Owing largely to the removal of the *espolones*, the cannon fire of the Christians was superior from the first; but this advantage was neutralized by the Turkish arrows, which did deadly execution on the troops who were attempting to board; Don John himself was slightly wounded. Twice the Spaniards got a footing on the decks of Ali's flagship, only to be driven back again with terrible loss. A third attempt carried them forward beyond the mast, and then, as he was leading on his janizaries to repel them, the Turkish commander fell dead with an arquebus shot in the forehead. A Malagan soldier pounced upon the body and brought it to Don John. The head was cut off and swiftly raised on the point of a lance, where it was plain to be seen by friend and foe. This incident determined the issue of the day. One final rush was sufficient to take the Turkish flagship. Its standard was hauled down and transferred to the galley of Don John. The banner of the Cross was hoisted in its place, and the air was rent with Christian cheers. One last desperate effort of the infidels to retrieve their loss was frustrated by the ready aid of Bazán and his reserves. By three o'clock in the afternoon the battle in the centre had been decisively won.[1]

Not so conclusive, however, was the victory of the Christians on the right, where Doria was opposed by the crafty

[1] Costiol, lib. ii, cap. xix; Stirling-Maxwell, i, pp. 414–417; Serrano, i, pp. 135 f.; Normann-Friedenfels, pp. 47 ff.

Aluch Ali and the swiftest vessels of the Turkish fleet. The
contest there began somewhat later than it had in the centre
and on the left, owing chiefly to the masterly manoeuvring
of the Turkish leader. Perceiving the damage that had
been done by the fire of the heavy galleasses to the other
parts of the infidel line, he skilfully eluded the pair in the
vanguard of Doria, and after baffling the chief galleys behind
them by wheeling first to one side and then to the other,
he finally bore away to the southwest as if to outflank his
adversary's right. In intercepting this manoeuvre, Doria
suffered the main body of his contingent to be drawn away
from the rest of the Christian fleet; a large hole was thus
opened between his left and Don John's right; and Aluch
Ali, seizing his chance, suddenly changed his course and
made with all possible speed for the gap in the Christian
line. So rapid were his movements that he succeeded in
getting through it, with the most of his ships, to the rear of
Doria and Don John; once there, he found himself close to
a small group of galleys of the Knights of St. John of Malta,
for whom he cherished rancor and profound contempt. In
a trice he succeeded in overpowering them. He captured
their banner and took their prior's ship in tow. Then,
seeing that the fight on the other wing and in the centre
was irretrievably lost, he started to escape to the open sea.
But at the same moment the Christian reserve, under Álvaro
de Bazán, bore down on him at full speed. To engage so
formidable an antagonist was under the circumstances
impossible, and the Turk had the wisdom to realize it.
He cut his prize adrift, and plied his oars with might and
main in one last desperate effort to get away. By the
merest hair's breadth he succeeded, with upwards of fifteen [1]

[1] Fernández Duro, ii, p. 159, makes it sixteen; Serrano, i, p. 137, puts it at
thirty.

of his best galleys, despite all efforts to prevent him on the
part of Bazán, who realized that the victory could never be
complete as long as this dangerous enemy was at large.[1]
The escape of the pirate was indeed a serious matter, far
more serious in fact, as the sequel was to show, than any
of the Christian leaders could have foretold. For the
moment, however, it seemed but a trivial misfortune; the
victors were all convinced that they had gained, as a contemporary put it, "the greatest triumph that had been won
in a thousand years."[2] Cervantes, who was present and
severely wounded in the fray, has rightly characterized it
as "the disillusionment of the world and of all the nations
who believed that the Turks were invincible upon the sea."[3]
Of the 300 or more infidel vessels which had entered the
fight, a bare 50 had got away; 117 had been captured by
the Christians, together with about 450 pieces of artillery.
Some 30,000 Turks had been slain, and at least one-fourth
of that number had been taken prisoners; and 15,000
Christian slaves had been liberated from captivity. On the
Christian side there had been between 7000 and 8000 killed,
and about 15,000 wounded; the loss of ships was insignificant — 15 or 20 at the most — and most of them were
Venetians.[4]

Great were the rejoicings in Italy and in Spain when
the glorious news of the victory arrived; in both peninsulas
the ensuing month was virtually given over to processions,
Te Deums, and ovations to the returning heroes. Titian,
then in his ninety-fifth year, did an allegorical painting
of it for the king of Spain, which is now in the gallery at
Madrid; two pictures of it by Tintoretto have perished,

---

[1] Defontin-Maxange, *Eudj' Ali*, pp.
130–151.

[2] Serrano, i, p. 138.

[3] *Don Quixote*, pt. i, cap. xxxix.

[4] Costiol, lib. iii, caps. i, iii; Stirling-
Maxwell, i, pp. 440 f.; Serrano, i,
pp. 137 f.; Fernández Duro, ii, pp. 160
f.; Normann-Friedenfels, pp. 52–66.

while two by Veronese are still to be seen in Venice.[1] The glad tidings reached Philip at San Lorenzo on the afternoon of November 8, while he was at vespers; and it was characteristic of him that he suffered no outward evidence of his joy to escape him, but ordered that the service be continued without interruption to the very end, when he commanded that a solemn Te Deum be sung.[2] Very different was the ecstatic welcome which the news received at the Vatican from the Pope, the real creator of the Holy League. Ever since the fleet had left Messina, Pius had been inspired with the belief that it was destined to return victorious. He longed to give the lie to the taunts of the sceptics, who had reminded him of the fate of the Holy Leagues of the Emperor's day. When his sublime faith was at last rewarded, he is said to have burst out, in his gratitude to the victor, with the words of the Evangelist, "There was a man sent from God, whose name was John."[3] The phrase, if it was ever really used, was doubtless but a momentary effusion of ardent thankfulness and joy; but it has a deeper and more permanent significance as well. Whether the disposition of the different units of the Christian fleet, the excellence of its cannon, or the superiority of the *tercios* to the janizaries, offers the best technical explanation of the victory, is for the naval and military experts to determine; the outstanding fact remains, that had it not been for the inspiration of Don John's leadership, and the help of the Venetians, there would not have been any campaign at all. The latter of these two essential elements was temporary,

[1] Pastor, xviii, pp. 446–448; Guglielmotti, *Storia della Marina Pontificia*, vi, pp. 255 ff.

[2] Cf. contemporary "Relacion de la batalla naval de Lepanto," in *D. I. E.*, iii, pp. 257 f.; J. Zarco Cuevas, *Documentos para la Historia del Monasterio de San Lorenzo el Real de El Escorial*, i, pp. 15, 51; José de Sigüenza, *Historia de la Orden de San Jerónimo*, 2ª ed., ii, p. 426.

[3] Cf. Pastor, xviii, p. 425; Stirling-Maxwell, i, p. 446; Fernández Duro, ii, p. 165.

uncertain, and, one might almost say, accidental; it had
been the product of the rage of the republic over the loss of
Cyprus, and could not be expected to last, for the interests
of the Venetians and the Spaniards were too radically
divergent to make it possible for them to be loyal allies
for long. But Spain's crusading enthusiasm, personified
by Don John, was a factor of much deeper and more permanent significance.[1] That enthusiasm had, indeed, been
somewhat dissipated and obscured in recent years by the
multiplicity of Spain's other interests, by her differences
with the papacy, and by numerous other minor considerations; but it had behind it an age-long tradition, and it
flamed out like a beacon at the hour of need. It was in
just recognition of Spain's major part in the splendid triumph
that had been so gloriously won, that the Sandjak, or grand
standard of the Turks, was handed over for safe-keeping to
the monks of the Escorial.[2] Not even in the Vatican could
it have found so fit a resting place.

Seldom, if ever, in the history of modern times have the
fruits of a fine victory been more shamefully wasted. "Now
we must take Jerusalem,"[3] was the cry of García de Toledo,
when the first news of Lepanto had come in. A combined
attack on Constantinople was also mooted; but before long
it was decided that the season was already too far advanced
for further offensive operations, and the first golden opportunity had been suffered to slip by. During the ensuing
winter, the old differences and jealousies between the allies
broke forth afresh. Spain and Venice could not agree as to
where the next blow should be planted; while Pope Pius was
attempting to bring them together, he was overtaken, on

---

[1] Fernández Duro, ii, pp. 165–167, and references there.

[2] Forneron, ii, p. 205; Zarco Cuevas, op. cit., i, pp. 15, 51.

[3] D. I. E., iii, p. 31.

May 1, 1572, by death; and though his successor, Gregory
XIII, seemed at first almost to surpass him in his enthusiasm
for crusading, he was unable to command the same confidence
on the part of the members of the League.[1] Philip II,
especially, seized every opportunity for delay; he was much
worried by the evidences of the hostility of France and of a
possible recrudescence of the ancient Franco-Turkish alliance. He was also beginning to be suspicious of Don John,
who now threatened to become too prominent and popular
to suit his taste. It is also significant that we find him, at
this very juncture, reverting to a project which had been
initiated two years before, of bribing Aluch Ali to desert the
Sultan; had not Selim given the corsair the supreme command of his fleet, which he succeeded, by the spring of 1572,
in raising to the number of some 135 galleys, it is not impossible that Philip's plots might have succeeded.[2] All this
naturally reacted most unfavorably on the attitude of the
Pope and the Venetians, who continued to urge active operations in the Levant. Gregory was outspoken in his con-
demnation of the Spanish monarch, while the republic began
seriously to consider the advisability of making a separate
peace with the infidel behind the backs of her allies, and of
utilizing the offers of France to facilitate this end.[3] But the
energy and enthusiasm of Don John would not suffer the
forces of the League to disperse without one more effort.
He finally secured the reluctant permission of Philip for the
mobilization of the Spanish squadrons. There was a tardy
reunion of the allies in August at Corfu, and a series of inconclusive minor operations against Aluch Ali and the Turkish
fleet up and down the western shores of Greece.[4] The near-

[1] Serrano, i, pp. 188–195.
[2] Forneron, ii, pp. 207 f., and references there.
[3] Serrano, i, pp. 251–268.
[4] Serrano, ii, pp. 1–118. Cf. also

Miguel Serviá's contemporary "Relacion de los Sucesos de la Armada de la
Santa Liga desde 1571 hasta 1574,"
in D. I. E., xi, pp. 359–454.

est to a decisive battle that occurred during the campaign took place on the anniversary of Lepanto off the harbor of Navarino; but the Turk refused to risk his ships in a prolonged engagement against superior forces, and prudently retired, when the enemy bore down upon him, under the protection of the guns of the fortress of Modon. A whole year had been lost, and nothing accomplished; the magnificent outburst of crusading ardor which had made possible the great victory of 1571 had been succeeded by the revival of the old suspicions and distrusts; and in the meantime the infidel had once more become formidable.[1]

If the wasting of the year 1572 was primarily due to the procrastinations of Philip, the dissolution of the League, which was to follow in 1573, must be charged first of all to the treachery of the Venetians. The issue of the campaign of 1572 had convinced the republic that the Spanish monarch would bear no share in any active offensive operations in the Levant, where all her interests lay. She had also observed that Don John had his eye fixed on Tunis, which did not concern her in the least. Throughout the winter months there were rumors and suspicions of her meditated treachery, both at Rome and at Madrid. They were strengthened by the refusal of the republic to arm as many galleys as heretofore for the coming campaign. The Pope was so much alarmed that he urged Philip to come in person to Italy as the sole possible way of saving the situation; and though the Prudent King could not bring himself to do this, he certainly showed far more energy and interest in the affairs of the League than he had exhibited in the preceding year.[2] But it was all in vain. The conviction of the republic that she could not herself derive any further advantage from

---

[1] Serrano, ii, pp. 119–150; Stirling-Maxwell, i, pp. 488–502; Fernández Duro, ii, pp. 169–185.

[2] Serrano, ii, pp. 198–284, *passim*, and references there.

continued adherence to her allies had made her abandonment of them practically certain in November, 1572; and
French influence and help facilitated her defection. On
March 7, 1573, she signed peace with the Porte, on such
terms as might have been expected to be made had the verdict of Lepanto been reversed; she tamely gave up Cyprus,
whose retention had been the chief inducement that had
caused her to join the League, and paid in addition an
annual indemnity of 100,000 ducats for three years to come.[1]
Gregory was furious when the news reached him a month
later, and the different Spanish representatives in Italy
scarcely less so; for a moment there was even talk of chastising the republic for her treachery.[2] But the wiser heads
soon realized that vengeance was, for the present, quite outside the sphere of practical politics, especially in view of the
state of affairs in France and the Low Countries; and Philip,
when he learned the facts, did not utter a word of reproach
against the deserters.[3] He could not afford to quarrel with
them, and he knew it; and even Gregory, before many
months had passed, came reluctantly to the same conclusion. It remained to be seen what the Pope and the
Spaniards could accomplish against the infidel without the
aid of the republic.

If the defection of the Venetians made it manifestly
impossible to attempt any extensive operations in the
Levant, it also removed the principal objection to Don
John's directing his efforts to some purpose more immediately
advantageous to Spain. Late in the summer it was decided
that the victor of Lepanto should be permitted to attack

[1] Serrano, ii, pp. 285–310; N. Jorga,
Geschichte des osmanischen Reiches, iii,
p. 156, and references there; treaty in
Dumont, Corps universel diplomatique,
v, 1, pp. 218 f.

[2] Pastor, xix, pp. 333–339; Fernández
Duro, ii, p. 186.
[3] Serrano, ii, pp. 332–334.

the city of Tunis, now occupied by the Turkish garrison installed there in 1569 by Aluch Ali, though the Spaniards still held on at La Goletta.[1] Don John left Sicily on October 1 for this purpose, with an armament of over 100 galleys, and some 20,000 troops; a week later he arrived off La Goletta, where he was welcomed like a conqueror. The Turks at Tunis, reading the signs, made haste to evacuate. Three days later the Spaniards entered the city almost without striking a blow, and set up the old sham Hafside dynasty there again in the person of Muley Mohammed, son of Muley Hassan, the protégé of Charles V.[2] But the fruits of this easy triumph were speedily lost through the failure of the victors to consolidate their gains. The usual story is that Philip had only consented to the expedition on condition that, after the expulsion of the Turks, the walls both of Tunis and of La Goletta should be completely destroyed, and the place evacuated; that he was unwilling to spend money on an outpost so remote; and that he was in mortal terror lest Don John, of whom he was becoming more jealous every day, should establish himself there as a semi-independent prince.[3] Others reject these allegations as groundless, and insist that Philip wished Tunis to be preserved.[4] Whatever the rights and wrongs of the point at issue, it is certain that Don John received no real support in his efforts to maintain what he had won. After the capture of Tunis, he gave orders for the preservation of the existing fortresses,

[1] Cf. *ante*, p. 126. On the intervening vicissitudes at Tunis cf. Stirling-Maxwell, ii, pp. 12 f., and Mercier, iii, pp. 106 ff.

[2] Cf. Placido Ragazzoni (1574) in Albèri, *Relazioni*, serie i, vi, pp. 471–475; M. Serviá in *D. I. E.*, xi, pp. 413–416; C. de C., ii, p. 205; U. Foglietta, *De Sacro Foedere*, etc., pp. 233–254; Mercier, iii, pp. 114–116; Stirling-Maxwell, ii, pp. 13–19.

[3] So, e.g., Forneron, ii, pp. 211 f., though the evidence in *D. I. E.*, iii, pp. 136–142, does not entirely bear him out.

[4] So, e.g., Fernández Duro, ii, p. 190; but to those who are familiar with Philip's methods of expressing himself, the document he cites in support of his views is hardly conclusive.

and for the erection of a new one; on his departure for
Sicily, two weeks later, he left an experienced officer in charge
of the work, together with a garrison of 8000 men; and on
his return to Sicily he besought Philip to send over yet more
troops and supplies. But he was everywhere met with the
most exasperating excuses and refusals, not only from the
king himself, but also from the royal representatives in
Italy.[1] Despite all his efforts, the place remained unfit
to stand a siege; and the Argus-eyed Aluch Ali, who, ever
since his flight from Lepanto, had burned for revenge, was
ready to seize his chance.

Fresh rumors began to reach Western Europe in the early
spring of 1574 of the preparation of another large fleet in
Constantinople, of which Aluch Ali was to have command;
and there could be no reasonable doubt what its destination
was to be. Don John saw the approaching peril and did his
utmost to avert it. He elicited orders from Philip — needless to add, too late — for the preparation of 100 sail at
Messina, and sent off some twenty galleys with men and
munitions to reënforce the garrison of La Goletta.[2] But the
enemy was too prompt and too powerful to permit him to do
more. On July 13, Aluch Ali appeared before Tunis with a
fleet of 230 galleys and a host of smaller ships.[3] There were
apparently as many as 70,000 troops on board under command of Sinan Pasha, the son-in-law of the Sultan. The
pasha of Tripoli and the inland tribes also furnished their
contingents, so as to blockade the fortress on the land side;
in all, the infidel armies numbered nearly 100,000 men.[4]
Against such overwhelming forces, the Christian garrisons
in La Goletta and the unfinished new fortress — still a 'cow-

[1] *D. I. E.*, xxiii, p. 238; xxviii, pp.
185–190; C. de C., ii, p. 234.
[2] Fernández Duro, ii, p. 191.

[3] Placido Ragazzoni (1574) in Albèri,
Relazioni, serie i, vi, p. 477.
[4] Fernández Duro, ii, pp. 191 f.;
Mercier, iii, pp. 116 f.

pen,' to use the picturesque language of the soldiers, rather than a fort [1] — were naturally insufficient, and the Turks began operations too swiftly to permit the larger reënforcements which Don John was painfully preparing in Sicily to arrive in time. On August 23, La Goletta was taken, and the garrison massacred, save for two or three hundred men, among them the commander, Portocarrero, who were enslaved; and the new fortress, after a heroic resistance, succumbed on September 15. The new fortifications were promptly blown up; a Turkish pasha was installed, with an adequate garrison, to organize the conquest after the infidel fashion; and in October Aluch Ali was back in Constantinople, bringing with him, in token of his triumph, some 300 Christian cannon, a number of distinguished captives, and finally Muley Mohammed, the last of the Hafsides.[2] The greatest of the Emperor's North African victories had been reversed, and the defeat of Lepanto at least partially avenged.

From 1574 onward, Philip lost all interest in fighting the hereditary foe. The papacy made several efforts to revive his crusading ardor, but in vain.[3] The loss of Tunis convinced the Spanish monarch that it was bad policy to spend money on the maintenance of remote outposts; the verdict of Lepanto had been at least sufficiently decisive to deter the infidel from annoying him by raids into the western basin of the Mediterranean on any such scale as had been customary in the days of his father; above all, the pressure of his multifarious projects and responsibilities in Western Europe was sufficient, during the remaining years of his rule,

[1] Fernández Duro, ii, p. 192.
[2] C. de C., ii, pp. 243–247; Mercier, iii, pp. 118 f.; Jorga, op. cit., iii, p. 158; C. A. Julien, Histoire de l'Afrique du Nord, p. 537; Defontin-Maxange, Eudj' Ali, pp. 163 f.
[3] Pastor, xix, ch. ix, passim.

to occupy all his time. One of these projects, the annexation of Portugal, was indeed, as we shall later see, to bring him temporarily into relations with the rulers of Morocco; but that was a minor affair, quite apart from the main problem of his attitude toward the Turks, and his handling of it was such as to demonstrate beyond any doubt that he had lost all enthusiasm for North African campaigning. Oran and Mers-el-Kebir he continued to hold,[1] despite the opinion of many of his counsellors that their maintenance cost more than it was worth; and their successive commanders continued to wage the same series of petty and fruitless wars with the neighboring tribes which had meant so much labor and pains to their predecessors.[2] It was entirely characteristic of the Spanish king that here, as in so many other of his affairs, he should have insisted on the policy of a rigid maintenance of the status quo. And it is interesting to observe that Philip's resolve to retain these two places prevented him, for several years, from obtaining the definite peace with the Porte which, despite all the threats and censures of the papacy, he had determined to seek since at least as early as 1575, when secret Spanish agents began to appear in Constantinople. By 1577, his efforts in this direction became more vigorous and definite; a certain Milanese called John of Marigiliano and an Albanian named Bruti were charged with the difficult task, only to be told that a treaty was impossible as long as the Spaniards kept Oran.[3] For three years more the matter hung fire. A report which

---

[1] And also, of course, certain outposts in Morocco, notably Melilla, which Spain had held since 1496 (cf. *ante*, Vol. II, p. 241), and Ceuta, which came to her with the annexation of Portugal; both of these places she retains today. Cf. Mercier, iii, pp. 308–310, 318 f., 343 f., 402, 438. Spain lost Oran and Mers-el-Kebir in 1708 (Mercier, iii, pp. 333–335), retook them in 1732 (*ibid.*, pp. 355–360), and evacuated them finally in 1792 (*ibid.*, pp. 432–436). She made a last fruitless effort to possess herself of Algiers in 1775 (*ibid.*, pp. 403–409).

[2] Mercier, iii, pp. 125 f.

[3] Charrière, *Négociations*, iii, pp. 705, 710–714, 733, 777 f.; Jorga, *Geschichte*, iii, p. 160; Pastor, xix, pp. 354 f.; Philippson, *Kardinal Granvella*, pp. 99 f.

reached Rome, in advance of the fact, in February, 1579, to the effect that peace had been actually concluded, elicited a final protest from Gregory XIII;[1] but Philip went steadily on his course, and on March 21, 1580, he at last attained his end. A revolt of the local Berber tribes against the Turkish representative in Algiers apparently convinced Sultan Murad III that he could ill afford to remain at enmity with Spain, whether she continued to occupy Oran or not, and he finally granted the Spanish representative a truce to last till January, 1581; after that it was twice renewed till 1585, when further serious fighting had ceased to be practically possible.[2] The whole negotiation was conducted in most extraordinary fashion. The Spanish representatives at Constantinople were treated rather as prisoners than as ambassadors, and they were constantly impeded by the counter-plots of the French and English;[3] but the enhancement of the power and territories of their master, through the annexation of Portugal and her colonies in the East and West, furnished an argument in their favor which the Turks found increasingly potent. Save for motives of religion, far less powerful than heretofore, Spain and the infidel had really little left to fight about. Each entertained a somewhat excessive respect for the power of the other. Both were exceedingly busy about other things. And the natural result was that though they were far from becoming friends, they ceased to be active foes.

Such was the rather sorry termination of a conflict which had gone on intermittently for over eight centuries, and in which the most ancient and permanent traditions of the

[1] Pastor, xix, pp. 354 f.
[2] Gioan Francesco Morosini (1581) in Albèri, *Relazioni*, serie i, v, pp. 327 f.; Jorga, iii, pp. 160 f.
[3] Charrière, *Négociations*, iii, pp. 850–895; Conyers Read, *Secretary Walsingham*, iii, pp. 225–228, 326–332; Edwin Pears, "The Spanish Armada and the Ottoman Porte," in the *English Historical Review*, viii (1893), pp. 439–466.

Spanish Empire were intimately bound up. The fact is worth emphasizing that the end came simultaneously with, and in some measure because of, the expansion of the Spanish Empire in other directions, an expansion which was to carry it to its greatest territorial extent. From the eighth to the thirteenth century Spain had made practically all her conquests at the expense of the infidel; from the thirteenth to the latter part of the sixteenth, she had advanced at the cost of infidel and Christian alike, and also of the aborigines of the Western Hemisphere; after 1580, the infidel really drops out of the picture; he is virtually forgotten in the pressure of other things. But what perhaps in the long run is even more significant than the coincidence of the cessation of war against the Turk with the annexation of Portugal and her dominions overseas, is the fact that the ensuing era of peace with the infidel is also that of the beginning of Spain's decline; when bereft of the ancient inspiration of crusading, she ceased to go forward and began to go back. She had more than done her part during the preceding century in maintaining the great struggle of the Cross against the Crescent. She had surpassed all other European nations in the carrying of the Gospel to the natives of the New World. But when it came to the assertion of her supremacy over her Christian neighbors to the north of her — the task which was to occupy her in the succeeding decades — she was destined to experience a series of bitter defeats; for her adversaries had attuned their lives to modernity, while she, in large measure, was still living in the past. It has often been pointed out that Spain's reverses in Western Europe were at least one reason why she ceased to carry on the struggle against Islam; and the observation is entirely justified by the facts. But it is also quite possible to turn the statement around the other way, and to maintain that the

fact that Spain had ceased to fight the infidel was in itself
a contributing cause of the disintegration of her mighty
empire, in that it deprived her of the most powerful of all the
incentives which had made possible her greatest triumphs
in the ages that had gone before.

BIBLIOGRAPHICAL NOTE

See note at the end of Chapter XXV, and add:

Sources. — On the rebellion at Granada and its suppression see the " Correspondencia de Felipe II y otros personajes con Don Juan de Austria desde 1568 hasta 1570 " in *D. I. E.*, xxviii, pp. 5–154; " Documents relatifs à la Guerre de Grenade," ed. R. Foulché-Delbosc in *R. H.*, xxxi (1914), pp. 486–523; the " Mémoire du Marquis de Mondéjar," ed. A. Morel-Fatio, on pp. 1–96 of *L'Espagne au XVI* et au XVII* siècle* (Heilbronn, 1878); Diego Hurtado de Mendoza, " Guerra de Granada," in *B. A. E.*, Historiadores de Sucesos Particulares, i, pp. 65–122 (on the vexed question of the authenticity of this, cf. Lucas de Torre y Franco-Romero in the *Boletín* of the R. A. H., lxiv (1914), pp. 461–501, 557–596; lxv (1914), pp. 28–47, 273–302, 369–415; also R. Foulché-Delbosc in *R. H.*, i, pp. 101–165, 338; xxxii, pp. 1–86; xxxv, pp. 476–538; and A. Morel-Fatio, " Quelques remarques," in École pratique des Hautes Études, section des sciences historiques et philologiques, *Annuaire*, 1914–15, pp. 5–50); Luis del Mármol Carvajal, " Historia del Rebelion y Castigo de los Moriscos del Reino de Granada," in *B. A. E.*, Historiadores de Sucesos Particulares, i, pp. 123–365; and " Sumario é Recopilacion," by Alonso de Castillo, in *M. H. E.*, iii, pp. 1–164. — For the Mediterranean campaigns, Pedro de Salazar's *Hispania Victrix* (Medina del Campo, 1570) covers the years 1546–65; Uberto Foglietta's composite volume, *De Sacro Foedere in Selimum Libri Quattuor* and *Variae Expeditiones in Africam, cum Obsidione Melitae* (Genoa, 1587; Italian translation, Genoa, 1598), gives an excellent contemporary picture of the sea fights and sieges down to the year 1574; and Alfonso de Ulloa's *Historia dell' Impresa di Tripoli, della presa del Pegnon di Velez, et del successo della Armata Turchesca venuta sopra l'isola di Malta, l'anno 1565* (Venice, 1566?) is a good general guide to the naval conflict of the years with which it deals. Vols. xiv and xxvii of the *D. I. E.* contain valuable contemporary documents and *relaciones* on the attack on the Peñon de Vélez in 1564; vols. xxix and xxx comprise the correspondence of Philip II with Don García de Toledo and others on the defence of Malta; and vols. iii, xi, and xxi give a number of contemporary *relaciones* of the Lepanto campaign and the ensuing events. From the manuscripts of the R. A. H. Cesáreo Fernández Duro published in the *Boletín* of the Academy, xii (1888), pp. 185–223, an anonymous contemporary account, without title, of the wars of Spain against the infidel from the days of the Emperor to the capture of Tunis in 1574 ; its object is to glorify Álvaro de Bazán.   The two *relaciones* (one by Álvaro de Sande) in C. Fernández Duro's *Estudios Históricos del Reinado de Felipe II* (Madrid, 1890), pp. 67–244, and the *Successi dell' Armata della M^{tà} C^{ca}* by Antonio Francesco Cirni (Florence, 1560) give vivid pictures of the disaster at Gerba.   Two little-known contemporary descriptions of the siege of Malta are *La Verdadera Relacion de todo lo que el anno de M. D. LXV. ha succedido en la Isla de Malta* by Francisco Balbi de Correggio (Barcelona, 1568) and *Deux veritables discours* on the siege of Malta by Pietro Gentile di Vendôme and Antonios Achélis, published in French and in Greek in 1567, and reëdited at Paris in 1910 by Hubert Pernot ; and the *Primera Parte de la Chronica del muy alto y poderoso Principe Don Juan de Austria*, by Hieronymo de Costiol (Barcelona, 1572), is important for the Lepanto campaign.   *La Liga de Lepanto entre España, Venecia, y la Santa Sede (1570–1573)*, by Luciano Serrano (Madrid, 1918–19, 2 vols.), and *La Lega di Lepanto nel carteggio diplomatico inedito di Luys de Torres*, by A. Dragonetti de Torres (Turin, 1931), are invaluable for the diplomatic negotiations between the signatories of the league ; both have excellent introductory summaries, which completely supersede the very inaccurate and biassed *Felipe II y la Liga de 1571* by Miguel Sánchez (Madrid, 1868).   The *Négociations de la France dans le Levant*, ed. Ernest Charrière in the *Collection de documents inédits sur l'histoire de France* (Paris, 1848–60, 4 vols.), is almost as indispensable for this period as for that which precedes it ; and Henry de Castries, *Les sources inédites de l'histoire du Maroc de 1530 à 1845*, première série, Dynastie Saadienne (Paris, 1905–26, 12 vols. and index), is the standard collection for the region and period with which it deals.

Later Works. — For the history of Spanish Protestantism Ernst Schäfer's *Beiträge zur Geschichte des spanischen Protestantismus* (Gütersloh, 1902, 3 vols.) is a final authority ; its principal conclusions are well summarized in vol. iii, pp. 411–479, of H. C. Lea's *History of the Inquisition of Spain* (New York, 1906–07, 4 vols.), which in turn virtually supersedes such older standard authorities as Llorente, Julio Melgares Marín, and Menéndez y Pelayo.   H. C. Lea's *The Moriscos of Spain* (Philadelphia, 1901) also renders it unnecessary for any save the specialist to delve in the older accounts of the rebellion of Granada, such as those contained in book vi of Jaime Bleda's *Coronica de los Moros de España* (Valencia, 1618), or in the second part of Ginés Pérez de Hita's more romantic than historical *Guerras Civiles de Granada* (best edition by Paula Blanchard-Demouge, Madrid,

1913–15, 2 vols.); Lea's book is a model of the best American scholarship of its day. Florencio Janer's *Condicion Social de los Moriscos de España* (Madrid, 1857) may still be consulted with profit. On the campaign of Gerba, the first 63 pages of C. Fernández Duro's *Estudios* are still valuable, but Charles Monchicourt's *L'Expédition espagnole de 1560 contre l'île de Djerba* (Paris, 1913) is the last word on the subject; it contains transcripts of a number of valuable documents and careful estimates of all the contemporary authorities. Ángel de Altolaguirre y Duvale's *Don Álvaro de Bazán* (Madrid, 1888) and Defontin-Maxange's *Eudj'Ali, corsaire barbaresque* (Paris, 1930) are both useful biographies for the ensuing period; both have adequate bibliographies, and the former contains 400 pages of published documents. — For the defence of Malta, Carlo Sanminiatelli Zabarella's *Lo Assedio di Malta, 1565* (Turin, 1902) and Félix de Salles's *Annales de l'Ordre de Malte* (Vienne, 1889), pp. 125–131, have superseded Giacomo Bosio's *Istoria della Militia di San Giovanni Gierosolimitano*, 2d ed., iii, pp. 487–716 (Naples, 1684), the Abbé R. A. de Vertot's *Histoire des Chevaliers Hospitaliers* (Paris, 1726, 4 vols.), and Edmond Jurien de la Gravière's *Les Chevaliers de Malte et la marine de Philippe II* (Paris, 1887, 2 vols.). Paul Herre's *Europäische Politik im cyprischen Krieg* (Leipzig, 1902) gives a good account of the diplomatic negotiations leading up to the formation of the Holy League. — On the campaign of Lepanto and the events which followed it, Sir William Stirling-Maxwell's *Don John of Austria* (London, 1883, 2 vols.) is not yet out of date, but the little monograph of Eduard von Normann-Friedenfels, entitled *Don Juan de Austria als Admiral der Heiligen Liga und die Schlacht bei Lepanto* (Pola, 1902), gives the best description of the formation of the rival fleets before and during the battle, and contains a number of valuable reproductions of contemporary pictures and charts. Those who are interested in the details of the naval construction of the period can find useful information on pp. 38 ff. of Gervasio de Artíñano y de Galdácano's *La Arquitectura Naval Española* (Madrid, 1920). The Venetian and papal sides of the story are adequately told in Paolo Paruta's *Storia della Guerra di Cipro*, ed. P. Rossi (Siena, 1827), which is a reprint of the second part of the author's *Historia Vinetiana* (Venice, 1605); in Camillo Manfroni's *Storia della Marina Italiana* (Rome, 1897); and in vol. vi of Alberto Guglielmotti's *Storia della Marina Pontificia* (Rome, 1887). C. Fernández Duro's *Armada Española*, vol. ii, N. Jorga's *Geschichte des osmanischen Reiches*, vol. iii, L. Pastor's *History of the Popes*, tr. Kerr, vols. xvi, xvii, and xviii, and E. Mercier's *Histoire de l'Afrique septentrionale*, vol. iii, are, of course, indispensable throughout. The last-named has been, to an extent, superseded by C. A. Julien's *Histoire de l'Afrique du Nord* (Paris, 1931), but the portions of Julien's book which are devoted to the period of Philip II are so brief that it is of little value for our purposes here. The list of works here given may be indefinitely extended by referring to the special bibliographies in the works of Serrano and of Monchicourt, cited above, and to the appropriate pages of Sánchez Alonso.

CHAPTER XXXIII

AMERICA AND THE PHILIPPINES

THE story of Spain in the New World is far less interesting during the reign of Philip II than under Charles V. The age of the greatest explorers and *conquistadores* is past; there are no adventures comparable to those of de Soto or Orellana, no feats of arms like those of Cortés and the Pizarros. The novelty of it all had begun to wear off, and the mother country was no longer fascinated by the Indies in the way that it had been in the Emperor's day.[1] Yet if measured by a less exalted standard, the progress of the Spanish rule in America under the Prudent King is by no means unimportant. There were, at least, several 'Phoenixes of the *conquistadores*'; such was Francisco de Ibarra,[2] who first brought effectively under Spanish control the regions comprised in the province of Nueva Vizcaya, roughly corresponding to the four northwestern states of the present republic of Mexico; such were Fray Agustín Rodríguez, Antonio de Espejo, and Juan de Oñate, who penetrated and began to colonize the southwestern portion of what is now the United States; such was also Sebastian Viscaino, who explored the Gulf of California, and later (after Philip's death) followed up the Pacific coast as far

---

[1] It is worth noting that the proportion of pages in Cabrera de Córdoba's *Felipe Segundo* which are devoted to the achievement of the Spaniards in the New World is far less than that in the contemporary histories of the reign of Charles V. Cf. also *infra*, p. 486.

[2] Cf. the admirable biography, *Francisco de Ibarra and Nueva Vizcaya*, by J. L. Mecham (Durham, N. C., 1927); its bibliography (pp. 240–250) will give ample indications to those who wish to pursue the story further.

as Cape Blanco in Oregon;[1] by these, and others like them, the area of the Spanish dominions in America was greatly enlarged. But it would be foolhardy to attempt to chronicle all these achievements in a work of the present size; we will therefore select three principal lines of development, each one of them typical of the Spanish method of dealing with a different problem of imperial domain, and try to portray them in some detail. These are, first, the settlement of Florida and conflicts with the French (1559–68), which indicate the attitude of the Spaniard toward the foreign infringer of his colonial monopoly; secondly, the Araucanian war, which shows how he fought the native Indian who refused to acknowledge the authority of the king of Spain; and thirdly, the refounding of Buenos Aires and the opening up of La Plata, an early stage of the long process of the transference of the economic centre of gravity of South America from the Pacific to the Atlantic coast.

The Spaniards, on the whole, had been grievously disappointed by the results of the expeditions that had hitherto been sent out to explore and subject the region which they called Florida.[2] The legend that it contained the fountain of eternal youth was not yet, indeed, wholly extinct, and Cabeza de Vaca, despite all the terrible privations that he had undergone there between 1528 and 1536, described

---

[1] The contemporary accounts of these and many other expeditions of the period may be found in *Spanish Exploration in the Southwest, 1542–1706*, ed. H. E. Bolton (New York, 1916); in H. R. Wagner's *Spanish Voyages to the Northwest Coast of America in the Sixteenth Century* (San Francisco, 1929); and in Baltasar de Obregon, *Historia de los Descubrimientos Antiguos y Modernos de la Nueva España, escrita*

año de 1584, ed. Mariano Cuevas (Mexico, 1924).

[2] Cf. *ante*, Vol. II, pp. 217 f.; III, pp. 523–531. To the Spaniards of that time Florida was an indeterminate area, stretching indefinitely inland from the northeastern shores of the Gulf of Mexico and the Atlantic coast from Cape Sable northward. Cf. *The Luna Papers*, tr. and ed. H. I. Priestley, i, p. xix.

it in his narrative as the "richest country in the world"; but as no tangible proof of these wonders had been forthcoming, men had generally gravitated to the verdict of Castañeda in 1543 that it was actually "full of bogs and poisonous fruits, barren, and the very worst country that is warmed by the sun." [1] Save for shipwrecks and certain sporadic and generally unsuccessful missionary endeavors, the Spaniards left the whole region virtually untouched during the ensuing seventeen years.[2]

At the time that the Emperor was giving place to his son Philip, there were signs of a great recrudescence of interest. The missionary appeal was always sure of a favorable audience at the court of the Prudent King; the second viceroy of Mexico, Luis de Velasco,[3] who had succeeded Mendoza in 1550, sent home pressing demands for the occupation of Florida; and Philip was the more inclined to listen to them because of his fear that if its settlement was not speedily effected there was grave danger of his being forestalled by the French. Ever since the expedition of Jacques Cartier to the 'codfish waters' in 1534–35, the dread of French competition in the New World had been felt very seriously at the Spanish court. The Emperor had laid stress upon it in his instructions to his son, and it had been reëmphasized in dramatic fashion, not only by the establishment in 1558 in the bay of Rio de Janeiro of the short-lived settlement of Nicolas Durand de Villegagnon, known as 'La France Antarctique,' [4] but also, much closer at hand, by a series of daring French raids on the Spanish

---

[1] Narrative of Castañeda, pp. 468, 545, in G. P. Winship, *The Coronado Expedition, 1540–1542* (Washington, 1896), an extract from the *Fourteenth Annual Report*, pt. 1, of the Bureau of Ethnology.

[2] *The Luna Papers*, tr. and ed. H. I. Priestley, i, p. xxi; Woodbury Lowery,

Spanish Settlements, 1513–1561, pp. 351–353.

[3] Lowery, *op. cit.*, pp. 353–356.

[4] *Cf. infra*, pp. 387 f. Paul Gaffarel, *Histoire du Brésil Français au seizième siècle* (Paris, 1878), is still a standard authority on this subject.

settlements on the shores of the Gulf of Mexico and the islands of the Caribbean Sea. Porto Bello, Cartagena, and Havana were perhaps the favorite points of attack, and much booty was taken.[1] It was noted, moreover, that these raids occurred not only at times when France and Spain were at war in Europe, but also in years when they were officially at peace; in other words, a brood of French corsairs and adventurers was apparently growing up which the home government was unable to control, and it was impossible to tell when or where they would next strike. Let them change their aims from piracy to colonization, and the scene of their activities from the region of the Gulf of Mexico to the hitherto unoccupied mainland farther north, and they might easily found a settlement which would imperil the Spanish monopoly of the New World. It may possibly be a slight exaggeration to speak of Philip as developing "the policy . . . of carrying expansion into the heart of the continent as a means of repelling the aggressions of his European rivals";[2] but there can be no doubt that the desire to anticipate the French was one of the principal motives that caused him, in December, 1557, to listen to the urgent pleas of Velasco, and order him, despite previous prohibitions, to "send out . . . to make new discoveries and settlements in Florida."[3] Velasco gave the post of governor of the prospective colony (October 30, 1558) to Tristán de Luna y Arellano, who had been resident in New Spain for some thirty years and was highly esteemed for his uprightness and efficiency.[4] Preparations to fit out an adequate expedition were pushed rapidly forward in the winter of 1558–59; in June, 1559, a fleet of thirteen vessels

[1] C. H. Haring, *Trade and Navigation between Spain and the Indies*, pp. 231–235.

[2] So Priestley, in introduction to *The Luna Papers*, p. xix.

[3] *Luna Papers*, p. 44.

[4] *Ibid.*, pp. 14–16, 32–52.

carrying some 1500 persons — men, women, and children, Spaniards, renegade Florida Indians, negro slaves, and Dominican friars —, 240 horses, and an abundance of ammunition and supplies, set sail with high hopes from Vera Cruz for the northeast.[1]

The expedition, however, was unlucky from the very first, and the result was to add one more to the already long list of disastrous experiences of the Spaniards in Florida. The adventurers made their first landing at what is now Mobile Bay; but, in the belief that a better place could be found farther eastward, they moved on some twenty leagues to Pensacola, where they finally established their base.[2] This was most unfortunate. Had they remained in Mobile Bay they could have ascended the Alabama River in boats, and made settlements in the rich lands along its banks within easy reach of the sea; as it was, the exploring expeditions which they sent out from Pensacola struck the comparatively poor pine lands farther south and eastward.[3] Some of the native Indians proved friendly and others hostile, and some of the adventurers became involved in the warfare of the local tribes. Provisions ran short; discontent became rife, and de Luna found it almost impossible to maintain discipline; after a year in Florida almost every one in the expedition was clamoring to return to Mexico. It was in the early months of 1561 that the miseries of the colonists reached their climax; on Palm Sunday a mutiny was narrowly averted through the devotion of the Dominican friars; and then two days later the long awaited succor arrived from Mexico with supplies sufficient to relieve present needs.[4] The relief expedition brought also, how-

[1] *Luna Papers*, pp. xxxiii–xxxv; Lowery, *op. cit.*, pp. 355–359.
[2] *Luna Papers*, pp. xxxiv f.

[3] G. R. Fairbanks, *Florida*, 2d ed. (Jacksonville, 1901), p. 60.
[4] *Luna Papers*, pp. xxxv–lxv; Lowery, *op. cit.*, pp. 357–374.

ever, a new governor, Ángel de Villafañe, commissioned by the viceroy to supersede de Luna, of whose leadership unfavorable reports had been received. As Villafañe had orders to occupy Cape Santa Elena [1] and trace the Atlantic coast, and as no one was anxious to remain at Pensacola, the settlement there was virtually abandoned. De Luna departed for Havana and then for Spain, in a vain attempt to reimburse himself for the expenses which he had personally incurred; and most of the rest of his company that remained accompanied Villafañe on his mission to Cape Santa Elena. On May 27, 1561, he reached it by sea, after touching at Havana on the way; he ascended a neighboring river [2] some fourteen miles, and formally took possession in the king's name; and in the next two weeks he reconnoitred the Atlantic coast northward as far as Cape Hatteras. But he found no country suitable for permanent occupation; his small fleet was in grave peril from storms; and finally, on July 9, he got back to Hispaniola. He had totally failed to establish a settlement, but he had also convinced himself that there was no danger that any other power would make the attempt. Moreover, he appears to have succeeded in persuading Philip that the region was safe from foreign intrusion, for on September 23 the king ordered the abandonment of all attempts to colonize the Atlantic coast.[3] The very next year was to prove that these calculations were entirely wrong.

The story of the first expedition of the French Protestant, Jean Ribaut, to the shores of Florida has been so often told

---

[1] On the different locations ascribed to the Punta Santa Elena, first discovered and named by Lucas Vásquez de Ayllón in 1526, cf. *Luna Papers*, pp. xx, xxvii, xxviii, and Lowery, *op. cit.*, pp. 355, 374, and references there. It certainly seems more likely that it was in what is now the southern corner of the state of South Carolina, near Saint Helena Island, than farther northward, near the mouth of the Santee.

[2] Probably the Savannah.

[3] Lowery, *op. cit.*, pp. 375 f., and references there.

that it is not necessary here to do more than repeat it in outline.[1] The adventurers were sent out through the efforts of the Admiral Gaspard de Coligny; they had two large ships and three small ones, carrying in all some 150 men, most of them ardent Calvinists; they sailed from Havre on February 16, 1562, and landed on May 1 at the mouth of the St. John's River.[2] There Ribaut erected a stone column with the arms of France engraved on it;[3] then he coasted northward, finally landing again at a point which most historians have now agreed in identifying as Port Royal Sound, South Carolina.[4] There he built a small blockhouse which he named Charlesfort, in honor of his king, and then, leaving twenty-eight of his most devoted followers to form the nucleus of a colony, he hurried back to France to get reënforcements.[5] But what is of greater interest for our present purpose is the accuracy of the information furnished to Philip in regard to this enterprise. His ambassador at the French court, Perrenot de Chantonnay, had got wind of the project long before Ribaut sailed, and sent home full details, laying horrified emphasis on the fact that those engaged in it were heretics and pirates, and had no official sanction from the government of France; Philip could only regard them as *corsarios Luteranos*.[6] This impression, moreover, was materially strengthened by the course of events after Ribaut's return. Civil war was raging in France at the time; and as Ribaut was consequently unable to get the help he desired, he crossed the

---

[1] The most famous account of it is, of course, that contained in Francis Parkman's *Pioneers of France in the New World* (Boston, 1865); it is not, however, entirely fair to the Spaniards. Cf. E. G. Bourne, *Spain in America, 1450-1580* (New York, 1904), pp. 188 f.

[2] Lowery, *Spanish Settlements, Florida, 1562-1574*, pp. 28-33; Carita Doggett Corse, *The Key to the Golden Islands* (Chapel Hill, N. C., 1931), pp. 7-10.

[3] Lowery, *op. cit.*, pp. 393 f.

[4] *Ibid.*, pp. 399-403, and references there.

[5] *Ibid.*, pp. 34-36.

[6] *Ibid.*, pp. 24-27, 31, and references there.

Channel in hopes of better fortune in England. He had no success there; in fact, his activities landed him temporarily in prison; but his doings were reported to Madrid by Quadra quite as fully as they had previously been by Chantonnay, and Philip's jealousy and resentment were fanned to a white heat.[1] The whole matter was frankly unintelligible to his meticulous and legalistic mind. That his exclusive right to the New World should be challenged by any one was hard enough to understand; but that his neighbors, with whom he was honestly striving to maintain amicable relations at the time, should permit rebels and heretics to trespass there, was utterly incomprehensible. Efforts to get satisfaction from Catharine and Elizabeth proved unavailing, and so finally, in May, 1564, a small expedition was sent out at Philip's order by the governor of Cuba, under Hernando Manrique de Rojas, to find and obliterate all traces of the French occupation of the Florida coast. It proved an unexpectedly easy task; for the remnants of the little colony which Ribaut had left at Charlesfort, rent by internal dissension and discouraged by loneliness and privations, had by this time deserted their post and gone home. On June 15 Manrique left the shores of the continent for Cuba, convinced that his enemies had departed for good. It was just seven days after he had gone that a second and far more formidable French expedition arrived.[2]

The newcomers, some 300 strong, had been sent out, like their predecessors, through the instrumentality of Coligny. Since Ribaut was still imprisoned in England, they were commanded by René de Laudonnière, one of Ribaut's companions on his first voyage. They established

---

[1] Lowery, *op. cit.*, pp. 34–39; *C. S. P., Spanish*, 1558–67, p. 536.

[2] Lowery, *Spanish Settlements, Florida, 1562–1574*, pp. 44–48, 54.

themselves at the mouth of the St. John's River at the point where Ribaut had planted the column with the arms of France;[1] there they built a redoubt which they called Fort Caroline.[2] But they were singularly unsuccessful both as colonists and as explorers. Within two months of their arrival insubordination became rife. On September 20 thirteen of their number took one of the ships and started off on a piratical cruise against the Spaniards in the West Indies; after seizing a shipload of gold and silver, they were themselves captured and taken to Havana, where they were forced to give information about the colony from which they had come. Other similar incidents, on a somewhat larger scale, followed in the succeeding months. To the French they made it evident that Laudonnière was not strong enough to control his followers, and that if the colony was to be saved he must be superseded by a better man; to the Spaniards they furnished convincing proof that the insolence of the *corsarios Luteranos* had reached greater heights than ever and that they must consequently be vigorously chastised.[3] The events of the year 1565, both in Europe and in America, were to bring the opposing theories of right and title to the New World into dramatic conflict with one another.

On March 20, at Madrid, Philip put his signature to an *asiento* creating Pedro Menéndez de Avilés *adelantado* of Florida, and appointing him captain-general of a fleet which was to carry 500 colonists to settle it.[4] Menéndez, who was at that time forty-six years old, was an Asturian of distinguished ancestry, who had already given high proof

---

[1] Which Manrique de Rojas had failed to find.

[2] Lowery, *op. cit.*, p. 58. Mrs. Corse (pp. 14 f.) puts the location of Fort Caroline on a small island at the mouth of what is now Shipyard Creek,

about four miles up the river from Mayport, where Ribaut first landed.

[3] Lowery, *op. cit.*, pp. 59–85, and references there.

[4] Printed in E. Ruidíaz y Caravia, *La Florida*, ii, pp. 415–427.

of exceptional valor, ability, and loyalty by the services
he had rendered his master both in the Old World and in
the New.[1] It was characteristic of him that he staked all
his private fortune on the success of the venture,[2] and that
he succeeded, before it set sail, in trebling its size. News
of counter-preparations in France emphasized the wisdom
of this course, and the expedition, when it finally departed
from Cadiz on June 29, consisted of ten ships carrying
1500 souls.[3] Seven weeks previously Jean Ribaut, released
from prison, had embarked at Dieppe with a fleet of seven
ships and a large number of followers,[4] to supersede Laudonnière and reënforce his colony. Coligny, as before, was the
moving spirit in the enterprise, but the queen-mother was
also cognizant of it, and though she was informed of the
preparations of Menéndez, and knew that his destination
was identical with that of Ribaut, she was fully prepared
to justify the latter's expedition on the ground that it was
directed to the Terre des Bretons, which had been claimed
by France since the time of Verrazzano, and whose southern
boundary was of course just as indeterminate as was the
northern limit of New Spain.[5] Ribaut's fleet was long
delayed by adverse winds. Not until August 28 did the
adventurers reach the mouth of the St. John's, where they
found the last remnant of Laudonnière's colony, utterly
disheartened and actually on the point of setting sail to
return to France;[6] had Ribaut arrived a day later he would
infallibly have found it gone. As it was, he had little
difficulty in inducing his countrymen to remain. Laudonnière accepted his demotion with dignity, and preparations

---

[1] Lowery, *op. cit.*, pp. 120 f., and
references there.
[2] Ruidíaz, *op. cit.*, ii, p. 64.
[3] Lowery, *op. cit.*, pp. 147–149.

[4] Probably about 300; cf., however,
Lowery, *op. cit.*, p. 96, note 3.
[5] *Ibid.*, pp. 114–117, and references
there.
[6] *Ibid.*, pp. 97 f.

were at once begun to refound and extend the settlement, when suddenly, on September 4, just one week after Ribaut's arrival, another large fleet was descried on the southern horizon. It was the advance guard of the expedition of Menéndez, which had also experienced bad weather in crossing the Atlantic, and had been obliged to put in at the West Indies for repairs. He had landed at last on the Florida coast, some twelve leagues to the southward of the Frenchmen, on the very day (August 28) that Ribaut had reached the St. John's, and had established a base which he called St. Augustine, in honor of the saint whose festival it was. He was now coasting northward in search of his foes.[1]

The story of the next six weeks is a sad chronicle of bloodshed. Menéndez immediately attacked four of Ribaut's ships which were lying outside the harbor and dispersed them. Two days later he was back at St. Augustine, where he landed his troops and munitions in preparation for a land attack on Fort Caroline. That attack was delivered in a pouring rain, in the small hours of the morning of September 20, and was completely successful. Ribaut, with the flower of the garrison, had gone off in chase of the Spanish fleet, so that the defenders, most of whom were in their beds, were in no condition to resist. One hundred and thirty-two were killed outright; fifty women and children and half a dozen drummers and trumpeters were taken prisoners;[2] the rest escaped into the forests,

---

[1] Lowery, *op. cit.*, pp. 154 f.

[2] "In a work [*La Reprinse de la Floride*, supposedly by Dominique de Gourgues] written in France some seven years later, and first published in 1586, it is related that Avilés hanged some of his prisoners on trees and placed above them the Spanish inscription, 'I do this not to Frenchmen, but to Lutherans'"; but this story, though it "found ready acceptance among the French of that period . . . is unsupported by the testimony of a single witness, and bears all the earmarks of an apocryphal origin." Lowery, *op. cit.*, p. 178, and references there. The *Reprinse* is published in *Voyages, relations, et mémoires originaux pour servir*

or swam out to the ships that remained in the harbor, and
Menéndez rechristened the place San Mateo. Eight days
later, after he had returned to St. Augustine, he got word
from some Indians that about 140 of Ribaut's men, the
remnants of the crews of two of his ships which had been
wrecked in the storm, were stranded on a marshy island
to the south of him. Taking some sixty men with him, he
advanced to a point on the mainland where he could be
seen; whereupon one of the Frenchmen swam over and
asked for a safe conduct to Fort Caroline. Menéndez in
his reply stated plainly that he was there as Philip's *adelantado*, commissioned to purge his Majesty's dominions of all
heretics. He bluntly refused to give the Frenchmen the
safe conduct they asked for, and furnished convincing
proof that Fort Caroline was already in his hands. When
they came back with the request for a ship and sailors to
take them back to France, he refused again, demanding
that they all of them give up their arms and place themselves at his mercy, "in order that he might do with them
as the Lord commanded him"; finally, he indignantly
rejected a ransom of 5000 ducats that was proffered if he
would spare their lives.[1] The Frenchmen, then, had no valid
reason for expecting anything but death at his hands; but
their situation was so desperate that they had no alternative
save to place themselves at his mercy. All their arms were
sent across to the mainland in a boat; then they themselves
were ferried over in groups of ten; once on the shore, their
hands were tied behind their backs, on the plea that otherwise they might overpower their less numerous captors.

à *l'histoire de la découverte de l'Amérique*,
ed. Henri Ternaux-Compans (Paris,
1837–41, 20 vols.), xx, pp. 301–366,
and the account of the inscription may
be found on pp. 357 f. Cf. also Charles
Samaran, "Dominique de Gourgues,"
in *Revue Historique*, cviii (1911), pp.
283–286.

[1] Francisco López de Mendoza, "Relacion," in Ruidíaz y Caravia, *La
Florida*, ii, pp. 461–465; Lowery, *op.
cit.*, pp. 421–425.

Ten of them, who were found to be Catholics, were sent by boat to St. Augustine; the rest, who confessed themselves Protestants, were given food and drink and were then started out on their march north to the Spanish camp four leagues away. After proceeding a few hundred yards they came to a line in the sand which Menéndez had drawn with his spear; at that point they were set upon by the Spaniards and butchered to a man.[1] Two weeks later, on October 12, the selfsame tragedy was reënacted, in the selfsame manner, and on the selfsame spot, the victims this time being Jean Ribaut himself and some seventy of his men, who found themselves in exactly the same predicament as their predecessors, and elected rather to throw themselves on the mercy of Menéndez than to face the certainty of death by starvation.[2] In early November, when the Spanish commander learned that the remnant of his enemies had gathered near Cape Canaveral, where they had built a fort and were constructing a ship to return to France, he advanced against them, and this time promised them their lives if they would surrender. All but five accepted the proffered terms, and Menéndez loyally kept his word.[3]

Before attempting to pass judgment on these events, it will be interesting to examine the story of the reception of the news in Europe. The Spanish king had learned about the preparations for Ribaut's second expedition in late March or early April, only a short time, if at all, before he had signed the *asiento* with Menéndez,[4] and Coligny, and also, in all probability, the queen-mother, knew all about the proposed voyage of Menéndez before Ribaut set sail. But neither Philip nor Catharine gave the other

---

[1] Lowery, *op. cit.*, pp. 193 f., and references there.
[2] *Ibid.*, pp. 194–204, and references there.
[3] *Ibid.*, pp. 214–218.
[4] *Ibid.*, p. 106.

any official notification of what had happened for many weeks to come. It was natural that the queen-mother should not do so. Since Ribaut had departed without her official sanction, she would do nothing to make it difficult for her to disavow him. Philip's motives for delay were somewhat different. The conference at Bayonne[1] was to take place in early June, and nothing must be suffered to mar the harmony of that reunion. Moreover, by the time that the conference had actually opened, Ribaut had already left, and Philip saw that the question would have to be solved rather by fighting in the New World than by diplomacy in the Old. He commanded Álava, Chantonnay's successor, not to say a word to Catharine about Menéndez until the latter had been gone so long that it would be impossible to recall or overtake him; as a matter of fact the Spanish ambassador did not notify the French court until November 23, probably at least a month after Philip had learned of the arrival of Menéndez in Florida, and six full weeks after Ribaut and his companions had been massacred.[2] On that occasion Álava bluntly demanded that the French withdraw; but Catharine skilfully avoided the issue by protesting that she had no intention of trespassing on Spanish soil, and was only seeking to colonize the Terre des Bretons. With the turn of the year, however, the news of the massacres and of the Spanish triumph had reached both Paris and Madrid, and there was no longer any point in further evasion or pretence; Philip's sole object now was to utilize the matter to discredit the cause of the French Huguenots. In mid-February at Madrid the whole story was retailed with brutal frankness to the French ambassador by the Duke of Alva, who justified the conduct of Menéndez at every point, and laid the whole blame for the tragedy on

[1] See below, pp. 261–265.   [2] Lowery, pp. 106–118.

Coligny; [1] on March 16, at Moulins, Álava staged a similar performance for the benefit of Catharine de' Medici.[2] The queen-mother had learned all the facts long before the Spanish ambassador related them to her, and was therefore the better prepared to hold her own in the interview; but though she fought "like an enraged lioness" in debate, and protested that "neither Turks nor Moors would have been guilty of so great a cruelty as the Spaniards had practised on the subjects of her son," she knew that for the present she was powerless to get redress. She could not afford to quarrel with Philip, and she realized it. Revenge, as the sequel was to prove, was to be obtained by a private adventurer.

More significant still was the reception of the news in Spain. Menéndez wrote a full account of his doings to the king, omitting nothing and palliating nothing, and Philip conveyed to him his full approval of the massacre; "as for the judgment you have executed upon the Lutheran corsairs," so his letter runs, "we believe that you have acted with entire justification and prudence, and we hold that we have been well served." [3] The whole Spanish court was delighted at the news, "more gladdened," said Fourquevaux, "than if it had been a victory over the Turk." [4] Clearly in the eyes of his compatriots Menéndez had every reason to be proud, and none whatever to be ashamed, of what he had done; and if the line of reasoning on which his actions were based fails to appeal to us today, we must remember that it would scarcely have been possible for him to have followed any other. His master's claim to the whole of the Western Hemisphere except Brazil, by

---

[1] Fourquevaux, *Dépêches*, i, pp. 59–62; Lowery, pp. 304–307.
[2] *Ibid.*, pp. 307–310.
[3] Philip to Menéndez, May 12, 1566,
in Ruidíaz y Caravia, *La Florida*, ii, p. 363.
[4] Fourquevaux, *Dépêches*, i, p. 56.

the bull of Alexander VI and the Tordesillas Line, as well as by right of priority in discovery and colonization, must have been in his eyes unimpeachable. The French were but common trespassers and pirates; that they were not officially supported by their government proclaimed as much, and the fact that most of them were Protestants made the matter even worse. He had treated them, indeed, with relentless severity; but the fact that his prisoners were more numerous than their captors gave his conduct the sanction of prudence, if not of humanity, and there is not the slightest reasonable evidence that he ever broke his word. The massacres he ordered have stained his reputation with a blot that it will never be possible to efface; but if he had been given a happier task, and a more favorable opportunity in which to display his talents, he might well have been numbered among the foremost of the great *conquistadores* who planted the banners of Spain in the New World.

The rest of the story of the Spanish settlements in Florida during the period of Philip II is not lacking in dramatic interest; but its practical importance for our purposes is comparatively slight, and we cannot do more than summarize it briefly here. After disposing of the French, Menéndez planned to devote his energies to exploring the interior, and also the Atlantic coast to the northward as far as Chesapeake Bay, where he believed he would find the longed-for strait leading to the Pacific; he also made persistent efforts to convert the Indians.[1] Ill fortune, however, attended his efforts. The natives were generally treacherous and hostile; the garrisons at St. Augustine and San Mateo were discontented and mutinous, and in May, 1567, Menéndez went back to Spain, where he success-

---

[1] Lowery, *op. cit.*, pp. 259–262.

fully vindicated himself against the reports of his detractors, received high honors and rewards at the hands of his king, but failed to get the prompt and effective assistance for his colony which he desired most of all.[1] And in the interim between his departure from Florida and his return thither in 1568-69,[2] the French took their revenge for the massacres of 1565. Rumors had reached France, through Fourque-vaux, of the wretched state of the Florida colony. Such a favorable opportunity to attack it might never come again, and since the Valois government was in no condition to give official sanction to such an enterprise, it was under-taken, instead, on his own initiative, by a restless patriot called Dominique de Gourgues, who, though in all prob-ability a Catholic, was determined to right the wrongs of his fellow-countrymen, and whose enthusiasm for fighting Spaniards had been fired by the maltreatment to which he had been subjected when a prisoner aboard their galleys.[3] On August 2, 1567, he set sail from Bordeaux with three ships and 180 men. He concealed the real object of his expedition even from his own followers, under the pretence that it was intended for a slave raid in North Africa; but on reaching the West Indies, he revealed to them its true purpose,[4] and in April, 1568, he accomplished it. He was greatly aided by the Florida Indians, who detested the Spaniards. A surprise attack, delivered while the defenders were "still picking their teeth"[5] after their midday meal, was completely successful. San Mateo and its two subsidiary forts were captured, most of the garrison being killed in the assaults; all of the rest, save a few who escaped, were hanged on the adjacent trees, under an inscription which read: "I do this not as to Spaniards, nor as to Marranos,

---

[1] Lowery, *op. cit.*, pp. 291 f.
[2] *Ibid.*, p. 345.
[3] *Ibid.*, p. 324.
[4] *Ibid.*, pp. 325 f.
[5] *Ibid.*, p. 329.

but as to traitors, robbers, and murderers." With this signal act of vengeance de Gourgues elected to rest content. St. Augustine, now keenly on the watch, he decided to leave alone, and on Monday, May 3, he set sail for France.[1] When he learned of the event, Philip was prompt to demand satisfaction from Catharine, which he naturally failed to get; but as the French showed no intention of following up their vengeance with renewed attempts to colonize, the matter was allowed to drop.

The history of the Florida colony during the rest of Philip's reign is a dreary chronicle of discouragement and destitution. Menéndez, the only person who had its interest really at heart, visited it for the last time in 1571,[2] but death claimed him in 1574 before he could accomplish anything in its behalf.[3] Six years later St. Augustine was raided by Sir Francis Drake. The natives, despite persistent attempts to civilize and convert them, continued to be both treacherous and hostile; no gold was found, and provisions were perpetually running short. At the time of Philip's death, it is probable that the total number of Spaniards in the colony did not exceed 300; and there is every reason to believe that they would have deserted their post, had it not been for the home government's unwillingness to leave it unoccupied, and for the zeal of the missionaries for the conversion of the Indians.

The contrast between the conditions which obtained in Southern Chile during the reign of Philip II and those that we have outlined on the coasts of Florida furnishes a significant illustration of the variety of the different problems

---

[1] Cf. Lowery, op. cit., pp. 329–336; Charles Samaran, "Dominique de Gourgues," in Revue Historique, cviii (1911), pp. 276–293.

[2] Lowery, op. cit., pp. 367–386.

[3] Ibid., p. 383; cf. also Colonial Records of Spanish Florida, i, pp. 2–115.

with which the Spaniards were confronted in their efforts
to establish their title to the New World. In Chile the
corsarios Luteranos, who had been their chief rivals in Florida,
counted for almost nothing. Sir Francis Drake, it is true,
passed through the Strait of Magellan in August, 1578,
ravaged the Chilean shores, got a rich booty at Valparaiso,
was repulsed at La Serena, and continued on up the coast.
His fellow countryman, Thomas Cavendish, followed after
him in 1587, neglected to relieve the starving remnants of
a small Spanish colony which had been planted a few years
previously in the Strait, landed at Quinteros, was defeated
in a skirmish with the inhabitants there, and sailed north
to Peru. Finally, seven years later, Sir Richard Hawkins,
who had inherited all his father's enthusiasm for plundering
the Spaniards, put Philip's subjects up in arms all the way
from Valparaiso northward to Atacames in Ecuador, where
he was finally assailed by an overwhelming force and captured.[1] But these were merely incidents, pirate raids of
the sort from which all of Philip's colonies suffered with
increasing frequency in the latter years of the reign, and
they only occasionally disturbed the Chilean Spaniards in
their efforts to accomplish what may be regarded as their
principal task. That task was the conquest and subjection
of the Araucanian Indians.

We have seen that the war against the Araucanians had

---

[1] Diego Barros Arana, *Historia Jeneral de Chile*, ii, pp. 465–471; iii, pp. 83–
95, 195–206; *The Hawkins' Voyages*, ed.
C. R. Markham (London, 1878), pp.
xxiv–xxvii, 83–349. Cf. here also the
contemporary poem called the *Discurso
de el Capitán Francisco Draque*, written
by Joan de Castellanos at Tunja in
1587, and first published by Ángel
González Palencia at Madrid in 1921.
It is principally devoted to the exploits
of the hero in the regions of the Gulf
of Mexico, where his raids were most
frequent, but pages 25–36 deal with his
doings on the Chilean and Peruvian
coasts. Reference should also be made
at this point to the volume edited in
1914 for the Hakluyt Society by Zelia
Nuttall, and entitled *New Light on
Drake*. It consists of a well selected
series of contemporary letters, deposi-
tions, and reports, mostly of Spanish
or Spanish-American origin, concerning
the activities of the Englishman on his
voyage of circumnavigation, 1577–80.

begun in the Emperor's day, and that the Spaniards had already had sufficient experience of it to learn that their foes were vastly more warlike than most of the American Indians, and that they had no desire to be converted or civilized, but were bent on maintaining their independence. The home government, however, had failed to learn that continuity of administration and personnel was essential to the successful prosecution of such an arduous struggle. Philip's perpetual jealousy of his subordinates, his haunting dread that they might somehow get out of hand and attempt to embark on enterprises of their own, manifested itself most clearly of all in the case of his remoter possessions; he dared not leave them undisturbed for any length of time, and his constant replacings of the governors of Chile caused disastrous interruptions of the campaign against the Araucanians. We have already seen that in 1557 Villagran and Aguirre, the two rival veterans of the early days of the conquest, had been displaced, at the order of Andrés Hurtado de Mendoza, viceroy of Peru, by Mendoza's son, García Hurtado, and that the young man had won splendid victories over the Araucanians in the course of the next two years.[1] But Philip could not bear to see so much power concentrated in the hands of a single family; so in 1560 he recalled both the viceroy and his son, and quite characteristically permitted the latter to be superseded by his ancient rival, Villagran.[2] The veteran, however, was much less successful against the Indians than the man he replaced; he suffered a series of disastrous defeats, and when he died in office, in June, 1563, his cousin and successor, Pedro de Villagran, was equally luckless. The latter's place was taken by Rodrigo de Quiroga, an adherent of the Mendozas, who

---

[1] *Ante*, Vol. III, p. 605.   [2] Barros Arana, ii, pp. 213-215, 258 f.

signalized his advent to power by a brilliant victory over the Araucanians.   Yet Philip, despite the good reports of Quiroga which he received, continued to be distrustful.   His next step was to confide the government of Chile to an audiencia of four *oidores*, which arrived and took office in 1567 ; but it was even more unfortunate than the Villagrans in its conduct of the war, and it was consequently suppressed in January, 1575, when Quiroga came back to power at the mandate of the crown, and did his best to retrieve the disasters of the preceding years.[1]   So it went on to the end of the chapter; the royal dread of the too successful *conquistador* being the only permanent element in the situation. No real continuity in office was allowed, and precious experience was thus suffered to go to waste.   News of a victory over the Indians was gratefully received at home, but it also constituted a strong reason for suspecting the victor; local jealousies were kept alive, nay even fostered, in order to prevent any faction from becoming dangerously predominant.   Small wonder, under all these circumstances, if the Araucanian war continued throughout the reign, without any decisive result.

It is not worth while to follow the ups and downs of the struggle.[2]   At the time of Philip's accession, the theatre of war was limited to a small tract between the Biobio and the Tirna, and that portion of it was usually known as the

[1] Barros Arana, ii, pp. 299–427, *passim.* The relationship of the governor of Chile to the viceroy at Lima varied rapidly in the ensuing years. In 1589 (*Recopilación de Leyes de las Indias*, lib. v, tit. i, ley iii) Philip orders the "gobernador" to be "subordinado al Virey," and recommends that they keep constantly in touch with each other; in 1597 (*ibid.*, lib. iii, tit. iii, ley xxx) he forbids the viceroys and audiencia at Lima to interfere in the government of Chile save in "casos graves y de mucha importancia." It was not till February 17, 1609 (*ibid.*, lib. ii, tit. xv, ley xii), that a regular audiencia was permanently established in Chile.

[2] Good accounts of it are given in R. G. Watson, *Spanish and Portuguese South America*, i, pp. 234–248, and in Barros Arana, iii, pp. 141–152, 189–212, 222–261.

guerra vieja because it dated from the Emperor's time; under Quiroga, the natives near Valdivia, Villarrica, and Osorno rose in arms, and the campaigns against them came to be called the *guerra nueva*. But the struggle was no nearer termination at the end of the reign than at the beginning. Indeed, the decade covering the last five years of Philip's life and the first five of that of his successor saw the Araucanians seize the offensive under one of their greatest chieftains, Paillamachu, and to such good effect that in 1603 the Spaniards had been practically ousted from all of the country south of the Biobio. The Spaniards had been obliged greatly to increase their forces during Philip's reign. Whereas Valdivia had made war with companies of a hundred men, his successors, forty years later, were commanding five times that number. But they could never get it into their heads that the Araucanians, unlike the majority of the South American natives, were not to be frightened into submission by a single defeat, and that after it had been inflicted on them, a series of desultory raids would be quite insufficient to keep them down; they consequently were often overwhelmed by the unexpected offensives of their foes. And if the Araucanians were slightly less numerous at the end of the reign than at the beginning, they had enormously increased the efficiency of their fighting machine. They learned from the Spaniards the value of defensive armor, of intrenchments, and of feigned retreats; they possessed horses,[1] which they used to the best possible effect; moreover, they showed signs of

[1] R. D. Carbia, *Manual de Historia de la Civilización Argentina*, i, p. 393, note. The common theory as to these horses, which were called *cimarrones*, is that they were the progeny of those brought over by Pedro de Mendoza in 1536 (cf. *ante*, Vol. III, p. 608) and abandoned by him when his settlement at Buenos Aires was given up. The horse had indubitably existed in America in the earliest times; but it had been extinct many thousand years before the Spaniards arrived.

appreciating the desirability of diminishing the horrors of warfare. Though they had not abandoned cannibalism at the end of the sixteenth century, they had begun to see that it was better to exchange their prisoners than to execute them. Altogether it is small wonder that in presence of foes so relentless, who were rapidly perfecting themselves in the methods of European warfare, the Spaniards returned battered and disheartened from the terrible privations and sufferings of the successive campaigns.

The halting progress of the Araucanian war had its inevitable reaction on the life of the Chilean colony. Besides being in large measure responsible for the frequent changes of administration, it made the whole settlement a debit rather than a credit item in the royal accounts. Instead of receiving gold and silver from it, Philip had to be constantly sending money thither to pay his troops. That his Spanish soldiers could not terminate the struggle victoriously and at once was something that passed his comprehension, and deeply galled his pride; it also served to arouse fresh suspicions, and confirmed his conviction that his representatives in Chile were somehow playing him false. In the colony itself the results were scarcely less lamentable. At the outset there had been much enthusiasm for the war, which was expected to end in a triumphal procession down to the Strait. Men served in it without pay, in the hope of being rewarded with *encomiendas*; in 1546 there had even been fears lest Santiago be depopulated.[1] Fifty years later all this was changed. It was almost impossible to get soldiers to fight. Desertion was frequent; nothing but high pay in cash would induce men to enlist, for there was little or no chance of obtaining booty in the war, and nobody cared any longer to possess landed

[1] Barros Arana, i, pp. 271–289.

estates which were certain to be raided by the Indians.
Mining activities, also, came almost to a standstill; agriculture and pasturage, though the climate was highly favorable
to them, were neglected; and the Spanish population, at
the end of the reign, did not reach 3000 souls.[1]

Altogether, the condition of the colony gave cause for
much anxiety and dissatisfaction, both in Spain and in
America, at the time of Philip's death. Perhaps the most
notable thing that was achieved during his reign on what
is now Chilean territory was the exploration of the Strait
of Magellan; and that was undertaken, not through the
efforts of the local Spanish authorities, but at the behest of
the viceroy of New Castile. The voyage of Drake in 1578
furnished the impetus for it, and the task was intrusted
to Pedro Sarmiento de Gamboa,[2] a Galician sailor of considerable repute. He returned to Spain, visited Philip
during the progress of the Portuguese campaign, and was
commanded by him to erect fortifications in the narrows;
but vile weather and the rivalries of his captains prevented
him from accomplishing all that had been hoped, and the
two small settlements which he established in the strait
perished wretchedly a few years later from starvation.[3]

While the Chileans were in the throes of the Araucanian
war, their more fortunate neighbors to the north of them
were able to make at least two fresh contributions to the
westward march of the Spanish Empire in the Pacific.
The first was the expedition which left Callao on November
19, 1567, under command of Álvaro de Mendaña, discovered
the Solomon Islands in the following February, and, after
several encounters with the cannibal natives, got back to
New Spain in March, 1569. Mendaña's failure to bring

[1] Barros Arana, iii, pp. 167–177.
[2] Cf. p. 219, note, below.
[3] Barros Arana, iii, pp. 59–82;
Carbia, *Manual*, i, pp. 451–464.

home gold made it difficult for him to get the government interested in the project of colonizing the archipelago, on which he had set his heart; but his indomitable resolution triumphed over every obstacle, and in April, 1595, more than a quarter of a century after his return from his first expedition, he set sail again, with four ships and 368 emigrants. This time, however, he was diverted from his original course by discovering the Marquesas group on the way, with the final result that he established his colony not on the Solomon Islands but in the New Hebrides. But the settlement was not destined to endure. Mendaña died within two months of his arrival; his followers were decimated by dissension and disease, and the survivors were only too thankful to find a refuge at Manila in 1596.[1]

In November, 1574, the Spanish pilot, Juan Fernández, in search of a means of shortening the voyage from Callao to Valparaiso by avoiding the adverse winds and currents that hugged the coast,[2] discovered the three small islands, some 350 miles to the westward, which ever since that day have borne his name.[3] There seems no good reason to give credence to the legend that on a subsequent voyage he reached out much farther into the west and possibly struck the shores of Australia or New Zealand, or even to believe the story that he established himself in the islands that he had found; for we know that he continued to direct

[1] For full accounts of these expeditions cf. *The Discovery of the Solomon Islands by Alvaro de Mendaña in 1568*, edited for the Hakluyt Society by Lord Amherst of Hackney and Basil Thomson (London, 1901, 2 vols.); Antonio de Morga, *The Philippine Islands*, tr. H. E. J. Stanley, pp. 65–74; and Georg Friederici, *Alvaro de Mendaña: Die Entdeckung der Inseln des Salomo* (Stuttgart, 1925).

[2] The voyage from Valparaiso to Callao took generally a month, sometimes less; the return trip was considered fast if it was accomplished in three.

[3] J. T. Medina, *El Piloto Juan Fernández* (Santiago de Chile, 1918), is the latest authority on this episode. He takes issue, in the matter of the date of it, with Barros Arana (iii, pp. 51–58), who places the discovery in 1583 or 1584.

navigation between Chile and Peru until at least as late
as 1593, and that there was no trace of any European
occupation of the archipelago of Juan Fernández when it
became, between 1704 and 1709, the home of Alexander
Selkirk, the prototype of Robinson Crusoe.

It will be remembered that with the dispersal in 1537–39
of the little settlement which Pedro de Mendoza had established at the mouth of the Rio de la Plata, the town of
Asuncion, far up the river in Paraguay, had become the
chief nucleus of Spanish activity in the southeastern portion
of South America.[1] Buenos Aires, however, was to be
refounded, this time permanently, during the reign of
Philip II, and the vast economic possibilities of the country
of which it is now the capital began for the first time to
be dimly foreseen.

The death, on October 3, 1556,[2] of the patriarch Martínez
de Irala, was a harbinger of stormy days for the little colony
at Asuncion. He had provided in his will that he should
be succeeded by his son-in-law, Gonzalo de Mendoza, who
was accordingly proclaimed *adelantado* without any opposition; but Mendoza died in the early summer of 1558, before
he had had a fair chance to get his administration started
or to nominate his successor, with the result that the inhabitants of Asuncion, taking advantage of a privilege which
had been granted by the crown to the settlers of the Rio
de la Plata in 1537, elected as their governor another son-
in-law of Irala named Francisco Ortiz de Vergara.[3] The
latter was a kindly soul, but totally deficient in talent for
ruling men. The first years of his administration were

---

[1] *Ante,* Vol. III, p. 608.
[2] R. Levene, *Lecciones de Historia Argentina,* 4ª ed., i, p. 91; Paul Groussac, *Mendoza y Garay,* p. 277.
[3] Levene, *Lecciones,* i, pp. 94–96; Groussac, pp. 278–284; Carbia, *Manual,* i, pp. 327, 358.

marked by Indian risings which he was quite unable to
suppress, and by discontent and insubordination on the
part of his own followers, who resolved to prevent his
obtaining the confirmation from the king or his viceroy
which would be necessary to give him permanent possession
of the office of governor. But it was chiefly as a result of the
expeditions that were sent out from Asuncion during the
period of his governorship, for purposes of exploration and
settlement, that a crisis in his fortunes and in those of
his colony was finally brought to pass.

We recall that the first hope of the early discoverers and
explorers of La Plata had been that it would prove the
entrance to a strait leading through to the Pacific ; and that
when that illusion had been dissipated, they continued to
lay plans for the utilization of the great river as a means of
shortening the route to Peru. During the period of Irala,
this idea rather fell into the background. He did little or
nothing to establish connections with the regions to the
westward, and Mendoza and Ortiz de Vergara were simi-
larly neglectful.[1] Many of their followers, however, had
larger vision. They longed to gain access to the mineral
wealth of the Andes. They wished to follow up the Pil-
comayo and ultimately get over the mountains to Cuzco.
The most dominant and ambitious figure among them was
a certain Nufrio de Chaves, a *conquistador* after the pattern
of Cortés and Pizarro, who, in 1561, signalized himself
by pushing through and founding the town of Santa Cruz
de la Sierra some sixty leagues to the west of the modern
Bolivian city which bears that name today. The forces
with whose aid he accomplished this object had been intended
by the governor at Asuncion for another purpose, so that his
action was tantamount to a declaration of revolt against

[1] Carbia, *Manual*, i, pp. 350–359.

Ortiz de Vergara. There were, moreover, rival claimants from Peru to the region where he proposed to establish himself; in fact he had been obliged, in 1560, to make a trip to Lima in order to get confirmation of his title from the viceroy. By 1564, however, he felt strong enough to return to Asuncion to pick up his family and belongings and face the wrath of the governor; for he was fully aware of the unpopularity of Ortiz de Vergara, and was convinced that if he offered the inhabitants a chance to return with him to the Andes, the majority would gladly accept it. And thus indeed it proved; in October, 1564, occurred the so-called 'exodus to Peru.' Almost all the *vecinos* of Asuncion cast in their lot with Chaves. Ortiz de Vergara himself came along, probably because he felt that it was the only way to preserve such measure of authority as was left to him; he had hopes, moreover, of getting confirmation in his office from the viceroy. In the course of their progress into the northwest, the inevitable occurred. Ortiz de Vergara was gradually elbowed aside and Chaves assumed his place; finally, when the expedition reached Santa Cruz de la Sierra, Vergara was informed that he could be permitted to go no farther. Chaves and the new ideas which he represented were fully in control.[1]

In the meantime certain constitutional changes had also been carried through, which served to focus attention on the territories to the east of the Andes, and lessen the measure of their previous isolation. On the ground that the lands under the jurisdiction of the audiencia of Lima were too extensive to permit of adequate administration of

[1] P. F. X. de Charlevoix, *Histoire du Paraguay* (Paris, 1757, 6 vols.), i, liv. iii; Carbia, *Manual*, i, pp. 355–361; Groussac, *Mendoza y Garay*, pp. 277–314; A. Audibert, *Los Límites de la Antigua Provincia del Paraguay*, pp. 75–90. Further bibliographical information in regard to the topics dealt with in this paragraph may be found in Carbia, i, pp. 400 f.

justice, the Council of the Indies, on April 20, 1551, had recommended to the crown the establishment of a new audiencia at the "villa de la plata que es en los charcas cerca de las minas de Potossi" — the city which today is called Sucre and is the capital of the Bolivian republic.[1] The suggestion had to be several times repeated before any attention was paid to it;[2] but finally, on September 4, 1559, at Valladolid, directly after his return to Spain, Philip gave orders that the new tribunal be set up, and on September 7, 1561, it was formally installed.[3] It at once became popularly known as the audiencia of Charcas, and it was composed at the outset of a *regente* and four *oidores*, who were to be presided over, in theory, by the viceroy of New Castile, and were restricted, in his absence, to functions exclusively judicial;[4] but when it was found, after two years' experience, that the viceroy was never able to attend, Philip provided, on August 16, 1563, for the creation of the office of a president, to be held by a resident member of the audiencia.[5] The territories that fell within its jurisdiction extended originally only for a distance of 100 leagues around the city of La Plata in which the audiencia sat;[6] but they were progressively enlarged in the immediately succeeding years, until they finally stretched from the Atlantic to the Pacific, and comprised what is today Bolivia and Paraguay,

---

[1] R. Levillier, *Audiencia de Charcas*, pp. 503 f.

[2] R. Levillier, *Audiencia de Lima*, pp. 63–67, 157 f.; idem, *Audiencia de Charcas*, pp. 505–510.

[3] *Recopilación de Leyes de las Indias*, lib. ii, tit. xv, ley ix; *Audiencia de Charcas*, pp. xviii, 23–35.

[4] *Audiencia de Charcas*, pp. 511 ff. Writing to Philip, on February 6, 1563, of its action in regard to the pacification of the Indians, the *oidores* tell how "vino una carta del visorrey e comysarios para que no entendiesemos en

otra cosa mas de en lo tocante a justicia entre partes." *Ibid.*, p. 93.

[5] *Audiencia de Charcas*, pp. 572 f. The new president was Pedro Ramírez de Quiñones, one of the four original *oidores*, who had had the title of regent before. It would appear, however, that one of these original *oidores* never actually took office (p. xxv), so that down to 1572 the audiencia was composed of Ramírez de Quiñones and three others; in that year, however, another *oidor* was sent out.

[6] *Audiencia de Charcas*, p. 17.

a good slice of the northern part of Argentina, a portion of Uruguay, and the Peruvian department of Puno.[1] The fact that the region committed to its charge had been carved out of territory hitherto under the jurisdiction of the audiencia of Lima must not be taken as an evidence that the viceroys had lost interest in the lands east of the Andes. Quite the contrary, it was the sole means by which they could hope to exercise any real control there, and prevent the inhabitants of the lower reaches of La Plata from becoming wholly autonomous; it was inspired by the principle of *divide et impera*. While apparently separating the destinies of the lands on the east from those on the west of the Cordilleras, it was really intended to hold them together; it was aimed, from a totally different angle, at the attainment of an end very similar to that which had inspired Nufrio de Chaves.[2] And certainly the new audiencia

[1] *Recopilación de Leyes de las Indias*, lib. ii, tit. xv, ley ix; J. M. Urquidi, *Nuevo Compendio de la Historia de Bolivia*, 3ᵃ ed. (La Paz, 1921), pp. 45 f.; *Audiencia de Charcas*, pp. 168 ff., 588–590, 676, 688 f. Audibert, *Los Límites de Paraguay*, pp. 83 f., maintains that the audiencia of Charcas had no jurisdiction over Paraguay till 1566.

[2] The same principle also inspired the foundation (November 29, 1563, cf. *Recopilación de Leyes de las Indias*, lib. ii, tit. xv, ley x) of the audiencia of Quito; it was composed of a president and four *oidores*, and comprised within the limits of its jurisdiction somewhat more than the territory of the present republic of Ecuador, reaching southward to Payta in Peru, and northward to Buenaventura in Colombia. Since the viceroys at Lima were unable to exercise any effective authority in the region in question, it was deemed wiser to establish a local jurisdiction. Cf. also E. Ruíz Guiñazú, *La Magistratura Indiana*, pp. 126–132.

The establishment of the audiencias of Charcas and Quito naturally brings up the whole question of the measure of independence enjoyed by such subordinate tribunals, and the nature of their relationship to the viceroys and the viceregal audiencias at Mexico and Lima. The matter is too complicated to be dealt with thoroughly in a footnote; but it may perhaps be summarized as follows. (1) In matters political and administrative the viceroy was the supreme authority in his viceroyalty, and all the subordinate audiencias and governors were in theory bound to obey him; but as a matter of fact the viceroy of New Castile was able to exercise this authority far more completely over the audiencias of Charcas and Quito than over the remoter ones, and the viceroy of New Spain, correspondingly, over that of Guadalajara, than over those of Santo Domingo and Guatemala; geographical proximity, in other words, was the real determining factor. (2) In matters of justice, the viceroy was forbidden to interfere with any of the audiencias in his viceroyalty; in this respect, moreover, they were all theoretically

rendered Chaves an important service by ridding him of his enemy Vergara, who was summoned to appear before it in the year 1566. After a long trial he was declared guiltless of the charges which had been brought against him, and was even temporarily restored to the headship of the settlement at Asuncion, pending the arrival of a new governor who had meantime been appointed, subject to the royal approval, by the viceroy. He professed himself, however, to be dissatisfied with this verdict, and went back to Spain to plead his cause before the Council of the Indies — needless to add, without success. From that time onward he subsides into insignificance; and when he came back to Asuncion in 1573 it was in a subordinate office in the government of his successor. Five years earlier his successful rival Chaves had met his death, the victim of a blow from an Indian *porra*, or war club, delivered from behind, by a member of a hostile tribe. He was a remarkable man, with qualities better suited to the age of the Emperor than to that of his son. Though cut off in the midst of his labors with his own objects only partially attained, his restless activity had at least been instrumental in reopening the whole problem of Peru and the La Plata basin.[1]

The man whom the viceroy had meantime selected to take over the government of Paraguay was a certain Ortiz de Zárate, who had come out with Blasco Núñez Vela in 1544, and remained there ever since. He had not been in any way involved in the various quarrels by which the settle-

equal, though the audiencias of Lima and Mexico sometimes heard appeals from the subordinate ones. Further information may be found in the *Recopilación de Leyes de las Indias*, lib. ii, tit. xv; in Solórzano Pereira's *Política Indiana*, lib. v, cap. iii, paragraphs 43 and 71; and R. Levillier, *Audiencia de Charcas, passim.*

[1] Carbia, *Manual*, i, pp. 360 f., 363; Groussac, *Mendoza y Garay*, pp. 277–314. Further information in regard to these events, which have been only very briefly summarized here, may be found in Audibert, *Límites del Paraguay*, pp. 75–90, and in Charlevoix, *Historia del Paraguay*, i, lib. iii, *passim*.

ment at Asuncion had been rent, and could consequently enter upon his new duties without favor or prejudice.[1] He promised, moreover, to spend 20,000 ducats of his own in fitting out the expedition which he was to lead into his new domain, and to bring with him 400 or 500 soldiers, 4000 cows, and as many sheep and goats; apparently, both he and the viceroy had at least some faint conception of the pastoral possibilities of the basin of La Plata. As the royal confirmation was necessary for his new office, he departed for Spain via Panama to obtain it. It therefore became necessary to send some one direct from Peru to Asuncion to represent him there during his absence. The choice for this difficult office fell on one Felipe de Cáceres, who had been active in Paraguayan affairs ever since the days of Cabeza de Vaca; in the end of 1568 he arrived at Asuncion. The four years of his rule there were chiefly remarkable for a violent struggle for supremacy between himself and the bishop of the diocese of La Plata,[2] who finally got him shipped off to Spain to answer before the Inquisition to a charge of atheism and blasphemy.[3] But Cáceres also succeeded during the period of his governorship in leading two reconnaissances down the Parana to the estuary of La Plata; he was firmly convinced that a new settlement should be made on the lower reaches of the river. As Cáceres himself was sent off to Spain directly after his return from the second of these expeditions, he was unable to carry his project into effect, but the work that he had initiated was to be continued by one of his subordinates. This was a certain Juan de Garay, a nephew of Ortiz de Zárate, then in his early forties, who had come out to Peru with his uncle in 1544, and had profited by "a long and active acclimatization" in South America. He

---

[1] Carbia, *Manual*, i, pp. 361 f.
[2] This had been established in July, 1547; cf. Carbia, *Manual*, i, p. 354.
[3] Of which, however, he was finally acquitted. *Ibid.*, i, p. 366.

had gone down to Asuncion in 1568 as a sort of lieutenant to
Cáceres, and accompanied him on both his trips to the lower
regions of the Parana.[1] He surpassed his chief in his enthusiasm for starting a settlement in these regions ; and his
ardor was still further quickened by the fear that if he did
not act at once he ran grave risk of being forestalled by
the Spaniards of Tucuman, who had founded the town of
Cordoba on July 6, 1563, and were now straining every nerve
to gain an outlet to the Atlantic.[2] The result was that
he immediately sought and obtained permission from the
authorities at Asuncion to equip at his own expense a new
expedition down the river, with the aid of which he founded
the town of Santa Fé, near the junction of the Parana and
the Rio Salado, on November 15, 1573.[3] It was there that
in the following February he received word, through an
Indian scout whom he had despatched for the purpose, of
the arrival of his uncle, Ortiz de Zárate, at the estuary of La
Plata.

Zárate had done well for himself during his sojourn in
Spain. By a *capitulación* agreed upon between himself and
the king on July 10, 1569, the terms of his tentative appointment by the viceroy had not only been confirmed but enlarged.[4] He was to be permitted to import African slaves into
his new domain, and it is highly significant that it was stipulated that of the 500 Spaniards whom he brought with him,
at least 100 should be workmen, artisans, and agricultural
laborers. Moreover, in addition to the post of governor
and captain-general, with an annual salary of 4000 ducats,
he was given the title of *adelantado* for himself and for his

---

[1] Groussac, *Mendoza y Garay*, pp. 211 f., 308.

[2] Carbia, *Manual*, i, p. 369.

[3] The actual site (cf. Carbia, i, p. 368) was apparently about twelve leagues to the northeast of the present city.

[4] Carbia, i, pp. 370–373 ; Groussac, p. 368, note.

descendants; he was vested, in other words, with a measure of hereditary authority in the territory which he proposed to colonize. It took him over three years to collect his followers and his armament. Not until September, 1572, was he able to set sail, and the delays and mishaps of the voyage were so numerous that he did not reach the mouth of La Plata till November 26, 1573. There, on the little island of San Gabriel, off the Uruguayan coast, and directly across from the modern city of Buenos Aires, he found a cross with a gourd hanging on it; in the gourd were letters telling of what had already been accomplished by .Cáceres and by Garay. Communication was speedily established with the latter, and there was fierce fighting with the natives on the north bank of the river. Zárate, who had promised the king to establish a settlement at its mouth, attempted to fulfil his obligation by founding a small outpost called San Salvador on the Uruguayan coast, which was destined to endure but a short three years. Finally he passed on up the river, and, leaving his nephew at Santa Fé, reached Asuncion on February 5, 1575. For nearly a year he devoted himself to the difficult task of restoring order after the internal quarrels and revolts by which the settlement had been rent, but death overtook him in the midst of his labors on January 26, 1576.[1]

Unutterable confusion ensued during the next three years. The heiress of Zárate was his daughter Juana, who was then residing at Charcas. Her representative at Asuncion was her cousin, Diego de Mendieta, a fatuous youth of some

---

[1] Carbia, i, pp. 375 f. A historical poem, *Argentina*, describing the glories of the region and the principal events of its history in this period, was written by a companion of Ortiz de Zárate, named Martín del Barco Centenera, and first published at Lisbon in 1602. It was reprinted, in facsimile, with notes and a scholarly introduction by Juan María Gutiérrez and Enrique Piña, at Buenos Aires in 1912. Cf. George Ticknor, *History of Spanish Literature*, 6th ed. (Boston, 1888, 3 vols.), ii, pp. 556 f.

twenty years of age, who soon earned the contempt of all the inhabitants, and in 1577 was turned loose to perish in the wilderness. In the meantime at the Ciudad de la Plata there ensued an unseemly rivalry between three ambitious men to secure the hand of Juana and the inheritance which went with it ; but the viceroy and the audiencia prevented the finally successful candidate from assuming the government, and soon after landed him in prison at Lima. The sole permanently important development of these miserable years was the steady growth of the power and prestige of Juan de Garay. In April, 1578, he was appointed legal representative of the government at Asuncion, and during the following year occupied himself chiefly with the difficult work of restoring order and fighting the neighboring Indians. When tranquillity was restored, in December, 1579, he prepared to carry through the unfulfilled task which was nearest his heart, the reëstablishment of a permanent settlement at the mouth of La Plata. This, indeed, was obligatory on him, as Zárate's successor, under the terms of the latter's *capitulación* with the king. In March, 1580, Garay left Asuncion at the head of an expedition of some sixty enthusiastic followers. Dropping down the river past Santa Fé, he finally selected a site on the south side of the estuary, sufficiently far from the shore to be safe from the danger of inundation, and three or four miles distant from the spot where, forty-four years before, Pedro de Mendoza had planted his temporary outpost ; the centre of it is today the Plaza 25 de Mayo in the city of Buenos Aires. The formal ceremony of establishing the municipality took place on Saturday, June 11, 1580, and in view of the fact that the next day was Trinity Sunday, it was called La Trinidad ; but the older name of Buenos Aires continued to be used to designate the port, and ultimately was to prevail as that of the city itself. The details of the story make interesting reading, particularly the fertility and extent of the surrounding *estancias* with which Garay rewarded his faithful followers. They gave happy promise of a future prosperity of which few Europeans could then have conceived. At any rate the settlement was now permanently established, never again to be abandoned, and Garay thus became the real founder of the future capital of the Argentine. The last three years of his life were chiefly spent in the less congenial tasks of maintaining authority at Santa Fé and Asuncion; and in the course of his journeyings to and fro between these places, he met his death in March, 1583, at the hands of hostile natives, while resting in the forest. He was the noblest figure in the early history of the Argentine, vigorous, far-sighted, upright, and fearless, explorer, conqueror, and master of men.[1]

The death of Garay ushered in a new period of disorder in the government of the settlements on the Rio de la Plata. Juan Torres de Vera y Aragón, the husband of Juana Ortiz de Zárate, and lawful heir, through her, of her uncle's office of *adelantado*, had by this time got out of prison, but was still prevented, by the hostility of the viceroy and the audiencia of Charcas, from entering his domains till the summer of 1587, and was only permitted to remain there till 1590. The sole event of importance which took place during his brief tenure of power was the founding (April 5, 1588) of the city of Corrientes. Discouraged by the opposition which he everywhere encountered, he retired to Spain and resigned his position in 1593; and from that moment the hereditary office of *adelantado* of the Rio de la Plata, which had been established in 1569 for Ortiz de Zárate and his successors, though it continued to exist in theory down to the year 1658 ,

[1] Carbia, i, pp. 381–389; Groussac, pp. 456–543.

became for practical purposes extinct, and the rule of that territory passed into the hands of a series of *gobernadores* appointed by the viceroy at Lima and confirmed by the crown.[1] Of these the most eminent was Hernando Arias de Saavedra, born of Spanish parents at Asuncion in 1561, and married to a younger daughter of Garay; he was the first creole to hold public office in the Argentine, and has even been called the first Argentine patriot.[2] He was really the foremost figure in the colony from the early part of 1592, when he was chosen by popular vote as the representative of the absent governor. Five years later he was raised to that office in his own right, and held it with intermissions down to the year 1617, when, largely as a result of his representations to the home government, the territories of the province of the Rio de la Plata were divided, and Paraguay was definitely separated from Buenos Aires.[3] His rule was not only marked by firmness and wisdom in matters political and administrative; still more was it notable for educational progress, and above all for the development of commerce. The enormous natural economic advantages of Buenos Aires began for the first time to be properly utilized, so that it speedily came to overshadow Asuncion; moreover, by the end of his life the old route across the isthmus of Panama had ceased to be the sole means of access to Peru, and traffic had been started from La Plata up the Parana and over the Andes.[4]

Other evidences of nascent realization of the possibilities of the Argentine had begun to multiply before the death of

---

[1] Carbia, i, pp. 389–397.

[2] Levene, *Lecciones*, i, p. 128.

[3] Pedro Lozano, *Historia de la Conquista del Paraguay, Rio de la Plata, y Tucuman* (Buenos Aires, 1873–75, 5 vols.), iii, pp. 304 f.; Levene, *Lecciones*, i, pp. 128–137. Both provinces continued to form a part of the audiencia of Charcas until the erection of the audiencia of Buenos Aires in 1661. Cf. *Recopilación de Leyes de las Indias*, lib. ii, tit. xv, ley xiii.

[4] Carbia, *Manual*, i, p. 398; Haring, *Trade and Navigation*, pp. 140–142.

Philip II. *Corsarios Ingleses* thought the settlements there
well worth the harrying, and in the winter of 1582 Edward
Fenton, after establishing himself on the island of Santa
Catalina off the Brazilian coast, made an effort to raid
Buenos Aires. The attempt, however, proved a miserable
fiasco, and the captain and crew of one of the ships that had
been intrusted with it were obliged, as the only alternative to
being killed by the Indians, to seek safety at the gates of the
very town that they had expected to sack.[1] The period is
also noteworthy for the activities of the missionaries. A few
frailes had accompanied the earlier expeditions to the basin
of La Plata from the time of Mendoza onward, but their
efforts had at first been almost completely restricted to the
settlements, and no serious attempts had been made to convert the natives. After the refounding of Buenos Aires in
1580, and partly as a result of it, the work of converting the
Indians was vigorously taken up. A body of eighteen Franciscans who reached the estuary of La Plata in January,
1583, deserve, perhaps, to be regarded as the pioneers; but
their activities were soon destined to be overshadowed by
those of the Jesuits, who, arriving in 1588, so successfully
extended their system of missions in Paraguay in the course
of the next thirty or forty years that they converted the vast
majority of the Guaranis, and obtained virtually exclusive
control of the whole region about Asuncion during the following century and a half. Though they never got actual possession of the government there, their influence remained
dominant in the colony until their expulsion in 1769. Perhaps most significant of all was the persistency of the efforts
of the new settlements on the eastern slopes of the Andes,
which had been founded by expeditions sent out from Chile

---

[1] Carbia, i, pp. 389 f.; also life of
Edward Fenton in *Dictionary of Na-*
tional Biography and references there,
for details.

and Peru, to break the ties that bound them to the audiencia of Lima, and unite their political and economic destinies with those of Buenos Aires. Tucuman, first exploited by Francisco de Aguirre in the Emperor's day,[1] succeeded in getting itself declared independent of Chile by a royal *cédula* of August 29, 1563, and placed under the jurisdiction of the audiencia of Charcas; between 1593 and 1595 it was even temporarily united with the government of the Rio de la Plata.[2] Economically speaking, its whole history during this period resolved itself into a series of efforts to obtain a direct outlet for its rich products via Buenos Aires to the Atlantic and to Spain. The story of the town of Mendoza farther south is much the same. Like Tucuman, it was founded in the early sixties by an expedition sent out from Chile; like Tucuman, it at once made every effort to get an outlet on the Atlantic and link its destinies with those of Buenos Aires. In matters commercial it attained its object, and before the reign of Philip II had closed, it succeeded in establishing connection with the future capital of the Argentine. Politically, however, it failed to gain its end, despite all the efforts to help it on the part of Tucuman, for it continued officially to belong to Chile down to the year 1776, when the natural frontier on the ridge of the Cordillera was finally and definitely established.[3] The old idea, that the political and economic centre of gravity of the Spanish domination in South America must necessarily reside in the mining regions on the Pacific slope, died hard; but even before the end of the reign of the Prudent King there were signs, if only those in authority had been able to read them, that the original emphasis was destined ultimately to be reversed.

[1] Cf. *ante*, Vol. III, pp. 604 f.   [3] Carbia, i, p. 447.
[2] Carbia, i, pp. 414–433.

The principles on which Philip guided the administration of the Indies throughout his reign are a faithful reflection of his own character and ideals, and of the precepts which his father had passed on to him. From first to last he played safe. His object was rather to make sure of what he had already inherited, and of the maintenance therein of the Spanish monopoly and of the absolute power of the crown, than to increase the extent of his transatlantic possessions. The *conquistador* is therefore relegated to second place; he is largely supplanted by the hardworking, reliable crown official, whose pole star was the establishment of the royal authority. There are, consequently, few innovations. Such changes as were made were really only the logical consequences of the ramifications and development of the system which had been founded by the Emperor; they solidified, but did not alter it. The absence of new ideas was ominous for the future; it was another proof of the completeness with which Spain was wedded to the old ways, while her neighbors to the north of her were launching out into modern ones. It showed an inability to go forward which was prophetic of going back.

The supereminence, under the crown, of the Council of the Indies, was fortified by a series of *Ordenanzas Reales para el Consejo de las Indias* which Philip issued on September 24, 1571,[1] and which formed the basis for practically everything that followed down to the advent of the Bourbons in the eighteenth century. By these ordinances the Council was given unlimited authority, under the king, in the territories committed to its charge; legislatively, executively, and judicially, it was made the counterpart, for the Indies, of the

[1] There is a copy of the original edition of these *Ordenanzas* in the British Museum, 8042.1; and most of their provisions are to be found in the *Recopilación de Leyes de las Indias.* Cf. also Solórzano Pereira, *Política Indiana*, lib. v, caps. xv–xvii.

Consejo de Castilla for Castile. As in the Emperor's day, it resided continually at the court, and met every day save on regular holidays, three hours in the morning, and two more in the afternoon. No business was to be transacted until at least three members were present, and not till then were the three hours of the morning session to be regarded as having begun to elapse.[1] The membership, which had been fixed by the Emperor in 1542 at eight, over and above the president, the attorney-general, two secretaries, and other minor functionaries, was now confirmed, twenty-nine years later, at the same figure by his son,[2] but it does not seem always to have been actually filled up; if we may trust the statement of Cabrera de Córdoba, there were but six regular councillors[3] at the time of the king's death in 1598. On the other hand, it would appear that the duties and responsibilities of the Consejo multiplied so rapidly in the latter part of Philip's reign that it became necessary, shortly after his death, to create two offshoots of it with special functions of their own. These were the *Consejo de Cámara de las Indias*, a committee of the Council itself, first created in the year 1600 to advise the king about all appointments to secular and ecclesiastical office, the distribution of pensions, and the exercise of the pardoning power in the New World;[4] and the so-called *Junta de Guerra y Armadas de Indias*, also set up in 1600, and composed of members of the Council of the Indies and of the Consejo de Guerra; its special function was to oversee the arming and despatch of the American fleets and to confirm nominations

[1] *Recopilación de Leyes de las Indias,* lib. ii, tit. ii, ley v.
[2] *Recopilación de Leyes de las Indias,* lib. ii, tit. ii, ley i.
[3] In addition to the president, secretary, and attorney-general. C. de C., iv, p. 332.

[4] Solórzano Pereira, *Política Indiana,* lib. v, cap. xv, paragraphs 18 and 19; Charles de Lannoy and Herman vander Linden, *Histoire de l'expansion coloniale des peuples européens* (Brussels, 1907–21, 3 vols.), i, p. 342.

sent up to it by the Casa de Contratación for the various posts and offices involved.[1] It thus served incidentally as an additional means of keeping the doings of the Casa at Seville under the supervision of the crown.

A few significant facts may be noted in regard to the presidents of the Consejo de las Indias during the reign of the Prudent King. There were eight of them in all,[2] beginning with Francisco Tello de Sandoval, who replaced Luis Hurtado de Mendoza on December 2, 1559, when the latter was called to the presidency of the Council of Castile; the average term, in other words, was a little less than five years, a considerably longer period than the law prescribed. Of the eight, no less than seven were *licenciados*, men of technical training in theology or law, and all of them had had previous experience in one or more of the great departments of state. Only the first two of them, however, had been members of the Council of the Indies before they were elevated to the presidency of it, and of this pair only one had ever been in America, namely, Francisco Tello de Sandoval, who had gone out to Mexico as *visitador*, and published the New Laws there in 1544.[3] The only other one of the eight presidents who had visited the New World was Pedro de Moya y Contreras, who had been sent out to set up the Inquisition in New Spain in 1570, became archbishop of Mexico in 1573, and served temporarily as viceroy there in 1584–85.[4] There seemed, in other words, to be little disposition on the part of the king to profit by the experience of those who had actually been on the ground. Philip was apparently more anxious to have the Council of the Indies act in consonance

---

[1] *Recopilación de Leyes de las Indias,* lib. ii, tit. ii, leyes lxxii–lxxxii; Haring, *Trade and Navigation,* p. 221.

[2] Cf. the list in Antonio Herrera y Tordesillas, *Descripcion de las Indias Occidentales* (Madrid, [1729]), i, p. 71.

[3] A. S. Aiton, *Antonio de Mendoza* (Durham, N. C., 1927), pp. 72, 96 ff.

[4] Lea, *The Inquisition in the Spanish Dependencies,* pp. 200–202.

with his own preconceived notions of what was for the best interest of his subjects in the New World than to permit it to be too well informed as to the actual facts. It is also clear that he proposed that the administration of his transatlantic domains should be kept closely in touch with the Inquisition. In addition to Pedro de Moya, three others of the eight presidents of the Council of the Indies during Philip's reign, the fourth, sixth, and last, had previously been members of the Consejo de la Suprema. The elimination of heresy was to be the government's first duty not only in the Old World but in the New.

In the year 1596 the ban which had hitherto officially excluded non-Castilian Spaniards from the Indies was formally lifted by a *pragmática* [1] removing the inhabitants of the realms of the crown of Aragon and Navarre from the category of *estranjeros*, and therefore conferring on them, by implication, if not directly, the privileges of emigration to the New World. It seems natural to attribute this gratifying change to the remodelling of the constitution of the eastern kingdoms in 1592,[2] which brought them much more closely than ever before under the control of the crown; Philip had no longer any reason to fear lest his transatlantic possessions might be contaminated by Aragonese 'liberties.' But it is doubtful if the *pragmática* of 1596 actually brought about any great change in the situation as it was. The royal right of granting special exemptions from the operation of existing laws had been so frequently utilized in the past for the benefit of desirable inhabitants of the eastern realms, that large numbers of them had already found their way across the Atlantic; and there was also the imperial decree of 1526, of which mention has been made in the preceding

---

[1] *Recopilación de Leyes de las Indias,* lib. ix, tit. xxvii, ley xxviii.　　[2] Cf. *infra*, pp. 595–598.

volume.[1] It is worth noting that the law of 1596 failed to take the Portuguese out of the category of *estranjeros*; indeed, a clause which was added thereto in 1614 specifically declared them to be in it; they continued, in other words, to be debarred from Spanish America, though naturally not from Brazil. Even after the annexation of Portugal and its colonies in 1581, Philip did not regard their inhabitants as quite in the same category with Spaniards.

While the personnel of the Council of the Indies remained practically unchanged during the period of Philip II, that of the Casa de Contratación at Seville[2] was considerably altered and enlarged. The first and obvious reason for this expansion was the enormous increase of the business that the Casa had to do; a second and subsidiary one, which really began to make itself seriously felt only in the latter half of the reign, was Philip's characteristic determination to extend the royal supervision down to the most insignificant details of the commerce of the New World, as well as of its government. Finally, the creation of new offices was not without its value as a financial expedient, for it is impossible to deny that, in Philip's later years, the minor positions went more often to the highest bidders than to those who best deserved them.[3]

There is every reason to suppose that the old inherited organization, under three officials, the treasurer, factor, and *contador*, with coördinate powers, had demonstrated its inadequacy before the death of Charles V. It must have been overwhelmed by the sudden increase of the work that

[1] Cf. *ante*, Vol. III, p. 629.

[2] It will be remembered that the Emperor's efforts to throw open the American trade to other Spanish ports had been a failure; in 1573 Philip definitely revoked his father's decree which permitted it; cf. *ante*, Vol. III, p. 629, n. 1. Apparently this revocation did not touch the Mediterranean ports, such as Malaga and Cartagena; but there is no evidence that they took advantage of the right which, by implication, they continued to possess.

[3] Haring, *Trade and Navigation*, pp. 46–58.

it had to perform during the last fifteen years of the Emperor's reign; in fact, it seems probable that Charles's absence from Spain and his preoccupation about other matters were the chief reasons why some remedy for the situation had not been found.   In any case we know that on October 7, 1557, some twenty-one months after Philip had taken the reins of government, a president was appointed for the Casa de Contratación.[1]   The first incumbent, Juan Suárez de Carvajal, only served a little more than a year, and the office thereafter remained vacant till 1579, when it was conferred on the licentiate Diego de Salazar.   After that, the succession remained unbroken down to the suppression of the Casa in 1790, and it is worth noting that all four of the remaining presidents under the Prudent King were, like their predecessors, *licenciados*, while the first three of the next reign were *caballeros de capa y espada*; the Prudent King could not get over his innate preference for the scholar over the man of action.   On the other hand, it is fair to add that during his reign, though not invariably under his successors, the rule requiring all presidents of the Casa to have had previous experience in the Council of the Indies was faithfully observed.[2]

The first duty of the president was to keep the Casa as a whole, and every department of it, in the closest possible touch with the Council of the Indies; for since it was resident at Seville, there was always the danger that it might strive to attain some measure of independence.   In order to accomplish this end, he was expected to supervise and coördinate the activities of the three offices into which the Casa from its inception had been divided;[3] to preside over the

[1] Joseph de Veitia Linaje, *Norte de la Contratacion de las Indias Occidentales*, lib. i, cap. 37, § 1.

[2] Veitia Linaje, lib. i, cap. 3, § 4; lib. i, cap. 37, § 2, 3, 4.

[3] Cf. *ante*, Vol. II, pp. 224-227.

tribunal of the Consulado ; [1] and to attend, and, if he was a *letrado,* to cast a vote in, the so-called *Sala de Justicia de la Casa de Contratación,* created in 1583 to deal with the steadily increasing amount of litigation which the activities of the Casa rendered inevitable.[2] This body, when it was first set up, was composed of only two *oidores,* but thirteen years later it became necessary to add a third. Its form and procedure were closely assimilated to those of the higher courts of the realm ; and the president, as *ex officio* member thereof, became, *ipso facto,* the indispensable connecting link between it and the older established administrative offices of the Casa. It was characteristic of Philip's fondness for courts and his determination to have justice done down to the minutest detail that this Sala should have been created and given such prominence by him ; and he doubtless felt that the right to participate in its proceedings was the greatest privilege that the president possessed. Nevertheless the administrative side of the work of the Casa increased, during his lifetime, even faster than the judicial ; we must therefore turn our attention to the expansion of the responsibilities of the offices of the treasurer and factor, and its results.

The work of the treasurer's department was more than doubled during the reign of the Prudent King, and its staff was in consequence greatly increased. Not only did it have to handle much larger amounts of money from the New World than in the Emperor's day ; it was made receiver of the proceeds of the rich silver mine of Guadalcanal, which had been discovered in 1555 on the border of Estremadura, and also, in 1579,[3] of all the *almojarifazgos* and *alcabalas* of Andalusia. What inference is to be drawn from the assign-

[1] Cf. *ante,* Vol. III, p. 625.
[2] Haring, *Trade and Navigation,* pp. 57 f., and references there.
[3] Haring, p. 47, and references there.

ment of the collection of these purely Spanish revenues to a body whose functions were theoretically restricted to amounts received from the Indies, it were difficult to determine. Probably the arrangement was made because, whatever the defects of the Casa, it was decidedly more efficient than the regular authorities of the *Hacienda*. Possibly it may also be taken to indicate a dawning realization of the necessity of reducing the excessive number of government officials, though this theory is sharply contradicted by the facts as they existed in other departments. In any event, the revenues received by the Casa from sources purely Spanish were but an exceedingly small fraction of the total sum it had to handle; it was chiefly through the increase of the amounts which arrived from the Indies that its responsibilities were enlarged.

The revenues which Philip derived from the New World mounted steadily during the course of the reign. All the expenses of the king's government in the Indies were paid out of these revenues before they left America; the sums received by the Casa de Contratación were thus only the surplus available for the use of his Majesty at home.[1] In 1554 they reached 223⅓ cuentos, in 1566, 252, in 1577, 445, in 1585, 700, and in 1598, 945.[2] The principal sources of them were the royal *quinto* (often more and sometimes less than one-fifth) of the yield of the American mines; sundry special

---

[1] Cf. C. H. Haring, "Ledgers of the Royal Treasurers in Spanish America in the Sixteenth Century," in *Hispanic American Historical Review*, ii (1919), pp. 181 f. In the decade 1553–63 only 628 of the 1523 *cuentos* received in New Spain were actually sent home to Seville. Cf. Archivo General de Indias, Contaduria, legajo 666.

[2] The estimated amounts set down in the official budgets are always considerably less than the amounts recorded as actually received by the Casa. The chief reason for this is probably that the former were reckoned on the basis of what had been received the year before. Moreover, the amounts recorded as actually received by the Casa included the *averia*, which the official budgets omitted, since it had to be forthwith paid back to the special *averia* account, which in 1590 reached 68 *cuentos*. Cf. Archivo General de Indias, Contratación, legajo 4556.

tributos de Indios y de Negros; the proceeds of the *alcabala*, which was extended by law to the Indies in 1558, and established there in fact at the rate of two per cent in 1574–76; [1] certain crown monopolies such as that of playing cards; [2] the *cruzada*; and the *almojarifazgos de los puertos* on both sides of the Atlantic; and the amounts derived from every one of these items increased between 1555 and 1598. The rate of the various imposts and taxes was steadily raised, and the gold, silver, and quicksilver mines of the New World yielded the crown between three and four times as much at the end of the reign as at the beginning.[3] In addition to the royal revenue from the New World, the Casa had also to handle the sums derived from the Indies by individual Spaniards. The latter averaged about two and one-half times as much as the former in the period under review.[4]

These totals are certainly impressive, and the rate of their increase during the reign is even more so. But what is far more noteworthy still is their relative smallness compared with the sums which Philip drew from European sources. According to the budget of 1554 the income derivable from the Indies was reckoned at less than 11% of the total amount due to the royal treasury; in 1566 at a little over 7%; in 1577 at 10%. In 1585 it rises to a little more than 25%, and in 1598 it only falls back to 22%,[5] but even at the very end

---

[1] *Recopilación de Leyes de las Indias,* lib. viii, tit. xiii, leyes i and xiv.

[2] Cf. *infra,* p. 441.

[3] Haring, *Trade and Navigation,* pp. 332–334; also E. J. Hamilton, "Imports of American Gold and Silver into Spain, 1503–1660," in the *Quarterly Journal of Economics,* xliii (1929), pp. 436–472.

[4] E. J. Hamilton, "American Treasure and Andalusian Prices," in the *Journal of Economic and Business History,* i (1928), p. 6.

[5] Archivo de Indias, Indiferente General, legajo 1805; Simancas Mss., sección 11, legajo 216. In my article in the *Revue Hispanique,* lxxxi, "A Note on the Finances of Philip II," which was written in the summer of 1930, though it was not published till 1933, I reckoned the American crown revenues as amounting, "on the average, during the first half of his reign, to a little more than six per cent of all the sums due annually to the royal treasury," but the documents in the British Museum on which this estimate was based happened to fall on three very lean years.

of the reign it is obvious that the American revenues did not constitute anywhere nearly so large a portion of Philip's income as has been popularly supposed. They did not even equal some of the more important single items in the list of the Spanish king's European resources. During the first half of the reign they averaged less than three-fourths of the sums derived from the ecclesiastical revenues in Europe (the *tercias, cruzada, subsidio, excusado,* and *maestrazgos*); only after 1580 did they begin to exceed them.[1] In 1554 they were only about two-thirds of the proceeds of the *encabezamiento* in Spain, in 1566 only a little better than one-half, in 1577 a little more than one-third. At the end of the reign, indeed, the current begins to flow the other way; the Indies yield 945 *cuentos* and the *encabezamiento* only 1035.[2] But it is evident that the legend that America constituted an inexhaustible treasure house for Philip cannot possibly be substantiated by the facts.

It was in the years 1564–66 that the organization of the sailings to and from America in two annual fleets was definitely and permanently set up. There had been foreshadowings of it, as we have seen, in the Emperor's day;[3] henceforth it was formally established, to last to the advent of the Bourbons.[4] On October 18, 1564, a set of ordinances was put forth providing for the annual despatch of two convoyed fleets, one for New Spain, the other for the Isthmus of Panama and New Castile; they subsequently became known as the Flota and the Galleons, and they averaged, in the latter years of Philip's reign, some seventy ships each.[5] The first was to sail in April for the Greater Antilles and the ports on the Gulf of Mexico; the second was to leave in

[1] Simancas Mss., sección. 11, legajo 216.
[2] Simancas Mss., sección 11, legajo 380.
[3] Cf. *ante*, Vol. III, pp. 631 f.
[4] Haring, p. 207.
[5] *Ibid.*, pp. 210–212.

August for the northern coast of South America and Nombre
de Dios.   Both were to winter in the Indies, and to repair to
Havana in March ; they were to leave for Europe not earlier
than the tenth of that month, and were generally expected
to sail home separately.   The details of these regulations
were not invariably observed.   The prescribed times of
sailing were not rigidly adhered to ; occasionally a year was
skipped, and it was only rarely that either of the fleets
arrived anywhere at the appointed times.   But the routes [1]
and schedules were at least sufficiently regular to enable the
pirates to swoop down on the fleets at the most awkward
possible moments, that is, to facilitate the very thing that
the Flota and the Galleons had been established to prevent,
with the result that increasing attention and expense had to
be devoted to convoy and armament.   At first it had been
the custom to rely on a few cannon and a handful of soldiers,
borne by each of the larger merchantmen of the fleet, but
the ships were so crowded with passengers and goods as to
be virtually useless when any fighting was to be done ; so in
1565 it was provided that the flagship of each fleet was to be
a galleon of at least 300 tons, with thirty-six cannon and
200 men, and it was never to encumber itself with merchandise of any kind, save when it rescued the cargoes of
wrecks.   The number of warships assigned for this purpose
gradually increased as the reign wore on, and their efforts
were supplemented by those of the so-called *Armada de la
Carrera de las Indias,* which patrolled the waters off the
Spanish coasts, and occasionally escorted the fleets across
the sea.   To us the system seems cumbersome and ineffective, a faithful reflection of Philip's excessive confidence in
the power of combination and weight, and of his inability
to see the value of manoeuvring and speed.   But it seems

[1] Cf. Haring, pp. 222–225, for details of these.

probable that it actually worked out, under the conditions prevalent at the time, rather better than the modern student would have reason to suppose. Despite all their foreknowledge of the dates and routes of the Spanish sailings, none of Philip's maritime enemies was ever able to capture an entire treasure-fleet. They had to content themselves with the cutting off of isolated vessels and minor squadrons. The Flota and the Galleons continued to maintain their sailings.

It will readily be seen from the foregoing paragraph that the provisioning, arming, and outfitting of the American fleets had become, under Philip II, a task far too heavy to be performed by the factor alone, who had had charge of it in the Emperor's day. The natural result was a large increase in his staff and the gradual distribution of his duties among a number of officials. Of these by far the most important was the purveyor-general of the armadas and fleets of the Indies, who was first appointed in 1588.[1] It was his duty to make sure that the ships themselves were in fit condition for the sea, and that they were fully supplied with provisions for the voyage; and he was expected to buy such commodities and to employ such labor as were necessary for these purposes. The matter of armament, however, still remained under the jurisdiction of the factor, who was aided, during the last twenty-five years of the reign, by an *artillero mayor*. The *Junta de Guerra y Armadas de Indias*, as we have already remarked, was not created until 1600.

On the other side of the Atlantic the consolidation and development of the system of viceregal administration inaugurated by the Emperor is by far the most significant fact of the period. Long lines of successors to Antonio de Mendoza were established under Philip II, both at Mexico

[1] Haring, p. 49.

and at Lima, and continued, with occasional interruptions, down to the era of the Revolutions.

Strictly speaking, there were but eight viceroys of New Spain between the departure of Antonio de Mendoza for New Castile in 1550 and the death of Philip II in 1598, and the same number in New Castile between Mendoza's death at Lima (July 21, 1552) and the end of the reign. In other words, the law of 1555, prescribing a three-year term,[1] was practically in abeyance. There were, moreover, three interregna in New Spain,[2] during which the government was carried on by the audiencia, and three of a similar nature in New Castile;[3] the second of this latter trio, which lasted from 1564 to 1569, amounted in fact to a suspension of the viceregal régime, for the home government was so disturbed by the succession of calamities[4] by which so many of the early viceroys of Peru had been taken off, that it determined to try the experiment of having the viceroyalty governed by the audiencia, under the able presidency of the licentiate Lope García de Castro, who had been a member of the Council of the Indies.[5] The longest term served by any viceroy in Philip's time was that of Velasco, 'the Emancipator,'[6] the successor of Antonio de Mendoza in Mexico, from 1550 to 1564; the next, that of Martín Enríquez de Almansa, who ruled New Spain from 1568 to 1580, and then was transferred

[1] Recopilación de Leyes de las Indias, lib. iii, tit. iii, ley lxxi.

[2] Between July, 1564, and September, 1566; between March and November, 1568; and between June, 1583, and September, 1584.

[3] Between July, 1552, and June, 1556; between February, 1564, and November, 1569; and between March, 1583, and November, 1586.

[4] Blasco Núñez Vela was beheaded by a black slave after the battle of Anaquito in 1546; Antonio de Mendoza had died in July, 1552, after a ten-

month term of office; and the Count of Nieva was murdered in February, 1564. Ante, Vol. III, p. 599; R. Levillier, Audiencia de Lima, pp. xxxvi, lxxi.

[5] Lillian Estelle Fisher, Viceregal Administration, p. 31; Sebastian Lorente, Historia del Perú bajo la Dinastía Austriaca, 1542–1598 (Lima, 1863), pp. 289 f.

[6] So called "for his first official act of freeing one hundred and fifty thousand Indian slaves." Lowery, Spanish Settlements, 1513–1561, p. 353.

to New Castile from 1581 to 1583 ; and there are at least four cases of terms shorter than two years.   Save for Enríquez de Almansa, the second Velasco, who governed New Spain from 1590 to 1595, was the only Mexican viceroy to be promoted during this period to the more dignified viceroyalty of Lima.

In general it is fair to say that under Philip the viceroys were carefully selected from men who in various ways had given proof of efficiency in the service of the crown.   There is no evidence of any tendency, such as appeared in the seventeenth century, to lay special emphasis on military qualifications ; if anything, Philip preferred the trained administrator to the soldier, and on one occasion he appointed a cleric.[1]   Most of his happiest choices, in both viceroyalties, were made from the great families of the Mendozas and the Velascos.   Of the former there were three, one in New Spain and two in New Castile, the last pair father and son,[2] and all of them of kin to the great Antonio de Mendoza of the Emperor's day ; of the latter there were two, father and son, in New Spain, and the son, as we have already seen, was promoted to New Castile.   But of all the viceroys appointed by the Prudent King, the greatest by far was Francisco Álvarez de Toledo, who was sent out to New Castile in 1569, when it was in utter confusion and disorder, and brought it back to peace and prosperity in the ensuing twelve years.   A brief summary of his career there will serve to give some slight idea of the conditions prevalent in Philip's American possessions in the middle years of his reign, and of the policies that were pursued in dealing with them.

[1] Pedro de Moya y Contreras, archbishop of Mexico, and viceroy there from 1584 to 1585.   He was also the first inquisitor in Mexico, and later president of the Council of the Indies.

[2] This son, García Hurtado de Mendoza, Marquis of Cañete, who ruled from 1590 to 1596, was very highly esteemed in Spain. Cf. C. de C., iv, pp. 17–23, 212–215.

Toledo had proved his value both as a diplomat and as a soldier before he was sent out to the New World, but Philip had no idea of leaving him a free hand in his new office.[1] His duties and responsibilities were specifically defined in an elaborate set of instructions given him on his departure. Perhaps the most important of all these instructions was that ordering him to make a tour of inspection of his viceroyalty, in order that he might become personally informed of its conditions and needs, and report them to the crown. He began to make that tour of inspection in October, 1570, taking with him as counsellors a Jesuit priest, a judge, and a licentiate. It covered in all over 5000 miles, and occupied him for more than five years, and its results were far-reaching and beneficent.[2] The two problems to which he gave his chief attention were the traditional ones : first, how to increase the output of the mines, and, secondly, how to better the conditions of the Indians.[3] Past experience had tended to show that neither could be solved save at the expense of the other; but Toledo was convinced that it would be possible to deal with them separately and satisfactorily, and succeeded in proving that he was right. New methods were established for the extraction of the silver from the ore by the use of mercury, which had been discovered at Huancavelica. A wise code of mining laws and regulations was drawn up and enforced; and a mint to stabilize the currency was established at Potosí.[4] These measures, and others, which Toledo adopted, were no small element in bringing about the

[1] *D. I. I.*, viii, pp. 217 f. This is a curious, though unfortunately incomplete account of Toledo's term of office, written in the first part of the seventeenth century, probably by one Tristán Sánchez. A. F. Zimmerman's *Francisco de Toledo* (the abstract of a University of Illinois doctoral dissertation, Urbana, 1928) contains a useful bibliographical note.

[2] *D. I. I.*, viii, pp. 243–256; Zimmerman, p. 8.

[3] The Pope wrote him a letter before his departure, emphasizing the importance of Christianizing the natives. *D. I. I.*, viii, pp. 214–216.

[4] *D. I. I.*, viii, pp. 282–287: *Relaciones de los Vireyes y Audiencias que han gobernado el Perú*, i, pp. 267–348.

gratifying increase, beginning about 1580, in the revenue which Spain was able to derive from the New World. At the same time the viceroy labored manfully to put an end to the maltreatment and exploitation of the loyal Indians. The chief means which he took to effect this end was to establish in the larger towns of his viceroyalty a system of *corregidores* and *corregimientos* modelled on that of Castile, and in the smaller ones, which were almost exclusively populated by natives, lesser officers called *corregidores de Indios*. Authority was thus gradually withdrawn from the *encomendero*, who had generally misused it, and placed in the hands of responsible officials, on whom the duty of caring for the welfare of the natives had been specifically laid, and who knew that they were likely to lose their positions if they neglected it.[1] The Indians were no longer victimized by the greedy lawyers and judges who had hitherto reaped rich harvests out of their ignorance; and special codes with special officers to administer them were provided to regulate their affairs. A scale of wages was established for them, and a census of their population was taken, so that the tribute due from them could be justly apportioned.[2]

But though Toledo was a sturdy champion of the rights of the loyal native, he would not tolerate any refusal to recognize the sovereignty of the Spanish crown. Tupac Amaru, the youngest son of Manco Inca of the days of the Pizarros, maintained an independent court in the mountains to the east of Ayacucho; it was a place of refuge for all sorts of undesirables, a potential centre of disturbance and rebellion. On his arrival at Lima, Toledo strove by peaceful

[1] Memorial of Toledo in *D. I. E.*, xxvi, pp. 143 f.; Zimmerman, pp. 8 f.; Ruíz Guiñazú, *La Magistratura Indiana*, pp. 301–311.

[2] *Relaciones de los Vireyes*, i, pp. 109–111, 155–266; Zimmerman, pp. 10 f.; Sir Clements Markham's introduction to Pedro Sarmiento de Gamboa's *History of the Incas*, pp. xv f.

means to induce the Inca to abandon this last vestige of the independence of his race; but Tupac refused to listen to him, and the viceroy reluctantly determined that it would be necessary to use force. An army was sent against the youthful Inca; he was captured, brought back to Cuzco, tried, found guilty on testimony the greater part of which was false, and, despite the passionate protests of almost all the inhabitants, both lay and clerical, of the city, suffered death at the hands of the public executioner in December, 1571.[1] The act has left a dark stain on the record of the viceroy. It has been characterized as a 'judicial murder,' and it gave Philip an excuse for cruelly turning against Toledo, when ten years later he became convinced that he was in danger of becoming too powerful.[2] But it was essential for the king's representative to make it evident, at the outset of his régime, that he had the power to enforce his will, and the rulers of the sixteenth century were not wont to be merciful to rebels.

Toledo was also much concerned with ecclesiastical affairs. The state of the clergy at the time of his arrival in New Castile cried aloud for reform. Churchmen, like laymen, had flocked across the Atlantic, primarily with the idea of enriching themselves. They neglected the principal duty which had been assigned to them, that of educating the Indians in the principles of the Christian faith; only a few of them, in fact, had even taken the trouble to learn the native languages, and most of them were both immoral and corrupt. There was every prospect, moreover, that these evils would be perpetuated, for the higher clergy in the New

---

[1] D. I. I., viii, pp. 262–282; Baltasar de Ocampo, Narrative of the Execution of the Inca Tupac Amaru, tr. and ed. Sir Clements Markham; C. R. Markham, History of Peru (Chicago, 1892), pp. 151–155.

[2] "You were sent to Peru to serve kings, not to kill them," is the phrase which tradition has placed in Philip's mouth. Porreño, Dichos y Hechos del Rey Felipe Segundo (Seville, 1639), fol. 15.

World had begun to usurp the royal right of patronage, and doled out the most lucrative posts to the highest bidders. One of the principal duties that had been given Toledo was that of reëstablishing the powers of the crown in this regard, and he lost no time in doing so. The king, in 1574, put forth an edict consolidating all the gains his representative had already made, and definitely providing for the future; and thereafter Toledo was able to bring about numerous salutary reforms.[1] Laws governing the conduct of clerics were promulgated and enforced. They were obliged to learn the Indian languages within a specific time, and if they did not succeed in so doing, they were deprived of their salaries.[2] Moreover in January, 1569, two months before Toledo left Spain for New Castile, Philip determined to establish tribunals of the Inquisition at Mexico and at Lima. The motive alleged by the king for this decision was the danger lest his transatlantic dominions should be contaminated by the taint of Protestantism, and French and English 'Lutherans' suffered death in the first two autos-da-fé: at Lima on November 15, 1573, and at Mexico on the 28th of the following February. It is hard to believe that the perils of heresy were as great as the Inquisitors, in order to justify their own vocation, almost invariably sought to make out; but the institution had proved its value as an instrument for the detection and punishment of clerical irregularities and as a means of fortifying the authority of the crown; and as such it was inevitable that Toledo should bid it welcome. He lent it his heartiest support during the entire period of his term of office, and established its power and supereminence in his viceroyalty after the fashion of the parent institution in Castile. The Indians, however, both in Mexico and in

[1] *D. I. I.*, viii, pp. 237–239; Zimmerman, p. 11.   [2] Zimmerman, p. 7.

Peru, were exempted from inquisitorial jurisdiction, and, despite numerous protests, remained subject to the authority of the bishops.[1]

The viceroy also rendered priceless service to New Castile and the Spanish Empire in a multitude of other ways; he seemed literally indefatigable and omniscient, and richly deserves the title of the 'Peruvian Solon.' He built roads, and aqueducts and canals to convey drinking water to the principal cities of the viceroyalty.[2] He established inns and hospitals, and set up regular military outposts at strategic points, so that it was safe, for the first time, for merchants and travellers to journey by the principal highways of his domains.[3] He fostered the lucrative culture of the cocoa leaf in the low hot valleys of the interior; yet he took great pains, at the same time, to put an end to the shocking maltreatment of the Indians who worked on the plantations.[4] The welfare of the native was never absent from his mind; moreover, he realized that there were many features of the ancient institutions of the days of the Incas which could profitably be utilized and preserved; some of his most happy regulations were inspired by a fusion of Spanish and native ideas.[5] The "Memorial" which he left for the instruction of his successors at his departure was regarded by them as an "authoritative text book," and one of them declared that "all future rulers of Peru were but his disciples."[6] And yet this greatest of all Philip's colonial

---

[1] D. I. I., viii, pp. 232 f.; J. T. Medina, Historia del Tribunal del Santo Oficio de la Inquisicion de Lima (Santiago de Chile, 1887, 2 vols.), i, pp. 47–55; H. C. Lea, The Inquisition in the Spanish Dependencies, pp. 198–214, 321–332.
[2] Fundacion Española del Cusco, edd. H. H. Urteaga and C. A. Romero (Lima, 1926), pp. 92–98.
[3] Zimmerman, p. 11.

[4] D. I. I., viii, pp. 260–262; Zimmerman, pp. 10 f.
[5] Markham, History of Peru, pp. 156 f.
[6] The Memorial is printed in D. I. E., xxvi, pp. 122–161, in D. I. I., vi, pp. 516–553, in Relaciones de los Vireyes y Audiencias que han gobernado el Perú, i, pp. 3–31 (this volume also contains most of Toledo's laws), and in Beltrán y Rózpide's Colección de las

administrators was deprived of his office without warning or reward. Though he had frequently asked to be relieved of his post, his requests had been invariably refused; but the very fact that he had been so successful had at last aroused the jealousy of his distant master, and in 1581 the viceroy of Mexico was suddenly sent down to Lima to supersede him. When Toledo got back to Spain, the king would not consent to receive him. He was accused and found guilty of having derived unlawful profit from his term of office, and in 1584 he died in his native town of Oropesa, broken hearted and worn out. Similar tragedies were to be frequently reënacted, with Philip's most notable European representatives as their principal victims, in the closing years of the reign of the Prudent King.

The sad story of Toledo's dismissal will serve as a salutary reminder of the all-important fact that Philip was quite as determined to keep all independent authority out of the hands of his subordinates in America as in Europe. In theory, the viceregal powers were fully as extensive during

---

Memorias o Relaciones que escribieron los Virreyes del Perú, i, pp. 71–107. A collection of similar *memoriales* left by the viceroys of New Spain is the *Instrucciones que los Vireyes de Nueva España dejaron a sus Sucesores* (Mexico, 1867). Another great service which Toledo rendered not only to his viceroyalty and to Spain, but to posterity, was to order the famous cosmographer and navigator, Pedro Sarmiento de Gamboa, to write his history of the Incas, of which the second part, the only one to be completed, was discovered in manuscript in the library of the University of Göttingen in the beginning of this century, and first published at Berlin in 1906, with a learned introduction by Richard Pietschmann, in the *Abhandlungen* of the Königliche Gesellschaft der Wissenschaften at Göttingen, phil.-hist. Klasse, neue Folge, vi, no. 4; an English translation, with notes by Sir Clements Markham, was also printed for the Hakluyt Society in 1907. It has been described as the "most reliable and authentic history of the Incas that has yet appeared," but it is marred by the fact that it was written mainly for the purpose of vindicating the viceroy's conduct in executing Tupac Amaru, and therefore takes the stand that the king of Spain was the rightful sovereign of the country, and the Incas but usurping tyrants; in a sense it may also be regarded as an answer to the pleadings of Las Casas. In the introductory epistle to the king, Sarmiento assures him that "the work done by your viceroy is such that the Indians are regenerated, and they call him loudly their protector and guardian, and your Majesty who sent him, they call their father." Cf. Markham's translation, pp. xii f. and 8.

the reign of the Prudent King as ever they had been in the days of his father; nay more, the viceroys were given by Philip, either temporarily or permanently, certain rights and duties which had not been accorded them in the New Laws. Such were the extraordinary powers with which they were invested in cases of rebellion, the authority to make treaties of peace with the native tribes, and the duty of maintaining the royal supremacy over the tribunals of the Inquisition.[1] Yet it would probably be a safe generalization to say that the viceroys of the latter part of the reign were not actually so strong in their independent authority as the earlier ones. Jealous though the Emperor had been of the aspirations for autonomy of his representatives across the sea, his son was vastly more so.　Moreover, by the end of the century the Spanish colonial system was working sufficiently well to enable the Spanish monarch to give his jealousy effect. Long as was the journey from the mother country to Mexico or to Peru in the latter years of the Prudent King, and likely as it was to be intercepted by the attacks of hostile corsairs, it was shorter, more regular, and more frequently made than it had been in the Emperor's day.　There was, in fact, what might be charitably described as a 'service,' and the king could consequently keep in touch with his representatives in the New World as his father had never been able to do. More and more meticulous were the instructions he sent out ; less and less were the viceroys permitted to settle matters on their own authority ; more and more were they commanded to send home information and wait for the royal orders as to how to deal with the existing facts.　The six interruptions, already noted, of the viceregal succession by the government of an audiencia, both in New Spain and New Castile, during

[1] Lillian Estelle Fisher, *Viceregal Administration*, pp. 19, 252 f.; *Recopilación de Leyes de las Indias*, lib. i. tit. xix, leyes xi, xii, xviii, xix, xxi, xxix.

the reign of the Prudent King, though each one of them had its immediate origin in specific events and conditions, may, perhaps, taken together, be interpreted as an evidence that Philip was not sorry to seize every opportunity to demonstrate that he could, if need be, govern his transatlantic dominions without the aid of viceroys.[1]

By far the most characteristic of all the methods employed by the Prudent King to keep watch on the doings of his representatives across the sea was the development during his reign of the *residencia* and *visita*.[2] For the present purposes it will suffice to describe the former, that is, the obligation incident on every official, from the viceroy down to the municipal *corregidor*, to continue to reside, for a specified period after the expiration of his term of office, at the place where he had exercised jurisdiction, in order that all those who considered themselves to have been aggrieved by any of his acts or decisions might prefer their complaints before the person or persons appointed to receive them. The *visita* was essentially only a *residencia* taken without notice at any time during the incumbency of the *residenciado*, and generally implying that things were not believed to be in good case. Philip, one of whose best qualities was a firm determination to see justice done to each and every one of his subjects, attached great weight to the *residencia*, "since experience had shown it to be most necessary as a means of repressing the arrogance of ministers";[3] more than one-third of the laws on the subject in the *Recopilación de Leyes de las Indias* are from his reign. They bear eloquent testimony to the excellence of his intentions, particularly in regard to the treatment of the Indians, who were to be given

---

[1] Cf. Fisher, *Viceregal Administration*, pp. 26–32.

[2] The main authority on these is Juan de Solórzano Pereira's *Política Indiana*, lib. v, cap. x.

[3] Solórzano Pereira, lib. v, cap. x, paragraph 14.

every chance to get their grievances heard.   They reveal his willingness to work hard and long, and to take infinite pains in order to secure his ends, and his desire and expectation that his subordinates do likewise.   But as the system actually worked in the New World, it probably produced more harm than good.   Dread of the oncoming test caused the magistrates to become timid, to act negatively rather than positively, to seek at every turn rather to avoid giving offence than to take vigorous measures for the public good. Whether or no the dictum of Solórzano that good judges ran more risk than bad ones can actually be substantiated, it is certain that the system tended to paralyze initiative, a defect which Philip would have been the last to appreciate.[1] Even worse was the waste of energy, money, and above all of time involved.   The number of officials employed in the taking of *residencias* was enormous, and their written reports filled scores of bulky tomes.[2]   The period occupied by the taking of the test evoked universal complaint, but nevertheless constantly tended to increase; even Philip was obliged to admit the evil, and in 1582 he put forth a law that the duration of the *residencias* of all lesser officials should not exceed sixty days.[3]   In the case of *residencias* of viceroys, however, he remained obdurate; nothing would induce him to set any time limit for them at all, with the result that a viceregal *residencia* became a synonym for eternity.   "In the year 1589," writes Solórzano,[4] "the *visita* of the Marquis of Villa Manrique, viceroy of Mexico, was committed to the bishop of Tlascala, and never ended at all; and in the margin

---

[1] Solórzano Pereira, lib. v, cap. x, paragraphs 18–21.

[2] Solórzano Pereira, lib. v, cap. x, paragraph 4.

[3] *Recopilación de Leyes de las Indias*, lib. v, tit. xv, ley xxix.   Other important laws governing *residencias* which were put forth in the reign of Philip II are leyes iii, v, vi, xi, xiv, xx, xxi, xxiv, xxv, xxviii, xxxiii, xxxvii, xl, and xliii in the same *título*.   There are forty-nine *leyes* in this *título de las residencias*.

[4] Lib. v, cap. x, paragraph 21.

of the *cédula* or commission of the same, there was written a note to the effect that this had happened because no time limit had been set, and that therefore it would be well to set one." But it was not until seventy-eight years later that this advice was taken; the law limiting the period of a viceregal *residencia* to six months was not put forth till the reign of Charles II in 1667.[1]

The *residencia* was indeed the quintessence of Philip's conception of good government. He saw only its virtues, and its virtues under ideal conditions; he refused to admit its faults as things actually worked out. There is evidence that his successors were far less enthusiastic for it than he. Philip IV was fully aware of its defects, and wished to substitute some other method of attaining the desired end; and Solórzano, whose great book was issued in 1629,[2] dilates on the evil effect of the appalling slowness of the *residencias*. "It is better," he declares, "to omit to ascertain and punish some things than to retard everything. A sovereign will never cure his republic with such medicine, if it brings with it greater ills and evils than those which it was intended to remedy."[3] And even earlier than this, in the reign of Philip III, the Marquis of Montesclaros, who was viceroy of Peru from 1607 to 1615, drew his famous parallel between "these *visitas* and the little whirlwinds which commonly blow up in the squares and the streets, with no other result than to raise the dirt, filth, and other refuse there, and let it fall down again on the heads of the people."[4]

It would be quite futile, in a book which attempts to cover as vast a field as does this, to describe all the other institutions in Spanish America at the close of the reign of the

---

[1] *Recopilación de Leyes de las Indias,* lib. v, tit. xv, ley i.

[2] In Latin. The first Spanish edition came out in 1648.

[3] Solórzano Pereira, lib. v, cap. **x**, paragraph 22.

[4] Solórzano Pereira, lib. v, cap. **v**, paragraph 19.

Prudent King. It must be remembered, moreover, that even the most important of them were but ephemeral; they were all to be swept away during the era of the Revolutions. If one bears this fact in mind, one is likely to conclude that the most notable achievement of the Spaniards in the New World was the conversion and civilization of the American Indians; and it was really in the reign of Philip II that this work was effectively begun. The foundations for it had indeed been laid by the Catholic Kings and the Emperor;[1] but the Spaniards of those days had been so much occupied with exploration and fighting that they had little time to spare for the gentler sides of their task. Under Philip, on the other hand, the Spanish colonial régime was definitely established, and the apostles of Spanish culture got their first real opportunity for effective work in the New World. One is tempted, at first sight, to characterize their methods of operation as negative rather than as positive. One is staggered by the number of restrictions on the sale of books and the setting-up of printing presses,[2] by the extent to which clerics were suffered to monopolize the conduct of instruction, by the barriers placed in the way of the study of the sciences, by the rigid control, through the monarchy and the church, of the intellectual development of the inhabitants of the New World.[3] These inhibitions, however, apply almost exclusively to what we should today call the higher education, and especially to the teaching of the children of Spanish parents in the universities; moreover, they were but the counterpart of the regulations in force at the

[1] Cf. Vol. III, pp. 662–664.
[2] *Recopilación de Leyes de las Indias*, lib. i, tit. xxiv, leyes i–xiv; V. G. Quesada, *La Vida Intelectual en la America Española* (Buenos Aires, 1910), cap. i.

[3] F. Barreda y Laos, *Vida Intelectual de la Colonia*, pp. 142–160; cf. also Irving A. Leonard, *Romances of Chivalry in the Spanish Indies, with some Registros of Shipments of Books to the Spanish Colonies* (Berkeley, California, 1933).

same time and for the same purposes in Spain, and therefore, in a sense, inherent in the transportation of Spanish cultural ideals across the sea. What is really more significant for our present purpose is the story of the progress that was made at the other end of the scale, in the elementary instruction of the Indians. From the nature of the case, it was bound to be inconspicuous, and we only get occasional glimpses of it here and there; but the efforts that were made to teach the natives Castilian [1] prove the eagerness of the king and of his representatives in the New World to raise his transatlantic subjects to the standards of European civilization. How much was accomplished in this direction before Philip's death it is obviously impossible accurately to determine, though the history of the seventeenth century leaves no doubt that much progress was made.[2] In this as in many other respects, some of the principal results of the reign of the Prudent King belong in the category of the imponderables.

It will be remembered that the group of islands in the Pacific in which the explorer Magellan had met his death, though situated well to the westward of the line of demarcation established by the treaty of Saragossa in 1529, had been virtually neglected by the Portuguese within whose waters they admittedly lay; but that in 1542 the Emperor had sent out an expedition from Mexico, which had further explored them, and had christened them the Philippines, in honor of the heir to the throne.[3] This expedition, however, had made no attempt to conquer or to colonize; it had merely asserted a legally invalid Spanish title by labelling the islands with a

---

[1] Quesada, *La Vida Intelectual en la America Española*, pp. 43–45, 74–77. The insistence of the Viceroy Toledo (cf. *ante*, p. 217) that priests in charge of the *doctrinas* should know the native dialects was principally a means to that ultimate end.

[2] *Ibid.*, pp. 131 f.

[3] Cf. *ante*, Vol. III, pp. 453–456 and map opposite p. 433.

Spanish name. The first serious effort to bring the archipelago under the dominion of the Spanish crown was not
made until twenty-two years later, in 1564.

The change of rulers and the pressure of affairs in Europe
are perhaps adequate to explain this long delay; but when
Philip got back to Spain after the conclusion of the treaty
of Cateau-Cambrésis in 1559, he at once took up the problem of Spain's possessions in the Pacific. It seems natural
to assume that the chief consideration which impelled him
to do so was the prospect that he might some day be able to
realize the dream of his ancestors by reannexing the kingdom
of Portugal, and thus acquire its dominions across the seas.
Obviously the time was not yet ripe; for the title of King
Sebastian could not be impugned, and Philip was not the
man to act without legal justification. On the other hand,
the Portuguese monarch had already given evidence of an
instability which augured ill for a long duration of his reign;
there was no prospect of a lineal heir, and if the opportunity
to act should suddenly arise, it would be of inestimable
advantage to the Prudent King to have an established base
in close proximity to the Portuguese dominions in the Orient.
At any rate, on September 24, 1559, Philip sent orders to
Luis de Velasco, the viceroy of New Spain, to organize and
send out an expedition for the discovery of the islands of the
West, "hazia los Malucos," but enjoined him to be particularly careful not to trespass on Portuguese territory.[1] On
the same day the king also wrote to a certain Augustinian
then resident in Mexico, named Andrés de Urdaneta, desiring him to accompany the expedition in the capacity of chief
navigator.[2] The reason for this choice was the fact that
Urdaneta had made a reputation for himself as a mathemati-
cian and cosmographer before he turned monk, and had

---

[1] *D. I. I.*, 2d ser., ii, pp. 94–97.   [2] *Ibid.*, pp. 98–100.

accompanied Loaysa's expedition to the Moluccas in 1525 and remained in the Orient till 1536. Urdaneta accepted in an interesting letter of May 28, 1560; [1] moreover, it seems to have been largely in order to please him that the supreme command of the expedition was given by Velasco to Miguel López de Legazpi, the scion of an ancient family of Guipúzcoa, who had lived in Mexico since 1532 : [2] a wise and generous man, who apparently sold most of his own property in order to help defray the costs of the enterprise.[3] His armada consisted of two galleons and two pataches, "the best that had been launched on the Southern Sea, and the stoutest and best equipped"; [4] they carried upwards of 350 persons, comprising soldiers, sailors, four Augustinians who accompanied Urdaneta in order to convert the heathen, and also a few servants. The expedition was practically ready in the end of 1563, and lay at Navidad awaiting orders to sail; but the illness of the viceroy, and a number of other delays of the typical Spanish brand, postponed its departure till November 21, 1564.[5]

Good fortune accompanied the adventurers on the voyage out. They touched at the Marshall and Ladrones groups, and solemnly took possession of them in the name of Spain.[6] When they reached the Philippines they were generally received by the natives in friendly fashion, as soon as they made it clear that they were not Portuguese.[7] On April 27–30, 1565,[8] they landed at Cebú, where Magellan had been

[1] D. I. I., 2d ser., ii, pp. 106–109.
[2] Ibid., p. 116; cf. also The Philippine Islands, ii, p. 83.
[3] Montero y Vidal, Historia General de Filipinas, i, p. 30.
[4] D. I. I., 2d ser., ii, p. 141; The Philippine Islands, ii, pp. 89 f.
[5] J. A. Robertson, "Legazpi and Philippine Colonization," in Annual Report of the American Historical Association, 1907, i, p. 149; Montero

y Vidal, i, p. 30; Fermín de Uncilla, "Felipe II y las Islas Filipinas," in Ciudad de Dios, xlvii (1898), pp. 186–202.
[6] Robertson, loc. cit., p. 151; The Philippine Islands, ii, pp. 108 f.; Montero y Vidal, i, p. 31.
[7] Robertson, loc. cit., pp. 151 f., and references there.
[8] The Philippine Islands, ii, p. 119; Montero y Vidal, i, p. 32.

given an amicable reception;[1] there, in the centre of the archipelago, Legazpi determined to establish his headquarters for the time being, and the discovery by one of his followers of an image of the Saviour, doubtless left there by the expedition of Magellan, was taken by all hands to be a highly favorable omen.[2]   In fact, the only serious misfortune which the adventurers had thus far encountered had been the desertion during the voyage out, on November 30, 1564, of Captain Alonso de Arellano with the patache *San Lucas*.[3] He had hurried on ahead of the rest to the Philippines, where he took aboard a cargo of cinnamon.   He had then hastened back to Mexico, in the hope of gaining for himself all the credit for the undertaking; and it was doubtless partly with the idea of checkmating his designs, as well as in compliance with the orders which had been given him at his departure, that Legazpi, on June 1, sent back his flagship, with Fray Urdaneta on board, to report what had already been accomplished.[4]   Urdaneta and Arellano finally encountered one another at court in Spain, where the former succeeded in establishing his case, while the latter was remanded to Mexico to be put on trial for his desertion.   Soon afterwards Urdaneta also returned to Mexico, and died there, at the age of seventy, on June 3, 1568.[5]   He was one of the noblest and most efficient clerics in the annals of the Spanish Empire beyond the seas, and deserves a large share of the credit for the enterprise which led to the conquest of the Philippines.

[1] Cf. *ante*, Vol. III, p. 434.

[2] Robertson, *loc. cit.*, p. 152. The fort around which the settlement was grouped was dedicated to the 'name of Jesus' in honor of the discovery of this image (*The Philippine Islands*, ii, pp. 120 f.).   The settlement itself was called San Miguel, "because it was founded on the day [May 8] of his apparition": *D. I. I.*, 2d ser., ii, pp. 336 f. It is today the town of Cebú;

cf. Haring, *Trade and Navigation*, p. 144.

[3] *D. I. I.*, 2d ser., ii, p. 222; *The Philippine Islands*, ii, pp. 105–107; Robertson, *loc. cit.*, p. 151.

[4] H. H. Bancroft, *History of Mexico*, ii, p. 600.

[5] *D. I. I.*, 2d ser., pp. 222 f., note; Montero y Vidal, i, p. 33.   Cf. also the life of Urdaneta in the *Enciclopedia Universal Ilustrada*, lxv, pp. 1406 f., and references there.

Meantime in the archipelago Legazpi and his followers were wrestling with the usual problems incident to the occupation and settlement of newly acquired lands. He had some difficulty in maintaining discipline among his own men; the example of Arellano had made many of them insubordinate, and severe punishments were necessary to hold them to their allegiance. There was also, curiously enough, great scarcity of provisions, and expeditions to the neighboring islands had to be organized to obtain them; but for the most part the natives showed themselves friendly and willing to supply the newcomers' needs. Ships passed back and forth several times in the course of the next three years between the archipelago and New Spain,[1] and Legazpi was particularly rejoiced when, on August 30, 1568, two galleons appeared from Acapulco with troops, munitions, and supplies. They arrived, indeed, in the nick of time; for in the very next month a Portuguese squadron came across from the Moluccas with the purpose of forcing the Spaniards to withdraw. After trying unsuccessfully to effect their ends by persuasion, they had recourse to arms, attempting to blockade the port of Cebú and destroying the villages of those natives who had befriended the Spaniards. Nothing, however, was accomplished by these means, and after three months the intruders retired.[2] The Spaniards were also much occupied with the repulse of piratical attacks from the native corsairs of Borneo and Jolo. At the same time they made steady progress with the exploration and conquest of the larger islands of the archipelago. Two expeditions were sent south to Mindanao, rather for the purpose of obtaining cinnamon than of making a settlement; and Panay, where

[1] A ship left the Philippines to carry letters to Philip on July 1, 1568: cf. *The Philippine Islands*, iii, pp. 29, 33.

[2] Accounts of this affair by Guido de Lavezares and Legazpi are given in *The Philippine Islands*, iii, pp. 30 f., 44–46.

the natives were generally friendly and willing to be instructed in the Christian faith, was brought under Spanish domination in 1569.[1]

Much more serious, however, proved the problem of gaining possession of the northern island of Luzon. Until it should be definitely in Spanish hands, the conquest of the archipelago could not be regarded as complete; and in the spring of 1570 a party of 120 Spaniards and a few native auxiliaries commanded by Martín de Goiti, Legazpi's campmaster, was sent out to reconnoitre.[2] Legazpi's grandson, Juan de Salcedo, who had come out from Mexico in 1567,[3] at the age of eighteen, and whose gallantry was afterwards to give him the name of 'Cortés of the Philippines,' also accompanied the expedition. Guided by a Moslem pilot, they reached Manila Bay, and at once perceived its advantages for the founding of a city; they were also received at first with great friendliness by the two local rulers, Soliman and Lacandola. The first named, however, proved treacherous. As soon as the newcomers were lulled into a sense of security he attacked them unawares, but fortunately the Spaniards were able to beat him off, and afterwards, assuming the offensive, to capture a fort which he had erected near by. In the course of these operations evidence was found that the natives had been aided in their resistance by the Portuguese.[4] Since it was obvious that the task of conquering Luzon would demand large reënforcements, the Spaniards after some further reconnoitring returned to Cebú. During their absence a letter had been received from Spain,

[1] Montero y Vidal, i, p. 35.
[2] The standard contemporary account of the conquest of Luzon is anonymous. It is printed in the *Archivo del Bibliófilo Filipino*, iv, pp. 1–37, and, in translation, in *The Philippine Islands*, iii, pp. 141–172.
[3] So *The Philippine Islands*, iii, p. 73,

note; Montero y Vidal, i, p. 34, makes it 1568.
[4] At least so Montero y Vidal, i, p. 36; I can find no evidence of it in the official contemporary account as given in *The Philippine Islands*, iii, pp. 73–104.

bringing the royal confirmation of Legazpi's title of governor and captain-general, and establishing his authority in his new domain.[1] He was occupied at the moment with the founding of a city at Cebú, and with the conversion of the natives there ; but the conquest of Luzon was of still greater importance, and so an expedition, under Legazpi's command, consisting of twenty-seven vessels, large and small, carrying 230 arquebusiers, was speedily organized, and left for the north on Easter Monday, April 16, 1571. After touching at Masbate and Mindoro on the way, Legazpi reached Manila on May 16.[2] When the natives knew that the governor had come with his entire force to settle the land, they burnt their villages and took flight ; [3] but Legazpi soon succeeded in getting in touch with them, and on discovering that he proposed to treat them well if they would recognize his authority, the majority soon decided to give him their allegiance. The rajah Soliman, indeed, continued to stir up trouble, but Goiti and Salcedo put down every insurrection. Meantime, on June 3, Legazpi "gave the title of city to this colony of Manila," whose name he left unchanged ; [4] and on the twenty-fourth he formally erected it into a municipality after the traditional Spanish pattern with *cabildo, alcaldes, alguaciles,* and *regidores* ; moreover he announced that in accordance with his Majesty's desire, he would give lands and *repartimientos* to those who wished to settle there.[5] In the course of the next year, Goiti and Salcedo brought most of the rest of the island under subjection. The Augustinians labored hard at the task of converting the natives, while Legazpi was chiefly occupied with the important matter of establishing and regulating com-

[1] *The Philippine Islands*, iii, pp. 62–66. The letter is dated at Madrid, August 14, 1569.
[2] Contemporary account in *The*

Philippine Islands, iii, p. 153.
[3] *Ibid.*, p. 153.
[4] *Ibid.*, pp. 173 f.
[5] *Ibid.*, p. 155.

mercial relations with the Chinese, whom he had found in large numbers on his arrival, and whose trade he was most anxious to get away from the Portuguese. He died on August 20, 1572, universally respected both by the natives and by his own people, one of the most attractive of Spanish empire builders, whose preference for peaceful rather than warlike methods stands out in agreeable contrast to the policies of most of the *conquistadores* in the New World.

On the death of Legazpi the government of the Philippines devolved upon his faithful lieutenant and camp-master, Guido de Lavezares, who had first visited the archipelago with Villalobos twenty-nine years before, and who had been acting as governor of Cebú while Legazpi was conquering Luzon.[1] Further progress was made in the conquest of the small islands during the three years of his rule, but the most notable events of that period occurred in connection with his dealings with the Chinese. The Spaniards were convinced that China possessed fabulous wealth;[2] they therefore strove their hardest to facilitate their own trade with it, to the prejudice of the Portuguese, who naturally did their utmost to prevent them. In an account of the Philippines which Lavezares sent back to Philip from Manila on June 29, 1573, he writes that "last year Chinese vessels came to this city to trade, and told us how the Portuguese had asked them not to trade with us, because we were robbers and came to steal and commit other depredations, so that these people wonder not a little if this be true. As the treatment accorded to the Chinese neutralizes these reports, more vessels came this year than last, and each year more will come."[3]   Even

[1] A. de Morga, *The Philippine Islands*, tr. H. E. J. Stanley, pp. 21 f.; Montero y Vidal, i, p. 70.

[2] Cf. the *carta-relación* written by Domingo de Salazar in 1590, which is printed in *Archivo del Bibliófilo Filipino*, iii, pp. 47–80.

[3] *The Philippine Islands*, iii, p. 182. Cf. also Cesáreo Fernández Duro, *Armada Española*, iii, pp. 59 f.

more important than the governor's direct efforts to encourage commercial relations between the Philippines and the Celestial Empire were the services which he rendered to both by his defeat of the famous pirate Li-Ma-Hong. This savage corsair, who had made so much trouble for the Chinese Emperor that he no longer felt safe on the shores of Asia, had determined to found an empire of his own in the Philippines, and in November, 1574, he appeared off Manila with a huge fleet and an army of soldiers and prospective colonists.[1] Salcedo, by far the best soldier that the Spaniards had, was absent at the time, with a large force, on an expedition farther north against Vigan, and the pirate's first assaults on Manila were only repulsed with great difficulty. But before Li-Ma-Hong could return to the attack with larger forces, Salcedo got back, and with his aid Lavezares defeated the invader, this time decisively, so that Li-Ma-Hong, abandoning his efforts against Manila, sailed away to the northward, in the hope of establishing a base for himself in Pangasinán. Salcedo, however, pursued him with a fleet, besieged him in the fortification that he had erected on the shore, and finally (August 3, 1575) completely routed his forces, so that the pirate, after murdering most of his men that remained alive, took flight, half famished, in a small canoe, and never ventured to molest the Spaniards again. It was a notable triumph, which greatly enhanced the reputation of Spain in the Orient, and a fitting culmination of the career of Juan de Salcedo, to whom the victory was chiefly due. He died March 11, 1576, of a fever, on his *encomienda* in Luzon, at the early age of twenty-seven, a striking exception to that decline of the fighting prowess of the individual Spaniard which is generally observable in the period of Philip II,

[1] Fernández Duro, *Armada Española*, iii, p. 56.

and was of such ominous portent for the future of the Spanish Empire.[1]

In August, 1575, Lavezares resigned his functions to Francisco de Sande, *alcalde* of the audiencia of Mexico, who had been sent out by the crown as governor of the Philippines, and six other royal representatives succeeded him in turn in that office before the death of Philip II.[2] We have no space to go into the individual achievements of each of these men, but a few general remarks may not be out of place. Their tenure of office was usually quite short, on the average less than four years, considerably less than the actual, if not the legal term of the viceroys of New Spain and of New Castile ; and its shortness is but one more of the innumerable evidences of Philip's perpetual fear lest his representatives in dominions so remote would tend, if allowed to remain long at their posts, to get out of hand, and strike out along lines of their own. There is also a significant alternation of the man of action and the constitutional administrator, of the soldier and the *letrado*, which may be taken as an evidence that Philip now regarded the conquest as virtually complete, and that consequently, in the Philippines as in the New World, he was tending to replace the *conquistadores* with men of less daring and greater dependence on himself. The fact that he became sovereign of Portugal and her dominions in 1580 relieved him from the fear of attack from his original

[1] Montero y Vidal, i, pp. 70–79; Fernández Duro, *Armada Española*, iii, pp. 55–59.

[2] Sande was followed in April, 1580, by Gonzalo Ronquillo de Peñalosa, who died in March, 1583. In May, 1584, the first audiencia (cf. below, p. 235) arrived, and lasted till May, 1590, when a new governor, Gómez Pérez Dasmariñas, came out with an order for its suppression. During the period of the audiencia its president, Santiago de Vera, was *de facto* governor of the Philippines. Dasmariñas was assassinated by the Chinese in October, 1593, and his son Luis took charge until June 11, 1595, when a new governor, Antonio de Morga, arrived from Spain. Morga, in turn, was succeeded (June 1, 1596) by Francisco Tello de Guzmán, who held office till May 8, 1598, when the audiencia was reëstablished. Cf. A. de Morga, *op. cit.*, pp. 22–91.

rivals in the Orient. Save for the peril from English and Dutch adventurers, which did not become serious until after his death, he and his representatives were henceforth free to devote themselves wholly to the problem of dealing with the natives, and with their neighbors in the adjacent islands and in China and Japan. Another noteworthy evidence, likewise paralleled in the New World, that the era of conquest was regarded as past, and that of assimilation to the Spanish Empire begun, was the establishment, in May, 1583, of the first royal audiencia of Manila.[1] It was set up as a result of advice to Philip from Gonzalo Ronquillo, who had been sent out as governor to replace Sande in 1580, and died in the Philippines in March, 1583; it was composed of a president, three *oidores*, and an attorney-general, but it led a very checkered existence in its early years.[2] In May, 1590, Gómez Pérez Dasmariñas, one of the most notable governors the Philippines ever had, brought out with him a decree for its suppression,[3] but after his murder in 1593 it was set up again, and continued, without interruption, till 1898.[4] A letter from the archbishop of Manila, written in 1624, assures us that the reason for its reëstablishment was the king's fear "lest in regions so remote the governors might become too absolute," [5] and there can be little doubt that he told the truth. The ups and downs of the early history of the audiencia at Manila were also closely connected with

[1] *Recopilación de Leyes de las Indias*, lib. ii, tit. xv, ley xi; *The Philippine Islands*, v, pp. 274–318; vi, pp. 35–44.

[2] Montero y Vidal, i, pp. 88–94; C. H. Cunningham, *The Audiencia in the Spanish Colonies as Illustrated by the Audiencia of Manila* (Berkeley, 1919), pp. 48–55.

[3] The decree is dated August 9, 1589. Cf. *The Philippine Islands*, vii, pp. 141–172, 208–211; Cunningham, *op. cit.*, p. 71.

[4] The date of the decree for its reëstablishment as given in *The Philippine Islands*, ix, pp. 189–192, is November 26, 1595; in the margin of the *Recopilación de Leyes de las Indias*, lib. ii, tit. xv, ley xi, it is given as May 25, 1596. The number of the *oidores* was raised, at the same time, to four. *Ibid.*, and Cunningham, p. 78.

[5] *The Philippine Islands*, ix, p. 191, note 28.

the development of the relationship between the Philippines and the viceroyalty of New Spain. The authorities at Mexico never ceased to look upon the archipelago as forming a part of their own domain, and resented any measure which tended to give it independence. The audiencia at Manila considered itself the symbol of such independence and coequal in all respects with that of New Spain, so that the two bodies regarded one another with hostility from the very first.[1]

On the side of exploration and relations with the adjacent Oriental powers, the last twenty-five years of the reign of the Prudent King witnessed numerous proofs of the mounting prestige of Spain in the Far East. In the Philippines themselves the most significant event of these years was the attempt to conquer and subdue the Moros of Mindanao, who had not yet acknowledged the authority of the Spanish crown. This task was undertaken in 1596 by a captain named Esteban Rodríguez de Figueroa, as a private enterprise at his own expense; the king in return gave him the title of governor, and full possession of the island for two lifetimes, provided he could accomplish his purpose.[2] He left Iloilo in April with a force of 214 men, and landed at Illana Bay, where he was generally well received by the natives; but on attempting to penetrate inland, he fell into an ambush and was slain. As his camp-master, Juan de Jara, was unable to carry through the conquest without reënforcements, the government at Manila sent out Juan de Ronquillo with a force of 400 men to help him. Meantime the Moros made every preparation to resist, and sought aid from the small island of Ternate farther south, whose inhabitants had been hostile to the Spaniards since the days of Magellan. But

---

[1] Cunningham, *op. cit.*, pp. 67–70.
[2] Montero y Vidal, i, p. 108; Fernández Duro, *Armada Española*, iii, p. 65, and references there.

Ronquillo defeated the ships that were bringing over the enemy contingent, and was well on his way to the subjugation of Mindanao, when he unaccountably lost heart, and, availing himself of an authorization received from Manila before the government there had been fully apprised of the victories he had won, abandoned his post and withdrew with all his troops.[1] Though he was officially acquitted by a court martial on his return, the consequences of his conduct were lamentable in the extreme. It encouraged the Moros and also the natives of the adjacent island of Jolo, all of whom were on the point of submitting to Spain, to persist in their struggle to maintain independence, and necessitated a number of subsequent expeditions and the loss of many lives, to complete the conquest of Mindanao during the ensuing years.[2]

More impressive were the demonstrations of Spanish power in the lands and islands beyond the limits of the archipelago. Many of these were made possible by embassies from native rulers to beg support against hated rivals, the same sort of situation as the Spaniards often utilized to their own advantage in North Africa and in the New World. Thus an appeal from the king of Borneo for aid against a brother who had dethroned him led, in 1578, to a Spanish expedition to that island, and the recognition of Spanish authority by the ruler whom it restored to power.[3] Requests for support from the king of Cambodia against his enemy, the king of Siam, brought Spanish troops to the mainland in 1596, and again in 1598; but though they greatly impressed the natives by their valor, they gained no

[1] Montero y Vidal, i, pp. 108–115.
[2] *Ibid.*, pp. 139 ff., *passim.*
[3] Cf. contemporary accounts in *The Philippine Islands*, iv, pp. 148–303; Montero y Vidal, i, pp. 82–84. The restored ruler was apparently once more dethroned by his brother, with Portuguese aid, in 1581, only to be again reinstated by the Spaniards.

permanent advantage.[1] Constant efforts were also made to subjugate the Moluccas and gain full control of the spice trade. These began with a large expedition sent out at Philip's command in 1582; but the climate, the consistent opposition of the inhabitants of Ternate, and the tradition of Portuguese hostility, which was kept alive till long after the annexation and evinced itself in native conspiracies and plots stirred up by Portuguese agency, prevented the full realization of these projects in Philip's day, and caused the deaths of many gallant men; moreover the reign was hardly over before the Dutch appeared to challenge the Spanish claims.[2] — With Japan there was an inconclusive and somewhat ridiculous exchange of communications. The Japanese emperor demanded that the Spaniards in the Philippines unreservedly acknowledge themselves to be his vassals, and was with difficulty persuaded that they had no intention of so doing. The Spaniards at Manila were equally determined to bring Christianity to Japan, and despatched a number of Franciscan friars for that purpose; but as both sides were resolved to maintain trade relations with one another, their political and religious divergencies did not lead to any fighting.[3] All these items go to prove that the Philippines had now become a solid outpost of the power of Spain in the Pacific. Her ability to hold them was no longer in any doubt. They were henceforth to be a base whence further expeditions could be sent forth, and whither all Spaniards in the Orient could repair for aid.[4]

During all the period of conquest and colonization the work of converting the natives went steadily forward. Indeed, it

[1] Montero y Vidal, i, pp. 101–105, 119–121; Fernández Duro, *Armada Española*, iii, pp. 135–150.

[2] Montero y Vidal, i, pp. 85–88, 98; Fernández Duro, *Armada Española*, iii, pp. 64 f.

[3] Montero y Vidal, i, pp. 96–98.

[4] As did, for example, the remnants of the expedition of Mendaña in 1596. Cf. *ante*, p. 185, and Montero y Vidal, i, p. 108.

would probably be safe to say that the missionary activities of the early Spaniards in the Philippines were even more vigorous and extensive than those of their compatriots in the New World. The Augustinians, as we have seen, were the first in the field, and down to 1577 had it all to themselves. In that year the first Franciscans arrived; [1] in 1581 the first Jesuits; [2] and six years later, the first party of Dominicans.[3] There was naturally keen rivalry among the different orders for the glory of making the largest number of converts, not only in the Philippines and in the adjacent islands, but also in China, which was visited by the Augustinians in 1575 and by the Dominicans in 1590; but the Jesuits resented the arrival of these newcomers as an invasion of their own domain, and in 1595 succeeded in putting a stop to it. They also managed to limit the monastic rivalries in the Philippines by having each of the different regions in the archipelago allotted to a separate order; moreover, they persuaded their general, Aquaviva, to erect the Philippines into a 'vice-province,' and to place one of the ablest of their leaders, Antonio Sedeño, at the head of it.[4] In the Philippines the society might be seen at its very best. Its members showed none of the unscrupulousness that gained them an evil name in Europe; they devoted themselves effectively and whole-heartedly to the accomplishment of a noble task. They were not satisfied with merely eliciting from the natives formal acceptance of a faith which they did not comprehend. They sought to instruct them not only to understand the tenets of the Christian religion, but also to live cleaner and better lives, and to practise the arts of a higher civilization.[5]

[1] Cf. anonymous "Entrada de la Seráphica Religión de nuestro P. S. Francisco en las Islas Philipinas" in *Archivo del Bibliófilo Filipino*, i, no. 3.

[2] *The Philippine Islands*, iv, p. 316, note 46; Montero y Vidal, i, p. 85, note.

[3] *Ibid.*, p. 89.

[4] *Ibid.*, pp. 76 f., 90, 107.

[5] One of the viceroys of Mexico is said to have remarked that "in every friar in the Philippines the king has a captain-general and an entire army." José Burniol, *History of the Philippines* (Manila, 1912), p. 85.

The progress of the archipelago during the last two decades
of the sixteenth century was also steady and rapid from the
economic point of view.   The era of restrictions such as had
fettered Spanish-American commerce since the time of the
Catholic Kings did not become fully operative in the Philippines until the seventeenth century, though the direct trade
of the archipelago with South America was apparently forbidden before 1590, while three years later that with Mexico
was limited to two ships a year, neither to exceed 300 tons
burden, a foretaste of what was to come.[1]   *Corsarios Luteranos*, the ubiquitous pest of the Spaniards in America,
were mostly out of the picture here.   A richly laden Manila
galleon was captured, indeed, off the western coast of Mexico,
in November, 1587, by Thomas Cavendish, who, after disposing of his booty and burning his prize, continued calmly
on across the Pacific, through the Philippines, and eluded
all attempts to intercept him;[2] but with this notable exception, the archipelago in this period was practically undisturbed by European sea-rovers.   The colonists, moreover,
were determined to prevent their happy lot from being ruined
by royal exactions.   In 1589 they persuaded the king to consent that a tenth, instead of the accustomed fifth, of the
gold collected in the Philippines be appropriated by the
crown, and that the natives be exempt from all payment.[3]
They were also desirous of uprooting the Portuguese tradition of enslaving the Filipinos, and their representations
procured a royal order that no one be permitted to make
new slaves, that the children of all existing slaves be born free,
and that any slave should be allowed to purchase his freedom
at a price to be fixed by the governor and the bishop.[4]

[1] Haring, *Trade and Navigation*,
pp. 144–149.
[2] Cf. the life of Cavendish in the
Dictionary of National Biography, and
references there.   The Spaniards called
him 'Candis.'
[3] Montero y Vidal, i, p. 91.
[4] Montero y Vidal, i, p. 92; also
The Philippine Islands, vi, pp. 157–

Altogether one derives the impression that at the end of the reign of the Prudent King the Philippines were both prosperous and happy.[1] There had been none of the revolting slaughter at the time of the conquest which stained the institution of Spanish rule in Mexico and Peru. The advance of commerce and civilization had been easier and more rapid. Natives and colonists were generally content, and as yet virtually undisturbed by the advent of European rivals. The archipelago had been acquired with far less effort than the American lands, and it appeared that correspondingly little work would be necessary to hold it and to raise it to the standards of European civilization. It exemplifies the contrast between the slacker, easier existence of the Orient, and the more strenuous life of the America of today, and makes a pleasing exception to the generally far less fortunate conditions which obtained in the rest of the Spanish Empire at the time of Philip's death.

233, and vii, pp. 141–172. Manila was erected into an episcopal see by Pope Gregory XIII in 1581, and raised to the rank of an archbishopric in 1595. Three other bishoprics were founded in the Philippines before the death of Philip II. Cf. Gams, *Series Episcoporum*, pp. 113–115.

[1] Fermín de Uncilla in *Ciudad de Dios*, xlvii (1898), pp. 201 f.

BIBLIOGRAPHICAL NOTE

It seems unnecessary to enumerate again those standard sources and secondary authorities on the Spaniards in America and the Pacific which have been listed in the bibliographical notes to Chapters XXVII–XXX in Volume III of the present work. The following, however, which are of special interest for the period under review, may be added here.

Sources. — The principal contemporary accounts of the struggle between the Spanish and French in Florida — various " Relaciones," the " Memoriales " and " Cartas " of Menéndez de Avilés, the " Memorial " of Gonzalo Solís de Merás, and the " Vida y Hechos de Pero Menéndez de Avilés " by Bartolomé Barrientos — are to be found in Eugenio Ruidíaz y Caravia's *La Florida, su Conquista y Colonización por Pedro Menéndez de Avilés* (Madrid, 1893, 2 vols.), and in Genaro García's *Dos Antiguas Relaciones de la Florida* (Mexico, 1902); but they have been so carefully analyzed and compared by the late Woodbury Lowery on pp. v–xv of his *Spanish Settlements within the Present Limits of the United States, Florida, 1562–1574* (New York, 1905), that it scarcely seems worth while to discuss them here. The most important original materials that have been published since Woodbury Lowery wrote are *The Luna Papers*, vol. i, tr. and ed. H. I. Priestley (Deland, Florida, 1928), and *Colonial Records of Spanish Florida*, tr. and ed. Jeannette Thurber Connor (Deland, 1925–30, 2 vols.); the first deals with the unlucky expedition of 1559–61, and the second contains some material on Menéndez de Avilés during the last four years of his life. The *Dépêches* of M. de Fourquevaux, ed. Célestin Douais (Paris, 1896–1904, 3 vols.), are of capital importance for the story of the reception of the news in Europe. — In South America Pedro Sarmiento de Gamboa's *History of the Incas* and Baltasar de Ocampo's *Execution of the Inca Tupac Amaru* are useful for the history of Peru; both were admirably edited, in translation, with notes and an introduction, by Sir Clements R. Markham for the Hakluyt Society in 1907. Markham translated Ocampo's work from a manuscript in the British Museum, and Sarmiento's from the first edition of the text, published with introduction and notes by Richard Pietschmann at Berlin in 1906. Roberto Levillier's *La Audiencia de Charcas, Correspondencia de Presidentes y Oidores*, tom. i, 1561–79 (Madrid, 1918), is a notable collection of documents, and is valuable for many other purposes besides that indicated by its title; and his *Audiencia de Lima*, tom. i, 1549–64 (Madrid, 1922), is also useful. The *Relaciones de los Vireyes y Audiencias que han gobernado el Perú*

(Lima and Madrid, 1867–72, 3 vols.) and Ricardo Beltrán y Rózpide's *Colección de las Memorias o Relaciones que escribieron los Virreyes del Perú*, tom. i (Madrid, 1921), are likewise indispensable for the matters with which they deal. — The most important sources for the history of the Philippines in this period are to be found in volumes ii-ix, xv, xvi, of *The Philippine Islands, 1493–1898*, edd. Emma Helen Blair and J. A. Robertson (Cleveland, 1903–09, 55 vols.); in volumes ii and iii of the *D. I. I.*, 2d series; and in the *Archivo del Bibliófilo Filipino, Recopilación de Documentos*, ed. W. E. Retana (Madrid, 1895–1905, 5 vols.). Most of what is given in Spanish in the last two of these collections appears in translation in the first, and a great deal more besides, particularly on constitutional, economic, and religious conditions, and the prefaces are also valuable; still it is often worth while to examine the originals. The standard contemporary history of the period is that of Antonio de Morga, *Sucesos de las Islas Filipinas* (Mexico, 1609; later edited by José Rizal, Paris, 1890, and W. E. Retana, Madrid, 1909). This is too brief to be of much value before the death of Legazpi; after that it is indispensable. I have used the translation of H. E. J. Stanley (Hakluyt Society, 1868); a later translation appeared in *The Philippine Islands, 1493–1898*, xv, xvi (Cleveland, 1904). — *The Discovery of the Solomon Islands by Alvaro de Mendaña in 1568*, edd. Lord Amherst of Hackney and Basil Thomson (Hakluyt Society, 2d series, no. vii, London, 1901, 2 vols.), is a useful translation of original Spanish narratives of Mendaña's expedition; and Zelia Nuttall's *New Light on Drake* (same series, no. xxxiv, 1914), Joan de Castellanos's *Discurso de el Capitán Francisco Draque*, ed. Ángel González Palencia (Madrid, 1921), and Martín del Barco Centenera's heroic poem *Argentina y Conquista del Rio de la Plata*, in twenty-eight cantos (Lisbon, 1602; edd. Juan María Gutiérrez and Enrique Peña, Buenos Aires, 1912), show the attitude of the Spaniard of Philip's day toward the English sea-rovers.

Later Works. — The two volumes of Woodbury Lowery, *The Spanish Settlements within the Present Limits of the United States, 1513–1561* (New York, 1901), and *The Spanish Settlements within the Present Limits of the United States, Florida, 1562–1574* (New York, 1905), supersede everything (including Parkman) that was previously written on the subject, and are destined to remain the standard authority for many years to come. For South America, volumes ii and iii of Diego Barros Arana's *Historia Jeneral de Chile* (Santiago de Chile, 1884–1902), Ricardo Levene's *Lecciones de Historia Argentina*, 4ª ed., i (Buenos Aires, 1919), the *Manual de Historia de la Civilización Argentina*, ordenado por R. D. Carbia, i (Buenos Aires, 1917), and H. C.

Lea's *The Inquisition in the Spanish Dependencies* (New York, 1908) are all standard works.   Useful monographs of a more special nature are Paul Groussac, *Mendoza y Garay, Las Dos Fundaciones de Buenos Aires, 1536–1580*, 2ª ed. (Buenos Aires, 1916); Alejandro Audibert, *Los Límites de la Antigua Provincia del Paraguay* (Buenos Aires, 1892); Lillian Estelle Fisher, *Viceregal Administration in the Spanish-American Colonies* (Berkeley, California, 1926);   Enrique Ruíz Guiñazú, *La Magistratura Indiana* (Buenos Aires, 1916);   V. G. Quesada, *La Vida Intelectual en la America Española durante los Siglos XVI, XVII, y XVIII* (Buenos Aires, 1910); Felipe Barreda y Laos, *Vida Intelectual de la Colonia* (Lima, 1909); J. T. Medina, *El Piloto Juan Fernández* (Santiago de Chile, 1918); and Georg Friederici, *Álvaro de Mendaña: Die Entdeckung der Inseln des Salomo* (Stuttgart, 1925).   The only modern work on the Philippines which deserves serious consideration is the *Historia General de Filipinas* by José Montero y Vidal (Madrid, 1887–95, 3 vols.).   Many of its statements are unsupported by any trustworthy evidence, and it is very careless in matters of chronology; with these reservations, however, it may be used to considerable advantage.   The names of many other works of too special a nature to be listed here will be found at the appropriate places in the footnotes.

CHAPTER XXXIV

SPAIN IN WESTERN EUROPE, 1559–78

THE story of Spain's foreign policy during the first two decades of the reign of Philip II revolves chiefly around the development of her relations with England and with France, while the course of her dealings with these two nations is at all times powerfully affected by the fluctuations of the struggle for the maintenance of Spanish authority in the Netherlands. The Low Countries, as has already been observed, were the focal point of Western Europe during the second half of the sixteenth century; and though no part of them attained recognized independence till long after the period covered by the present chapter, it will be clearer to treat of them in connection with Spain's foreign affairs than to consider them, where they perhaps more logically belong, as a part of the internal problems of the Spanish Empire.

Taking the period in question as a whole — that is, the twenty years that elapsed between the return of Philip to Spain in 1559, and the assumption by Cardinal Granvelle of the post of chief minister in 1579 — it is fair to say that the dominant principle of the Spanish monarch's foreign policy was to avoid aggressive action, and to preserve the status quo; politically speaking, he was content to maintain that attitude of 'sturdy defensiveness' which had been recommended to him by his father. In matters of religion, there was indeed a somewhat different tale to tell. So deep was the king's detestation of heresy that whenever he was offered an opportunity to suppress it, he found it next to impossible to hold his hand; and so close was the fusion of religion and politics in the period under review, that a blow for the faith was often difficult to distinguish from a move for the aggrandizement of Spain. But on the whole, during the first half of his reign, Philip did not play the aggressor. He asked nothing better than to leave his French and English neighbors alone, provided they would forbear to breed trouble for him and to imperil Catholicism by concessions to heretics. Certainly he contemplated no further conquests at their expense.

There were of course many ebbs and flows. It is interesting to observe, as the panorama gradually unfolds itself, how closely those ebbs and flows corresponded with the character of the successive administrations of the Low Countries. When Philip's representatives there were conciliatory, Spain's relations with England and France, if not cordial, were at least tolerable; whenever the Netherlanders were up in arms, there were echoes of the conflict both in London and in Paris. We shall therefore do well to begin our investigation of this complicated period with an examination of the state in which Philip left his Burgundian dominions when he departed for Spain in 1559.

Two preliminary observations are indispensable in order to enable the modern reader to envisage the problem of these Burgundian territories as it presented itself to the Spanish king; and the first is concerned with their geographical extent. So largely is the interest of the period concentrated in the Low Countries, that one is likely to forget that the lands which Philip had inherited from his Burgundian forbears included not only the seventeen provinces of the Netherlands, corresponding roughly to modern Belgium and Holland, but also the Free County of Burgundy to the southward. The two blocks of territory were separated by many miles, and a journey between their respective capitals, in the sixteenth century, occupied an average of fourteen or fifteen days.[1] The administrations of the two holdings had drifted steadily apart under the Emperor, and were now, for all practical purposes, separate. It is true that the Spanish monarch's representative in the Low Countries was also in theory chief ruler under the crown of Franche Comté; but as that representative continued to reside in Brussels and never visited Besançon or Dôle, his practical importance in the county was almost nil, and his functions passed to the royal agents on the ground.[2] On the other hand, one cannot afford to lose all sight of the southern holding while one studies the more dramatic events in the Netherlands. If administratively speaking they had now, for all practical purposes, fallen apart, they had their roots in a common past. Many of the great houses whose scions were to play prominent roles in the approaching struggle in the Low Countries traced their origins back to Franche Comté. The Granvelles came from Besançon, and William the Silent inherited the name of Orange from that of the foremost family in the county, whose last direct descendant was his elder cousin, René, slain before St. Dizier in 1544. Moreover, Franche Comté was an indispensable link, a military route for the passage of Spanish troops to the seat of trouble in the Netherlands; and it was, finally, a reservoir from which Philip was able to draw both funds and supplies wherewith to put down the rebellion in the North. Though we shall hear of it infrequently in the succeeding pages, we cannot afford to forget its existence.

In the second place it is essential that the reader be

[1] Lucien Febvre, *Philippe II et la Franche-Comté* (Paris, 1911), pp. 69–71.   [2] *Ibid.*, pp. 71–75; Forneron, iii, pp. 390 f.

reminded that the only picture of a Spanish dependency in Europe which was available as a model and guide for Philip II at the time that he took over the reins of government from his father was the picture of the Spanish dependencies in the Mediterranean and in Italy. The only overseas possessions which Spain had thus far held in Europe were the Balearics, Sicily, Sardinia, Naples, and Milan, the first three of which had been acquired by the realms of the crown of Aragon before the days of their union with Castile, the fourth at least partially so, while the fifth had fallen in during the period of Charles V.[1] The methods by which they had been administered varied somewhat, of course, in detail, according to local conditions and traditions;[2] but, *mutatis mutandis*, one may safely say that the guiding principle had been increasingly, throughout the list, that of the establishment and increase of monarchical authority, at the expense of every local custom or institution which ran counter to it. The application of that principle, moreover, had been considerably intensified since the union of the crowns. It was an integral part of the process of Castilianizing Italy to which reference has already been made. It was the essence of the political atmosphere in which Philip's life was lived; and it is difficult to see how, in dealing with his Burgundian dominions, he could possibly have been expected to follow any other. The experience of the next century was conclusively to prove that the Netherlanders would not submit to what the Italians had been willing to put up with, that the geographical position of the Low Countries made them far harder to handle than any of the Mediterranean dependencies, and, above all, that the power of Protestantism in the North destroyed every remaining

[1] Cf. *ante*, Vol. III, pp. 268–272.

[2] The traditions of Milan were of course rather imperial than Spanish; it cannot be regarded as quite in the same class with Sicily, Sardinia, and Naples.

ground for regarding them as parallel cases. But when we consider the task which the Emperor had bequeathed to Philip and the nature of the instructions which he had left behind, we can scarcely be surprised that the Spanish monarch at the moment of his accession was practically blind to the first two of these considerations; as for the third, that is, the increasing power of heresy in the Low Countries, it but constituted in his eyes another and most cogent reason for following the traditional policy of absolutism and suppression. There can be no reasonable doubt that the image of Spain's Mediterranean and Italian dependencies, particularly Naples and Milan, in the state in which they had been handed over to him by his father, exercised a powerful influence in the determination of Philip's policy and methods in regard to the Netherlands; and that consideration should serve at least to mitigate the severity of the judgments we pass upon him, when we look back upon the tragic history of Spain in the Low Countries from the vantage ground of the knowledge and experience of the twentieth century.

On his departure for Spain, Philip confided the regency of his Burgundian dominions, which Mary of Hungary had laid down in 1555, to his half-sister, Margaret of Parma, then in her thirty-eighth year. She was the illegitimate child of the Emperor Charles V by the daughter of a cloth-weaver of Flanders, and the first eleven years of her life had been spent in the Low Countries; but in 1533 she had been sent off to Italy to be married, first (February 29, 1536) to Alessandro de' Medici, and then, after his assassination a few months later, to Ottavio Farnese, the grandson of Pope Paul III. By these two unions she had become deeply involved in Italian politics, and particularly in the interminable questions arising out of the conflicting claims to

Parma and Piacenza.   Her husband had allied himself with France in the recent war in order to enforce what he regarded as his rights there, and though officially reconciled with the Hapsburgs in 1556, was still by no means satisfied; indeed one of the reasons why Philip had selected Margaret as his regent in the Low Countries was his belief that her desire to obtain full realization of her husband's territorial ambitions in Italy would induce her to place herself unreservedly at the disposal of the government at Madrid.[1]   At the time that she took office there her point of view was no longer native but foreign.   She had even forgotten how to write French. She was, in fact, a living and present reminder of many of the characteristics of which the inhabitants complained in the king.   Her intellectual and administrative gifts were by no means remarkable.   Hard-working and methodical, but neither attractive nor brilliant, she was not comparable for one moment with either of her two great predecessors.[2]

But the power was by no means exclusively in the regent's hands.   Officially, indeed, she was invested with all the authority inherent in the king himself; but secret instructions obliged her, in all matters of importance, to take the advice of a committee of three persons, of whom by far the most important was Granvelle; the Spanish name, the *Consulta*, by which this special committee soon came to be known, is at once indicative of the work which it was expected to perform and a significant comment on Philip's way of doing things.   The trio that composed it were all members of the old Council of State, which still remained, in theory at least, the official advisory body of the regent; outwardly nothing had been changed.   But practically the

[1] Cf. *ante*, Vol. III, p. 280. Cf. also   Rachfahl, *Margaretha von Parma*, pp.
Pirenne, iii, pp. 380-383, and F.   17 ff.

[2] Pirenne, iii, pp. 383 ff.

Consulta usurped all the functions of the Council, whose other three members, Egmont, Orange, and Glajon, were simply elbowed aside, until they became, by the force of events, the leaders of the national opposition. Philip's plan, in other words, was to Hispanicize the government of the Low Countries by stealth, in order, if possible, to avoid revolution. He was determined to subvert their most cherished liberties, both political and religious, to reduce them to a state of subjection to the home government comparable to that of the Spanish dependencies in Italy; but he desired, if possible, to achieve his end without a fight. He hoped to conceal the true meaning of his policy from the watchful eyes of the Netherlanders themselves, by leaving the outward fabric of their ancient form of government untouched, and accomplish his own ends by working under ground.[1]

It was an impossible programme, as the sequel was to show. The differences between Philip and his subjects were far too deep seated, at least in those portions of his Burgundian dominions where religious grievances were superadded to political, to be settled otherwise than by the arbitrament of war; but revolution did not really break out during the regency of Margaret of Parma. The period of her rule was that of indispensable preparation for the scenes of bloodshed that were to follow; but the outstanding fact of it, when viewed by itself, is that the government succeeded in preserving peace. A large measure of this success was attributable to the fact that Philip, at Margaret's advice, made certain reluctant concessions to the popular demands. He had no intention of permanently abiding by them; but as it immediately became evident that the Netherlanders could

---

[1] E. Gossart, *L'Établissement du régime espagnol dans les Pays-Bas*, pp. 25 ff.; Pirenne, iii, pp. 384 ff.

not be hoodwinked into passive acquiescence in his policy of Hispanicization, there was no other alternative if he was not prepared to fight. The first of these concessions was the sanctioning of the departure of the last detachment of the detested Spanish *tercios* (January 10, 1561); another was his decision, three years later, to recall Granvelle, whom the opposition regarded as the source of all their woes; without his support, the Netherlanders were convinced that the much more pliant Margaret could be induced to grant them their desires.[1] That Philip was willing to grant as much as this is an evidence of the predominance at the time of Ruy Gómez and the peace party in the Royal Council at Madrid;[2] but there were other points on which the king showed himself less complaisant, and it is significant that it was in matters religious that his hostility to compromise was most manifest. Not only did the 'placards,' or edicts, against all forms of heresy, a legacy from the days of his father, increase in severity and scope; there were also ominous innovations. In May, 1559, before his departure for Spain, he had obtained from Pope Paul IV a bull erecting fourteen new bishoprics in the Netherlands over and above the six existing ones. The right of appointment to these bishoprics was vested in the king, who would obviously nominate with a view to his own ends, and regardless of the claims of the Burgundian nobles; moreover the measure had an important bearing upon the political situation, for the new prelates would all have seats in the States-General, and constitute the nucleus of a monarchical party there. Mission after mission was despatched to Madrid to protest against this new departure, and, above all, to demand the removal of Granvelle, who was popularly supposed to be responsible

[1] Gossart, *L'Établissement*, pp. 36 ff.; Philippson, *Kardinal Granvella*, pp. 11 f. [2] Pirenne, iii, p. 409. The Duke of Alva was furious at the king's leniency. Cf. *Correspondance de Philippe II*, i, p. 272.

for it ; but though Philip in 1564 'permitted the Cardinal to retire,' the new bishoprics continued without change.[1]

The bitterness caused by Philip's religious policy was much increased by the fact that at the very time that he succeeded his father the guidance of the heretical party in the Netherlands passed from Lutheran to Calvinist hands. The doctrines of the Genevan reformer had made their first appearance in the Low Countries during the closing decades of the Emperor's reign. They slipped in at first almost unperceived ; but once they had got a foothold, they gained ground with astonishing rapidity. They were eagerly seized upon by the urban capitalistic centres, to which the implications of Calvin's economic teachings were particularly welcome ; the progress of the French Huguenots was another element in their favor ; before long the more passive Lutherans were simply elbowed aside, and the programme of the heretics in the Netherlands became aggressively militant.[2] In October, 1561, there was an heretical outbreak in the town of Valenciennes, which required the use of regular troops to put it down ; and from that time onward the discontent, though sometimes latent, grew steadily stronger until the day (April 5, 1566) of the famous interview with the regent when the petitioners were given the name of 'Beggars,' which was to be their rallying cry for years to come. Margaret, on this occasion, showed that she appreciated the seriousness of the crisis and the need of compromise. She promised to present to the king the requests of his subjects, and to moderate, pending his reply, the severity of the 'placards.'[3] For a moment it seemed possible that Philip would also yield ; but the prospect of royal concessions, instead of allaying the excitement in the Netherlands,

---

[1] Pirenne, iii, pp. 397 ff.
[2] Pirenne, iii, pp. 357, 411–425.
[3] Pirenne, iii, pp. 439 ff.

served only to augment it. Preachers harangued excited
congregations, and lashed them into paroxysms of rage
against the existing régime. There were outbursts of
iconoclasm and desecrations of churches.[1] Before long it
became evident that some of the revolutionists would not
be content with liberty to exercise their own faith, but were
even intent on the destruction of Catholicism. Such a
programme as this was, of course, totally inadmissible, even
to the somewhat temporizing nature of the regent; at the
first news of the revolt of the iconoclasts she nominated the
Count of Mansfeld as governor of Brussels, placed herself
under his protection, and soon succeeded, with his help, in
collecting several regiments of soldiers in the Empire.[2]
There was fighting, in the first three months of 1567, outside
Antwerp and Valenciennes, and the government was everywhere victorious.[3] Margaret was alive to the danger of
pushing her triumph too far. She fully realized that the
rebels were too much in earnest to be permanently discouraged by a few trifling reverses; and she wrote to Philip
urging him to seize the moment of his victory as the psychological opportunity to be generous to the defeated foe.[4]
But Philip had no intention of taking her advice. His
previous concessions had been but temporary and reluctant;
he was resolved that the liberties of the Netherlands should
be crushed under the heel of Spain, and above all that every
vestige of heresy should be obliterated. The events of the
first seven years of Margaret's regency had convinced him
that these ends could not be attained by subterfuge and
deceit, as he had originally hoped, and that, much as he
deplored it, strong measures were indispensable. He had,

[1] Rachfahl, *Margaretha von Parma*,
pp. 182 ff.; Gossart, *L'Établissement*,
pp. 49 ff.
[2] Rachfahl, *op. cit.*, pp. 206 ff.
[3] Bernardino de Mendoza *Comentarios*, lib. i, caps. xv, xvi.
[4] Kervyn de Lettenhove, *Les Huguenots et les Gueux*, i, pp. 468 f.

in fact, taken the first of these measures in the autumn of 1566, when he ordered the Duke of Alva to repair to Lombardy and conduct to the Low Countries the Spanish troops which were concentrating there.[1] On the 9th of the following August the vanguard of his *tercios* arrived in Brussels, and four months later the regent departed for Italy, leaving the terrible Duke as her successor in title as well as in fact.[2]

When contrasted with the regencies of the Emperor's day, the rule of Margaret of Parma seems a troublous period, and it certainly saw the sowing of the seeds of future miseries; but compared with that of the Duke of Alva which followed, it appears as a time of tranquillity and peace. Such at least was the light in which contemporaries regarded it. Save for the few who knew the whole story, the dominant fact of the situation was that, though Philip had been offered grievous provocation, he had not yet really shown his teeth. It served to strengthen the impression, already prevalent among his fellow sovereigns, that, if possible, the Spanish monarch was determined to avoid war.

The course of the relations between Spain and France during these same years (1559–67) is difficult to characterize in brief space. So complicated were the issues involved, so bewildering the interaction of religious and political motives, so numerous the *dramatis personae*, and so quick the shifts of scene, that consistency in the following out of any logical policy was practically out of the question for either of the two courts. The situation, in other words, was such as offered Philip an admirable opportunity for the exercise of his talents for concealment and intrigue. Renewal of the

[1] Alva's first commission was dated December 1, 1566, and was replaced on January 31, 1567, by a much more rigorous one. *Correspondance de Philippe II*, ii, pp. 600–602, 619–622.

[2] Pirenne, iii, pp. 460 f.; iv, p. 8; Rachfahl, *op. cit.*, pp. 258–267.

Hapsburg-Valois conflict as it had been in the Emperor's day was now out of the question; the disrupted state of France rendered it impossible for her to wage it, and unnecessary for Spain to undertake it. The real question in the eyes of the Spanish government was how much profit could be made, by diplomacy and craft, out of the civil and religious struggle on the soil of its ancient foe.

As befitted long-standing enemies who had but recently made peace, the rulers of France and Spain were deeply distrustful of one another. Each was determined to be precisely informed about the ongoings at the other's court, and anxious, if possible, to exert influence in the other's councils. The method used by Philip to attain these ends in France was a far-reaching system of political espionage, first installed by the Duke of Alva when he repaired to Paris, after the treaty of Cateau-Cambrésis, to represent his master at his marriage to Elizabeth of Valois, and later developed and perfected by Thomas Perrenot de Chantonnay, the younger brother of Cardinal Granvelle, who was the ambassador of the Prudent King at Paris from August, 1559, to February, 1564.[1] On the other side, the queen-mother, Catharine de' Medici, who, after the death of Henry II in July, 1559, gave the French government such measure of continuity as it was to possess for thirty years to come, expected that her daughter Elizabeth, who was finally sent south to her Spanish husband in the winter of 1559–60, would soon have his full confidence, and send home all she learned; it was also hoped that she would be able to influence him in a way favorable to France. The princess, on her departure, was furnished with a magnificent wardrobe and all manner of appliances for increasing her charms and rendering her attractive to Philip; but all

[1] C. S. P., Foreign, 1558–59, p. 442; Forneron, i, pp. 218, 290; Courteault, Blaise de Monluc, p. 483.

these carefully laid plans of the queen-mother were brought to naught by the attack of small pox which Elizabeth suffered shortly after her arrival, and which rendered it impossible for her husband to have anything to do with her for several months to come.[1]   When at last Elizabeth got well, and was able to take up her duties as queen of Spain, it was made clear to her that she was expected to forget the land of her birth and become solely devoted to that of her adoption. Such a shift of allegiance cost her many a pang, and rendered her mother furious; but under the circumstances in which she found herself, there was no possible escape.[2]   At the outset, then, everything seemed to promise that the power which Philip would be able to exercise in France would far outweigh any influence which the French government might be able to exert in Spain.   Only in the Low Countries was the Spanish power really vulnerable, and the possibilities of that region were as yet unrevealed.

During the brief reign of Francis II (July, 1559–December, 1560) the queen-mother was temporarily in the background, and the government was controlled by the two uncles of the king's wife, Mary queen of Scots — Francis, Duke of Guise, and the cardinal of Lorraine.   In matters religious their policy was wholly in accord with the views of Philip II; but he cherished a grudge against them because of their achievements in the recent war,[3] and he was in mortal terror lest they should manage to effect a permanent union of France and Scotland.   He did not venture to express his views openly, for opposition to the Guises would mean dalliance with heretics; but there can be no doubt that during the year which succeeded the treaty of Cateau-Cambrésis there were several occasions on which he secretly

[1] Forneron, i, pp. 217 ff., and references there.

[2] *Ibid.*, i, pp. 221, 315–318, and references there.

[3] Cf. *ante*, pp. 11 f.

hoped for the success of John Knox, the Lords of the Congregation, and of those who supported them in England, and it is certain that he was greatly relieved by the news of the conclusion of the treaty of Edinburgh (July 5, 1560), whose object was to prevent the annexation of Scotland to France.[1]   Six months later, however, the whole situation was suddenly changed by the death (December 5, 1560) of Francis II, the consequent elimination of the Guises from the government, and the return thither of Catharine de' Medici as regent for Charles IX.   Philip's fears for Scotland were now entirely allayed; but the peril of Protestantism, to which the queen-mother showed herself alarmingly tolerant, loomed larger than ever before.   And it was not merely by the danger that heresy might become definitely established and recognized in France, intolerable though that would be, that Philip's fears were roused.   There was also every prospect that the contagion would infect his own dominions in the Netherlands and threaten the subversion of his own authority there.   As early as August 9, 1560, while the Guises and their policy of peace were still in the saddle, Granvelle had written Gonzalo Pérez that with things in the state in which they were in France, it was a miracle that matters were no worse in the Low Countries;[2] what then was to be expected with Catharine de' Medici in power? Obviously at all costs the Reformation must be put down, and from the beginning of the year of 1561 Philip bent all his efforts to that end.

These efforts, however, took the form of a vast campaign of bribery and intrigue; on no account did Philip propose to be dragged into open war.   At the outset he attempted to turn against Catharine de' Medici a project which she had

[1] Forneron, i, pp. 122 ff., 224 ff., and   [2] *Correspondance de Philippe II,* references there; Froude, vii, pp. 177,   i, p. 191.
194, 204, 216–218, 264 f.

once favored for the purpose of embarrassing him : namely, a plan to prevail upon him to give up to Anthony of Bourbon the Spanish portion of Navarre. There had been, as we have already seen, some doubts as to the legitimacy of the methods by which Spain had acquired that territory in the days of Ferdinand the Catholic;[1] the emperor's 'instructions' and 'political testament' contained passages which might be interpreted to indicate that he had conscientious scruples about retaining it;[2] there was a possibility that Philip might take the same view. Bourbon's case was, at least, sufficiently strong to put the Spanish king in a very embarrassing position if he refused to give it consideration ; and it was in the hope of causing him such embarrassment that Catharine supported it. But Philip utilized the situation to his own advantage. He knew that Bourbon was both vacillating and imprudent, and that his Protestantism was no proof against his desire for personal aggrandizement ; and for the next two years he negotiated with him, tantalizing him with offers, not indeed of Navarre, but of Sardinia, of Tunis, and even of the Balearics in lieu of it, in the hope of inducing him to take vigorous measures for the defence of Catholicism in France.[3] These projects were all suddenly terminated by Bourbon's death, October 26, 1563, as a result of wounds received at the siege of Rouen ; but the fact that before March, 1562, he had consented to 'receive instruction' in the Roman Catholic faith, from a teacher recommended to him by Jesuits,[4] and that in the following May he had published a proclamation expelling all Huguenots from

[1] Cf. *ante*, Vol. II, pp. 345–347; also Forneron, i, pp. 230–233, and references there.
[2] Cf. *ante*, Vol. III, pp. 406 ff.; Armstrong, *Charles V.*, ii, pp. 360 f.; Laiglesia, *Estudios*, i, p. 117; *Archiv für österreichische Geschichte*, xciii, pp. 237 ff.

[3] Forneron, i, p. 260, and references there; Giovanni Michiel (1561) in Albèri, *Relazioni*, serie i, iii, pp. 435 f.; Michele Soriano (1562), *ibid.*, iv, p. 145; J. W. Thompson, *Wars of Religion*, pp. 131 f., and references there.
[4] Thompson, p. 132.

Paris,[1] gives reason for believing that if the unworthy sovereign of French Navarre had continued to live, he might well have become a pensioner of the king of Spain.

Another affair, which began in 1562, and continued for several years to come, though it ultimately effected little save to augment the suspicion and distrust of Catharine de' Medici toward the Spanish government, is too characteristic of the methods of Philip II to be entirely omitted. This was the attempt of the Prudent King to take advantage, for his own purposes and for the advancement of Catholicism, of the vanity and sensitiveness of Blaise de Monluc. That gallant but unmanageable old soldier, "the real creator of the French infantry," had been deeply aggrieved by the inadequate fashion in which his services to the French crown had been rewarded. He was also convinced — or at least pretended to be — that the position of the church was gravely imperilled by the policy of toleration of heresy on which the queen-mother had embarked. In October, 1562, the rumor was current that he was planning to deliver the whole of Guienne into the hands of the king of Spain.[2] The person who was doubtless responsible for turning his thoughts in this direction was a certain Captain Felipe de Bardaxi, who had been condemned as a heretic by the Spanish Inquisition in 1558, but had escaped to France and got employment in the army of Monluc. His valor and skill won him the confidence of his new chief, with whose character and cupidity he soon became acquainted, and it occurred to him to make use of the situation in which he found himself for the advantage of Spain, and as a means to the rehabilitation of his own fortunes.[3] Philip was prompt to profit by the opportunity, for this was just the kind of undertaking that

[1] C. S. P., Foreign, 1562, no. 107, sect. 16.
[2] Courteault, Blaise de Monluc, pp.
471, 483; C. S. P., Foreign, 1562, no. 932, sect. 9.
[3] Courteault, pp. 484 ff.

appealed to him. Its conduct was placed in the hands of
Bardaxi's cousin, Juan, one of the army of secret spies which
the Prudent King maintained in France; and it is characteristic of Philip's methods of procedure that his regular ambassador at Paris, Chantonnay, was kept totally in the dark in
regard to the whole affair.[1] Though no document has been
found to prove it, there can be little doubt that Monluc
became a pensionary of the Spanish monarch from the very
moment that his attitude was known. He had a secret
interview with Juan de Bardaxi at Toulouse in February,
1564. He sent Philip a long memorial dilating on the many
advantages that would ensue from Spanish intervention in
Southwestern France, and Philip replied with an elaborate
letter in which he begged Monluc to continue to inform him,
and to see if Damville, the new governor of Languedoc,
could not possibly be induced to participate in a Catholic
uprising.[2] At this juncture proceedings were suddenly interrupted by a summons to Monluc to return to Paris to face
accusations of treasonable correspondence, put forward by
the secret agents of Catharine de' Medici. Quite characteristically, he flatly denied all the charges that had been
made, nay, even demanded that his traducers be punished,
and Catharine, who had many reasons for wishing to avoid
a public scandal, thought it wiser, under all the circumstances, to accept his word. She even consented to go
through the motions of a trial of the chief of his accusers.
Meantime Monluc shamelessly continued his correspondence
with Philip and Bardaxi, and in a letter to the last named,
written October 27, 1564, put forward the plan of a meeting
between the Spanish monarch and Catharine for the discussion of a joint programme for the suppression of heresy in
France. Such was the first suggestion of the famous inter-

[1] Forneron, i, p. 299.   [2] Courteault, pp. 486, 488, note 1.

view which was to take place, June 14–July 4, 1565, at Bayonne.[1]

The idea of such an interview had been cherished by the queen-mother ever since her daughter Elizabeth had been sent south to marry Philip II.[2] If she could induce the Spanish monarch to pay her a formal visit on French soil, it would proclaim to the world that her authority was firmly established, and that she was regarded as a real bulwark of the Roman Catholic church. It was doubtless these very same considerations that determined Philip not to go, and his resolve was confirmed at the last moment by a report that reached him of a threatened renewal of the ancient alliance between the government of France and the infidel Turk.[3] On the other hand, the queen-mother's invitation offered him an opportunity, which he could ill afford to neglect, to extend his own influence in French affairs; he therefore sent his wife Elizabeth and the Duke of Alva to represent him at the interview which Catharine had proposed. It was a strong combination. The queen-mother's passionate devotion to her children would induce her to do everything possible to please her daughter Elizabeth, who had now become so completely Hispanicized that there was no danger that she would be too complaisant. Alva had already proved himself equally competent at bullying and intrigue, and knew well which method to select in order to attain his ends.[4] The instructions they received dealt almost exclusively with the affairs of religion. They were to propose a 'holy alliance' of the two governments against their heretical subjects and the elimination of all ministers

[1] Courteault, pp. 487–489.
[2] Mariéjol in Lavisse, vi, 1, p. 90.
[3] Forneron, i, p. 321; Erich Marcks, *Die Zusammenkunft von Bayonne*, pp. 169 ff.

[4] Excerpts from Alva's letters to Philip are printed in Forneron, i, appendix d, pp. 418–421.

and counsellors who would not do their utmost to advance the faith.[1]

Catharine, on her side, came to Bayonne with objects primarily political and dynastic. Her only real interest was the preservation of her own authority, and that of her children who should succeed her; and one of the most obvious methods of attaining this end was to strengthen the family ties between the Valois and the Spanish Hapsburgs. She wished to marry her daughter Margaret to Don Carlos, and her son, the future Henry III, to Philip's younger sister Doña Juana, the widow of Prince John of Portugal. But neither of these schemes appealed to Philip II. The state of Don Carlos's health was a sufficient reason for refusing, at that juncture, to consider any marriage for him; in case he should get well there were other princesses who would make far better matches for him than Margaret de Valois. There were also numerous objections, particularly in the matter of the dowry, to the union which the queen-mother proposed between Henry of Anjou and Doña Juana; and, finally, Philip was convinced that his own position was so strong, and that of Catharine, comparatively speaking, so weak, that he could well afford to insist on the 'Holy League' which he had so closely at heart, without making any concessions whatever in return.[2] The Prudent King, moreover, had by this time completed all his arrangements for keeping secret watch on Catharine and checking the results. Monluc was at Bayonne, and in close touch with Alva; so also was the new Spanish ambassador, Francisco de Álava, who had replaced Chantonnay in February, 1564, and had by

[1] Mariéjol in Lavisse, vi, 1, pp. 90 f. The best monograph on the interview is still that of Erich Marcks, *Die Zusammenkunft von Bayonne* (Strasburg, 1889). François Combes, *L'entre-vue de Bayonne et la question de la Saint-Barthélemy* (Paris, 1882), prints some interesting documents preserved at Simancas.

[2] Marcks, *op. cit.*, pp. 194 ff.

this time perfected the system of spies and underground information which had been initiated by his predecessor.[1] But Catharine was both wily and obstinate. She pretended to be amazed that Philip should be so disturbed by the state of religion in France; she was profuse in her promises to take vigorous measures against heresy as soon as it could be demonstrated that such measures were needed; but it was impossible to pin her down to any definite engagement to act at a specified time. Whenever Alva sought to bring the conversation to this point, she skilfully shifted it over to her own dynastic projects. Two weeks of diplomatic thrust and parry had no other result than to convince each party that the other was not to be trusted. There were, indeed, a number of affecting interviews, and suitable exchanges of courtesies and honors;[2] and these outward evidences of cordiality, coupled with a series of violent edicts, in the ensuing weeks, against the printers of Protestant books,[3] made such an impression upon the uninformed mass of the Huguenots, that a legend arose, which has not been wholly eradicated today, that the project which bore fruit seven years later on St. Bartholomew's day originated at Bayonne. But the principals at the conference were not deceived.[4] Philip and Catharine were really further apart at the end of the interview from which so much had been hoped, than they had been when it began.

Two events which took place in the succeeding months, neither of them, apparently, in any way connected with the

---

[1] Courteault, pp. 483, 486 ff.; Forneron, i, pp. 342 ff.

[2] Marcks, pp. 192 ff.

[3] Forneron, i, pp. 330 f.

[4] The letter of Philip to Cardinal Pacheco at Rome (August 24, 1565), which is printed on pp. 39-49 of F. Combes's *L'entrevue de Bayonne*, might be taken to indicate that the Spanish king deluded himself into thinking that he had got something out of the interview for a couple of months after its close; but he cannot have deceived himself much longer.

conference at Bayonne, are significant indications of the
way in which the wind was blowing. The first, which has
been already described in detail,[1] need only be mentioned
here, namely, the massacre, by Pedro Menéndez de Avilés,
in September, 1565, of the French Protestant colony on
the shores of Florida. The patent or *asiento* authorizing
Menéndez to undertake the expedition which produced this
tragic result was dated March 20, 1565,[2] and the first rumor
of it which reached France is to be found in a letter written
just two weeks later to Charles IX by Saint-Sulpice, his
ambassador at Madrid, to tell him that it had been decided
to send Menéndez to the shores of Florida with a good fleet
and 600 men to fight the French and put them to death.[3]
It is true that the fleet did not actually set sail until June 29,
when the conference at Bayonne was practically over;[4]
but the plan of sending it had been devised before the meeting
had even been arranged; and though Spanish slowness
delayed Menéndez's departure until the meeting had been in
session for a fortnight, the two events are to be regarded
as entirely separate. There were justifications for the massacre, in Spanish eyes at least, other than the mere fact
that Ribaut and his companions were heretics; for the
Frenchmen were also trespassers on land that was indubitably Spanish under the bull of Alexander VI and the treaty
of Tordesillas; but naturally this line of reasoning found
no adherents among the Huguenots, who clamored loudly
for revenge when the news was known. Catharine protested and demanded reparation; but Philip's position was
too strong to make it possible for her, officially at least, to

[1] Cf. *supra*, pp. 169-173.
[2] *D. I. I.*, xxiii, pp. 242–258.
[3] E. Cabié, *Ambassade de Jean
Ébrard, Seigneur de Saint-Sulpice*, p.
364; cf. *C. S. P., Foreign*, 1564–65,
no. 1168, sect. 4.

[4] E. G. Bourne, *Spain in America*,
pp. 180 ff., and references there.
Forneron, i, p. 340, wrongly puts the
date of Menéndez's departure in May.

translate her words into deeds.[1] If vengeance was to be
obtained it would have to be through private means.

Vengeance for the slaughter of Ribaut's colony naturally
suggests the name of Dominique de Gourgues, who sailed on
his own responsibility from Bordeaux on August 2, 1567,
accomplished his end, and was back in France on the sixth
of the following June; the story of that enterprise has
already been fully told.[2] For the present we are chiefly
concerned with another expedition, which departed from the
same port almost exactly one year earlier, and is generally
understood to have been a retort to the Florida massacre;
this was the famous seizure of the Portuguese island of
Madeira by Captain Peyrot de Monluc.[3] This restless
fighter, the second son of Blaise de Monluc, found life empty
and tiresome in France after the termination of the First
Civil War by the Pacification of Amboise (March, 1563).
He longed to distinguish himself by some notable feat of
arms, and cherished plans for a descent on the Portuguese in
Africa; there was even talk of his going as far as Madagascar.[4] Coligny, in his capacity of admiral of France, gave
him hearty support, in spite of Peyrot's sturdy Catholicism;
but the king and the queen-mother were far more cautious,
and it was not until the news of the Florida massacre had
been received that Peyrot stood any real chance of being
allowed to put to sea. It seems doubtful, in fact, if he had

[1] Antoine, Marquis Du Prat, *Élisabeth de Valois*, pp. 206–208; Forneron,
i, p. 341; Fourquevaux, *Dépêches*,
ed. Douais, i, nos. 4–7, 15, 16, 19, 21,
23–26, 28, 29, 38, 43, 47. Fourquevaux's complaints of Spanish "longueur
de respondre aux articles par moy
presentez" are very significant. He
hoped to get something out of Eboli,
but was told "que l'ordinaire de ceste
court est de proceder lentement en
toutes chozes." *Dépêches*, i, p. 116.

[2] Cf. *supra*, pp. 177 f.

[3] Cf. E. Falgairolle, "Une expédition
française à l'île de Madère en 1566,"
in Académie de Nîmes, *Mémoires*, 1894,
pp. 67–95; P. Gaffarel, "Peyrot
Monluc," in *Revue historique*, ix, pp.
273–332; Courteault, pp. 495–497.

[4] Gaffarel in *Revue historique*, ix,
pp. 291 ff. In the spring of 1566 there
was a prospect that he would be sent
to the Baltic to aid King Frederick II
of Denmark against King Eric XIV of
Sweden; but the plan was soon abandoned. *Ibid.*, pp. 300–304.

any definite idea of where he was going before April, 1566 ; but his plans took shape rapidly in the succeeding weeks, possibly as a result of the representations of two members of a family named Menin, well known in Guienne, one of whom had suffered on the sea at the hands of the Portuguese, while the other had been taken prisoner by the Spaniards in Florida, and brought back by them to Madrid, where he told his tale to the French ambassador, Fourquevaux. It would seem natural to trace the connection which indubitably existed between the Florida massacre and the expedition of Peyrot to the activities of these Menins.[1] At any rate, Peyrot's plans were sufficiently well known, in the weeks before he set sail, to elicit vigorous protests from the Portuguese and Spanish ambassadors.[2] It would appear that he had made private arrangements to be joined, directly after he left Bordeaux, by a squadron of sixteen English vessels, which, together with the seven that he furnished himself, brought his armament up to twenty-three.[3] Cruising southward, the expedition encountered violent storms ; when it came in sight of Madeira it was short of water and supplies ; solely with the idea of replenishing its stock it put into the port.[4] But the inhabitants, doubtless because of the rumors of the expedition which had been circulated for months before, were convinced that it was Peyrot's intention to conquer the island. Without the slightest warning they launched a furious attack, and though Peyrot had,

---

[1] Du Prat, *op. cit.*, pp. 430–433; Gaffarel in *Revue historique*, ix, pp. 293 f.

[2] Gaffarel in *Revue historique*, ix, pp. 299 f.

[3] It is certain at least that sixteen English vessels participated in the expedition (Gaffarel, *loc. cit.*, p. 313), and, unless their meeting with Peyrot was purely accidental, some sort of prearrangement must be assumed.

Whether Elizabeth knew anything of the matter, even unofficially, may well be doubted, and it is worth noting that all the contemporary English accounts of the expedition speak of it as a purely French affair. Cf. *C. S. P., Foreign*, 1566–68, nos. 786, 810, 822, 824, 827, 843, 852, 859; *C. S. P., Domestic*, 1547–80, p. 287.

[4] Gaffarel, *loc. cit.*, pp. 312–314.

apparently, promised the French government before his departure that he would never play the aggressor, he felt amply justified in defending himself. On the water the combat was speedily terminated in favor of the invaders; the land fighting which ensued took somewhat longer, but ended with the same result. There was much bloodshed and wantonness, and Peyrot himself was numbered among the slain, but the close of the day found his comrades who survived him in undisputed possession of the island of Madeira. They did not, however, remain there long. As Peyrot had kept his ultimate objective secret, there were naturally all sorts of different opinions as to what should be done next. Many desired to attempt conquest and piracy on a large scale, but feared the displeasure of the home government. Those who preferred to remain at Madeira were in terror of the vengeance of the king of Portugal; and the final result was that after a few weeks the invaders evacuated the island and returned to Europe.[1]

The whole affair had been utterly haphazard, and typical of the maritime enterprises of that day and generation. There was a terrible explosion of wrath at Lisbon when the first news of Peyrot's conquest came in. The government prepared to take summary vengeance, and the lives of the French and English residents in the Portuguese capital were in grave danger.[2] But Catharine was prompt to disavow Peyrot; the news that his expedition had voluntarily departed from Madeira helped to mollify the Portuguese; before the end of the year all the excitement had blown over. What is of most interest for our purpose is the attitude of Philip towards the whole affair. Officially it was none of his business. The harm had been actually done to Portugal

---

[1] Gaffarel, loc. cit., pp. 314–316. To show that their courage was still good, they captured two Flemish barques and two Biscayan ships on the way.

[2] Ibid., pp. 317 f.

and not to Spain; moreover, there was every reason
to believe that Peyrot's ultimate objective had been in
Portuguese and not in Spanish waters, and yet Philip took
the matter up with the French government just as vigorously
as if he himself had been the injured one.[1] In so far as
Peyrot's expedition could be regarded as an act of vengeance
for the Florida massacre — and it is fair to add that the numbers and cruelty of Menéndez's Portuguese followers on that
occasion lent color to such a view — the king of Spain was
perhaps warranted in resenting it. It may be further added
that a Madeira in French and English hands would have
constituted a menace to his treasure fleets which Philip could
not have been expected to ignore. Yet is it not also reasonable to regard the vigor with which the Prudent King espoused the quarrel of his western neighbor as an earnest of
the project, already half formed in his mind, to extend his
influence over the destinies of the Portuguese empire, as a
foreshadowing, in fact, of the events of 1578–81?

So the year 1566 passed off without an open rupture between France and Spain. In view of the number and bitterness of the issues between them, it is really remarkable that
it should have been avoided, and a tribute to the firmness of
the determination of both Philip and Catharine to keep the
peace. And now new causes of irritation appeared to com-
plicate a situation already difficult enough. The new
Spanish ambassador Álava was most offensive to the queen-
mother; so perfect was the network of spies at his command
that she felt herself caught like a bird in the fowler's snares.
His insolence in demanding apology and reparation for
piracies which she had not sanctioned became more intolerable from day to day; worst of all, he was obviously draw-

[1] Gaffarel, *loc. cit.*, pp. 318 f. Fourquevaux's description of the way in
which the news was received by the
Spanish court is given in his *Dépêches*,
i, pp. 136 f.

ing closer to the Guises, and laying the foundations of the League which a decade later was to disrupt France.[1] When it became known that the Duke of Alva was to be despatched to the Netherlands, the Huguenots demanded that war be declared. The Calvinist alliance which Philip feared so much seemed about to be established; 6000 Swiss troops were raised for the defence of France. But despite all these provocations and inducements, Catharine could not bring herself to the point of fighting. The fate of the Protestant rebels in the Low Countries was a matter of profound indifference to her, provided her own authority could be firmly maintained in France, and for the moment she was persuaded that this end could be best secured by keeping peace with Spain; indeed she actually furnished provisions for Alva's *tercios* as they passed north, just beyond her eastern frontiers, in the summer of 1567.[2] It was a bad mistake, as the sequel was to show. Catharine's difficulties and complications, already great, were to become vastly greater as soon as the new régime was definitely established in the Low Countries.

The relations of Philip II and Queen Elizabeth of England, during the period we have just been considering, present striking points, both of similarity and difference, to his contemporaneous dealings with Catharine de' Medici. In both cases there is a long and varied list of mutual gravamina, both political and religious, and at the same time a firm determination on the part of both sovereigns — though for very different reasons — that peace must at all costs be preserved. In both cases the course of events is intimately bound up with the development of the revolt in

[1] Forneron, i, pp. 346 f.; and also Thompson, *Wars of Religion*, p. 304, note.
[2] Mariéjol in Lavisse, vi, 1, p. 94.

the Low Countries.   In both cases Philip had to do with
rulers who were far more ready than he to sacrifice religion
to politics.   On the other hand, the fact that England had
now officially gone over to Protestantism, and that she was
for the most part internally at peace and united, constituted
difficulties for the Spanish monarch in his dealings with
Queen Elizabeth which did not obtain in his relations with
Catharine de' Medici.   There was no longer any marriage
tie to unite the Tudors and the Hapsburgs.   Philip's spy
system could not work so effectively across the Channel as
it did in France.   And finally, though Philip was slow to
discover it, the lapse of time was conclusively to prove that
the queen of England, though capable of the most tortuous
diplomacy to secure her immediate ends, had a policy and a
programme far more patriotic and consistent than the dynastic strivings of the queen-mother of France, that she was,
in fact, by far the abler woman, who was destined in the end
to be Spain's most dangerous foe.

At the outset the prospects for friendly relations between
England and Spain could scarcely have been worse.   Not
only had the new queen insulted Philip by refusing his
proffer of marriage ; she had scandalized him by daring to
abandon Rome and

"mould new mode of old Christianity" ;[1]

from the bottom of his heart he longed to have her punished.
Yet on the other hand, it was obvious that he could not
undertake her chastisement himself.   His mind, for the
time being, was set, as we have already seen, on keeping the
peace, and getting back to Spain ; clearly under all the circumstances it was a case for temporizing.   So in the spring
of 1559, before he left the Low Countries for the last time,

---

[1] Camoens, *Lusiads* (tr. R. F. Burton), canto vii, stanza 5.

Philip installed in London a new ambassador, Álvaro della Quadra, bishop of Aquila, bold, skilful, and unscrupulous, with instructions to watch events and report frequently.[1] His first letter, May 10, 1559, to the Duke of Alva, closes with the following significant sentence: "Religion here now is simply a question of policy, and in a hundred thousand ways they let us see that they neither love nor fear us."[2]

Philip's determination to proceed cautiously in England, and to make sure of his ground before taking any definite steps to punish the enormities of the queen, received ample justification in the following July. The sudden death of King Henry II brought his son Francis II to the throne of France, and Francis was married to Mary queen of Scots. France and Scotland were thus united more closely than ever before; but that was by no means all. In addition to being queen of Scotland and of France, Mary was also, in case Elizabeth should die without issue, the lawful heiress of the throne of England; nay more, in the eyes of all true Catholics, she was actually the rightful queen of England at that very moment, for it was a motto of the Counter-Reformation that no heretic should be allowed to reign. All these circumstances powerfully affected the position of Philip II. If, as the lay champion of the Counter-Reformation, he supported Mary and Francis in an attempt to dethrone Elizabeth, he would be contributing enormously to the political aggrandizement of the Valois monarchy, of which, though he had just made peace with it, he continued to be deeply jealous and distrustful. Much as he was offended by the conduct of the English queen, he could not afford to give vent to his indignation. Rather it might even be a case of his being obliged to lend covert support to that

[1] C. S. P., Spanish, 1558-67, nos. 30, 33. Quadra had been in London for some time before, as one of the staff of his predecessor the Count of Feria.
[2] Ibid., no. 32.

detestable heretic, in order to ward off the political peril of the absorption of the whole of Great Britain by France.[1]

This complexity of circumstances furnishes the key to the story of the relations of Philip to Elizabeth down to the month of December, 1560, when the death of Francis II broke up the Franco-Scottish alliance and liberated England from a truly deadly peril. Throughout those crucial eighteen months the policy of Elizabeth was that of masterly inaction. She played the Hapsburgs off against the Valois, and vice versa; she coquetted with the Scottish Protestants; she committed herself to no one, and grew steadily stronger through the rivalries of her various foes. Philip, during the same period, was also inactive, but to far less good purpose than was the queen of England; he never got the lead out of her hand. He sought to bind her to the house of Hapsburg by proposing that she should marry one of his cousins, the Archdukes Ferdinand and Charles of Austria.[2] He flirted with a scheme of sending a Spanish force into Scotland on the plea of the necessity of suppressing heresy there, but really, of course, to keep watch on the French, and then, after the French were disposed of, to aid and abet a rising of the English Catholics.[3] But nothing would induce him to listen to the pleas of Quadra that he interfere boldly and vigorously in England, or to his assurances that so good a chance would never come again.[4] Doubtless the Spanish ambassador overstated his case. Until the Valois peril was removed by the death of Francis II, Philip was, of necessity, practically immobilized. The really extraordinary thing is

[1] A. O. Meyer, *England and the Catholic Church under Queen Elizabeth*, p. 58, even speaks of Spain in this period as "the ally of the English, and therefore also of the Scotch, Reformation."

[2] *C. S. P.*, *Spanish*, 1558-67, nos. 26, 28, 29, 30.

[3] Froude, vii, pp. 191 ff.; A. Teulet, *Relations politiques de la France et de l'Espagne avec l'Écosse*, ii, pp. 52-142, *passim*.

[4] *C. S. P.*, *Spanish*, 1558-67, no. 91.

that when that danger was passed in midsummer, 1561, with the return of the queen of Scots, widowed but independent, to her native land, the habit of inaction had become so fixed with the Spanish king that he could not avail himself of the fact that his hands were no longer tied. Once more Quadra urged him to strike, to grant vigorous support to Mary Stuart, since she was no longer bound to France, and to stir up a Catholic rising in England. He even ventured to tell Philip that the English Romanists had "lost all hope, and complain bitterly that through their placing all their confidence in your Majesty and trusting to you entirely, they have failed to avail themselves of the friendship of the French." [1] But it was all in vain. Nothing would induce the Prudent King to risk a fight; the most he would do was to play with a project for definitely binding the queen of Scots to the Hapsburgs by arranging a marriage between her and Don Carlos.[2] Whether, in view of the state of the prince's health, Philip had any real intention of carrying through this project may well be doubted; but Quadra flung himself into the negotiations for it with such feverish energy that the strain they entailed proved too much for his constitution, and in August, 1563, he died.[3]

There is no point in following the course of Philip's policy with respect to the internal affairs of England during the next few years; it is a tale of promises and projects unfulfilled, of endless procrastination, and complete ineffectiveness. More than ever he was convinced that, no matter what provocation was offered him, he could not under any circumstances afford to appeal to arms; and the character and instructions [4] of his next ambassador, Diego Guzmán de Silva, who was sent to replace Quadra at London after

[1] C. S. P., Spanish, 1558–67, no. 150.
[2] Ibid., nos. 215, 216, 218, 230, 239.
[3] Ibid., no. 240.
[4] Ibid., nos. 244, 248.

an interval of six months, are the best possible evidence of it. The new Spanish representative was a far gentler person than his two predecessors; it has been well said of him, moreover, that he came not to impose a policy, but to ask for a redress of grievances.[1] Some of these were standard topics of complaint which had to do with the internal situation, such as, for instance, the matter of the very mild disabilities of the English Catholics, and are of little interest for us here; but there were two others of much wider import which powerfully affected the development of the Spanish Empire, and therefore demand at least passing consideration. The first of these was the embargo which England had laid on the products of the Low Countries; the second was the menace of the Elizabethan pirates.

The distrust between England and Philip's government in the Netherlands, and the sympathy of the English Protestants for the cause of the rebels there, had already begun to manifest itself in a series of restrictive enactments and counter-enactments which had practically brought to a standstill the anciently established and mutually indispensable commercial relations of the two countries.[2] The Netherlanders were unquestionably the side that suffered most, for without English wool their manufactures were ruined, whereas England had various alternative outlets for her raw material and goods; moreover, many of the Flemings had already taken refuge across the Channel, and had been liberally aided by Elizabeth in setting up their industries in England. Hitherto Philip had answered every one of Elizabeth's prohibitions with some kind of retaliatory

[1] *C. S. P.*, *Spanish*, 1558–67, introduction, p. li.

[2] *Statutes of the Realm*, 5 Elizabeth, cap. 7, and 8 Elizabeth, cap. 3, 6; William Cunningham, *The Growth of English Industry and Commerce in* *Modern Times* (Cambridge, 1912), i, p. 25. *C. S. P.*, *Spanish*, 1558–67, no. 248, gives an excellent picture of the situation as seen through Philip's eyes.

act; but now he was convinced that he was getting the worst of the argument, and he ordered Guzmán to arrange "for the conference to settle the whole question . . . in the friendly spirit anciently existing between the two countries and their rulers." [1] But the queen was in no hurry to accept the suggestion. Difficult though the situation was, she was far less worried by it than was Philip; and she knew enough of the character of the Spanish king to realize that a conference was bound to be useless unless she was prepared to grant more than she gained. To ruin the commerce of the Low Countries was, after all, one of the most effective ways of holding the Spanish power in check there; and she had already plainly perceived that unless it was held in check the safety of England would be endangered. And so Guzmán was put off with excuses, and the situation went from bad to worse.[2]

If Philip was powerless to remedy the conditions that had arisen with regard to the commercial relations of the Netherlands and England, he was somewhat better prepared to oppose the activities of the English sea-rovers. The naval enthusiasm of Tudor England, carefully nurtured by Henry VII and Henry VIII, was now beginning to reach its full fruition; and in view of the strained relations, political, commercial, and religious, between the English and Spanish governments, it naturally manifested itself at the expense of the subjects of the Prudent King. Piratical seizures in the Channel were no longer the exception but the rule. Single galleons plying between Antwerp and Cadiz were an easy prey.[3] Elizabeth gave no official sanction to these outrages, but on the other hand she carefully avoided putting a stop to them. The rovers, moreover, were now

---

[1] C. S. P., Spanish, 1558–67, no. 248, p. 359.

[2] Froude, viii, pp. 449 ff.

[3] C. S. P., Foreign, 1561–62, no. 324;

C. S. P., Spanish, 1558–67, no. 249; Froude, viii, pp. 438 f., and references there.

venturing out into more distant waters. In June, 1563, Hugh Tipton, an Englishman resident at Seville, reported to Sir Thomas Chaloner, Queen Elizabeth's ambassador at Madrid, a characteristic occurrence. A Spanish vessel, homeward bound from Porto Rico, met with two small ships, whose crews "killed two or three of her men, and hurt divers, and robbed them of 3000 pieces of money, ten chests of sugar, 200 great hides, and all their ordnance, cables, and anchors. . . . They carried away the pilot of the Spanish ship." Tipton was confident that "if they do more hurt, all the English goods here will be embargoed," and assured his Spanish friends "that they were Scots and Frenchmen, and some Englishmen among them, a sort of thieves gathered together to go a robbing." [1] Scores of other similar instances are recorded in the correspondence of the time. And that was by no means all. It was in October, 1562, that Sir John Hawkins made his first voyage to the West African coast in search of negro slaves, of whom, after plundering a number of Portuguese vessels, he obtained a goodly number, together with rich merchandise. With this booty he crossed over to the West Indies, where he exchanged it for hides, ginger, sugar, and pearls. With the greater part of this treasure he himself returned to England, but two of his vessels he despatched to Seville to dispose of their cargoes there. Naturally Philip did not relish this daring infringement of his monopoly of the trade of the New World; the ships which Hawkins had sent to Seville were seized and their cargoes confiscated, and their crews only escaped imprisonment by flight. Hawkins's efforts to recover his property were unavailing; and the episode led directly on to his much more famous expedition in the year 1565, in

[1] C. S. P., Foreign, 1563, no. 944. Cf. also infra, p. 279. Chaloner had been sent as ambassador to Spain in October, 1561. Though popular there, he was unable to settle outstanding disputes, and was recalled in 1564.

which he visited not only West Africa and the Caribbean, but also the French colony on the shores of Florida, and the coast of Newfoundland on his way home. His relations to the Spaniards, uncordial, to put it mildly, during his first venture, became openly and avowedly hostile during his second.[1]

Such escapades as these were quite undreamed of in the philosophy of Philip II. Their irregularity, their utter lawlessness, the evident delight which they afforded their perpetrators, were utterly abhorrent to his formal, slow-moving mind. But he was not without his means of retaliation. Boycotts and embargoes, indeed, would obviously avail him nothing, but in the Inquisition he possessed a weapon of defence as characteristically Spanish as the piracies of the sea-rovers were English. In the latter part of the Emperor's reign, the Holy Office had been instructed to use special vigilance at the seaports, doubtless in order to prevent heretics and heretical books from seeping into the realm.[2] Its minions were fully informed in regard to the arrival and departure of every foreign ship, and they utilized the 'supereminence' of the institution which they served to invoke the aid of all the local authorities in the accomplishment of their allotted task. The result was that, from the very beginning of the reign, a goodly number of Englishmen found their way into Spanish prisons, where they were not seldom so cruelly treated that they died. The fate of the crews of certain English ships captured in the harbor of Gibraltar in November, 1563, may be cited as an example. Two hundred and forty men had been incarcerated on that occasion, and when the studiously deliberate investigation of the whole affair had been concluded, there were but eighty

[1] J. A. Williamson, *Sir John Hawkins*, pp. 81–116.

[2] Lea, *Inquisition of Spain*, iii, pp. 505 f.; Froude, viii, pp. 439 f.

left alive to be sent home.[1] The situation, of course, was made vastly worse in the exaggerated reports that found their way back to London, but it certainly was such as befitted less a state of formal peace than one of war. When, in January, 1564, the climax was reached with a definite order from Philip for the arrest of every English ship in Spanish harbors, together with their crews and owners,[2] it was really remarkable that hostilities were not openly declared. But, as usual, both sovereigns preferred to play safe. Both of them had their hands full of other things, and could ill afford to risk a fight; and so the settlement of outstanding disputes was placed in the hands of a commission of plenipotentiaries which met at Bruges in the early part of 1566, but totally failed to accomplish its purpose.[3] One year later, in the summer of 1567, just as the period under review was drawing to a close, an event occurred in Plymouth Harbor, far more indicative of the way the wind was really blowing than any effort to settle existing Anglo-Spanish difficulties at a council table — a foreshadowing, in fact, of what was to occur in that self-same harbor in the summer of 1588. Sir John Hawkins was there, getting ready for a new expedition to the Indies, in reckless defiance of the protests of Philip's ambassador, when seven Spanish ships, flying the flag of Castile, entered the port. There was no reason to think that they had come with any hostile intent, though their failure to salute the queen's ships was certainly discourteous; but Hawkins promptly fired into them, forced

[1] C. S. P., Foreign, 1563, nos. 1424, 1465, 1483, 1488, 1508, 1525, 1526, 1541, 1561; 1564–65, nos. 21, 22, 59, 87, 179, 226, 342, 376, 505, 552, 595, 611, 641, 900; letter of Guzmán to Philip, June 5, 1564, calendared in J. Paz, Catálogo, p. 121, no. 439; Froude, viii, p. 446; supra, p. 112.

[2] C. S. P., Foreign, 1564–65, no. 80.

English sailors considered the breaking of peace "by ymbargo" that "which of all kindes of defiances is most reproved, and of least reputation." Sir Richard Hawkins, in The Hawkins' Voyages, ed. Markham, p. 318.

[3] C. S. P., Spanish, 1558–67, p. 417, note.

them to lower their colors, and refused to listen to their commander's subsequent expostulations.[1]   However much Philip and Elizabeth were determined to avoid war, it was impossible to quench the spirit that was ultimately to force their hands.

The stage is now set and the chief characters placed for the great drama that was to be enacted in Western Europe in the ensuing thirty years.   Peace had been kept, chiefly because Philip was resolved that it should be kept ; but there was more than enough incendiary material in the Netherlands, in France, and in England, to feed a tremendous conflagration.   In the next act of the play, the Spanish monarch becomes somewhat more aggressive ; the flames of war burst forth in the Low Countries; and the relations of Spain with France and with England proceed from bad to worse.

This next act lasts from 1567 to 1573, and is epitomized in the name of Philip's new regent in the Netherlands during those years : Fernando Álvarez de Toledo, better known as the Duke of Alva.   His appointment itself was adequate evidence, for those who knew the facts, that Philip was done with making concessions there.   The king, as was his habit, tried his best to conceal his hand, and to make men think that the policy of the days of Margaret of Parma was to continue unchanged ; but no one familiar with Alva's character and past record could have had any real doubts that he was being sent to the Netherlands for the purpose of Hispanicizing them, both politically and religiously, to an extent that had never been contemplated before : of erecting them, in fact, into a regular *presidio*, whence the Spanish monarchy,

---

[1] J. A. Williamson, *Sir John Hawkins*, pp. 132–135.   It is perhaps needless   to add that Hawkins was reprimanded for his conduct by the queen.

undisturbed by further revolt, could assert its predominance over England, France, and the Empire.[1] Moreover, there could be no real question that the methods by which this result was to be attained were to be primarily those of repression and violence. That Alva had made his reputation as a soldier proclaimed as much, as did also the fact that he was the first of the Hapsburg representatives in the Low Countries who was not related by blood to the royal family. And, finally, his own character and antecedents were directly the opposite to those of the people over whom he was sent to rule. He was the typical Castilian grandee, proud, intolerant, and disdainful; they were the scions of traders and artisans, hard-working, democratic, and boisterous. He had not forgotten how at the age of twelve he had seen his own country insulted and impoverished by the Flemings in the train of Chièvres;[2] he had waited for years for an opportunity for revenge. Waiting and remembering were in fact two of his strongest points. They made him a fit instrument of the policy of Philip II.[3]

For a full month after his arrival in the Low Countries the new regent held his hand. It may have been in compliance with the royal instructions; more likely it was in order to make absolutely sure of ultimate success; certain it is that during the interval the whole population was oppressed with the conviction that some terrible and mysterious catastrophe was impending.[4] Then suddenly, beginning on September 9, 1567, the blows began to fall. On that day the two chief rebel leaders, Egmont and Hoorn, were arrested at Brussels.

[1] Pirenne, iv, pp. 4 f.; Gossart, L'Établissement du régime espagnol, pp. 79–81.

[2] Cf. ante, Vol. III, pp. 26–33.

[3] Cf. the account of his first interview with Margaret of Parma, August 26, 1567, in Correspondance de Philippe II, i, pp. 566 f. A more favorable picture of Alva is given in the Contribución al Estudio de la persona del III Duque de Alba (Madrid, 1919), the discourse by his descendant the Duque de Berwick y de Alba upon his entry into the R. A. H.

[4] Pirenne, iv, p. 9; Gossart, pp. 83 ff.

Twelve days later, when the news had reached Spain, their representative there, the Baron de Montigny, who had been lulled into security by the false promises of Philip, was likewise seized and confined in the *alcazar* of Segovia.[1]   At the same time there was set up in the Netherlands the famous Council of Troubles — better known as the Council of Blood — a body of seven, dominated by three Spaniards, whose function it was to prepare the sentences of those whom the government had decided to have punished.   It superseded all other courts and jurisdictions; it overrode all privileges and liberties, both personal and national; like the Revolutionary Tribunal of 1793, it sacrificed everything on the altar of *raison d'état*.   On January 4, 1568, 84 persons were executed, on February 20–21, 108, on March 20, 55.[2] All the property of the victims was forfeited to the crown; it was intended that the new policy of blood should more than justify itself as a financial measure.   On June 5, 1568, the climax was reached with the execution of Egmont and Hoorn in the public square in Brussels.   Though their countrymen were too terrified, too dumfounded to protest at the time, the event had the merit of making the issue clear.[3] After that there could be no doubt that the day of compromises and palliations was passed, that two irreconcilable systems were confronting one another, and that one or the other must ultimately succumb.

Meantime William of Orange, more cautious than Egmont and Hoorn, had escaped the clutches of Alva, and was organizing an army of resistance in the Northeast.   The

[1] *Correspondance de Philippe II*, i, pp. 572–575, 578 f., 581.

[2] The contemporary estimates of the total number of Alva's victims in the Low Countries vary from 6000 to 18,000; but it seems clear that the first figure is far nearer the truth than the second. Cf. Pirenne, iv, p. 10, note; Hugo Grotius, *Annales* (Amsterdam, 1658), p. 60.

[3] Pirenne, iv, p. 13.   The standard Protestant account of the tragedy is that of Motley, *Rise of the Dutch Republic*, part iii.

Lutherans of the Empire gave him considerable support. French and English Calvinists rallied to his standard. It was evident that there was plenty of sympathy for his cause in the neighboring lands, even though the policies of their governments might not permit formal expression of it. But Orange on the battle field was far inferior to Orange at the council table. His forces, led by his heroic brother, Louis, count of Nassau, were successively defeated by Alva's veterans at Dahlen (April, 1568) and Jemgum (July 21); by November the rebel army had been virtually dispersed, and Orange himself had taken refuge in Picardy.[1] Then Alva was convinced that he had triumphantly and permanently finished the work he had been sent to do. The people, so he assured the king, were the easiest to govern in the world, if one only knew how to treat them.[2] He had statues of himself erected at Antwerp [3] and at Brussels. He even ventured to send 1500 horsemen into France to aid Catharine de' Medici against the Huguenots, and to reply to the piracies of the English in the Channel by arresting all the subjects of Elizabeth in the Low Countries. It looked as if the dream of Philip was about to come true; instead of constituting a danger point to Spain and a vantage ground to her foes, the Netherlands promised soon to become a mighty fortress from which he could overawe the entire North of Europe. The king indeed was less fully convinced than was his representative of the advantage of indefinite prolongation of the policy of severity. Since February, 1569, he had been in favor of granting a general pardon, but it was not until seventeen months later that Alva could be brought to con-

---

[1] This story is told in detail on pp. 213–447 of vol. iii of F. Rachfahl's *Wilhelm von Oranien und der niederländische Aufstand*, the most recent and exhaustive treatment of the subject.

[2] *Correspondance de Philippe II*, ii, p. 79.

[3] For a description of this see Gossart, *L'Établissement*, pp. 117 f.

sent to it; moreover, when the pardon was finally issued, it was so full of exceptions, both general and specific, that it virtually amounted to a fresh proscription. One example of its operation will suffice : it was precisely three months after the day on which it was put forth that Montigny, who had languished in his Spanish prison since September, 1567, was secretly strangled in the castle of Simancas.[1]

But Alva's conception of his task in the Netherlands was not solely one of torture and massacres. He proposed to prevent the recurrence of 'troubles' in the future by a radical alteration of the constitution of the Low Countries, which should convert them into a docile dependency of the Spanish crown after the pattern of Naples and Milan. Absolute extirpation of heresy was, of course, the indispensable preliminary to this. The new bishoprics, provided in 1559, were now fully organized and set up, and their occupants charged with the duty of hunting out Lutherans and Calvinists. Alva was delighted to have them employed in this fashion, for it tallied with his conception of the duty of the church to lend its full support to the state.[2] At the same time every effort was made to Hispanicize the government, and to abrogate or nullify local privileges and liberties. Alva proposed to bring everything to the feet of his master. It was observed that when a vacancy occurred in any of the councils he did not hurry to fill it. His plan, as he explained in a letter to the king, was to let the unoccupied places accumulate until, by providing for a large number of them at once, he could Hispanicize the personnel of the administration *en bloc*; "under the system of successive nomina-

[1] Pirenne, iv, pp. 16 f.; Gossart, *L'Établissement*, p. 306.

[2] Pirenne, iv, pp. 17 f. As another means of preventing heresy, matriculation at foreign universities was forbidden; and there was even talk of founding colleges for Spaniards at the universities of Louvain and Douai, and for Flemings at Salamanca and Alcalá. *Correspondance du Cardinal de Granvelle*, ed. Piot, iv, pp. 35 f.

tions," so he wrote to Philip, "those who remain corrupt those who come in, just as happens when one throws a flask of good wine into a cask of vinegar." [1] Most fundamental of all, however, was his financial policy. To have the Spanish monarchy in any sense dependent for its revenues, as it still was in the Low Countries, on the vote of the national assembly, was to Alva's mind intolerable. With Philip's full approval, he now proposed to remedy this defect in characteristic Spanish fashion by forcing the Estates to sanction the permanent establishment in the Netherlands of an *alcabala* or tax on sales, at the rate of five per cent on real and ten per cent on personal property. There was also to be a single impost, at the rate of one per cent, levied once and for all on all property in the land. The Estates were summoned to Brussels on March 21, 1569, to consent to these exactions, and all the resources of treachery and intimidation were brought into play in order to bend them to the royal will. The levy of the hundredth penny, after many protests, was finally sanctioned and at once put into operation; by February, 1571, it had yielded 3,300,000 florins.[2] To the *alcabala*, on the other hand, the deputies were resolved not to submit. Not only would its establishment mean the subversion of their most cherished liberties; they also clearly perceived, what Philip and Alva were unable to comprehend, that it ultimately spelt economic ruin, that the measure which the king and his adviser had adopted as the shortest way to replenish the royal exchequer was really only killing the goose that laid the golden eggs. They finally succeeded in inducing Alva to accept for a period of two years (August 13, 1569–August 13, 1571) a lump sum of 2,000,000 florins per annum in lieu of the *alcabala*, which

[1] *Correspondance de Philippe II*, ii, p. 360; Pirenne, iv, pp. 18 f., and other references there.

[2] Pirenne, iv, pp. 20–23, and references there.

they dreaded most of all. When that period had expired, the Duke refused to consider the prolongation of it, and within a few weeks the *alcabala* was in full swing.[1] Thereupon ensued a scene of wild confusion. The business world was paralyzed. Merchants left the country in swarms. Contracts were cancelled right and left. Rents fell to one-sixth of their former value. The textile industry was so hard hit that Alva could not find enough blue cloth in all Brussels and Antwerp to enable him to renew the furnishings of his own palace. But he was absolutely deaf to any kind of remonstrance. He would not listen to the advice of his own clergy, or of Francisco de Álava, the Spanish ambassador at Paris, when they warned him of the dangers of the course he was pursuing. As for the rage of the masses, he felt sure that it could be safely ignored. "This people," so he once wrote to Philip, "is always such as Julius Caesar depicted it." [2]

Before we take up the course of the revolution which Alva's brutality and ineptitude unchained in the Netherlands in the spring of 1572, it is essential to consider the effect of his presence in the Low Countries on the relations of Spain to France and to England.

It is easy enough to see, after the lapse of three centuries and a half, that one of Philip's gravest errors was his failure to realize that the England of Queen Elizabeth constituted a far more serious menace to the integrity of the Spanish

---

[1] Pirenne, iv, p. 23; *Correspondance du Cardinal de Granvelle*, ed. Piot, iv, p. 93.

[2] *Correspondance de Philippe II*, ii, pp. 209 f.; *Correspondance du Cardinal de Granvelle*, iv, pp. 100, 126, 149, 305; Gossart, *L'Établissement*, pp. 211 ff., 297 ff. Alva doubtless refers to Caesar's characterization of the Gauls as prone to sedition, yet inconstant in adversity. *De Bello Gallico*, lib. iv, cap. 5: "infirmitatem Gallorum . . . quod sunt in consiliis capiendis mobiles, et novis plerumque rebus student"; lib. iii, cap. 19: "mollis ac minime resistens ad calamitates perferendas mens eorum est"; also lib. iii, caps. 1, 10.

Empire than did the France of the last three Valois kings.
We think of the former as passing through one of the most
notable periods of its history, united at home under one of
the greatest sovereigns of all time, reaching out to lay the
foundations of a far-flung colonial and commercial empire,
inevitably destined, for reasons political, religious, and
economic, to come into violent collision with Spain, both in
the Old World and in the New.   We think of the latter as
internally disrupted by civil and religious strife, a prey to
factions, without any consistent policy either at home or
abroad.   But when we come to consider the situation as it
presented itself to the Spanish monarch, we shall not be at
a loss for reasons to explain why he continued so long to
underestimate England and to exaggerate the danger from
France.   The latter, in the first place, was the hereditary
foe, the constant enemy, for over sixty years past, not only
in the Old World but also in the New.[1]   Secondly, it intervened between Spain and the Low Countries, and constituted an annoying barrier to communication between them.
Thirdly, its recent tendency towards Protestantism, though
less marked than that of England, was probably even more
alarming to Philip; for it was perilously close to his own
borders, and he could not endure the idea of having a heretic
on his flank.   England, on the other hand, seemed much
more remote, and principally occupied with its own affairs.
It had, moreover, been recently Spain's ally against France;
Philip had even cherished hopes of bringing it permanently
under Hapsburg control.   So rapid had been the oscillations
of its religious policy during the previous half-century that its
complete re-Catholicization did not seem by any means out
of the question.   Spain had not "yet learned to think of
Elizabeth's government as strong, nor of the Elizabethan

[1] Cf. *ante*, Vol. III, pp. 525 f., 631, 634 f.

settlement in England as stable." [1] The exploits of the
English sea-rovers were regarded by the Spaniards more in
the light of the irritating pranks of an extremely naughty
boy than as the first evidences of the upcoming of the greatest naval power of modern times. Before 1568, when the
attention of Queen Elizabeth's government was primarily
focussed on the affairs of Scotland, there had been, perhaps,
some real basis for this point of view; but with the defeat
and flight to England of Mary queen of Scots, the situation had entirely changed. Elizabeth began to consider the
problem presented by the Netherlands far more seriously
than ever before. New voices, like that of Sir Francis Walsingham, were beginning to make themselves heard in her
councils,[2] and causing her to consider the probable consequences of Alva's obvious intention to erect them into a
Spanish *presidio*. We discern the first faint glimmerings of
the dawn of a new era in English foreign policy, which was
ultimately to bear fruit in the defeat of the Spanish Armada.

But Philip was still determined to adhere, if possible, to
the policy of 'sturdy defensiveness' in his foreign relations
which had been commended to him by his father. If the
Tudor and Valois monarchs would only leave Alva to carry
out undisturbed in the Netherlands the new programme
which he had been sent there to initiate, he had as yet no
intention of making trouble for them. But the Duke soon
became aware that his doings in the Low Countries were
arousing deep hostility on both sides of the Channel. Moreover, like his master in Madrid, he was at first inclined to
believe that he was in considerably more danger from France
than from England. William of Orange and his brother
Louis were in close touch with the leaders of the French

---

[1] J. R. Seeley, *Growth of British Policy*, i, p. 153.

[2] Conyers Read, *Mr. Secretary Walsingham*, i, pp. 54 ff.

Huguenots. There were rumors that Condé had made the peace of Longjumeau (March 23, 1568), which had terminated so unexpectedly the so-called Second Civil War, in order to be free to interfere in the Low Countries; and it was only five months later that William signed a secret treaty with Condé and Coligny in which they promised each other mutual assistance, offensive and defensive, until they should have gained their ends.[1] The Third Civil War in France broke out, it is true, directly afterwards, and the Catholics won impressive victories at Jarnac (March 13, 1569) and at Moncontour (October 3, 1569); but their Protestant foes refused to be discouraged, and at the peace of St. Germain-en-Laye (August 8, 1570) obtained important concessions for their faith. Still more alarming to the Duke of Alva was the palpably anti-Spanish attitude of Charles IX, who, after having remained for ten years a puppet in his mother's hands, was now beginning to demand a share in the direction of affairs. Louis of Nassau had two conferences with him in July, 1571, in which he besought him to intervene to deliver the Low Countries from their Spanish oppressors, and the king gave him most encouraging replies. Even Catharine for the moment seemed to have succumbed to the anti-Spanish trend. She had been much irritated by Philip's refusal, after the death (October 3, 1568) of Elizabeth of Valois, to wed as his fourth wife the latter's younger sister, Margaret. She was at present planning to marry Margaret to Henry of Navarre, and her son, Henry of Anjou, was seeking the hand of the queen of England. Finally, there were mysterious activities in the harbors of Nantes and Bordeaux. Ships were being prepared. No one seemed to know exactly what was to be done with them, but Alva was persuaded that they were destined for

[1] Mariéjol in Lavisse, vi, 1, pp. 99 f., 105, 109.

some enterprise which boded ill for his master. Even the news of Don John's great victory at Lepanto (October 7, 1571) did not serve to frighten the French into an abandonment of their anti-Spanish attitude. The Duke was convinced that a blow would soon be struck, and struck in all probability at Spain in the Netherlands.[1]

The prospect of English hostility, on the other hand, he affected, at first, to regard as far less serious. He realized that Elizabeth, like his own master, loved to temporize. He recognized her natural reluctance to countenance any revolt against monarchical authority, even though the monarch in question might be her bitterest foe. He knew that she was well aware that the maintenance of the wool trade between England and the Low Countries was wellnigh indispensable to both. He was glad to learn that she had assured the Spanish ambassador, in August, 1568, that she was delighted at the news of his victory over the rebels.[2] There were, of course, a host of other bits of evidence which pointed in the opposite direction. In October, 1567, only two months after Alva had reached Brussels, Hawkins had set sail on another freebooting expedition into American waters, which was destined to eclipse all his previous impertinences.[3] We have already described the treatment accorded to Dr. John Man, the English ambassador at Madrid, because of his demand that he be permitted to have the Anglican service performed at his house without fear of interference by the Holy Inquisition; never again was Elizabeth to have an official resident representative at the court of the Prudent King.[4] Then, in December, 1568, had ensued the

[1] Mariéjol in Lavisse, vi, 1, pp. 111–120, passim; Pirenne, iv, p. 29.

[2] Froude, ix, pp. 321 f.; C. S. P., Spanish, 1568–79, nos. 36, 37, 45; E. F. Benson, Sir Francis Drake, pp. 95 f.

[3] Williamson, Sir John Hawkins, pp. 145 ff.; Froude, ix, pp. 358–362.

[4] Cf. ante, pp. 79 f. Envoys extraordinary, however, continued occasionally to be sent, as, e.g., Sir Henry Cobham, who was in Spain on special

seizure by the English government of a fleet of Spanish treasure ships bound for the Low Countries, which had sought refuge in Plymouth and Southampton from the pirates of the Channel. Alva was prompt to retort with the counter-seizure of all English property in the Netherlands, and the arrest of the English residents there; and Elizabeth in turn retaliated by imprisoning in his house the new and very aggressive Spanish ambassador to London, Guerau de Spes, whom Philip had despatched in the previous August to replace the more complaisant Guzmán de Silva.[1] By midsummer, 1569, however, the tension had slackened again; and, as an evidence of her hope and belief that peace could be preserved, Elizabeth restored the Spanish ambassador to liberty.[2] There appeared, in other words, to be no sequence or system to her aggressions; most of them might even have been charitably construed rather as the acts of lawless individuals than of the English government. To Alva's formal mind they were, for that very reason, doubly abhorrent, but as yet they did not seem to him to indicate the existence of any settled policy of war. Without question they merited condign punishment; but it seemed likely that such punishment could be administered quite as effectively and much more cheaply by conspiracy and intrigue than by hostilities open and avowed.[3]

The consequence was that the next two years of English history (November, 1569, to December, 1571) witness a

---

missions for the queen in 1570 and in 1575.

[1] C. S. P., Spanish, 1568–79, nos. 68, 70; Froude, ix, pp. 366–376. The correspondence between Alva and Guerau de Spes is printed in full in vols. v and vi of Kervyn de Lettenhove's Relations politiques des Pays-Bas et de l'Angleterre. Cf. also C. Read, "Queen Elizabeth's Seizure of the Duke of Alva's Pay-Ships," in the Journal of Modern History, v (1933), pp. 443–464.

[2] Froude, ix, p. 475.

[3] An excellent account of the ebbs and flows of Anglo-Spanish relations in these years is to be found in vol. i, chap. i, of P. O. von Törne's Don Juan d'Autriche. A briefer one is given in chapter vi of E. Gossart's L'Établissement du régime espagnol.

series of Catholic plots against the Queen and the government, of all of which Philip and Alva were cognizant and to some of which they lent active encouragement. The situation in England was highly favorable to such attempts. The Romanists were discontented owing to the enforcement of the penal laws. The captive Scottish queen furnished an excellent rallying cry. Guerau de Spes was in London to pull the wires. But even with all these advantages, and also the conviction that they were fully justified in any means that they might use to effect the deposition of an heretical queen, Philip and Alva acted neither effectively nor in unison; and their slackness was a grievous disappointment both to Guerau de Spes and to the English Catholics.[1] The king throughout was apparently more anxious for vigorous action than was the Duke.[2] The latter was primarily interested in the recovery of his treasure ships by negotiation, and did not wish to risk it by getting involved with aristocratic conspiracies in which he had little faith. Not until the Northern Earls should prove their mettle by liberating Mary queen of Scots from captivity would he consent to send them support;[3] and as they were unable to accomplish this, an opportunity which, if vigorously seized at the outset, might have yielded good results, was suffered to slip by unimproved. On February 25, 1570, Pope Pius V launched a bull of excommunication against Elizabeth, and strove to induce Philip and Alva to undertake the execution of it. De Spes and the English Catholics were fully convinced that, with aid from across the Channel, their success was assured; but both the king and his representative in the Low Countries continued to hang back. They complained, with some justice, that they had not been consulted before-

---

[1] Froude, ix, pp. 523 f.   [2] Törne, *op. cit.*, i, pp. 42 f.
[3] *Ibid.*, p. 87.

hand in regard to the bull, or even notified that it was to be put forth; nothing would induce them to follow it up with a vigorous attack.[1] In the winter of 1570–71 a third opportunity — in some respects the most favorable that had yet occurred — was presented by the machinations of the Duke of Norfolk and of the papal agent Ridolfi; de Spes and the English Catholics were more urgent than ever; the captive Mary "committed her cause to Spain." This time Philip was persuaded that the moment had come to strike.[2] On Saturday, July 7, 1571, there was held in Madrid a famous meeting of the Consejo, in which it was decided that Elizabeth must be assassinated, and ways and means were discussed. Orders also were despatched to Alva to have a fleet and an army in readiness, that he might be able to invade at the critical juncture.[3] But the Duke was more cautious than ever with regard to England at the very moment that his master had grown more bold. He was worried by rumors that reached him of the intimacy of certain malcontents of the maritime provinces of the Netherlands with the English privateers; he was impressed with the ease with which the government of Elizabeth had weathered the previous storms. If the assassination of the queen could be actually accomplished, he agreed that an invasion should be attempted forthwith; until that event, he insisted, it would be perilous to move,[4] and his hesitation made a profound impression on the mind of the king. Neither the resolutions of the Spanish war council nor the pleadings of Spes could induce Philip to give the word for an invasion; he placed the conduct of his policy with regard to England entirely, for the moment, in Alva's hands. And so the year 1571 ended

[1] Törne, op. cit., i, pp. 93–96.
[2] Törne, i, pp. 101–108, and references there; A. O. Meyer, op. cit., pp. 236 f.
[3] Törne, i, pp. 109–113, and references there; Froude, x, pp. 250–259; Mignet, Marie Stuart, 3e éd., ii, p. 145.
[4] Törne, i, pp. 113 f.

with nothing accomplished.   Elizabeth was not assassinated, and England remained uninvaded.

From their comfortable conviction that the Netherlanders would never venture to revolt, and from their hesitant machinations against the governments of England and of France, Philip and Alva were suddenly aroused by the astonishing news that on April 1, 1572, the town of Brill, at the mouth of the Meuse, had been seized and occupied by the famous 'Beggars of the Sea.' [1]

Broadly speaking, this disaster was in large measure due to the same error of judgment that had given the keynote to the foreign policy of Philip during the five preceding years: namely, his tendency to overestimate the danger from France and to underestimate that from England.   So preoccupied had been the Duke with the perils of invasion from the southwest that he failed to keep track of what had been happening in the ports of Holland and Zealand.   The inhabitants of these seacoast towns were among the bitterest of his enemies.   His character and his programme, political, economic, and religious, were utterly detestable to them.   Their own native independence and disregard for authority were stimulated by the example of the English privateers, with whom, ever since 1568, they had been increasingly closely in touch; even Queen Elizabeth had been induced to grant them covert encouragement and support, and they possessed what amounted to a base at Dover.[2]   At the outset the Duke had practically ignored them.   Later on, in 1571, as we have already seen, he began to take the matter somewhat more seriously; he entered into negotiations

[1] Pirenne, iv, p. 29; P. Geyl, *The Revolt of the Netherlands (1555-1609)*, p. 116.

[2] P. J. Blok, "De Watergeusen in England (1568-72)," in *Bijdragen voor Vaderlandsche Geschiedenis*, derde reeks, ix, p. 251 (1896).

with Elizabeth on the subject, at the very moment that he was plotting for her assassination, with the result that in the end of February, 1572, the chief of the Dutch pirates, William de La Marck, sometimes known as the Sire de Lumey, was ordered to leave the realm.[1] The news of his expulsion relieved Alva's worst fears for the moment; he felt confident that such danger as there had been from England was now at least temporarily past; he reverted once more to the problem presented by the situation in France. But the future was to prove that his calculations were entirely wrong. Precisely how far the government of Elizabeth was implicated in the events that followed the expulsion of La Marck will probably never be known; but the available documents make possible the hypothesis that she so timed her official compliance with Alva's request as to convert it into the first effective blow against his government in the Netherlands.[2] At any rate, La Marck had no sooner quitted Dover than he swooped down on a convoy of Spanish traders which was approaching the narrows of the Channel, seized two of the largest vessels, and flung their crews overboard. A few days later he appeared off Brill, which he captured, as we have seen, with the utmost ease.[3] And the capture of Brill was only a beginning, merely the signal for the unchaining of the forces of revolution. During the next ten days four other seaport towns rose in sympathetic revolt against the Spanish authorities; particularly important was the accession of Flushing to the ranks of the insurgents, for it controlled the mouth of the Scheldt, and was therefore the key to Antwerp. So horrible were the excesses committed by the rebels [4] that at first William of

[1] Froude, x, pp. 371–373.
[2] *Ibid.*, p. 373, and document there cited.
[3] *Ibid.*, pp. 373 f.

[4] Cf. Hubert Meuffels, *Les Martyrs de Gorcum* (Paris, 1908), in the series *Les Saints*. On the seizure of Rotterdam by the Spaniards and the ensuing

Orange hesitated to recognize them; but his hand was ultimately forced by the march of events, and by the urgency of his councillors, one of whom even ventured to issue, without showing it to him, a manifesto in his name, in which William assumed the title of stadtholder or representative of his Majesty in Holland, Zealand, Friesland, and Utrecht, and called on all men to bear aid in the revolution.[1] Louis of Nassau and his Huguenot allies were prompt to utilize the situation for their own advantage; in the latter part of May they seized Mons and Valenciennes. Alva at Brussels was at his wit's end which way to turn; but, still believing that the most serious danger was that from France, he turned his face to the southwest, and in the latter part of July sat down before Mons, while his son, Don Fadrique, defeated and cut to pieces a force of 4000 men which had been despatched to its relief. Needless to add, the rapidity of the progress of the Northern revolt, already spectacular, was now still further increased; one town after another declared for the insurgents. In Zealand only Middleburg held out for the Spaniards; in Holland, only Amsterdam and Schoonhoven.[2] The revolution even penetrated into Friesland and Gelderland.

Then suddenly, in the twinkling of an eye, the entire situation changed. On September 5, while he was still in front of Mons, Alva received sure news of the massacre of St. Bartholomew twelve days before. Catharine had reversed her policy once more. She had made away with Coligny and most of the rest of the Protestant chiefs, together with several thousands of their adherents.[3] All the

sack and massacre, see Bernardino de Mendoza, *Comentarios*, lib. v, cap. vii; Motley, ii, p. 358, and references there.

[1] Pirenne, iv, p. 31; Kervyn de Lettenhove, *Documents inédits relatifs à l'histoire du XVIe siècle*, p. 166.

[2] Pirenne, iv, p. 32.

[3] Full accounts of the copious literature on the massacre are to be found in Thompson, *Wars of Religion*, p. 452, note, and in Pastor, xix, pp. 482–512, notes. Modern scholarship has fully

long-laid plans of Orange and his brother for securing the support of the Huguenots for their cause were knocked on the head,[1] at least for the time being. Alva had been saved in his extremity by what had happened in the very country whence he and his master had apprehended their gravest peril.

The report of the massacre naturally spread consternation among the Protestant states of Europe. Philip is reported to have laughed when he heard the news,[2] which was celebrated at Rome with processions and rejoicings.[3] The defensive league which had been created between the governments of Elizabeth and Charles IX by the treaty of Blois in the previous April was now succeeded in England by preparations for war; never had the Counter-Reformation seemed so menacing before. But the panic was excessive, as the sequel was to show. The massacre was not an indication of any settled policy on the part of Catharine de' Medici; it was but a crowning demonstration, if such were needed, that she could not be trusted to follow one. Disembarrassed of Coligny, whose ascendancy she could not abide, she made peace offerings to his coreligionists, both at home and abroad.[4] As was natural under the circumstances, these peace offerings were either flatly rejected or else treated with justifiable distrust, with the consequence that for some months to come France was practically eliminated as an international force. None of her neighbors was in a condition to attack her, and none of them would venture to accept her alliance.

disproved the old idea that it had been long premeditated.

[1] Orange himself characterized the massacre as a "coup de massue."

[2] So at least says Froude, x, p. 409, but I can find no contemporary evidence to prove it. Cf. also Antonio Benítez de Lugo, "Contento y Regocijo de Felipe II por la Matanza de los Hugonotes," in *Revista de España*, cxxxv (1891), pp. 356–372, 416–433.

[3] Pastor, xix, pp. 499–507.

[4] Forneron, ii, pp. 341–346.

For Alva, of course, the massacre meant that his south-western frontier was temporarily safe. Mons capitulated on September 21,[1] and the Duke was free once more to return into the North, and deal with the revolt that was gathering headway there. But before letting loose the full flood of his vengeance on the rebels, he determined, with characteristic caution, to deprive them of their last hope of the continuance of the English aid which had proved so in-dispensable to them in the past; here again he gave tardy proof of his dawning realization of the latent perils of the hostility of Britain. Outwardly he seemed to have ample justification and also an excellent opportunity for casting down the gauntlet before the government of Queen Eliza-beth. Ten months before she had mortally offended Philip by ordering his ambassador, Guerau de Spes, to take his de-parture within four days.[2] She had secretly supported the rebels in the Low Countries. And now her loss of the French alliance made her presumably less able to resist a Spanish attack. If the massacre of St. Bartholomew could only be completed by the subversion of English Protestant-ism, it seemed that the triumph of the Counter-Reforma-tion would be achieved. Yet, just at the very moment that men expected him to declare war, the Duke of Alva moved heaven and earth to obtain a treaty of peace.[3] His first duty and desire was to crush the Sea Beggars; and the sur-est way to do that was to cut off the help they got from Eng-land. Certainly it was no time to undertake a crusade; better, far better, take advantage of Englishmen's horror of the massacre of St. Bartholomew to impress them with the

---

[1] On the extraordinarily lenient treat-ment of its garrison cf. Froude, x, p. 424, and Forneron, ii, pp. 344 f., and refer-ences there.

[2] Törne, *Don Juan d'Autriche*, i,

pp. 117 f., and references there.

[3] Cf. his letter to Philip of March 18, 1573, in *Correspondance de Philippe II*, ii, pp. 320–322.

superior moderation of Spain. And so, with the reluctant approval of his master, Alva went to work to secure a settlement of all outstanding difficulties with the English government, and obtained it at last on March 15, 1573, by the so-called Convention of Nimwegen, providing for the reëstablishment of commercial intercourse between England and the Low Countries for a period of two years, for the abandonment by each of the rebels against the government of the other, and for the repression of the pirates in the Channel.[1] At last the Duke was free to wreak his vengeance on the Beggars without fear of interference from without.

There is no need to recount the story of that vengeance here: the sack of Mechlin, the massacre at Zutphen, the heroic resistance of Haarlem, and the comparatively lenient terms, whose good effect was forthwith destroyed by the first of those mutinies of Philip's unpaid soldiery which were destined to play havoc with the Spaniards in the Low Countries.[2] On this occasion the Netherlanders were goaded into a last desperate resistance by the outrages committed by their conquerors, and they were encouraged to persist in it by the fact that the discipline of Alva's *tercios* had utterly broken down. The town of Alkmaar defied all the efforts of Don Fadrique to take it. The Spanish fleet suffered a significant defeat in the Zuyder Zee,[3] and the Spanish garrison barely succeeded in maintaining itself in Middleburg, the last outpost in Zealand that remained in Alva's hands.[4] As long as the Duke had continued to be victorious, Philip was determined to maintain him in office, despite Alva's repeated requests for recall. Now, however, that it seemed to have

---

[1] Kervyn de Lettenhove, *Relations politiques des Pays-Bas et de l'Angleterre*, vi, introduction, p. xii, and text, p. 680; *Correspondance de Philippe II*, ii, pp. 318 f.; Read, *Walsingham*, i, p. 308.

[2] Pirenne, iv, pp. 40–44.
[3] Bernardino de Mendoza, *Comentarios*, lib. x, caps. iv, v.
[4] Pirenne, iv, p. 44.

been demonstrated that no amount of bloodshed or expense
could avail to quell the revolt, he began to consider the
advisability of a change.   On October 15, 1573, he notified
the Duke of his intention to supersede him ; a month later,
Don Luis de Requesens, who had been appointed his successor, arrived in the Netherlands ; before the year was over
Alva had departed for Spain.[1]   He carried with him, needless to add, the execrations of the entire population which
he had so outrageously misruled.   The chief result of his
term of office had been to identify the government of Spain
which he represented with the most intolerable of tyrannies
in the Netherlandish mind ; indeed, he had made ultimately
inevitable the ruin of the Spanish Empire in Northern Europe.   Yet as even the Devil should be given his due, so it is
but fair that two points should be noted in Alva's favor.[2]
The first is the clearness of his perception, in the latter
months of his rule, of the dangers to Spain in the Netherlands from England ; had his views in this matter been
heeded by the king, it was not impossible that the defeat of
the Spanish Armada might have been avoided.   The second
is that the worst and most disastrous of his mistakes were
virtually forced upon him by the emptiness of the Spanish
treasury.   In Philip's inability to give his *tercios* their regular pay lay the basic reason for that long series of atrocious
mutinies, which, initiated in Alva's time, reached its horrible
culmination in the 'Spanish Fury' at Antwerp in 1576.   The
fact that the Spanish government was determined to make
the Low Countries pay the costs of their own Hispanicization was what finally unchained the forces of revolution.[3]

---

[1] Pirenne, iv, pp. 44 f.

[2] Cf. *Contribución al Estudio de la Persona del III Duque de Alba*, by the Duque de Berwick y de Alba (Madrid, 1919).

[3] It has been well said that the real object in sending the Duke to the Netherlands was not so much that he might punish rebels as that he might impose new taxes.   Nevertheless, with all his exactions it had been necessary

The primary cause of it, in other words, was economic, though it was to need the additional impetus of Calvinism to give it victory in the Northeast. The blighting *alcabala*, with its various developments and ramifications, proved a cancer that was destined to eat away the very vitals of the Spanish Empire.

Luis de Requesens, whom the king, after long hesitation, had selected to succeed Alva in the Low Countries, was of ancient Castilian lineage, and the son of a favorite tutor of Philip's boyhood days. He had already been ambassador to Rome and governor of Milan, when, at the age of forty-six, he was despatched to the Netherlands. He was in failing health at the time of his appointment, and did his utmost to induce the king to confer it upon someone else; but Philip was obdurate, for he discerned in Requesens a man who would continue unabated the policy of Hispanicizing the Netherlands to which he had now committed himself — "a reliable man, who would tolerate no diminution of the authority of the crown." The methods by which Requesens proposed to attain his ends were certainly much gentler than those of his predecessor, though things so fell out that he never got a fair chance to apply them; but the fundamental principles on which the Spanish administration was based remained, in all essentials, exactly what they had been before.[1]

As far as relations with France and with England are concerned, the period of the rule of Requesens is singularly empty; no event of decisive importance in international

between 1567 and 1572 to send on 8,000,000 florins from Spain. On all this, cf. Pirenne, iv, p. 45, note 1, and references there.

[1] Pirenne, iv, pp. 47–49; A. Morel-Fatio, "La Vie de Don Luís de Requesens," in *B. H.*, vi (1904), pp. 210–213; F. Barado y Font, *D. Luis de Requesens y la Política Española en los Países Bajos* (Madrid, 1906).

affairs occurred during his tenure of office. Europe was taking a breathing spell after Alva, and before the still more arduous years that were to follow. The effects of the massacre of St. Bartholomew continued to dislocate the foreign policy and nullify the international influence of France. At home she was disturbed by "factions, edicts, and Estates"; abroad she was much preoccupied with the unusual problem of getting an errant king back from Poland. With England Spain had inherited a temporary understanding, owing to the efforts of the Duke of Alva in 1573; and though neither party observed it with perfect loyalty, and there were consequently complaints and recriminations on both sides,[1] there was never any real prospect of serious trouble. Both Philip and Elizabeth were content, for the time being, with the maintenance of the status quo. We turn, therefore, to the progress of events in the Netherlands themselves.

Requesens was convinced that the sole possible way to win back the Low Countries to their allegiance was to proclaim a general pardon for past offences, and to rescind the most unpopular measures — such as the imposition of the tenth penny — which had recently been enacted by the government of Philip II. But Alva, who stayed on in Brussels for a month after Requesens's arrival, had no use whatever for such a policy as this. On his return to Spain he laid his views before the king, who had previously accepted the ideas of his successor, and the natural result was a long period of hesitation. Not till March 10, 1574, did Philip

---

[1] Read, *Walsingham*, i, pp. 306 ff. It is to be said that in the autumn of 1574 Pedro Menéndez de Avilés, of Florida fame, was given command of an expedition which had been prepared at Santander for the invasion of England; but the plague prevented it from ever sailing and carried off Menéndez. Cf. *Archivo Histórico Español*, ii, p. v. Apparently the affair created little or no interest at the time; I can find no mention of it in the contemporary documents.

send his royal permission to proclaim the general pardon.[1]
Meantime Requesens was obliged, much against his will, to
continue the war against the rebels which had been bequeathed to him by his predecessor, and thereby convinced
men, quite erroneously, that he was fully as blood-thirsty
as Alva had been before him. The course of the struggle was
at first inconclusive. The surrender of Middleburg to the
Prince of Orange (February 18, 1574) deprived the Spaniards
of their last stronghold in Zealand; but this reverse was
fully compensated for by the crushing defeat (April 14)
inflicted by Sancho de Ávila and some 8000 Spaniards at
Mook, near Grave, in the valley of the Meuse, on an army
of German mercenaries which Louis of Nassau was bringing to his brother's aid; Louis himself met death on the field
of battle. The effect of this victory, however, was neutralized in turn by the disgraceful conduct of the Spanish soldiery who had won it. Furious at their failure to get their
regular pay, they determined to recoup themselves by the
plundering of Antwerp, and as it was utterly impossible to
reëstablish discipline by force, Requesens was obliged to
negotiate with the mutineers in order to save Antwerp from
being sacked.[2] All this, of course, reacted most unfavorably
on his own policy of conciliation. When he proclaimed the
general pardon at Brussels on June 5, and followed this two
days later by an offer to abolish the *alcabala* in return for a
generous subsidy, his concessions fell painfully flat. No
one seemed to care to take advantage of them; men interpreted them, rather, as a confession of weakness on the part
of the government, and derived from them encouragement to
persist in their rebellion. One of Requesens's chief counsel-

[1] *Correspondance de Philippe II*,
iii, pp. 33–37; Pirenne, iv, pp. 50
ff.
[2] Pirenne, iv, pp. 51–53; *Correspon-*
dance de Philippe II*, iii, pp. 55–67;
Motley, *Rise of the Dutch Republic*, ii,
pp. 543–550.

lors went so far as to tell him bluntly that "one can not do in the Netherlands what one does in Naples and Milan."[1] The falsity of the parallel on which Philip had based his policy in the Low Countries was now mercilessly and publicly exposed.

Meantime, on October 3, 1574, there had occurred the relief of Leyden by the cutting of the dykes. It was in some respects the most brilliant achievement of the entire war, and a crowning demonstration of the fact that although the Spaniards might still be invincible in a land battle, they had not learned all the possibilities of utilizing the sea.[2] This event, together with the parlous state of Requesens's finances, led to a fresh effort to secure peace by negotiation at the so-called conferences of Breda in February, 1575; but the commissioners would not trust one another without the giving of guarantees which neither side was disposed to concede, and the question of toleration for Calvinism proved an insurmountable stumblingblock to agreement.[3] In the following summer and autumn the hopes of the Spaniards were raised by a temporary return of fortune on the field of battle. They possessed themselves of all the islands between the northern outlet of the Scheldt and the Meuse and thus separated Zealand from Holland.[4] But the rebels were by no means discouraged by this reverse; quite the contrary, at the very moment that it was taking place, the Estates of Holland and Zealand took the decisive step of ceasing to put forth their edicts in the name of Philip II. Hitherto

---

[1] *Correspondance de Philippe II*, iii, p. 119.

[2] *Correspondance de Philippe II*, iii, pp. 169, 174 ff.; Robert Fruin, *The Siege and Relief of Leyden*, translated by Elizabeth Trevelyan (The Hague, 1927). Professor G. M. Trevelyan, in his introduction to this book, declares that the relief of Leyden claims "an equal place with the Defeat of the Armada as having given the decisive check to the conquest of Europe by the Spanish Monarchy and by the Catholic Reaction. Leyden was the first event to stem the tide."

[3] Pirenne, iv, pp. 57 f.

[4] *Ibid.*, pp. 58 f.

they had preserved the fiction of loyalty to the Spanish monarch, and maintained that their rebellion had been directed solely against the representatives he sent out; now they resolved to have done with shams and offer their sovereignty to some other prince. But for the time being it was impossible to induce any one to accept it. Neither Elizabeth of England nor Henry III of France was willing to take the risk of openly defying the government of Spain.[1]

Such was the perilous state of affairs in the Low Countries when on March 5, 1576, Requesens died of a fever. He had never had an opportunity to carry out his own ideas; even if he had, it would probably have been too late. So destitute was he at the time of his death, that his funeral had to be postponed for several days because of the impossibility of finding money to pay the expenses of it.[2]

It was the first time that a royal governor of the Low Countries had died in harness, the first time that the continuity of the Spanish régime had been broken; eight months elapsed before Requesens's successor could be appointed and reach his post. For Philip that interim was one long agony of suspense. The only representative of his authority in the Netherlands that was left standing was the Council of State — composed, it is true, exclusively of Catholics officially loyal to the Spanish crown, but also convinced, save for its secretary, Roda, that Philip's policy had been utterly wrong, and must be radically changed if the Low Countries were to be preserved. With such half-hearted officials on the spot, it was clear that the king was for the time being powerless; it was also equally obvious that a golden opportunity was thereby offered to the rebels to

[1] Motley, *Rise of the Dutch Republic*, iii, pp. 42–47.

[2] Pirenne, iv, p. 60, and references there.

strengthen their position; and under the able leadership of William of Orange they were prompt to take advantage of it. In any history of the Low Countries, the events which occurred between the death of Requesens and the arrival of his successor are of capital importance, and must needs be recounted in detail; here it must suffice to summarize them in brief. Another furious mutiny of the Spanish *tercios* broke out in the summer of 1576; it centred in Brussels, and was caused, like its predecessors, by the determination of Philip's soldiers to obtain, at the expense of the inhabitants on whom they were quartered, the pay which the royal treasury was unable to afford.[1] This mutiny put all the Catholic southwestern districts up in arms, and gave William of Orange the chance to bring forward a plan for the union of all seventeen provinces in a common effort to expel the Spaniards. Hitherto he had tried to effect his ends through Holland and Zealand, backed by the support of England and of France; now for the moment, at least, it was evident that foreign aid was not forthcoming, and without it Holland and Zealand were powerless by themselves. Only by a united movement of all the Netherlands could he hope to accomplish his purpose, and, with the instinct of the statesman, he seized the psychological moment to act. After vainly attempting to persuade the Council of State to see the justice of his cause and to lend him its support, he succeeded, on September 4, in arresting the most refractory of its members, thereby removing it from Spanish control and hurling defiance at the government of Madrid.[2] Before the month was over, a meeting of the States-General of the Low Countries was assembled at Brussels, on the invitation of the Estates of Brabant, and the departure of

---

[1] Pirenne, iv, pp. 66 f.; Motley, iii, pp. 90–93; P. Geyl, *Revolt of the* pp. 78–81. *Netherlands*, p. 146.

[2] Pirenne, iv, p. 73; Motley, iii,

the Spanish soldiers was unanimously demanded.[1] Realizing that there was no chance of Philip's voluntary compliance with this request, the Estates promptly took steps towards the raising of a national army. In carrying out these measures there were collisions with the royal troops, which culminated, on November 4, in another 'Spanish Fury' at Antwerp, more terrible by far than any of its predecessors; over 7000 were killed, and there was an orgy of pillage and rapine.[2] The news of it naturally made the rebels more desperate than ever; it caused the religious differences between the Catholic Southwest and the Protestant Northeast to dwindle into temporary insignificance, in comparison to the unanimous determination to shake off the yoke of Spain. On November 8, there was solemnly proclaimed in the city that bears its name the instrument known to history as the Pacification of Ghent. It provided for an armed alliance of Catholics and Protestants to expel the Spanish troops, for the subsequent convocation of the States-General to settle the question of religion, for the suspension of the 'placards' and other edicts against heresy, for the liberation of prisoners condemned by the Council of Blood, and for the restoration of confiscated property to its lawful owners. Never had the Spanish authority in the Low Countries been challenged in such fashion before.[3]

Meantime Philip had been anxiously considering the question of Requesens's successor. He was still convinced that he must continue to conciliate, and the exigencies of the situation and the advice of his Council all pointed to his half-brother Don John of Austria as the obvious man for the vacant place. The fame that he had won at Lepanto was still fresh in men's minds; his charming personality could

---

[1] Pirenne, iv, pp. 75 ff.
[2] *Ibid.*, p. 78; *Correspondance de Philippe II*, v, pp. 19–22.
[3] Pirenne, iv, pp. 79–81; Motley, iii, pp. 124–127.

be counted upon to effect much; he was not, like Alva or
Requesens, an unmitigated Castilian; unlike them, also, he
would satisfy the oft-expressed desire of the Netherlanders
that the royal representative in the Low Countries should
have royal blood in his veins.[1] As far back as 1574
Requesens had advised Philip to send him there, and the
Council at Madrid had been of the same mind. But Philip,
as usual, had been doubtful and hesitant. He was profoundly jealous of his half-brother, whose brilliant achievements and far-reaching schemes for the future aroused his
deepest suspicions. He could not rid himself of the idea
that Don John was possessed with the desire to carve out
for himself an independent realm, and aspired to renounce
all allegiance to Spain. Now, however, in view of the crisis
with which he was confronted in 1576, Philip was forced to
admit that Don John was the sole possible solution. On
April 8 he wrote to his half-brother, who was in Naples, that
it was his desire that he "should take wings and fly to the
Low Countries," and that in order to save the delay of a
journey to Spain for a preliminary interview, full instructions would be sent forward to meet him as he passed north
through Lombardy.[2]

But Don John was by no means eager to comply with the
royal command. The task of bringing order out of chaos in
the Netherlands did not appeal to him in the least. His
mind at that moment was filled with a daring scheme for invading England, dethroning Elizabeth, and replacing her
with Mary Stuart, whom he hoped to make his wife; and he
had no intention of proceeding to the Low Countries until he
had obtained Philip's formal consent to the prosecution of

[1] Pirenne, iv, p. 84; Stirling-Maxwell, *Don John of Austria, passim*;
Törne, *Don Juan d'Autriche*, ii, pp.
6-12.

[2] Stirling-Maxwell, ii, pp. 115 f.;
Törne, ii, pp. 13-16.

that magnificent plan.[1] For this purpose it was necessary to return to Castile, and he did so, arriving at Madrid in early September, in defiance of the king's order to go direct from Naples to the Netherlands. Philip, of course, gave him the permission he desired, though it was hedged about with numerous conditions and reservations;[2] he then proceeded to emphasize the instructions that had been drawn up for the guidance of Don John in the Low Countries. Conciliation was everywhere to be the keynote. In order to maintain true religion and the authority of the Spanish crown, Philip was now prepared to surrender on every other point at issue: to remove the Spanish troops, to rescind all innovations that had been set up since the arrival of the Duke of Alva, and to leave the administration of the government as far as possible in the hands of the Netherlanders themselves. Not only in essentials but in details was Don John adjured to take the utmost care not to give offence; he was to speak French, not Spanish, and to avoid selecting his mistresses from among the principal families of the land.[3] In order to dissipate any possible idea that he intended to follow a policy of compulsory Castilianization, it was decided that he should enter his new dominions by traversing France on horseback, disguised as the servant of his only attendant, Ottavio Gonzaga, the son of the old viceroy of Milan. It was on the evening of November 3, 1576, that the pair finally crossed the frontier into Luxemburg — one short day before the 'Spanish Fury' at Antwerp and only five before the signature of the Pacification of Ghent.[4]

It would scarcely have been possible to arrive at a more inopportune moment, and it was but a few days before Don

---

[1] On the details, see Törne, i, pp. 161–188; ii, pp. 60–109.

[2] *Ibid.*, ii, pp. 46 ff., and references there.

[3] *Correspondance de Philippe II*, iv, pp. 450–464; Törne, ii, pp. 47–51.

[4] Pirenne, iv, p. 83.

John discovered the full measure of his impotence. The revelation of his identity failed to procure him respect. The spectacle of the unrestrained licentiousness of his mother, Barbara Blomberg, who had been living in the Netherlands for the previous twenty-five years,[1] served to remind men that he was a bastard, even if also the son of a king. The local authorities, whose existence he recognized and with whom he attempted to negotiate, showed that their sympathies were rather with the States-General than with him. On every hand he met the same reply; until the Spanish troops were sent away no talk of conciliation was possible; and within two months of his arrival he wrote to Philip to say that a rupture was inevitable, and that he must have more men and funds.[2] On the other hand, he could not bear to relinquish his schemes for the invasion of England, in which he was assured of papal support; and he continued to labor to win peace in the Low Countries, in order that he might use the troops that would thereby be released for the prosecution of the great plan on which his heart was set.[3] Meantime in the camp of the rebels the inevitable rifts began to appear. The statesmanship of Orange, with united action as its constant watchword, had produced great things in the heat of the universal resentment at the 'Spanish Fury' at Antwerp. Now, however, in the calmer days that followed, the effects of the particularistic aims of the different provinces, and, above all, of the great gulf between the Catholic Southwest and the Protestant Northeast, inevitably made themselves felt. By the beginning of January, 1577, the rebels were gradually dividing into two groups, alike, indeed, in the unanimity of their demand for the withdrawal of the Spanish soldiery, but differing in that one of

[1] P. Herre, *Barbara Blomberg*, pp. 31–74.

[2] Pirenne, iv, p. 87; *Correspondance de Philippe II*, v, pp. 39–46.

[3] Törne, ii, pp. 110–113.

them, which had its chief strength in the Southwest, regarded that removal as a preliminary to the reëstablishment of Catholicism and reconciliation with Spain, while the other, inspired by Orange, and chiefly recruited from Holland and Zealand, cherished plans for the establishment of Protestantism and the overthrow of the authority of Philip II. Don John was enough of a statesman to discern that the widening of this breach was essential to the success of his own plans, and that the surest way to widen it was through concessions. On February 12, therefore, by an instrument which has always borne the singularly inappropriate title of the Perpetual Edict, he formally agreed to the majority of the Netherlanders' demands, and especially to the departure within twenty days of the Spanish troops.[1] But in the arranging of the details of that departure all his hopes were dashed. It had been his purpose to remove them by sea, in order, no doubt, to use them against England; but this could scarcely be done without their passing through Holland and Zealand, where all the seaports were, and Holland and Zealand obstinately refused to permit them to traverse their territory.[2] The upshot of the matter was that in the month of April the Spanish troops departed to the southward by land for Italy; and Don John, his grand project all scattered to the four winds of heaven, wrote Philip to beg on bended knees to be recalled.

The king, however, paid no heed to his desires; eighteen months more of "weariness, and death"[3] at the age of thirty-three were all indeed, as Don John had foreseen,

---

[1] Pirenne, iv, pp. 90 f.

[2] Pirenne, iv, p. 91; Seeley, *Growth of British Policy*, i, pp. 157 ff.; Read, *Walsingham*, ii, pp. 355–358; Törne, ii, pp. 114 ff. Apparently Elizabeth also warned Don John "that she feared lest the removal of his troops would mean that they were intended to deliver the Scottish Queen."

[3] The phrase is that of his secretary Escovedo; cf. *Correspondance de Philippe II*, v, p. 187.

that were destined to be left to him. The history of this brief phase is complicated and not particularly important, save in so far as the attitude of the outside powers is concerned; we must therefore hurry as rapidly as possible over the internal history of the revolt and the attempts that were made to suppress it.   The keynote of the period is increasing distrustfulness between Don John and the rebels. All the effect of the concessions he had made in the Perpetual Edict seemed to have been forgotten in the unseemly quarrel over the method of the departure of the Spanish troops. He was formally welcomed at Brussels, indeed, according to the ancient ceremonial, on May 12, 1577; but the States-General only recognized his official title by a majority of one vote; each side seemed convinced that the other was meditating treachery.[1] So alarmed for his personal safety did Don John become that he soon retired from Brussels, and finally, on July 24, possessed himself, by a *coup-de-main*, of Namur; thence he wrote desperately to Philip to assure him that a peaceful solution to his difficulties was impossible, and that the Spanish troops must forthwith be sent back, in order to enable him to seize the offensive.[2] It took a long time, as usual, to persuade the Prudent King to reverse his policy, but finally it was done; in early December the vanguard of the *tercios* began to file back into Luxemburg, where Don John welcomed them with open arms. The only way in which he could now retrieve his fallen fortunes was by a military victory, and he knew it; and on January 31, 1578, at Gembloux, near Namur, the army of the rebels delivered itself into his hands in a fashion which plainly demonstrated that, however antiquated the Spanish

---

[1] Pirenne, iv, p. 93. The letter of Ottavio Gonzaga to Antonio Pérez, written from Brussels on May 30, 1577, is very significant; it may be found in the *Correspondance de Philippe II*, v, pp. 379 f.

[2] *Correspondance de Philippe II*, v, pp. 182–185.

methods of governing, the Spanish army still remained
master on the battlefield.[1] It was a rout rather than a fight.
There were few slain but a multitude of runaways, and an
enormous amount of munitions and supplies was destroyed.
But Don John had not enough troops to enable him to follow
up his advantage and strike direct at Brussels. He had to
content himself with gathering in some minor cities to the
south. Meantime the skill of William of Orange reconstituted the rebel party, and provided for it, as we shall soon
see, the immediate prospect of effective foreign aid. He
utterly refused to be discouraged, and under his inspiration
the rebel army soon began to gather itself again. The lesson
of these events was not lost on Don John. Even his victories on the field of battle seemed but to serve to reanimate
his foes. His dreams of glory had vanished. He had become an object of suspicion to the master whom he had
but reluctantly consented to serve; his health was ruined,
and he was in despair. Death came to his rescue at last,
on October 1, 1578, in his camp at Bouges near Namur.[2]

We revert to the story of the relations of Spain to France
and England, and more especially to their effects on the
situation in the Netherlands. Under Requesens, as we have
already seen, these matters subside into insignificance, but
under Don John they return to the centre of the stage; indeed, it would probably be safe to say that the chief importance of the brief rule of Philip's half-brother in the Low
Countries was that it brought once more into view the ultimate possibility of foreign intervention. The widespread

[1] Pirenne, iv, pp. 115 f.; Stirling-
Maxwell, ii, pp. 291–294.

[2] Stirling-Maxwell, ii, pp. 312–339;
Pirenne, iv, p. 123; cf. also the summary of the letter of Francisco Dorante,
Don John's confessor, announcing his
death to the king, on pp. 129–133 of
*Les bibliothèques de Madrid et de l'Es-
curial: notices et extraits*, ed. L. P.
Gachard (Brussels, 1875) in *Collection
des Chroniques Belges*.

fame and ambitious projects of Don John really rendered this inevitable.

It was natural, in view of the commercial treaty of 1573, and of Don John's own designs against the government of Queen Elizabeth, that the question of Spain's relations with England should come prominently to the fore. It was a sordid tale of plot and counterplot.[1] Elizabeth was still far from converted to the view of the more radical of her counsellors that she should take a vigorous stand in favor of the rebels. On the other hand she was fully alive to the necessity of keeping close watch on the situation in the Low Countries, and also of forestalling any independent intervention on the part of France. Messengers more or less secret had passed to and fro between her and Orange, to be treated, each in turn, as the exigencies of the moment should dictate;[2] but, save for promises of a loan, and one downright cash payment of £20,000, the queen of England had insisted on keeping her hands free. With Don John also she remained outwardly friendly, though she had surprisingly full information in regard to his designs against her throne;[3] when she complained of the presence of certain suspicious persons about Don John's court, he wrote her (March 7, 1577) a letter of explanation, which, despite the raised eyebrows of her counsellors, she professed to accept with good grace.[4] A little later Don John received a friendly visit from Sir Philip Sidney, homeward bound from his formal embassy of 'condolence and congratulation' on the recent change of rulers in the Empire.[5] The undercurrent of spying and reporting continued indeed unabated on both ends, but after the departure of the Spanish troops, and the con-

[1] Törne, ii, pp. 60 ff., *passim*.
[2] Read, *Walsingham*, i, pp. 339 ff.
[3] Cf. *ante*, p. 308.
[4] *C. S. P., Foreign*, 1575–77, nos.

1322, 1366; Stirling-Maxwell, ii, pp. 208 f.
[5] Stirling-Maxwell, ii, pp. 228 f.

sequent probability that her own throne would remain secure, it became increasingly plain that Elizabeth was not yet prepared to take sides. Of Orange and his adherents, as of all other rebels, she entirely disapproved. She was ready to make use of them, in case it should be absolutely necessary to do so, in order to enable her to defend her own shores, and she certainly did not propose to have them become the cat's paw of France; but as neither of these two contingencies seemed imminent, Elizabeth relapsed into the old congenial game of marking time.[1]

The story of the relations of France to Spain in the Low Countries during this period is also inconclusive for the time being, though ominous for the future; it centres from first to last around the person of the last of the Valois, the younger brother of Henry III, the Duke of Alençon and Anjou.[2] In the early spring of 1576 this wretched scion of royalty had burst into prominence by successfully leading a party of 'Malcontents' in France, and extorting from the crown terms highly favorable to the Huguenots by the celebrated peace of Monsieur (April 27); it was on this occasion that he received the duchy of Anjou as a part of his reward, and thereafter he was generally known as the Duke of Anjou, without the title of Alençon which he had borne before. Since he had struck such a shrewd blow for the new faith in France, it was but natural that he should attract the favorable attention of Orange. On May 6, 1576, two months after the death of Requesens, a document[3] was drawn up, under Orange's direction, stating the terms under

[1] Her letters to the States, during this period, which are printed in extenso in Kervyn de Lettenhove's Relations politiques, ix, x, and xi, are a faithful mirror of her 'masterly inactivity.'

[2] The principal source for the dealings of the Duke with the Low Countries is the Documents concernant les relations entre le Duc d'Anjou et les Pays-Bas (1576–1584), edd. P. L. Muller and Alphonse Diegerick in nos. 51, 55, 57, 60, and 61 of the nieuwe serie of the Werken of the Historisch Genootschap of Utrecht.

[3] Cf. Kervyn de Lettenhove, Les Huguenots et les Gueux, iv, pp. 50–54.

which the Estates of Holland and Zealand were willing to accept Anjou as their count and hereditary sovereign. For some time the Duke hesitated. He was fully alive to the perils of any enterprise against the government of Philip II; he had no real love for Protestantism; he dreaded the disapproval of Queen Elizabeth, whom he had aspired, since 1572, to make his wife.[1] But the consequences of the 'Spanish Fury' at Antwerp were a telling argument for immediate action; from that moment, as has been well said, the Duke "regarded the Low Countries as his certain prey." His secret agents began to flood the Netherlands, and, on October 19, a correspondence began between him and the rebels which was practically uninterrupted until the day of his death.[2] It is unnecessary to follow all the ebbs and flows during the governorship of Don John. The main things they proved were the inadequacy of Anjou's abilities and the shallowness of his character; at one moment, indeed, he came near to being utilized as an opponent of Orange to the advantage of Spain.[3] Elizabeth did her best to checkmate him at every turn. Not yet did he make war against Spain in the Netherlands, as was later the case, with her approval, in order to save her the trouble of doing so herself, and in some faint hope of winning her hand; for the present she seemed bent on keeping him out of them altogether.[4] It looked, in fact, as if the ancient jealousies of France and England might come to the rescue of the Spanish Empire once more, and at a time when its leaders were far less competent than in earlier days. But it was not destined to be so. The period of Don John was not to close

---

[1] Read, *Walsingham*, i, pp. 176, 206-210.

[2] *Documents concernant les relations entre le Duc d'Anjou et les Pays-Bas*, i, pp. 9 ff.

[3] Pirenne, iv, p. 119.

[4] For the moment she supported the Calvinist Count Palatine, John Casimir, against him. Cf. Pirenne, iv, pp. 118 f.

without witnessing the definite achievement of one more
stage, slight, perhaps, in itself, but significant in its implications for the future, along the road to foreign military
intervention against Spain in the Netherlands. Fear that,
unless they came to terms with him themselves, he might be
betrayed into doing harm to their cause, led the States-
General, under Orange's guidance, on August 13, 1578, to
put their signature to a definite treaty with Anjou. The
Duke was to maintain in the Netherlands, at his own expense, an army of 10,000 foot and 2000 horse for three
months; he was to take the title of 'Defender of the Liberties of the Low Countries' against the tyranny of the
Spaniards and their adherents; but he was, for the time
being, to bear no part in their government. If Philip should
be deposed, the Estates promised to place him first in the
line of succession. If they should make peace with the king
of Spain, they would recognize their great indebtedness to
him, and reward him accordingly.[1]

After such a long and complicated tale as this chapter
has had to tell, it may be worth while to devote a couple of
paragraphs to a summary of results, more especially as the
attention of the reader in the ensuing pages is to be invited
to the state of affairs in a very different corner of Europe.

The outstanding fact had been the progress of dissatisfaction and revolt in the Netherlands. Philip had accepted
them, much against his will, from a sense of filial duty, and
in flat defiance of the most obvious dictates of racial, geographical, and political expediency. He had alternately
tried terrorism and conciliation, and had miserably failed in
both. Revolution had broken out and was progressing, and

---

[1] *Documents concernant les relations entre le Duc d'Anjou et les Pays-Bas*, i,
pp. 408–414.

was attracting the favorable attention of France and England, not so much because of any sympathetic comprehension on their parts of the aims of the revolution itself, as because of the opportunity it offered them to put a spoke in the wheel of Spain.   France was much less menacing than she had been twenty years before, when she had been fighting Philip under a strong and powerful king and supported by the see of Rome; on the other hand, though she might now be internally weak and disrupted, she possessed an opportunity to strike at Spain in the Low Countries which had not been available for her in the days of Henry II, and the tradition of hostility between the Hapsburgs and the Valois was by no means yet extinct.   With England the situation was infinitely worse.   A score of years earlier Philip had been king consort there, the husband of a queen who gloried in the fact that it had been vouchsafed to her to restore her errant subjects to the see of Rome.   Now he had been thrust forth, rebuffed, and insulted by the heretic government established after the death of Mary Tudor, and was regarded as an open enemy by the mercantile and seafaring portion of the population, however much the cautious lady who occupied the English throne might choose to preserve the appearances of friendship.   But here too the ancient traditions came in — though in this case their operation was the reverse of that in the case of France — to cloud the issue as it presented itself to Philip's mind.   The Anglo-Spanish tradition, for nearly a century past, had on the whole been one of amity and alliance, and Philip, who was far more alive to the significance of historical precedent than to inherent probabilities for the future, could not bring himself to believe that the old ties would be easily snapped.   He underestimated the latent peril from the Tudors even more than he overestimated the more open menace from the Valois.

A brief glance over the rest of Europe will serve to make still clearer the picture as Philip saw it in the last months of the year 1578. Save for the 'plague spot' in the Netherlands and its attendant vexations, his outlook was exceedingly bright. The Counter-Reformation had run its first triumphant course; indeed, the elements were all at hand which were soon to produce a fresh recrudescence of it. Spain and the 'rechristianized' papacy were once more moving hand in hand; there might be minor squabbles and conflicts of jurisdiction, but there could be no doubt that Rome now looked to Madrid for support and guidance, and to Philip as her lay champion, in a manner and to an extent that she had never done before. The imperial throne, after two occupants who had tended to be disagreeably lenient to heretics, was now held once more by a fanatical Catholic, and Spain's Italian possessions were generally in good order. The navy of the Turks had been laid low at Lepanto, and Spanish maritime supremacy erected in its place. The Philippines had been conquered and annexed, and the Spanish-American colonial régime was operating satisfactorily, according to the standards of that day and generation. And finally, in midsummer, 1578, two short months before the death of Don John of Austria, it so happened that an opportunity had suddenly presented itself to gain for the Spanish monarchy an extension of territory which would cause its predecessors to seem but puny in comparison — an extension, which, if obtained, would make the Spanish Empire by far the largest that the world had ever seen. The winning of this great prize occupied most of the next few years of the life of Philip II. Its successful accomplishment carried him to the climax of his power, and will demand our attention during the ensuing chapter.

BIBLIOGRAPHICAL NOTE

See notes at the end of Chapters XXIV and XXXI, and add:

Sources. — In addition to the *D. I. E.* (in which the items concerning the Low Countries during the period of Philip II are well analyzed by Theodoor Bussemaker on pp. 356–442 of the ninth volume of the third series of *Bijdragen voor Vaderlandsche Geschiedenis*, The Hague, 1896), the *Calendars of State Papers, Foreign*, and *Spanish*, and other standard sources, the following more special collections may be mentioned: the *Correspondance de Marguerite d'Autriche avec Philippe II* (1559–65), ed. L. P. Gachard (Brussels, 1867–81, 3 vols.), continued by J. S. Theissen in the *Publications* of the Historisch Genootschap of Utrecht (i, 1565–67, = troisième série, xlvii, 1925, of the *Publications*); the *Correspondance de Philippe II sur les affaires des Pays-Bas* (to 1577), ed. L. P. Gachard (Brussels, 1848–79, 5 vols.); the *Correspondance du Cardinal de Granvelle, 1565–1586*, edd. Edmond Poullet and Charles Piot (Brussels, 1877–96, 12 vols.), in *Collection de Chroniques Belges*; *Documents concernant les relations entre le Duc d'Anjou et les Pays-Bas*, edd. P. L. Muller and Alphonse Diegerick, in vols. 51, 55, 57, 60, and 61 of the nieuwe serie of the *Werken van het Historisch Genootschap gevestigd te Utrecht* (Utrecht, The Hague, and Amsterdam, 1889–99); " Apuntamientos para la historia del Rey don Felipe Segundo de España, por lo tocante á sus relaciones con la Reina Isabel de Inglaterra, desde el año de 1558 hasta el de 1576," ed. Tomás González, in R. A. H., *Memorias*, vii, pp. 249–467; the *Relations politiques des Pays-Bas et de l'Angleterre sous le règne de Philippe II* (to 1579), ed. J. M. B. C., Baron Kervyn de Lettenhove (Brussels, 1882–1900, 11 vols.), in *Collection de Chroniques Belges*; *Relations Politiques de la France et de l'Espagne avec l'Écosse au XVIᵉ siecle*, ed. Alexandre Teulet (Paris, 1862, 5 vols.): the *Ambassade en Espagne de Jean Ébrard, Seigneur de Saint-Sulpice, de 1562 à 1565*, ed. Edmond Cabié (Albi, 1903); and the *Dépêches de M. de Fourquevaux, ambassadeur du Roi Charles IX en Espagne, 1565–1572*, ed. Célestin Douais (Paris, 1896–1904, 3 vols.). — The *Catálogo de Documentos Españoles existentes en el Archivo del Ministerio de Negocios Extranjeros de París* by Julián Paz (cf. *supra*, p. 70) gives summaries of the most important papers which it lists; and it is particularly rich in material on the field covered by the present chapter. The " Comentarios de lo sucedido en las Guerras de los Países-Bajos, desde el año de 1567 hasta el de 1577," by Bernardino de Mendoza, is a vivid narrative of the military events of those years, in which the author took an active part. He kept a careful diary of his experiences, and based his book thereon. The first Spanish edition was published at Madrid in 1592, the year after his retirement from the post of ambassador at

Paris. The most convenient Spanish edition is in *B. A. E.*, Historiadores de Sucesos Particulares, ii, pp. 389–560, and there is an excellent French translation (Brussels, 1860–63, 2 vols.) in the *Collection de mémoires relatifs à l'histoire de Belgique*.

Later Works. — The great difficulty of the task of envisaging the history of this period as seen by Philip II is that nearly all the standard books about it have been written from the viewpoint of his enemies. In the seventeenth century, indeed, a number of works appeared on the Spanish side — such as Cardinal Guido Bentivoglio's *Della Guerra di Fiandra* (Cologne, or Rome, 1632–39, 3 vols.) and Famiano Strada's *De Bello Belgico* (Rome, 1632–47). Both these books were widely read at the time, and were translated, wholly or in part, into English and other languages, but by the nineteenth century they had been wellnigh forgotten, and were principally replaced by such strongly Protestant ' classics ' as J. A. Froude's *History of England* (London, 1856–70, 12 vols.) and J. L. Motley's *Rise of the Dutch Republic* (New York, 1856, 3 vols.). The best of the more recent works, however, are not so biassed as these : Henri Pirenne's *Histoire de Belgique*, vols. iii and iv (Brussels, 1907, 1911), Ernest Gossart's *L'Établissement du régime espagnol dans les Pays-Bas* (Brussels, 1905) and his *Domination Espagnole dans les Pays-Bas* (Brussels, 1906), and J. H. Mariéjol in Lavisse, *Histoire de France*, vol. vi, pt. 1 (Paris, 1911), are all notable for their accuracy and detachment. Pieter Geyl, *The Revolt of the Netherlands (1555–1609)* (London, 1932), is the most recent presentation of the subject. Among the monographs of a more special nature that I have found most useful are Felix Rachfahl, *Margaretha von Parma* (Munich and Leipzig, 1898) ; J. M. B. C., Baron Kervyn de Lettenhove, *Les Huguenots et les Gueux* (Bruges, 1883–85, 6 vols.) ; Paul Courteault, *Blaise de Monluc, historien* (Paris, 1908), which contains a useful bibliography on pp. xxi–xlviii ; Edmond Falgairolle, " Une expédition française a l'île de Madère en 1566," in Académie de Nîmes, *Mémoires*, viie série, xvii (1894), pp. 67–95 ; Conyers Read, *Mr. Secretary Walsingham and the Policy of Queen Elizabeth* (Oxford, 1925, 3 vols.) ; P. O. von Törne, *Don Juan d'Autriche et les projets de conquête de l'Angleterre* (Helsingfors, 1915–28, 2 vols.) ; A. O. Meyer, *England and the Catholic Church under Elizabeth*, translated by J. R. McKee (London, 1916) ; and R. Lechat, *Les réfugiés anglais dans les Pays-Bas espagnols durant le règne d'Élisabeth* (Louvain, 1914) ; this last book is now difficult to obtain, but summaries of its earlier portions (to 1580) may be found in the *Annuaire* of the University of Louvain, 1911, pp. 479–484 ; 1912, pp. 448–464. Numerous other works of a more special nature are cited, in appropriate places, in the footnotes.

CHAPTER XXXV

THE ANNEXATION OF PORTUGAL

WE have several times remarked that Philip, in obedience to the wishes of his father, had made it the object of his policy during the first twenty years of his reign rather to guard his inheritance than to attempt to enlarge it. Whatever his methods, it is impossible to deny that the struggle which he was carrying on in the Netherlands and its attendant quarrels with England and with France were all of them, in his eyes, of a distinctly defensive character; he was but putting down rebels and those who aided and abetted them. Even Lepanto, if envisaged historically, could scarcely be regarded as an aggression; moreover, the benefits of the victory were shared by the whole of Western Europe. The sole real extensions of territory that Spain had achieved in the first half of Philip's rule were the enlargements of his American possessions and the acquisition of the Philippines, and these had not been won at the expense of any European power; they were simply the logical fulfilment of Spain's high destiny to carry the Cross to the heathen. Down to the year 1578 Philip could honestly maintain that he had played a strictly defensive game.

This predominantly defensive character of the king's political programme was accurately reflected in the choice of his most intimate advisers. The Emperor, it will be remembered, had left him a full account of the merits and defects of his various counsellors, and had warned him against the danger of giving any one of them full sway; but, down to his death in July, 1573, it was Ruy Gómez da Silva, Prince of Eboli, who enjoyed Philip's confidence more than any one else, and Eboli's policy was in general that of the maintenance of the status quo. Ruy Gómez was of an ancient Portuguese house, and had come to Spain, while yet a child, in the train of the Empress Isabella. At her desire he had been detailed to the household of the baby Prince Philip; he had helped to dress and to undress the heir to the throne; he had accompanied him wherever he went, and usually slept in his room; there naturally grew up the closest intimacy between them.[1] In 1553, as a further mark of the royal favor, he was permitted to contract marriage with Anna, the daughter of the Prince of Melito, of the great house of Mendoza; as the bride, however, was less than thirteen years old at the time of the wedding, she was separated from her husband, in accordance with the common custom of the time; not till the end of 1559, when Silva came back with Philip from the Netherlands, did the pair live together as man and wife. They had ten children in the next twelve years.[2]

It was but natural, then, that on Philip's return to Spain the Prince of Eboli should become his principal adviser.[3] Of his absolute devotion to the king there could be no doubt. Their views on the conduct of the government coincided. "Ruy Gomez and [his] faction . . . rule all alone," wrote an English observer in 1563; he "does more than all" the rest, reported another in 1565.[4] Until 1567 the Duke of

---

[1] Muro, *La Princesa de Eboli*, pp. 23–25; Forneron, i, pp. 235 f.

[2] Muro, pp. 18–32. She was the granddaughter of the Count of Melito, who was viceroy of Valencia under Charles V. Cf. *ante*, Vol. III, pp. 106–112. She was second cousin to Diego Hurtado de Mendoza, the famous statesman and author, to Antonio de Mendoza, the first viceroy of New Spain, and to Bernardino de Mendoza the ambassador. Vol. lvi of the *D. I. E.* contains numerous documents concerning her career.

[3] Michele Soriano (1559) in Albèri, *Relazioni*, serie i, iii, p. 381.

[4] *C. S. P., Foreign*, 1563, no. 1192; 1564–65, no. 1629.

Alva might possibly have maintained that he headed a war party in the Council in opposition to him; but when in that year the Duke was sent off to the Netherlands, the ascendancy of Eboli became more obvious than ever.[1]   Ruy Gómez was in fact the only minister the king ever had who was really permitted to exercise any measure of independent authority.   But Eboli was not satisfied with the establishment of his own preëminence; he laid his plans to pass it on, after his death, to those who shared his views on the conduct of the government.   First it was his creature the secretary Francisco de Eraso, whose career was ultimately ruined by his peculations.   Then for a brief space it was Cardinal Espinosa, whose insolence mounted so high that he was insulted in full Council meeting by the king, went home to his bed, and died the next day.   Bernardo de Fresneda, bishop of Cuenca, and confessor to the king, was another of the same school.[2]   But by far the most famous and ablest of them all, and the one who came nearest to succeeding to the place which became vacant on Eboli's death in 1573,[3] was the fascinating Antonio Pérez, the illegitimate son of Gonzalo Pérez, archdeacon of Sepúlveda, who had been a favorite of the Emperor and was recommended by him to Philip II.[4]

This Pérez was born in 1534, and eight years later received a patent of legitimacy from Charles V.   He was given an excellent education, both at Alcalá and beyond the Pyrenees, and was early associated with the work of the government, where his keen intelligence, wealth of expedients, and almost unlimited capacity for hard work soon won him favorable

---

[1] C. S. P., Foreign, 1566–68, nos. 1816, 1969, 2109, 2125, 2475; and references in Forneron, i, pp. 236 f.

[2] Forneron, i, pp. 237–239, and references there.

[3] On July 29, according to Muro, p. 35, note.

[4] Mignet, Antonio Perez et Philippe II, p. 11.

attention. More and more did Eboli depend upon him; more and more did he instil into him his ideas; more and more obvious did it daily become that it was Pérez who was destined ultimately to fill his place and continue his policy. Philip had been thoroughly won over to him by the time that Eboli died. Men marvelled at the way in which the young upstart was suffered to beard the Duke of Alva at the royal dining table; and the canny ones took note of the fact that it was Pérez who decided, when the despatches of the day were deciphered, what matters were to be communicated to the Council, and what matters were to be reserved for the king. It was also by Pérez that the evil custom of the sale of public offices, which had rapidly increased since the days of the Emperor, was for the first time erected into an established system; he was intrusted with the distribution of the plums, and was liberally rewarded by the recipients.[1] So rapid a rise not unnaturally made him enemies.[2] After he had been in the saddle two or three years, the elements began to combine which were destined to effect his overthrow, and ultimately to give a new and totally unexpected trend to the development of the Spanish Empire.

The events which led to the murder of Juan de Escovedo, the confidant of Don John of Austria, on the night of March 1, 1578, and the effects which it produced, have been recounted many times, in different ways, by many different historians. There is no lack of material bearing on the case; the sole real difficulty is what to believe. The story that is told by Mignet,[3] Gachard,[4] and Forneron,[5] and

---

[1] Juan Beneyto Pérez, *Los medios de Cultura y la Centralización bajo Felipe II* (Madrid, 1927), pp. 93, 109.

[2] Mignet, *Antonio Perez et Philippe II*, pp. 11 f.

[3] *Ibid.*, pp. 74 ff.

[4] *Don Carlos et Philippe II*, p. 207, note 3.

[5] *Histoire de Philippe II*, iii, pp. 52 ff.

received the most general acceptance until the latter part of the nineteenth century, lays the original blame at the door of the Princess of Eboli. It represents her as having been the mistress of Philip, as well as the wife of his chief minister; it emphasizes the fact that one, at least, of the children she had supposedly borne to her husband was strikingly like the king; it then goes on to point out (what no one, except Froude, denies) that after the death of her husband she also became the mistress of Pérez, whom she vastly preferred to Philip, that their liaison was discovered one day in dramatic fashion by Escovedo, and that Pérez felt it necessary to have him made away with in order to prevent him from reporting the facts to the king. Finally it describes how Pérez, by a diabolically clever series of false reports and insinuations, so succeeded in poisoning Philip's ear against Escovedo, that he ultimately obtained a formal written order to have him assassinated, thus converting what had been a grave peril to his own position into an actual strengthening of it; for he now had evidence which he could hold *in terrorem* over the king, if ever the latter should seem inclined to abandon him.[1] But other eminent historians, among them Ranke, Froude, and Lafuente, have rightly pointed out that it was not very likely that a woman who had become the mother of ten children within the space of twelve years, and wore a black patch over her right eye,[2] should have been capable of commanding the allegiance both of the king and of his chief minister.[3] They also emphasize the fact that the circumstances under which Pérez was subsequently to write

[1] Cf. documents in Pidal, *Philippe II, Antonio Perez, et le royaume d'Aragon*, i, pp. 350–385.

[2] A good reproduction of her portrait by Sánchez Coello forms the frontispiece to Muro's *Princesa de Éboli*.

[3] Froude (*The Spanish Story of the Armada and other Historical Essays*, pp. 19, 118 f.) is particularly violent in his denunciation of Mignet's views; cf. also Muro, *La Princesa de Éboli*, pp. 249 f.

his *Relaciones* make it difficult to put faith in their veracity; but they are confronted, in turn, with the serious difficulty of explaining the reasons for the murder of Escovedo. In general, they take the line that Pérez suddenly became jealous of Escovedo's prominence at the court, and so worked on Philip's dread of his influence with Don John that he finally persuaded the king to give orders to have him put out of the way, and this is perhaps the least improbable solution;[1] at any rate the deed was done; six armed men, all hirelings of Pérez, lay in wait for Escovedo in the streets of Madrid at night, killed him with a single thrust,

[1] Cf. here M. A. S. Hume, "El Enigma de Antonio Pérez," in his *Españoles é Ingleses*, pp. 167–203; and A. Lang, "The Murder of Escovedo," in his *Historical Mysteries*, pp. 32–54. Major Hume's theory is that Philip, for political reasons, ordered Escovedo's assassination in the autumn of 1577; that, before it could be accomplished, he ceased to desire it, but neglected to countermand the order, and that Pérez, six months later, when he became anxious for private reasons to get rid of Escovedo, made use of the royal command, which Philip no longer wished fulfilled, to shield him from the consequences of his crime. P. O. von Törne's *Don Juan d'Autriche et les projets de conquête de l'Angleterre*, ii, pp. 173–176, is also well worth reading on the murder of Escovedo. Törne steers clear of any investigation of the relations of Philip and Pérez to the Princess of Eboli, but he emphasizes the fact "que l'hostilité de Perez envers son collègue était de date assez récente," and later, that "le malheureux a su quelque chose qui était désagréable pour Perez, et c'est évidemment cette connaissance fatale de faits dont, le cas échéant, il pourrait se servir pour nuire à celui-ci, qui a fini par perdre notre secrétaire si malencontreux. L'exposé que Mignet donne sur cette question nous semble tout à fait concluant." Cf. also Angela Valente,

"Un Dramma politico alla corte di Filippo II," in the *Nuova Rivista Storica*, viii (1924), pp. 264–303, 416–442, to which further reference will be made on p. 346.

Two books have been recently published, one, in 1910, by José Fernández Montaña, *De Cómo Felipe II no mandó matar á Escobedo*, the other, in 1929, by Louis Bertrand, *Philippe II, une ténébreuse affaire*, which bring forward a number of arguments to show that the king was guiltless of complicity in the assassination of Escovedo. It is true that it is possible to throw doubt on the authenticity of the famous marginal annotation in Philip's hand (printed in Pidal, *Philippe II, Antonio Perez, et le royaume d'Aragon*, i, pp. 358, 360) on which the strongest evidence of the king's guilt rests; it is also undeniable that it is possible to read a variety of different meanings into it (cf. Bertrand, pp. 89 f.). On the other hand, to maintain that Philip was morally incapable of such an act — and this after all is the fundamental contention both of Fernández Montaña and of Bertrand — seems to us absurd. (Cf. G. Muro, *Vida de la Princesa de Éboli*, pp. 74 f.) The absence of conclusive evidence of his guilt would doubtless make it impossible to convict him today in a court of law; but it is certainly difficult to believe that he was wholly innocent.

and reaped their promised reward. The position of the king's minister now seemed established beyond the possibility of further challenge.[1]

But the inevitable jealousies were speedily aroused. No one was particularly anxious to avenge Escovedo,[2] but many coveted for themselves the place that Pérez had obtained, and resolved to utilize the situation for the purpose of depriving him of it.[3] Perhaps the most dangerous of these aspiring rivals was the crafty Mateo Vázquez de Leca, a miserable orphan of Seville, who had made a name for himself as an informer, and subsequently became one of the secretaries of the famous *Junta de Noche*;[4] he convinced himself that, by insinuating that Pérez had persuaded Philip to sanction the murder of Escovedo under false pretences, he would ultimately be able to undermine the influence and position of the minister with the king. But it was a long time, as usual, before Philip could be induced to act, and the blow finally fell when it was least expected. All through the spring and early summer of 1579 he continued to assure Pérez of his confidence and friendship; on the night of July 28 he labored with him over sundry papers until ten o'clock, and ordered him to return for further work on the following morning. An hour after he had left the king, Pérez was arrested and taken to the house of one of the royal *alcaldes*. Shortly afterwards the Princess of Eboli, who had gone out with the intention of passing the night at Pérez's house, was informed of what had happened, and made haste to return to her own home, to find the royal *alguaciles* awaiting her at her door. She was speedily sent off to the Torre de Pinto, three leagues south of Madrid,

[1] Mignet, pp. 92–99.
[2] Save possibly his son, who comes into the picture ten years later; cf. *infra*, p. 575.
[3] Mignet, pp. 424–430.
[4] Forneron, iii, p. 263, and references there.

where she suffered so cruelly that she finally obtained
permission to repair to her own castle of Pastrana and remain
a prisoner there.[1]

Philip had not struck in this dramatic fashion without
careful preparation and forethought. The arrest of Pérez
was more than the end of a ministry; it marks the termination of a whole policy and system of government, which
for lack of a better name we may call the Eboli system.
The essential principle of that system, as we have already
pointed out, had been the maintenance of the status quo;
it was the principle which Charles V had recommended to
Philip in his instructions; it was the principle which Eboli,
under Philip's guidance, had developed; it was the principle which Pérez had inherited from Eboli. Now it was to
be thrown over and exchanged for a different policy, more
positive, more adventurous, more imperial. This exchange
and its consequences, moreover, mark a deep dividing line,
not only in the reign of Philip II, but also in the whole
history of the development of the Spanish Empire; in a
sense it was the beginning of the push over the precipice.
We have summarized the unedifying story of the personal
jealousies and secret intrigues which furnished the background for it as seen from Madrid; now we can turn to the
far more significant task of seeking to discover what the
deeper reasons for it were. The murder of Escovedo was
by no means the only, or even the most important, cause, of
the ruin of Antonio Pérez. Just at the time when the events
we have been recounting reached their climax, a new opportunity for imperial aggrandizement had presented itself to
Philip, which he was determined to embrace, and which he
was convinced from the outset would render indispensable

[1] *D. I. E.*, i, pp. 95 f.; vii, pp. 268 f.; Mignet, pp. 133–135; Forneron, iii, pp.
70–73, and references there.

to him the services of a man of much larger vision than the lover of the Princess of Eboli. Exactly one year after the murder of Escovedo, and four months previous to the arrest of Pérez, Philip had written to Rome to call Cardinal Granvelle across to Spain to bear aid in the tremendous task of annexing the empire of Portugal. It was not without significance that he was unable to find a Spaniard to help him in the solution of a problem so exclusively Iberian.[1]

We have not encountered Cardinal Granvelle since the early days of Margaret of Parma and the *Consulta* in the Netherlands, whence it will be remembered that he had been given permission to 'retire' in the year 1564. The next twenty-one months he spent in his native city of Besançon in Franche Comté, vainly striving to busy himself with the patronage of letters and art, and really eating his heart out for lack of a political office in which he could give free scope to his talents for ruling men.[2] A rather reluctant command of Philip, and the call of the conclave for the choice of a successor to Pope Pius IV, gave him an excuse for departing for Rome in the last days of 1565. The election of Pius V took place while he was on his way there, but after his arrival he found useful and honorable employment in connection with the preparations for the great effort against the Turk which was to culminate so gloriously at Lepanto ; no small share of the credit for that great victory belongs, in fact, to him. From Rome, in April, 1571, he was sent to Naples to assume the office of viceroy left vacant by the death of the Duke of Alcalá ; and there, during the next four years, he wrestled manfully with the proverbially various and vexatious problems associated with the administration of that most difficult of Spain's Italian dependencies. When

[1] Cf. Martin Philippson, *Ein Ministerium unter Philipp II.: Kardinal Granvella am spanischen Hofe (1579–* *1586)*, p. 86.

[2] Philippson, *Kardinal Granvella*, pp. 13–16.

in May, 1572, a new conclave was called at Rome to elect a successor to Pius V, he hastened thither, and within nineteen hours of his arrival brought about the unanimous choice of Gregory XIII. One reason, indeed, why Granvelle was so successful in Naples during the next three years was because his services to the new pontiff gave him amity and coöperation in a quarter in which, according to the Neapolitan tradition, there had always been hostility and distrust.[1] His friendship with Gregory, moreover, was of the utmost value to him when in the spring of 1575 he was sent back to Rome to give help and advice to the resident Spanish ambassador. So high did he stand in the confidence of the Pope that he soon took precedence over all the rest of Philip's representatives on the ground. The king was forced to recognize the value of his services and the wisdom of his counsels as he had never done before, and asked his opinion with increasing frequency and insistence.[2]

Granvelle was at this time some sixty years old.[3] His character had been tested by prosperity and adversity, and his knowledge of mankind had been ripened by experience. He had been brought up to believe that the incontestable supremacy of the house of Hapsburg was a cornerstone of the development of Europe, indeed, almost an essential to the maintenance of civilization, and he never wavered in that faith. If his own dominant characteristic was a fondness for ruling, he never dreamed of trying to exercise it except for the advancement of his Hapsburg master; of his loyalty to the dynasty there could be absolutely no doubt. That the supremacy of the Hapsburgs should have become of recent years so inseparably associated with Spain was

[1] Philippson, *Kardinal Granvella*, pp. 21 f.

[2] *Ibid.*, pp. 24 f. He was a violent opponent of Alva's policy in the Low Countries.

[3] He was born August 20, 1517. Philippson, p. 3.

doubtless in his eyes a misfortune. He would have preferred the picture as it was in the early part of the Emperor's
reign, with the centre of gravity north of the Pyrenees;
in view of his origin, that could scarcely have been otherwise. But it was not in Granvelle's nature to waste time
and energy in vain efforts to alter established facts. Fate
had decreed that the policy of the house of Hapsburg
should be directed, for the time being at least, from Madrid
and the Escorial; from Madrid and the Escorial it was
therefore necessary to take orders. The most he could permit
himself to do was to caution his sovereign against the
dangers of too rapid an Hispanicization of the principles and
personnel of the government of the Low Countries. Now,
however, in midsummer, 1578, an event had occurred which
threw the affairs of the Netherlands, hitherto all-prominent,
into the background; the centre of interest was to shift from
the Low Countries to the Spanish peninsula.[1] The next
act in the great drama of *Austriae est imperare orbi universo*
was to be performed on Iberian soil, and it was the irony of
fate that the Burgundian Granvelle, who had proved
insufficiently Spanish to satisfy his sovereign in the Netherlands, should have been selected, to the exclusion of aspiring
Spanish rivals, to bear aid in the gathering in of the Portuguese inheritance. Was it because twenty years of the
Eboli system had exterminated the generation of great
empire builders in Spain that Philip found it necessary,
now that a fresh opportunity for vast expansion suddenly
revealed itself, to bury all his inherited prejudices against
foreigners, and to call in, to help him grasp it, a chief minister
from outside?

[1] There is an interesting paragraph
by Mariéjol in Lavisse, vi, 1, pp. 205 f.,
pointing out how in 1578 Philip suddenly became conciliatory in his dealings with England, with France, and
with the rebels in the Low Countries,
in order that he might concentrate his
resources on Portugal.

Ever since the attainment in the twelfth century of independent national existence by the kingdom of Portugal, the sovereigns of Castile had persistently striven to reannex it. During the thirteenth and fourteenth centuries they sought, for the most part, to gain their end by war; but the battle of Aljubarrota was a lesson not easily forgotten, and from 1385 onward they generally preferred to have recourse to the pleasanter method of marriage. John II of Castile married a Portuguese princess, who became the mother of Isabella the Catholic. Isabella, the eldest daughter of the Catholic Kings, married Affonso, the son of King John II of Portugal, and after his death in 1491, his cousin King Emmanuel the Fortunate; after her death in 1498, Emmanuel married her younger sister Maria, and after Maria's death in 1517, he took as his third wife her niece Eleanor, the sister of Charles V. Charles V's wife was his first cousin Isabella of Portugal, the daughter of Emmanuel of Portugal and of his second wife Maria; and Philip II's first wife was also his own first cousin, Maria, the daughter of his aunt Catharine and of the Portuguese King John III. But despite all these efforts to unite the two dynasties, a Portuguese heir, with an unimpeachable title, had hitherto been invariably on hand to keep all Castilian claimants from the Lusitanian throne. During the first twenty years of the reign of Philip II it was his nephew Sebastian, the son of his sister Joanna and of his first wife's brother John, that blocked the hopes of the Prudent King for a reannexation of the western realm.

There can be no doubt that the ambitions of the Castilian sovereigns to gain control of the destinies of Portugal were enhanced by the speed at which the value of the prize increased before their eyes. Portugal in the days of Aljubarrotta had been but a little strip along the west coast of the Iberian Peninsula; now, in the days of Philip II, it had become one of the mighty empires of the world.[1] The genius of Henry the Navigator had furnished the inspiration; the capture (1415) of Ceuta across the Strait of Gibraltar gave a starting point; by the time that Columbus had discovered the New World, the Portuguese had occupied the Azores, the Madeira group, and the Cape Verde Islands; they had slowly felt their way down the west coast of Africa, establishing trading posts as they went; they had rounded the Cape of Good Hope and reached Algoa Bay in 1486. In the next two decades their advance was more rapid still. We have already spoken of Cabral and of his discovery of Brazil, and of the Tordesillas Line by which Portugal was given title to it,[2] but that, in the eyes of the Portuguese of that day, was only a subsidiary affair; the Spaniards, after all, had got ahead of them in the West; what they desired was to find an eastern route to India and the Spice Islands. In addition to circumnavigating the Cape of Good Hope, they had begun to investigate the possibilities of getting to the East by the Red Sea. In 1488, Pedro da Covilham had crc sed from Aden to Cananore, whence he had passed on to Calicut and Goa, and thence recrossed to Sofala in Africa. Then in 1497 came the great voyage of Vasco da Gama, the reaping of the fruits that had been sown by undaunted predecessors. Rounding the Cape of Good Hope in November of that year he passed up the east coast of Africa, covering the still unexplored stretch between Algoa Bay and Sofala and completing its circumnavigation.

[1] The events recorded in the next four paragraphs are so well known that it scarcely seems worth while to give extended references for them in footnotes. One of the best modern accounts is that of Charles de Lannoy and Herman vander Linden, in their *Histoire de l'expansion coloniale des peuples européens*, i, Portugal et Espagne (Paris and Brussels, 1907); and it contains (pp. 437–447) an admirable "Liste des ouvrages consultés," for the guidance of those who wish to pursue the subject further.

[2] Cf. *ante*, Vol. II, pp. 202–204, 212 f.

Then, from Melinde, where he obtained a pilot, he crossed
in twenty-three days to the Malabar Coast near Calicut,
where the jealousy of the Arab traders already established
on the spot prevented his being given the most cordial of
receptions; thence he passed north to Cananore and Goa,
and finally got home to Lisbon in September, 1499.   It was
a magnificent achievement, and a fit subject for the greatest
of Portuguese epics, but if it was to be utilized to the full
extent of its possibilities, it was essential to follow it up.
The unfriendliness of the rajah of Calicut promised to spell
the ruin of the great scheme on which the Portuguese
sovereigns had already staked their fortunes, namely, to
seize the monopoly of the commerce of the Eastern Seas,
and to prevent all others from navigating thereon; and the
lesson was reënforced by the experience of Pedro Alvares
Cabral, who, after touching at Brazil (April, 1500), had also
made his way to Calicut.   In his case there had been far
more than latent hostility there; actual fighting had taken
place.   The inference was obvious.   A great military
demonstration was imperative, and in February, 1502,
Vasco da Gama was again sent out to make it.   Quiloa on
the East African coast and Calicut in India were successfully bombarded.   Rival fleets were burnt and their crews
tortured.   Cochin, Quilon, and Cananore were forced at
the cannon's mouth to renounce all commercial relations
except with the Portuguese.

Such action was not merely an affront to the rulers
of East Africa and the Malabar Coast; it was a challenge
to all those who had traded with them hitherto.   The
interests of the sultan of Egypt were affected, as were those
of the merchants of Arabia and even of the republic of
Venice.   Hostilities on a far larger scale were inevitable
in the near future; and in order to be fully prepared for

them King Emmanuel sent out, in the spring of 1505, a fleet of twenty ships, with 1500 soldiers. Command was given to an experienced soldier, Francisco de Almeida, who was granted the title of viceroy of the Indies and was to hold office for three years. Those three years were filled with wellnigh uninterrupted fighting against African and Asiatic foes. Almeida was almost uniformly successful; so much so, in fact, that in 1508, when his term of office had expired, he refused to yield his authority to Affonso de Albuquerque, who had been sent out to take his place. Not till after he had established the supremacy of Portugal in India by defeating the Egyptian fleet in February, 1509, in a great battle off Diu, did he consent to hand over his authority to his successor. Albuquerque was the greatest of all the Portuguese empire builders. Less cautious than Almeida, he believed that his country was destined to be the mistress of the East, and he was convinced that in order to hold the Indian Ocean it was essential to obtain undisputed possession of all its principal ports, and especially of those which controlled access to it. He put this idea into practice on his voyage out to India. As he passed up the East African coast, he discovered Madagascar, which had hitherto been unperceived; in August, 1507, he seized the island of Socotra, and constructed a fort there. Ormuz in the next year he took but could not hold; but in February, 1510, he possessed himself of Goa, and made it the chief centre of Portuguese power in the East. The following year he went on to Malacca, which he seized, thus gaining control of the access to the Spice Islands; thereafter he returned to the Malabar Coast, and in March, 1515, put the cap-stone on the edifice of his former achievements by definitely establishing the Portuguese power at Ormuz. Nine months later he died at Goa, in the

heart of the great empire whose chief founder he may claim
to be.

None of the viceroys who succeeded Albuquerque during
the next sixty years was anywhere nearly his equal; but
their average level was distinctly high, and under them
the work of extending and solidifying the Portuguese
establishments steadily progressed. Various efforts, not
particularly successful, were made to explore Africa;
enough was discovered of Abyssinia to put an end to the
famous myth of Prester John, which had been generally
believed in Europe for centuries past. Portuguese navi-
gators also penetrated to the heads of the Red Sea and the
Persian Gulf; it was by them that the persistent delusions
as to the color of the former were finally and definitely
dispelled. More notable still were their achievements in
the Far East. In the years after Albuquerque's seizure of
Malacca the Portuguese circumnavigated Sumatra, passed
on to Java, Amboina, and the Moluccas, visited New
Guinea and Borneo, and, in all probability, touched the
northern coast of Australia. They also followed up the
shores of Asia to the northward. In 1518 they were at
Canton, and in the next three years they sent ambassadors
to Nanking and Peking. In 1542 they landed in Japan,
and seven years later St. Francis Xavier began his efforts
to establish the Christian religion there. But while the conversion of the natives was one of the chief objects of these
early builders of the Portuguese empire, they did not attack
the problem in quite the same way as did the Spaniards in
the New World. Official Christianization was in their
eyes indispensable for every one with whom they proposed
to do business, in other words, for those who lived in or near
the great centres of Portuguese power on the coast. No
deviation or backsliding was tolerated, hence the cruel

persecutions which got the Portuguese such an evil name in the days to come. On the other hand, they made little effort to provide for the instruction of those that they had brought into the fold, and they scarcely troubled themselves at all about the natives of the back country. This policy was but the religious expression of the fundamental conception of the Portuguese Empire as an empire for trading purposes and little more. Provided its founders were conceded the monopoly of the commerce of the lands and the seas that fell within their line of demarcation, they were not, for the most part, anxious to assume further responsibilities. They made few serious attempts to penetrate into the interior of the lands on whose shores they had established themselves. They had no idea of forcing the local rulers and their peoples to acknowledge themselves subjects of their own home government in the way that the Spaniards had done in the New World ; payment of a tribute was the utmost that they demanded. They trusted to a vast chain of coastal fortresses and trading posts to enable them to keep the commerce of the Orient exclusively in their hands, and with that they were content.

These scattered holdings were divided for purposes of administration into seven different provinces, comprising together the so-called *Estado da India*, and stretching around in magnificent succession from the Cape of Good Hope to Japan.[1] The viceroy, who resided at Goa, had practically absolute power under the crown ; he is correctly described

[1] Cf. here J. Suárez Inclán, *Guerra de Anexión en Portugal*, ii, pp. 170 f. ; Gioan Francesco Morosini (1581) in Albèri, *Relazioni*, serie i, v, pp. 298–311. B. M., Add. Ms. 29,444, fols. 276–289, is an Italian "Discorso di Portogallo," describing the country and its dependencies at the time of Sebastian ; it begins "Possiede il Re Sebastiano di Portogallo Pº di questo nombre . . ." On fols. 288 v–289 the author gives a summary of the annual revenues of the king, amounting to 2,650,000 ducats. Of this sum Portugal and Algarve provided 1,000,000 ducats only ; the Atlantic islands, 200,000 ; the Indian and African possessions, with imposts on the spice trade and other commerce, 1,450,000.

by a contemporary writer as the "true king and God of India." All the local authorities were responsible to him; the *residencia* which he was obliged to undergo at the expiration of his term of office was really a farce, for the consequences of making a complaint were likely to be so serious that it was the part of wisdom to refrain. The entire system was honeycombed with corruption. The pursuit of wealth was the universal aim, and every other consideration was sacrificed to it. Bribery became so common that it ceased to be regarded as a crime. If there was no other way of attaining the desired end, it was always possible to leave the native trader unpaid.

These conditions had their inevitable reaction on Portugal herself. In the first place, the colonial establishment which she was attempting to maintain was greatly in excess of her capabilities; the call for sailors and soldiers denuded the countryside and brought agriculture and pasturage to a standstill. The desire to participate in the trade of the Orient contributed in another way to produce the same results. Every one was determined to get to Lisbon, which was the centre of it; the population of the capital increased by leaps and bounds, and its luxury and wealth were the marvel of all beholders. But this outward splendor failed to conceal from the keener minds the unsoundness of the foundation on which it rested. The country was flooded with African slaves, and manual labor was more and more despised. The best blood in the nation had been drained away across the seas; the army that was left at home was scarcely worthy of the name. Finally, King Sebastian, last scion of the house of Avis, was the despair of all who still hoped to escape Castilian bondage. He had succeeded his grandfather John III in 1557, at the age of three, but from his childhood onward "he had lacked the greatest blessing that a ruler can have, namely a wise man at his side in whom he could put his trust." [1] Though by no means destitute of fine qualities, he was a perfectly impracticable king. Leaving the government largely in the hands of others, he disciplined himself by rigorous military training and the severest forms of asceticism. The sole national enterprise which could evoke his enthusiasm was the project of a crusade against the infidels of Morocco; moreover, as all efforts to arrange a marriage for him proved unavailing, there was no hope of an heir to take his place.[2]

It will be readily believed that Philip, who prided himself on the accuracy and completeness of his information on the course of events in every corner of Europe, had kept in intimate touch with everything that had occurred in Portugal since his return to Spain in 1559. The closeness of the relationships between the courts of Lisbon and Madrid gave him an excellent excuse for doing this, and the Portuguese origin of the Prince of Eboli furnished him abundant means; but the instrument which he chiefly made use of for the purpose was his Portuguese counsellor, Cristóbal de Moura. Moura had come to Spain in 1554, at the age of sixteen, in the train of the Princess Joanna, the sister of Philip and the mother of Sebastian, after the death of her husband John, the son of King John III. Like his compatriot Eboli, he had risen rapidly in the favor of the Spanish monarch; he was made a knight of Calatrava and later of Alcántara, and given a variety of important posts about the court;

[1] Jeronimo Franchi di Conestaggio, *Dell' unione del Regno di Portogallo alla Corona di Castiglia* (Genoa, 1585), fol. 10. The latest biography is by Antero de Figueiredo (6th ed., Lisbon, 1925).

[2] Cf. Diogo Barbosa Machado, *Memorias para a Historia de Portugal, que comprehendem o Governo del Rey D.* *Sebastião* (Lisbon, 1736–51, 4 vols.); Antero de Figueiredo, *D. Sebastião*; and José, Conde de São Mamede, *Don Sébastien et Philippe II* (Paris, 1884). Original material on the various efforts made to arrange a marriage for Sebastian will be found in the B. M., Add. Mss. 28,403–28,407.

but, as the years went on, it became increasingly obvious
that his principal sphere of usefulness would be in connection
with the developments in his native land. In the autumn
of 1565 he was sent thither to discover the truth of reports
which had reached Madrid to the effect that Sebastian was
sexually impotent. He was also very useful in helping to
settle various differences which had arisen between those
who were managing the government of Portugal during
Sebastian's minority — his grandmother Catharine, his
great-uncle Cardinal Henry, and his cousin Antonio, the
prior of Crato; and he kept Philip fully informed of all
the successive proposals which were made for Sebastian's
marriage.[1] The policy of the Prudent King all through
this early period was perfectly consistent. He was determined, when the time came, to possess himself of the Portuguese inheritance. On the other hand, he had no intention of hurrying the inevitable, or of putting in his claims
before his rights were clear. His sole object for the present
was to keep himself fully apprised of all that was going on,
and to be certain that nothing was done to the prejudice of
his own lawful interests.

It was Sebastian's enthusiasm for crusading that brought
matters to the final crisis; for the conquest and conversion
of the Moors across the Strait of Gibraltar became, as he
grew up, the one absorbing passion of his life. He made
a reconnoitring expedition to Morocco in 1574, and would
doubtless have started campaigning there and then, had it
not been for the opposition of his grandmother Catharine
at home, and the refusal of his uncle Philip to furnish him
with the support for which he asked. On his return to
Portugal he at once set about making ready for a renewal
of the attempt. In December, 1576, there was held the

---

[1] Danvila y Burguero, *Cristobal de Moura*, pp. 109–133.

famous interview between him and the Prudent King at
the monastery of Guadalupe in Estremadura, rich in crusading traditions and in memories of the battle on the Salado.
Once more Sebastian begged for his uncle's coöperation,
and the latter did his utmost to dissuade his nephew from
his intended enterprise, or at least from taking command of
the expedition himself.[1] But Sebastian refused to listen
to counsels of caution; he went back to Lisbon and continued
his preparations. The death (February 15, 1578) of his
grandmother Catharine served to remove what had been
a principal restraining influence, and the remonstrances
of Philip's new ambassador, Juan de Silva, were impatiently
waved aside. The situation in Morocco, indeed, was
certainly such as augured well for his projects. The Turkish
suzerainty there had not been established in any such
fashion as at Tunis or at Algiers. The throne was disputed
between a number of hostile claimants, none of whom
bore any love to Constantinople, though some were not too
proud to solicit its aid in effecting the dethronement of a
hated rival. Since 1573 the legitimate sovereign, Abou-
Abd-Allah Mohammed, had been sustaining an unequal
contest against his two uncles, Abd-el-Malek and Abu-el-
Abbas, who were supported against him by the Porte. So
well had they succeeded that Mohammed, after several
vain efforts to gather his adherents and induce them to

---

[1] There is reason to think that this
interview was originally arranged by
Sebastian's counsellors, who were themselves unable to induce him to abandon
his project, but hoped that his
"unkle . . . the Kinge of Spayne by
his autoritie and experience might
diswade him from that soe chargeable
and daungerous an enterprise." Cf.
Castries, Angleterre, i, pp. 190 f.
There is no trustworthy evidence that
Philip gave Sebastian any real encouragement, though the latter apparently
went back to Portugal believing that
his uncle was going to help him; cf.
Bernardo da Cruz, Chronica, caps.
xxxvi–l, passim; and Conestaggio,
fols. 13 v ff. The Duke of Alva
and the Marquis de los Vélez, who
were present at the interview, were
of the opinion that Philip could not
possibly persuade Sebastian to give up
his expedition, but that he might try
to get it postponed to another year.
Castries, Angleterre, i, pp. 223 f.

make a stand, had passed over to Spain to get the aid of Philip II in the recovery of his dominions. During the spring of the year 1577, he and his victorious kinsmen across the Strait bid against one another for the friendship of the Spanish monarch; but Philip, who was fully alive to the perils of North African campaigning, was determined from the outset not to support the dispossessed claimant. Despite the fact that his enemies were, ostensibly at least, in alliance with the Porte, he felt that it was safer to let them alone, and urged Sebastian to follow his example.[1] But the Portuguese king remained deaf to Philip's advice. His crusading ardor was deeply stirred. The fact that the actual rulers of Morocco were supported by Constantinople was in his eyes an added reason for attacking them, and the promise of Mohammed that, in case he was successful, he would turn over the port of Arzila to his Christian allies, did the rest. Sebastian threw himself heart and soul into preparations for an expedition in the following spring. He was undismayed by the difficulty of finding soldiers to accompany him and of collecting the necessary funds. He applied to Philip for help, and obtained a certain amount of munitions and supplies; nothing, however, would induce the Prudent monarch to furnish the detachment of troops which was requested; the state of affairs in the Low Countries was made an excuse. Until the last moment Philip continued to urge, through his ambassador, Silva, that the enterprise be abandoned, or, at least, that Sebastian himself should not take part in it in person; if it ended, as he foresaw, in disaster, he was determined that the fault should not be laid at his door.[2] But Sebastian continued to ignore

[1] Castries, Angleterre, i, pp. 191, note 1, 341.

[2] Philip's counsellor Benito Arias Montano, who had previously been advocating a policy of conciliation in the Low Countries, was also sent to Lisbon in February, 1578, at once to remonstrate against the North African

his uncle's remonstrances.   In June, 1578, he finally got his
army together — a motley horde of some 20,000 Portuguese,
Italians, and Germans; on the 25th, amid magnificent
ceremonies, the expedition left Lisbon.   After a five days'
wait at Cadiz it landed at Arzila, where Mohammed, who
had gone on ahead to make preparations, was awaiting it
with but an insignificant portion of the troops that he had
promised to provide.

The story of the next few weeks is briefly told.   The
rashness of Sabastian was only equalled by his ineptitude.
He took no pains to establish his base on the coast, or to
guard his lines of communications.   Insulting messages
which reached him from his enemies confirmed him in his
determination to seek them out wherever they were, no
matter what the risk.   He declared that he wished to "conquer with peril"; if any one advised caution he attributed
it to cowardice.   The taunts of his foes made him abandon
the strong position which he occupied near the coast, and
advance inland across a stream which was spanned by a
single bridge; no sooner had he reached the other side than
a squadron of the enemy's cavalry circled around behind
him and cut off all retreat.   Finally, on August 4, 1578, the
hostile armies encountered one another on the great plain of
Alcazar-el-Kebir.   During the first moments of the conflict
one of the two rival uncles of the infidel pretender, who had
been seriously ill for weeks before, died in the litter in which
he had been brought to the fight; but the fact was so well
concealed and the plan of the battle had been so carefully
laid that the Christians were in headlong retreat before

expedition, and to extend the good
name of the Spanish king.   "No hablo
de la cuestion sucesoria, pero tomó
nota de los juicios favorables a Felipe
II . . . muy tenidos en cuenta despues . . . de Alcazarquivir."   Cf. Luis

Morales Oliver, *Arias Montano y la
Política de Felipe II en Flandes* (Madrid,
1927), pp. 303–312; also *D. I. E.*,
xli, pp. 127–418, and Forneron, iii,
pp. 371–377.

the fact was known. A panic seized Sebastian's forces; within two hours they were scattered in ignoble flight. Many were cut down by the weapons of their pursuing foes; more were drowned in the river that barred their retreat, among them, in all probability, Sebastian himself, who, though the Portuguese for a long time refused to believe his death, was never seen alive again; his protégé, Mohammed, also perished in the waves. Mohammed's surviving uncle, Abu-el-Abbas, gathered in all the fruits of the victory and established his dynasty in Morocco in such fashion that it was not to be challenged for years. So weary were the Christians of North African campaigning that there were numbered among those who came to congratulate him on the establishment of his authority, if we may believe the contemporary Moorish chronicle, both representatives of Philip II and also of the regency in Lisbon.[1]

The sad news reached the Portuguese capital on August 17,[2] and eleven days later Sebastian's great-uncle, the Cardinal Henry, the last male scion of the house of Avis whose descent was unquestionably free from the taint of illegitimacy, was proclaimed king; but as he was then in his sixty-seventh year and bound by his clerical vows of celibacy, it was obvious that his reign could be only the briefest of

[1] The best contemporary published accounts of the battle of Alcazar-el-Kebir are those in Conestaggio, fols. 25–50, and in Bernardo da Cruz, caps. lxvi–lxx; cf. also Castries, Angleterre, i, pp. 329–338. The best modern ones are, perhaps, those of Suárez Inclán and Durand-Lapie. On the various pretenders who took advantage of the popular belief that Sebastian was not dead to impersonate him, cf. Victor de Heaulme, *Dom Sébastien et les mystères de la bataille d'Alcaçar* (Paris, 1854); Miguel d'Antas, *Les faux Don Sébastien* (Paris, 1866); J. L. d'Azevedo, *A Evolução do Sebastianismo*

(Lisbon, 1918); Adriano Anthero, "Os Falsos D. Sebastião," in his *Os Falsos Principes* (Porto, 1927), pp. 87–141.

[2] Danvila y Burguero, p. 328. Philip got the news five days earlier, and, at least outwardly, showed great grief. Cf. *D. I. E.*, vii, pp. 229–234; Castries, Angleterre, i, p. 304; and S. I., i, pp. 28 f. He also wrote to the Marquis of Santa Cruz on August 13, commanding him to bear aid to the Portuguese in North Africa; cf. Altolaguirre y Duvale, *Álvaro de Bazán*, p. 262.

stop-gaps.[1] The opportunity, in other words, which Philip
and his predecessors had long desired seemed now at last to
have actually arrived; for the Spanish monarch, as the son
of the Empress Isabella, the eldest daughter of Emmanuel
the Fortunate, had unquestionably the best legal right to
the Portuguese throne as soon as Cardinal Henry should die.
But there were many rival claimants.[2] First of all there was
Antonio, the illegitimate son, by a converted Jewess, of
Louis, the brother of Cardinal Henry and the Empress
Isabella. Antonio had entered the order of the Knights of
St. John of Malta and was prior of the rich commandery of
Crato; he had accompanied Sebastian to North Africa, and
was for the moment a prisoner in the hands of the Moors,
but he finally escaped in the autumn of 1579, and was to be a
thorn in the side of the Prudent King for many years to
come.[3] More immediately dangerous was Catharine, the
younger daughter of Cardinal Henry's younger brother
Edward, a woman of high abilities and ambition; but her
worthless husband, the Duke of Braganza, was ultimately
to ruin her chances, and her son, the Duke of Barcelos, was
in the hands of the king of Spain.[4] There were also three
other candidates from abroad; Ranuccio Farnese, the son of

[1] J. M. Rubio, *Felipe II y Portugal*,
pp. 112 f.

[2] Conestaggio, fols. 50 v ff.

[3] Bernardo da Cruz, cap. lxxxii;
Paul Durand-Lapie, in *Revue d'histoire
diplomatique*, xviii, pp. 275–281.

[4] Angela Valente, in the monograph
cited on p. 327, note 1, maintains that
a principal cause for the imprisonment
of Pérez and of the Princess of Eboli
was their conduct in connection with
the affairs of Portugal. She represents
the Princess as being less the lover than
the *cliente* of Pérez ("nella lista di
coloro che pagavano al segretario regale
i suoi illeciti favori, la vedova di
Ruigomez occupa il primo posto");
and she cites a letter from Giovanni di
Bologna, chaplain to Philip II, to
Cardinal Farnese, of October 17, 1579,
to show that the Princess wished to
marry her daughter to the son of the
Duke of Braganza, and therefore
revealed to the Duke Philip's plans in
regard to Portugal, which had been
communicated to her by Pérez. There
may well be much truth in this contention. Certainly Pérez had all the
threads of the Portuguese project in
his hands to the day of his arrest;
so conversant was he, in fact, with all
its details, that he was referred to about
the Court as 'el Portugues.' Cf.
here also Muro, *La Princesa de Éboli*,
p. 150.

Alexander of Parma, whose mother, Maria, was a sister of Catharine of Braganza; Emanuel Philibert, duke of Savoy, who was the son of Cardinal Henry's elder sister Beatrice;[1] and, finally, Catharine de' Medici, who claimed descent from the mediaeval Portuguese King Affonso III and his repudiated wife, Matilda, Countess of Boulogne. None of these, however, had any idea of seriously prosecuting their claims; they only put them forward in the hope of extorting from the Spanish king counter-concessions which might prove useful to them in Italy and elsewhere.[2] So strong in fact, during the first weeks of Cardinal Henry's rule, did Philip believe his position to be, that he began to cherish hopes of gaining his ends without a fight.

Much depended, of course, on the attitude of the Portuguese themselves, and Philip spared no pains to turn it in his favor. Foreseeing the probable outcome of Sebastian's expedition, he had taken his first measures before his nephew's death; thereafter he redoubled his efforts. Legists, theologians, and professors were drafted from all over Europe to demonstrate the justice of his cause.[3] Letters were written to Lisbon and the other principal cities of Portugal to express his sorrow at the death of Sebastian, to remind them of his close relationship to the house of Avis, and to profess his affection for the Portuguese.[4] But he found the most efficient instrument for the attainment of his ends in Cristóbal de Moura. Moura was convinced that the sole possible salvation for Portugal lay in reunion with Castile.

---

[1] On the claims and purposes of Emanuel Philibert, see Arturo Segre and Pietro Egidi, *Emanuele Filiberto* (Turin, 1928), ii, pp. 271-273, 277.

[2] Durand-Lapie, *loc. cit.*, pp. 275-278; Philippson, *Kardinal Granvella*, p. 87.

[3] Durand-Lapie, p. 278; *D. I. E.*, xli, pp. 383-386.

[4] E.g., Madrid, Library of the R. A. H., est. 27, gr. 3ᵃ, 80, fols. 11 f., "Carta a la ciudad de Lisboa," March 14, 1579; printed from a manuscript at the Escorial in *D. I. E.*, vii, pp. 238-240; English translation, B. M., Cotton Ms. Nero B. I, fol. 188, printed (in part) in Castries, *Angleterre*, i, pp. 340 f.

His intimate knowledge of his native land told him where and how the most effective blows could be struck, and he was furnished with an abundance of money, most of which he used to gain popularity for his master by ransoming the prisoners who had been captured at Alcazar-el-Kebir; the rest of it he distributed in well placed bribes.[1] The evidence in regard to the measure of success which these efforts attained is most contradictory, but it seems probable that they counted for much. At the outset there was undoubtedly much opposition; for the age-long struggle of the Portuguese to maintain their independence made them naturally regard the Castilians in the light of hereditary foes; "rather would we become Frenchmen, Englishmen, or even Turks than Spaniards," said the Portuguese ambassador in Madrid to the Venetian envoy Morosini in February, 1579.[2] But in the ensuing months the tide began to turn the other way. In November Antonio of Crato, who had just got back from his captivity in North Africa, wrote in deep discouragement to the French ambassador, Saint-Gouard, that "the king of Castile is certain to reign over the Portuguese; all of them have been won over to this solution."[3] And in February, 1580, the writer of the Fugger news letters from Lisbon declared that "the struggle cannot last long, for all the best people here are in favor of Spain, but dare not let it be seen. . . . When the King of Spain appears here with his army he will be better received than he expects. . . . I fancy the authorities set up in this country have an understanding with the Spaniards. I have no doubt that Spain will take possession of Portugal, as is fitting. I hope that then there will be better government and better business."[4]

[1] Danvila y Burguero, *Cristobal de Moura*, pp. 335–366.
[2] Philippson, *op. cit.*, p. 89.
[3] Forneron, iii, p. 99.
[4] *Fugger News-Letters*, second series, pp. 37 f.

Meantime, in the winter of 1578-79, it became evident that the Portuguese problem, though apparently exclusively Iberian, could not be solved without affecting the course of European politics beyond the Pyrenees. So mighty were Philip and Spain that any further increase of their power was bound to be regarded with dread by the other European states, all of which were eagerly looking for an excuse which would justify their interference in opposition to the Prudent King. Such an excuse was finally furnished by the news that Cardinal Henry, who, though at first anxious to prevent the succession of the Spanish monarch, was by no means wholly friendly to any of the other pretenders, had resolved to seek dispensation at Rome from his vows of clerical celibacy, in the hope that he might possibly be able himself to produce an heir; though this was regarded in Madrid as practically out of the question, it was also apparently believed there that, in case the dispensation were secured, it was possible that the aged claimant might be provided with a pregnant wife.[1] At any rate Philip was determined to prevent, if possible, the granting of this dispensation, and sent envoys to Rome to effect that end. Pope Gregory was thus placed in an exceedingly awkward position.[2] It had been his hope to keep entirely out of this difficult Portuguese affair, for he was unable to determine which side he hoped would win. On the one hand, he dreaded to see the power of Spain, already excessive, still further enhanced; on the other, he was reluctant to offend Philip II, whose support was essential to his policy in other parts of Europe.[3] The situation was further complicated by the French, who did their utmost to advance the granting of Cardinal

---

[1] Bernardo da Cruz, cap. xcviii; C. de C., ii, p. 515; Philippson, pp. 88 f.

[2] Pastor, xix, pp. 358 f.

[3] Philippson, pp. 90-93. Philippson remarks upon the policy of the Jesuits in supporting the pretensions of Philip II in order to secure his favor.

Henry's dispensation;[1] it was also much affected by
the fact that the term of the clerical subsidy in Spain,
indispensable to Philip, expired in 1579, and that Gregory
obstinately refused to renew it; indeed, the Pope persisted
in his refusal until November 6, 1581, when he yielded in the
hope of securing Philip's support in the affairs of England.[2]
The Prudent King's contemporaneous policy of seeking
peace with the infidel, the status of the Neapolitan *exequatur*,[3]
and a host of other traditional points of difference between
Rome and Madrid became involved in the problem; but
Philip, though he showed himself willing to yield on a number
of minor details, adhered rigidly to all his chief contentions;
and nothing would induce him to hear of a plan, which was
put forward at one stage of the proceedings, to place the
final decision of the whole Portuguese question in the hands
of the Pope.[4]

Such then was the situation of Spain's foreign and internal
affairs which determined Philip, on March 30, 1579, to call
Cardinal Granvelle from Rome to the position whence he had
already determined to dismiss the lover of the Princess of
Eboli. The tone of the letter, countersigned by Pérez himself, which summoned Granvelle is very urgent; "I need your
person and your help," so it runs; "The sooner you come
the happier I shall be."[5] Granvelle, when he first received
it, was in some doubt if it would be wise for him to accept.
He had never been popular with Castilians, and he was by
no means certain exactly how Philip intended to utilize him;
but personal ambition and loyalty to the house of Hapsburg
decided the issue, and on April 20 he wrote to the king that

---

[1] H. Léonardon, *loc. cit.*, p. 40.

[2] Philippson, p. 380; Pastor, xix, p. 364.

[3] Pastor, xix, p. 362; and cf. p. 472, below.

[4] Philippson, p. 95; Forneron, iii, pp. 101 f.; Pastor, xix, pp. 358–361.

[5] Philippson, p. 62; *Correspondance du Cardinal de Granvelle*, ed. Piot, vii, pp. 352 f.

he would soon be on his way to Madrid.[1] In Genoa he met with Juan de Idiáquez, who was to be the companion and continuer of his work; Idiáquez was thirty-nine years old at the time, and had been called home from the Spanish embassy at Venice to bear aid to the cardinal in the accomplishment of the great task that awaited him. Such were the delays of travelling in those days that it was not until July 8 that the pair reached Barcelona, whence they were ordered to proceed at once to the Escorial.[2] When word reached Philip that they had actually landed, he made haste, as we have already seen, to dispose of Pérez and the Princess of Eboli, on July 28–29; a few days later he received the cardinal "as a deliverer" at San Lorenzo.[3] The last vestiges of the old defensive Eboli peace party had been destroyed. Philip was to have the priceless aid of an able, energetic, and aggressive statesman in the launching of his new policy of imperialism.

It naturally took Granvelle some months to get used to the details of his new office. Moreover, he was particularly careful to seek to give the appearance of keeping his hands off Portuguese affairs, in order to avoid rousing the jealousy of the Spaniards, who could not understand why Philip had selected a Burgundian as his principal adviser. Not until matters came to a crisis with the death of Cardinal Henry in the following year did the new minister take the lead in the question of the hour; the last five months of 1579 were really a period of preparation for the moment when decisive action should become necessary.[4] Ostensibly they were filled with a struggle of opposing factions around the throne of Cardinal Henry, whose hopes of a dispensation from Rome had by this time vanished, and who was consequently

---

[1] *Correspondance du Cardinal de Granvelle*, ed. Piot, vii, pp. 376 f.
[2] Philippson, pp. 67–69.
[3] *Ibid.*, pp. 69–71.
[4] *Ibid.*, p. 121.

faced with the problem of deciding to which of the rival
candidates for the succession he should lend the advantage
of his own support. In the preceding April he had summoned the Portuguese Cortes to Lisbon, to select eleven
judges to pronounce upon the validity of the conflicting
claims.[1] As was natural, Philip replied by assembling
another body of legal lights at Madrid to give their verdict
on the same question.[2] The Portuguese body decided in
favor of Don Antonio, of whose legitimacy, despite all the
evidence to the contrary, they professed themselves satisfied;
but Cardinal Henry, who bore no love to the prior of Crato,
and whose hostility to him was further enhanced by the
representations of the envoys of Philip II, refused to accept
this verdict, and banished Antonio from his court.[3] The
Spanish jury, as had been inevitable from the first, gave its
decision in favor of the claims of the Prudent King. During
the early autumn, the sentiments of Cardinal Henry veered
steadily more and more in the direction of the Spanish
candidacy. The influence of his Jesuit confessor, who had
been won over to Philip's cause, counted for much, as did
the rumors which reached him of the military preparations
which the Spaniards were making to enforce their claims,
if necessary, by the sword.[4] But the partisans of Antonio
were loud in their disapproval, and finally in the end of
October Cardinal Henry, who felt that his days were now
numbered, and was desirous above all of having the matter
peacefully settled before he died, took the advice of the Pope,
and once more summoned the Portuguese Cortes to
Almeirim, in the hope of arriving at a solution satisfactory
to all concerned.[5] When the assembly met on January 9,
1580, the cardinal came out strongly for the claims of

[1] Durand-Lapie, *loc. cit.*, p. 145.
[2] *Ibid.*, p. 278.
[3] *Ibid.*, p. 284.

[4] Bernardo da Cruz, caps. cvi–cviii;
Durand-Lapie, p. 288.
[5] *Ibid.*, p. 288.

Philip II;[1] most of the clergy agreed, and also the majority of the nobility, whom Moura had won over by his bribes. But the representatives of the people, still unable to endure the thought of subjection to a Spanish monarch, begged the cardinal to nominate his own successor, and promised to accept any one he should select, provided only he should be a Portuguese; and when Henry refused, they produced historical precedents to prove that, on the extinction of the male line of Portuguese kings, it belonged to the Cortes to settle the succession to the throne.[2] Apparently they still desired that the choice should fall on Antonio, who was in hiding at the time, but whose claims were so strong that Philip offered him an annual pension of 50,000 ducats and a governorship[3] if he would renounce them. Finally, on January 31, 1580, the event that had been so long expected occurred, and the old king-cardinal died after a reign of one year, five months, and five days. He left behind him a regency of five members to govern the realm until his successor should be chosen. Of the five, three were already won over to the support of Philip, and though they did not dare openly proclaim their position for fear of arousing the popular wrath, they saw to it that nothing effective was accomplished towards putting the kingdom in a state of defence against him.[4]

The irresolution and disruption of the government of Portugal had given Philip time to prepare his forces for the trial of strength which now seemed inevitable; and it was in the acceleration of these preparations that Granvelle rendered his first and greatest service. The king's new minister had seen from the outset how essential it was to be ready to invade as soon as Cardinal Henry should die,

[1] Philippson, pp. 116 f.
[2] Durand-Lapie, pp. 288 f.
[3] Ibid., p. 290.

[4] Philippson, pp. 120–123; Durand-Lapie, pp. 291–293; Danvila y Burguero, Cristobal de Moura, pp. 545–566.

before opposition could be organized, and had busied himself
with the task of making preparations to that end.[1] First of
all he attacked the problem of the Spanish national finances,
which had been left in sorry condition by the administration
of Antonio Pérez. Not only was the treasury empty, it was
burdened by enormous debts; peculation was rife; the
Castilian grandees were in league with the foreign bankers
to cheat the government out of the revenues that were
justly due to it, and the prospects for the future were even
darker than the existing conditions.[2] All this was gall and
wormwood to Granvelle, who lost no time in telling his
worries to the king; but although Philip admitted the facts,
he could not be induced to take any effective measures
for reform. Money must somehow be found to pay for the
army,[3] and to supply Moura in Portugal with the means of
bribery; but it was not to be by the stopping of corruption
or the curtailment of expenses in other directions.[4] The
only method which Philip comprehended was that of further
mortgaging the future; and Granvelle, whose knowledge of
the principles of sound finance was as much in advance of
his times as that of his master was behind them, must have
been deeply cast down at the prospect. Not even these
financial discouragements, however, could avail to shake
his faith in the necessity for preparedness.[5] He fully
realized that foreign influences hostile to Spain were already
at work in Portugal, and that the only way to make certain
of success was to be ready to strike both by land and sea as
soon as the fitting moment should arrive. Numerous efforts

[1] Philippson, pp. 121–123, and references there.

[2] Cf. *infra*, p. 438, note 2.

[3] B. M., Egerton Ms. 122, fol. 92 v: "Entretenia el Rey Catholico en este tiempo el exercito de España con mas trabajo y maior gasto que en otras provincias se tuviere, porque con no ser la tierra muy abundante, era forçoso proveer los bastimientos de lexos."

[4] Forneron (iii, p. 105) says "Plus un ducat n'est envoyé aux Pays-Bas," but he does not state his authority.

[5] Philippson, pp. 122–126.

were made by the foreign representatives at Madrid to persuade the Spanish government that there would be no occasion for fighting; of these the majority — particularly those of France — were intended to lull Philip into a false sense of security and thereby give the Portuguese a chance to prepare to resist him;[1] the Holy See, on the other hand, exhorted Philip to submit the case to papal arbitration.[2] Until the death of Cardinal Henry these efforts had had some effect, and despite all the energy of Philip's new minister the military preparations had advanced but slowly. But after January, 1580, when the crisis became imminent and Granvelle's position and influence were securely established, a gratifying change took place. In the immediately succeeding months the Castilian nobles displayed real patriotism and began to raise little armies at their own expense, while the cities contributed troops, ships, and funds. The Portuguese enterprise was supported by the nation.[3]

The choice of a commander-in-chief was the hardest problem of all. Public opinion demanded the Duke of Alva, who, though he had been sent into retirement on his estates at Uceda after his return from the Low Countries in 1573, was universally conceded to be the best soldier in Spain; but Philip's resentment against him was still so deep that it is doubtful if he would have got the place without the intervention of Granvelle. So effective, however, was the cardinal in finding means of accommodating the various differences that still kept the king and the proud Duke at odds,[4] that on February 22, 1580, Alva received his appoint-

---

[1] Léonardon, p. 42.
[2] Pastor, xix, pp. 358 f.
[3] Philippson, p. 126.
[4] Cf. *D. I. E.*, vii, pp. 464–524, "Documentos sobre las causas que dieron motivo á la prision de D. Fadrique, hijo del Duque de Alba, y tambien á la del mismo Duque" (1578); S. I., i, pp. 89–92.

ment to the command of the invading force.[1] It was
further decided that Philip and his family should accompany
the army to the Portuguese frontier, in order that he might
appear in his new kingdom the moment that it should seem
best for him to do so; on March 4 he left Madrid on his
way to Guadalupe. Fearing the machinations of the other
sovereigns of Europe, he refused permission to their representatives to accompany him, and insisted that they should
stay on at the capital, where Granvelle remained in charge.[2]

Three months more, however, were to elapse before Alva
led his army across the frontier.[3] The intervening time
was filled with plots and intrigues, and Spanish hopes that
Philip after all might possibly be recognized without opposition. At first there seemed some reason to believe that this
would be the case. The five regents left by Cardinal Henry
were generally useful to the cause of the Prudent King;
three of them, as we have already seen, had been won over
to him by bribes; they pretended to organize an army of
resistance in order to satisfy the malcontents, and at the
same time sowed disorder in the realm, so as to make such
resistance impossible.[4] Queen Elizabeth, who had been
asked by the Portuguese for help against the Spaniards,
gave honeyed words but did nothing; such an adventure was
far too remote to appeal to her practical and parsimonious
mind. [5] French opposition promised to be more dangerous; but for a time it was largely nullified by indecision
as to whether Antonio or the Duke of Braganza would be
the better candidate to support,[6] and by fears of the possible

[1] D. I. E., xxxii, pp. 15–17. The
formal commission as captain-general,
dated June 12, 1580, is printed in
D. I. E., xxxii, pp. 151–160, and in S. I.,
ii, pp. 368 f.
[2] Philippson, pp. 129–131.
[3] Ibid., p. 175; Léonardon, p. 44;
Durand-Lapie, p. 299.

[4] Forneron, iii, pp. 107–109, and
references there; Durand-Lapie, pp.
291–296.
[5] Philippson, p. 163; C. Read, Walsingham, ii, p. 42.
[6] Léonardon, pp. 43 f.

results of the Huguenot capture of Cahors (May 31, 1580). More serious for the moment was the opposition of the Pope, who was now resolved that his rights as supreme arbiter in a case of disputed succession should be formally recognized; he decided to send a legate, Cardinal Alessandro Riario, to Portugal for the purpose of asserting them.[1] But the difficulties and dangers of the journey were such that Riario did not reach Barcelona until June 12; we shall note a little later how he fared from that point.[2]

As far, then, as the outside powers were concerned, the situation in the early months of 1580 was not unfavorable to Philip. All of them, for different reasons and in different degrees, disliked the prospective enlargement of the dominions of the Spanish king, but none of them was actually in a position to give practical effect to its feelings. In Portugal, however, it became obvious, as the spring wore on, that it would be impossible for Philip to enter upon his new inheritance without some use of military force.[3] He promised all sorts of concessions to the Portuguese, in regard to the maintenance of their independent institutions and officials, as soon as he should be recognized as king. All the immemorial principles of Spanish separatism were to be maintained; another entity was to be added to the Spanish Empire, but there was to be no merging of the new body in the old.[4] Moura and the other Spanish representatives in Portugal surpassed themselves in the energy and skill they exhibited in their efforts to win over the Portuguese to the cause of their master; and Philip kept postponing, against

[1] Philippson, pp. 164–166; Pastor, xix, pp. 359 f. The instructions to Riario (April 14 and 18, 1580) are summarized in Ricardo de Hinojosa, *Los Despachos de la Diplomacia Pontificia en España*, i (Madrid, 1896), pp. 279–285.

[2] *Infra*, p. 364.
[3] Philippson, p. 168.
[4] Bernardo da Cruz, cap. ci, "Como elrei de Castella buscou todos os mêos pera escusar guerras com Portugal."

Granvelle's advice, the day of the invasion for which every preparation was now complete, in the hope that the Portuguese would accept him of their own free will.[1] There were negotiations with representatives of the five regents at Guadalupe in late March and early April, but nothing came of them.[2] Philip would not submit his claims to arbitration, as the regents desired, even with what amounted to a preliminary assurance that the verdict would be given in his favor ; he stood out for the form as well as the substance, and insisted that his rights were so clear that it was useless to call them in question.[3] Such an attitude was incomprehensible to those who still opposed him. It encouraged them to prepare for resistance ; in late April and May the French ambassador at Madrid, the Seigneur de Saint-Gouard, redoubled his exertions to bring about the intervention of his master against the Spanish king.[4] By this time it had become evident that if resistance were actually to be offered the official leader of it must be Don Antonio. He had now issued from his place of concealment, so that his presence in the realm was generally known ; he had a gallant manner, and ability to arouse popular enthusiasm, and his bastardy, of which irrefutable proof had been recently brought to light, did not trouble his partisans in the least. His sole possible rival, the Duke of Braganza, derived all his claims from his wife ; he was, moreover, the last man in the world to fight an uphill battle. As soon as he saw that the cards were going against him, he began haggling with Philip over the price that should be paid him in return for a renunciation of his rights, and apparently was ultimately satisfied with a collar of the Golden Fleece. Antonio, on the other hand, was unwilling to accept the offers which were made

[1] Danvila y Burguero, pp. 605 ff.
[2] Philippson, p. 168.
[3] Durand-Lapie, pp. 294 f.

[4] Philippson, pp. 172 f.; Guy de Bremond d'Ars, *Jean de Vivonne* (Paris, 1884).

him through Moura. The Spanish monarch bid higher and higher for his submission, but Antonio would be satisfied with nothing short of the post of Philip's representative in Portugal and the right to nominate the chief officials in the Portuguese dominions beyond the sea — with what amounted, in fact, to recognition as a sort of second king; and this Philip refused to grant. Antonio made capital for himself at home out of the failure of the Spanish monarch to bribe him; henceforth it was inevitable that he should become the standard-bearer of the cause of national independence.[1]

On April 16 Philip sent the Portuguese an ultimatum. If they would recognize him officially as their lawful king within twenty days, he would keep all his previous pledges to them; if not, they must be prepared to feel the full weight of his displeasure and vengeance. At the expiration of the appointed time, he ordered his army to concentrate on the Portuguese frontier near Badajoz. The Castilian cities sent on their contingents. By ship came Spanish veterans of the Sicilian, Neapolitan, and Lombard *tercios*, a large force of Valencians, three *coronelías* of Italian infantry, and a strong regiment of Germans. The whole army counted some 35,000 infantry, 2100 cavalry, and 136 pieces of artillery.[2] The Duke of Alva was most graciously received by Philip at Merida; the monarch repressed any feelings of personal resentment that he continued to cherish, in order to give his commander-in-chief the advantage of appearing to enjoy the full confidence of his king. A fleet was also collected in the harbor of Cadiz under the Marquis of Santa Cruz; its assigned function was to sail around Cape St. Vincent, capturing such ports as it could on the

---

[1] Danvila y Burguero, pp. 587–589.
[2] S. I., ii, pp. 361–367; *D. I. E.*, xxxiv, pp. 287–304; Isidro Velázquez

Salmantino, *La Entrada que en el Reino de Portugal hizo Don Philippe* (Lisbon, 1583), fols. 31–35.

way, and coöperate with the army of invasion against Lisbon. The Spanish representatives at the Portuguese capital were recalled and made their preparations to depart, though most of them did not actually leave the country until after the invasion had begun.[1] A final attempt of the regents to find a peaceful solution failed miserably, and on May 21 the king and his whole court transferred themselves to Badajoz.[2] A league thence, at Cantillana, Alva assembled his legions in a great camp, where they were reviewed, on June 13, by the king and queen, the Cardinal-Archduke Albert of Austria, and the commander-in-chief.[3] The proximity of so great a force caused the Portuguese fortress of Elvas to yield on June 18 without resistance.[4] Villa Viçosa was occupied by an advanced detachment on the 22d.[5] On June 27 the main army broke camp and, under the eyes of the king, crossed the frontier in battle array.[6]

Had Philip followed Granvelle's advice,[7] and struck two months earlier, he might well have encountered no resistance at all; as it was his delays had given his opponents a chance, though an inadequate one, to prepare. Most of the impetus was furnished by the patriotic zeal of the masses, the monks, and the lower clergy, but the encouragement and direction of the representatives of the king of France also counted for much. Saint-Gouard was rude and defiant toward Philip, and openly urged his master to declare war; when the Prudent King refused to receive him, he made ostentatious preparations to depart, thus threatening a breach of diplomatic relations.[8] Efforts also were made at Paris to

[1] Philippson, pp. 168 f.; Danvila y Burguero, p. 598.
[2] Philippson, p. 170.
[3] Erich Lassota, Tagebuch, p. 26; C. de C., ii, pp. 595 f.
[4] Danvila y Burguero, pp. 616 f.; Velázquez Salmantino, Entrada, fol. 42 v; S. I., i, pp. 232–235.
[5] Hilario González, loc. cit., p. 107; S. I., i, pp. 236–239.
[6] Lassota, pp. 27 f.
[7] Philippson, p. 171.
[8] Philippson, pp. 169–173.

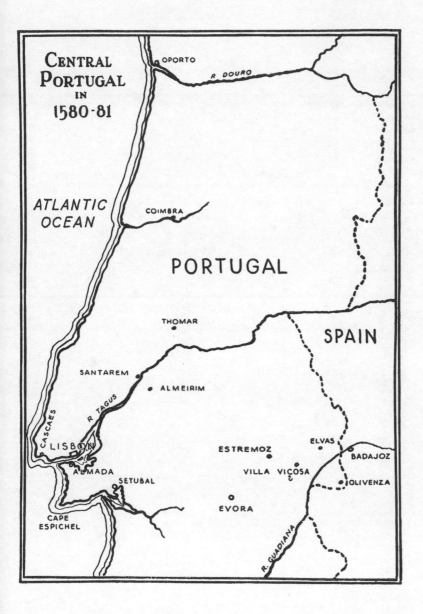

CENTRAL
PORTUGAL
IN
1580-81

ATLANTIC
OCEAN

OPORTO

R DOURO

COIMBRA

PORTUGAL

THOMAR

SPAIN

SANTAREM

ALMEIRIM

R TAGUS

CASCAES

LISBON

ALMADA

SETUBAL

CAPE
ESPICHEL

ESTREMOZ

VILLA VIÇOSA

EVORA

ELVAS

BADAJOZ

OLIVENZA

R. GUADIANA

secure the coöperation of Queen Elizabeth on behalf of the
Portuguese; a French ship which arrived at Plymouth,
having on board a thousand arquebuses and a quantity of
powder intended for Portugal, was permitted to depart
without hindrance.[1] More useful still to the Portuguese
cause was the action of Jean Pierre de Abbadie, the French
secret agent in Portugal itself, and of Pierre Dor, the French
consul at Lisbon.[2] In coöperation with the papal nuncio
Frumento, they labored to check a last movement on the
part of some of the patriots to transfer their allegiance to the
Duke of Braganza. The latter, they insisted, had better be
completely ignored; only by concentrating on the prior of
Crato was there any chance of success; Dor even went off
to France to get aid for Antonio's cause.[3] Meantime
sporadic levies began to collect. If, as seems likely,
Antonio's adherents were in the minority, they were more
vocal and more active than the partisans of the Spanish
king. There were boasts that Philip's foreign soldiers were
few, and that the Portuguese had defeated the Castilians
before and had no doubt of their ability to do so again; if
necessary, they were prepared to call in the Moors from
North Africa to their rescue. But it was not until news
came of the surrender of Elvas that the friends of Antonio
took the decisive step of proclaiming him to be their lawful
king. On June 18 the bishop of La Guarda pronounced a
vehement discourse at Santarem, urging all men to support
him. On the following day the popular enthusiasm had
reached such a height that it was felt safe to hold a solemn
service of recognition in the church; Frumento was present
to lend to the ceremony the approbation of the Holy See.

[1] D. I. E., xci, p. 488; C. S. P.,
Spanish, 1580–86, p. 35 (June 11,
1580); Philippson, p. 174.
[2] Philippson, p. 172; Guy de Bremond d'Ars, Jean de Vivonne, pp. 120–
122.
[3] Philippson, p. 172.

Thereafter the new monarch proceeded to Lisbon; and despite the obvious disapproval of the upper nobility, he at once showed his mettle by ordering the five regents out of the town of Setubal, where they had taken refuge, and which they had plotted to hand over to the Spanish fleet.[1]

In the meantime the Spanish army under Alva continued its practically unobstructed advance into Portugal, while Philip and his wife remained behind at Badajoz. Olivenza,[2] like Elvas, surrendered without a fight. In the first days of July the Duke and his forces were before Estremoz, where Moura, who could no longer remain safely in Portugal and was making the best of his way back to Spain, brought them precious information of the state of the kingdom.[3] The Spanish fleet left Cadiz on July 8 and soon got possession of Lagos and other places near by. A little later it established communication with Alva and his army before Setubal. On July 18 that strong fortress surrendered after a nominal resistance.[4] There was much plundering and cruelty to the defenceless inhabitants, particularly in the suburbs of the town; the Italians apparently were the worst offenders, and Alva, who had been ordered by Philip to prevent such things, caused some of the guiltiest to be beheaded.[5] From Setubal there were three possible methods of advancing on Lisbon: (1) to turn northward and cross the Tagus where it narrows at Santarem; (2) to make directly for Almada, opposite Lisbon, and be carried over by the fleet; and (3) to sail around to Cascaes, west of the

[1] Philippson, pp. 176–178; Danvila y Burguero, pp. 616–624; S. I., i, pp. 226–248; Damião Peres, O Govêrno do Prior do Crato, pp. 5–16; Durand-Lapie, pp. 296 f.

[2] On the position of this town see ante, Vol. I, p. 106, note 3.

[3] S. I., i, pp. 273 f.; D. I. E., xxxii, pp. 189–198.

[4] Conestaggio, fols. 149 ff.; Lassota, Tagebuch, pp. 28 f.; Velázquez, Entrada, p. 46; H. González, loc. cit., p. 109; S. I., i, pp. 305–342; Altolaguirre y Duvale, Álvaro de Bazán, pp. 98–100.

[5] D. I. E., xxxii, pp. 285 f.

capital, and attack it from there.[1] The first was abandoned because of the bad roads and the distance involved, and because the army would necessarily lose the support of the fleet. The second was judged too dangerous because of the batteries on the opposite shore. The third was accordingly adopted, with a feint to the north to make the enemy believe that the Spaniards intended to cross at Santarem.[2] The enterprise was not free from peril, for the coast near Cascaes was so high and difficult that a landing could have been prevented with ease,[3] and a reverse at that moment and in that place would have had an enormous effect upon the popular mind. But the Portuguese were incapable of realizing their opportunity, and the disembarkation was effected without striking a blow. The neighboring fortresses soon fell in succession, and the prisoners captured were treated with pitiless severity. Diogo de Menezes, Antonio's general-in-chief, a scion of one of the most important families in the land, was condemned to a traitor's death; the same fate was decreed for the alcalde of Cascaes; the common soldiers were sent to the galleys, and Philip formally approved of it all. It has been well said that Alva reckoned quite as much on the terror of his hangman as on the power of his armies, as he approached the Portuguese capital.[4]

The advance of the Duke's army naturally had an immediate reaction, highly favorable to Spain, on her diplomatic relations with the other European states.[5] Granvelle did his utmost to delay the mission of the papal legate Riario; it must have given him grim satisfaction to be able to utilize

[1] H. González, p. 110.

[2] S. I., i, pp. 344 ff.; H. González, pp. 110–112; J. M. Rubio, *Felipe II y Portugal*, pp. 279 ff.

[3] Conestaggio, fols. 157 ff.; Lassota, p. 30; Morosini in Albèri, *Relazioni*, serie i, v, pp. 307 f.; Philippson, pp. 178 f.; S. I., i, pp. 352–377.

[4] *D. I. E.*, xxxii, pp. 368 f.; xxxv, pp. 65–69; Philippson, p. 179; Durand-Lapie, pp. 300 f.

[5] Philippson, pp. 179–185.

the very same Spanish slowness, which had so often caused him misery in the past, for the actual furtherance of the ends he had in view. Riario was held at Barcelona by illness until June 21. Sumptuous entertainments were arranged for him at every town through which he had to pass on his way from Barcelona to Castile; not till the middle of July did he reach the Portuguese frontier.[1] By that time, of course, all thoughts of a peaceful solution at the arbitration of the Pope had been abandoned. Antonio had now been formally recognized by the Portuguese as their king, and Granvelle lost no time in informing Riario that the only sure method by which further effusion of blood could be prevented was to persuade the nation to give its allegiance to Philip. The new Spanish representative at the Vatican, the Count of Olivares, laid the same considerations before Gregory XIII, and with such good effect that Frumento, who had taken sides with Antonio, was recalled, while Riario was commanded, in case Antonio did not abandon his 'usurped claim' to the disputed throne, to leave Portugal and take up his permanent residence at the court of Spain. Gregory had thus been converted, in a few weeks, from a potential arbiter of the Portuguese succession into an obedient instrument of the policy of the Prudent King.[2] French machinations against Spain were also checked at the same time. A new Spanish ambassador, de Tassis, was dispatched to Paris on the death of his predecessor, Vargas, to deal with the situation there.[3] He soon found that Henry III and his mother were so much discouraged by the news of the advance of Alva's army that there was no longer any chance of their interfering, unless they should be supported by Queen

---

[1] Hinojosa, pp. 286 f.

[2] Philippson, p. 182; S. I., ii, pp. 161–165. P. O. von Törne, *Ptolémée Gallio* (Helsingfors, 1907), pp. 181–185, gives a careful analysis of the changes in Gregory's policy.

[3] Cf. p. 609, *infra*.

Elizabeth.[1] But this was quite out of the question. The Portuguese representative in London, Antonio de Castilio, had by this time gone over completely to the side of Spain, and coöperated with his Spanish colleague, Bernardino de Mendoza, to thwart the efforts of the special envoy João Rodrigues de Sousa, whom Antonio had sent to ask Elizabeth's aid. He was not even permitted to have access to her, and she openly declared, in the early part of August, that she now regarded Philip as the actual ruler of Portugal.[2]

Meantime, in Portugal itself, the military verdict was finally delivered in the latter part of the same month, in favor of the Prudent King. While Alva had been advancing from Cascaes on Lisbon, the Spanish grandees whose domains lay close to the Portuguese border had invaded the realm with another army of some 30,000 men, which they had raised at their own expense. Before the end of August they gained possession of all the principal cities in the southern part of the kingdom.[3] Their advance relieved the Duke of all anxiety lest he should be attacked from behind; the secret negotiations in which he had continued his master's efforts to bribe Antonio into peaceful submission had by this time definitely failed; [4] and on August 24, he advanced to the bridge of Alcantara just outside Lisbon,[5] where the enemy had gathered a force of some eight or ten thousand men to defend the ravine that separated the invading army from the capital. They were a mixed rabble, hurriedly collected, monks, tradesmen, and artisans, "fitter to fight with words than with arms," and impotent to withstand the

[1] Philippson, pp. 182 f.
[2] Philippson, p. 183.
[3] Philippson, p. 185; S. I., i, pp. 418–421; Rubio, pp. 301 f.
[4] Rubio, pp. 287 f.; D. Peres, op. cit., pp. 80–85.
[5] The bridge of Alcantara was on the spot now occupied by the Estação

Alcantara Terra, opposite the Palacio Real das Necessidades, where the tiny Ribeira de Alcantara flows underground to the Tagus. The site of the battle was far nearer the bank of the river than it is today; since that time an enormous amount of made land has been filled in below.

methodical attack of Alva's superior forces.[1]   On the 25th the Duke sent forward Prospero Colonna with his Italian arquebusiers "to open the ball" with an assault on the bridgehead, while Sancho de Ávila led on his Spaniards by the side ridges to take the defenders on the flank.   Everything was covered by a devastating artillery fire from the land and from the fleet, most of it directed against the bridge, and the rest against the houses of Lisbon.   After a brief resistance, the Portuguese broke and fled, leaving fully a thousand of their number dead or wounded on the field; on the Spanish side the casualties numbered less than a hundred.   Antonio, who bore himself like a hero and was wounded in the forehead, strove gallantly but vainly to rally the fugitives; finally, seeing that all was lost, he leaped on a horse with his follower, the Count of Vimioso,[2] and rode off up the Tagus to Santarem.   At the same time the remnant of the Portuguese fleet made haste to surrender to the Marquis of Santa Cruz.[3]

The outrages which had already got the Spanish soldiery such an ugly name at Setubal had been continued as they advanced on the capital.   Philip had expressly forbidden Alva to permit his men to plunder,[4] and the Duke did his utmost to prevent it, but without success.   "The disorders which are occurring here," so he wrote to the king on August 6 from Cascaes, "are such as I never thought to see, nor would have believed possible among soldiers.   I have done everything I can to stop them, but without success; for disobedience and disrespect are rife, and it is all the fault

[1] Philippson, p. 185; C. de C., ii, pp. 611, 613.

[2] On Vimioso see J. M. Rubio, "Don Francisco de Portugal, Conde de Vimioso, adversario de Felipe II," in *Revista de Historia*, xvi (1927–28), pp. 58–72, 81–91.

[3] C. de C., ii, pp. 612–614; *D. I. E.*, xxxii, pp. 453–459; *C. S. P., Foreign*, 1579–80, p. 480; S. I., ii, pp. 1–30; H. González, pp. 114–116.

[4] *D. I. E.*, xxxii, pp. 450–452; xxxv, pp. 61–63.

of the officers, for I assure your Majesty that there is not a
colonel, a camp-master, a captain, nor any other commander
who is doing his duty as he ought to do it, and that they
ought all to be suspended from their functions." [1]   At Lisbon it was much the same.   The capital surrendered unconditionally on the evening of the battle of Alcantara, and had
every reason to expect merciful treatment; but Alva,
though he preserved the inner part of the city from harm,
was unable to keep his men from working their will in the
suburbs.[2]   The king was apparently kept in ignorance of
what had occurred on this occasion, for he wrote to the Duke
of Medina Sidonia on August 28 that Lisbon had surrendered
without bloodshed or sack, as he had desired.[3]   Unfortunately the evil example which his enemies had set him was
followed by Antonio in the ensuing weeks.   Though he had
failed at Lisbon, the prior still had hopes of reconstituting
his party in the North.   He established himself at Coimbra,
and sought to terrorize all men into joining him by his cruel
maltreatment of those who refused.[4]   Even Sancho de
Ávila, the ' butcher of Antwerp,' who was sent, in late September, to dislodge him, was amazed when he found what had
occurred.   In view of all these things it was no wonder that
the last phases of the campaign, which virtually ended in
October when Ávila entered Oporto, evoked the bitterest
hatreds on both sides.   Most of Philip's earlier efforts to
conciliate the Portuguese were forgotten; the ancient enmi-
ties were revived, and Antonio began to become, to an extent that he had never been before, a national hero, and

[1] *D. I. E.*, xxxii, pp. 368 f.   Cf. also
D. I. E., xxxi, p. 296.

[2] J. M. Rubio, *Felipe II y Portugal*,
pp. 297 f.

[3] *D. I. E.*, xxvii, pp. 370 f.   Cf. *infra*,
p. 476, note 2.

[4] S. I., ii, pp. 71 ff., 157 f.;   *C. S. P.*,

Foreign, 1579–80, no. 488;   Juan
Beneyto Pérez, *Los Medios de Cultura
y la Centralización bajo Felipe II*,
p. 123.   Forneron's account (iii, pp.
114 f.) of this phase of the campaign
is grossly inaccurate.

the personification of the cause of escape from Castilian bondage.

The correspondence of Philip with Alva and his other representatives in Portugal during the months of September and October is an accurate reflection of all these things. Instead of drastic commands to check the outrages of his own soldiery, the Prudent King issued savage orders for the punishment of all who continued to resist him.[1] To make sure that there was no undue leniency, he sent a number of Castilian judges into Portugal to carry with them, into a country where there could be no ties of kinship or friendship, the full rigor of the Spanish law.[2] Above all he insisted that Antonio should be taken, or at least that he should not be suffered to escape from the realm;[3] he offered a reward of 80,000 ducats for his delivery alive or dead.[4] But Alva made little effort to carry out the royal commands. He remained at Lisbon, busying himself with the reform of the administration of the city, and the ceremony of the solemn proclamation of his master as king of Portugal on September 12;[5] and Antonio was given the opportunity to escape. Barred by a tempest from his intended flight by sea, he sought refuge with a few companions in the wild hills of Northern Portugal.[6] His friends there were loyal to him in his hour of need; and the prior, who was at his best when personal courage was needed, was successful, after months of hair-breadth escapes, in getting passage in a Dutch ship from Setubal to Calais.[7] In a manifesto, published four years later at Leyden,[8] he gives some account of his adven-

[1] *D. I. E.*, xxxi, pp. 303 f.

[2] Philippson, p. 188, and references there.

[3] *D. I. E.*, xxvii, pp. 371 f.

[4] Antonio de Herrera, *Cinco Libros de la Historia de Portugal,* fol. 135; Philippson, p. 187; Durand-Lapie, p. 305.

[5] C. de C., ii, pp. 615 f.; Rubio, pp. 300 f.

[6] Durand-Lapie, pp. 304–306.

[7] He arrived there June 9, 1581.

[8] A small quarto of 79 pages: *Explanatio veri ac legitimi iuris quo Serenissimus Lusitaniae Rex Antonius eius nominis primus nititur ad bellum*

tures during that perilous time : how he wandered in disguise from one peasant's hut to another, often recognized, yet never betrayed ; how he spent whole days in the reeds with the water up to his chest, and how his wounds and his illnesses often made him despair. We may well believe that the story lost nothing in the telling, but there is no reason to doubt that the main lines of it are true. Philip was so enraged when he learned that his prey had escaped that he ordered the execution of Beatrice González, the devoted woman to whose energy Antonio owed it that he was finally got on board ship.[1] Nor did Philip exaggerate the importance of Antonio's escape ; to the day of his death the prior continued to breed trouble for Spain. He carried to the sovereigns of northern Europe a highly colored account of the conquest of Portugal, and of the difficulty and cruelty with which it had been accomplished. He assured them that the most effective of all the ways in which they could satisfy their hatred of Philip would be to lend him their aid in an attempt to recover his throne. He converted what had been originally an Iberian affair into a matter of vital interest to all the states of Europe, and linked the conquest which carried the Spanish Empire to its greatest territorial extent with the forces which were to combine to effect its dissolution.

While Alva and his *tercios* were overrunning Portugal, Philip had remained behind on Spanish soil at Badajoz. Astrologers had insisted that the year 1580 was certain to be unlucky, and Philip was not above listening to their prognostications. An epidemic of catarrh was also raging, and the king was stricken down by it. At one moment he was

Philippo Regi Castellae pro regni recuperatione inferendum. Leyden, Plantin, 1585. Translations into English and Dutch were published in the same year.
[1] Durand-Lapie, p. 306.

convinced that he was going to die, and when, finally, he did get well, his recovery was universally attributed to the audacity of his physician, Valles, "who ventured to purge him during a conjunction of the moon."[1] His wife, Anne of Austria, who had accompanied him to Badajoz, was less fortunate, for she died on October 26, 1580, at the age of thirty-one, and the whole court was plunged in grief.[2] But the need of Philip's presence in Portugal was so obvious that it was impossible for him to delay his departure long; on December 5 he left Badajoz for Elvas, with his kinsman, the Archduke Albert of Austria, whom he had practically adopted as a son and who had recently[3] been made a cardinal. Only a small number of ministers and courtiers accompanied him, in order that the more places should be left free for his Portuguese subjects.[4] At Elvas he was received with appropriate ceremonies by three Portuguese bishops and a number of the prominent nobles of the land, and he was convinced by their protestations of loyalty that he would be universally welcome in his new kingdom. It was here at Elvas that the Braganzas, through a representative, swore allegiance to Philip as lawful king of Portugal;[5] it was also here that Philip conferred his first real favor on the Portuguese by abolishing the line of custom houses that separated their country from Castile.[6] Finally, it was from Elvas that the new king issued a summons to the Portuguese Cortes to meet in the following April at Thomar[7] in order that the formal ceremony of recognizing him might take place, and that the representatives of the three estates

[1] C. de C., ii, p. 616.

[2] Philippson, pp. 189 f.; D. I. E., vii, pp. 336 f.

[3] In May, 1577. D. I. E., vii, pp. 189–194.

[4] S. I., ii, p. 159; Lavisse and Rambaud, Histoire générale, v, p. 68.

[5] Correspondance du Cardinal de Gran-velle, ed. Piot, viii, p. 232; D. I. E., xl, pp. 380–382; Escorial, Ms. "Felipe II. La Entrada en Portugal y la Posesion que tomó del Reyno"; cf. Zarco Cuevas, Catálogo, iii, p. 542.

[6] S. I., ii, p. 160; Philippson, p. 208.

[7] Selected in preference to Lisbon on account of the pestilence.

might receive in return such favors as it should please him to grant.[1] The usual delays prevented the assembly from actually meeting until April 16; and Philip, who left Elvas for the westward on February 28, spent the intervening weeks to excellent purpose in efforts to win the affection of the Portuguese.[2] At the advice of Moura, he distributed a number of favors and dignities to the more important nobles; he took pains to dress and cut his beard after the Portuguese fashion, and forced the Castilians who accompanied him to do likewise.[3] In the last days before his departure from Elvas, he gave audience to the papal legate, Riario, and received his assurance that the Pope had now come round to full approval of the very solution in Portugal which he had been sent out to prevent.[4]

The meeting of the Cortes of Thomar was a notable occasion, and the contemporary historians exhaust themselves in describing the costumes and ceremonies of the day.[5] The king solemnly swore before the three Portuguese archbishops of Braga, Lisbon, and Evora to observe all the laws, customs, and privileges of the realm in the same form that they had been observed by his predecessors; thereafter he received, one after the other, the oaths of fidelity of the nobles, clergy, and representatives of the third estate. On the following day, with similar ceremonies, Philip's eldest surviving son, Diego (born July 12, 1575, died November 21, 1582) was

[1] Philippson, p. 208; Alessandro Brandano, *Historia delle Guerre di Portogallo* (Venice, 1689), pp. 20–22.

[2] S. I., ii, p. 165.

[3] J. Beneyto Pérez, *Medios de Cultura*, p. 122.

[4] S. I., ii, pp. 161–164.

[5] Cf. Bib. Nac. Madrid, Ms. cc. 42, fols. 169–173: "Relacion de los señores y perlados y procuradores de las cibdades y villas llamadas al juramento," etc., etc.; and "Relacion de lo sucedido en el juramento." The latter ends as follows: "Las galas de los portugeses no fueron muchas, aunque las mas fueron de la casa de Verganza. El Duque salio de Rojo y su Hijo de Blanco. Los castellanos fueron todos vestidos de Rajallana [a coarse gray cloth] por mandado de su Mag[d] . . ." Also B. M., Add. Ms. 20,932; Herrera, *Cinco Libros*, fols. 140–144; C. de C., ii, pp. 632–635; S. I., ii, p. 167.

solemnly recognized as his father's heir and successor.[1] A
sweeping act of pardon followed, from which some fifty
partisans of Antonio were specifically excepted;[2] of these
the most prominent were João de Portugal, bishop of La
Guarda, and the Count of Vimioso. Opinion naturally
differed between Castilians and Portuguese as to the gen-
erosity of this course, but we are at least assured by Velázquez Salmantino that in the succeeding period Philip successively cancelled the exceptions, so that in the end the pardon
was practically universal. We are also informed that he
refused to listen to the advice, given by some of the more
rancorous of his Castilian followers, that he should suppress
the ancient university of Coimbra on account of its ardent
support of the cause of his rival.[3]

But the proceedings of the Cortes of Thomar are by no
means so significant for the purpose of the student of history
as is the statement of the principles on which Philip determined to govern his newly conquered realm; this statement
was finally issued at Lisbon as a *carta patente* on
November 12, 1582.[4] The concessions contained in this
document were really replies to the petitions of the Cortes
of Thomar in the preceding year;[5] but the basis of them
was a set of 'fundamentals,' agreed upon between the
late Cardinal Henry and the Spanish representatives, the
Duke of Osuna and Cristóbal de Moura, at his court, a
short time before the cardinal's death, when he had decided
in favor of the right of Philip to succeed him on the Por-

[1] S. I., ii, p. 168; *D. I. E.*, xl, pp. 400–
403.
[2] The list of names is given in Lassota,
Tagebuch, pp. 45 f.; and *D. I. E.*, xl,
pp. 399 f.
[3] Conestaggio, fol. 203; Velázquez
Salmantino, pp. 85–104; C. de C.,
ii, pp. 634 f.; S. I., ii, pp. 166–169;
Rebello da Silva, ii, p. 622; Danvila
y Burguero, p. 677. Moura was
Philip's intimate adviser throughout
all this time; S. I., ii, p. 166, declares
that "todo el peso del Gobierno gravitó
en este período sobre Don Cristóbal de
Mora."
[4] Rebello da Silva, ii, p. 628, note;
Danvila y Burguero, p. 677.
[5] Herrera, *Cinco Libros*, fols. 147–
149; C. de C., ii, pp. 634 f.

tuguese throne.[1] They summarize the basic principles on which Philip's administration of his new kingdom was henceforth to be founded.

Besides his oath to maintain all the laws, privileges, and customs of the realm, Philip promised that he would never hold the Portuguese Cortes outside the kingdom, and that no legislation affecting Portugal should be permitted in any assembly which met beyond its frontiers.[2] He also gave his word that he would confer the office of viceroy or governor only on Portuguese or on members of the royal family; that all greater and lesser offices of justice, finance, and administration should be given only to Portuguese and never to foreigners; that all the ancient posts in the kingdom should be maintained for Portuguese occupants, as they had been in the days of his predecessors, and that the same principles should apply with regard to all other offices, great and small, on the land and on the sea, already existing or to be created in the future; and that all garrisons stationed in Portugal should be composed exclusively of Portuguese. He also agreed that the commerce of India and Guinea and of the other Portuguese colonies, already discovered or to be discovered in the future, should be continued as at present and in no wise changed; that the officials in charge of it should continue to be Portuguese and should sail only in Portuguese ships; that all gold and silver coined in Portugal should be stamped with the arms of Portugal and with no other; that all prelacies, abbeys, benefices, and other ecclesiastical preferments in the realm should be conferred only on Portuguese, and that the same principle should govern

---

[1] Cf. *supra*, p. 352; also Rebello da Silva, ii, pp. 622 f.; Danvila y Burguero, pp. 676 f.

[2] B. M., Add. Ms. 20,934, fols. 135 v–137, "Privilegios que el Rey Dom Felipe Segundo de Castella jurou cumprir y manter a Portugal" (this document is not listed in Gayangos); Herrera, fols. 147–149; Rebello da Silva, ii, pp. 623–628.

in regard to the office of inquisitor general, the commander-
ies, pensions, and functions of the Military Orders (in which
there was to be no innovation whatsoever), and the priory
of Crato ; and that there should be no *tercias* or other taxation payable by the Portuguese clergy to the state, nor any
request for bulls to permit the same. He promised that he
would not make any royal grant of any city, town, place, or
jurisdiction within the realm to any one save to Portuguese ; that crown estates which had become vacant should
not be absorbed into the royal domain, but should be re-
granted to some relative of the previous tenants or to some
other well-deserving Portuguese ; Castilians and other foreigners, however, who were at that time resident in Portugal,
or had been servants of earlier Portuguese kings, were not
excluded from this privilege. Nobles were to come into the
enjoyment of their *moradias* [1] at the age of twelve, and
Philip and his successors were to receive every year "two
hundred Portuguese servants who should also have their
moradias" ; those who had not the privilege of nobility were
to serve in the armed forces of the kingdom. Philip also
promised, for himself and his successors, that whenever they
came into Portugal they would not demand compulsory
entertainment [2] as was the custom in Castile, but would
follow the usages of Portugal ; and that when his Majesty
or his successors were outside the kingdom they should
always have with them one prelate or other ecclesiastic, one
official of finance, one secretary, one chief chancellor, and two
oidores, all of Portuguese birth, who should jointly compose
a Council of Portugal, with whose aid all the business of
that realm should be transacted in the Portuguese lan-

---

[1] On *moradias*, 'livings' or court
pensions, see the references in J. A. de
Figueiredo, *Synopsis Chronologica de
Subsidios para a Historia da Legislação*

Portugueza (Lisbon, 1790), ii, pp. 165,
196.

[2] "No se tomen casas de aposento."

guage.[1] All chief civil magistracies and other judicial positions
were to be filled from within the realm, as was at present the
case, even though his Majesty should be absent, and the same
principle was to apply to all financial posts; all matters of
justice and finance were to be determined and carried out
within the realm as hitherto.   The service in the royal
chapel at Lisbon was to be continued according to the custom of previous reigns; Portuguese were to be admitted to
the offices of the royal household, "in accordance with the
Burgundian custom," on the same basis with the Castilians
and his Majesty's subjects of other nations; the queen was
usually to have Portuguese women among her principal
ladies.   "For the benefit of the whole people of the kingdom," all frontier customs between Castile and Portugal
were to be abolished, and merchandise was to pass freely in
both directions as was done before the imposition of the
duties actually being levied at the time,[2] and every facility
was to be given for the importation of Castilian grain into
Portugal; and Philip promised to give 300,000 *cruzados*,
of which 120,000 were to go for the ransom of captives,
150,000 to be placed at the disposal of the chamber of Lisbon, and the rest to be used for the relief of the victims of
the pestilence.   The king also agreed that in providing for
the fleets of India, and the other squadrons required for the
defence of the realm, for the chastisement of corsairs, and
for the security of the frontiers of Africa, he would, after
consultation with the representatives of his new realm, take
such measures as should seem most wise, even if they involved the giving of aid by his other kingdoms, and great
increase of expense to his royal treasury.   Finally, though it

[1] On the *Consejo de Portugal* see
Danvila y Collado, *Poder Civil*, ii,
p. 438; Rebello da Silva, v, pp. 397 f.
[2] I.e., under the law of January 23,
1559 (*Nueva Recopilación*, lib. ix, tit.
xxxi, ley 1), "Que declara los derechos
que se han de pagar en los puertos
secos entre Castilla y Portugal."

was recognized that in view of the multitude of other realms
which it had pleased God to give him, it would be impossible
for Philip to live continually in Portugal as the Portuguese
would have liked, yet he promised to do his utmost to reside
there as long as he could ; and that when no other more important consideration intervened to prevent it, he would
allow his son and heir to visit Portugal, in order that he
might be brought up there in part, and get to know and love
his future subjects.[1]

These certainly look like large concessions ; and in general
it may be said that Philip continued to observe the most
important of them, in letter at least if not entirely in spirit,
to the day of his death.   In some particulars he even went
beyond what he had promised, as in the establishment of a
court of appeal at Oporto for the convenience of the northern
provinces.[2]   It appears, however, that in 1593 he restored
the frontier customs between Portugal and Castile ;[3] and the
Count of Ericeira enumerates several other infractions of the
privileges of Thomar, among them being the occupation of
the fortresses of Portugal by Castilian troops.[4]   It would
have been too much to expect of the Prudent King that he
should even admit the possibility of any country being
worthy of comparison with his beloved Castile ; in his choice
of officials to help him govern his newly conquered realm, he
generally selected those Portuguese who had been notoriously Castilianized, like Moura ; and he availed himself of
the stipulation that he might send a member of his own
family to represent him in Lisbon by selecting as his first
appointee to that office the Archduke Albert of Austria, who

---

[1] See the comments of J. Beneyto
Perez, *Los Medios de Cultura y la
Centralización bajo Felipe II*, pp. 122 f.,
on these "excesivas . . . concesiones."

[2] Pedro de Mariz, *Dialogos de Varia
Historia* (Lisbon, 1674), p. 529.

[3] C. de C., iv, p. 93; cf. *Nueva
Recopilación*, lib. ix, tit. xxxi, ley 1.
The annual return from these was
reckoned to be thirty *cuentos*.

[4] *Historia de Portugal Restaurado*
(Lisbon, 1679–98), i, pp. 36–38.

was his cousin, his nephew, his brother-in-law, and in later years his son-in-law. But it is difficult, save in the matter of the customs, to find cases of direct violation of his pledge of 1582 that cannot be plausibly excused as measures of military necessity or public emergency. The first clear instance of the imposition of the Castilian tax came in 1636, during the reign of Philip IV and as a result of the policy of Olivares; and four years later the revolution broke out which was to end in 1668 with the acknowledgment by Spain of Portuguese independence. The contrast between the policy of Philip the Prudent and that of the masterful and ambitious minister of his grandson is very marked. Olivares imposed the tax which brought on the catastrophe largely, without doubt, in order to satisfy the needs of the moment — such was ever his way; but perhaps it is not entirely fanciful to see in his action something more than merely that. There is evidence that enough of the spirit of contemporary France had penetrated his mind to convince him that the principle of constitutional separatism, which, as we have often remarked, underlay the whole fabric of the Spanish Empire, was no longer practicable or wise, and that some sort of closer administrative union between the different scattered states and colonies that composed it had become imperative. He had visions of doing something such as the Bourbons did with the Spanish Empire in the eighteenth century, after some of its most burdensome limbs had been lopped off; but he had not the ability to carry through his programme, and the experiment ended in disaster.[1] Philip II, on the other hand, was far too deeply imbued with the ancient traditions of his native land to think for one moment of embarking on any such hazardous adventure as

[1] On the policy of Olivares and its results, see Martin A. S. Hume, *The* *Court of Philip IV*. (New York and London, 1907), pp. 159–162.

this. The principle of the maintenance of the constitutional separatism of the different states that composed the Spanish Empire in Europe had never been violated, from the days of the little Pyrenean Christian realms in the early period of the Reconquest down through the gradual acquisition of the Mediterranean and Italian dependencies, of the Netherlands and of Franche Comté; it had even begun to permeate the administration of the Spanish territories of the New World. Now that at last Philip had obtained what he probably coveted most, the sole portion of the Iberian peninsula which had escaped his forefathers, and whose reacquisition had virtually been bequeathed to him by them as a duty, he never dreamed of depriving it of its own independent form of government. The concessions which he had made, partly no doubt in deference to the wishes of his new subjects, were fully in line with his own preconceived ideas as to how his new territories should be managed. The measure of autonomy which the Portuguese demanded and received was in some respects more complete than that of the realms of the crown of Aragon, of the Mediterranean and Italian states, and of the Burgundian lands, notably in the stipulations for the exclusion of Castilians from the government and the provisions against the introduction of Castilian taxation; but that was merely the more perfect carrying out of the oldest and most fundamental principle of the administration of the Spanish Empire. The terms on which Portugal had finally been superadded to the vast agglomeration of separate states, now comprised in that huge and unwieldy organism, were fully in accord with the most ancient traditions of its upbuilding.[1]

[1] J. Beneyto Perez, *op. cit.*, pp. 124 f., maintains that Philip's Castilian subjects were deeply dissatisfied at the extent of the autonomy that he had granted the Portuguese, and declared that when he had the power in his hands he should have taken measures to fuse the two kingdoms.

The acceptance of Philip as the lawful sovereign of the different colonies of which the vast Portuguese empire was composed was effected, save for one notable exception, with an ease and absence of turmoil, which is perhaps chiefly significant in demonstrating how slight were the changes which the advent of the new dynasty brought about. The concessions hitherto enumerated, which Philip had made in 1581, guaranteed that there should be no real alteration in the methods or the personnel of the administration of the Portuguese empire; the colonies remained colonies of Portugal, which under Castilian rule continued to retain as before the monopoly of their commerce for the benefit of its own ports.[1] The Portuguese colonies for the most part showed themselves utterly indifferent to the change of dynasty. What mattered it to them to what family their sovereign belonged, or whether he resided in Lisbon or in Madrid, in Cintra or in the Escorial? And, moreover, at first sight there seemed to be many positive advantages in becoming the subjects of the most powerful monarch on the face of the earth; in case of danger they hoped to be assured of effective protection. In Brazil, furthermore, there was a special consideration in favor of the recent change, for it would insure the peaceful termination of those boundary disputes between the Spanish and Portuguese colonies in

---

[1] The only considerable reform in the central administration of the Portuguese colonies which was attempted by Philip II was the substitution in 1591 for the old and unsatisfactory office of the *vedores da fazenda* of a central Council of Finance (*conselho da fazenda*) to manage the revenues of the kingdom and its dependencies. It was divided into four sections, of which one dealt with the affairs of Portugal itself; the second with those of the Indies, West Africa, and Brazil; the third with those of the Military Orders and the islands of Madeira and the Azores; and the fourth with those of Morocco and the accounting. It was a good move in the direction of much needed centralization, but it did not go far enough; in 1604 it was in turn replaced by a Council of the Indies which extended its authority to matters civil, judicial, and religious, as well as financial. Cf. Lannoy and vander Linden, *Histoire de l'expansion coloniale*, i, pp. 84–85; also Rebello da Silva, iii, pp. 280 f.

South America which had already begun to loom large as a possible danger for the future.   As things ultimately developed these happy expectations were never realized. Within less than a decade of the annexation of Portugal, Spain's naval power had been broken; the maritime and commercial nations of Western Europe were swift to seize the golden opportunity to dismember her vast empire for their own advantage, and the Portuguese colonies, which had most recently been brought into the combination, were among those that suffered most; instead of being protected, they were specially singled out for attack.   But the first results of this adverse development, which was ultimately destined to obliterate all the favorable ones, were not felt until the very last part of the reign of the Prudent King, and its full effects were not visible until a much later time.   The Portuguese empire continued to flourish during the years immediately following the Spanish conquest, though the storm clouds were beginning to gather thickly on the horizon. It took Europe another long half century to realize how utterly Spain's vitality had been sapped, and down to the peace of Westphalia in 1648 her diplomats played the game of bluff to perfection.

It would be futile to attempt any detailed narrative of the course of events in the different parts of the Portuguese empire during the seventeen years of Philip's occupation of the Portuguese throne, but some of the outstanding facts may be briefly set down.   For the purposes of the short summary which alone is possible here, we may safely omit the Portuguese colonies on the west coast of Africa;   the tendency was rather to neglect them in this period and to concentrate instead on the Orient and on Brazil.[1]   We will begin, then, with a glance at the fate of those scattered terri-

[1] Lannoy and vander Linden, i, p. 103.

tories, extending from the Cape of Good Hope around to China and the Spice Islands of the Pacific, which acknowledged the authority of the Portuguese viceroy at Goa.

That office was held by six different incumbents between 1581 and 1598; all of them, in accordance with the promises of Philip at the time of his accession, were of ancient Portuguese families, and the period of their rule is chiefly filled with struggles with rebellious natives and Turkish pirates from Mombasa in East Africa to the Moluccas.[1] The new king's accession was proclaimed without resistance at the church at Goa on September 3, 1581,[2] and from that time onward his representatives seemed wholly absorbed in extending the possessions of their new sovereign, and in defending what had already been acquired. In 1585 they attempted without success to utilize the rivalries of the kings of Tidore and Ternate in order to regain possession of the fort which they had once possessed on the latter island; but a little later they beat off an attack on their establishment at Malacca by the king of Johore, and afterward destroyed the city of Johore and forced its ruler to flee for his life.[3] At the same time they convincingly reasserted their authority over Mombasa and their East African establishments, an action which was made imperative by the imminent danger of a Turkish advance into that region; they also erected a powerful fortress at Muscat to strengthen their control over the entrance to the Persian Gulf.[4] Perhaps the most notable achievement of the period was the proclamation of Philip, in 1597, as king of Ceylon.[5] Various uprisings by

[1] F. C. Danvers, *The Portuguese in India* (London, 1894), ii, pp. 42–120; Rebello da Silva, iii, pp. 148–169.

[2] Danvers, ii, pp. 25 f.

[3] Cf. *ante*, Vol. III, pp. 439 f.; Danvers, ii, pp. 63 f., 70–73.

[4] Danvers, ii, pp. 68 f.; cf. also J. Strandes, *Die Portugiesenzeit von* *Deutsch- und Englisch-Ostafrika* (Berlin, 1899), pp. 142–162.

[5] On Portuguese Ceylon see P. E. Pieris, *Ceylon: the Portuguese Era* (Colombo, 1913–14, 2 vols.), and the same, *Ribeiro's History of Ceilão* (Colombo, 1909). The latter work contains a translation of most of João

Christianized as well as non-Christian natives had given the viceroys adequate excuse for vigorous interference there. At the outset their efforts were most unsuccessful. They were driven from Kandy by a rebel Cingalese, who had previously embraced Catholicism and been baptized with the name of Don John. This leader, who now styled himself Wimala Dharma, reverted to the religion of his fathers in order to win the support of the priesthood, and announced that he was in possession of the *dalada*, or sacred tooth of Buddha, which was regarded as a proof of his right to the throne.[1] In the rest of the island, however, the Portuguese were more fortunate; and when its lawful king, who was a more permanent convert to Christianity, died at Colombo in May, 1597, it was found that he had appointed King Philip to be his heir. The Spanish monarch's power extended nominally over the whole of the island save Kandy,[2] where he had been repulsed, and Jaffna, where the authority of a local ruler was still recognized.[3] There was a solemn ceremony of recognition and allegiance, in which the inhabitants, though stoutly refusing to permit the introduction of Portuguese laws and customs, promised absolute loyalty to their new master, provided he would observe and respect the native ones. On one point alone were they willing to make any concessions; the priests and religious orders were to have full liberty to preach the Catholic faith and make what converts they could.

Such is the brighter side of the picture, as seen from the standpoint of Philip and his representatives, and down to the death of the Prudent King it was unquestionably the

---

Ribeiro's history, completed in 1685, and summaries of other early treatises.

[1] Danvers, ii, p. 91.

[2] Kandy remained a thorn in the side of the Portuguese throughout the reign of the apostate Don John. Danvers, ii, pp. 97 f., 111 f.

[3] Danvers, ii, p. 98.

most prominent one; but before the reign ended, the first signs had appeared of the advent in the Orient of other powers, whose presence was ultimately to spell ruin for the Spanish Empire in that part of the world. Five years after Philip's recognition as king of Portugal, he was at open war with the Dutch, who were supported — if somewhat half-heartedly — by England. Reports of the rich cargo of the Portuguese carrack *San Filippe*, which had been captured by Sir Francis Drake, in June, 1587, on its way back from Goa to Lisbon, were not slow to reach Holland, and convinced her of the profits that could be derived from the Far East;[1] the existence of a state of war with Spain, and the seizure in 1585 of all Dutch ships in Spanish and Portuguese harbors, gave her ample excuse for invading the Oriental monopoly of her ancient foe. The States-General made matters difficult by issuing a series of prohibitions against trade of all kinds with Spain or Portugal or with any lands or islands which acknowledged the authority of their king; but these prohibitions were never very strictly enforced, and it was, moreover, easy to evade them by the device of sailing under a neutral flag. Precious information as to routes, trade winds, quicksands, and the course of commerce were furnished by Jan Huygen van Linschoten, the son of a West Frisian burgher, who had resided for two years in Lisbon, and thirteen in India. Finally, in April, 1595, a number of Dutch merchants provided the funds for the despatching of four ships to " the countries lying on the other side of the Cape of Good Hope."[2] The expedition was not entirely successful. It was detained for five months at Madagascar by storms and illness, sailed thence direct for Java, and on June 22, 1596, reached Bantam. The natives, doubtless inspired by the Portuguese, gave the newcomers a hostile

[1] Danvers, ii, p. 66; *infra*, p. 520.   [2] Danvers, ii, p. 106.

reception; fighting ensued; the Dutch captain, Cornelis Houtman, was captured and had to be ransomed. Thence the invaders proceeded to the Moluccas, where one of their vessels became unseaworthy and was abandoned; the crews also were sadly reduced, and the survivors were lucky to get home with three ships in July, 1597. But though the cargo they brought back was insufficient to pay for the expense of the expedition, it was more than adequate to demonstrate the wealth of the Orient.[1] New 'companies' for similar experiments were rapidly formed; and in the following year — the year of Philip's death — no less than twenty-two Dutch vessels sailed for the East Indies. Three years later, in March, 1601, these different companies were amalgamated, under government direction and support, into a single body, the Dutch East India Company, and from that moment onward the ruin of the Spanish-Portuguese monopoly in the Orient became a certainty.[2] Philip's ill-omened Burgundian inheritance and the methods by which he had attempted to retain it were to have consequences of which he would never have dreamed.

The Count of Ericeira, in his *Portugal Restaurado*, tells us that Philip offered to his rival, the Duchess of Braganza, the whole of Brazil and the title of king of it for her husband, in return for their abandonment of all claim to the Portuguese throne, and that she refused.[3] Since Braganza was subsequently bought off by a collar of the Golden Fleece,[4] this story, if true, certainly throws a curious light on the slight importance attached in those days by Europeans to their

[1] P. J. Blok, *History of the People of the Netherlands*, iii, pp. 271 f.
[2] The English East India Company was incorporated in 1600 and entered at once into active competition with the Portuguese and Dutch. Danvers, ii, pp. 108–110.
[3] *Historia de Portugal Restaurado*, i, p. 16.
[4] Rebello da Silva, iii, pp. 10 f.

transatlantic possessions; and the tale is particularly amusing when one contrasts it with the action of the descendants of that same Duke and Duchess of Braganza in the early part of the nineteenth century.[1] The descriptions[2] of Brazil that have come down to us from the time it passed into Spanish hands would indicate that it was a land which any ruler ought to have been proud to possess. The principal settlements were at São Salvador (now Bahia), Pernambuco, Olinda, and São Vicente. The first named boasted a population of 800 inhabitants, of whom 100 enjoyed incomes of over 5000 *cruzados*; and the whole *reconcavo*, or coast line of the surrounding bay, some 2000, exclusive of Indians and negroes. There were sixty-two churches in the city and district, and the country for miles around was covered with plantations. There were fifty-seven sugar works in the neighborhood, whose annual export amounted to 2400 hogsheads, and oranges and lemons, cocoa and ginger, were grown in enormous quantities. Cattle raising was also extensive and successful. Horses and cows, sheep and goats were brought over from Europe and the Cape Verde Islands and flourished in their new home. The other settlements were somewhat smaller. There were various insect scourges and much disease. The morals of the community at large were not good, and the enormous impor-

---

[1] In 1807–08 John VI (then regent) of Portugal fled before the advancing armies of Napoleon to Brazil, which he found so much more attractive that it was only with great difficulty that he was forced, thirteen years later, to return. After his death in 1826 his son, the Emperor Pedro, attempted for a short space to control, from its quondam colony, the destinies of the mother country.

[2] Cf. Heinrich Handelmann, *Geschichte von Brasilien* (Berlin, 1860); the manuscript *noticias* summarized in Robert Southey, *History of Brazil* (London, 1810–19), i, pp. 316 ff., and R. G. Watson, *Spanish and Portuguese South America during the Colonial Period* (London, 1884), i, pp. 250 ff.; the works of Gabriel Soares and Fernão Cardim (1584–85) summarized in F. A. de Varnhagen, *Historia Geral do Brazil*, 2d ed., i, pp. 357 ff.; George Buchanan, *De Sphaera* (1584), lib. iii, vv. 560 ff.; Carlos França, "Os Portugueses do seculo XVI e a Historia Natural do Brasil," in *Revista de Historia*, xv (1926), pp. 35–74, 81–128, 161–166.

tation of negro slaves did not work altogether to the advantage of the colony.[1]   Yet the prevailing impression one receives is of a happy and prosperous life, predominantly agricultural and pastoral in its interests, and far less strenuous than that of the Spanish colonies farther westward.

The government until about the middle of the sixteenth century had been almost entirely in the hands of a number of captains-proprietors, each of whom had been given a stretch of coastline extending north and south for a distance of fifty leagues, and the land westward therefrom stretching indefinitely inland;   each exercised exclusive criminal and civil jurisdiction within his captaincy, though appeals could be sent home to Lisbon in case of capital punishment.[2] Naturally the fortunes of these captaincies varied widely in accordance with climatic conditions, fertility of the soil, and the abilities of the grantees;   but six of them were ultimately converted into permanent settlements.   Beginning with the reign of John III (1521–57) the power of the captains-proprietors was considerably restricted.   The local magistrates whom they had hitherto nominated themselves were gradually replaced by royally appointed officials sent out from Lisbon.   Finally, in 1549, some measure of unity and cohesion was given to the scattered settlements by the appointment of the first royal governor, Tomé de Sousa, with supreme supervisory power over all the authorities on the ground.[3]   He established himself at Bahia, which thenceforth became a sort of capital of the entire colony, and did his best to carry out the elaborate instructions which had

---

[1] Cf. Paul Leroy-Beaulieu, *De la colonisation chez les peuples modernes*, sixième éd. (Paris, 1908), i, pp. 52 f.
[2] T. C. Dawson, *The South American Republics* (New York and London, 1903–04), i, pp. 319 ff.; João Ribeiro, *Historia do Brasil*, 10ª ed. (Rio de Janeiro, 1923), pp. 65 ff.
[3] Handelmann, *Geschichte von Brasilien*, pp. 75–85.

been given him by the home government for the regulation
of the conduct of the captains-proprietors. But as he had no
direct jurisdiction over any one of them, his efforts and those
of his successors resulted rather in paralyzing local initiative
than in effecting healthy centralization;[1] so that at the
accession of Philip II Brazil was still rather a loose federation
of different settlements than a single colony.

It would not seem that the Prudent King or his successors
effected any very serious change in the situation as they
found it in 1581. Three new captaincies were set up;
Parahyba in 1585, Sergipe in 1589, and Rio Grande do Norte
in 1597.[2] A certain number of improvements, particularly
in the administration of justice, were introduced in the different captaincies, and various attempts were made to check
non-residence and decentralization and to establish an official
hierarchy. But the period of the Hapsburg rule in Portugal
was too short and too disturbed to permit of much permanent
achievement in this line; and when Portugal regained its
independence in 1668, the government of Brazil was not
essentially different from what it had been when the Spaniards assumed control.[3]

The narrative history of Brazil during the period of Philip
II is largely that of conflicts with hostile powers, who, after
the Spaniards had got possession of it, redoubled the efforts
which they had made in Portuguese days to gain for themselves footholds on its attractive coasts. It was in the year
1555 that the first serious attempt in this direction had been
made by a party of French Huguenots, sent out under
Nicolas Durand de Villegagnon by Admiral Gaspard de
Coligny to found what was proudly called 'La France

---

[1] Lannoy and vander Linden, pp.
92 f. In the middle of the sixteenth
century the captains-proprietors were
only rarely resident in their captaincies.

[2] Handelmann, *op. cit.*, pp. 120–127.
[3] Handelmann, *op. cit.*, pp. 115 f.;
Lannoy and vander Linden, p. 93.

Antarctique.' [1] They established themselves at what is now Rio de Janeiro, kept on good terms with the Indians, and were unmolested by the Portuguese for at least four years. But Villegagnon proved a traitor to his employers. He quarrelled with the Huguenots, gave up his command, returned to France, and went over to the Guises; meantime in 1558 the Portuguese had sent out a new and vigorous governor, Men de Sá, who nine years later (1567) completed the expulsion of the intruders.[2] The French, however, were not willing to relinquish without further effort all claims to the place where they had gained such a promising foothold, and the accession of Philip to the Portuguese throne gave them an excellent excuse for renewing their attempts. They established a trading post at Parahyba, whence the task of ousting them was intrusted in 1583 to Philip's admiral, Diego Flores Valdés, on his way back from a vain effort to secure control of the Strait of Magellan. After some delay the work was successfully accomplished, and the French did not again venture to appear in South America until the seventeenth century.[3]

More troublesome by far were the incursions of the English, who, though they had previously traded in Brazil, had never gone there as enemies until the initiation of the Spanish régime.[4] Their subsequent expeditions thither were naturally of an increasingly hostile nature and became a part of the general maritime struggle of Spain and England all over the world. In December, 1582, Captain Edward Fenton, ostensibly bound for the Strait of Magellan and the Far East, came to anchor, with a small squadron, off Santa

---

[1] Cf. Robert Ricard, "Le Brésil dans la littérature française au XVIème siècle," in Revista de Historia, xi (1922), pp. 123–134.

[2] Justin Winsor, Narrative and Critical History of America, viii, pp. 391–394;

Ribeiro, Brasil, pp. 121–129.

[3] Southey, i, pp. 350–352.

[4] Ibid., p. 352. Captain William Hawkins of Plymouth, father of Sir John Hawkins, made a voyage to Brazil as early as 1530.

Catalina Island. His objects were apparently peaceful; but the contemporaneous exploits of Drake made the Spaniards suspicious and they proceeded to attack him. An inconclusive moonlight engagement followed, in which one of the Spanish ships was sunk, and the English finally escaped to the open sea.[1] In 1586 another squadron, fitted out by George Clifford, Earl of Cumberland, and commanded by Captain Robert Widrington, entered the port of Bahia and remained there for six weeks. Despite the sturdy defence of the place by the converted Indians of the adjoining country, who did notable things with their bows and arrows, the marauders succeeded in doing a considerable amount of damage.[2] Five years later Thomas Cavendish made a rather futile attack on the town of Santos, burnt São Vicente, returned to Santos again, where he was treated even more roughly than before, and finally lost a large portion of his men in an attempt on Espirito Santo; so deeply was he cast down by this last repulse that he died, it is said, of grief on the voyage home.[3] Most notable of all was the expedition commanded by Captain James Lancaster in 1594–95. Its objective was Pernambuco, where there happened to be a number of heavily laden East Indiamen. The place was taken and the booty captured; but while Lancaster was loading his vessels for the voyage home he was constantly harassed by attacks from the Portuguese, who strove to cut off his water supply, floated fire-ships down the river to dislodge him, and, finally, established a battery at the mouth of the harbor to prevent his escape. The destruction of this work cost the English a considerable number of men, but their expedition finally got home in safety, and the wealth

[1] J. S. Corbett, *Drake and the Tudor Navy*, i, pp. 356–360, and references there; Watson, *Spanish and Portuguese South America*, i, p. 254; *supra*, p. 198.

[2] Southey, i, pp. 356 f.

[3] *Ibid.*, pp. 359–364; cf. Barco Centenera, *Argentina*, cantos xxvii. xxviii.

it brought with it was unquestionably an incentive to the formation of the English East India Company.[1] Both Holland and England, Spain's most dangerous potential enemies, had thus got a good taste of the possibilities of commercial and colonial expansion at her expense before the end of Philip's reign.

Very different was the story of the establishment of Philip's power in the Azores. Though less valuable than the East Indies or Brazil, they were destined to give the Prudent King more trouble than all the rest of his Portuguese acquisitions put together. Their geographical location involved them in the current of European politics more intimately than the Asiatic and American lands, and they remained a thorn in Philip's side till the end of his days. And the first note of warning in the Azores was sounded by the efforts of his rival Antonio of Crato, in league with the French.

Of the nine islands of which the archipelago is composed, São Miguel, the largest of the group, was the only one which had immediately acknowledged Philip and been occupied by the Spaniards.[2] Terceira, the next in importance and size, gave convincing evidence of its loyalty to the cause of Antonio, who, before he fled from Portugal, had sent thither one of his adherents, Cyprião de Figueiredo, to make the most of the situation; he was aided by the Franciscan friars, while the local Jesuits, against the almost unanimous desire of the rest of the clergy, vainly attempted to advance the cause of Spain.[3] The Spaniards in São Miguel neglected

[1] *Voyages of Sir James Lancaster*, ed. C. R. Markham for the Hakluyt Society (London, 1877), pp. 35–56; Southey, i, pp. 364–371. Lancaster commanded the first fleet despatched by the English East India Company to Asiatic waters, 1601–03.

[2] At the beginning of 1581; cf. S. I., ii, p. 177; *Archivo dos Açores*, i, p. 468.

[3] Conestaggio, fols. 194 ff., 207 ff.; S. I., ii, p. 175.

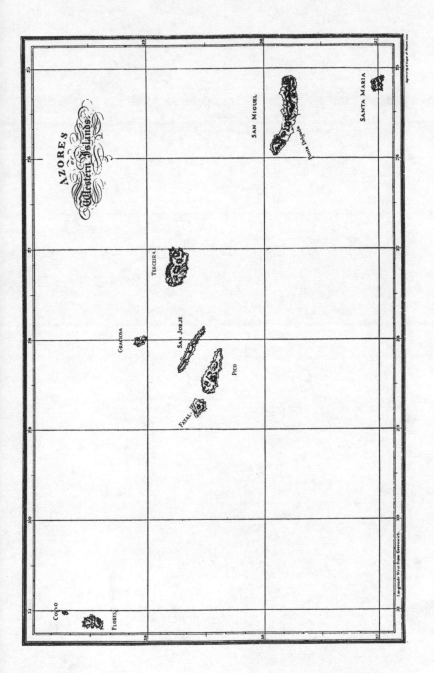

AZORES or Western Islands

SAN MIGUEL

Ponta Delgada

SANTA MARIA

TERCEIRA

GRACIOSA

SAN JORJE

PICO

FAYAL

CORVO

FLORES

Longitude West from Greenwich.

the situation in Terceira until after Antonio's partisans had gained full control there;[1] moreover, the Terceirans succeeded in persuading the inhabitants of the seven lesser islands to follow their example and take sides against the Spanish king. When Antonio finally succeeded in getting away from Portugal to France, it was reasonably clear that his best hope of recovering his dominions was by gaining full control of the Azores and establishing a base there. The archipelago was a rendezvous for fleets from America and from the Orient;[2] in more ways than one it was a focal point, where all sorts of trouble could be bred for Philip of Spain. Antonio had carried the crown jewels of Portugal away with him; knowing the fondness of the queen of England for precious stones, and the enthusiasm of her sea-rovers for maritime adventure, he attempted to interest Elizabeth in his cause.[3] But that wary lady was not yet ready for overt action. Drake and Hawkins were anxious to utilize the opportunity to the utmost; a subscription list was opened and many contributions were sent in; but the royal approval was long withheld, and the small squadron which was finally permitted to sail never saw action against the Spaniards. But Antonio had another string to his bow. While he had been negotiating with Queen Elizabeth, his agent, the Count of Vimioso, had been active in France, where he found a situation much more favorable to his master's plans. Matters there had developed in anti-Spanish fashion since 1578. The Huguenots were enthusiastic for Antonio's cause; the queen-mother's own claims to the Portuguese throne were enough to insure her sympathy and support; another good omen was that on

[1] S. I., ii, p. 176, note 1.

[2] *Ibid.*, ii, pp. 179–183. Juan Bautista de Tassis, Philip's ambassador at Paris, called the Azores "the key to the New World." C. Fernández Duro, *La Conquista de las Azores*, p. 9.

[3] Read, *Walsingham*, ii, pp. 55–57.

August 17, 1581, the Duke of Alençon-Anjou had seized Cambray, almost from under the nose of Alexander of Parma. For the sake of appearances it was judged wise that King Henry III should remain officially ignorant of all plans to aid Antonio; but as a matter of fact he was fully apprised of them, and desired that they be carried out. It was not, however, until the early summer of 1582 that the expedition was ready to start. It was composed of some sixty ships with upwards of 6000 soldiers, beside the crews, under command of Catharine de' Medici's favorite general, the condottiere Filippo Strozzi.[1] It left the port of Belle-Île on June 16 and carried Antonio, Vimioso, and also an efficient and perfidious Spanish spy, by the name of Miguel Vaez, whom the pretender, in his innocence, believed to be the most loyal of his followers.[2]

Philip was fully informed of all these preparations. His ambassador at Paris was a marvel of efficiency in the use of secret informers and spies, and everything he learned and did was duly laid before his master.[3] But the Prudent King as usual was determined if possible to avoid a fight. In early May, 1581, he despatched to the Azores one Ambrosio d'Aguiar Coutinho, a Portuguese who had been won over to his service, to see if he could not persuade the inhabitants of Terceira and the smaller islands to acknowledge the authority of Spain; but the effort completely failed.[4] In the next two months two small fleets were sent out, under Pedro de Valdés and Lope de Figueroa, primarily in order to get in touch with the East Indian and American fleets which were due at the Azores at that time, and prevent them from being persuaded to join with the rebel Terceirans;

[1] C. Fernández Duro, *Conquista de las Azores*, pp. 34 f.
[2] So at least Forneron, iii, p. 147, though he cites no evidence.
[3] Cf. S. I., ii, p. 178.
[4] *Ibid.*, pp. 175–177.

secondly, for the purpose of continuing the attempts of
Coutinho to win over Terceira without a fight; and thirdly,
in case these efforts failed, to attack Terceira by force of
arms. Largely by good luck, the first of these objects was
successfully attained; but the attempts to gain the second
and third were miserable failures, and the defeat that Philip's
forces sustained in their operations against the Terceirans
encouraged the islanders to persist in their resistance.[1] The
accounts which the crestfallen commanders brought back
to Lisbon,[2] together with the news that kept pouring in of
the progress of hostile preparations in France, sufficed to
convince the Prudent King that the Azores could never be
won without a far greater military and naval effort than he
had contemplated hitherto; and he forthwith ordered the
Marquis of Santa Cruz to be ready to sail in April, 1582, in
the hope that he might be able to anticipate the French.[3]
The expedition did not get away till July 10 nor reach the
Azores till the 21st, six days after the arrival of the enemy.
It was, however, a far more imposing armament than its
predecessors. It was composed of two galleons, the *San
Martin* and the *San Mateo*, nineteen galleys, and sixteen
smaller boats, and carried, according to the official muster
roll, something over 8000 soldiers. It seems clear, however,
that the number of ships and of fighting men who actually
got to the Azores was considerably less.[4]

The French had already landed 1500 of their men at
Ponta Delgada in São Miguel. They had successfully
repulsed a sortie by the garrison of the castle, which they
were besieging when the Spaniards arrived. Neither side
was apparently in any hurry to begin to fight. The French

---

[1] S. I., ii, pp. 183 ff.; C. Fernández
Duro, *Conquista*, pp. 12 ff.

[2] Fernández Duro, pp. 199–209.

[3] S. I., ii, pp. 200 f.; Fernández

Duro, pp. 22 f., 234–251.

[4] S. I., ii, pp. 211–213, 392–394;
Fernández Duro, pp. 23 f.

had underestimated the size of the enemy's fleet; their commanders were at odds with one another, and they had hopes of the arrival of help from England which never came; Santa Cruz was also expecting reënforcements, and for nearly a week scarcely a shot was fired. Finally, at dawn on July 26, the *San Mateo*, which had manoeuvred itself into an isolated position between the two fleets, was attacked by several of the best French ships at once; an hour later the combat had become general, and lasted for five hours. The Spaniards strove to grapple and board, while the French tended in general to trust to cannonading; but their guns were not sufficiently powerful to enable them to do this with success; their seamanship was inferior; and despite the fact that they had more ships, the Spaniards were ultimately victorious. Strozzi and Vimioso were killed; a number of the less ardent of the French commanders, and also Antonio, sought refuge in ignominious flight; two of their ships were burned, four were sunk, and four more fell into the hands of the victors; some 2000 of their sailors and soldiers met their deaths, and upwards of 390 more, including seventy-six *caballeros*, were taken prisoners. On the Spanish side the losses were considerably less, amounting in all to 224 dead and 553 wounded, though the list included some of the most noted soldiers and sailors of the time.[1] It was a gallant and well fought battle,[2] and Santa Cruz won universal praise for engaging so powerful an enemy in a place where if he had met defeat he could not possibly have escaped;[3] but his

[1] The best contemporary authorities on the battle are Conestaggio, fols. 233 ff. (on which Herrera's *Cinco Libros* and C. de C. are chiefly based), and the despatch of Stanislaus Fogelveder, Polish ambassador at Madrid, in Lassota's *Tagebuch*, pp. 59–64. The standard modern accounts are those of C. Fernández Duro, *La Conquista de las Azores*, pp. 38–48, of S. I., ii,

pp. 228–252, and of Altolaguirre y Duvale, pp. 109–113, 348–350. Conestaggio calls it a "crudelissima battaglia," and Herrera (*Historia del Mundo*, ii, p. 488) characterizes it as "de las mayores que se han visto en el mar Oceano."

[2] S. I., ii, p. 252, note 1.

[3] *Ibid.*, ii, p. 247.

victory was stained by a deed of savage cruelty which he perpetrated five days later. Deaf to the murmurs of his officers and men, who cherished no rancor against their valiant foe,[1] he caused all the prisoners who had fallen into his hands to be taken on shore and executed in cold blood. The gentlemen were beheaded and the common sailors and soldiers hanged, "for the service of God, of the king our master, and of the king of France," as he put it in his report to Philip.[2] In the last six words of that quotation is to be found — if there be one — the sole possible justification of this barbarous deed. Santa Cruz did not regard his opponents as honorable foes, but as lawless pirates who had gone off on a marauding expedition without the sanction of the French government;[3] they were therefore beyond the pale, and their execution was but ridding their king of a pack of dangerous criminals. It is as hard for us today to palliate the act as it is to exculpate Menéndez de Avilés for his slaughter of the followers of Jean Ribaut; but the theory that really underlay both deeds was the same, namely, that by papal donation all land and water west of Europe belonged without exception to Spain, and to Portugal which had now been annexed to Spain, and, consequently, that all foreigners

[1] On this point cf. Conestaggio, fols. 239 v–240 r: "Questa sentenza parue crudelissima a tutti coloro che la vdirono, e massime a' soldati Spagnuoli, . . . onde alcuni de soldati lasciati i rispetti da parte diceuano, che non era bene fondata la sentenza, per non essere fra il Catolico e'l Cristianissimo Rè salda nè inuiolata pace; anzi guerra, ne coloro esser corsali nè ladri, ma valorosi soldati: . . . E che se bene fra l'vna corona e l'altra si dissimulauano molte cose scusandosi il Re Cristianissimo hor con la Madre, hor col fratello, esser tutte fintioni di principi; ma non lasciar per questo di esserui publica guerra, le leggi della quale diceuano non esser si rigorose che comandino impiccarsi tutti i prigioni. . . . [Il Marchese] rispose esser espresso ordine del Re Cristianissimo che fossero puniti nella vita tutti quei Francesi, che contra le cose del Re Catolico pigliassero l'armi . . ."; and so the sentence was executed.

[2] D. I. E., vii, p. 356; Fernández Duro, pp. 48–50; S. I., ii, pp. 252–255. "Pronunciavit esse ruptores foederum, Turbatores quietis publicae, fautores Rebellium Hispaniae Regis, Pyratas et latrones, his enim ipsis verbis utitur in Decreto . . . Nero tam crudelis non fuisset." Fogelveder in Lassota, Tagebuch, p. 64.

[3] Cf. ante, p. 392.

who trespassed thereon did so at their own peril. That Santa Cruz could describe the act as a service to the king of France only proves that he refused to believe that the French government could officially sanction such intrusions.[1] The protests of his men showed plainly that they did not understand his reasoning or accept its logical consequences; but we know that Philip approved, as he had of the massacre in Florida.[2] According to present-day standards, he was wholly and unquestionably wrong; but in passing judgment on him and on his admiral it is but fair that we should bear in mind the theories and principles of the times in which they lived.

If Santa Cruz was barbarous in his treatment of his prisoners, he was also neglectful of his opportunities to utilize to the full the victory that he had won. It would seem obvious that he should have seized the moment when the inhabitants of Terceira were dismayed at the rout of their French allies to take possession of the island and hold it for Spain, and Philip, when he learned of the victory that his admiral had won, was most anxious that he should do so.[3] The king's message, however, did not arrive on time; Santa Cruz returned to Lisbon, and his failure to complete the conquest of the archipelago encouraged Spain's enemies to try again. Once more the tireless pretender gained the sympathy and support of Catharine de' Medici and Henry III. Another expedition was despatched in May, 1583, under command of Aymar de Chaste, governor of Dieppe and first cousin of the Duke of Joyeuse, and in June Santa Cruz had to be sent back to the islands to beat him off.[4] This time the invaders made

[1] C. Fernández Duro, *La Conquista de las Azores*, pp. 49–52; Altolaguirre y Duvale, pp. 144–146; E. G. Bourne, *Spain in America*, pp. 186 f.
[2] Bourne, *op. cit.*, p. 187; S. I., ii, p. 254; C. Fernández Duro, *op. cit.*, pp. 49–51, and references there.
[3] S. I., ii, pp. 261–265.
[4] S. I., ii, pp. 271–326; C. Fernández Duro, pp. 69–88, 366–467; Altolaguirre y Duvale, pp. 115–125, 360–405; *Archivo dos Açores*, ii, pp. 104, 220–247.

considerably less trouble than in 1582, though Terceira and the lesser islands were not completely in Spanish hands until the end of August ; the real importance of this second expedition against the Azores lies in the influence which it exerted upon the future. On the one hand its reports, doubtless grossly exaggerated, of the heroism of the islanders' resistance to the Spaniards, caused all Philip's enemies to select the archipelago as the most favorable place to attack him in the stormy years which were to follow. On the other, the belief, current in Spain, that there had been an English contingent [1] in Chaste's force, caused Philip's admirals to believe that they had beaten two enemies at once, and led them greatly to underestimate the naval resources of Queen Elizabeth. We shall revert to this phase of the story in another place. The Azores, at least, had been conquered in 1583, and with them the last stronghold of the independence of Portugal, and when Santa Cruz got back to Cadiz in the middle of September, 1583, he was received with enthusiasm by the multitude and was heartily thanked by his sovereign.[2]

Not such was Philip's reception of the news of the death of his old general, the Duke of Alva, which occurred at the Portuguese capital on December 11.[3] After the actual fighting had been finished, the king had no more use for him.

[1] This English contingent, if it was present at all, was not more than a couple of hundred soldiers; cf. Bib. Nat. Paris, Ms. 16,108, fol. 166 ; C. Fernández Duro, *La Conquista de las Azores*, pp. 70, 454. The note to Forneron, iii, p. 160, is not convincing. It deals, of course, with the first expedition against the Azores (the quotation it gives is from pièce 9 and not pièce 5 of Ms. K. 1561 of the Archives Nationales), and it seems to show, if Philip read the information sent by Vaez, that he at least realized that there had been no English ships in Strozzi's force, and not, as Forneron would have it, the reverse. Whether or not Santa Cruz believed that he had beaten Englishmen as well as Frenchmen in 1583 does not appear, but it is evident from his famous letter to Philip of August 9, 1583 (cf. Altolaguirre y Duvale, pp. 400 f.), that he regarded an expedition against England as but a logical consequence of the conquest of the Azores. Cf. also below, p. 516.

[2] S. I., ii, pp. 322 f.; Fernández Duro, p. 93. The Cortes of Madrid, on receipt of the news of the victory, voted Philip the *servicio extraordinario* before he asked for it. *Actas de las Córtes*, vii, pp. 88–92 (August 22, 1583).

[3] S. I., ii, pp. 267–270.

Since the autumn of 1580 he had withdrawn more and more authority from him and handed it over to others; on the other hand, he refused all Alva's requests for permission to retire.[1] Despite all the Duke's services to the Prudent King and to his father, despite the fact that he had organized and led the army that had conquered Portugal, Philip was unable to forgive the past or forget his ancient grudge; and even the Portuguese were profoundly shocked when he gave open demonstration of his ingratitude by dining in public, in defiance of precedent and tradition, on the day following the death of the greatest of his generals.[2]

In the middle of February, 1583, Philip bade good-by to the kingdom which he had won, and in which he had resided for more than twenty-six months, and returned to his beloved Spain, which he was never again to leave. On the whole, he had good reason to look back with satisfaction on the work that he had accomplished since Cardinal Henry's death. The change from a generally defensive to a comparatively aggressive policy, which he had made at that time, and which was exemplified by the calling of Cardinal Granvelle to the post of chief minister, seemed to have been fully justified by the results it had produced. He had put the capstone on the edifice that had been erected by Ferdinand and Isabella by uniting the Iberian Peninsula under a single sceptre for the first time since the days of the Visigoths.[3] Moreover he had done it, as he loved to do, with relatively little fighting; compared with the last two conquests — Granada and Navarre — by which the Spanish dominion of the peninsula had been rounded out, the annexation of Portugal had been almost

[1] J. M. Rubio, *Felipe II y Portugal*, pp. 313–315.
[2] S. I., ii, p. 268.
[3] "Bolvio España a la perfeccion antigua." José de Sigüenza, *Historia de la Orden de San Jerónimo*, 2ª ed., ii (Madrid, 1909), p. 461.

bloodless.   From the imperial standpoint his achievement was more remarkable still.   The acquisition of the Portuguese colonies carried the Spanish dominions to their greatest territorial extent, so that they now constituted the most extensive empire that the world had ever seen.[1]   The Portuguese colonies, as we have already pointed out, were for the most part really only coastal trading posts.   Little effort had thus far been made to penetrate into the interior and subdue the native inhabitants ; it is, therefore, perhaps scarcely fair to regard the lands in which the Portuguese had established themselves as belonging to Portugal in the same sense that Spain's American possessions belonged to Spain.   On the other hand, the Portuguese had a far better claim to them than any other European nation.   They had been unquestionably the first on the ground ; they had, moreover, at least in the eyes of all good Catholics, valid rights under the papal bull of demarcation and the Tordesillas Line ; and if we adopt this method of measurement, and call all the lands on the shores of which they had established themselves Portuguese, the acquisition of these territories by the Prudent King caused the Spanish dominions to cover considerably more than half of the habitable surface of the globe. When we reflect that eight and a half centuries earlier the domains of Philip's predecessors had been restricted to an indeterminate patch of ground in the rocky fastnesses of the Asturias, we can not but marvel at the rapidity, the grandeur, and most of all at the continuity of the develop-

---

[1] "Una Monarquía la mas enstendida, y dilatada que se ha conocido en el mundo, pues comprehende en efecto otro mundo, muchas veces mayor que el que antes se havia descubierto, y poblado en Europa, Africa, y Asia, mediante el qual se puede hoy dár por todo el Orbe una vuelta en contorno, sin salir nunca de los terminos del feliz, y augusto Imperio de V. M."

Juan de Solórzano Pereira, "Razones que se ofrecen para que el real y supremo Consejo de las Indias deba preceder al que llaman de Flandres" (1629), in his *Obras Posthumas* (Madrid, 1776), pp. 178 f.   It is characteristic of Solórzano's scholarship that he supports his statement with a large page and a half of references.

ment by which that little kingdom had been extended south-ward, eastward, westward, and eastward again, until at last it could be said to encircle the earth. Measured by the extent of the territory over which he theoretically held sway, Philip was the most powerful monarch that the world has ever known.[1]

But the attainment of such unprecedented greatness was the signal for the beginning of decline. Spain's resources, Spain's knowledge of economics and of the principles of successful colonial administration, most of all Spain's traditions and her conception of the work in the world that she was destined to perform were not such as augured well for her ability permanently to retain and develop such gigantic possessions. Her empire had become so top-heavy that it was almost inevitable that it should fall with its own weight. And the jealousy which her preponderance naturally aroused among her neighbors rendered what was inherently probable an absolute certainty. That jealousy, it is true, was of comparatively recent origin. The reconquest of the Iberian peninsula from the infidel had for the most part been accomplished with the blessings and applause of Spain's neighbors to the north. The Mediterranean empire of the realms of the crown of Aragon had been won in the thirteenth, fourteenth, and fifteenth centuries without provoking the active enmity of any of the European powers save France. French hostility was also the only serious menace to the

---

[1] Some people have wondered that he did not celebrate his triumph by removing his capital from Madrid to Lisbon; certainly the latter was by far the more attractive, and vastly better fitted to be the focus of a world empire. Such, however, was not Philip's way; moreover, if he had transferred his residence to Portugal he would have been in grave danger of losing the realms of the crown of Aragon, Ramón de Mesonero Romanos on p. 43 of his *El Antiguo Madrid*, i (Madrid, 1881), says that it would have been "altamente impolítica" for Philip "desnacionalizar su capital y trasladarla al pueblo conquistado . . . medida que . . . hubiera dado entónces por resultado la inmediata separacion de la coronilla aragonesa, ó que el curso del Ebro marcára, come ahora los Pirineos, el límite del territorio español."

development of Spain under the Catholic kings. The treacheries of Ferdinand in his later years had certainly served to put his neighbors on their guard; but down to the accession of Charles V it is safe to say that Spanish expansion, both in the Old World and in the New, had proceeded without evoking any general sentiment of suspicion or distrust among the rest of the European states. Under the Emperor, of course, all was changed. The union in one hand of the Hapsburg and Trastamara dominions, and the uncovering of the resources of the Western Hemisphere, had combined to make the Spanish Empire appear for the first time in the light of a universal menace. The unholy Franco-Turkish alliance and the calmness with which it was regarded by the rest of Europe proclaimed as much; and England and the papacy, both of which in the days of Ferdinand and Isabella had been rather pro-Spanish than pro-French in their inclinations, gave ominous signs of veering around to the other side. The Emperor, as we have seen, had been acutely conscious of the danger, and in the latter years of his reign had done his best to avert it by advising his son to follow a policy of 'sturdy defensiveness'; and down to the year 1578, save in his dealings with the infidel, Philip had generally acted upon his father's advice. Then, finally, there had come this God-given opportunity for the annexation of Portugal and for the completion of the task which his ancestors had striven vainly to perform. To achieve it would necessitate indeed an abandonment of 'sturdy defensiveness' and the resumption of the comparatively aggressive. On the other hand, there was no question that Philip had the best legal claim to the Portuguese throne; moreover, he proposed, if he possibly could, to enforce that claim without a fight. Last of all, he regarded the Portuguese question first and foremost as a *cosa de España*, a purely Iberian matter, in which his neighbors north of the Pyrenees were in no wise concerned, and in which he hoped and believed that they would not venture to interfere. But it was just in this last hope that he was doomed to disappointment. Had it not been for Portugal's colonial empire, the case might have been otherwise, for Portugal herself was regarded by the rest of Europe with comparative indifference; but her possessions in the Orient and in the Occident made her annexation by Spain an affair of the whole world. Their acquisition by Philip threatened to give the Prudent King the same kind of monopoly in Brazil and in the East Indies that he already claimed to possess in the Spanish dominions in America, and thus to enable him to control the trade of the globe: to do just what sundry *corsarios Luteranos* — Dutch, French, and English — were firmly resolved to prevent, and were striving with might and main to persuade their respective governments to give them official support in preventing. The struggle over the Azores, though the Prudent King had been ultimately successful there, was really of ominous signifiance. As soon as the official policy of Philip's neighbors to the north of him, particularly of England, should align itself with the activities of the sea-rovers whom they still for the most part continued to disavow, the advance of the Spanish Empire was certain to be arrested, and the stately process of its territorial aggrandizement, which had gone on virtually unchecked since the beginnings of the Reconquest, to be succeeded by disintegration and decline.

BIBLIOGRAPHICAL NOTE

As the subject treated in the foregoing chapter is presumably less well known to most English-speaking readers than those dealt with in the rest of this volume, it has seemed worth while to append a somewhat fuller bibliographical note. The sources and literature on Antonio Pérez will be found at the end of Chapter XXXVIII.

See notes at the end of Chapters II, XXVII, XXXI, XXXIV, and add:

Manuscript Catalogues and Manuscripts. — In addition to such well known works as the various manuscript catalogues and indices of Gayangos, Morel-Fatio, Zarco Cuevas, and Julián Paz, described in the bibliographical note to Chapter XXXI, the Conde de Tovar published a useful *Catálogo dos Manuscritos Portugueses ou relativos a Portugal existentes no Museu Britânico* at Lisbon in 1932; but it should be added that there are a number of important documents in the Museum which escaped both the Conde de Tovar and Gayangos. Two of the most important unprinted manuscripts on the period in question are the *Descripcion de las cosas sucedidas en los reinos de Portugal, desde la jornada que el rey D. Sebastian hizo en Africa, hasta que el . . . rey . . . D. Felipe . . . quedó universal y pacífico heredero de ellos*, by Diego Queipo de Sotomayor, which is to be found in the Biblioteca Nacional at Madrid, Ms. G. 161, and is described by Julián Suárez Inclán in his *Guerra de Anexión en Portugal*, i, p. xviii, and p. 43, note, and the *Comentario que trata de la infeliz jornada que el Rey Don Sebastian hizo en la Berberia el año de 1578* by el Capitan Luis de Ojeda, also in the Biblioteca Nacional, Ms. pp. 21, fols. 1–87. The student should be warned that there are numerous manuscript chronicles and accounts, usually set down as anonymous, in the great libraries of Madrid, Paris, and London, which turn out, on investigation, to be but copies, summaries, or translations of contemporary printed works. The manuscript volume in the British Museum numbered Egerton 522 (cf. Gayangos, i, p. 601, where the name 'Juan de Villegas' is incorrectly stated to be appended to it) is a case in point; it is nothing more nor less than a Spanish translation of the well known work of the Genoese Jeronimo Franchi di Conestaggio entitled *Dell' unione del regno di Portogallo alla Corona di Castiglia*, first published at Genoa in 1585 (cf. below).

Printed Sources and Contemporary Chronicles. — Volumes xxxii–xxxv of the *D. I. E.* are devoted to the story of the annexation of Portugal. Valuable material on it may also be found in Albèri's *Relazioni degli Ambasciatori Veneti*, serie i, v, and appendix volume;

in the *Correspondance du Cardinal de Granvelle*, ed. Piot, vols. viii-x, xii ; and in the *Foreign, Spanish*, and *Venetian Calendars*. *Les sources inédites de l'histoire du Maroc*, ed. H. de Castries, and *Négociations de la France dans le Levant*, ed. E. Charrière, vols. iii, iv, are indispensable for the campaign of Alcazar-el-Kebir. Cesáreo Fernández Duro published the most important documents on the conquest of the Azores on pp. 179–504 of his book on that subject (Madrid, 1886), and the collection known as the *Archivo dos Açores* (Ponta Delgada, 1878–) may also be used to good advantage. The *Fugger News-Letters, 1568–1605*, ed. by Victor von Klarwill and tr. by Pauline de Chary (London, 1924), and the same, 2d series, tr. by L. S. R. Byrne (London, 1926), shed much light on the sentiments of the Portuguese in regard to Philip's candidacy for the throne. — Of contemporary accounts the most important are (1) Jeronimo Franchi di Conestaggio, *Dell' unione del Regno di Portogallo alla Corona di Castiglia*, first published in Genoa in 1585 ; at least five more Italian editions, two in Latin translation, one in Spanish, four in French, and one in English appeared before 1642. Conestaggio afterwards became chaplain to Philip III and archbishop of Capua and died in 1639. Some people have attributed his book to Juan de Silva, Count of Portalegre, the loyal friend and supporter of Philip II, but there does not seem to be enough evidence to justify this theory (cf. on this J. Suárez Inclán, *Guerra de Anexión en Portugal*, i, pp. xv-xvii). Conestaggio's book covers the years 1578 to 1583. In his opening paragraph he states that he was himself present at the greater part of the events he describes, and had the most trustworthy information in regard to the rest ; furthermore, that he was free from the trammels which often prevent the historian from telling the truth, since he was not a native of the Iberian peninsula nor vassal of any king or prince. On the fly-leaf of the British Museum copy of the edition of 1589 there is written, however, the following significant sentence: "Hier. Franchi Conestaggius Genuensis natione anno 1585 in gratiam Serenissimi Regis Philippi de Portugalliae cum regno Castellae unione libellum in lucem edidit ; in cuius compositione Angelum auricularem (ut certo scivimus de eiusdem Conestagii familiaribus) habuit Christophorum a Moura, qui bene noverat quomodo Jupiter duxerat Junonem. Speculum tyrannidis Phil. Reg. Castellae in usurp. Portug." The book is distinctly pro-Spanish, and was never popular in Portugal. (2) Bernardo da Cruz, *Chronica de elrei D. Sebastião*, edited by A. Herculano and A. C. Payva and first published at Lisbon in 1837, subsequently, in two volumes, in 1903. The author accompanied the expedition to North Africa in 1578, but got back and lived through 1580 ; his book goes on to just before the Cortes of Almeirim. (3) Isidro Velázquez Salmantino, *La Entrada que en el Reino de Portugal hizo la S. C. R. M. de Don Philippe*, published at Lisbon in 1583; the author of this very rare volume describes himself as "andante en Corte." It contains 160 small quarto folios, and relates what Velázquez regarded as "casos dignos de cuento" from the death of Sebastian to Philip's formal entry into Lisbon. It gives some interesting military data, but is chiefly a glorification of the Prudent King, and an assertion of his right to the Portuguese inheritance. (4) The *Diarium* of the Silesian Erich Lassota of Steblau, edited by Reinhold Schottin from the manuscript preserved at Bautzen and published at Halle in 1866; a Portuguese translation of the Iberian section of the diary was issued at Coimbra in 1913. Lassota joined the German contingent of Philip's army of invasion in Italy, landed at Cartagena, February 7, 1580, and served for four years in Portugal and the Azores. This book is described as a "fiel cronologia de sucesos y acontecimientos que presenció el autor." (5) Antonio de Herrera, *Cinco Libros de la Historia de Portugal y Conquista de las Islas de los Açores en los años de 1582. y 1583*. (Madrid, 1591). This is largely based on Conestaggio (*not*, as Forneron, iii, p. 92, note, has it, Conestaggio on it); and most of it reappears in Herrera's *Historia del Mundo* and in Cabrera de Córdoba's *Historia de Felipe Segundo*. For further information in regard to source material, cf. J. Suárez Inclán, *op. cit.*, i, pp. i-xxiv, and C. Fernández Duro, *La Conquista de las Azores en 1583* (Madrid, 1886).

Later Works. — Of the standard histories of Portugal those of L. A. Rebello da Silva (Lisbon, 1860–71, 5 vols.), volumes i, ii, and the first two chapters of volume iii, and of Fortunato de Almeida (Coimbra, 1922–29, 6 vols.) deserve first mention; the collaborate *História de Portugal* edited by Damião Peres (Barcelos, 1928–   ) has thus far only reached 1580 in three volumes; the fourth, by J. M. de Queiroz Velloso, is expected shortly, and I have had the privilege of examining some of the early pages of it in manuscript. The best authority on the story of the annexation, particularly from the military point of view, is still Julián Suárez Inclán, *Guerra de Anexión en Portugal* (Madrid, 1897–98, 2 vols.); the most valuable monographs on the subject that have been subsequently published are those of Francisco, Marques de Sousa Viterbo, *O Prior do Crato e a Invasão Hespanhola de 1580* (1897), of Julián María Rubio, *Felipe II y Portugal* (Madrid, 1927), and of Hilario González, "Felipe II y la Conquista de Portugal," in the *Boletín* of the Real Academia de Bellas Artes y Ciencias Históricas de Toledo, x (1928), pp. 93–116. Alfonso Danvila y Burguero's *Cristobal de Moura* (Madrid, 1900), Martin Philippson's *Ein*

Ministerium unter Philipp II.: Kardinal Granvella am spanischen Hofe (Berlin, 1895), and Henri Léonardon's "Essai sur la politique française dans la question de la Succession de Portugal," in École des Chartes, *Positions des thèses*, 1889, pp. 39–53, are all indispensable for the political and diplomatic aspects of the problem.   Juan Caramuel Lobkowitz, *Philippus Prudens Lusitaniae, Algarbiae, Indiae, Brasiliae, Legitimus Rex demonstratus* (Antwerp, 1639), is typical of the arguments in favor of the Spanish claim that continued to be put forth down to the revolution of 1640. Some indication of the enormous amount of literature on Sebastian, the false Sebastians, and *Sebastianismo* will be found in the footnotes to pp. 340 and 345.   Paul Durand-Lapie wrote an interesting account of the life of Antonio in the *Revue d'histoire diplomatique* for 1904–05 (xviii, pp. 133–145, 275–307, 612–640; xix, pp. 113–128, 243–260) under the title of "Un roi détroné réfugié en France," and Damião Peres, *1580: O Govêrno do Prior do Crato* (2d ed., Barcelos, 1929), is the most recent account of his career in Portugal.   C. Fernández Duro's *La Conquista de las Azores en 1583* (Madrid, 1886) is the standard authority on that subject; it has, moreover, an excellent bibliography and numerous documents.

There is crying need for a modern work on the Portuguese colonies during the Philippine period.   At present one has to glean one's information about them, in large part, from such books as the general histories of Brazil by F. A. de Varnhagen and Heinrich Handelmann, and the *Histoire de l'expansion coloniale des peuples européens* by Charles de Lannoy and Herman vander Linden.

BOOK VIII

THE TURN OF THE TIDE

CHAPTER XXXVI

THE GOVERNMENT OF SPAIN UNDER PHILIP II

THE reign of Philip II was not a period of far reaching institutional innovations. Save for the remodelling of the constitution of the kingdom of Aragon in 1593, which followed as an inevitable consequence of the suppression of the great rebellion stirred up there by Antonio Pérez, the Prudent King was content, in matters internal as well as foreign, to preserve all the essential features of the system which he had inherited from his predecessors. Maintenance and increase of the royal power were the dominant principles throughout; yet, in theory at least, the institutional autonomy of the component parts of the Spanish Empire was scrupulously preserved.[1] Philip was too deeply imbued with the traditions of Spanish separatism to dream of erecting a centralized government such as the Bourbons were to bring with them across the Pyrenees in the early years of

---

[1] A little book, *De Titulis Philippi Austrii Regis Catholici*, by Jacobus Mainoldus Galeratus of Cremona, which was published at Bologna in 1573, gives Philip's list of titles (fol. 9 v) as follows: "Philippus Secundus, Rex Catholicus Hispaniarum, Utriusque Siciliae, Hierusalem, Hungariae, Dalmatiae, Croatiae, Sardiniae, Corsicae, Maioricarum, Insularum Canariae, Orani, Insularum Indiarum, Terrae Firmae, et Maris Oceani. Archidux Austriae. Dux Burgundiae, Mediolani, Lotharingiae, Brabantiae, Lemburgi, Lucemburgi, Geldriae, Athenarum, et Neopatriae. Marchio Sacri Romani Imperii, Oristani, et Gotiani. Comes Barcinonis, Ruscinonis, Cerretaniae, Flandriae, Artesiae, Hannoniae, Hollandiae, Selandiae, Namurci, Zutpheni, Burgundiae, Habspurgi, et Tyrolis. Dominus Cantabriae, Molinae, Frisiae, Mechliniae, Ultraiecti, Transisalanae, et Gruningae." Full explanations of the origins of all the titles are given on the succeeding pages. Cf. also Sir Robert Bruce Cotton, *A Briefe Abstract of the Question of Precedency betweene England and Spain* (London, 1642), and B. M., Harl. Ms. 1858.

the eighteenth century. On the other hand his preference for Castile — for he was even more a Castilian [1] than a Spaniard —, coupled with the financial resources derived from the wealth of the Indies, gave that part of his dominions a preponderance over the rest still greater than that which it had attained in the Emperor's day. Even the remodelling of the constitution of Aragon, to which reference has just been made, though it was rendered possible by exceptional circumstances, is really to be regarded as but a step in the great process of the progressive Castilianization of the Spanish Empire.

Yet if the underlying principles remained the same, the methods of their application were somewhat changed; and the changes were chiefly due to the differences in the personalities of Philip II and of Charles V. The fact that Philip never left the peninsula after his return thither in 1559 is of fundamental importance in the history of the internal government of the Spanish Empire; for he was thus able to concentrate on the details of administration with an intensity which had been quite out of the question for his perpetually travelling father. The energies which Charles had spent on foreign campaigns Philip believed to have been largely wasted, and he was fond of pointing out that the imperial armies had won greater victories under the command of de Leyva, Colonna, and Pescara than under that of the Emperor himself.[2] Such matters, in his opinion, should be

---

[1] And a north-central Castilian too; he was rarely seen in Andalusia. He was at Cordova in 1570 for the meeting of the Cortes there, and he visited Seville in the same year (C. de C., ii, pp. 56–58). On the other hand I can find no evidence to support the statement of Bratli (p. 101) that he went to Granada and Almeria at this time, and the story (*ibid.*, p. 75) that he accompanied his mother's corpse to Granada in 1539, as a boy of twelve, is not borne out by the accounts in the "Journal des Voyages de Charles Quint" in *Collection des Voyages des Souverains des Pays-Bas*, edd. Gachard and Piot, ii, pp. 150–151, or in Javier Vales Failde, *La Emperatriz Isabel* (Madrid, 1917), pp. 298 f.

[2] Giovanni Micheli (1557) in Albèri, *Relazioni*, serie i, ii, p. 338.

delegated to professional soldiers, always provided, of course, that they kept as constantly and closely in touch with Madrid as distance and the difficulties of communication would permit, and never deviated a hair's breadth from the instructions that he sent them.[1] The time that Philip saved from travel he spent in intimate and meticulous supervision of the internal administration of his Spanish realms. He proposed to know and direct everything that concerned them. The accuracy and extent of his information were the wonder of his contemporaries. Elaborate lists and statistical tables were perpetually being drawn up for him; his secret agents sent him constant reports of existing conditions in every municipality and diocese, and of the instruction given at the universities.[2] He was far better informed of the state of his revenues than any of his ministers of finance. If any one applied to him for a place, he had his record by heart.[3] Most of what he learned he kept to himself. It was part of his theory of political life that the rank and file of the government servants should work in water-tight compartments, each keeping to his narrow path, ignorant of the activities of his colleagues; an atmosphere of secrecy, and consequently of suspicion, pervaded everything. Even the king's most intimate counsellors were told only what Philip in his supreme wisdom decided that it was well for them to know. If, perchance, they should happen to learn more, the king was sure to hear of it, and they would be likely to lose their posts; Antonio Pérez is a case in point. To himself alone Philip reserved the stupendous responsibility of knowing and coördinating every-

---

[1] Philip's Italian subjects wished him to follow the example of his father in this regard. Cf. Bib. Nac. Madrid, S. 28, Ms. 6413, fols. 1–11, "Discurso al Rey Philipe exortandole que deue ir en persona a la gerra."

[2] J. Beneyto Pérez, *Los Medios de Cultura y la Centralización bajo Felipe II*, pp. 75 ff.

[3] C. de C., ii, pp. 556–560; Ranke, *Die Osmanen und die spanische Monarchie*, dritte Auflage, p. 149.

thing, and then, in his omniscience, of making the final decision.

Philip's principles and methods of government are admirably illustrated by the manner in which the great system of councils, inherited from the Catholic Kings and Charles V, which formed the heart of the Spanish Empire under the house of Hapsburg, was enlarged and modified during his reign.

The Consejo de Estado, or Council of State, remained, as in his father's day, officially at the head of the list, and the contemporary writers exhaust themselves in their descriptions of its dignity and preëminence. It dealt with foreign affairs and international relations, "with the loss, gain, and just conservation of kingdoms and states, three principal points so different from the evil objects and opinions to which Machiavelli refers."[1] Its membership, however, was considerably modified. The non-Spanish element, which in the Emperor's day had been at times preponderant, was now completely eliminated. After Philip's return to the peninsula in 1559 the Council was composed almost exclusively of Castilians; when Granvelle entered it twenty years later, he did so by virtue of being president of the Council of Italy, whose chief, together with the president of the Council of Castile, was generally given a seat there.[2] Unlike the Council of Castile, the number of its members was not fixed, but depended, like the choice of the individuals that composed it, on the will of the king. It had no rules or traditions of action or deliberation, nor were the limits of its competence strictly defined. Philip

[1] Gabriel Lobo Laso de la Vega, "Relacion muy puntual de todos los Consejos," Bib. Nac. Madrid, Ms. 5972, fols. 88–119.

[2] Gounon-Loubens, pp. 153, 160; Danvila, ii, pp. 364 f.; Lobo Laso de la Vega, ms. cited; Ranke, *Spanische Monarchie*, p. 233.

was officially the president of it,[1] but apparently never attended its meetings. He preferred to communicate with it through his secretaries,[2] and to be informed of its deliberations by a *consulta*.[3] He still further diminished its real efficiency by using it as a stage for his favorite game of playing off the heads of rival factions against one another. It was the chief scene of the struggles between Eboli and Alva, until the time of the latter's departure for the Netherlands in 1567.[4] Its official 'supereminence' over the other Councils and its exclusively Castilian membership gave the king an admirable opportunity of serving notice on his fellow sovereigns that the Spanish Empire was governed from Madrid; but there, for practical purposes, its importance came to an end. If a really vital question of foreign policy was to be settled, it was Philip himself who made the decision. The Council might be made to seem, in the eyes of the masses, to share the responsibility, but the shrewder observers were not deceived. Writing of it in 1557, the Venetian Federico Badoero said: "At the court the opinion about this Council is that it is not the source of such advice, deliberations, and performances as make for the honor and advantage of the king . . .; for there seem to be no written rules or customs to produce order in its deliberations or decisions, nor is membership in it either convenient or dignified; and the result is a decline in the vitality of its discussions." [5]

With the Council of Castile, or Consejo Real, on the other hand, the picture is almost precisely reversed. Despite the fact that it had been invested since 1480 with the supreme legislative, executive, and judicial power, under the crown,

[1] Lobo Laso de la Vega, ms. cited; Gounon-Loubens, p. 154.

[2] Gounon-Loubens, p. 153.

[3] Ranke, *Spanische Monarchie*, p. 185.

[4] *Ibid.*, pp. 188–198; Gounon-Loubens, pp. 150, 159 f.

[5] In Albèri, *Relazioni*, serie i, iii, p. 247.

within the realm, and that its president ranked next to the monarch,[1] it had suffered a decline both in the number and in the competence of its membership during the closing *Wanderjahre* of the Emperor's reign. So fearful was Charles of a usurpation of his own authority during his many absences from Spain, that he had allowed it to dwindle from sixteen to eight or nine; moreover he chose his councillors on the basis of loyalty and absolute obedience, rather than on that of independent ability and initiative.[2] This policy, coupled with the enormous amount of work with which the Council was charged, resulted in a staggering accumulation of unfinished business; even before Philip returned to the peninsula the Cortes were insistent in their demands for a reform. In 1551 they asked that the number of councillors be augmented by six, "since they are so old and infirm at the time of their appointment that they cannot perform the work that is laid before them."[3] In 1555 they begged for the establishment of another *sala* in the Consejo, to deal with the most important suits.[4] In 1555 and 1558 they requested that the councillors be given larger salaries.[5] In 1559–60 they complained that the great increase in the duties of the Council had become the occasion of excessive delays, and they reiterated their previous demands for an increased membership, and for the creation of a special *sala* to hear cases of great importance.[6] Philip was well disposed to listen to these requests. Having resolved to reside in Spain and never to travel abroad, he had no need to fear lest the Council become too independent in his absence; and so deep was his affection for his native Castile, and so high his sense of duty to her, that he was

---

[1] B. M., Cotton Ms. Vesp. C. VI, fol. 6 v.
[2] Cf. *ante*, Vol. III, pp. 146 f.
[3] *Cortes*, v, p. 497.
[4] *Cortes*, v, pp. 634 f.
[5] *Cortes*, v, pp. 632, 736.
[6] *Cortes*, v, p. 811.

determined that she should have, under his constant supervision, the best administration which he was capable of
devising.

His first step towards the improvement of the existing
conditions was to issue, as regent, just prior to his departure
for England in the summer of 1554, the so-called ordinances
of Corunna, defining more precisely the limits of the jurisdiction of the Council, and also investing it for the first time
with the increasingly important function of censorship and
regulation of the press.[1] On his return to the peninsula in
1559 he immediately complied with the request of the Cortes
that the number of councillors be increased ; from that time
onward until the end of the reign there were sixteen of them
in addition to the president.[2] In regard to the other matters
in which the Cortes demanded reform, he showed himself
less complaisant. Not till the very last years of his life could
he be brought to see that the same body could not reasonably
be expected to act both as a supreme administrative council
and as the highest court of the realm, and to initiate the
process, already long overdue, of dividing the Consejo into
separate *salas*, each with a special function of its own. It
is commonly said that the division of the Council into four
separate chambers was postponed until the reign of Philip
III, who reorganized it by a royal *cédula* of January 30,
1608 ;[3] but in justice to his father, it should be pointed out
that orders to that effect were issued by the Prudent King
almost exactly ten years before. By *pragmáticas* of February
14 and 17, 1598,[4] Philip decreed, "in order to improve and
accelerate the despatch of business," that the president and
five other councillors should constitute a *sala de gobierno* for

[1] *Nueva Recopilación*, lib. ii, tit. iv,
leys 31–49 ; Gounon-Loubens, p. 187.
[2] B. M., Cotton Ms. Vesp. C. VI,
fol. 6 v ; *Nueva Recopilación*, lib. ii,
tit. iv, ley 1.

[3] Gounon-Loubens, p. 189, note ;
Danvila, ii, pp. 571 f.
[4] Bib. Nac. Madrid, Mss. CC. 85
and 89, sueltos 18,722³⁶ and 18,729¹⁷.

executive and administrative affairs; and that the remaining eleven members of the Council should be split into three sections: the first, with five members, being intrusted with "public affairs which demanded speedy action, with *pleytos de mil y quinientos*,[1] and with *residencias*," while the other two, with a membership of three each, were to occupy themselves exclusively with matters of justice. The names of the members who were to constitute each *sala* were specifically set down in the decree, and there was the usual wealth of detailed instructions in regard to hours and methods of procedure, and the spirit that should animate the members. Whether or not these *pragmáticas* were immediately carried into effect is another question; from the fact that the ordinances of 1608[2] so closely resemble them, it looks as if they were not. On the other hand Lobo Laso de la Vega, writing in 1607, speaks of the Council as being divided into five or six *salas* according to the pleasure of the president;[3] from this one would infer that Philip's ordinance of 1598 was informal and permissive, rather than definite and authoritative, and that the presidents of the Council availed themselves of it or not as they saw fit. In any case it seems clear that Philip the Prudent learned, before he died, the lesson which the *procuradores* had so often attempted to teach him, though he practically took the whole of his lifetime in the process.

In view of his reverence for the church and for the law, it is somewhat surprising to find Philip at the beginning of his reign departing from the precedent, set by his father, of always appointing a cleric to the presidency of the Council

[1] Cf. *ante*, Vol. III, p. 183, and *infra*, pp. 456 f.

[2] *Nueva Recopilación*, lib. ii, tit. iv, ley 62.

[3] Lobo Laso de la Vega, ms. cited: "cinco salas y algunas vezes seys, conforme el Presidente los reparte." In this reckoning Lobo Laso doubtless counted the Cámara de Castilla, which was given separate existence in 1588; cf. *infra*, p. 418.

of Castile.[1]   Juan de Vega, viceroy of Sicily, who was given
the post on April 18, 1557, died December 19, 1558, and
Cristóbal Vaca de Castro, who had brought order out of
chaos in Peru, filled in, as an interim appointee, for the next
three years; finally, in 1561, the office was conferred on
Luis Hurtado de Mendoza, second Marquis of Mondéjar,
who had distinguished himself as a foe of the Comuneros
forty years before, and who had been president of the
Council of the Indies from 1546 to 1559.   It was doubtless
chiefly the universal prevalence of hate of the legists,[2] and
his own desire to show his sympathy with his subjects'
wishes, that led Philip to make these appointments.   In the
case of Mendoza he may also have wished to serve notice
that he now regarded the monarchy as so firmly established
that it no longer had anything to fear from its ancient
enemies the grandees.   But the forces of tradition and
precedent were not slow to reassert themselves.   After
Mendoza's retirement in 1563 Philip again gave the job to a
cleric, Juan Rodríguez de Figueroa, and on his death in 1565
to a licentiate, Diego de Espinosa, who proved a miracle of
vigor and efficiency during his seven years of service; of
Espinosa's four successors, all but one, the Count of Barajas
(1583–92), were also either legists or clerics.[3]   Their respect
for precedent and routine was more agreeable to Philip than
the more modern methods advocated by such men as
Barajas, who ventured to send him a vigorous memorandum
on the delays and confusion "which render intolerable the
office of president of this Council. There is no order of
precedence," he continued, "in the cases that come before it,

[1] Cf. *ante*, Vol. III, p. 146.
[2] Cf. C. de C., i, pp. 42 f.: "los
profesores de letras legales . . . grandes
dificultadores de lo político," etc.
[3] Cf. Gil González Dávila, *Teatro de
as Grandezas de la Villa de Madrid*

(Madrid, 1623), pp. 360–402, "Vidas
de los Presidentes de Castilla"; and
Bib. Nac. Madrid, Sección de Manuscritos, no. 10,923, tom. 38, pp. 193–198,
"Breve, curiosa, y ajustada Noticia de
los Presidentes de Castilla."

save the memory of those councillors who have to deal with them . . . so that it is necessary for all who have suits to be tried to pace up and down the courtyard and struggle with one another to get nearer the door of the Council in the hope that they may be the next to be called before it . . . and though there are functionaries called *porteros*, they do not know whom to call, nor how to forewarn their advocates, and when they go to seek for them, they are either not to be found, or else they arrive late, so that many cases go by default for lack of a defence."[1] It may possibly have been this remonstrance which induced Philip, in 1588, somewhat to lighten the burden of the Council's labors by definitely giving separate existence for the first time to the so-called *Cámara de Castilla*, established for the distribution of crown pensions, privileges, and appointments both lay and clerical. Hitherto the Cámara had been but a section of the Council; now it became an independent body of four members, though the president of the Council always had the right to sit and vote there.[2] But save for this comparatively minor change, which was really only the logical consequence of what his

[1] B. M., Add. Ms. 28,361, fol. 236.
[2] Cf. *ante*, Vol. III, pp. 148 f.; Danvila, ii, pp. 432–434; Gounon-Loubens, p. 175; *Códigos Antiguos*, p. 1039; Lobo Laso de la Vega, ms. cited: "En el se qualifican los servicios, qualidades, sciencias, sufficiencia, experiencia, costumbres, y virtudes de las personas que pretenden todo lo qual embian al Rey en su consulta proponiendos e los por sus grados, el qual nombra los que el mas es servido y le parecen mas convenientes y aproposito. Suelen en esto los Reyes de su parte hazer diligencias para satisfazerse de las personas a quien proveer. I a la verdad ninguna provision se havia de hazer donde no precediese este examen, muy cuydadosa y apretadamente porque sin hazerlo assi no se si aseguran la consciencia de todo punto ni aun la opinion.

Desta excelente y loable advertencia usava Phelippe 2.º con su prudencia, sagacidad, y cordura, dexando al mundo exemplo assi desta como de otras disposiciones suyas, y como aquel que mientras vinió no perdió de la memoria lo que sobre este caso el glorioso Emperador Carlos V su padre le dexo encomendado entre aquellos 64 capitulos escriptos de su mano y letra para espejo de su govierno, conservacion, quietud, y aumento de su monarchia, que tantas advertencias, exemplo, doctrina, y utilidad de estado y Govierno contienen con tan christianos y altos fundamentos, los quales ningun Principe del mundo para ser perfecto devria ygnorar sin perderlas un punto de la memoria mayormente el que sabe quan necessario es en ella un virtuoso y costante a quien imitar."

father had done before him, Philip did nothing to remedy the existing situation in the Consejo down to the *pragmática* of 1598, by which he divided it into *salas*.[1] The spectacle that the Council presents, down to the very end of the reign, is that of a body of universal competence, under the king, in matters legislative, administrative, and judicial, but so hopelessly ill-organized and overloaded with work, particularly on the judicial side, that efficiency in action was impossible.

A new ramification of the great conciliar system was the creation, in the year 1555,[2] of a Council of Italy, distinct from that of Aragon. It seems clear that hitherto the Council of Aragon had exercised a certain measure of jurisdiction over the Mediterranean and Italian lands belonging to the Spanish crown. Certainly it had every historical justification for so doing, for all these lands save Milan had been conquered for the Spanish Empire from the eastern kingdoms, and enjoyed some measure of consciousness of a common past. But the process of Castilianizing these Mediterranean and Italian territories had now advanced so far that Charles and Philip felt justified in giving formal expression to it; moreover they were probably not sorry to do something towards obliterating the memory of the mediaeval Aragonese Empire, whose animating spirit had been so different from that of the larger agglomeration in which it had been swallowed up and over which they now held sway. The new Consejo de Italia, whose organization was further perfected by Philip in an ordinance of the year 1579,[3] resided at the court of Spain and was composed, at

---

[1] "Relacion de la orden que su Magestad manda que segue en la division de el Consejo Real." Bib. Nac. Madrid, Sección de Manuscritos, CC. 85 and 89, sueltos 18,722[36] and 18,729[17].

[2] Bib. Nac. Madrid, H. 3, suelto 18,718[51], "Institucion del Consejo de Italia separándole del de Aragon"; also Lobo Laso de la Vega, ms. cited. Cf. also Danvila, ii, pp. 216 f. Gounon-Loubens, p. 357, following Herrera, makes the date 1556.

[3] Danvila, ii, p. 217.

the end of the reign, of a president,[1] the treasurer-general of the realms of the crown of Aragon [2] (the sole vestige of the ancient Aragonese connection that was allowed to remain), and six regents, three of them Spaniards, and three Italians,[3] one each from Sicily, Naples, and Milan; apparently the administration of Sardinia, like that of the Balearic Islands, was allowed to remain in the hands of the Council of Aragon.[4] The functions of the Council were "to deal with the government of Italy, to make *mercedes de Ventajas* [5] to the soldiers quartered there, to provide officers of justice for the cities, and grant titles to magnates, all in consultation with his Majesty. Only in this Council are the affairs of Italy taken up." [6] The Council of Aragon, in the meantime, continued to perform similar functions for Aragon, Catalonia, Valencia, and the islands of the Western Mediterranean. It was composed of a president, who had the title of vice-chancellor, the treasurer-general of the realms of the crown of Aragon, who was not necessarily a native of any one of them, and six *oidores*, two of them Aragonese, two Catalans, and two Valencians; there were also a number of royal secretaries and other special officials. As in the Emperor's day, it remained constantly in attendance on the sovereign; but whereas this had meant, under Charles, that it travelled all over Europe and got a cosmopolitan point of view, it resulted, under Philip, in its remaining almost perpetually

[1] B. M., Cotton Ms. Vesp. C. VI, fol. 6 v: "es Presidente del el Principe de Melito duque de Francavilla."

[2] Ibid.: "el Conde de Chinchon."

[3] Lobo Laso de la Vega, ms. cited; B. M., Cotton Ms. Vesp. C. VI, fols. 6 v–7.

[4] The same mss.; Carlos Riba y García, *El Consejo Supremo de Aragón en el Reinado de Felipe II* (Valencia, 1914), p. xcviii; Antonio Ballesteros y Beretta, *Historia de España* (Barcelona, 1918–   ), iv, 2, p. 18. Sar-

dinia comes into the picture but little in Philip's time. Tiepolo (1567) says "non è cosa di molta importanza per esser quasi deserta, e importa più la spesa che il benefizio." Albèri, *Relazioni*, serie i, v, p. 137.

[5] Grants of additional pay (*paga d'avvantaggio*). Girolamo Ramusio (1597) in Albèri, *Relazioni*, appendice, p. 345.

[6] B. M., Cotton Ms. Vesp. C. VI, fol. 7.

at Madrid or the Escorial, subject to the same process of Castilianization which is observable everywhere else.[1]

The composition and functions of most of the other Councils — Gabriel Lobo Laso de la Vega enumerates no less than eleven of them in all — will be taken up in connection with our examination of the special duties with which they were respectively charged. But it may not be amiss to insert one brief word here about the Council of the Orders, of which no mention has been made since its inception in the days of the Catholic Kings.[2] The extent of its responsibilities and the amount of property which it controlled may be judged by the fact that no less than twenty-two of the eighty-eight *corregimientos* into which Castile was divided were placed wholly under its jurisdiction and withdrawn from that of the Consejo Real.[3] Its regular members were a president and four *oidores*, all of whom must be *cavalleros limpios*, and wear the garb of Santiago, Calatrava, or Alcántara.[4] It was to determine all suits arising on the lands of the Orders (the audiencias having no jurisdiction there) ; to make certain of the *limpieza* of all those on whom his Majesty proposed to confer the honor of membership therein ;[5] to punish *comendadores* who violated their rules ; and to make recommendations for all minor appointments and offices depending on them.[6] One gathers from contemporary documents that the ancient dignity and prestige of the Castilian aristocracy had been

---

[1] Lobo Laso de la Vega, ms. cited; B. M., Cotton Ms. Vesp. C. VI, fol. 8; Riba y García, *El Consejo Supremo de Aragón*, pp. xvii f.

[2] Cf. *ante*, Vol. II, p. 117.

[3] B. M., Cotton Ms. Vesp. C. VI, fol. 7 v; cf. C. de B., lib. v, cap. xi.

[4] B. M., Cotton Ms. Vesp. C. VI, fol. 7.

[5] Agustín Álvarez de Toledo, "Discurso sobre los Consejos," in Archivo Histórico Nacional, Madrid, Sección de Manuscritos, Q. 104, Ms. 5791, fols. 157–190: "Uno de los mayores mas proprios y principales cuydados deste Consejo ha de ser conservar la nobleza de España, no consintiendo que se pierda ni manche ninguna casa ni familia por Livianas occasiones . . ."

[6] B. M., Cotton Ms. Vesp. C. VI, fol. 7 v.

suffered to decline in the Emperor's day,[1] and that the Council of the Orders was expected to restore them. Nothing, of course, was to be done without consultation with the king, who, as chief of all three Orders, had a special interest in the work of this Council, "which is less universal than that of any of the rest."

The history of the Castilian Cortes in the reign of the Prudent King has usually been painted in doleful colors. It has been justly pointed out that the abstention of the nobles and clergy after 1538 had reduced the national assembly to a single chamber, composed of thirty-six representatives of eighteen different cities, chosen, usually by lot and sometimes in rotation, from certain privileged families or categories of the municipal magistracy, and in such fashion that royal interference and manipulation were easy to exercise should the crown so desire.[2] It has also been made clear that their ineffective procedure, and their failure to make redress precede supply, still further sapped the vitality of the Castilian Cortes; that they made no use, for the assertion of their own privileges, of their traditional right to withhold official recognition of a new sovereign, or of the heir to the throne, or to refuse to grant the *servicio*. Moreover they permitted Philip, early in his reign, to subvert another ancient prerogative which the national assembly had successfully maintained in the Emperor's day, namely, that of refusing to consent to the revocation of laws passed in pre-

---

[1] Agustín Álvarez de Toledo, ms. cited; "Mayormente por que no pareze de pequeña consideracion no ser justo que la relajacion de los tiempos passados en estas materias hago en estos daño irreparable en los quales se trata tan differentemente. Medium tenuere beati."

[2] Cf. *ante*, Vol. II, pp. 126–131, and Vol. III, pp. 156–180. On the organ-

ization and procedure of the Cortes see the *introducción* by Tomás Muñoz to the *Actas de las Córtes*, i, pp. vii–xxiii. The president of the Council of Castile was also president of the Cortes; but he was present only at the formal opening session and when he had occasion to transmit to the *procuradores* the propositions and messages of the king.

vious Cortes: "If it be my pleasure," declared the Prudent King in 1555, "I shall annul, without the Cortes, the laws made in the Cortes; I shall legislate by *pragmáticas* and I shall abolish laws by *pragmáticas.*" [1] All this would seem to show that the functions of the national assembly had practically dwindled to the voting of taxes, and that it exercised that function solely in accordance with the will of the king.

Yet there are certain other considerations which point to the conclusion that this picture has been somewhat overdrawn. Philip's attitude towards the Castilian Cortes, in the first place, was in some respects less hostile and suspicious than was that of his father. Despite the progressive Hispanization of his point of view, Charles's interests, during the greater part of his life, had been rather international than Iberian. He wished to get his money without delay, and to use it, often for non-Spanish purposes, without being bothered by petitions and discussions; hence all but a very few of the fifteen meetings of the Castilian Cortes during his reign were finished in less than three months. With Philip it was a very different story. His interests were predominantly Spanish and Castilian. Though he did not doubt that he was vastly wiser than the representatives of the nation, he was by no means averse to hearing their views. Indeed, he rather liked to dally in solitude [2] over the petitions of the *procuradores* before he answered them; it was a most obvious method of obtaining the information for which he always hungered. Noncommittal replies or point-blank refusals were indeed their usual fate, but at least Philip seemed to give

---

[1] *Cortes*, v, p. 677. Cf. also my article on "Control by National Assemblies of the Repeal of Legislation," in the *Mélanges Bémont*, pp. 437–458; and *ante*, Vol. III, p. 169.

[2] Though never in consultation with any of the *procuradores* themselves.

When the Cortes of 1570–71 asked him to listen to two or three of their representatives, in order that they might inform him of the reasons for the petitions that had been preferred, he unhesitatingly refused. *Actas de las Córtes*, iii, pp. 363 f.

them careful consideration; he did not answer the *cuaderno* of the Cortes of 1583 till sixteen months after they had closed, nor that of the assembly of 1588–89 until three full years after its dismissal. Doubtless this is largely to be ascribed to his incorrigible slowness; certainly it was 'poor business'; but it also shows that he felt his subjects' desires to be worthy of attention. Another significant fact in the same connection is the progressive lengthening of the sessions of the Cortes under the Prudent King. The earlier ones were comparatively brief, as in the Emperor's day; but those of 1579, 1583, and 1588, continued, with intermissions, for an average of over two years, while the last one, which met at Madrid in the spring of 1592, was still in session when the king died.[1] Apparently Philip longed for the advice and consolation of the representatives of his people in the avalanche of misfortune, both at home and abroad, with which, at the last, they had been overwhelmed together.[2]

If the *procuradores* were gratified by the changed attitude of the monarch, they were also determined to do their utmost to maintain all the vestiges that still remained of the ancient parliamentary liberties. In this it was inevitable that they should encounter the opposition of the crown, for though Philip was anxious to be apprised of his subjects' desires, he was none the less firmly resolved to keep all the real power in his own hands. The principal barrier in the way of his having what his Tudor contemporaries called a 'tractable parliament' was the *poderes*, or instructions to the *procuradores*, by which the municipalities whom they represented attempted to prescribe their conduct in the Cortes;

---

[1] Danvila, ii, pp. 326–334, 347–350, 357–361. There is no basis for the theory that the sessions were prolonged in order to enable the king to get more money. The Cortes complained of the lengthened sessions in 1585, but only on the ground of the expense to the cities and the *procuradores*. *Actas de las Córtes*, vii, pp. 811 f.

[2] Cf. here Danvila, v, pp. 598–695.

and Philip strove his hardest, from the very beginning of his reign, to convert these *poderes* into what today would be called 'blanket powers.' In 1560 he commanded the cities to amplify the instructions to their delegates, so that in addition to recognizing Don Carlos as the heir to the throne, they might be empowered to hold a regular session of the Cortes;[1] at the opening of the Cortes of 1566 he forced the *procuradores* to swear that their *poderes* were "unlimited and unrestricted."[2] In 1573 we find him sending instructions to local *corregidores* and theologians to use all their efforts to effect the same end (in this case he even appears to have attempted to influence the voting in the *ayuntamientos*).[3] In 1592 the same measures were still more intensively applied; the king did not even shrink from employing the confessional.[4] On such occasions, it is perhaps needless to add, the royal objects were always ultimately attained; but the fact that the king was forced to have recourse to such methods in order to effect his ends shows that the ancient spirit of parliamentary independence was not by any means wholly extinguished. Another characteristic, if wholly futile, method by which the *procuradores* sought to keep alive the memories of a glorious past, was the vigorous maintenance of the time-honored struggle for precedence between the delegates of Burgos and of Toledo.[5] In 1563 this virtually attained the proportions of a rough-and-tumble fight, and the king was obliged to intervene to restore order.[6]

The *cuadernos* also contain abundant evidence that the *procuradores* were determined that all their ancient rights

---

[1] Danvila, ii, p. 280.
[2] *Actas de las Córtes*, ii, p. 13.
[3] Danvila, ii, p. 320.
[4] Danvila, ii, p. 357.
[5] Cf. my article, "The Cortes of the Spanish Kingdoms in the Later Middle Ages," in *American Historical Review*, xvi (1911), p. 482, note 29, and references there.
[6] *Actas de las Córtes*, p. 19.

and privileges should be constantly reasserted in principle, even if they were pitiably unable to effect their reëstablishment in practice. They constantly complain of the infringement of their prerogatives by the imposition of new taxes and the alienation of the royal patrimony without their consent, and they harp on the excessive number and exactions of the royal tax-collectors.[1] They show their jealousy of the way in which the Consejo de Castilla had usurped their legislative authority, and they demand that no new law or *pragmática* be made by the king alone while the Cortes are in session.[2] They never hesitated to tell Philip just what they thought of his own manner of life and of work. In 1559, after the king's return from the North, their old fears of Burgundian luxury, inherited from the Emperor's day, made them protest against the expenses of the royal court and table,[3] "since there is in such matters no inviolable law save the example which your Majesty is pleased to give";[4] and when further observance of their new sovereign's way of living relieved them of all fears in this regard, they changed their tune and begged his Majesty to take less responsibility on his own shoulders in the despatching of business, and to restrict his activities to the conduct of foreign affairs and of

---

[1] *Actas de las Córtes*, ii, pp. 301–306, 400–402; iii, pp. 356–358; v, pp. 17–19; vii, pp. 819 f.; ix, pp. 384–386; xi, pp. 513–515; xvi, p. 664. The third petition of the *cuaderno* of 1571 is particularly significant: "Por los Reyes de gloriosa memoria, predecessores de vuestra Magestad, está ordenado y mandado por leyes hechas en Córtes, que no se crien ni cobren nuevas rentas, pechos, derechos, monedas, ni otros tributos particulares ni generales, sin junta del Reyno en Córtes, y sin otorgamiento de los procuradores dél, como consta por la ley del Ordenamiento del señor Rey Don Alonso y otras. Y en las Córtes próximas passadas se hizo relacion á vuestra Magestad de cómo por averse sin esta órden criado é impuesto algunas nuevas rentas y derechos y hecho crescimiento de otras muchas en estos Reynos, se les avia seguido tanta carga y carestía en las cosas necessarias para la vida humana, que eran muy pocos los que podian vivir sin gran trabajo, por ser mayor el daño que con las dichas nuevas rentas se avia recebido, que el provecho y socorro que dellas se avia sacado." *Actas*, iii, pp. 356 f.

[2] *Cortes*, v, pp. 762 f.; *Actas de las Córtes*, iv, pp. 529–531; v, pp. 311–322, 512 f.; vi, pp. 810 f.; xvi, pp. 638 f.

[3] *Cortes*, v, p. 809; *Actas de las Córtes*, i, p. 400; Häbler, pp. 118, 130 f.

[4] *Cortes*, v, p. 809.

war, which thereby would be more expeditiously decided.[1] And in theory at least, Philip made no objection to these assertions of parliamentary power. In 1569 there were published at his command the *Leyes del Reyno*,[2] commonly cited as the *Nueva Recopilación*, the seventh *título* of whose sixth book contains thirteen laws — the first of them of the reign of Alfonso XI — in which all the principal powers of the Cortes, in legislation and in finance, are specifically stated to be in force, and the privileges and methods of election of the *procuradores* are fully described. It gives a pretty illustration of the wide gulf between theory and fact which had always characterized the government of Castile, of her fondness for recalling the memories of the past, and vainly attempting to weave them into the life of a totally altered present.

The attitude of the Castilian Cortes towards the course of foreign affairs during the reign of the Prudent King was naturally quite different from what it had been in the time of his father, and the obvious cause of the change was Philip's constant residence in the peninsula. Under the Emperor one of the chief worries of the *procuradores* had been his preoccupation with non-Spanish matters, and they vigorously protested whenever they thought that he was sacrificing their interests to those of the house of Hapsburg.[3] With the accession of Philip these fears were of course relieved. The national assembly generally approved of his foreign policy, which until 1584 was successful rather than the reverse; even in the Netherlands, where in some respects the strain was heaviest, the struggle could now be represented chiefly in the light of a religious war, and when it was a question of the suppression of heresy, the Castilian was

---

[1] *Actas de las Córtes*, x, p. 501.
[2] See p. 455, *infra*.
[3] Cf. *ante*, Vol. III, pp. 170–172.

never found wanting. At the end, of course, there was disaster everywhere, but the *procuradores*, like Philip, were convinced that it was the hand of God that caused it. They could commiserate with their sovereign, but they did not venture to offer him advice.[1] The fact that they ceased to attempt to influence the course of foreign affairs left them the freer to occupy themselves with internal ones; to these, and particularly to matters economic, they devoted virtually their exclusive attention. Whether their knowledge of such affairs was greater or less than that of the king to whom their petitions were addressed is a question which is easier to ask than to answer. Certain it is, only, that their viewpoint was predominantly local, while his was perforce far more national and universal, and that both were tragically out of touch with the modern policies and ideas which were beginning to take root in the more enlightened countries to the north of them.

Of all the grievances of which the *procuradores* demanded redress, the most oft repeated was the financial and economic condition of the realm. The *procuradores* were for the most part convinced, at least in the early part of the reign, that Spain had it in her to be a really prosperous country, if only her natural resources were properly fostered, the royal exactions limited, and foreign competition restrained. "Though there exists in Spain," so runs the eighty-fourth petition of the Cortes of 1559,[2] "plenty of iron, steel, wool, silk, and other raw materials of industry, we are so far behind other nations in our capabilities of utilizing them that they are taken away to foreign realms, where they are manufactured and whence

---

[1] It is true that in 1593 one *procurador* went so far as to suggest that if Philip would suspend his "justas y continuas guerras," it would be possible to defend the coasts against corsairs and pirates and lighten the unendurable load of taxation. *Actas de las Córtes*, xii, p. 448.

[2] *Cortes*, v, pp. 849 f.

they are sold back to us at exorbitant prices"; the *procuradores* therefore requested that these "necessary and useful arts" be introduced into Castile, distributed among the *pueblos*, and put in charge of "practical and intelligent persons, who should be encouraged by governmental privileges and exemptions as long as it should seem desirable."[1] Petitions for the maintenance and increase of agriculture and pasturage, for the enforcement of the laws about hunting and fishing, for the restriction of luxury and costly raiment, and for the limitation of the rates of interest, are to be found in every one of the *cuadernos* of the reign;[2] and protests against the alienation of the *patrimonio real*, against the sales of lands and patents of nobility, and against the imposition of new taxes and the raising of the rates of the *encabezamiento* and *alcabala*[3] occurred with increasing frequency as the years rolled by. As late as 1576 we find a demand that the debts of the Emperor be promptly paid.[4] The taking of money out of the realm, "as if we were Indians," was another fertile source of complaint; such action was directly in contravention of the laws of the land, but Philip, like his father before him, sold numerous privileges to violate them, and the petitions of the *procuradores* could not induce him to desist.[5] Another matter on which he was more ready to listen to their demands was the annulment of the letters of naturalization which his father had granted to Englishmen, Flemings, and Genoese, "who came with their ships to the prejudice of the native Spaniards," and had got into their hands the carrying trade

---

[1] Cf. Danvila, ii, p. 284; Colmeiro, Introd., ii, pp. 279 f.

[2] *Cortes*, v, pp. 769 f., 818, 846–848, 864; *Actas de las Córtes*, i, p. 400; ii, p. 464; iii, pp. 34 f., 369; iv, pp. 464 f., 472–474, 476 f., 480 f., 495–497; vi, pp. 860 f.; vii, pp. 832, 834 f.; ix, pp. 393 f., 396 f., 448–450.

[3] *Cortes*, v, p. 809; *Actas de las Córtes*, iii, pp. 368 f.; vii, pp. 817, 820 f., 823 f.; xi, pp. 513–515, 543 f.; xvi, pp. 630, 668.

[4] *Actas de las Córtes*, v, p. 73.

[5] *Cortes*, v, pp. 820 f.; *Actas de las Córtes*, xi, pp. 521–524, 535.

of the realm.[1]   We also find him, in 1588, agreeing to the
absolute prohibition of the importation of foreign silk,
because of its bad quality, and of "baubles, glassware, dolls,
knives, and other similar things of no use to human life"
which came in from France.[2]   In theory the king shared the
conviction of his subjects that Spain was quite capable of
providing for her own needs.   In practice the immediate
exigencies of the royal exchequer obliged him to violate or
ignore many of the recommendations whose underlying
principles he fully approved.   Under such circumstances it
was impossible to follow any consistent policy, and at the
end of the reign there was wellnigh universal chaos.   The
story of the duties on the Portuguese frontier affords a pretty
illustration of this.   At the beginning of the reign the *procuradores* demanded free trade in cloths with the western
kingdom, and a little later the abolition of the customs
houses which had recently been established on the border.[3]
Down to the time of the annexation in 1580–81, Philip did not
feel that he could afford to comply with these requests, and
when at last he became king of Portugal, the ensuing
abolition of the duties was but temporary.   In 1593 his financial embarrassment caused him to reëstablish the customs on
a frontier which, politically speaking, had ceased to exist.[4]

In the early years of the reign the *procuradores* were much
exercised over the lack of adequate coast defences of the
Mediterranean shores of Spain, the insecurity of commerce,
and the frequency of the visits of Moorish pirates.   "The
greatest commerce of the world," declare the *procuradores*,
"was that of the Mediterranean Sea, which bore the trade
of Flanders and France with Italy and Venetians, Sicilians,
Neapolitans, and with all Greece, and Constantinople too,

---

[1] *Cortes*, v, pp. 836–838.
[2] *Actas de las Córtes*, xi, pp. 521–524.
[3] *Cortes*, v, pp. 763–765, 822; cf.

Nueva Recopilación, lib. ix, tit. xxxi,
ley 1 (January 30, 1559).
[4] Cf. *supra*, p. 376, note 3.

and all the Morea and all Turkey, and of all them with Spain, and Spain with them. All this has ceased, because now the Turkish and Moorish corsairs are so much lords of the sea that not a ship sails from the Levant that does not fall into their hands; and so great are the captures which they have made, as well of Christian captives as of estates and goods, that the riches which the said Turks and Moors have won, and the great destruction and desolation which they have made upon the coast of Spain, are alike beyond comparison and number." [1] No one dared live within four or five leagues of the shore, and much land suitable for agriculture and sheep raising was consequently wasted. After the battle of Lepanto, these complaints are less frequent,[2] and, in the later years of the reign, there is less notice than one would naturally expect of the depredations of the English sea-rovers on the coasts of the Atlantic; doubtless the *procuradores* realized that Philip was by this time as powerless to prevent them as he had been to control the tempests which had completed the destruction of the Armada. The increase and prosperity of the Granadan Moriscos, "who neither go to war nor enter the church," [3] was another fertile source of complaint, particularly in the latter part of the reign; the way was well paved, before the death of the Prudent King, for the edict of expulsion of September, 1609. But Castile's proverbial loyalty to the faith did not prevent her representatives from constantly protesting against the many abuses of ecclesiastical jurisdiction. Petitions against the amount and

---

[1] *Cortes*, v, pp. 857 f. Cf. also *Actas de las Córtes*, ii, pp. 428, 453 (*cuaderno* of 1567, pets. xvi, xlix).

[2] The fifty-ninth petition of the *cuaderno* of the Cortes of 1583–85 (*Actas de las Córtes*, vii, p. 830), for the authorization of privateering, speaks of "the losses inflicted by sea and land" by "the enemies of our holy Catholic faith"; but the enemies most in mind at that time were probably the English and the French.

[3] *Actas de las Córtes*, xi, pp. 542 f.; "erecen en tanto número, por ser gente que no va á la guerra, ni se meten en religion"; cf. xvi, pp. 689–693. Cf. the report of Doctor Liébana (1582) in F. Janer, *Condicion Social de los Moriscos*, p. 272.

inalienability of the property of the church are frequent, down to the session of 1586, when repeated failure to gain the ear of the king caused the *procuradores* temporarily to desist; and the same demand occurs again in 1598.[1] Almost equally numerous are the protests against the abuse of the interdict by the *juezes ecclesiasticos* whenever the secular authorities attempted to defend their own jurisdiction.[2] In 1588 and in 1592 there are vigorous complaints against the excesses of the Inquisition;[3] in the first of these cases the king promised improvement, but the repetition of the protest makes it evident that he did not keep his word.[4] He showed just as much zeal in defending the 'supereminence' — and the abuses — of his favorite tribunal at home, as he exhibited in guarding against the attempts of the papacy to control it from abroad.

It is also evident that the *procuradores* were much concerned over the decline of the pristine fighting qualities which had characterized the Spaniards in mediaeval times, and enabled them in the Emperor's day to perform prodigies in the conquest of foreign lands. In the fifteenth petition of the Cortes of 1576 it is pointed out that the Military Orders of Santiago, Calatrava, and Alcántara had been established in these kingdoms in order to fight the Moors, but that ever since the infidel had been expelled from the peninsula, the Knights had given themselves up to a life of ease, and had forgotten the profession of arms. They recommend that in order to prevent the further progress of this evil, the

---

[1] *Actas de las Córtes*, i, pp. 352–354; ix, pp. 434–437; xvi, pp. 627 f., 672 f.

[2] *Cortes*, v, pp. 756 f.; *Actas de las Córtes*, i, pp. 403 f.

[3] In the *proposición* to the Cortes of Madrid in 1563, Philip had specially emphasized the "favor y ayuda" which had been given to the "ministros del Santo Oficio," as the sure means of bringing Spain back to "la fé católica y obediencia de la iglesia romana en la pura limpieza é integridad y religión que conviene y se puede desear." *Actas de las Córtes*, i, pp. 22 f.

[4] *Actas de las Córtes*, xi, pp. 520 f.; xvi, pp. 654 f.; Lea, *The Inquisition of Spain*, i, p. 485.

Orders be established on the frontiers of the Spanish territories in Africa, where the Knights should be obliged to reside, and where those who especially distinguished themselves against the Moors should be rewarded with *encomiendas*.[1] The request, ten years earlier, that military exercises and tournaments be introduced in place of bull-fights,[2] is another phase of the same story; as are petitions that prompt measures be taken for the improvement of the breed of horses.[3] The manners and customs of the students at the universities also gave food for thought. The seventy-third petition of the Cortes of 1558 [4] makes it evident that the rector of Alcalá was powerless to repress the excesses of youth. In 1598, the *procuradores* demand that the printing and reading of obscene literature be forbidden.[5] Apparently the representatives of the realm feared that Castile was no longer producing the type of manhood which had made possible her glorious past.

There was only one meeting, during the reign of the Prudent King, of any of the separate Cortes of the different realms of the crown of Aragon, and that was the famous session of the Cortes of Aragon at Tarazona in 1592, rendered necessary by the 'troubles' stirred up by Antonio Pérez; the consideration of it will be reserved till a later chapter. There were, however, two meetings of the General Cortes of the eastern kingdoms in 1563 and in 1585, at Monzon, to which a few words must be devoted here. The fact that there were but two sessions of this assembly in Philip's reign, in contrast to six in that of his father (under whom there were also held five meetings of the separate Cortes of

---

[1] *Actas de las Córtes*, v, pp. 33–35.
[2] *Ibid.*, ii, p. 454.
[3] *Cortes*, v, pp. 850 f.; *Actas de las Córtes*, iii, pp. 93, 161, 162 f., 208–211; xvi, p. 638.
[4] *Cortes*, v, pp. 772 f.; cf. also J. Beneyto Pérez, *Medios de Cultura*, pp. 75–77.
[5] *Actas de las Córtes*, xvi, p. 675.

the different kingdoms), is but another of the innumerable proofs of the Prudent King's incorrigible Castilianism. He never visited his eastern realms save in order to get their formal recognition of an heir to the throne, or to obtain *donativos*, and it is needless to add that the latter were significantly small in contrast to the revenues which he derived from the Cortes of Castile. The constitutional machinery of these Eastern assemblies, and the limitations which they were still able to impose upon his royal authority, must have been gall and wormwood to him; and, as we shall later see, he utilized the first opportunity to subvert them.

It will be remembered that these General Cortes of the realms of the crown of Aragon were, in effect, merely a juxtaposition of the assemblies of the three eastern kingdoms, each of which dealt separately with the affairs which immediately concerned it, and not seldom continued its sittings in its own capital after the close of the joint meeting at Monzon.[1] But there is such a striking similarity in the proceedings of all three that we are dispensed with the necessity of following them separately. Like those of Castile, they showed singularly little interest in the course of foreign affairs, despite the fact that both in 1563 and in 1585 the *proposición real* was largely occupied with what had been accomplished abroad.[2] Local matters, particularly the impartial administration of justice and the restraint of the excesses of the Inquisition, in which they rightly discerned a potential instrument of Castilianization as well as of extirpation of heresy, were their principal cares;[3] even the ancient cosmopolitanism of the county of Catalonia seems to have vanished away. It was quite characteristic

---

[1] Danvila, ii, p. 298, and *ante*, Vol. I, pp. 483 f.; Coroleu and Pella, *Las Córtes Catalanas*, pp. 361-370.

[2] Danvila, ii, pp. 297, 342; Coroleu and Pella, pp. 362 f., 366 f.

[3] Danvila, ii, pp. 292, 296 f., 299, 301, 336, 338.

of them that in 1563 the Cortes of Monzon began by formally erecting into a law of the land, with some amplifications and improvements, the provisions of the *pragmática* by which Philip, eight years before, had reconstituted the Council of Aragon and separated from it that of Italy.[1]   Matters legal and constitutional, many of them of the most trivial practical importance, were, as ever, the chief preoccupation of the stiff-necked Aragonese ; and even in maritime Catalonia and Valencia, where enthusiasm for trade had generally taken the precedence of insistence on the technicalities of the law, there is evidence of a tendency in the same direction ; a dread of Castilianization was common to all three realms. On matters financial and economic, there is surprisingly little legislation or complaint.   There is much more, as would be expected, in the session of 1585 than in that of 1563–64, but nothing comparable to what is to be found in the *cuadernos* of the Cortes of Castile.   One gets the impression that the ancient rights and privileges of the eastern kingdoms were still sufficiently vital to afford considerable protection against the exactions of the crown.   Though they were probably quite as well able to pay as Castile, Philip preferred to continue to impoverish the kingdom of his choice, rather than to take the trouble to fight the battles in Aragon, Catalonia, and Valencia, which an attempt to secure a more equitable distribution of the burden of taxation would have necessitated.

Taken as a whole, the history of the different Spanish Cortes in the reign of the Prudent King is that of a series of heroic efforts to keep alive the memory of the constitutional rights and privileges of an earlier age, which no longer had any place in the monarchical atmosphere of the sixteenth century.   In practice, as we have seen, these efforts were

[1] Danvila, ii, pp. 291 f.

unavailing. In Castile Philip's power was so firmly intrenched that in any difference of opinion with the *procuradores* he always emerged victorious. With the Cortes of the
realms of the crown of Aragon, where the popular liberties
were so much more strongly established, he followed, until
circumstances forced him to abandon it, the policy of avoiding a decisive issue. Yet it would be a grave error to regard
the national assemblies of the Spanish kingdoms in the
reign of Philip II as wholly without significance. Their
records give us the best picture at present available of the
popular aspirations and desires. They show the importance
of keeping alive the forms of constitutional liberty, even
though the animating spirit be lost. If they fall far below
the Parliaments of Queen Elizabeth, they counted for more
than the contemporary *États-Généraux*. Not until the
degenerate successors of Philip the Prudent had ceased to
perform the functions of royalty did the Cortes of the
Spanish kingdoms disappear from the picture.

The foregoing paragraphs will doubtless have made it
clear that the really fundamental problems of the reign of
Philip II — even though the king was unable to realize it —
were those of finance and economic conditions. We have
therefore to investigate the state of the royal exchequer, and
the ability of the king's subjects to replenish it.

The body with the supreme authority under the crown
over the management of the royal finances, which Philip
inherited from his father, was officially known in the Emper-
or's day as the *Contaduria Mayor,* and was composed, as we
have seen, of two *contadores mayores* and two *contadores
mayores de cuentas,* aided by eight or ten special officials.[1]
In 1554, while he was still Prince of Asturias, Philip enlarged

[1] Cf. *ante,* Vol. III, pp. 190 f.

it by the addition of three *letrados,* "to hear and determine all cases which should arise" in connection with the work of the *contadores*; and the organization was further perfected by a royal ordinance of October 28, 1568.[1] There also appears, beginning with the year 1523, a body with the official name of the Consejo de Hacienda.[2] Originally composed of six persons, it is described, in the middle of Philip's reign, as consisting of a president, three of the senior *oidores* of the Consejo Real, and an unspecified number of "contadores mayores de su magestad"; obviously its function was to bring the Council of Castile into closer touch with the problems of the exchequer.[3] Its relations to the Contaduria are defined in a *pragmática* of November 20, 1593,[4] in which the Consejo de Hacienda was charged with the general supervision of the entire financial system, with the task of drawing up estimates of receipts and expenses for each ensuing year, and, as the former never equalled the latter, with the cumulatively onerous and impossible duty of inventing new sources of supply; to the *contadores* was assigned the management of the details of the collection of the different kinds of revenues, while the councillors continued to sit on all cases arising in connection therewith.[5] To all intents and purposes the Hacienda and the Contaduria,

[1] *Nueva Recopilación,* lib. ix, tit. ii, ley 1; Gounon-Loubens, p. 275, and references there. B. M., Cotton Ms. Vesp. C. VI, fol. 8, describes this body as composed, in 1575–77, of two *contadores mayores* and twelve *contadores.*

[2] The statement of Laiglesia, referred to in Vol. III, *ante,* p. 191, that the name Consejo de Hacienda cannot properly be given to this body in the Emperor's day, is wrong. Cf. Simancas Mss., Consejo y Junta de Hacienda, legajo 9.

[3] B. M., Ms. Vesp. C. VI, fol. 7 v; *Cortes,* iv, p. 376; *Nueva Recopilación,* lib. ix, tit. i, ley 14 (1524), and lib. ix,

tit. vii, ley 21 (1523, 1525); C. Espejo, "Sobre Organización de la Hacienda Española en el Siglo XVI," in *Cultura Española,* vi, pp. 403–428; vii, pp. 687–704; Danvila, ii, p. 435; Gounon-Loubens, pp. 276 f.

[4] *Nueva Recopilación,* lib. ix, tit. ii, ley 2.

[5] Simancas Mss., Diversos de Castilla, nos. 1406, 1810; Espejo, "El Interés del Dinero en los Reinos Españoles," in *Archivo de Investigaciones Históricas,* i (1911), pp. 506 f. Espejo characterizes the councillors and the other officials of the treasury as "gente insuficiente é incapaz."

though officially separate, were but closely interrelated divisions of a single body, at the time of Philip's death; and the *pragmática* of Philip III, by which the two were definitely fused in 1602, did little but legalize an existing state of affairs.[1]

But the Contaduria and the Hacienda were after all but obedient instruments of the royal will; it was primarily at Philip's own door that the blame is to be laid for the dismal financial history of the reign. In justice to him, it should be made plain at the outset that the situation which his father had bequeathed to him was beset with difficulties. Certainly he himself had no knowledge of or interest in finance. He expected the money to be furnished by others. His treasury, in fact, was the only portion of the government service which he did not meticulously superintend; it was the exception that proves the rule.[2] Moreover, in addition to the extent of his possessions and the expense inevitable to the maintaining of them, over and above the totally disproportionate share of the burden of Spanish taxation which fell on Castile, he had been left with a debt generally estimated at 20,000,000 ducats.[3] What was even worse, his father had set him a bad example of financial recklessness and mortgaging of the future. He had seen the borrowing of vast sums at high rates of interest from foreign bankers. He had watched the development and extension of the evil system of *juros,* and of the even more ruinous practice of the sale of public offices.[4] On the other hand he had inherited

---

[1] Danvila, ii, p. 573; *Códigos Antiguos de España,* pp. 1239 f.

[2] "Razon tiene su Magestad de dezir que el Emperador . . . jamas tuvó tanto dinero junto para emprender cosas; pero assistia en persona, y no era tan largo, como han sido los ministros que despues han sido empleados, que han consumido poços de oro, y hecho poco . . . en las entrañas siento

que nos vamos á visto de ojos perdiendo y ne alcanzo remedio: con esta provision de dinero, temo que en otro mes no despacharemos." Idiáquez to Granvelle, January, 1580, in *Correspondance du Cardinal de Granvelle,* ed. Piot, viii, p. 2.

[3] *Ante,* Vol. III, pp. 196 f.

[4] J. Beneyto Pérez, pp. 109 f., and references there.

in Castile a national assembly which still maintained, in theory at least, that no new tax could lawfully be imposed without its consent, while the Cortes of the realms of the crown of Aragon had practically succeeded in erecting that theory into a fact. The Castilian *procuradores* continued, indeed, throughout the reign to vote him *servicios*, as they had done ever since 1542, to the annual amount of 150 *cuentos*. In 1570 they even added an extra 150 for the marriage of his Majesty to Anne of Austria, though the *procuradores* of Granada roundly declared on this occasion that their constituents would not contribute, and that they only voted in order that others might pay.[1] The realms of the crown of Aragon contributed scattering *donativos*.[2] But these sums, as the sequel will show, were insignificant in comparison with Philip's annual expenditures. Certainly the financial problems which Philip inherited were of the hardest. In view of the disasters which overwhelmed him in later years, they could justly be described as insoluble. Had he succeeded in maintaining the status quo, or even an approximation thereto, it would be unfair to blame him. But his actual record was almost unbelievably worse than that of his father before him. Not only were all the ancient and most ruinous imposts maintained and increased; many new ones were superadded, in defiance of the law of the land, and the tax-paying capacity of the realm was exhausted. In 1557 and again in 1592 the number of municipal offices was increased in order that they might be sold for the profit of the crown. Important posts in the national government could also be obtained at a price, and the children of clerics

[1] Danvila, ii, p. 313; Gounon-Loubens, p. 278, and references there.
[2] Danvila, ii, pp. 298, 304, 336, 344. B. M., Cotton Ms. Vesp. C. VI, fols. 81 v and 86 v: "Vale cada un año a su Magestad los reynos de Valencia, Aragon, y Cathaluña sin otros servicios que suelen hacer, 200,000 ducados . . . esto no se cobre sino quando el Rey va a tener Cortes en los dichos Reynos."

bought patents of legitimacy right and left.[1] The *juros*, and the sums borrowed at exorbitant rates from foreign bankers, mounted by leaps and bounds; on two occasions Philip was forced to make what amounted to a declaration of bankruptcy. Mortgaging the future was the sole policy which he could comprehend — always deluding himself with the belief that the scales were bound to turn. But the great victory which he confidently expected never came, and in the end he left his successor with a debt four times as great as that which his father had bequeathed to him.[2] A brief summary of the history of the successive financial expedients which he adopted will serve to show the steps by which an originally bad situation was suffered to get infinitely worse.

The process began even before his return to Castile. The war with France and the papacy cost heavily; neither the Netherlands nor the Italian dominions were able to help him; like his father before him, he was driven back on Castile and the Indies. In 1558 he took a step which the Emperor had often considered, but never actually adopted, namely, the extension by law of the *alcabala* to New Spain and New Castile.[3] In the same year the export of Castilian wool was subjected for the first time to a heavy duty (*derecho de lanas*);[4] in 1561 it was calculated to yield 80,000 ducats; and in 1577, 150,000, of which 130,000 were pledged in advance

[1] J. Beneyto Pérez, pp. 109 f.; Antonio Sacristán, *Municipalidades de Castilla y Leon* (Madrid, 1877), pp. 415–434; M. J. Bonn, *Spaniens Niedergang während der Preisrevolution des 16. Jahrhunderts* (Stuttgart, 1896), pp. 88–101.

[2] The official figures, as given in the archives at Simancas, are 79,734,415 ducats; cf. Simancas Mss., Consejo y Junta de Hacienda, legajo 380. The usual estimate (e.g., Häbler, p. 134) makes it 20,000,000 ducats larger.

[3] Cf. *supra*, p. 208; and Häbler, p. 119. Actual collection of the *alcabala* in the Indies did not begin till 1574–76.

[4] *Nueva Recopilación*, lib. ix, tit. xxxii; *Cortes*, v, p. 735; Häbler, pp. 66, note 26, 119; Klein, *The Mesta*, p. 46, and references there. After various changes, the duties were fixed in 1566 at one and a half ducats a bale for exports to Flanders and four ducats for Italy, France, Navarre, Aragon, Valencia, and Portugal.

(*empeñado en juros*).[1] In 1559 a line of custom houses was
established on the frontiers of Portugal, which had hitherto
enjoyed free trade with Castile; and duties at the rate of
ten per cent were enforced on all exports and imports, as on
the confines of Aragon, Valencia, and Navarre.[2] In the
same year Philip decreed that all gold, silver, and quicksilver
mines in Spain should be turned over to the crown;[3] he
also bought back the *diezmos de la mar*, or customs revenues
of the Biscayan ports, from the Constable of Castile, to
whose family they had been granted for over a hundred
years, and raised the rate. In 1561 they were calculated to
be worth 48,000 ducats; in 1577, 150,000.[4] In these same
years the royal monopoly of playing cards, which had been
established, in theory at least, from a much earlier date,
was for the first time rigidly enforced; in 1577 it netted over
53,000 ducats.[5] And in 1564 all the salt pits of the realm
were incorporated into the royal domain; thirteen years
later they yielded the king's treasury an annual income of
250,000 ducats.[6]

All these, however, were but trifling beginnings. They
may have infringed the letter of the law of the land, but
Spain was so glad to get back her king that the Cortes
hardly made a complaint; indeed their protests did not

[1] B. M., Cotton Ms. Vesp. C. VI, fol.
85 v; Vesp. C. VII, fols. 216 f.

[2] *Nueva Recopilación*, lib. ix, tit. xxxi,
ley 1; Gounon-Loubens, p. 304.

[3] *Nueva Recopilación*, lib. vi, tit.
xiii, ley 4 (January 10, 1559).

[4] B. M., Cotton Ms. Vesp. C. VI,
fol. 85; Vesp. C. VII, fols. 216 f.;
Simancas Mss., Diversos de Castilla,
no. 1406; C. de C., i, p. 168. Apparently there was litigation about these
diezmos de la mar. Cf. "Memorial de las
Finanças de España en los años 1560 y
1561," in *Papiers d'état du Cardinal de
Granvelle*, ed. Charles Weiss, vi, p. 161:
"los diezmos de la mar que tenia el

condestable, aunque hay pleyto en
ello, mas todavía se ponen aquí . . ."

[5] B. M., Cotton Ms. Vesp. C. VI,
fol. 86 v. On the history of the royal
monopoly of playing cards in Spain and
the Indies cf. José Canga Argüelles,
Diccionario de Hacienda (Madrid, 1833),
ii, p. 357; Häbler, p. 119, note 21;
Forneron, i, p. 247; *C. S. P., Foreign*,
1564–65, no. 1676; *Recopilación de
Leyes de las Indias*, lib. viii, tit. xxiii,
ley xv.

[6] B. M., Cotton Ms. Vesp. C. VI,
fol. 85; Espejo, "La Renta de Salinas,"
in *R. A.*, tercera época, xxxix (1918),
pp. 48 f.

become violent until ten or fifteen years afterwards.[1]   Nevertheless the year 1561 did not close without a fresh innovation, immediately much more lucrative, though ultimately far more harmful, than any of Philip's previous ones.   It will be remembered that under an arrangement inherited from the Emperor's day, the cities of Castile had been paying in annually to the royal treasury a lump sum of 334 *cuentos*, called the *encabezamiento*, in lieu of the crown's abandonment of its right to the *tercias* and *alcabala*.[2]   This *encabezamiento* was already the largest item in the royal income, but Philip was determined that it must be still further increased. Chiefly on the plea that it was the king's prerogative to raise the rate of the *alcabala*, whose abandonment by the crown was the principal basis upon which the *encabezamiento* rested, he now proposed to the *procuradores* an increase in the latter which should bring its annual yield up to 456 *cuentos*, besides certain payments in kind; and the *procuradores* accepted the arrangement in return for Philip's solemn promise to alienate no more of the royal domain and to impose no new taxes.[3]   The repartition of the payment of this increased *encabezamiento* among the different localities was made in accordance with the results of a special investigation of the state of the population and the resources of the various parts of the realm.   No pains were spared to make the apportionment as fair as the excessive demands of the crown would permit, and any community or individual who so desired was granted exemption from the *encabezamiento* in return for direct payment of the *tercias* and *alcabala*.[4]   In 1561 Philip obtained from Pope Pius IV a

[1] Häbler, pp. 120, 122.
[2] Cf. *ante*, Vol. III, pp. 160–164.
[3] Gounon-Loubens, pp. 283 f., and references there; *Actas de las Córtes*, ii, p. 305. For further details in regard to the "condiciones con que

estos Reinos tomaron a su cargo, por encabeçamiento general, las Rentas dellos" cf. Juan Gutiérrez, *Opera* (Lyons, 1730), iii, pp. 347–371.
[4] Gounon-Loubens, p. 285.

yearly subsidy (*subsidio*) of 300,000 ducats, increased in the following year to 420,000, for the preparation of a fleet to fight the Turk; [1] and in 1571 Pius V permitted him, on the same plea, to collect for the royal coffers the tithe due to the church from the house in each parish which paid the highest tithe.   This new tribute, called the *excusado,* yielded in 1577 the sum of 293,000 ducats.[2]   In 1566 the *almojarifazgos* and other customs duties were greatly increased.   It seems safe to say that between Philip's accession and 1573 the revenues of the state approximately doubled.[3]

Much more, however, was still to come.   In 1571, and again in 1573, the representatives of the government informed the Cortes that the ordinary income of the realm for the ensuing five years had already been spent in advance, and that the outstanding debts were perilously near 50,-000,000 ducats; [4] some new and drastic method must forthwith be devised in order to meet the existing situation.   After various proposals and counter-proposals had been made and had failed, Philip intervened (November 9, 1574) with a proposal to the *procuradores* for a new and greater increase in the *encabezamiento* which should raise its annual yield to 1395½ *cuentos;* [5] ten months later (September 1, 1575) he issued a royal decree declaring all interest on state debts to be suspended until new means of liquidating them could be found.[6]   As these two drastic measures marked the

[1] Pastor, xvi, pp. 359 f. The subsidy was granted at first for five years; in 1562 the period was lengthened to ten.

[2] The original grant, made July 15, 1567, was of the tithe of the third house in value in each parish. The grant of May 21, 1571, was for five years only; but it was continually renewed, and in 1757 was made perpetual. The papal nuncio assured Philip that the change from the third to the first house would double or treble the value of the grant. Canga

Argüelles, *Diccionario de Hacienda,* i, p. 454; *Códigos Antiguos,* p. 915, ley 1, notes 1, 2; Ricardo de Hinojosa, *Diplomacia Pontificia,* i, p. 178, note; B. M., Cotton Ms. Vesp. C. VI, fol. 86.

[3] Häbler, p. 122.

[4] *Actas de las Córtes,* iii, pp. 21 f., 311–319; iv, pp. 21–23, 283–287; Häbler, p. 122.

[5] *Actas de las Córtes,* iv, pp. 300 f.

[6] For the text of the decree cf. B. M., Cotton Ms. Vesp. C. VI, fols. 142–156. See *Actas de las Córtes,* iv, p. 411, for

beginning of the utter bankruptcy. with which the reign closed, it is worth while to follow the results of them in some detail.

Let us begin with the *encabezamiento*. The *procuradores* made difficulties, of course, but Philip was not to be denied. He exerted every influence, lawful or unlawful, that he could bring to bear, and finally got the Cortes to sanction the measure.[1] But the actual collection of the funds proved to be a far harder matter. As soon as the new rates had been announced, a large majority of the Castilian cities exercised the right which they indubitably possessed, of refusing to accept the *encabezamiento*, and reverting instead to the payment of the *alcabala*; the government soon found that the sums which it could derive from the places which had elected to follow this method of procedure were often only a half, and sometimes only a third, of the amount which it had reckoned that it would gain. This fact, together with the protests which the new rates evoked on every hand, caused Philip, in 1577, to diminish the total amount of the *encabezamiento* to 1018½ *cuentos*, besides the payments in kind, where it remained, save for an increase of fifteen *cuentos* in 1590, until the end of the reign.[2] Even with this modification, the government had the utmost difficulty in persuading the Castilian cities to accept the *encabezamiento* in place of the *alcabala* and *tercias*; and Ávila, Granada, Cordova, and Toro stood out against it till the very end.[3] Philip had indeed succeeded in more than trebling the yield of the largest of the various sources of the government revenue during the

the story of its announcement to the *procuradores*. Cf. also Ballesteros, *Historia de España*, iv, 2, pp. 206 f.; Espejo, "El Interés del Dinero en los Reinos Españoles," *loc. cit.*, pp. 497–501.

[1] Häbler, pp. 125 f., and references there; Gounon-Loubens, pp. 285 f.;

Actas de las Córtes, iv (see index thereof, s. v. *Encabezamiento general*).

[2] Häbler, pp. 125, 127, note 37; *Actas de las Córtes*, v, adicional, p. 613; documents in Gutiérrez, *Opera*, iii, pp. 371–403.

[3] Häbler, p. 126, note 35.

course of his reign, but in so doing he had wellnigh exhausted the tax-paying capacity of his realm. The blighting effect of the *alcabala*, which was the chief basis on which the system of taxation rested, was first revealed in its fulness during the reign of the Prudent King.

As for the decree of suspension of payments, September 1, 1575, its first obvious effect was to cause a panic among all those to whom Philip owed money both at home and abroad, and to ruin Spanish credit in Europe.[1] There had been previous occasions, notably in 1557 and 1560, when he had been unable to discharge his obligations, and many of the German bankers on whom his father had relied had already begun to fight shy of investments in Spain; but now the Genoese, who had hitherto stood by him, refused to lend him another ducat. For some time after the issuance of the *decreto*, Philip was utterly unable to borrow funds. At all costs he must take measures to reëstablish his credit abroad; and in 1577 he temporarily succeeded in so doing by the arrangement known as the *medio general*.[2] This consisted, in brief, of the issuance of new pledges in place of the old ones, to all the state's creditors, from the foreign bankers to the holders of *juros*, by which the said creditors were promised their interest at varying rates out of the regular revenues of the crown. For the time being the expedient served the purpose for which it was intended, for Philip was thereby enabled to borrow money again; but ultimately it left him worse off than before, for the sole principle that underlay it continued to be the same old vicious one of mortgaging the future. Larger and larger were the proportions of the government revenues that were drawn off from the treasury

---

[1] Ballesteros, iv, 2, p. 207; Espejo, *loc. cit.*, p. 501; memorial of the Genoese and others in reply to Philip's decree, B. M., Cotton Ms. Vesp. C. VI, fols. 157–164.

[2] Espejo, *loc. cit.*, p. 501; Häbler, p. 126; Ballesteros, iv, 2, p. 207.

by the king's various creditors, smaller and smaller his actual receipts; and finally in 1588 he reached the nadir of his fortunes, when instead of the great victory to which he had so confidently looked forward as the sole means of relieving his embarrassments, came the news of the defeat of the Invincible Armada. It had cost him, so he plainly told the Cortes, 10,000,000 ducats.[1] This time he frankly admitted his own inability to meet the situation, and told the *procuradores* that they must find means to help him out ; and the result was the first imposition, in 1590, of the tax that came subsequently to be known as the *millones*.[2] In the form that it was voted by the *procuradores* in that year (Granada, Segovia, and Soria standing out) it consisted of a direct contribution of 8,000,000 ducats, the collection to be spread over a period of six years ; but when the term had expired, and the amount had been paid in, it was prolonged, this time at the rate of 500 *cuentos* per annum, for four years more.[3] In theory the Prudent King, who died in 1598, should only have had the benefit of the first two of these four years ; but the actual state of affairs is revealed by the fact that his son, on his accession, explained to the *procuradores* that the income of the last two had already been spent in advance. Moreover even the *millones* did not save Philip from the necessity of issuing a second decree of suspension on November 29, 1596,[4] and the object of this one, as has been justly remarked, was no longer to reëstablish the royal finances, which now were past praying for, but solely to get easier rates on the sums already borrowed.[5]

The foregoing paragraphs will have made it abundantly

[1] Häbler, p. 127. The *Actas de las Córtes*, x, p. 118 (June 9, 1588) puts the cost of the Armada which had left Lisbon in the latter half of May and of that "que tenia hecha y junta en Flandes" at 900,000 ducats per month.

[2] Häbler, p. 128.
[3] Häbler, p. 129, and references there.
[4] Espejo, *loc. cit.*, p. 502, note 1.
[5] Häbler, p. 129.

clear that the most serious drain on the Spanish exchequer was the payment of the interest on the various crown debts; it even exceeded the 'extraordinario,' or sums appropriated for foreign diplomacy and wars. There are all sorts of different ways in which the total of it can be reckoned up, but in any case it is clear that before the *decreto* of 1575 it amounted to at least one-third of the regular income, and at the end of the reign to two-thirds;[1] in other words, at the time of Philip's death, considerably less than half of the state revenues were actually at the disposal of the government. The rate of interest paid to the foreign bankers and other *asentistas* steadily rose until it was arbitrarily scaled down in 1575 by the *decreto*. Under the Emperor it probably varied from five to twenty per cent. In the first half of his son's reign, it was certainly far nearer the latter extreme than the former.[2] After 1575, of course, the rates which the government consented to pay cannot any longer be taken as an index of the measure of its solvency. For this we must look to the number of individuals and of banking houses, both in Spain and abroad, whose trust in it had been rewarded by financial ruin.

From our consideration of the state of the royal exchequer under Philip II, it is natural to turn to that of the general economic conditions in Spain; and a few words must be devoted at the outset to the much vexed question of the state of the population during the reign of the Prudent King. An abundance of material on the subject has come down to us, for Philip was even fonder than his predecessors of taking periodical *censos de población*, both for his own private infor-

---

[1] Cf. Simancas Mss., Memoriales de la Cámara de Castilla, legajo 444; Häbler, p. 130.

[2] Cortes, v, p. 820; Espejo, *loc. cit.*, pp. 411, 497. As early as 1566 the rate of exchange with Italy was already so high "que era una vergüenza"; one paid 422 maravedis instead of 350 for an Italian ducat. Espejo, *loc. cit.*, p. 490.

mation, and for the purposes of royal taxation. These *censos*, buried for over two centuries in the archives of Simancas, were discovered, and many of them published, in 1829, by a painstaking scholar named González, and one of the most complete of them, taken in the year 1594, gives materials from which the entire population of Spain at that date has been estimated as 9,034,410.[1] This impressive total is less than two-thirds of that usually given for the population of contemporary France; but it is twice as large as that of England and Wales in the same period.[2] Certainly it seems extraordinarily high in comparison with some of the modern estimates,[3] and in view of the reiterated complaints of the Cortes of the period about the depopulation of the rural portions of the realm.[4] Yet further consideration inclines one to believe that there are valid reasons for accepting it. The density per square mile is only half that of the population of France, and but fifty-seven per cent of that of England and Wales; and the depopulation of the rural districts can be adequately explained on the theory of urban concentration.

A further analysis of the figures of González throws light on the way in which the inhabitants were divided among the different portions of the realm. Old and New Castile, with the northwest provinces and the ancient kingdom of Leon, are given a total of 6,020,915, with an average density of over sixty per square mile; Murcia and Andalusia get 1,656,790, with an average density of thirty-nine; Aragon,

---

[1] *Censo de Poblacion de las Provincias y Partidos de la Corona de Castilla en el Siglo XVI*, ed. Tomás González (Madrid, 1829), especially pp. 90, 97, 388; Gounon-Loubens, pp. 49–53; A. P. Usher, "The History of Population and Settlement in Eurasia," in *Geographical Review*, xx (1930), p. 121, and letter of June 12, 1930.

[2] Usher, *loc. cit.*

[3] As, e.g., in Ballesteros, iv, 2, p. 144.

[4] As, e.g., in *Actas de las Córtes*, xv, pp. 748 f.; cf. also Albert Girard, "Le chiffre de la population de l'Espagne dans les temps modernes," in *Revue d'histoire moderne*, iii (1928), pp. 420–436; iv (1929), pp. 3–17; the same, "La répartition de la population en Espagne dans les temps modernes," in *Revue d'histoire économique et sociale*, xvii (1929), pp. 347–362.

378,710, Catalonia, 336,970, Valencia, 486,860, and Navarre, 154,165; in Aragon there were barely twenty-one souls to the square mile.[1] These figures are, of course, primarily significant as evidence of yet another phase of that Castilianization of the Iberian peninsula to which we have so often referred; but they also show that, within the limits of the western kingdom, the inhabitants preferred the pasture lands of the north, and the cities of the central plateau, to the fertile valleys of the Guadiana and Guadalquivir. In other words, they seem rather to confirm than to contradict what we can gather from other sources in regard to the decline of Spanish agriculture. There is evidence that the population declined in the closing years of the century.[2] In 1597 a deputy in the Cortes declared that in nothing were the Spanish realms so poor as in people.[3]

The reign of the Prudent King witnessed a new phase of the age-long struggle between the rival interests of agriculture and pasturage in Spain. The various privileges which the Emperor had granted to the Mesta had sufficed to establish it in a position of unquestioned preponderance for the rest of the century. Philip had little to do save to confirm the existing arrangements, and the Cortes apparently recognized the futility of attempting to alter them; there is a notable absence of petitions on the subject in the *cuadernos* of this reign, in comparison with those of the preceding and succeeding ones.[4] But if the state of the grazing interests remained, relatively speaking, happy under Philip II, that of the tillers of the soil became much worse. The petitions of the Cortes and the testimony of contemporaries bear wit-

---

[1] These figures have been worked out by Professor A. P. Usher from the tables in González, especially those on pp. 90, 97, 388.

[2] Girard, in *Revue d'histoire moderne*, iii, p. 430.

[3] Martín de Porras of Burgos, August 23, 1597. *Actas de las Córtes*, xv, p. 540.

[4] Ballesteros, iv, 2, pp. 154 f.; Klein, *The Mesta*, pp. 331–337.

ness to it at every turn.[1] Year by year we learn of fertile
fields being abandoned,[2] of real wealth "vanishing in papers
and contracts" ;[3] in 1593 the Cortes deplore the depopulation
of these "richest realms in Europe, in such fashion that
almost every year there is sterility and lack of food, because
the laborers have faded away, and two-thirds of their number
are missing."[4] The causes of the decline were doubtless
numerous. The departure of the Moriscos after the Granadan rebellion,[5] emigration to the Indies, the wars of Italy and
the Low Countries,[6] and a series of blights and scant crops
were all, no doubt, partially responsible for the decay ; but
there can be no question that the greater part of the blame is
to be laid at the door of the government. The need of encouraging agriculture became increasingly imperative as the reign
progressed, but the means that were adopted to effect it were
most inadequate. Philip could not be made to realize its importance. His attention was exclusively occupied with the
increase of the yield of the *alcabala* and the *encabezamiento*,
to which the comparatively self-supporting farmer contributed little or nothing, and he generally refused or ignored
the petitions that were addressed to him for the relief of the
sad state of the tillers of the soil.[7] The experiment, which
had been tried and failed before, of fixing the price of agricultural products was repeated at the request of the Cortes
in 1558 ; but when, eight years later, the *procuradores* had

---

[1] Häbler, pp. 36 f.; Ballesteros, iv,
2, pp. 146–156; Espejo, *Carestía de la
Vida*, pp. 69–73.

[2] Valencia was obliged to import grain
from Sicily. Ballesteros, iv, 2, p. 146.

[3] Ballesteros, iv, 2, p. 153.

[4] *Actas de las Córtes*, xiii, p. 136.

[5] The depopulation of Granada was
remedied, to a certain extent, at the
expense of other parts of Spain. Over
12,000 Asturian, Galician, and Castilian
families removed thither. Ballesteros,
iv, 2, p. 153.

[6] *Actas de las Córtes*, xv, p. 749
(November 23, 1598) : "há casi ciento
y seis años que se descubrieron las
Indias, y escomenzó la conquista del
Reyno de Nápoles, y desde entonces
acá, todos los años han ido flotas para
poblar lo uno, y armadas de gente de
guerra para las que ha habido fuera
del Reyno, que siendo muchas cada
año, muy pocas son las que á él vuel-
ven." Cf. p. 656, *ibid.*

[7] Häbler, p. 37.

discovered their mistake, and begged that the schedules be abolished, Philip refused; the rates were maintained and steadily increased until the end of the reign.[1] It is needless to add that the scarcity and consequent dearness of food became increasingly serious problems as the reign progressed. An eminent specialist has calculated that the price of wheat in Spain increased, during the sixteenth century, 456 per cent, and that of wine 500 per cent.[2] To an extent, of course, it is only fair to regard this rise as but a part of the general price revolution contemporaneously in progress all over Europe,[3] but it was certainly far greater than it would have been if the general financial policy of the government had been more wise. It was the tragedy of the situation that Philip's foreign loans deprived Spain of the wealth of the Indies at the very moment she needed it most. After she had brought it across the Atlantic it flowed through her as water through a sieve to profit other lands; and she was left without resources to meet the increased costs which the achievements of her own empire-builders had been largely instrumental in creating.

On the side of industry and commerce the story is scarcely less depressing. Presumably the depopulation of the fields was counterbalanced to some extent by an increase in the size of the cities, and there have been those who have maintained that the decade 1550-60 was a thriving period for Spanish manufacture and trade.[4] But there can be no question that the period as a whole saw a rapid decline. The *procuradores* at the outset demanded protection against foreign competition in the form of prohibitions of the admission into the realm of goods manufactured abroad, and

---

[1] Häbler, p. 36; Ballesteros, iv, 2, p. 147.

[2] Espejo, *Carestía*, p. 125.

[3] Cf. E. J. Hamilton, "En période de révolution économique: la monnaie en Castille (1501–1650)," in *Annales d'histoire économique et sociale*, iv (1932), pp. 140–149, 242–256.

[4] Häbler, pp. 66 f., and references there.

of the exportation of raw material from Castile.   They also requested that the Castilians be given the opportunity to become acquainted with the newest and best methods of manufacturing.[1]   In theory Philip approved of this programme, and gave orders for the carrying of it out;[2] but before long the immediate needs of the royal exchequer became so pressing that everything gave way before them. Philip could never understand that no king can be really rich unless he has a wealthy nation behind him.[3]   We have seen that in order to get more revenue, he levied heavy export duties on Castilian wool in 1558, and he increased them in 1562 and 1566 ;[4] but in spite of these imposts, which one would expect to find helpful to the native clothiers, woollen goods of foreign manufacture constantly made their appearance in Spain, either as a result of the revocation of the *pragmáticas* forbidding their importation, or by virtue of special licenses to transgress the established laws granted by the government in return for pecuniary rewards.   The silk industry, which had been one of the glories of Granada, was by this time almost ruined by the progressive increases of the *rentas* to which it had been subjected,[5] while the raising of the rates of the *encabezamiento* and *alcabala* after 1577 cramped all commercial activity within the realm;[6] the only notable exception was Seville, whose prosperity was kept alive and increased by the trade with the American colonies.[7]   The effects of the *decreto* of 1575 were also most harmful to Spanish commerce abroad, for the foreign merchants whose loans Philip had declared his inability to pay revenged themselves, at least in part, by cancelling their contracts with the Spanish

---

[1] *Cortes*, v, pp. 849 f.;   Colmeiro, *Introd.*, ii, pp. 279 f.
[2] *Ibid.*, p. 280.
[3] Häbler, p. 65.
[4] Cf. p. 440, *supra*, and note 4.

[5] Häbler, p. 85.
[6] *Ibid.*, p. 73.
[7] *Ibid.*, pp. 75–77, and references there.

export houses. Every effort the king made to lighten his financial burdens left him, and also his subjects, worse off than before.

Amid all these evidences of economic disintegration and decay, it is refreshing to note that in one respect the Prudent King was actually in advance of his day and generation. He may be justly called the first of modern sovereigns to have established a postal service for the use of the general public. A *correo* for the despatch of royal letters and mandates throughout the different Hapsburg dominions in Europe had been organized and set up in the Emperor's day under the direction of the de Tassis family, and there was another for the Indies administered by Lorenzo Galíndez de Carvajal.[1] Under Philip the existing facilities were greatly expanded. It seems probable that the credit for originating the idea of a postal service for general use belongs to one Francisco de Cuevas, who in the early years of the reign established a *correo ordinario* at Burgos; but we may well believe that the king, with his passion for detailed information in regard to everything that was taking place all over Europe, did his utmost to forward and develop it. In 1580, with the hearty support of Granvelle, there was established a fortnightly service for general use between Rome and Madrid; the charge was two *reales* (i.e., about two-elevenths of a ducat) for every ounce of paper.[2]

We have several times remarked that Philip II was essentially a law-loving man. Of this his whole policy, both foreign and internal, affords convincing proof. Such acts as the free and easy piracies and pillagings of the English sea-rovers were beyond his understanding. Whenever he

---

[1] Cf. Cayetano Alcázar, *Historia del Correo en América* (Madrid, 1920).

[2] Ballesteros, iv, 2, pp. 192–195, and references there.

himself assumed the offensive he took meticulous pains to justify his actions in the eyes of legal experts; the care with which he established and fortified his lawful rights to the Portuguese throne on the death of his nephew Sebastian is perhaps the most striking of the many instances of it that have come down to us.[1] The same quality is even more plainly observable in his conduct of internal affairs. He justified his own most arbitrary acts on the ground that as king by right divine he was himself the ultimate source of all law; on the other hand, he was most insistent on the literal observance of existing legislation by everybody else. Like his great-grandmother, Isabella the Catholic, he was determined that even-handed justice should always be available to the humblest of his subjects. He was zealous for the punishment of every sort of violence and crime. He filled his realms with innumerable agents, charged to detect and report all infringements of the laws. Indeed, the keynote of his whole system of internal administration was strict and constant surveillance.

If Philip expected his subjects to observe the laws, it was obviously essential that they should know what those laws were; but at the time of his accession this could not be fairly expected of them. The many defects in the most recent existing code, the *Ordenanzas Reales* of 1484, and the enormous number of new elements that had come into play during the Emperor's reign, had created legal chaos in Castile long before Philip assumed control. The Cortes, as we have already seen, had been loud in their complaints,[2] and at least as early as the year 1537 Charles had taken the first measures for the drawing up of a new code.[3] The first three of those to whom the work was intrusted all died before the end of his reign; a fourth was so busy in the Consejo

[1] Cf. *ante*, p. 347.   [2] Cf. *ante*, Vol. III, pp. 173 f.   [3] Danvila, ii, p. 201.

Real that he was unable to finish the task; and it was finally completed, early in Philip's reign, by the licentiate Bartolomé de Atienza,[1] also of the Consejo, and therefore presumably in close touch with the king. It was formally approved by a royal *cédula* of March 14, 1567, wherein it was specifically stated that it was to be exclusively used by all judges and tribunals of the realm, even though its provisions were contradicted by the earlier codes; and it was first published at Alcalá de Henares on January 11, 1569.[2] It was principally composed of "laws made in Cortes," but it also included some 300 *pragmáticas* and *cédulas* issued on the royal authority alone, as well as a few *autos acordados del Consejo*. Both its content and the method of its establishment as the law of the land afford the plainest evidence that the king regarded himself as possessed of supreme legislative power, independent of the national assembly. It was by far the most important legal compilation in Spain since the days of the *Partidas*, and it continued, with periodical additions, to be the law of the land down to the publication of the *Novísima Recopilación* in 1805.[3]

The supreme judicial tribunal of the realm remained under Philip, as it had been under his predecessors, the Royal Council of Castile. We have already examined the course of its development during the reign; here we need only remark that the vast number of cases which were permitted to come before it afford additional proof of the fondness of the king for everything pertaining to the law, and of his resolve, in so far as it was humanly possible, to

[1] Danvila, ii, p. 403.

[2] The work appeared in many subsequent editions down to 1777; our references are to the edition of 1640. The title, originally simply *Leyes del Reyno*, appears from 1581 as *Recopilacion de las Leyes destos Reynos*. The name *Nueva Recopilación*, by which it is usually cited, does not appear in the title, but is found in the royal *cédula* of approval: "las dichas leyes, y nueva Recopilacion, y reduccion dellas." M. and M., ix, p. 252; *Los Códigos Españoles concordados y anotados*, vii, pp. xv f.

[3] Danvila, ii, pp. 404 f.

keep himself in close touch with its interpretation and administration. Next below the Consejo came the four great regional courts of the realm — the Chancillerías of Valladolid and Granada, and the Audiencia of Galicia, inherited from the days of the Catholic Kings, and the much more recent Audiencia of Seville, established in 1556; ten years later Philip set up a fifth tribunal at Las Palmas in the Canaries, whose inhabitants had hitherto resorted in important cases to the Chancillería of Granada.[1] The two chancillerías continued to maintain their ancient preëminence over the more recent audiencias; "the greater part of Spain has recourse to them in the districts committed respectively to their charge."[2] The membership of each, namely, sixteen *oidores*, divided into four *salas*, inherited from the Emperor's day, does not seem to have been altered by any law in the reign of the Prudent King; but a document of the eighth decade of the century describes each as composed of "twelve *oidores*, a president, and four *alcaldes*, and three *alcaldes de hijosdalgo*," all of them appointed by the president of the Council of Castile;[3] doubtless the accumulation of suits necessitated a gradual increase in the number of the magistrates. The same document gives interesting details in regard to jurisdiction and procedure; it is particularly enlightening as to the method of appeal from the Chancillería to the Sala de Mil y Quinientos in the Consejo, and reveals exactly why and how the latter got its name. No such appeal could be made if the amount at stake was less than 4000 ducats. The appellant must deposit

---

[1] *Nueva Recopilación*, lib. iii, tit. iii, ley 1. The Emperor had created an audiencia at Las Palmas by *cédula* of December 7, 1526, but there is no evidence that it performed its functions during his lifetime. Cf. Danvila, ii, p. 441. It was provided that in the more important civil and criminal cases there might be an appeal from the Audiencia of the Canaries to the Audiencia of Seville. *Nueva Recopilación*, lib. iii, tit. iii, ley 4.

[2] B. M., Cotton Ms. Vesp. C. VI, fol. 9 v.

[3] B. M., Cotton Ms. Vesp. C. VI, fols. 9, 9 v, 10.

1500 *doblas* beforehand, and if the verdict of the higher court went against him, he was obliged to pay one-third of the 1500 *doblas* to the Cámara Real, another third to the judges who gave the verdict, and the rest to his opponent in the suit.[1] There were certain very definite limitations to the jurisdiction of the chancillerías. By *pragmáticas* of 1561 and 1568 they were forbidden to take cognizance of any case arising out of the decrees of the Council of Trent, such matters being exclusively reserved for the Consejo Real; and the seventy-fourth petition of the Cortes of Madrid in 1583 was erected into a law which inhibited them from concerning themselves with "lo que se huviere vendido" in the Consejo de Hacienda.[2]

The Audiencias of Galicia and of Seville were lesser bodies. The area of their jurisdiction was smaller, and they were forbidden to deal with cases of *hidalguia*; in other respects their competence was virtually identical with that of the chancellerías. The former was composed of a regent, four *oidores*, and four *alcaldes*; in the latter the number of the *oidores* was six. We also find a Consejo de Navarra — obviously rather a court than a council — with full jurisdiction over all cases arising in that realm. It was composed of a regent, six *oidores*, and four *alcaldes*, and there was no appeal from its decisions to the Sala de Mil y Quinientos.[3] — There is no evidence of any important alteration in the existing judicial arrangements in the eastern kingdoms down to the time of the 'troubles' in Aragon in 1591.

Yet the composition and activities of the higher courts of the realm, important though they be, give a far less characteristic picture of Philip's conception of government than

---

[1] B. M., Cotton Ms. Vesp. C. VI, fols. 9, 9 v, 16 v. 1500 *doblas* = 2000 ducats of 11 reals each (fol. 16 v).

[2] *Nueva Recopilación*, lib. ii, tit. v, ley 79.

[3] B. M., Cotton Ms. Vesp. C. VI, fol. 9 v.

the methods by which justice was administered in the municipalities. Here we find the most perfect exemplification of his resolve that royally appointed officers should carry the king's will into every corner of the realm, of his fondness for fusing administrative and judicial functions, and of his passion for complete and accurate information in regard to everything that was taking place throughout the length and breadth of the land. The heart of the whole system was the *corregidor* and the *residencia*: both described, during his reign and shortly afterwards, with a wealth of detail, by two of the greatest of contemporary legists, Jerónimo Castillo de Bovadilla and Juan de Solórzano Pereira, who gloried in tracing back the origins of both of them to the days of the Creation and of the Garden of Eden.[1]

The institution of the *corregidores* was common to all the Iberian kingdoms,[2] but it was so much more highly developed in Castile than elsewhere that it will suffice to examine its workings in the sixty-six [3] *corregimientos* into which that realm was officially divided in the reign of the Prudent King. The office itself underwent several significant changes in Philip's day, some of them in contravention of the law of the land. In the first place the appointment of the *corregidores*, which had hitherto remained in the hands of the crown, was now actually made by the president of the Council of Castile.[4] According to Castillo de Bovadilla, this change (which had gone into effect before 1578) was due to the popular outcry against the inefficiency of some of the appointees;[5] but we may also take it as an evidence of the closeness with which Philip kept in touch with the Consejo Real. It was obviously an advantage to have its members make preliminary

[1] C. de B., lib. i, cap. ii, no. 2; cf. *ante*, Vol. I, p. 233, note 2.
[2] C. de B., lib. ii, cap. ix, no. 7.
[3] *Ante*, Vol. II, p. 147, note 3.
[4] B. M., Cotton Ms. Vesp. C. VI, fol. 10.
[5] Lib. i, cap. iii, no. 4.

investigations of the fitness of the candidates, while it was, of course, inconceivable that any final appointment should be made of which the king did not approve. In the second place, it is to be noted that the period of incumbency, long since fixed at one year, with the provision that it might be extended to two,[1] was suffered gradually to prolong itself beyond the legally established limit. Such prolongations had not been unknown in the Emperor's day;[2] but under Philip they ceased to be the exception and became the rule. The *corregidores* continued, indeed, to be appointed for one-year periods, as the law required; but at the expiration of that time, the term was often extended for two, three, or even more years, or until a successor were despatched, so that at the close of the reign it was not uncommon for *corregidores* to remain in office for five years or longer.[3] The Cortes heartily disliked the change, as productive of corruption and perversion of justice, and the *procuradores* vigorously demanded that the laws be observed;[4] but there is no evidence that any attention was paid to their complaints. The constant changes which the literal enforcement of the law would have demanded became increasingly repugnant to the careworn king; moreover, the shorter term which the Cortes desired gave the incumbent scant time in which to become acquainted with conditions in his *corregimiento*, or effectively to maintain the power of the crown.[5]

The *corregidor*, like the sovereign he represented in the district committed to his charge, was at once a judicial and

---

[1] *Nueva Recopilación*, lib. iii, tit. v, ley 4.

[2] *Ante*, Vol. III, p. 185.

[3] C. de B., lib. i, cap. ii, no. 13; cf. B. M., Cotton Ms. Vesp. C. VI (1561–67), fol. 62, "El Presidente del Consejo Real pone los corregidores en la Ciudad o Villa del Rey de tres en tres años, o mas, o menos, como sirve y hasse su officio cada uno." This is probably a chance average by a contemporary observer.

[4] *Actas de las Córtes*, xii, p. 582 (August 27, 1593).

[5] A *corregidor* could not be connected with the city of his jurisdiction by residence, birth, or marriage. The same rule applied to his *tenientes* and *alguaciles*. B. M., Cotton Ms. Vesp. C. VI, fol. 17.

administrative officer. In almost all the accounts of his office which have come down to us more space is devoted to his functions as a judge than to his duties as an executive. "He represents the person of the king," so runs a contemporary description of his powers, "and may sit in judgment and mete out punishment for any sort of crime . . . and condemn the guilty party to confiscation, or death, or the galleys, or a fine to be paid to the Cámara del Rey, and in all such cases the *corregidor* has a free hand, even though the accused be a titled lord or a noble of the realm."[1] The *corregidor*, moreover, was generally selected from the *letrado* class, though *corregidores de capa y espada* (or *sin letras*, as they were sometimes called) were not unknown, and it would appear from the eighty-seventh petition of the Cortes of 1571 that the *procuradores* preferred the latter type, particularly for the frontier towns.[2] The *corregidor's* one, two, or three *tenientes*, whom he himself appointed subject to the approval of the Consejo Real,[3] were also invariably *letrados* ;[4] and in case the *corregidor* himself was not a legist, he was obliged to relinquish the exercise of his judicial functions to his *teniente*.[5] All this is an interesting comment on the predilection of the Spanish monarchs for the judicial side, on their faith in the efficacy of the Roman law as essential to the maintenance of civilized society ; and certainly no previous Spanish sovereign had ever exhibited that predilection as plainly as the Prudent King. But the picture cannot be complete without some account of the various administrative functions which the *corregidor*, as the years went on, had

[1] B. M., Cotton Ms. Vespasian C. VI, fol. 15; also Gounon-Loubens, pp. 208 f.

[2] *Actas de las Córtes*, iii, pp. 418 f.

[3] *Actas de las Córtes*, vi, pp. 831 f. (Cortes of 1579–82, pet. 28) ; *Nueva Recopilación*, lib. iii, tit. v, ley 11.

[4] B. M., Cotton Ms. Vesp. C. VI' fol. 15 v ; *Nueva Recopilación*, lib. iii, tit. v, ley 10.

[5] C. de B., lib. iii, cap. xiv, no. 3; Gounon-Loubens, p. 208.

gradually been permitted to superadd to his primarily judicial ones, and which carried his office, in the latter half of the sixteenth century, to the climax of its prestige. It was with good reason that Castillo de Bovadilla describes him as being "with the exception of the sovereign, the highest authority in the community which he governs."[1]

As ruler, under the king, of the district committed to his charge, the first duty of the *corregidor* was to see to the enforcement of all royal *pragmáticas* and decrees, and to maintain in all respects the authority of the crown. He was to make himself acquainted with the local ordinances, to enforce those that were good, and to see that unsuitable ones were revised or abolished, though he could not take action to that end save in conjunction with the municipal *regimiento*.[2] He was expected to visit each year all the communities in his *corregimiento*, including the *villas eximidas*;[3] to make sure that justice and good government were well maintained;[4] to see that roads, walls, bridges, and other public works were kept in good repair,[5] that the streets and markets were kept clean, and that the district was well supplied with meat, fish, and other provisions, at reasonable prices;[6] and to prevent the unauthorized construction of castles or other fortifications.[7] He was to guard the royal prerogatives from any encroachment on the part of the

---

[1] C. de B., lib. i, cap. ii, no. 31.

[2] *Nueva Recopilación*, lib. iii, tit. vi, ley 14; C. de B., lib. iii, cap. viii, no. 155.

[3] These *villas eximidas* had been permitted to retain a larger measure of self-government than the other urban communities in the realm. But under Philip II the *corregidor* of the district, or his *teniente*, began to be employed as the agency for the maintenance of royal supervision over them. Once the *corregidor* received instructions to visit a *villa eximida* the principle of the *visita* by that official was established and his successors were authorized to continue to perform that function without further notification. Cf. C. de B., lib. v, cap. x, nos. 5, 6, 7; Gounon-Loubens, p. 207.

[4] *Nueva Recopilación*, lib. iii, tit. vi, ley 6.

[5] *Ibid.*, lib. iii, tit. vi, ley 18.

[6] *Ibid.*, lib. iii, tit. vi, ley 14; C. de B., lib. iii, cap. iii, no. 12.

[7] *Nueva Recopilación*, lib. iii, tit. vi, ley 18.

clergy or ecclesiastical courts, and see to it that no papal
bull or indulgence was published in his *corregimiento* except
in the form and manner prescribed by law.[1]

The most interesting and significant light on the position
which the *corregidor* actually occupied in the district committed to his charge is afforded by the state of his relations
to the *ayuntamiento*. At first glance it would seem that no
efforts were spared to preserve all the high traditions of
Castilian municipal autonomy. On his arrival, the *corregidor*, who had already taken oath before the Consejo Real,[2]
had to be sworn into office a second time by the local
ayuntamiento, before being permitted to enter upon his
duties.[3] Though the *corregidor*, or in his absence, his
teniente, alone possessed the right to convene and adjourn
the *ayuntamiento*,[4] he had no vote there save in the case of an
even division,[5] and there are a number of specific instances
during Philip's reign in which the Royal Council and the
chancillerías gave orders that the *corregidores* abide by the
decisions of the *ayuntamiento*,[6] though no general legislation
to this effect was ever enacted. Moreover, if the matter
under discussion in any way concerned his own discharge of
his functions, the *corregidor* was always required to withdraw,
leaving his *teniente* in his stead ; [7] and the *regidores* reserved
the right to meet privately if they desired to formulate
complaints against him to the crown.[8] These and other
passages in Castillo de Bovadilla make it perfectly clear
that, whatever the powers inherent in his office, the
corregidor had no legal right to dominate the *ayuntamiento*.[9]
But it is also evident that, in the monarchical atmosphere of
the sixteenth century, the prestige of his royal appointment

[1] *Nueva Recopilación*, lib. iii, tit. vi, leyes 16, 37.
[2] *Ibid.*, lib. iii, tit. vi, ley 1.
[3] C. de B., lib. iii, cap. vii, no. 18.
[4] *Ibid.*, lib. iii, cap. vii, nos. 11, 14.
[5] *Ibid.*, lib. iii, cap. vii, no. 66.
[6] *Ibid.*, lib. iii, cap. viii, no. 172.
[7] *Ibid.*, lib. iii, cap. vii, no. 51.
[8] *Ibid.*, lib. iii, cap. vii, no. 13.
[9] *Ibid.*, lib. iii, cap. vii, no. 72.

gave the *corregidor* an initial advantage in cases of conflict with the *ayuntamiento* which was nearly always sufficient to turn the scale in his favor. He possessed extensive jurisdiction over the persons and actions of the *regidores*, both during the meetings of the *ayuntamiento* and outside, and not seldom sent them to prison for misconduct.[1] Whenever they exercised their privilege of holding meetings in his absence, the tendency of the government was to regard such action as a usurpation of authority; Castillo de Bovadilla was very much against it.[2] The right of the *corregidor* to bring up any matter that he chose for the consideration of the *ayuntamiento* gave him an invaluable initiative in the deliberations of that body;[3] and the records of the Cortes of the reign furnish abundant evidence that, whatever the regulations by which he was theoretically bound, he not seldom acted in opposition to the wishes and decisions of the *regidores*.[4] He was not only the principal executive, but also the supreme judge in the district committed to his charge; and as the authority of the crown which he represented became increasingly potent, it was inevitable that he should continue, in practice, to usurp a steadily increasing proportion of the powers which under the law of the land still belonged to the *concejos*. When one remembers, in addition to all this, how many of the local offices were sold to the highest bidders, the decline of the Castilian cities ceases to cause surprise.[5]

It will be readily believed that if Philip was willing to let the ancient municipal liberties and privileges of his kingdom become gradually weakened through the extension of the authority of the *corregidores*, he was also determined to make certain that the *corregidores* were zealous and just in the

[1] C. de B., lib. iii, cap. vii, nos. 53–57, 64, 65.
[2] *Ibid.*, lib. iii, cap. vii, no. 51.
[3] *Ibid.*, lib. iii, cap. vii, no. 67.
[4] E.g., Cortes of Madrid, 1579–82, pet. 29 (*Actas de las Córtes*, iv, pp. 832 f.).
[5] Danvila, ii, pp. 451–453; J. Beneyto Pérez, *Los Medios de Cultura*, pp. 107–110.

performance of their duties, and, above all, that they remained implicitly obedient to the commands of the crown. For this double purpose the instrument at his disposal was the *residencia*. Probably no other existing institution in Spain, save, possibly, the Inquisition, was dearer to Philip than this. It seemed to be made expressly to promote the cardinal principles of his system of government : to secure even-handed justice for each and every one of his subjects, to make certain that no royal official misconducted himself in any way, or neglected or exceeded his instructions from the crown, and to give the monarch constant and detailed information, duly attested and in writing, of everything that was occurring throughout the length and breadth of the land. We have already examined the workings of the *residencia*, particularly that of the higher officials, in the Indies. A few words may be added here in regard to its operation, at the lower rungs of the ladder, in Spain.

The Emperor, as we have already seen, had tended to neglect it. He had been altogether too busy with international affairs, and on Philip's accession there was crying need of reform.[1] Under Charles the *residencia* of an outgoing *corregidor* had been usually taken by a special *juez de residencia* or *pesquisidor*, sent down for the purpose; not until he had completed his task, which sometimes required ten months or a year, could the new *corregidor* enter upon his office, and once there it was his first duty to take the *residencia* of the *juez*.[2] The Cortes resented this practice and complained of it, petitioning that the *ad interim* jurisdiction of the *juez de residencia* be abolished, and that new *corregidores* be immediately appointed on the expiration of the term of the outgoing ones.[3] Philip acceded to this

[1] *Ante*, Vol. III, pp. 185 f.
[2] C. de B., lib. v, cap. i, no. 32; Gounon-Loubens, p. 248.
[3] *Cortes*, iv, p. 436 (Toledo, 1525, pet. 55); v, pp. 511 f. (Madrid, 1551, pet. 27).

request, at least in part; but the result was that for some
time to come only *letrados* were appointed as *corregidores*,
displacing the *corregidores de capa y espada* whom the
representatives of the nation in general preferred, and that
the first months of their term of office were almost exclusively
occupied with taking the *residencias* of their predecessors.[1]
The defects of this system became so immediately obvious,
that in 1564 the experiment was tried of sending out special
juezes de residencia with all new *corregidores*, thus leaving
the latter free for the performance of their regular duties;
in 1592 this practice became general throughout the
realm.[2] No sooner had the change been made than
the *procuradores* began to clamor for a return to the earlier
system; the remedy, in their eyes, had proved worse than
the disease.[3] There were numerous complaints that the
juezes de residencia failed to fulfil their duties, that bad
corregidores got off scot free, while good ones were not
given adequate recognition for their services; above all,
there were protests about the unnecessary expense. At the
beginning of the reign the cost of the *residencias* was borne
by the crown,[4] but as the years went on and the financial
situation grew more and more precarious, Philip gradually
began to shift the burden from the royal treasury to the
shoulders of the *residenciados*, and ultimately to those of the
community itself;[5] and when it came to paying heavily for
a process of whose value to themselves they were increasingly
doubtful, it was not unnatural that the *concejos* should draw
back. Even Castillo de Bovadilla was of one mind with the
procuradores on this matter, and vigorously protested

[1] C. de B., lib. v, cap. i, no. 33;
Actas de las Córtes, ii, p. 463 (Madrid,
1566, pet. 66).
[2] C. de B., lib. v, cap. i, nos. 33, 37;
Gounon-Loubens, p. 250.
[3] *Actas de las Córtes*, ii, pp. 463 f.

(Madrid, 1566, pet. 66); xii, pp. 581 f.
(August 27, 1593); xiv, pp. 174 f.
(July 7, 1595).
[4] C. de B., lib. v, cap. i, no. 251.
[5] *Ibid.*

against the abuses of the *juezes*, above all the way in which they prolonged the legal period of the *residencia* — thirty days — in order to fill their own pockets.[1] But Philip refused to make any change. The very cumbersomeness, the delays, of the system initiated in 1564 appealed to him; if it gave rise to corruption it was doubtless regrettable, but that, as he once said, was "simply one of those evils inevitable in all human affairs." And it is but fair to add that there were many cases in which the system worked well. The practice, initiated at the close of the reign, of appointing ex-*corregidores* of proven ability as *juezes de residencia* did much to improve the efficiency of the institution.[2]

There were a multitude of meticulous regulations in regard to the conduct of a *residencia*. It was duly proclaimed beforehand, so that every one in the *corregimiento* might be given an opportunity to make complaints,[3] which could be preferred during the whole period of the *residencia*, down to the latter part of the reign, when it was ordered that they must be presented during the first twenty days of it.[4] The *pesquisa secreta*, or private examination of witnesses by the *juez de residencia*, occupied the first part of the proceedings. The *corregidor* provided the *juez* with a list of persons who might be expected to bear him a grudge, and who therefore should be excluded from the *pesquisa*; but apparently some of these persons were almost invariably summoned by the *juezes*, on the principle that the truth could be more easily ascertained from the enemies of the *residenciado* than from his friends.[5] There was a list of standard questions, forty-three in number, which were regularly to be put to the

[1] C. de B., lib. v, cap. i, no. 35.
[2] C. de B., lib. v, cap. i, no. 37.
[3] *Nueva Recopilación*, lib. iii, tit. vii, ley 10; C. de B., lib. v, cap. ii, nos. 11–23.

[4] C. de B., lib. v, cap. i, no. 24; *Nueva Recopilación*, lib. iii, tit. vii, at end, auto 101, fol. 25.
[5] C. de B., lib. v, cap. 1, nos. 61–76.

witnesses at the *pesquisa*; they indicate the high measure of Philip's interest in the political and economic well-being of the municipalities, and, still more, the universal prevalence of bribery and corruption.[1] At the end of the *pesquisa* the outgoing *corregidor*, who was required to remain at his post during the whole period of the *residencia*,[2] was apprised of the charges preferred against him, and permitted to present his defence, whereupon the *juez de residencia* rendered judgment. If the *residenciado* was found guilty, the almost invariable penalty was a fine. If it only amounted to 3000 *maravedis* or less, he was obliged to pay it before appealing to the Consejo Real; if more, payment was suspended, provided good security could be found, pending the decision of the Consejo, to which a full report of the *residencia* was always sent within fifteen days of its completion.[3] No matter what its outcome, the case had to be reviewed by the highest court of the realm before the *residenciado* could be reappointed to office, and in case the outgoing official had been found guilty by the *juez de residencia*, he always had the right to appear before the Consejo to plead his case on appeal.[4] No wonder that the Royal Council, with this addition to the multitude of its other responsibilities, had more work on its hands than it could properly perform.

We pass for a few moments to the administration of the Italian dependencies, whose Castilianization, which had begun in the Emperor's day, reached its climax in the reign of his son. The independent establishment of the Consejo de Italia, to which reference has already been made, constituted the first and most important step in this direc-

---

[1] C. de B., lib. v, cap. i, no. 260; *supra*, p. 439.
[2] *Nueva Recopilación*, lib. iii, tit. vii, ley 23.
[3] *Nueva Recopilación*, lib. iii, tit. vii, leyes 17, 20; C. de B., lib. v, tit. i, no. 254.
[4] *Nueva Recopilación*, lib. iii, tit. v, ley 12; lib. iii, tit. vii, ley 17.

tion; the course of the internal history of Sicily, Naples, and Milan,[1] and the names of their viceroys are further manifestations thereof. Five of Philip's nine representatives in Sicily were of Castilian lineage; so also were eight of the nine in Naples, and nine of the ten in Milan.

It was, of course, in Sicily that Philip encountered the most serious difficulites in erecting the type of well ordered despotism, managed from afar, which was so dear to his heart; and it was with good reason that his biographer Cabrera de Córdoba characterized the island as "fatal contra sus vireyes." [2] When the inhabitants, proud of the 'liberties' which they had inherited from Norman and Hohenstaufen times, rose in protest or revolted against the policies which Philip from Spain imposed upon his representatives at Palermo and Messina, the usual outcome was that the monarch abandoned his viceroy and retired him; then another was sent out and the conflict began anew.[3] The Sicilians were far better equipped to wage such conflicts than were either the Neapolitans or the Milanese. Barons, clerics, and cities were zealous for the maintenance of their ancient privileges; when the three orders were united in Cortes, the viceroys had to use deceit and corruption in order to obtain the *donativos*.[4] But the viceroys, on their side, were

[1] On Sardinia see p. 420, above.

[2] C. de C., i, p. 280. The same view finds even earlier expression in Scipio di Castro's "Avvertimenti al Marc' Antonio Colonna quando andò Vice Rè di Sicilia" (1577), in Comin Ventura's *Thesoro Politico* (Milan, 1600–01), ii, pp. 450–483, which begins: "Il Governo di Sicilia è stato fatale a suoi governatori dall' anno 1490. fin' all' anno 1571." Ranke enumerates (pp. 319 f.) the successive misfortunes of Philip's viceroys Juan de Vega (1547–57), the Duke of Medina Celi (1557–65), the Marquis of Pescara (1568–71), and Marcantonio Colonna

(1577–84). When the Count of Olivares (1592–95) was welcomed with royal honors at Messina, the historian notes that he was accompanied by his predecessor, "cosa non piu veduta in Sicilia." Giuseppe Buonfiglio Costanzo, *Historia Siciliana* (Venice, 1604), p. 663.

[3] G. E. di Blasi, *Storia Cronologica dei Vicerè, Luogotenenti, e Presidenti del Regno di Sicilia*, 3ª ed. (Palermo, 1867), pp. 196–265.

[4] Scipio di Castro, "Avvertimenti," *loc. cit.*, pp. 457–470, sections "Della natura de Siciliani" and "Della forza del Parlamento"; Ranke, pp. 310–312.

well armed for the fray. The administration of justice was largely in their hands, for they appointed the judges, most of whom held office for only two years, and naturally did everything in their power to please the king's representative in order to be continued at their posts; the viceroys, moreover, made good use of *letrados*, of the typical Castilian variety, to extinguish the memory of the ancient liberties of the realm.[1] There were also unending conflicts between the viceregal government and the Inquisition, which had won here for its officials immunities far beyond those which were permitted in Spain herself. In 1577 the viceroy declared that there were 25,000 familiars, and that they included all the nobles, the rich men, and the criminals.[2] When one adds to these considerations the important fact that Sicily still continued to be rent by a multitude of family feuds inherited from its checkered past, and that the whole political structure, from the viceregal palace to the lowest of the courts, was honeycombed with corruption, one ceases to wonder that the island was in constant turmoil.[3] The real source of trouble was at Madrid and the Escorial, for no sort of government of which Philip approved would ever have been tolerable to the liberty-loving Sicilians; the curious thing is that the Prudent King should not have afforded any consistent support to his representatives on the ground. Whether it was his preoccupation with other cares, or his haunting dread lest his representatives in his various dominions should get out of hand, it is difficult to say; the fact remains that when complaints against his Sicilian viceroys

[1] Ranke, p. 314.
[2] See Lea, *The Inquisition in the Spanish Dependencies*, pp. 27–34.
[3] Ranke, pp. 315 f. The judges had no other remuneration than the fees of the litigants, called *candles*, and ¡t was jocosely remarked that the decision went to him who could throw most light upon the case. Cf. also Michele Soriano (1559) in Albèri, *Relazioni*, serie i, iii, p. 353: "la discordia invecchiata è come un' infermità velenosa sparsa per tutto il corpo," etc.

reached the Consejo de Italia, they were on the whole rather welcomed than the reverse. For Philip, as for his father before him, Sicily constituted one of the most unceasing of minor cares; indeed, at certain crises of their Mediterranean campaigns, it might have been characterized as a major one. But as neither of them was able to spend sufficient time or energy on it completely to extirpate its ancient liberties, they preferred, as in so many other cases, to leave an unsatisfactory situation alone.

In Naples there is a totally different tale to tell. Its historical background, as we have already had occasion to observe, was far more favorable to royal absolutism than that of the island to the south of it; the *Seggi* of the city of Naples took the place of the ancient Neapolitan parliament; [1] the size of the revenues which it annually paid in to the crown, and the rate at which they increased, are significant indications of the extent of the royal power.[2] Its viceroys were granted a measure of authority which was vouchsafed to no other representative of the Spanish crown beyond the limits of the Iberian peninsula; [3] and the very exceptional fact that their *residencias* were seldom if ever taken may plausibly be explained on the theory that their power was so firmly established that nobody ventured to complain of them. Like their master at Madrid, they were surrounded by a series of councils whose members did their will. Contemporaries remarked on the resemblance between the Consiglio de Santa Chiara and the Consejo Real de Castilla. The Camera della Sommaria controlled matters relating to taxes,

---

[1] Cf. *ante*, Vol. II, p. 310, and references there.

[2] Between 1561 and 1577 the revenue of Naples appears to have increased from 1,200,000 to 2,400,000 ducats, while that of Sicily remained unchanged at 1,000,000 ducats. B. M., Cotton Ms. Vesp. C. VI, fols. 85–89; Vesp. C. VII, fols. 216 f. The sale of titles of nobility yielded a large income to the crown. Girolamo Ramusio (1597) in Albèri, *Relazioni*, appendice, p. 317.

[3] Ranke, pp. 340 f.

feudal tenures, and the royal patrimony. The Consiglio Collaterale — or 'papacy of doctors'' as Lippomano called it, because it was the centre of everything — was modelled on the Spanish type of *consulta* which was so dear to Philip's heart; it was composed of two Spaniards and two Italians, but one of the Italians was always at the king's court.[1] The government was particularly successful in playing off against one another, to its own advantage, the rival interests of nobles, clergy, and the third estate; and it had at its disposal a large standing army, always in readiness to suppress revolts. Altogether the situation in Naples must have been far more satisfactory to Philip than that in any other of the Spanish dependencies overseas.

The only really dark spot in the Neapolitan picture, as it presented itself in the eyes of the Prudent King, was the danger lest his own authority and that of his viceroys might be threatened by the encroachments of the power of the Popes, who had claimed, since the eleventh century, to be overlords of the realm. This danger was particularly acute at the beginning of the reign, owing to the events of the pontificate of Paul IV. It prolonged itself during the succeeding years in struggles over the publication of certain decrees of the Council of Trent extending the jurisdiction of the clergy[2] over the laity, of which Philip wholly disapproved, and against which he waged constant war in all his dominions, and still more over the bull *In coena Domini*, which limited the king's power to impose taxes upon the clergy of his realms. The obvious weapon which Philip possessed against these dangers, and "the brightest jewel of

---

[1] Ranke, pp. 335 f.; Girolamo Lippomano (1576) in Albèri, *Relazioni*, serie ii, ii, pp. 276 f.

[2] Who were very numerous. Cf. "Discorso Político intorno al governo di Napoli di Incognito Autor," in Bib. Nac. Madrid, Sección de Manuscritos, Q. 135, Ms. 5972, fols. 41–61, "Un' altra causa de mali del Regno e la moltitudine de Preti, frati, e Religiosi."

his Neapolitan crown," was his right to withhold the royal *exequatur*, without which no papal decree could be published within the kingdom; and a *pragmática* of August 30, 1561, shows that the king proposed to make the fullest possible use of it, despite vigorous papal protests that the terms of his investiture did not permit him to do so.[1] It became a question, in other words, whether the monarchy or the papacy should be able to win the majority of the Neapolitans to its support, and the decision of this issue was highly favorable to the crown. The nobility, many of whose domains had been acquired at the expense of the church, were in mortal terror of being deprived of them, and rallied loyally to the king; so also did the third estate, who feared that the clerical exemptions from taxation demanded by the Pope would serve materially to increase their own burdens. As for the clergy, though on the one hand they wished to emancipate themselves from the control of the king, they dreaded, on the other, too much domination by the Pope, and Philip succeeded in manipulating these conflicting interests in such fashion that the mass of the Neapolitan clerics gave their allegiance to the crown. The influence of Cardinal Granvelle, both at Naples and at Rome, and the fact that the papacy was so dependent on Spain at the time of the campaign of Lepanto, were both potent factors in determining the issue. Thus the monarchy obtained well-nigh unanimous national support in its struggle against the papal pretensions, so that by the end of the reign there was practically nothing left of them, save the privilege of annually receiving from Philip's viceroy at Naples a present of a white palfrey on the feast of Saint Peter and Saint Paul.[2]

The pages in the preceding volume devoted to the administration of Milan in the Emperor's day render it unnecessary

[1] Ranke, pp. 332 f.   [2] Ranke, p. 334.

for us to do more, at this point, than to notice certain changes in the situation there which came to pass during the reign of his son. Measured by modern standards it was doubtless a period of decline. On the other hand the fact remains that in the first half of the seventeenth century the Milanese looked back with fond memories to the rule of the Prudent King, and wished that he could be brought back again to live till the end of the world.[1]

The obvious explanation of this apparent paradox lies in the political situation in Western Europe during the three different periods concerned. Under the Emperor, and again in the time of the Thirty Years' War, Milan was the scene of constant fighting, but the reign of Philip was a calmer interlude when the strife was diverted to other lands. Charles's ordinances in regard to the duchy, as we have already had occasion to observe, were quite as liberal as the military exigencies of the moment would permit. He defended the privileges of the Senate and the communes, and when, under Philip, the military pressure had been removed, it would have been reasonable to expect an extension of these privileges. But that was not the way of the Prudent King. His own authority and that of his viceroys must at all costs be preserved, and it is significant and characteristic of him that he forthwith provided the latter with a *consulta*, in which the generals of the local troops and the heads of the different tribunals were equally represented, and their respective interests played off against one another.[2] He attacked the rights of the Senate as vigorously as his father had defended them, bitterly complaining that it exceeded its jurisdiction, and he arbitrarily deprived it of many of its ancient prerogatives.[3] Another accompanying feature of the period is a further decline of the liberties of the

[1] Ranke, p. 365.   [2] *Ibid.*, p. 364.   [3] *Ibid.*, p. 350.

communes, whose *consiglios* steadily diminished both in membership and in prestige. The only exception to the rule was Cremona, who not seldom refused to guarantee the *donativos* demanded by the viceregal agents. Occasionally her example prevailed over that of her more complaisant neighbors, who postponed their action until they learned what hers was to be, and it is incidentally worth noting that while the annual revenues from the royal treasury in Naples apparently increased between 1561 and 1577 from 1,200,000 ducats to 2,400,000 ducats, those in Milan remained constant at 800,000.[1]

The opposition which the monarch occasionally encountered, in matters financial, from the municipalities was but trifling compared with that which he met, at least during part of the reign, at the hands of the Milanese archbishops. In so far as the public liberties within the duchy were preserved at all, it was indeed largely due to the conflict of the highest spiritual and temporal authorities there.[2] The protagonist of this struggle was the celebrated Carlo Borromeo, nephew of Pius IV and hero of the Counter-Reformation, who was raised to the see of Milan in 1560, at the age of twenty-one, though he did not actually arrive in his archbishopric until 1566. Under him the pristine glories of the see of Ambrose were revived. At the outset there seemed no prospect of his colliding with the civil authorities; but when he began to occupy himself with the conduct of the laity, over whom he attempted to exercise a supervision comparable to that of Calvin over the Genevese, the government complained that he was exceeding his jurisdiction, and open war was soon declared. The moral ascendency of Borromeo gave him a tremendous initial

[1] Ranke, pp. 360–363; B. M., Cotton Ms. Vesp. C. VI, fol. 87; Vesp. C. VII, fol. 216,   [2] Ranke, pp. 358 f,

advantage, and he was fearless in his use of the power of excommunication; but the viceroy was also strong in the possession of military resources, and for some years there was a battle royal between them.[1] As long as Borromeo was in office the side that he represented was consistently victorious, and Philip's viceroy, the Duke of Alburquerque, was reduced to the extremity of seeking absolution at the hands of Pope Pius V.[2] But after Borromeo's death in 1584 the tide turned the other way. His successors were quite unworthy of him, and when one of them proposed to excommunicate Juan Fernández de Velasco, the ablest of all Philip's representatives in the Milanese,[3] the Pope not only refused to support him, but even gave orders that the excommunication be not pronounced. From that time royal authority was permanently reëstablished. Though the power of the archbishop may have henceforth constituted an annoyance, it never really threatened.[4]

Philip's reign saw no important modification in the organization of the Spanish army which he had inherited from his father. The rebellion of the Granadan Moriscos (1567–71), which necessitated the recall of a number of veterans from Italy to suppress it, showed the imperative need of a new *alistamiento* for the increase of the available forces within the realm; but it was not till 1590 that the plan for it was approved by the Consejo and put into active operation.[5] Twenty-three new *tercios* for service abroad were created by

---

[1] Ranke, pp. 352–354; Lea, *Inquisition in the Spanish Dependencies*, pp. 123–135. It is to be noted that popular opposition kept Philip from establishing the Spanish Inquisition in Milan; but the papal and episcopal inquisitions worked together with such harmony and vigor that, as Lea remarks, the Milanese profited little by their victory over the king.

[2] Ranke, p. 354.
[3] See biographical sketch in Pedro Salazar de Mendoza, *Origen de las Dignidades Seglares de Castilla y Leon* (Toledo, 1618), fols. 130 v–131.
[4] Ranke, pp. 358 f. A formal *concordia* between the secular and ecclesiastical jurisdictions was established in 1615.
[5] Danvila, ii, p. 449.

Philip between 1566 and 1597, but many of these had only temporary existence, especially those formed for the acquisition of Portugal.[1] The plain fact of the matter was that though Philip was obliged to use soldiers, he never really liked them ; this, and his inability to pay his troops on time,[2] were the underlying reasons for the decay of the ancient military spirit of Spain, which is one of the most significant phenomena of the period. Lack of leadership was also doubtless a contributory cause of the decline. Philip would gladly have Castilianized the command of his army, like everything else, but the material was not at hand. Alva was the last of the great Spanish soldiers of the Emperor's day, and the Prudent King mistrusted the foreigners by whom he was succeeded, particularly Alexander of Parma.[3]

Yet the terror of the infantry created by Gonsalvo continued to hold Europe in its grip till the end of the Thirty Years' War. The most eloquent testimonies to its efficiency were paid in the Emperor's time ;[4] but there is plenty of contemporaneous evidence, in Philip's day and even later, that other nations still regarded it as unconquerable, and the consensus of modern opinion ranks it higher than any other army in Europe down to the peace of Vervins in 1598. Doubtless its deficiencies would have been sooner revealed

[1] Ballesteros, iv, 2, pp. 89 f.

[2] Ballesteros, iv, 2, pp. 83–85. Apparently the outrages of the Spanish soldiery in the Netherlands — largely due, as we have seen, to lack of pay — had got Philip's army such an ugly reputation before 1580, that he determined, if possible, to prevent their recurrence when he invaded Portugal. The elaborate edict of Cantillana (June 28, 1580: printed in S. I., ii, pp. 383–388) was put forth to effect this end, but the conduct of Alva's *tercios*, after they had crossed the frontier (cf. *ante*, p. 362), would seem to afford convincing proof that it actually accomplished nothing. Yet the soldiers murmured that they had won a kingdom in fifty-eight days as the kingdom of Heaven is won, that is, by fasting on bread and water. Conestaggio (1585), fol. 199 v. On conditions in the later years of the reign and the mutinies of the unpaid troops, see two studies by Philippe van Isacker, "L'organisation et la situation de l'armée espagnole aux Pays-Bas" and "Les mutineries militaires aux Pays-Bas à la fin du XVIᵉ siècle," in University of Louvain, *Annuaire*, 1907, pp. 389–393 ; 1909, pp. 469–480.

[3] Cf. Forneron, iv, pp. 42–44 ; *infra*, pp. 619 f.

[4] Ballesteros, iv, 2, pp. 80, 82, 92.

had the campaigns which it fought in the Netherlands and in Northern France been of larger size, so that considerations of strategy could have come into play ; but rarely, if ever, were more than 40,000 men engaged. On land, at least, the Spanish forces maintained their preëminence.[1]

On the sea, of course, there was another tale to tell. After the defeat of the Armada the naval forces of the realm were, at least temporarily, paralyzed ; and if another fleet of fighting ships was constructed in the Spanish ports before the end of the reign,[2] it was accomplished rather despite than because of the wishes of the king. The fact is that Philip never comprehended, until too late, the importance for his empire of the control of the sea, and neglected to take the most obvious measures to maintain it.[3] The petitions of the Cortes on the subject were largely disregarded. The naval activities of the northwestern ports, which had been so successfully revived by his father, were suffered once more to decline. The king preferred to purchase or hire his ships in foreign lands, rather than to stimulate his own subjects to construct them at home.[4] He liked fighting on the sea even less than on the land, and the economic possibilities of a strong navy never dawned on his horizon at all. There was also lamentable deficiency of sailors and sea-captains. No foreigner comparable to Andrea Doria entered the Spanish

---

[1] Cf. Clonard, *Historia Orgánica de las Armas de Infantería y Caballería Españolas*, iv, p. 215, where the zenith of the military glory of Spain is put at the capture of Antwerp. See, however, the *Actas de las Córtes* on the unsatisfactory condition of the national defence in the later years of Philip's reign, particularly xii, p. 182; xv, pp. 64–68, 612–618.

[2] *Infra*, p. 558. In the last days of Philip the Spanish naval forces, besides the northern squadrons operating against English, French, and Dutch, comprised the 'light fleet' of eighty galleys, nearly all stationed in the Mediterranean, with their arsenal at Barcelona, and the 'heavy fleet,' twelve galleons at Lisbon and as many at Seville with the necessary complement of smaller vessels, for the protection of the trade to the East and West Indies. Agostino Nani (1598) in Albèri, *Relazioni*, serie i, v, p. 488.

[3] C. Fernández Duro, *Armada Española*, iii, pp. 173–182.

[4] Ballesteros, iv, 2, p. 104.

service during his reign, and Álvaro de Bazán was the last of
the old Castilian sea-dogs.   The dying-out of the great race
of empire-builders in Spain is perhaps exemplified more
tragically than anywhere else in the story of the decline and
fall of her navy and her consequent loss of the command of
the sea.

If Philip hated to fight, he dearly loved to negotiate ; his
reign is the greatest of all periods in the history of Spanish
diplomacy.   Firm foundations for its triumph and prestige
had been laid by the Catholic Kings, but under the Emperor
most of the important posts had been given to Flemings and
Italians, while the Spaniards were elbowed aside ; in no
branch of the government service was there a better excuse
for Philip to pursue his favorite policy of Castilianization.
We may well believe that he did not suffer the opportunity to
escape him ; though the foreign element was not absolutely
eliminated, all the really important ambassadors of the reign
were of ancient Castilian lineage, and Spanish diplomacy was
once more in Spanish hands.   The average level of his representatives abroad, particularly in France and in England,
was exceedingly high ; the best of them, such as Álava and
Bernardino de Mendoza,[1] challenge comparison with the
greatest names among the ambassadors of modern times.
Many of their methods were doubtless such as would not be
tolerated today.   They spied, and they plotted.   They started
insurrections and even commanded rebellious troops ;[2]
but the ethics of their profession had not yet been
established ; they were really no worse, but merely more
effective, than their rivals and contemporaries of other lands.

[1] See the monograph of A. Morel-
Fatio, "D. Bernardino de Mendoza,"
in *B. H.*, viii (1906), pp. 20–70, 129–
147.

[2] Ballesteros, iv, 2, pp. 115 f., and
references there.

To their efforts and activities it was primarily due that the magnificent bluff of Spanish preponderance was so successfully maintained for a long half century after the Prudent King had been in his grave. They furnished notable examples, to be followed in the succeeding generations by such men as the masterful Gondomar at the court of James I, and the haughty Peñaranda at the Congress of Westphalia. Their achievements seem the more remarkable when we consider that they, like the army and the navy, were perpetually in difficulties because of the shortage of funds. Bernardino de Mendoza had to pawn his jewels and his silver in the service of his master before finally returning from Paris to Madrid.[1]

The prevailing impression of the majority of foreign visitors to the Spain of Philip II was unquestionably that of the power and prestige of the Roman Catholic church. There were clerics everywhere, and their influence seemed all-pervasive. Yet it would be a grave error to conceive of the government of the Prudent King as 'priest-ridden' in the ordinary sense of the term; his conception of the monarchy was far too exalted to permit of that. We have already had occasion to point out how zealous he was to defend his royal prerogative against papal encroachments. Like many other strong monarchs in the history of Europe, he expected Rome to reward his unswerving loyalty to the faith with virtual control of the church within his own dominions. His ideal was to have church and state march hand in hand, both under his own guidance, and each lending to the other its indispensable support.

If we keep these fundamental ideas clearly in mind, it is easy to see the reason for Philip's well known predilection for

---

[1] Ballesteros, iv, 2, p. 116; Morel-Fatio, *loc. cit.*, p. 62.

the Spanish Inquisition. It seemed to embody the main
principles of his life. On the one hand it was the relentless
foe of heresy and dangerous innovation; on the other it
fortified the absolutism of the crown. In the latter part of
the Emperor's reign it had not been in a flourishing state.
Charles's many absences had not helped it, and the avaricious
Inquisitor-General Hernando de Valdés, who had evaded his
share of the forced loan demanded of the clergy, was perilously near disgrace. Something was desperately needed to
restore his prestige and that of the institution over whose
activities he presided, and in 1557–58 that need was at least
temporarily supplied by the discovery of the two small Protestant communities in Seville and Valladolid, to whose
extirpation he devoted himself in 1559. The number of
victims, both reconciled and relaxed, was not very great;[1]
but the work was so thoroughly done that, save for a few
sporadic instances, we hear nothing more of Spanish Protestantism during the remainder of the reign; indeed the
chief significance of the whole episode was that it served to
tide the Inquisition over a danger point in its existence, when
it threatened to perish for lack of fuel to feed its flames. But
Valdés was not yet satisfied. At all costs he must make
certain of the support of the Prudent King. He also was most
desirous to feed fat an ancient grudge against a man who had
recently and most unexpectedly been elevated to a post which
he had coveted for himself, Bartolomé de Carranza, since
1557 archbishop of Toledo, and Carranza, accordingly, was
accused before the Suprema of having expressed heretical
opinions in his Commentaries on the Catechism. There was
not the slightest basis for the charge. Carranza was an
ardent advocate of reform within the church. That he had no
sympathy with Protestantism is proved by his career in Eng-

---

[1] See pp. 78 f., *supra*.

land, where, if we may believe his boast, he burnt, reconciled, or drove from the realm 30,000 heretics, and brought back 2,000,000 souls to the faith.[1] But Valdés was fortunate in being supported in his attack by Melchior Cano,[2] who enjoyed the unlimited confidence of the king, and he finally succeeded in poisoning Philip's ear against Carranza. Not only did the king suffer the trial to proceed ; when the papacy intervened, he did his utmost to prevent the case from being sent to Rome. That it was sent there at last, after a delay of seven years, that the final verdict was so much milder than the Inquisition desired, and that Valdés was ultimately forced to resign his position, are, for our present purposes, comparatively unimportant ; the main fact that demands our attention here is that the affair committed Philip irrevocably to the cause of the Holy Office against all who attacked it both at home and abroad, as the strongest bulwark of the omnipotence of the crown. From that time onward its 'supereminence' was doubly assured, and it was utilized at will, not only for the extirpation of potential enemies of the church, but for the suppression of political unrest.[3]

The influence of the church was naturally predominant, as it was in all other Catholic countries during the age of the Counter-Reformation, in education and in learning, in culture and in art. The universities were largely controlled by Jesuits and Dominicans, who regulated the subjects taught and the methods of teaching them. But it would be quite wrong to think of the reign of the Prudent King as a period of intellectual stagnation. On the contrary it is characterized throughout by a burning interest in scholar-

[1] Lea, *History of the Inquisition of Spain*, ii, p. 49. Carranza had been sent to England with Philip in 1554, became confessor to Queen Mary, and labored earnestly for the reëstablish- ment of Roman Catholicism, particularly at Oxford.
[2] Cf. *ante*, p. 58.
[3] Lea, *Inquisition of Spain*, ii, pp. 48–90.

ship; it ushers in, even if it does not last to see the culmination of, the golden age of Spanish literature.[1] That
such things should have been possible in an atmosphere of
unquestioned clerical predominance, is but one of a number of
convincing refutations of the theory, not yet extinct, that the
tendencies of the Romish church have always been obscu-
rantist.[2] That they should have occurred in an age of
political and economic decline is but another illustration of a
phenomenon observable in many other countries, at many
other epochs, ever since the days of the Roman Empire.
The greatest periods of intellectual and artistic development
have tended on the whole to follow rather than to coincide
with those of the most notable political achievement.

The greatest works of scholarship in the reign were produced in the field of history, theology, and law; nearly all of
them were of the ponderous, monumental type which was to
become prevalent throughout Western Europe in the seventeenth century. In history the greatest names are those of
Ambrosio de Morales (1513–91) and of Jerónimo de Zurita
(1512–80). The former was appointed to the post of official
chronicler in 1563, and continued the work of Florian de
Ocampo; the latter was secretary of the Inquisition, and in
1548 was elected the first *coronista* of Aragon by the unanimous vote of the Cortes.[3] Both are notable for their patient
zeal in the search and use of manuscripts and inscriptions, and
for their daring rejection of unproven legends; indeed they
may be justly regarded as the founders of critical historical

[1] "In der Literatur wurden die
Spanier unter der Regierung Philipps
II. erst recht das herrschende Volk
Europas." Martin Philippson, *West-
europa im Zeitalter von Philipp II.,
Elisabeth, und Heinrich IV.* (Berlin,
1882), p. 373. On the influence of
Spanish literature in France at this
time see J. Mathorez, "Les Espagnols
et la crise nationale française à la fin

du XVIe siecle," in *B. H.*, xviii (1916),
pp. 97–100.
[2] A concise summary of the repres-
sive influence of the Spanish Inquisition
on the literature of this period is given
by Philippson, *op. cit.*, p. 375.
[3] Ballesteros, iv, 2, pp. 316, 321;
D. J. Dormer, *Progressos de la Historia
en el Reyno de Aragon, y Elogios de
Geronimo Zurita* (Saragossa, 1680).

scholarship in Spain. And there were also a host of lesser lights.[1] On the borderline between history, theology, and political science stands the imposing figure of the great Jesuit Juan de Mariana (1535–1624), whose work was largely done in the reign of the Prudent King, though most of it was published in that of his successor. He was a paragon of learning, and a master of Spanish prose. To characterize as 'scientific'[2] a history which begins with the statement that "Tubal, the son of Japheth, was the first man that came to Spain" seems to us excessive; but when Mariana deals with contemporary affairs his views become at least modern, if not positively revolutionary. In his treatise *De Rege et Regis Institutione*, which was published in 1599 with the sanction of the Spanish crown, he justified the slaughter of tyrants in extreme cases; and when Ravaillac, who was popularly supposed to have been influenced by the book, assassinated Henry IV in 1610, it was burnt by the public executioner in Paris.[3] In theology the outstanding figures are those of the Jesuits, Luis Molina (1535–1600) and his follower Francisco Suárez (1548–1617), who attempted to reconcile the doctrine of predestination with the ideas of the freedom of the will then current in the church of Rome. Suárez also earned an unenviable fame in England in the succeeding reign by his treatise against the oath of allegiance which James I demanded of his subjects.[4] And since theology and law marched hand in hand in the Spain of the Prudent King, it is not surprising to find priests like Suárez distinguishing themselves also in the field of international

[1] Many of these are mentioned in the bibliographical notes in the present and the preceding volume.

[2] So Ballesteros, iv, 2, p. 321.

[3] Ticknor, *History of Spanish Literature*, 6th ed., iii, pp. 206–214; Georges Cirot, *Mariana historien* (Bordeaux, 1905); John Laures, *The Political Economy of Juan de Mariana* (New York, 1928).

[4] Ballesteros, iv, 2, pp. 266, 314; *Encyclopaedia Britannica*, 14th ed., s. v. "Suárez."

jurisprudence. A notable precedent for their activities in this direction had been set them during the Emperor's reign by the noble Dominican friar Francisco de Vitoria, who has been called, with but slight exaggeration, "one of the precursors of the League of Nations"[1]; and his example was eagerly followed by the writers of Philip's day. Grotius owed much to Suárez's *Tractatus de Legibus ac Deo Legislatore*, in which the theory of the divine right of kings is refuted and the essential equality of all men is maintained. Balthazar Ayala's *De Jure et Officiis Bellicis et Disciplina Militari* (1582) is a notable attempt to mitigate the horrors of war.[2] Probably the most learned legal writer of the day — he has sometimes been called the Spanish Bartolus — was the Toledan, Diego de Covarrubias y Leyva (1512–77), professor of canon law at Salamanca. He wrote on the Council of Trent and on many legal topics, but he was by no means exclusively a scholar, for he held judicial posts at Burgos and Granada, was bishop of Ciudad Rodrigo and of Segovia, and finally rose to the presidency of the Council of Castile.[3]

The ascendency of the church is also plainly discernible throughout the reign in the realms of poetry and imaginative prose. The works of Santa Teresa de Ávila, of San Juan de la Cruz, of Fray Luis de León, and of Fray Luis de Granada furnish perhaps the most striking examples of it; and though Fernando de Herrera, who was far greater than any of them, cannot be classed as a strictly religious poet, he attains his highest successes when celebrating the triumphs or mourning the defeats of the Christians in warfare against

[1] Salvador de Madariaga, *Spain* (New York, 1930), p. 48.
[2] A reproduction of the first edition, with introduction by John Westlake and English translation by J. P. Blake, has been issued by the Carnegie Institution of Washington (1912, 2 vols.).
[3] Ballesteros, iv, 2, p. 358.

the infidels.[1] But all these names, and many others besides, pale into insignificance in comparison with those of Cervantes and Lope de Vega, both of them realists of transcendent genius, wholly emancipated from ecclesiastical limitations, who carried the fame of the Spanish story and the Spanish drama throughout the four quarters of the globe. Neither of them can be said to belong to the age of Philip in quite the same sense that Spenser and Shakespeare belonged to that of Elizabeth.[2] Cervantes did not begin Don Quixote till after 1591, and the first part was not published till 1604 or 1605; and the first work of Lope saw the light in the very year of the death of the Prudent King. Yet it was under Philip II that both men had the various experiences and adventures, both at home and abroad, which furnished the material for what they subsequently wrote. Cervantes was wounded at Lepanto, suffered cruel captivity as a galley slave at Algiers, and collected taxes in La Mancha; Lope served in the Invincible Armada. Both knew their country in the height of its glory as well as on the threshold of its decline, and they have immortalized its splendor and its tragedy, its comedy and its pathos, and, most of all, its unlimited variety, for the benefit of all the succeeding generations of mankind.

Architecture, sculpture, and painting, on the other hand, are almost totally dominated, during Philip's reign, by the influence of the church of the Counter-Reformation. The king, as we have already had occasion to observe, took a lively interest in the fine arts and directed them; the Escorial is the mirror in which his tastes are most accurately reflected. In architecture the leading figure is that of Juan de Herrera

---

[1] Henry Butler-Clarke, *Spanish Literature* (London, 1893), pp. 118–121. Herrera's best works are the *Canción á Lepanto* and the *Pérdida del Rey Don Sebastián y su Ejército.*

[2] Cervantes died on Saturday, April 23, 1616, according to the new style; Shakespeare just ten days later, Tuesday, April 23, old style.

(1530 ?–97), a master of the construction of edifices "conformable to the sombre thoughts of the monarch"; and it was largely as a result of his influence that the plateresque style, which had held the forefront of the stage in the Emperor's day, almost completely disappeared in the reign of the Prudent King.[1] In sculpture and painting the tale is much the same. The names of Philip's favorite artists, both native and foreign, have been given in another place,[2] and we have also seen that they painted numerous portraits; but fond though the king was of pictures from real life, he cared most of all for representations of sacred subjects, of the contemplative or ecstatic qualities exhibited in the works of his most characteristic religious painter, Luis de Morales, and later in those of Murillo. One curious fact is the paucity of pictures or sculptures showing the achievements of the Spaniards in the New World. Possibly it may indicate that contemporaries did not regard the American possessions as playing a part in the Spanish Empire as considerable as that which is usually ascribed to them today, though the wealth of historical material about the American lands may plausibly be adduced as evidence on the other side.

In music the reign of Philip was veritably a golden age. Its greatest name is that of Tomás Luis de Victoria (1540–1613 ?), whose hymns entitle him to a place with Palestrina in the forefront of the composers of the era of the Counter-Reformation.[3] Secular melodies were also much in vogue, and it was an essential part of a gentleman's education to know how to play the guitar[4]; but in music as in almost all other activities of the time the power of the church remained transcendent.

[1] Ballesteros, iv, 2, pp. 432–435.
[2] Cf. *ante*, pp. 45 f.
[3] Ballesteros, iv, 2, pp. 484 f.
[4] *Ibid.*, p. 486.

Spanish history is full of contrast and contradiction — at no period more than in the reign of Philip II. Regarded from the modern standpoint, in which economic considerations are so preponderant, the age of the Prudent King seems emphatically to be an age of decay ; yet even in its last and most tragic decade it produced men of genius whose names will survive forever. Certainly Philip did not stifle the life of his people. The most notable figures in Spain's military and political annals were indeed gone, but from their ashes there had arisen a generation of men of letters which has seldom been equalled and never surpassed, and the greatest of all painters was to follow close behind. At the moment that the sceptre of empire was slipping from her grasp, Spain won the crown of immortality in literature and in art.

BIBLIOGRAPHICAL NOTE

Practically all the printed material that has been utilized in this chapter has been described in the bibliographical notes to Chapters V, X, and XXIII, and in the Note on the General Authorities at the beginning of this volume; the principal exceptions to this statement are Juan Beneyto Pérez, *Los Medios de Cultura y la Centralización bajo Felipe II* (Madrid, 1927), Carlos Riba y García, *El Consejo Supremo de Aragón en el Reinado de Felipe II* (Valencia, 1914), and other lesser monographs which have been cited only once or twice. It therefore seems appropriate to devote this note to a description of the most important manuscripts from which material has been drawn.

Of these the greater part have been found in the Sección de Manuscritos in the Biblioteca Nacional at Madrid, in the Archivo Histórico Nacional, in the archives at Simancas, and in the British Museum. The most generally useful documents that I have found are as follows: (1) Agustín Álvarez de Toledo, "Discurso sobre los Consejos," in the Archivo Histórico Nacional, Q. 104, Ms. 5791, fols. 157–190, and also in the Biblioteca Nacional, Sección de Manuscritos, E. 31, Ms. 904, fols. 99–138, where it is entitled "El Govierno de Spaña." Álvarez de Toledo was a prominent *licenciado* at the court and a member of the Councils of Castile and of the Indies (cf. C. de C., ii, p. 449; iii, pp. 445, 546; iv, p. 332; B. M., Add. Ms. 28,344, fol. 317), and wrote his "Discurso" during the reign of Philip II.   (2) The "Relacion de la orden que su Magestad manda que segue en la division de el Consejo Real" (February, 1598) in the Biblioteca Nacional, Sección de Manuscritos, CC. 85 and 89, sueltos 18,722 [36] and 18,729 [17]. (3) Gabriel Lobo Laso (or Lasso) de la Vega (1559–1615), "Relacion muy puntual de todos los Consejos Superiores y Tribunales Supremos que residen de ordinario en la Corte de España, con las Audiencias y Chancillerias q'ay en España y en las Indias Occidentales, con el número de plazas y officiales que cada qual de los referidos tiene y de lo que trata," in the Biblioteca Nacional, Sección de Manuscritos, Q. 135, Ms. 5972, fols. 88–119.   The author served in various capacities at the court of Philip II and Philip III, and was widely known as a writer in prose and verse (cf. James Fitzmaurice-Kelly, *Historia de la Literatura Española*, 4ª ed. (Madrid, 1926), p. 260; *Enciclopedia Universal Ilustrada*, xxix, p. 941).   He wrote his account in 1607. (4) The "Ordenanzas del Consexo de Hazienda, y Conttaduria maior de Hacienda, y Conttaduria maior de Cuenttas, fechas en 20 de Noviembre de 1593," in the Biblioteca Nacional, Sección de Manuscritos, S. 43, Ms. 6587, fols. 1–30; most of this is printed in the *Nueva*

Recopilación, lib. ix, tit. ii, ley 2.　(5) The "Advertencias de Don Scipion de Castro á Marco Antonio Colona nombrado por Virrey de Sicilia," in the Archivo Histórico Nacional, Q. 104, Ms. 5791, fols. 233–250; this is probably a translation from the Italian; the treatise is printed in that language in Comin Ventura's *Thesoro Politico* (Milan, 1600–01), ii, pp. 450–483.　On Scipio di Castro and his works see Alessio Narbone, *Bibliografia Sicola* (Palermo, 1850–55), ii, p. 388; iv, p. 28; B. M., *Catalogue of Printed Books*, xvi, col. 209.　(6) The "Discorso Politico Intorno al Governo di Napoli di Incogniti Autor" (probably written between 1667 and 1670), in the Biblioteca Nacional, Sección de Manuscritos, Q. 135, Ms. 5972, fols. 41–61.　(7) Archivo General de Simancas, Diversos de Castilla, nos. 1227, 1406, 1760, 1810, which contain much useful financial information and advice from Philip's various agents.　(8) British Museum, Cotton Ms. Vespasian C. VI (cf. Gayangos, *Catalogue*, i, pp. 683–686), especially fols. 6–10, 15–23, 37–39, 62–63, 85–89, and 122–130, a contemporary *relación*, presumably by a royal secretary, of the different phases of the political and economic institutions of Spain, and of the state of the king's finances.　It appears from internal evidence to have been written between 1575 and 1577, and I have found it of the highest value. (9) British Museum, Cotton Ms. Vespasian C. VII (cf. Gayangos, *Catalogue*, pp. 679–681), "Acta inter Angliam et Hispaniam, 1516–1588," chiefly relating to the reign of Philip II.　This is particularly valuable for financial matters; cf. my "Note on the Finances of Philip II" in *R. H.*, lxxxi (1933).　Numerous other manuscripts of too special a nature to be inserted here are cited in the appropriate places in the footnotes.

CHAPTER XXXVII

THE INVINCIBLE ARMADA

WE have already had occasion to observe that a great change had been effected in the policy of Philip of Spain between the years 1578 and 1580. The dismissal of the last remnants of the old Eboli peace party, the summoning of Cardinal Granvelle from Rome, and the vigorous prosecution of the Spanish claims to the throne of Portugal were all symptoms of the fact that the Prudent King no longer proposed merely to rest on the defensive, but was prepared to take the lead into his own hand. And this change did not find its sole expression in his dealings with the problems of the Iberian peninsula; it was also reflected in his attitude toward England and France, and most of all in his treatment of the rebels of the Low Countries, which continued, for at least a decade more, to be the focal point of the international politics of Western Europe. Save for the six years of Alva's rule, the keynote of Philip's policy there had hitherto, on the whole, been conciliation. His representatives on the ground may not always have been able to give effect to it, but that at least was the line they were told to take. Now, however, Philip had become convinced, particularly by the news of the treaty which the rebels had made, August 13, 1578, with the Duke of Anjou, that more vigorous action was imperative, unless the Low Countries were to be lost; and in the successor whom he selected for Don John of Austria he found an able and effective instrument for the accomplishment of his purpose.

Alexander of Parma, who was given the post, was born in Rome on August 27, 1545, the son of Ottavio Farnese and Margaret of Parma, the illegitimate daughter of Charles V, who was to be regent in the Netherlands from 1559 to 1567. At the age of eleven, he became attached to the court of Philip II in the Low Countries. Three years later he returned with the Prudent King to Spain, and was educated there with Don Carlos and Don John.[1] But he never became thoroughly Hispanicized. His character and outlook on life continued, to the end of his days, to be those of the Italian soldier and statesman of the Renaissance. He followed the precepts of Machiavelli's *Prince*, and also of Castiglione's *Cortegiano*. Primarily a soldier, he did not hesitate to expose his person on the battlefield, when by so doing he could reanimate the drooping spirits of his men, but he never pushed his courage to the point of foolhardiness, and had no patience with those who did. With his military talents, moreover, he united the qualities of true statesmanship. He knew when to fight and when to treat, and possessed rare gifts in handling men ; in this last respect he offers a curiously close parallel to his great rival, William of Orange ; if he was less genial and friendly, he had greater dignity and distinction. He never underestimated the power of his potential foes, nor blinded himself to their virtues. In his letters to the king one finds none of those expressions of contempt and disdain for the Netherlanders which are so painfully frequent in the correspondence of his predecessors.[2] Last of all, he was firmly resolved to make a brilliant success in the great task to which Philip had called him, and of which, unlike Don John, he fully comprehended both the difficulties and the importance. He knew that the eyes of Western

[1] L. van der Essen, *Alexandre Farnèse,* i, pp. 1–82.

[2] *Correspondance du Cardinal de Granvelle,* ed. Piot, ix, pp. 96, 122.

Europe were focussed upon him.   He hoped to terminate,
definitely and victoriously, the great contest which his
Spanish predecessors had only embittered and prolonged.[1]
The situation in the Low Countries, at the time of his
advent to power, was so ticklish that, for the time being at
least, it was obvious that he must act with the utmost
caution.   The military power of the rebels had been greatly
increased by their treaty of the previous August with the
Duke of Anjou, while the immediate prospect of the
annexation of Portugal rendered it impossible for Parma to
get more troops from Spain.   Clearly he must have recourse
to diplomacy and avoid war.   Equally clear was the object
which his diplomacy must seek to attain, namely, the reopening of the breach between the Protestant Northeast and the
Roman Catholic Southwest, which the ineptitude of Don John
had almost healed ; to the Orange motto, *L'union fait la force*,
he must oppose the classical *Divide et impera*.   The state of
affairs after the death of Don John was not unfavorable to
the attainment of this end.   Few Protestants or Catholics
could be brought to give hearty support to the policy of
toleration as a means to political coöperation, enunciated in
the draft for a religious peace which William of Orange had
submitted to the Estates on July 10, 1578 ; and the Protestant minority in the Walloon provinces, urged on by the
Calvinists of Ghent, were now convinced that, by a little
forcing of the pace, they could carry all the southwestern provinces into the camp of the Reformation.   An account of their
attempt and failure to accomplish this, and of the futile intervention in the Low Countries on their behalf of the firebrand
Count Palatine John Casimir, is not necessary for our purposes here ;[2] suffice it to say that by clever utilization of the

[1] *Correspondance d'Alexandre Farnèse avec Philippe II*, ed. Gachard, pp. 25–29 ; Pirenne, iv, pp. 176 f.

[2] Motley, *Rise of the Dutch Republic*, iii, pp. 336 f., 375 f., 385–389.

jealousies and resentments of the Catholic leaders in the rebel army, which had been defeated by Don John at Gembloux, Farnese convinced most of the southwestern provinces that the "barbarous insolence and tyranny of the sectaries exceeded that of the Spaniards," and paved the way for their acknowledgment, at the price of liberal concessions, of the sovereignty of the Spanish king. The Union of Arras, concluded January 6, 1579, between the deputies of the Estates of Artois and Hainault and the city of Douai, "to bring about a general reconciliation with the Catholic King, our natural lord and sovereign," was the first triumph of his diplomacy, [1] and on May 17 following, in the instrument known as the peace of Arras, the terms of that reconciliation were arranged.[2] They demanded, in brief, the reëstablishment of all the autonomous privileges of the Netherlanders which Philip and his regents had attempted to subvert. The foreigners were to depart; the government was to be carried on by the Netherlanders themselves, and the king was to be represented only by a prince of the royal house; short of renouncing the sovereignty of the Spanish crown, it would have been impossible, politically speaking, for him to have conceded anything more. But in reality the peace of Arras was a victory for Philip in disguise. In the first place it provided for the exclusive maintenance, in the provinces that accepted it, of the Roman Catholic faith, and thereby made irreparable the breach with the Protestants of the Northeast. In the second, by removing political grievances, at the same time that it satisfied the conservatives in religion, it caused the latter to look to Spain as their champion in a way that they had never done before. And certainly Philip had need

---

[1] *Actes des États Généraux*, ed. Gachard, ii, pp. 454–460; *Correspondance d'Alexandre Farnèse avec Philippe II*, pp. 63–76.

[2] *Actes des États Généraux*, ii, pp. 522–536.

of all the advantages that it furnished him. On January 23, 1579, seventeen days after the Union of Arras, there had been formed the Calvinist Counter-Union of Utrecht. This comprised the seven northeastern provinces of the Low Countries ; and the Protestant towns of Flanders and Brabant, of which the most important were Antwerp, Brussels, and Ghent, soon cast in their lot with it. Its objects were the maintenance of the Reformed religion and enfranchisement from the sovereignty of Spain.[1] The Netherlands were now divided into two irreconcilably hostile groups, and Philip was henceforth to have the alliance of the one in his efforts to subjugate the other. The problem with which he was hereafter to be confronted in the Netherlands was doubtless hard enough, but he owed it to the diplomacy of Alexander of Parma that it was not infinitely worse.

The very fact that Parma had shown such efficiency made him an object of suspicion to the Spanish king, for Philip dreaded the concentration of political and military authority in the hands of such a man. He took advantage of the provision in the peace of Arras which stipulated that the royal representative in the Netherlands should be of royal blood to withdraw the administration of the Low Countries from Parma, and place it once more in the hands of his mother Margaret, who returned in the early summer of 1580 to the office that she had laid down in 1567 ;[2] it was the king's plan that her son should continue only to command the army. But Parma did not propose to be treated in such fashion as this. He knew that, under the existing circumstances, it would be fatal to separate the military from the political con-

---

[1] P. Geyl, *Revolt of the Netherlands*, pp. 161–179. At Brussels the Catholics outnumbered the Protestants; but the hatred of the Spaniards was such that the latter got the power into their hands. Pirenne, iv, p. 161.

[2] Pirenne, iv, pp. 154, 179 f. The treaty of Arras had given Parma the right to retain his position, provisionally, for a period of six months.

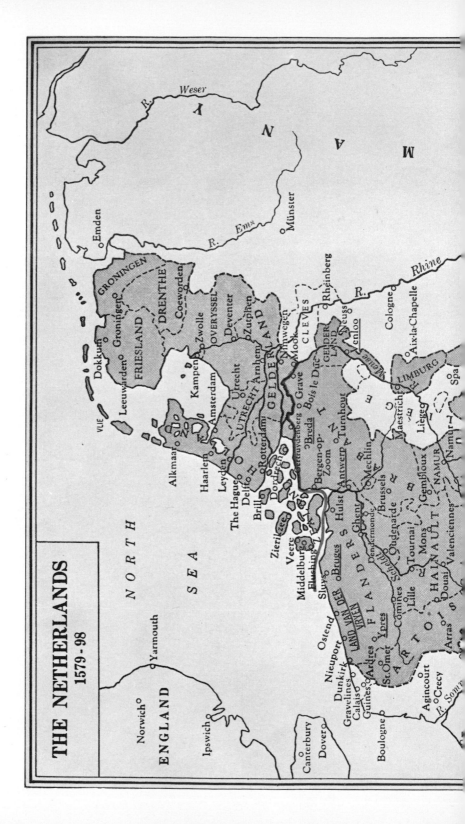

THE NETHERLANDS
1579-98

Weser

R.

Y

N

A

M

Emden

R. *Ems*

Münster

Rhine

GRONINGEN

Groningen

DRENTHE

Coeworden

Rheinberg

Cologne

Dokkum

Leeuwarden

FRIESLAND

Zwolle

OVERYSSEL

Deventer

Zutphen

Nimwegen

CLEVES

Neuss

Aix-la-Chapelle

GELDER LAND

Venloo

Spa

VLIE

Kampen

Utrecht

Arnhem

GELDERLAND

Grave

LIMBURG

Alkmaar

Amsterdam

UTRECHT

Mook

Bois le Duc

Maestricht

Haarlem

Leyden

Geertruydenberg

Breda

Turnhout

Liege

Namur

Rotterdam

Delft

Dordrecht

Bergen-op-Zoom

Antwerp

Mechlin

Gembloux

NAMUR

The Hague

Brill

Hulst

Dendermonde

Brussels

Zierikzee

Ghent

Oudenarde

Tournai

Mons

HAINAULT

Valenciennes

Veere

Bruges

Comines

Lille

Douai

Middelburg

FLANDERS

Flushing

Sluys

LAND VAN DER VRYEN

Ypres

A

R

T

O

I

S

Arras

NORTH

SEA

Ostend

Nieuport

Dunkirk

Agincourt

Crecy

Gravelines

Calais

Guines

Ardres

St. Omer

Boulogne

R. *Somme*

ENGLAND

Norwich

Yarmouth

Ipswich

Canterbury

Dover

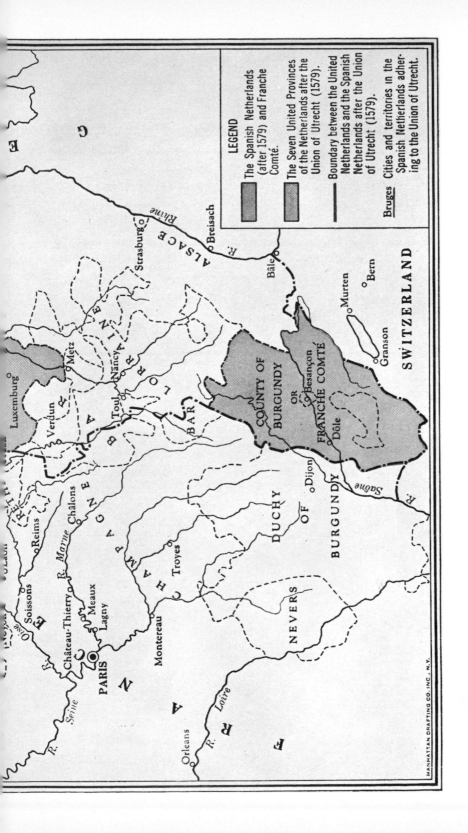

LEGEND

The Spanish Netherlands (after 1579) and Franche Comté.

The Seven United Provinces of the Netherlands after the Union of Utrecht (1579).

Boundary between the United Netherlands and the Spanish Netherlands after the Union of Utrecht (1579).

Bruges Cities and territories in the Spanish Netherlands adhering to the Union of Utrecht.

GE

Luxemburg

Strasburg

ALSACE

R. Rhine

Breisach

Metz

Verdun

Nancy

Toul

LORRAINE

BAR

Reims

Soissons

Châlons

R. Marne

Château-Thierry

Meaux

Lagny

CHAMPAGNE

Troyes

Montereau

PARIS

R. Seine

R. Oise

NEVERS

Dijon

DUCHY OF BURGUNDY

COUNTY OF BURGUNDY OR FRANCHE COMTÉ

Besançon

Dôle

R. Saône

Bâle

Granson

Murten

Bern

SWITZERLAND

F R A N C E

R. Loire

Orleans

trol, and he was determined to regain the latter. He had a number of painful interviews with his jealous mother,[1] but expediency was so plainly on his side that she and Philip were ultimately obliged to give way. In December, 1581, the provisions of the peace of Arras were violated by his official reinstatement in the government of the Low Countries — an interesting evidence of the futility of the concessions it vouchsafed to the Netherlanders in comparison with the solid advantages which it obtained for the king.[2] Meantime, while Parma plotted to regain political control, he continued his military preparations. Until May, 1579, when the peace of Arras was signed, he could still use foreign troops, and though Spaniards were no longer available, he purchased the services of some 30,000 Germans; with their aid he captured the city of Maestricht on the Meuse, after a four months' siege, on June 29. This triumph was stained by outrages reminiscent of those of the days of the Duke of Alva; nevertheless, it caused several towns which had hitherto wavered between the two camps to declare for reconciliation with Spain.[3] In the succeeding months Parma was obliged, under the terms of the peace of Arras, to send off his foreign mercenaries and create a new army out of the loyal Catholics on the ground. It was a puny force in comparison with the German levies whom he had been obliged to dismiss, and it failed miserably in an attempt to keep the Duke of Anjou from getting into the Netherlands and relieving Cambray.[4] But lack of support from France, and desire to visit Queen Elizabeth of England, prevented Anjou from pushing his advantage; in October, 1581, he took his departure, and thus gave Parma a chance to attack Tournai, the sole important

---

[1] *Correspondance du Cardinal de Granvelle*, ed. Piot, viii, pp. 364–367.

[2] Pirenne, iv, pp. 179 f.

[3] *Correspondance d'Alexandre Farnèse*, pp. 106 f.; Pirenne, iv, p. 160.

[4] August 19, 1587. *Documents concernant les relations entre le Duc d'Anjou et les Pays-Bas*, ed. P. L. Muller and A. Diegerick, iv, pp. 163–180; Pirenne, iv, p. 176.

city in the Southwest which remained friendly to the Union of Utrecht. The place fell on November 30, 1581, and the terms of its capitulation, in sharp contrast to the horrors enacted at Maestricht, are a significant evidence of the fact that Parma and the more enlightened outlook and policy which he represented were now firmly in the saddle. The garrison was permitted to march out with the honors of war. The citizens, in return for a levy of 200,000 florins, were allowed to remain unmolested in their persons and goods. Even the Protestants in Tournai were given leave to remain there if they would live 'without scandal,' which doubtless meant without openly professing their faith, and those who would not submit to these conditions were permitted to sell their property and depart. On the other hand, all demands for the maintenance of the Pacification of Ghent were peremptorily refused. Parma did not propose to let Tournai be the instrument of mending the great breach which he had been at such pains to create.[1]

Before carrying the history of the revolt of the Netherlands into the stormier years that were to follow, we must take time to draw France and England into the picture. The simplest way to do this will be to retrace our steps for a bit and follow the career of the Duke of Anjou, who had now become the chief link between the rebels in the Low Countries and those outside powers from which they hoped to get support.

Since his treaty with the Estates in August, 1578,[2] the Duke had done little to justify the hopes of further assistance to the rebels in the Low Countries which he had then held out. Neither his brother nor his mother would support him whole-heartedly. They were reluctant to sanction anything which savored of open defiance of the king

---

[1] Pirenne, iv, pp. 181 f.   [2] Cf. *ante*, p. 317.

of Spain; moreover, they both of them had use for Anjou in France, where his mediation (November 26, 1580) was successful, as it had been four years before, in terminating that rather ridiculous phase of the intermittent struggle between the Huguenots and the Catholics which is generally known as the *Guerre des Amoureux*.[1] But the Duke did not relinquish his projects in the Low Countries. Indeed the chief reason why he had consented to act as a mediator in the civil strife in France was that he hoped thereby to strengthen himself for his intended enterprise abroad; and meantime the rebels continued their negotiations with him. The success of Parma's diplomacy made his help more than ever indispensable to them. William of Orange was convinced that without it they were lost. On September 19, 1580, their representatives came and found him at Plessis-les-Tours, where they got his signature to a treaty in which it was stipulated that he should be made "prince et seigneur" of the Netherlands as his predecessors of the house of Burgundy had been; and that, in return, he should bring with him to the Low Countries the alliance and support of the king of France.[2] But here the Duke was promising far more than he could perform. Henry III, it is true, had given him much encouragement in words. On the eve of the treaty of Plessis-les-Tours he protested that he would help his brother *jusques à sa chemise*. On the day of the peace which ended the *Guerre des Amoureux* he even put his signature to a secret pact to the same effect, but this time his promise was made conditional on the Duke's being "effectually received and admitted to the lordship" of the Low Countries;[3] in

---

[1] Mariéjol in Lavisse, vi, 1, pp. 199 f.

[2] *Documents concernant les relations entre le Duc d'Anjou et les Pays-Bas*, iii, pp. 469–493; Mariéjol in Lavisse, vi, 1, pp. 207 f. The treaty was ratified by the Duke at Bordeaux on January 23, 1581: Pirenne, iv, p. 175.

[3] Kervyn de Lettenhove, *Les Huguenots et les Gueux*, v, p. 599; Mariéjol in Lavisse, vi, 1, pp. 207 f.

other words, it was so phrased as to give every opportunity for indefinite postponement. Meantime Anjou began to collect his army of invasion — a motley band, for the king, alarmed by the protests of the Spanish ambassador, did everything possible to put obstacles in his way; but the Duke was so confident of success that he continued to go boldly forward. Finding it impossible to restrain him, Henry and Catharine now determined to make the best of the situation as it was, and to draw from it what advantage they could. With this idea in mind they gave the Duke just such support as they hoped would induce Philip to pay them a high price for abandoning him, and it was with a similar idea in mind that they espoused, at the same time, the cause of Antonio of Portugal.[1] But the king and queen-mother did not even persist in this new policy. The support they gave the Duke was so half-hearted and ineffectual that he only succeeded in revictualling and strengthening Cambray; then, as his cavalry, made up of gentlemen volunteers, had "only enlisted for a summer's amusement,"[2] he disbanded his forces, and departed for England to press his suit for the hand of Queen Elizabeth.

The net effect of these long months of backing and filling, as far at least as Franco-Spanish relations were concerned, had been very slight. If Anjou was to be a potential trouble-maker for Philip, it was evident that he would not receive, for the time being, the cordial support of France. If he were to become really dangerous, it would be through the backing of

---

[1] It has been well said of Catharine that her idea was "to put an end to all differences, as in a comedy, by a marriage"; and she had plans at this stage for the settlement of all outstanding questions between France and Spain by wedding Anjou to a Spanish Infanta. On August 5, 1581, she made the Duke promise, in case she succeeded in her scheme, to abandon his enterprise in the Low Countries and restore his conquests there; on September 23 following, the French ambassador at Madrid was instructed to propose a match between Anjou and one of the daughters of the Prudent King. Mariéjol in Lavisse, vi, 1, p. 209.

[2] Motley, Rise of the Dutch Republic, iii, p. 525.

England, and a chief reason why he had gone forward so boldly with his projects in the Low Countries in the face of the half-heartedness of his brother and his mother was because he had recently been encouraged to believe that he could obtain it.

Ostensibly, at least, the state of the relations of Spain and England had changed for the better since we last considered them. After having been vacant for more than six years, the post of resident Spanish ambassador at London was filled once more in March, 1578.[1]

Don Bernardino de Mendoza,[2] whom Philip selected for the task, was one of nineteen children of Alonso Suárez de Mendoza, the third count of Coruña, and Juana Ximenes de Cisneros, a niece of the great cardinal; he was born in Guadalajara in 1540 or 1541. Before he had reached his twenty-first year, he had been given a command in the royal forces; he served at Oran, Peñon de Vélez, and Malta from 1563 to 1565. In 1567 he attached himself to the Duke of Alva, and accompanied him into the Low Countries, where he demonstrated his ability and usefulness in many ways; such in fact was his mastery of the military and political situation there, that when he was sent back to Madrid in the spring of 1573, on the proverbially difficult errand of extracting more men and money from the king, he succeeded, after a stay of only two weeks, in obtaining them.[3] From that time forward he was a marked man, and when, in December, 1577, Elizabeth sent Philip a demand that he make peace with his subjects in Low Countries, the king seized the opportunity to despatch Mendoza as resident ambassador to London with

[1] *C. S. P., Spanish*, 1568-79, no. 483.

[2] Not to be confounded with his elder contemporary Bernardino de Men-

doza, captain of the galleys, several times mentioned in Vol. III.

[3] Cf. A. Morel-Fatio, "D. Bernardino de Mendoza," in *B. H.*, viii (1906), pp. 20-70, 129-147.

his reply. His selection, incidentally, was an interesting evidence of the extent to which every one realized that the fate of Anglo-Spanish relations was bound up with the Netherlands, and of the firmness of Philip's determination that his official representative in England should be fully apprised of the situation there. Mendoza did not bring with him any specific answer to the point on which Elizabeth had demanded satisfaction, and his failure to do so made his first interviews with the queen rather stormy;[1] but in general his instructions[2] were to be conciliatory. When, in August, 1578, the death of King Sebastian at the battle of Alcazar-el-Kebir opened the prospect of Spain's annexing Portugal, the king's anxiety to maintain good relations with England was substantially increased. He was going to have need of all his resources at home. Any dissipation of his energies would be fatal.

There was, however, another side of the picture. Mendoza himself was too hot-blooded to be an entirely willing instrument of the policy of watchful waiting which his master desired him to pursue; incidents occurred almost every day which ruffled his dignity and infuriated him. Important events, moreover, began to occur soon after his arrival in London, which could not fail to strain the relations between England and Spain. The Jesuit mission for the subversion of Elizabeth's throne, of which Campion and Parsons were the leaders, began its work in 1580, and continued to be a menace until December, 1581;[3] though it was despatched by a Pope with whom Philip was at odds,[4] and carried out by members of an order of which he disapproved, it was naturally regarded by Englishmen as an expression of

---

[1] *C. S. P., Spanish*, 1568–79, nos. 483–487.

[2] Cf. *D. I. E.*, xci, pp. 181–190, and *C. S. P., Spanish*, 1568–79, nos. 475–476.

[3] A. O. Meyer, *England and the Catholic Church under Queen Elizabeth*, pp. 189–214.

[4] Cf. *ante*, p. 62.

Catholic hatred, and Philip, the acknowledged lay head of the forces of the Counter-Reformation, inevitably came in for a generous share of the odium which it aroused.[1] It was also believed that Philip was fomenting rebellion in Ireland.[2] Moreover, on December 13, 1577, Sir Francis Drake had set sail on the memorable voyage which put a girdle around the globe; even before his return (September 26, 1580) news had reached Europe of his depredations in the Spanish settlements in the New World. Mendoza remonstrated — more vigorously, in fact, than Philip, in his desire to avoid war, would have approved. The queen countered with queries in regard to the purpose of a great armament which was being assembled at Cadiz; when Drake got back, she refused to give up any of the plunder which he had brought with him, while some of her counsellors mortally offended Mendoza by offering him a good bit of it as a bribe if he would smooth matters over with the Spanish government.[3] There was, finally, the question of Don Antonio of Portugal. In June, 1580, he had sent an envoy to Elizabeth to ask for her recognition and support of his claims, and though the queen was not yet prepared to commit herself, their correspondence continued; by April, 1581, her secretary, Sir Francis Walsingham, had been won over to the pretender's cause, and two months later Antonio himself arrived in England, where preparations to aid him were at once begun.[4] Every

[1] There seems to be no trustworthy evidence that either Philip or Mendoza gave any direct aid to Campion or Parsons. The phraseology of the paragraph in Mendoza's letter to the king of November 7, 1581 (*C. S. P., Spanish*, 1580–86, no. 160), in which he tells of his efforts to save Campion's life, is highly significant in this connection.

[2] Froude, xi, pp. 205 f.; Read, *Walsingham*, ii, p. 24.

[3] *D. I. E.*, xci, pp. 530–534; xcii, pp. 166–168; *C. S. P., Spanish*, 1580–

86, nos. 60, 159; Froude, xi, pp. 387–404, 442. Mendoza's phrase "fingí una carta" is translated by Froude (xi, p. 442) as "I have forged a letter," and by Major Hume in the *Calendar* (no. 159) as "I pretended that I had a letter." The context seems to make it clear that Froude's rendering is the more nearly correct; but perhaps "I concocted" would have made Mendoza's meaning plainer still.

[4] Read, *Walsingham*, ii, pp. 42 f., 51, 55, 83.

effort was made to conceal the facts, but Mendoza soon got
wind of them and reported to Philip, who wrote to Elizabeth
demanding that Don Antonio be given up; it was doubtless
largely for that reason that Antonio, shortly afterwards, was
allowed to cross over to France. Elizabeth did not want
war any more than Philip; but the force of events was driving them further and further apart, and the Spanish ambassador at London found it increasingly difficult to accommodate himself to the temporizing policy of his master.[1]

Such, then, was the situation when the Duke of Anjou
arrived in London from the Low Countries in November,
1581.[2] He was by this time a familiar figure in England.
He had been put forward, as we have already seen, as a suitor
for Elizabeth's hand in 1572, and though rebuffed at the time,
he had never abandoned hope; six years later, when he first
began seriously to interest himself in the fate of the Netherlands and needed her help there, he returned to the charge
once more. In August, 1579, he paid her a secret visit, and
was on the whole encouragingly received;[3] on the other
hand, she could not then be persuaded to give him any
assurance that she would vigorously support him in the Low
Countries. But now, in 1581, conditions had radically
changed. In addition to all the other events of the intervening two years which had threatened to make trouble between
Spain and England, the victories, both military and diplomatic, of Alexander of Parma imperilled the fate of the
revolt in the Netherlands, which it was essential that Elizabeth, for her own safety, should keep alive. Hitherto she
had had hopes that France could be brought to perform that
important service for her, but now there seemed much less

---

[1] *C. S. P., Spanish*, 1580–86, nos. 112, 121, 127, 139; *C. S. P., Foreign*, 1581–82, no. 314.

[2] Froude, xi, pp. 444 f.; Read, ii, p. 89.

[3] Read, i, pp. 176, 206–210, 376–422, *passim*; ii, pp. 19–24.

chance of this; the air was full of rumors of a Franco-Spanish understanding, and of the possibility that Anjou might wed a Spanish bride. The inference was obvious. Elizabeth must herself lend aid to the rebels in the Low Countries; she must also encourage Anjou's matrimonial aspirations to whatever extent it might prove necessary, in order to prevent him from seeking another wife. The first she did with extreme reluctance; the second more willingly — for it rather amused her —, until Anjou, actually convinced that she was in earnest, forgot about the Netherlands and threatened to outstay his welcome in England; then indeed she was hard put to it to get rid of him. She had sent him £30,-000 before he reached London, largely as a means of encouraging him to come. He got £10,000 more from her while he was there, and the promise of another £50,000 after he should return to the Netherlands, whither he finally departed in February, 1582.[1] She had bribed him to come in order to bind him to her cause; she had bribed him to go in order to keep him at his task. Nevertheless, despite all the attendant tergiversations and histrionics, this second English visit of the Duke of Anjou marks an epoch in the history of the relations of Philip and Elizabeth. It was the beginning of the end of her policy of marking time. Henceforth she was to be obliged, though most reluctantly, to take sides with increasing definiteness against him.

Meantime in Spain the influence of Cardinal Granvelle was steadily gaining ground, and Philip, in spite of himself, was being driven every day to the adoption of a more aggressive policy against his numerous foes. In his dealings with France and England, the king contrived, indeed, for a little longer to preserve the status quo, for in this phase of Spain's foreign relations the cardinal had not yet actively intervened;

---

[1] Read, ii, pp. 76-100.

but the success of the Portuguese campaign was a telling argument in favor of more vigorous action, and the place where, next after Portugal, the cardinal was most anxious that vigorous action be taken was in the Low Countries. The events of the year 1579, and above all, Parma's astonishing success in splitting the Netherlands into two hostile camps, and in winning back the southwestern one to its allegiance to the Spanish monarchy, convinced him that, by a little forcing of the pace, the whole rebellion could be crushed, and the Spanish power reërected beyond the possibility of overthrow; with that once accomplished, Spain could make her own terms with England and with France. His correspondence in 1580, both with Philip and with Farnese, is full of pleas for severity and repression.[1] To treat or conciliate any longer, he averred, would make the Netherlanders kings and Philip their subject. The effect of his representations was speedily evident. On March 15, 1580, there was formally drawn up, and in the following June published, the famous ban of the king against William of Orange, in whom Philip had now recognized the chief source of all his difficulties. It declared him to be a traitor and an enemy of his country. It put a price of 25,000 gold crowns upon his head, and promised the successful assassin forgiveness of any and all crimes that he might have previously committed, and if he were not already noble, a coat of arms.[2] It was answered, before the end of the year, by the famous 'Apology' of William of Orange,[3] and again on July 26, 1581, by the solemn deposition of Philip from the sovereignty

[1] *Correspondance du Cardinal de Granvelle*, ed. Piot, viii, *passim*; Philippson, *Kardinal Granvella*, p. 243, and references there.

[2] P. J. Blok, *History of the People of the Netherlands*, tr. Oscar Bierstadt and Ruth Putnam, iii, pp. 151 f.; Motley, iii, pp. 492 f.; Pirenne, iv, pp. 167 f.

[3] Pirenne, iv, p. 168, calls the Apology "le plus beau peut-être, et, à coup sûr, le plus prenant, en même temps que le plus habile des pamphlets du XVIᵉ siècle."

of the Low Countries by the representatives of the Estates of
the provinces of the Union of Utrecht, assembled at the
Hague.[1] Save for Holland and Zealand, which stoutly
refused to have any other ruler than William the Silent and
their own provincial estates, the Duke of Anjou was now the
official *prince et seigneur* of the rebel provinces, under the
terms of the treaty of Plessis-les-Tours. When he returned
to the Netherlands from England, in early March, 1582, he
was received with all honors by the States General, convened
at Antwerp, and formally welcomed as their new sovereign.[2]
It was evident that before long he and Parma must come to
blows.

Neither side, however, was as yet so confident of success
as to be willing to be the first to appeal to arms. Anjou had
many difficulties in smoothing over the dissensions between
the different factions of which his motley following was
composed. Despite the wise advice and loyal support of
William of Orange, he could not quiet the complaints of the
Calvinists against the exercise of Catholic rites by his own
immediate suite, or allay the suspicions of the Flemings
against the French.[3] Parma, on his side, was even less ready
for battle; he had not as yet enough money or enough men.
And so it came about that the months after Anjou's return to
the Low Countries were chiefly memorable for a series of
attempts by Philip and his representatives to remove their
principal enemies by assassination. The years 1582 to 1584
are the great era of murderers and hiring of murderers in the
reign of the Prudent King. The resources of diplomacy had
been exhausted. If war, which Philip still dreaded, was to
be avoided, there seemed to be no other way. In the Low

[1] Motley, iii, pp. 504–508; L. P.
Gachard, "La déchéance de Philippe
II," in Académie Royale de Belgique,
Bulletins, deuxième série, xvi (1863),
pp. 573–591.
[2] Blok, iii, p. 161; Geyl, p. 183.
[3] Pirenne, iv, pp. 182 f.

Countries the publication of the ban against Orange had, of course, furnished the king and Parma with a host of applicants for the ugly task for which it promised reward. The first of them to make the attempt was the Basque, Jean Jaureguy, who tried to kill William with a pistol on March 18, at Antwerp, and was slain by the prince's attendants on the spot.[1] Orange was badly wounded, but finally recovered; the incident, however, did great harm, for the time being, to the cause of the Duke of Anjou, for the mass of the population, with their memories of Coligny and St. Bartholomew, were at first convinced that the plot was of French origin, and were with difficulty brought to understand that it was Spain that was really to blame.[2] In the following summer, an Italian by the name of Baza, and a Spaniard, Salcedo, were caught in an attempt to poison both Orange and Anjou, and confessed that they had both been hired by Parma for the purpose;[3] and three other plots to kill Orange, all of them instigated by Philip or his minions, were detected and foiled before the final and successful one in July, 1584. And it was not merely in the Netherlands that the Spanish government planned to use hired assassins. In England Mendoza, egged on by the Jesuits, Creighton and Parsons, got closely in touch with all the disaffected Catholics in the realm, and dabbled in plots for the murder of Elizabeth. In this case it seems probable that Philip rather sought to restrain than to encourage the efforts of his ambassador. Despite the decision of the Consejo in 1571,[4] he could not bring himself to regard the assassination of a reigning, if heretical, sovereign, like the queen of England, in quite the same light as that of an arrant rebel like William of Orange;

---

[1] Motley, iii, pp. 538–549.

[2] *Ibid.*, iii, p. 540; Blok, iii, p. 162.

[3] Motley, iii, p. 558; *Correspondance de Guillaume le Taciturne*, ed. L. P. Gachard

(Brussels, 1847-66, 6 vols.), vi, pp. lxxii-lxxviii.

[4] *Ante*, p. 293.

on the other hand, it would appear that he gave his endorsement to a scheme for that purpose which originally emanated from the Duke of Guise.[1] In any case, the confession that was racked out of Francis Throgmorton in November, 1583, showed that Mendoza had been sufficiently implicated in various treasonable designs to make it undesirable that he should remain any longer in England ; in January, 1584, he was ordered out of the realm.[2] The post that he left vacant in London was not to be filled again during the lifetime of the Prudent King, and Mendoza was promptly transferred as Spanish ambassador to Paris.

While Philip's campaign of assassination was developing, the weakness and incompetence of the Duke of Anjou became more and more painfully evident. Seldom, if ever, in history has a hard-pressed nation called in a more unworthy deliverer. The troops which he had raised in France were almost useless, and totally failed to prevent Parma from capturing Oudenarde [3] (July 5, 1582) ; moreover, it soon became clear that Henry III would not send him any more, for the Valois court had by this time turned against him. Since it was thus obvious that Anjou would be unable to redeem his promises in the treaty of Plessis-les-Tours, the Netherlanders felt themselves absolved from the necessity of keeping theirs. Though the urgency of Orange, who still felt that the French alliance was the only hope of salvation, had persuaded them to give him official recognition as their sovereign lord, they showed him no real respect, and soon refused to obey him ; by midsummer, 1582, the queen of England began to complain of the scant support accorded to her lover.[4] The treatment that the Netherlanders gave Anjou not unnatu-

[1] Read, ii, pp. 382–384, and references there; A. O. Meyer, *England and the Catholic Church*, pp. 258 ff.

[2] *D. I. E.*, xcii, pp. 528–532; *C. S. P., Spanish*, 1580–86, no. 366.

[3] Pirenne, iv, p. 182, and references there.

[4] *Archives de la Maison d'Orange-Nassau*, première série, viii, pp. 120–122.

rally embittered his feelings towards them.   He had no real
use for them, save as a means to enable him to wear a crown.
With their aims and ideals, both political and religious, he
was almost as unsympathetic as was Philip of Spain.   The
situation, so he told his French followers in January, 1583,
had become intolerable, and there were but two ways out of
it.   Either he must retire from the Netherlands for good,
which would disgrace him, or he must assert his authority
there in such fashion that it would not be questioned again.[1]
A plan was therefore concocted whereby his French troops,
which he had brought into the Low Countries in order to
fight the Spaniards, should simultaneously seize possession
of the principal towns in Flanders at the expense of the
native garrisons.   Detachments were despatched to deal
with the smaller places; Antwerp the Duke reserved to
himself as his 'special prey.'   On January 17 he gathered
3000 of his men before its walls on the pretext of holding a
review; at midday, while the burghers were at dinner, a
signal was given, and the French rushed into the city shouting *Ville gagnée!   Tue, tue!*[2]   A furious street fight ensued,
and many were slain, but Orange was on hand to quiet the
tumult, and if need be, organize resistance; by night time
order had been restored and Anjou's treachery foiled.   Needless to add, this 'French Fury' at Antwerp was the end of
his career in the Low Countries.   For five months more he
hung on at Dendermonde, where his adherents had obtained
control, and where Orange continued to negotiate with him
in a last desperate attempt to conserve the French alliance;
by the end of June, however, it became evident that nothing
could be done, and Anjou, on the pretext of consulting his
mother and getting help from Henry III, retired to France
amid the execrations of his former subjects, and died there

[1] Motley, iii, pp. 560 f.   [2] Motley, iii, p. 566.

(June 10, 1584) of consumption.[1] One month later William of Orange fell a victim, in his house at Delft, to the bullet of the Burgundian Balthazar Gérard,[2] and the Netherlanders were left leaderless to face the vengeance of Parma.

The latter, in the meantime, had been getting everything in readiness; now, at last, he was prepared to launch the great campaign which he had resolved to postpone until he should be certain of success. The year 1582 had been most fortunate for him. Taking full advantage of the universal contempt for Anjou, and the conviction that he would be unable permanently to give the land the peace for which it longed, he persuaded the Estates of Artois and Hainault to permit him to transgress that section of the peace of Arras which forbade the use of foreign soldiers in the land. The cessation of hostilities on the Portuguese frontier came in the nick of time; by the month of August three of Philip's best *tercios* arrived from Spain, and were reënforced shortly afterwards by a few regiments from Italy.[3] Against these the rebels had but a bare 6000 men in the field. The rest were occupied in garrison duty; militarily speaking, the game was now in Parma's hands. Yet even now he took no risks. Like the master whom he served, it was ever his policy to make assurance doubly sure. The eyes of all Europe were focussed on him; it would never do to fail. The years 1583 to 1585 were to be golden years in the reign of the Prudent King. His power and prestige continuously marched on from one great triumph to another, and the chief element in his success was the careful, methodical, systematic advance of Alexander of Parma in the Low Countries.

[1] Blok, iii, pp. 166 f., 173; Pirenne, iv, pp. 183 f., 188. Forneron, iii, p. 205, note 1, insists that the date of Anjou's death was June 11.
[2] Forneron, iii, pp. 213–219, and references there; Motley, iii, pp. 608–614; Pirenne, iv, pp. 187 f.: "un crime inutile."
[3] *Correspondance du Cardinal de Granvelle*, ed. Piot, ix, pp. 273 f.

Obviously, for Parma, the primary problem lay in the fortified rebel towns of Flanders and Brabant; not until he had finished with them would it be safe to go on into the Northeast. The only question was whether he should lay siege to them or starve them out, and careful reflection soon convinced him that the latter was the preferable alternative. He knew by bitter experience "how much money and blood are spent in sieges, and how after all the sacrifices, success is by no means assured."[1] He knew, on the other hand, that the wealth of the Netherlands lay in the cities, and that without them the countryside could not support itself. The cities, in other words, must be taken, but they must be taken by the slow and certain methods of starvation and blockade; he must rely on his engineers rather than on his officers. He must, in the first place, close all the rivers so as to cut off the most obvious means of communication with the adjacent countries and the sea. He must erect blockhouses at strategic points, and keep constantly on the watch for unexpected convoys of supplies.[2] These methods, by the spring of 1583, were already in full operation. Ypres, in January of that year, was the first large city to be cut off, and finally surrendered in April, 1584. Bruges followed on the 20th of the following May. Ghent, which came next on the list, offered a tragic spectacle of futile heroism, desperate and prolonged, but no effective resistance. When the inhabitants learned of the murder of William of Orange, they sent their condolences to Maurice of Nassau and congratulated him on being there to lead them against the tyranny of Spain. They told each other heart-rending tales of Spanish Catholic bigotry and cruelty. The slow inexorable processes of famine, however, it was impossible to defy; on September 17, 1584, Ghent bowed to

---

[1] Fea, *Alessandro Farnese*, p. 144.   [2] Pirenne, iv, pp. 184 f.

the inevitable.[1] Brussels followed on March 10, 1585, and here, as in every other case, men noted with wonder and admiration the extreme liberality of the terms which Parma offered to the inhabitants of the vanquished towns.[2] It was Tournai all over again, and even more. General pardon, preservation of all the ancient customs, trifling indemnities (in the case of Brussels the amount was remitted entirely), were the order of the day. The Protestants were dumfounded to discover that one of whom they had heard such dreadful things could be so generous, and Parma, as he had doubtless intended from the first, made much capital for himself within the walls of still defiant Antwerp.[3] All exercise of the reformed religion was indeed strictly forbidden, but the Protestants were given two years in which to decide whether or not they would conform. Certainly no servant of Philip II could have been expected to concede more; indeed Parma was so disturbed lest his master should find him too lenient and disavow him, that he wrote a full explanation of his policy to Madrid.[4]

Meantime, beyond the limits of the Low Countries, the diplomacy of Spain had been proceeding with marvelous success. The rebels still continued, after the flight of Anjou, to pin their hopes on France, and on April 25, 1584, they had recognized Henry III as his successor in the sovereignty of the Low Countries. But the king of France was in no position to assume such an arduous responsibility. Even in the more promising years that had preceded, he had been by no means enthusiastic for his brother's cause; now,

[1] Pirenne, iv, pp. 185–187, and references there; Vázquez in *D. I. E.*, lxxii, pp. 457 ff.

[2] On an interesting attempt at reconciliation made by Parma in 1585–86 through the canon Gilles de Gottignies, see Charles Piot in Académie Royale de Belgique, *Bulletins*, troisième série, xxix (1895), pp. 979–989.

[3] Pirenne, iv, pp. 187, 190.

[4] Belgium, Commission Royale d'Histoire, *Compte rendu des séances*, 3e série, xiii, pp. 102–109.

far from taking up the cudgels against Spain in a foreign
land, he found himself obliged to seek measures of defence
against her at home. On the last day of the year 1584,
Philip played the card that he had held up his sleeve for so
long, and amply revenged himself on the Valois for their
lukewarmness in religion, by allying himself with the Guises
in the treaty of Joinville, against the French crown and
the heretic Bourbon who was there to claim it as soon as
Henry III should have passed to the grave.[1] French opposition to Spain in the Low Countries could be safely ignored
for the next few years; the Valois were amply occupied at
home.

And now the eyes of all Europe were turned on Antwerp.
Until Antwerp was taken, Philip could not call himself
undisputed master of the provinces of the Union of Arras;
and until rebellion was utterly crushed in the provinces of
the Union of Arras, Parma could not safely attack the chief
strongholds of his master's enemies farther north. The city
was garrisoned by a strong force of Netherlanders, French
Huguenots, and Scots, ably led by Orange's devoted friend
Marnix, and all of them enthusiastic for their cause; moreover, it was so situated that the mere methods of starvation
and blockade, which Parma had employed so successfully at
Ghent and Brussels, would not suffice to compel its surrender.
It possessed a number of exterior forts, from which sallies
could be effectively made against beleaguering armies. More
important still, the Scheldt, on which it stands, was so
broad that Parma's few small ships were unable to guard it,
and as long as the Scheldt remained open, provisions could
not be cut off.[2] But Parma's engineers were fully equal to
the occasion; only give them time, and they promised that

[1] Mariéjol in Lavisse, vi, 1, p. 241; *universel diplomatique*, v, 1, pp. 441–
text of the treaty in Dumont, *Corps* 443.

[2] Pirenne, iv, p. 189.

the Scheldt should be closed. And so, in September, 1584, the long process began, methodical, unrelenting, inevitable, after a fashion that must have delighted the heart of the Prudent King. Clearly some sort of a barrier or *estacada* must be built across the river. The difficulty was that the cannon of the forts of Antwerp commanded the chief approaches to all available points, so that the enterprise was generally regarded as impracticable. But the Spaniards were able, at this crisis, to utilize the peculiar characteristics of the Low Countries against the Netherlanders, almost as effectively as the Netherlanders, in former years, had utilized those same characteristics against them. The 'canal of Parma,' dug with infinite labor across the marshy land of Waes, made it possible to bring the necessary materials to the desired point in flatboats. On February 25, 1585, the *estacada* was finished, the Scheldt closed, and Antwerp's principal avenue of supplies cut off.[1] The fall of Brussels, on March 10, the failure of Holland and Zealand to send effective relief, and the increasing conviction that Henry III could do nothing for them, all served at the same time to dishearten the garrison and the inhabitants of the beleaguered city ; the civil and military authorities were at loggerheads. Every effort was indeed made to break down the *estacada* and reopen the Scheldt. Floating batteries and infernal machines were sent down the river whenever there was a favorable wind and tide ; but after the most formidable of them all, constructed by the Italian Gianibelli, had failed in April, 1585, permanently to accomplish its purpose, it became evident that starvation could not long be delayed.[2] The slow inexorable advance of Parma's besieging forces in the next few weeks, the capture of the Kowenstyn dike on May 26, and of Mechlin on July 17, served to convince the

---

[1] Pirenne, iv, pp. 189 f.   [2] Vázquez in *D. I. E.*, lxxiii, pp. 7 ff.

most obdurate that surrender was now inevitable.[1] On August 17 Antwerp capitulated, on terms essentially similar to those which had been granted to Brussels and Ghent, though the period of grace granted to the Protestants, in which to turn Catholic or leave the land, was extended in this case to four years. Never had Parma shown himself greater than in victory. Never did he forget that his ultimate object was not to terrorize the Low Countries into unwilling submission, but rather to win them back gladly to their allegiance. When he made his formal entrance into the conquered city, he took pains to keep his Spanish and Italian officers away. His escort was solely composed of the scions of the most ancient families of the land. It was like the *joyeuse entrée* of a national prince in the good old Burgundian days.[2]

It has been well said that the capture of Antwerp marks the climax of the career of Alexander of Parma; it might also be characterized with equal truth as the apogee of the reign of the Prudent King, and perhaps indeed of the power and prestige of the Spanish Empire.[3] We have already had occasion to point out the great strength of Spain's position in 1578–79, but now it was far stronger still. In the intervening years the conquest of Portugal and of the Portuguese Empire had been converted from a dream into an accomplished fact. France had been immobilized, and the larger and more important part of the Low Countries had been won back to allegiance. Militant Catholicism was once more in

---

[1] The standard Spanish account of the siege is F. Barado y Font's *Sitio de Amberes, 1584–1585* (Madrid, 1891).

[2] Pirenne, iv, pp. 192 f., and references there; Fea, pp. 237 f.

[3] Philip was so delighted at the news that he woke his daughter Isabella at midnight to tell her about it. Cf. *C. S. P., Venetian*, viii, no. 284. "D'une chose puis-je assheurer vostre Altèze," wrote Granvelle to Margaret of Parma from Monzon on September 20, 1585 (*Correspondance du Cardinal de Granvelle*, ed. Piot, xii, pp. 103 f.) "que ny de la baptaille de Sainct-Quintin, ny de la Navale [which it is natural to interpret as Lepanto, despite Piot to the contrary], ny de la conqueste de Portugal, ny de la Tercera, ou aultres bons succès passez, Sa Majestén'a monstré tant de contentement, comme il ha faict de cecy d'Anvers."

the saddle, with Philip as its acknowledged lay leader. Hopes were even cherished that Protestantism might be utterly stamped out. Never had Spain seemed so majestic, so invincible. The world was apparently at her feet.

Four years later the picture had wholly changed, and England was to be the chief instrument in effecting that tremendous reversal. We therefore return to the relations between Philip and Queen Elizabeth, which we left in the month of January, 1584, when the Spanish ambassador Bernardino de Mendoza was ordered out of the realm.

The story of the conversion of the Prudent King to whole-hearted approval and support of a vigorous Spanish attack on England will probably never be fully known, but it seems certain that the process was not complete till late in the year 1585.[1] At the outset he had shown no inclination to proceed vigorously against the realm in which he had reigned as king consort from 1554 to 1558. The Anglo-Spanish tradition was, as we have seen, on the whole, distinctly amicable, and despite his initial rebuff by Queen Elizabeth, Philip cherished high hopes, during the first half of his reign, that England might ultimately be brought back into the Roman fold without a war. England seemed to him, moreover, to lie somewhat outside the orbit of European politics. Certainly he had many other more immediately pressing responsibilities. Even if he should attack and conquer her, there was grave question whether or not he would be any better off. He would doubtless be able to re-Catholicize the kingdom, at least on paper, but he could not set up a Spanish government there. The legal heiress of Elizabeth was Mary queen of Scots. Philip, a stickler for legality, would be in honor

---

[1] Philippson, *Granvella*, pp. 515 f.; J. R. Seeley, *Growth of British Policy*, Read, *Walsingham*, iii, pp. 216 f.; i, p. 179.

bound to place her on the English throne, and in view of the
Scottish queen's maternal ancestry and affiliations, her
accession in England would redound to the benefit of Spain's
traditional enemy, France.[1] All these, and other considerations, combined to make the Prudent King hold back, when
his ambassadors and admirals urged him to attack in force.
He dabbled indeed in Catholic plots, and gave the discontented English Romanists large promises of Spanish support.
In February, 1580, he even concluded an offensive alliance
against Elizabeth with the grand duke of Tuscany and the
Pope.[2] But when it came to giving actual effect to these
proposals, he could not be induced to move. Three years
later it was the same story over again. When the Marquis
of Santa Cruz had defeated the second of the two squadrons
which the pretender Antonio had sent to the Azores,[3] he
wrote (August 9, 1583) to Philip urging an immediate and
vigorous attack upon England;[4] indeed, his letter to the
king is generally regarded as the initial step in the preparations for the sending of the Spanish Armada.[5] But Philip
was not yet prepared to do much more than "take his
admiral's proposal into consideration." He wrote him,
indeed, a letter of thanks, and spoke vaguely of certain indispensable preliminary orders to be issued.[6] He also sounded
Alexander Farnese at the same time in regard to the feasi-

[1] Seeley, op. cit., i, p. 201. On the
other hand, cf. Articles of the Con-
federates in the League against the
queen of England (February 18, 1580)
in C. S. P., Venetian, vii, no. 826.

[2] C. S. P., Venetian, vii, no. 826.

[3] Cf. ante, p. 397.

[4] Fernández Duro, La Armada Invencible, i, pp. 241–243; cf. Altolaguirre
y Duvale, Álvaro de Bazán, pp. 129 f.

[5] The views of Santa Cruz on this
matter were shared by most of Philip's
statesmen and generals. In 1580 Mendoza wrote from London that the
English fleet could not withstand a

quarter of the Spanish maritime forces.
D. I. E., xci, p. 473. Parma expressed
the same idea in different words. It
was known, he said, that the queen
of England could not arm more than
forty ships; as for the boasts of the
English captains, he made little of
them, since at the battle of the Azores
it was observed that their ships were
the first to run away. Herrera, Historia
General del Mundo, iii, p. 65. See also
p. 397, note 5, above.

[6] Fernández Duro, Armada Invencible,
i, pp. 243 f.

bility of the plan, and received from him a characteristically cautious reply. The letters they exchanged are particularly interesting as evidence of how closely the attack on England and the suppression of the revolt in the Netherlands were connected in the minds of the king and of his nephew, and of the way in which they both regarded the former, from the very outset, as a land and a naval expedition combined.[1] But for the time being nothing more was done. During the year 1584 the whole project was apparently dropped again.

In the autumn of 1585 fresh rumors of an 'English expedition' began to fill the air. Lisbon was to be the rendezvous for the various contingents; the king, if his health permitted, was to go thither in person to superintend things. Gradenigo, the Venetian ambassador, was at first inclined to believe that it might all "be only a ruse to induce the Pope to grant the bull of crusade";[2] but things developed before the close of the year in such fashion as to convince him that this time Philip really meant business. The greatest of Drake's plundering expeditions, to Vigo, Santiago, Santo Domingo, Cartagena, and Florida, had left Plymouth on September 14; full reports of its first depredations had already reached the Spanish court, and exceeded anything that had been heard of *corsarios Luteranos* before.[3] Hot on the heels of this came word of the expedition under the Earl of Leicester which Queen Elizabeth had finally consented to send to the relief of the Netherlands.[4] We may well believe that this conjunction of events roused fury in the heart of

[1] Gossart, *Domination espagnole*, pp. 158 f.

[2] *C. S. P., Venetian*, viii, nos. 288, 292.

[3] *C. S. P., Spanish*, 1580–86, nos. 387, 391, 409, 413, 444, 447, 465, etc.; *C. S. P., Venetian*, viii, nos. 290, 300, 304, 305, 308, 321, 334, 358, 416; E. F. Benson, *Sir Francis Drake*, pp. 188–203; *Papers Relating to the Navy during the Spanish War, 1585–1587*, ed. J. S. Corbett, pp. 1–96; Joan de Castellanos, *Discurso de el Capitán Francisco Draque* (1586), ed. Ángel González Palencia (Madrid, 1921).

[4] Leicester left England December 8, 1585. Read, iii, p. 130, and reference there.

the Spanish king. He had been patient, infinitely patient, vastly more patient than his soldiers and sailors could possibly comprehend, in suffering the insults and injuries of England. He had hoped against hope that "time would cure all things," but it seemed, instead, to have made them decidedly worse. His mounting prestige and accessions of territory and power had neither impressed nor terrified the English pirates as he had expected; quite the contrary, they had but stimulated them to unprecedented outrages. His heretical sister-in-law had hitherto confined her activities on behalf of the rebels in the Low Countries to vague promises of encouragement and lending of money. Now she had despatched an expedition of 6000 men to their relief; she was assuming the role which France had been obliged to lay down. Small wonder if Philip was at last convinced that the game of patience had been played out, and that the great enterprise, which he had hitherto postponed and postponed in favor of every other item on his vastly overloaded programme, must be undertaken whole-heartedly and at once. When the Marquis of Santa Cruz wrote to him a second time on January 13, 1586,[1] again advising him to fit out and dispatch an expedition against England, the king ordered his secretary, Idiáquez, to request him to draw up a plan of campaign.[2]

Two months later the Marquis sent in his preliminary estimates, gigantic in size, meticulous in detail; not only Spain and Portugal, but also all the Italian and Mediterranean possessions were to bear their share of the tremendous burden. There were to be 150 ships in all, not counting *urcas de carga* and *navios pequeños*; of these nearly one-third were classified as galleasses or galleons, and the rest as *naves gruesas* or armed merchantmen; the total tonnage was estimated at 77,250. The fleet was to carry with it no less

---

[1] Fernández Duro, *Armada Invencible*, i, pp. 244–247.   [2] *Ibid.*, p. 247.

than 55,000 infantry, of whom 28,000 were to be Spaniards, 15,000 Italians, and 12,000 Germans; there were also to be 1600 horse and over 4000 artillerymen.   The land forces on board were, in fact, to be twice as numerous as the sailors; evidently, even in the mind of such an old salt as Santa Cruz, the real purpose of the Armada was to convey the invincible Spanish army to a point where it could engage, either on the decks of the ships or on shore, with the land forces of the foe. The whole cost of wages, armament, ammunition, and supplies for eight months, was reckoned at 3,801,288 ducats; of this 1,211,769 was to be levied in Naples, Sicily, and Milan, thus leaving 2,589,519 to be charged to the crown of Castile.[1]

Philip approved the plan; and by the spring of 1586 there were signs of great activity in all the ports and shipyards of Spain, Portugal, and the Spanish possessions in Italy.   No one was to be allowed, according to the king's instructions, to know exactly what the object of all the preparations was,[2] but it must have been clear to every one that some great enterprise was afoot.   Those preparations were not permitted to go on undisturbed.   News of Drake's depredations in the Indies reached Philip in April, and he promptly commanded Santa Cruz to sail thither and take vengeance; but before the admiral could depart, word came that the pirate had got safely back to England, and Santa Cruz remained at home.[3]   In the summer of 1586 five London merchantmen, returning from the Levant, decisively defeated and put to flight Philip's Sicilian squadron of two frigates and eleven galleys, which had been lying in wait to intercept them off the little island of Pantellaria.[4]   A year later the king received

[1] Fernández Duro, *Armada Invencible*, i, pp. 250–319.

[2] Fernández Duro, *Armada Invencible*, i, pp. 27 f.; Herrera, *Historia General del Mundo*, iii, p. 62.

[3] Altolaguirre y Duvale, *Álvaro de Bazán*, pp. 134–136.

[4] A. O. Meyer, *England and the Catholic Church under Queen Elizabeth*, pp. 307 f., and reference there.

an even more disagreeable and dramatic reminder of the daring insolence of the *corsarios Ingleses*. In April, 1587, Drake appeared off Cadiz, sailed straight into the harbor, sank or burned eighteen of the ships that were lying there, and captured six more, all laden with provisions and munitions of war. He then passed along the coast of Algarve, pillaging as he went, and established a base at Cape St. Vincent. Through May and early June he cruised in the adjacent waters, capturing despatch boats and preventing concentrations, and, finally, possessed himself of a Portuguese East Indiaman, the *San Filippe*, said to have been the largest merchantman in the world, with a cargo worth more than 250,000 ducats,[1] with which he returned in safety to England.[2] Small wonder if Philip's great machine was paralyzed by such whirlwind tactics as this. And just at the moment that the Spanish monarch was in most desperate need of vigorous and aggressive advice and support, he was deprived by death of the most efficient of his servants. On September 21, 1586, Cardinal Granvelle, who, ever since his summons to Spain in 1579, had headed the war party in the royal councils, and had ardently supported the expedition against England, succumbed at last to the attacks of a fever which he had gallantly fought off during the three preceding months. His influence, during the last four years of his life, had been considerably less powerful than in the days of the annexation of Portugal, when for a brief space he had literally managed everything ; the king, as usual, had grown jealous of his chief minister, and withdrew much of the authority with which he

[1] On the effect of this capture in turning the attention of English merchants to the East India trade, see J. K. Laughton in the *Dictionary of National Biography*, v, p. 1341. Cf. also p. 383, *supra*.

[2] *C. S. P., Venetian*, viii, nos. 510, 512, 513, 514, 518, 519, 521, 522; Fernández Duro, *Armada Invencible*, i, pp. 29, 334 f.; *Papers Relating to the Navy during the Spanish War*, ed. Corbett, pp. 97–314; E. F. Benson, *Sir Francis Drake*, pp. 204–220; *supra*, p. 383.

had been previously invested. On the other hand, it is undeniable that the vigorous, aggressive line of action which the cardinal personified had remained the basis of the royal policy, even after its originator had been elbowed aside; the king might make the actual decisions, but the guiding principle of them was still Granvelle's. Whether Philip would have consented to avail himself of the cardinal's administrative genius in the final stages of the preparations of the Armada had Granvelle lived, may well be doubted; but the fact remains that his death removed the only man in Spain really capable of effectively directing the organization of the vastest enterprise that the Prudent King was ever to undertake.[1]

The loss of Granvelle and the ravages of Drake were not the only misfortunes that Philip suffered during the period when the Armada was being got ready to sail. The state of Spain's foreign relations was a constant anxiety to him; and he was particularly disquieted by the attitude of Pope Sixtus V. At Rome, of course, he had emphasized the fact that the Armada was to be sent primarily for the purpose of bringing England back to the Catholic fold; it was to be the realization of a plan that had been cherished by the Holy See ever since the accession of Queen Elizabeth. It was to be the fulfilment of the motto of the Counter-Reformation, "No heretic shall be allowed to reign."[2] Obviously, under these circumstances, Philip felt that he had the right to expect the hearty approval and support of the Pope in his great adventure; he counted on him, moreover, for a liberal contribution in funds. But Sixtus V was inclined to view the matter in a somewhat different light. He did not conceal from himself the fact that, politically speaking, the expedition, if successful, would redound chiefly to the benefit of

[1] Philippson, *Granvella*, pp. 621–626.   [2] Philippson, pp. 520–527.

Spain, and that her preponderance, already intolerable, would thereby be so much further enhanced that Rome would henceforth have to take her orders from Madrid.   He recognized that England under the 'new Jezebel' was rapidly becoming the chief stronghold of heresy; but at the same time he was fully alive to the great qualities of Elizabeth, and he still cherished the hope that she might be induced by peaceful means to return to Rome.[1]   There was a long period of diplomatic thrust and parry between the Pope and Philip's representative at the Vatican, the Count of Olivares, in the winter of 1585–86.   It showed, on the one hand, how deep was the distrust between Spain and the Holy See; on the other, it made it evident that neither could afford to bid the other defiance.[2]   Before Christmas, 1585, the Pope had been prevailed on to grant Philip for seven years all the revenues of the bull of crusade, which amounted annually to 1,800,000 crowns.[3]   But on his side, Sixtus not unnaturally felt that he had a right, in return for such a liberal contribution, to expect that Philip would get something promptly done.   He was loud in his complaints of the Spanish monarch's interminable delays and of the fact that the great undertaking was again and again postponed.[4]   It would be difficult to conceive of two personalities less fitted to understand one another and effectively coöperate than the brilliant, fiery, impetuous pontiff, and the slow-moving, meticulous, Prudent King.

The situation was, of course, still further complicated by the state of affairs in England itself.   Mary queen of Scots, the legal heiress of Elizabeth, and in the eyes of all good Catholics the lawful queen of England, had been a prisoner

---

[1] Pastor, xxii, pp. 33 f.
[2] Philippson, pp. 521–527; Pastor, xxi, pp. 262–266.
[3] Ibid., xxii, pp. 47 f.
[4] Ibid., p. 48; Philippson, pp. 526–532.

in her cousin's kingdom ever since her flight from Scotland in 1568. She had been the centre and rallying point of all sorts of conspiracies against Elizabeth's life and throne; men marvelled that she had been permitted to live. But Elizabeth was deeply loyal to her grandfather's idea that the crowns of England and Scotland must some day be united. Provided she herself was permitted to live out her own days in peace, she was fully prepared to have Mary succeed her; and the fact that Mary's son, the future James I, had gone over to Protestantism in 1585 naturally tended to confirm the English queen's resolution. Mary, on the other hand, was so angered at her son's defection from the cause of Rome that she made haste to disinherit him. On May 20, 1586, she wrote to Bernardino de Mendoza at Paris that she formally handed over all her rights to the English succession to his master the king of Spain; [1] and a month later Mendoza transmitted to Philip a genealogical chart for the purpose of making clear to him that he, as a direct descendant of Catharine of Lancaster, the daughter of John of Gaunt, who had married Henry III of Castile, was himself, next after the Stuarts, the lawful heir of the crown of England in his own right. [2] All this naturally had far reaching effects on the policy and plans of the Prudent King. He was, by nature, deeply respectful of precedent and law. One of the things that had made him hesitate so long over the enterprise against England was the reflection that, if successful, it would redound to the political advantage of the Stuarts, and also indirectly, owing to their French affiliations, to that of his most powerful continental rival. Now, after Mary queen of Scots should die, the Stuart claims would lapse and Spain would reap the reward she so richly deserved. Of course these same facts would make Sixtus hold off, for they

---

[1] *C. S. P., Spanish*, 1580–86, no. 442.   [2] Philippson, p. 537.

would redouble his dread of Spanish preponderance; but James's conversion to Protestantism was a telling argument on the other side. Unless the Pope supported the expedition, there was every probability that England and Scotland would be permanently lost to Rome. So forcibly, in fact, was this latter argument advanced by Olivares at the Vatican that by midsummer, 1586, the Pope declared himself prepared to grant 500,000 *scudi* out of the papal treasury, and 2,000,000 more from the revenues of the Spanish clergy, if Philip would add another 2,000,000 of his own.[1]

By the summer of 1587, however, the state of affairs had been considerably clarified. Philip's preparations were by this time so well under way that Sixtus could no longer doubt that he really meant business; and the execution of Mary queen of Scots on February 8/18[2] served to force Pope and king, despite all their mutual suspicions, into closer alliance against England.[3] One of the chief causes of Philip's long delays had been the fact that Mary had been permitted to live so long. If England, through her means, could be brought back to the Roman fold without a war, he would be spared the necessity of the invasion which he never really desired to undertake. Mendoza, in Paris, when first informed of the schemes that lay at the bottom of the Babington plot, wished to halt all the projects of attack until the issue of the conspiracy had been determined.[4] Now, however, that the plotters had been foiled, and Mary's head

---

[1] Pastor, xxii, p. 48.

[2] The Gregorian Calendar, or new style, introduced October 5/15, 1582, had by this time replaced the Julian Calendar in Spain and most of the Catholic countries of Europe, while England retained the old style until 1752. In this book the new style is followed from the time that it was accepted in Spain; so that such events as the different battles between the rival fleets in the Channel are dated ten days later than they are in histories of England.

[3] An excellent account of Philip's reception of the news and of its effect on his position is to be found in Kervyn de Lettenhove, *Marie Stuart* (Paris, 1889, 2 vols.), ii, pp. 435–440.

[4] Pastor, xxii, p. 38; Kervyn de Lettenhove, *Marie Stuart*, i, pp. 350 f.

had fallen, there remained no alternative to war. Then, in
the second place, the removal of the Scottish queen made
Philip, at least in his own eyes, the lawful king of England,
and, in view of the situation across the Channel at that
juncture, the possession of England would be invaluable to
him. He made haste to demand of the Holy See that he
himself be invested with the English crown, and when Sixtus
demurred, he asked that it be given to his daughter, Isabella
Clara Eugenia — thus reviving all the Pope's fears of an
intolerable Spanish preponderance.[1] On the other hand, the
execution of the Scottish queen was a deed of blood which the
church of Rome was in honor bound to punish and avenge.
The faint hopes which Sixtus had once cherished that France
might be used for that purpose had now been shattered;
only by availing himself of the services of the king of Spain
would it be possible for him to accomplish his purpose.[2] So,
on July 29, 1587, a definite treaty was drawn up between the
Holy See and the Spanish crown. Sixtus promised a subsidy
of 1,000,000 *scudi*, on condition that the expedition should
set sail before the end of the year. Philip, if successful, was
to nominate for England, subject to papal approval and
investiture, a king pledged to restore and maintain the
Roman Catholic faith.[3] How fully the treaty would have
been observed, had the great enterprise been successful, may
be open to question; but it seems clear that for the present
Philip had succeeded in getting the Pope into line.

During all the period covered by these negotiations it had
become increasingly plain that the Spanish invasion of England was to take the form of a land and a naval expedition
combined, and that the fleet which was being prepared in the
Spanish ports was to act in coöperation with the Spanish

[1] Pastor, xxii, p. 50.
[2] *Ibid.*, p. 32.
[3] *Ibid.*, p. 51; text of the treaty in

A. O. Meyer, *England and the Catholic
Church under Queen Elizabeth*, pp. 520–
523.

forces in the Netherlands. It will be remembered that
Philip had consulted Alexander of Parma as to the feasibility
of the enterprise years before, in 1583, when the idea was still
nebulous.[1] In the following year he placed a large measure
of the direction of it in Parma's hands ;[2] apparently, at this
stage of the proceedings, it was only to his nephew in the Low
Countries that the Prudent King ventured to open his whole
heart with regard to the invasion of England. Parma was
even more certain than Philip that the conquest of Britain
and the suppression of the revolt in the Netherlands were
but parts of the same problem ; England was the head and
Holland and Zealand the neck and arms of the same body.[3]
The expedition of the Earl of Leicester, though barren of
immediate results, had still further emphasized the closeness
of the connection, and Parma must have been delighted to
receive from his uncle a letter written on December 29, 1585,
in which Philip declared that without full possession of a
port in the Low Countries nothing could possibly be accomplished against England.[4] But when it came to giving effect
to this idea, it was a very different story. No decision could
be reached for a long time as to what port should be selected
for the purpose. Parma's capture of Sluys, in August, 1587,
seemed momentarily to settle the matter ; but Parma, like
Sixtus, had expected the invasion to take place in 1587. He
had calculated on a rapid concentration and the effects of a
surprise. By the postponement of the expedition to 1588 his
enemies were given time to make counter-preparations and
prevent the flatboats which had been constructed in the heart
of Flanders from ever reaching Sluys at all. There were also

[1] E. Gossart, *Domination espagnole
dans les Pays-Bas*, pp. 158 f. ; *supra*, pp.
516 f.

[2] R. Lechat, *Les réfugiés anglais dans
les Pays-Bas durant le règne d'Élisabeth*,
p. 143.

[3] Lechat, *op. cit.*, p. 143 ; Kervyn de
Lettenhove, *Marie Stuart*, i, p. 346.

[4] Gossart, *op. cit.*, p. 160 ; Forneron,
iii, p. 301 ; Fea, p. 280.

numerous threats of a diversion in the form of an attack from
the Huguenots in France.   Though no such attack ever took
place, the fear of it was a constant anxiety to the duke.
But all these troubles paled into insignificance in comparison
with the increasing difficulty of coöperating with Madrid.
Philip's counsellors had worked on their master's well known
fear lest distant subordinates should get too independent in
order to discredit Parma.   They insisted that he had vast
ambitions of his own and was aiming solely to fulfil them.
By the winter of 1587–88 Philip was often at cross purposes
with the only man to whom four years before he had been
willing to give his full confidence; he sent him neither the
money nor the reënforcements on which the duke had
counted.   In Parma's eyes, from the very first, the Spanish
army in the Low Countries had been the vital factor in the
whole affair, and the sole function of the Armada was to be
to insure its safe transportation to England.   In Philip's
mind the enterprise still took the shape of a land and a naval
expedition combined, but the naval part of it had by this
time assumed far greater relative importance than he had
originally intended or Parma ever desired.[1]

Parma was not the only one of Philip's servants whose
efficiency and independence made them objects of suspicion
to their master; there still remained one more, the last of the
old sea-dogs of Lepanto, Alvaro de Bazán, the venerable
Marquis of Santa Cruz.   One of the chief reasons why the
king had steadily tended, since the beginning of 1586, to lay
more and more weight on the fleet and the naval side of the
expedition, and less and less on the Spanish regiments in the
Low Countries, was that the former, in Spain and Portugal,
was more or less under his eyes, and therefore subject to his
control.   He demanded that every smallest detail of its

---

[1] Gossart, *Domination espagnole*, pp. 158–163, and references there.

preparation, provisioning, and armament be referred to himself for final decision; never before had he pretended to such unlimited omniscience.[1] All this was gall and wormwood to Santa Cruz. He was well aware that he knew more of naval affairs than any man in Spain, and that the king was almost totally ignorant of them; to be bound hand and foot by instructions from the Escorial was intolerable to him. Yet in spite of all the difficulties with which he was beset, he gallantly carried on his work; and it is vastly to his credit that he had got practically all the fleet concentrated at Lisbon and ready to sail, when death overtook him on February 9, 1588.[2] The king was by no means sorry to be rid of him. The Marquis was not only far too independent, but also much too popular to suit his taste; in any case, his removal gave Philip the opportunity to place in command of the Armada a man of whom it may truthfully be said that such was his ignorance of naval affairs that he had no alternative save blindly to obey the commands of his sovereign. Alonso Pérez de Guzmán el Bueno, Duke of Medina Sidonia, who was given the post,[3] was the richest peer in Spain. He was thirty-eight years old at the time of his appointment, and had been married since 1572 to the daughter of Philip's old minister, Ruy Gómez, and the Princess of Eboli. He was dumfounded when he learned that the king had selected him, and protested, with pathetic truthfulness, that he had no qualifications whatsoever for the post;[4] but Philip insisted, and of course ultimately had his way. It was characteristic of him that in a crisis like the present, when time was of the

---

[1] The *avisos* which Philip received from his spies in France and England, during the summer of 1587, reveal the excellence of his information as to what was happening there. Many of them are printed in the *Archivo Histórico Español*, ii, pp. 21 ff.

[2] Fernández Duro, *Armada Invencible*, i, pp. 160 f. His correspondence with Philip during the months before his death is printed in the *Archivo Histórico Español*, ii, pp. 43–137, *passim*.

[3] *D. I. E.*, xxviii, pp. 378–383.

[4] Fernández Duro, *Armada Invencible*, i, pp. 429 f.

essence, he permitted six full weeks to be wasted in futile correspondence with his new admiral; Medina Sidonia's formal appointment as 'captain-general of the Ocean Sea' was not issued until March 21. With it was sent a long letter of instructions, which reveals, if nothing else, how completely the king had now assumed control. Some of the topics with which those instructions deal shed a flood of light on the workings of Philip's mind. One example will suffice: Medina Sidonia was ordered to take special care to prevent his soldiers and sailors from swearing, and from gambling because it led to swearing.[1]

The Duke had been ordered to set sail as soon as possible; he had hoped, in fact, to get away by the end of March, in order to avoid the strong north winds which blow down the Portuguese coast in the later spring. But as soon as he had arrived at Lisbon, it immediately became evident, even to his inexperienced eye, that another long postponement was inevitable. Most of the provisions that Santa Cruz had got on board had by this time gone bad; it was essential to replace them. More alarming still was the shortage of munitions, especially of powder. Not only was there not nearly enough on board, it was apparently almost impossible to purchase any more; the king, as usual, was loath to grant any money, and there was much talk of cheating, if not of treason, on the part of the purveyors and contractors.[2] Such were a few of the more immediate practical problems with which Medina Sidonia was confronted, and his confusion became worse confounded still when in early April he received a letter from Philip instructing him in the ways in which the forthcoming campaign was to be fought.[3] Coöperation with

[1] D. I. E., xxviii, pp. 383–392; Fernández Duro, Armada Invencible, i, p. 424; Archivo Histórico Español, ii, pp. 144 ff., passim.

[2] Fernández Duro, Armada Invencible, i, pp. 439–528, passim.
[3] Ibid., ii, pp. 5–15.

Parma and the transportation of his veterans to England
were, of course, to be the keynote of it. But Parma was
now virtually blockaded by the Dutch, and besides, the sailing of the Armada had been so often postponed that there
was no longer any possibility of effecting the surprise on
which he had counted; the English had had every opportunity to forecast Philip's plans, and were aiding their Dutch
allies to forestall them. The Armada, so the king directed,
was to remain in close formation, and never to separate in
pursuit of a fleeing foe. It was to fight at close range, while
the English would be certain to shoot from a distance; how
this was to be effected in view of the enemy's recognized
superiority in speed Philip could not define, but doubtless
God would take care of it. Throughout the entire paper one
finds evidence that the king was convinced that only a small
portion of the English fleet was at Plymouth and that the
main body of it would be encountered in the narrows of the
Channel, where it would certainly be stationed in order to
keep watch on Parma. The Armada was therefore to proceed
directly to the narrows and get control of them before it
attempted to gain a base in England. At the time (April 1)
that the king wrote these instructions, the disposition of the
enemy fleet was, indeed, very much what he had supposed.
Drake, Hawkins, and Frobisher were at Plymouth, but Lord
Howard of Effingham, who was, officially at least, the English
commander-in-chief, was still, with some of his best ships,
patrolling Calais Roads. By mid-April, however, it had
become obvious that a much smaller squadron, under Lord
Seymour, was quite adequate to the task of watching Parma.
It was also evident that Howard could be more useful farther
westward; and on May 23, long before the Armada finally
left the coasts of Spain, all of the really effective vessels in
the English fleet were united in Plymouth Sound. The

sequel will show that this change was to be of primary importance in determining the issue of the campaign.[1]

Submerged by the steadily rising tide of conflicting orders and demands, Medina Sidonia struggled bravely, if incompetently, on; by May 10 everything was at last as nearly ready as he was able to get it. The Armada, when finally united, was considerably less imposing than the estimates of Santa Cruz had called for two years before. There were now 130 vessels as against 150, and of these only 73 could be fairly regarded as fitted to take their place in the battle line; the rest were lighter craft and hulks. The total tonnage was now 57,868 instead of 77,250; the *gente de guerra* had diminished from 63,890 to 19,295; the *gente de mar y de remo* had shrunk to 10,138;[2] and all these figures were to be still further lessened before the Armada got into contact with the English fleet. It was divided into a number of territorial squadrons, Portuguese, Castilian, Andalusian, Italian, etc., according to the custom of the time, each of them commanded by an officer of experience and distinction; Juan Martínez de Recalde, Miguel de Oquendo, Martín de Bertendona, and Pedro de Valdés were perhaps the most eminent. Diego Flores Valdés, who had already made a name for himself in American waters,[3] sailed with Medina Sidonia on his

[1] J. S. Corbett, *Drake and the Tudor Navy*, ii, p. 150.

[2] Fernández Duro, *Armada Invencible*, ii, p. 66; Corbett, *op. cit.*, ii, pp. 163–165; W. F. Tilton, *Die Katastrophe der spanischen Armada*, pp. 24 ff. There is also in the British Museum (192. f. 17) a copy of an exceedingly rare pamphlet of 42 folio pages by one Pedro de Paz Salas, entitled *La Felicissima Armada que el Rey don Felipe nuestro Señor mandó juntar en el puerto de la Ciudad de Lisboa en el Reino de Portugal. El año de mil y quinientos y ochenta y ocho*. It was published at Lisbon on May 9, 1588, "por Antonio Alvarez, Impresor"; and bound in with it are a set of colored plates which belong to a *Discourse concerning the Spanish Fleet*, translated from the Italian of Petruccio Ubaldini. Cf. Corbett, *Drake and the Tudor Navy*, ii, pp. 444–450, and Fernández Duro, *Armada Invencible*, ii, p. 505. It is annotated in an English hand which the British Museum Catalogue attributes to Lord Burleigh, and was used by John Strype (cf. *Annals of the Reformation*, iii, p. 519). A Simancas copy of what appears to be the same pamphlet is reprinted, without title page or name of author, in *Archivo Histórico Español*, ii (1929), pp. 384–435.

[3] Cf. *supra*, p. 388.

flagship, the *San Martin*. The king had commanded that in
all questions of tactics the Duke should defer to his advice,
so that he became, in fact, the real commander of the
Armada.   Why Philip selected him must always remain a
mystery, for all the other squadron commanders had more
experience and better fighting records than he.[1]

None of the many comparisons that have recently been
made between the fighting strengths of the Armada and of
the English fleet is wholly satisfactory, because conditions
shifted so rapidly during the ten days in which they were in
contact; but they all tend to emphasize the important fact
that the Armada was by no means so much the larger as used
to be popularly supposed.[2]   Though the Spaniards had at
least thirty more vessels than their foes when first they met
off Plymouth Sound, the superiority was much less than it
seemed, for they were not able, as were the English, to
develop all the offensive power they had; and by the time
that Seymour had joined with Howard and Drake off
Gravelines, it seems clear that the English were actually more
numerous than the Spaniards.   In tonnage the Armada was
indeed greatly superior, at least on paper; but the Spanish
system of tonnage measurement was so different from the
English that it now appears that the amount of their
superiority should be reduced by at least one-third.
Furthermore, that superiority, such as it was, became, under
the circumstances under which the fight was to be fought, a
positive disadvantage; for the Spaniards, rising tier on tier
out of the sea, both fore and aft, till the "ocean groaned
under their weight," made a far easier mark than the English
vessels, which were high out of water only at the stern and
cut very low in the bows.   The greater weatherliness of the

---

[1] Corbett, *Drake and the Tudor Navy*,
ii, pp. 163–165.

[2] *Ibid.*, pp. 188–202; Tilton, *Kata-*
strophe, pp. 24–44; *State Papers Relating
to the Defeat of the Spanish Armada*,
ed. J. K. Laughton, i, pp. xxxix-lii.

English ships, perhaps the crucial factor in the whole campaign, was also largely ascribable to the same cause. The proportion of soldiers to sailors on the Armada was far larger than on the English fleet, but this again, as things actually worked out, was destined to do it more harm than good. In weight, range, and efficiency of gun power the English were clearly preponderant.[1] Had the Spaniards been able, as they hoped against hope, to lure their foes into an old-fashioned encounter of ramming and boarding, on the lines of the battle of Lepanto,[2] they might have had a chance. Under the conditions which the English were able to impose upon them, they were foredoomed to failure.

But it was not in Philip's nature to foresee new things. Parma from the Netherlands kept urging him to send the Armada on, and finally communicated some measure of his impatience to his master; the king was now anxious to have the great enterprise begin. There might still be practical deficiencies in leadership, munitions, and supplies, but every single man in the Armada had a certificate stating that he had confessed and been absolved, and monks and nuns had encouraged the commander with assurances of divine help.[3] On May 14 Medina Sidonia reported to the king that the fleet had begun to drop down the Tagus to Belem; on the 30th he had put to sea.[4] The wind on that day was a mere zephyr from the northeast, but the Armada was unable to make way against it. On June 1 it had drifted down to the south of Cape Espichel;[5] not till a fortnight later did it regain the latitude of Lisbon. Meantime the results of bad

[1] Tilton, *Katastrophe*, pp. 29 f.; Fernández Duro, *Armada Invencible*, i, pp. 75-77; *State Papers Relating to the Defeat of the Spanish Armada*, i, pp. xliv–xlvii.

[2] Rightly characterized by G. de Artíñano y de Galdácano (*Arquitectura Naval Española*, p. 79, note) as "la postrera gran batalla en que *predominan* las remeras."

[3] Froude, *Spanish Story of the Armada*, pp. 26, 28.

[4] Fernández Duro, *Armada Invencible*, ii, pp. 97–99, 105 f.

[5] *Ibid.*, pp. 106 f.

provisioning had become tragically apparent. The food
stank, and the water was foul; 500 of the men were already
down with dysentery; the crews complained, and the officers
were in despair.[1] On June 10, the wind shifted to the southwest, and the Armada at last got fairly started to the north;
but the sickness on board continued to increase, and when,
on the 19th, the wind became a gale, there was nothing for
it but to put in at Corunna.[2] At first only forty of the ships
were able to make the port; for despite the king's insistent
orders that the fleet keep close together, the wind had
scattered it. Not till more than two weeks later could it
be collected again, and when the crews got on shore, large
numbers of them deserted.[3] The Duke was despondent. He
feared that the news of his plight would reach England, and
that *corsarios* would be sent to capture his battered ships.[4]
On June 24 he wrote to Philip, advising the abandonment of
the enterprise.[5] But the king would not hear of it; on July
5 and 12 he sent vigorous letters[6] to the Duke, promising
to provide him with everything he needed, but commanding
him to set sail at the earliest possible moment. The vice-
admiral and the generals, too, were all opposed to giving up.

---

[1] Fernández Duro, *Armada Invencible*,
ii, pp. 107–112, 117–124.

[2] *Ibid.*, pp. 121–124.

[3] *Ibid.*, p. 121, note, and reference
there.

[4] *Ibid.*, pp. 131–134. Medina Sidonia's fears were fully justified by the
facts. Howard had joined Drake with
his best ships at Plymouth in the first
week of June; both were confident
that if permitted to make a dash at the
coasts of Spain, they could prevent the
Armada from ever putting to sea. On
the 9th they made a first attempt, but
the winds were contrary; and on the
16th they returned. The next two
weeks were wasted in petitions to the
hesitant Elizabeth and her Council to
be allowed to try again; finally the
queen yielded, and on June 30 they

sallied forth once more. For two
weeks the winds proved contrary, and
the best they could do was to lie in a
long line off Ushant, awaiting the
coming of the foe; finally on July 17, it
started to blow from the north, and
again they started southward in search
of their prey. Two days later they
were nearly across the Bay of Biscay
and almost in sight of the Spanish
coast; then the fickle north wind died
away, and finally veered into the southwest; they were forced to put back,
and the Spaniards were saved. Cf.
Corbett, ii, pp. 165–181, for details.

[5] Fernández Duro, *Armada Invencible*,
ii, pp. 134–137.

[6] *Ibid.*, pp. 150–154, 184–186; also
Archivo Histórico Nacional, ii, pp. 208–
226.

Valdés was particularly insistent, and Recalde seized the opportunity to make a final though futile appeal to Philip to modify his instructions, and permit the fleet to secure a port on the English coast before advancing to the narrows of the Channel.[1] Meantime fresh food and good water had been taken on board. The necessary repairs were made, and the gaps in the crews were filled up. Every man on the fleet confessed and received the sacrament again; and finally, on Friday, July 22, the Armada made a fresh start out of Corunna. This time the wind blew strong out of the southwest; in the next three days the fleet had crossed the Bay of Biscay and reached the mouth of the English Channel.[2] There they encountered another storm, which scattered them and sent most of the galleys and the flagship of Recalde flying for refuge into the nearest French ports; but on Friday, the 29th, the majority of the stragglers had been collected again.[3] The wind now blew gently from the southwest, as the fleet came in sight of the Lizard. On the following day, at two o'clock in the afternoon, Medina Sidonia, convinced that the crucial hour had at last arrived, determined to reënact the great scene that had inspired the Christians on the eve of Lepanto. A standard, displaying Christ crucified on the one side, and the Virgin Mary on the other, was run up at the masthead of the flagship; three pieces of artillery were shot off, "and every man in the fleet knelt down and prayed our Lord to give us victory over the enemies of his faith."[4]

But the crisis which the Duke anticipated was not to come. While he knelt with his followers on the deck of his galleon,

---

[1] Fernández Duro, *Armada Invencible*, ii, pp. 141–149, 169–172.

[2] *Ibid.*, pp. 172–221, *passim*.

[3] Letter of Medina Sidonia to Philip, July 29, 1588, in *Archivo Histórico Español*, ii, pp. 252–255.

[4] Fernández Duro, *Armada Invencible*, ii, pp. 220 f., 374. For an account of the ships lost in the gale of July 27, see Corbett, *Drake and the Tudor Navy*, ii, p. 189, note.

it was actually occurring, if not already past. Early on the Friday afternoon, Captain Fleming of the *Golden Hind* had burst in on Drake and his officers, who were playing their historic game of bowls on Plymouth Hoe, with the news that the Armada was already off the Lizard, and slowly proceeding before the southwest wind toward Dodman Point.[1] The Spaniards, in other words, now threatened to catch the English in the very predicament in which the English had so often sought to catch them : cooped up in a narrow harbor, with the breeze blowing full into the mouth of it, where a vigorous attack, prepared with fire-ships, could scarcely fail of complete success. There was but one way to meet the situation, namely, to get to sea at once, and to the windward, if possible, of the Armada, where the superior gunnery and sailing qualities of the English ships would be fully available ; and this, despite the obvious perils of uncovering the threatened port, Drake and Howard determined at once to do.[2] On the Friday night the ships were warped out of the harbor ; on Saturday morning the best of them were beating out of Plymouth Sound. In the early afternoon fifty-four of them had almost reached Eddystone, where for the first time they caught sight of the Spaniards. At the same moment the wind died down, and rain and fog came on, so that there was nothing further to be done save to lie still under bare poles in order that the enemy might not see them. On the Armada, in the meantime, a council of war was being held, in which the expediency of attacking Plymouth in defiance of Philip's instructions was ardently debated. What decision was reached we cannot surely tell, for the accounts are very contradictory.[3] At any rate, when sunset at last revealed

---

[1] Corbett, *op. cit.*, ii, pp. 187 f.

[2] *Ibid.*, pp. 203 f.

[3] Cf. the *relación* of Alonso Vanegas in Fernández Duro, *Armada Invencible*, ii, pp. 370 ff. ; letter of Pedro de

Valdés to King Philip, Englished, in *State Papers Relating to the Defeat of the Spanish Armada*, ii, pp. 133–136 ; Corbett, *op. cit.*, ii, pp. 205 f., 442 ff.

the English fleet a few miles to the leeward, off Eddystone,
the Duke immediately came to anchor, for he was convinced that he must keep the weather gauge in the attack
which he confidently expected on the following morning.[1]
But this was just what the enemy was determined at all
costs to prevent. Soon after sundown, the southwest wind
rose once more, and the English ships again made sail. The
main body of them stood south, out to sea, across the front of
the Armada, but apparently the Spaniards never saw them;
their attention was distracted by eight other ships which were
beating dead to windward, between the left wing of the
Armada and the shore. Consequently the Duke made no
effort at all to prevent his right flank from being turned, and
at daybreak on the Sunday morning he was dumfounded to
discover the pick of his daring foes reunited in safety to the
windward of him.[2] The position had been assumed which,
skilfully maintained and improved by Drake and his
followers during the next ten days, was ultimately to transfer from Spain to England the sovereignty of the seas. It
was the decisive manoeuvre of the entire campaign.

It used to be said that the Armada advanced up the
Channel in the form of a huge crescent, convex side to the
fore, and this conception has been confirmed by numerous
contemporary charts and drawings and by the tapestries in
the House of Lords. But recent research has made it
abundantly clear that this was not the case. The basic idea
on which Philip's elaborate instructions and Medina
Sidonia's orders were founded was that the Armada would be
exposed, as it sailed up the Channel, to attacks in both front
and rear: in the rear from Drake and his ships who were
known to be in Plymouth, and in front from the main body

---

[1] Corbett, *op. cit.*, ii, p. 207.   [2] Fernández Duro, *Armada Invencible*,
ii, pp. 274 f.; Corbett, ii, pp. 208 f.

of the English fleet, which the Spaniards confidently believed
would be awaiting them in the narrows.   Even after Medina
Sidonia learned, on Sunday morning, the 31st, that Howard
had joined forces with Drake, he could not get it into his
head that practically the whole fighting force of his enemies
was behind him.   He therefore adhered to his original formation.   He himself, on the flagship *San Martin*, led the vanguard or 'main battle,' consisting of two squadrons of his
best galleons, each strengthened by a galleasse ; in the centre,
directly behind him, were the hulks and the victuallers ; and
behind them, in turn, a strong rearguard of four squadrons,
of which the two hindmost were placed on the extreme left
and right, and each protected by a galleasse.   As all the
attacks of importance were to come from behind, it will be
readily seen that the adoption of this formation virtually
wasted a large proportion of the Duke's best ships, because
they could not get into the fight ; it will also serve, at least
partially, to explain the origin and persistence of the idea of
the crescent formation, since it was like a crescent that the
Armada must have appeared when seen by the English from
behind.   The English tactics, on the other hand, were
devised with the idea of making the fullest possible use of the
two unquestioned points of English superiority, namely,
better sailing ability and better gunnery ; having got the
weather gauge, they were prepared to take every possible
advantage of it.   Their fleet, in brief, was drawn up in a
single long line — *en ala*, as the Spaniards called it —, which
tacked back and forth across the rear of the weathermost
Spanish ships, keeping them perpetually under fire, but
resolutely refusing to come to close quarters.   Such a refusal,
of course, confirmed the Spaniards' conviction that the English were cowards, but that was about all the comfort that
they got from it.   The fact, of course, was that their enemies

had turned a fresh page in the book of naval strategy. The Duke and his followers were confronted with a situation with which they were powerless to deal.[1]

The first contact of the two fleets outside of Plymouth on Sunday, the 31st, was to give an inkling of the way in which these rival tactics worked. As the west wind bore him along opposite the mouth of the Sound, Medina Sidonia stood in shore, partly perhaps with the idea of threatening the port, more probably, however, for the purpose of cutting off the slower English ships, which had not been able to come out with Howard and Drake on the Saturday morning, and which now were attempting to get to sea and join the main fleet. But Howard and Drake made no move to intercept him; they were resolved at all costs to preserve the weather gauge, and so all they did was to attack the Spanish rear guard. They contented themselves, moreover, for the most part, with cannonading at long range, but the effects of their fire were so deadly that most of the Spanish ships crowded down on Medina Sidonia; only the gallant Recalde had the nerve to come up in the wind and face the foe. For two hours he stood his ground, virtually isolated from the rest of the Armada, while Medina Sidonia made futile efforts to beat up to his rescue. But these efforts merely gave a golden opportunity to the English squadron coming out of the Sound; it worked to windward and soon rejoined the main fleet. Even with this reënforcement, Drake and Howard were unwilling to risk a general engagement, at least at close quarters; when Medina Sidonia finally succeeded in rallying his galleons to the relief of the battered Recalde, they simply discontinued the fight. No great damage had been done to either side, but it was ominously evident that the English could henceforth dictate just how and when all future

[1] Corbett, *op. cit.*, ii, pp. 209–221, and references there.

encounters were to be fought. Meantime the wind and the tide had carried both fleets to the east of Plymouth. The Spaniards could do no further damage there, and practically all the effective force of their enemies was reunited to the windward of them.[1]

Monday, August 1, passed by without any important event.[2] On the morning of Tuesday, the second, the two fleets, their relative positions unchanged, had reached the waters off Portland Bill, when the wind, for the first and only time in that memorable week, hauled into the northeast and gave the Spaniards the precious weather gauge; they consequently made ready to attack. The action that ensued was complicated in the extreme, but not productive of serious results; it was, on both sides, a day of lost opportunities. The efforts of the English to get to windward enabled Medina Sidonia to cut their fleet in two; but then, instead of concentrating on the slower or inshore part, which he might have compelled to engage in a contest at close quarters, such as all the Spaniards desired, he foolishly gave chase to the swifter seaward portion, which he was totally unable to catch up with. The long-range cannonading of the English proved its effectiveness once more, and the smoke from their heavy discharges had the additional advantage of concealing their position from the Spaniards. In the afternoon the wind shifted back again into the southwest, and Medina Sidonia's flagship, which was momentarily isolated in a heroic attempt to protect the westernmost ships of the Armada, received terrible punishment from the batteries of Howard and Drake.

[1] Cf. *diario* of Medina Sidonia in Fernández Duro, *Armada Invencible*, ii, pp. 230 ff.; the *relación* of Alonso Vanegas, *ibid.*, pp. 376 ff., and the two *relaciones* in *Archivo Histórico Español*, ii, pp. 255–258, 267–270; also Corbett, ii, pp. 222–226, and Froude, *Spanish Story of the Armada*, pp. 42 f.

[2] The incident of Drake's leaving his place in the line to capture the disabled flagship of Pedro de Valdés is rather a part of English than of Spanish history, and need not be recounted here. Cf. Corbett, ii, pp. 230–235.

The comments of the Spanish narrators on the fight of that day are bitter in the extreme; they felt that they had had victory within their grasp, and then had been unaccountably deprived of it. There was talk of treachery and cowardice, of the unwillingness of those ships "in which there was no *caballero* or person whom the seamen respected" to go to the rescue of the Duke and his *capitana*; above all, it had been finally proved to them "that it was impossible to board if the enemy did not so desire."[1] The first of these difficulties was dealt with at once; sergeant-majors visited each ship in the Armada to learn how every man was doing his duty;[2] but the second, from its very nature, was irremediable. The Armada continued on its eastern course, in substantially the same formation as before, while the enemy, now considerably augmented by ships that had come out to join it from the various ports which it had passed, was henceforth divided into four separate squadrons, headed respectively by Howard, Drake, Hawkins, and Frobisher. Each was directed to follow the same tactics which had been used hitherto by the entire English fleet, tacking back and forth astern of the Spanish rear guard, and pouring in volleys at long range; the only difference was that henceforth the assault was to be delivered in four places at once.[3]

Wednesday, the third, was a day of calm, in which neither of the fleets could make any appreciable headway. Recalde was apparently the target of some heavy cannonading, and at one moment the English threatened to surround and cut off his *capitana*; but when Medina Sidonia bore up to his support, the action was immediately discontinued.[4] In the

---

[1] The best accounts of this engagement will be found in Fernández Duro, *Armada Invencible*, ii, pp. 233–235, 256–258, and 381–384. Cf. also Corbett, ii, pp. 236–244.

[2] Fernández Duro, ii, p. 258.
[3] Corbett, ii, pp. 244 ff.
[4] Fernández Duro, *Armada Invencible*, ii, pp. 384–386.

late afternoon the west wind rose again, and the Spaniards came in sight of the Isle of Wight, where they had by this time decided, in defiance of Philip's instructions, to try to establish a base and await the arrival of Parma.[1] The action that ensued on the morrow, to the south of Dunnose, is again very difficult to comprehend, principally because none of the contemporary accounts distinctly states the precise direction of the wind; it seems most probable, however, that it was more nearly south than west. This would account for the fact that the port squadrons of the English fleet, which got to the north of the left rear of the Armada in order to prevent a possible attempt to land, were temporarily deprived of the weather gauge; the Spaniards were confident that they had one of the English *capitanas* at their mercy "when nine light boats got her under way again and took her out of our hands with such speed that it was a thing of wonder to see."[2] "We attacked, and got near them, and they fled," goes the account of the master of one of the Seville ships; "they were broken in two parts and the victory assured, when the enemy's *capitana* turned upon our fleet, and the galleon *San Mateo*, on the point of our weather wing, gave way to it, and retreated into the main body of the Armada. Seeing this, the enemy took heart, and attacked the said wing with his whole fleet or the greater part of it, and got us into a corner, in such fashion that if the Duke had not gone about with his flagship, we should have been vanquished that day instead of the victors that we were."[3] This account makes it clear that while the rear port squadrons of the Armada had been occupied with the English ships which had got between them and the shore, their vanguard had been vigorously attacked by the starboard squadrons of their enemies under Drake and

[1] Fernández Duro, *Armada Invencible*, ii, pp. 221 f.
[2] Vanegas in Fernández Duro, *Armada Invencible*, ii, pp. 386.
[3] *Ibid.*, pp. 275 f.

Hawkins, who had kept the weather gauge, and as usual had been completely successful; the phrase "got us into a corner" doubtless refers to the possibility, of which the English had planned to take full advantage, that the Armada might be driven upon the dangerous banks called the Owers. Medina Sidonia's pilots were also alive to this peril. To remain where he was would bring certain disaster; to pass on to the east meant the abandonment of all his hopes of establishing a base on the Isle of Wight; but of the two evils the latter was obviously the less. So he signalled to his scattered ships to re-form around him, and by the middle of the afternoon he was once more headed straight east for Calais, his terrible foes hanging relentlessly on his heels.

The rest of that day and night and the following morning both fleets continued on their eastward course, and there was no action worthy of the name. But if one reads between the lines in the various contemporary *relaciones*,[1] it is only too evident that the Spaniards were deeply disheartened. They had looked forward to the action off the Isle of Wight as critical. Once more they had thought that victory was theirs; then it had been suddenly snatched away from them by tactics with which they were powerless to cope, and they had been driven past the point where they had hoped to establish their base. They had lost seven good ships since leaving Corunna, and had seen their enemies constantly reënforced as they sailed up the Channel. Their powder was getting short. There were a number of dead and wounded; and though Medina Sidonia had proved himself both loyal and gallant in the way that he had come to the rescue of his hard-pressed friends, it was only too evident that he was no seaman.[2] Still if Parma and his veterans were awaiting them at

[1] Fernández Duro, *Armada Invencible*, ii, pp. 238 f., 258 f., 268, 276, 386.

[2] The verdict of Fernández Duro on the Duke (i, pp. 90–92) is more severe than mine.

the narrows, the game was not yet lost.   Means would surely
be found to guard their transfer across the Channel, and no
man doubted that if a Spanish army was once landed on English soil, the defences of their enemies would fall like a house
of cards.   Message after message had been despatched to
Parma, ever since the fleet had left Lisbon, begging him to
be ready,[1] but so far there had been no definite word from
him, and on Saturday morning, the sixth, when the Armada
had reached Calais Roads, Medina Sidonia sent him a final
appeal to come out with his flatboats.[2]   But Parma, as we
shall later see,[3] had no mind to do this.   He was on hand,
indeed, as he had promised Philip that he would be, but he
resolutely refused to put to sea till the fleet should be able to
protect him, and that, for the moment, was obviously impossible.[4]   The hopelessness of the Armada's position was at
last fully revealed.   Medina Sidonia could not beat back to
the westward.   To drift on past Calais and Dunkirk was to
abandon all remaining hope of transporting the *tercios* — the
fundamental object of the entire expedition — not to speak
of the danger of being driven aground on the treacherous
shoals farther east.   To remain where he was would
obviously be perilous, as the governor of Calais took pains
to point out to him, but under the circumstances, there was
no other alternative.   And so, at five o'clock on the Saturday
afternoon, the Duke came to anchor, and signalled to the
rest of the fleet to do likewise.   At the same time the
Spaniards, already deeply disheartened, were still further
cast down by observing a group of thirty-six enemy ships,
which had been lying to leeward, and which they erroneously
believed to be commanded by Hawkins, beat up around their
north flank, and join forces with the rest of the English fleet.

[1] Fernández Duro, *Armada Invencible,*
ii, p. 237.
[2] *C. S. P., Spanish*, 1587–1603, no. 368.
[3] Cf. *infra,* p. 622.
[4] *C. S. P., Spanish*, 1587–1603, nos.
374, 380.

It was, of course, the squadron of Seymour, who had been told off to watch Parma, but who now, seeing that he could no longer be of any use in the position to which he had been originally assigned, had very wisely decided, in the face of conflicting orders, to get to windward of the enemy at all costs and unite with Howard. Such was his contempt for the failure of Medina Sidonia to make any effort to prevent this obvious move, that one of his ships poured a broadside at close range into the northern flank of the Armada as he sailed by, and then passed on, while the two rear galleasses 'returned thanks' with their stern culverins. The whole of the English fleet, which had also come to anchor, was now within cannon-shot to the windward of the Armada.[1]

Sunday, August 7, passed off without any important engagement, but while the English spent it profitably in devising means whereby they might dislodge their foes, the Spaniards could do nothing but worry and wait. Messages from Parma made it plain that the Dutch blockade of the Flemish ports would render it impossible for him to send out the ammunition and provisions of which the Armada was now in desperate need, and he persisted in his refusal to move his troops or his flatboats until the Armada should be ready to protect them. The enemy divined the Spaniards' discouragement at the plight in which they found themselves, for he seized the opportunity to intimate his contempt for them in characteristic fashion. At four in the afternoon a pinnace from the English fleet bore down on the *capitana real*, fired four shot into her at close range, went about and got away with no damage to herself but a culverin-shot through her topsail. "Its daring," comments the author of the *relación* which records the incident, "was very notable,

---

[1] Fernández Duro, *Armada Invencible*, ii, pp. 238 f., 260, 387 f.; Corbett, ii, pp. 262–265.

and more than ever we saw how with their very good and very light ships they could come and go as they pleased, the which we could not do." [1] But much worse was soon to come. How far the position in which the two fleets now were had been foreseen in England, it is of course impossible to say; but we know that the exploit of Gianibelli at Antwerp in 1585 had been noised abroad all over Europe, that Gianibelli was in England at the time with letters of introduction to Sir Francis Walsingham, and, finally, that Walsingham had sent orders and material for the construction of fire ships to Dover some days before the Armada reached Calais Roads. It certainly looks as if some plan of dislodging the Spaniards by the use of vessels filled with combustibles had been carefully considered by their relentless foes. [2] In any case, the conditions on Sunday night were as favorable as could be desired for such an attempt. The west wind had risen, and the tide was boiling up the channel. So fearful, in fact, were Howard and Drake that such an opportunity might never come again, that they decided not to waste time by sending in to Dover for the fire-ships which had been got ready there, but to sacrifice eight of their own smaller vessels for the purpose. [3] Shortly after midnight the 'hell burners' were set adrift, and came flaming down on the huddled mass of the Armada, "spurting fire and their artillery shooting," so runs the Spanish account of it, "which was a horror at night time, and when all of our ships had to have two anchors out." Medina Sidonia did not dare remain where he was; he could not weigh; and so in despair he gave orders for the cables to be cut, and the Armada, with the ships that composed it running afoul of each other in helpless confusion, drifted on out of the narrows of the Channel toward the shoals of Dun-

---

[1] Fernández Duro, *Armada Invencible,* ii, pp. 282 f.

[2] Read, *Walsingham,* iii, pp. 320 f.
[3] Corbett, ii, pp. 268 f.

kirk. The eight fire-ships, in the meantime, had burned themselves out, and had become harmless; "yet they had accomplished," as the Spanish narrator bitterly remarked, "what the enemy had neither been able nor ventured to do with 130 sail."[1]

When dawn, on the Monday morning, revealed to the English admirals the plight of their Spanish foes, they promptly gave chase, intent on dealing a knockout blow before the Armada had had a chance to re-form. In order to prevent this, and also because his pilots told him that he was getting perilously near the Flanders banks, Medina Sidonia came up in the wind, facing his pursuers, and signalled to the rest of the fleet to do likewise; some fifty of them managed to obey and gather around him, and it was by these that the battle of Gravelines was fought. The English remained true to the tactics that they had so successfully followed during the preceding week. They refused to grapple and board, and shot into their foes at the water line. The Spaniards, of course, were as powerless as ever to prevent this, or to bring on a battle of the sort that they wished to fight; though under the circumstances it was impossible for them to win, it cannot be denied that their courage was superb. All the accounts by Spanish eyewitnesses ring with special praises of the heroism displayed by the Portuguese galleons, the *San Felipe* and the *San Mateo*; the glory, be it noted, goes wholly to the generals and soldiers on board them; there is not a word about the sailors. Both placed themselves in the hottest of the fight. Each was surrounded by over a dozen of the enemy's ships, and fought them off for hours "without help except from God." Offers of quarter were contemptuously refused.[2] But finally the weather,

[1] *Relación* in Fernández Duro, *Armada Invencible*, ii, p. 283.

[2] "Carta del Padre Geronimo de la Torre," in Fernández Duro, *Armada Invencible*, ii, pp. 404 f.

which had been so favorable to the English during the previous ten days, came temporarily to the rescue of the hard-pressed Spaniards. In the late afternoon a terrific squall of wind and rain blew up, so that further firing was impossible; moreover, while the English came up in the wind and faced it, the shattered Spaniards were unable to do this, and simply drifted to leeward, with the result that the two fleets became separated; after the squall had passed, the fight was virtually over. But despite the fact that it had been interrupted by the elements, the battle of Gravelines had been decisive. The Armada had been driven past the point where it had hoped to unite with Parma, and there was practically no hope of its regaining it. The only real question now was what proportion of the fleet would be able to get safely back to Spain.[1]

For, though Philip's great Armada had itself become innocuous, it was by no means out of danger of destruction. All Monday night the wind blew hard out of the northwest, and when the Spaniards discovered their position on Tuesday morning, it became evident that they were being rapidly driven down on the treacherous shoals to the eastward. Medina Sidonia and a few of his best ships made desperate efforts to weather them, but the bulk of the Armada was unable to do this. A mile or more away the English hung relentlessly on their windward quarter, content to watch them pass on to their inevitable fate. The Spaniards took soundings again and again — eight fathoms, six fathoms, five fathoms; the pilots vowed that such large ships had never passed that way before; clearly they were now at the mercy of God, and officers and men betook themselves to prayer. But, sometime about noon, when they were all expecting death at any moment, "it pleased God to work the miracle" for which

[1] Corbett, ii, pp. 290–292; Fernández Duro, i, pp. 103 ff.

they had besought Him. The wind eased off a point or two, and began to blow out of the southwest. The Spaniards were just able to avoid the shoals, and in the early afternoon they had got together again in some kind of formation in the deeper waters of the North Sea. For the moment, at least, they were safe, and the English had been robbed of their prey.[1]

Later in the day Medina Sidonia called a council of war on board his flagship, to determine what was next to be done.[2] A few of his officers believed that when the wind shifted, it might be possible to return to Calais Roads and engage the English again. The Duke himself, who was certainly no coward, would have been glad to do so, had it not been for the fact that the ammunition was practically exhausted; but without powder and ball it was evident that they could not fight. Some of them were in favor of passing on to a point in Norway to spend the winter and refit; but the Duke did not like the idea of seeking refuge in the territory of strangers; moreover, it would never do to leave the Spanish coasts unguarded. The only alternative then was to get home as quickly as possible, and with the least possible loss; and with the wind in the west and the enemy between them and the narrows of the Channel, the only way to get home was to sail up to the north beyond the Orkneys, and thence around the west of Ireland to Spain. Even this course had its dangers. The provisions were almost as short as the ammunition, and the water supply was the lowest of all. They had brought with them many horses and mules to drag the artillery after it had been landed in England, and these they might now have killed and eaten in order to appease their hunger; but instead they elected to throw some eighty

[1] Fernández Duro, *Armada Invencible,* i, pp. 105 f., 172–174; ii, pp. 393 f.; Corbett, ii, pp. 292–296.

[2] Fernández Duro, i, p. 106; ii, pp. 394–396.

of them overboard in order to husband their water supply.
All this, and the fact that they were now in full retreat, took
the heart out of officers and men. Investigation revealed
that there had been numerous cases of cowardice and insubordination. A court-martial was held, and twenty were condemned to death. Of these, however, only one was actually
executed, being hung from the yard-arm of a pinnace; the
others were let off with degradation and minor penalties
"through the great clemency of the Duke."[1] During
Wednesday and Thursday, the 10th and the 11th, the English continued to pursue. They thought that the Spaniards
would never dare return home with nothing accomplished,
and feared lest they might possibly combine with the Catholics in Scotland. On Friday, however, it became evident
that the Armada was bent on flight, and the English
abandoned the chase. They were almost as short of powder
as their foes, and the queen was most reluctant to pay for
any more. Now that the danger was over, her parsimony
asserted itself; and as the surest way of preventing any
further activities on the part of her fleet, she peremptorily
summoned Howard to attend in his place at her Council.[2]

The misfortunes of the Armada were not yet at an end.
Its homeward journey was beset by gales. As far north as
the Orkneys the fleet held together; but when it started to
beat westward into the Atlantic, the ships that had suffered
most in the fighting were unable to keep up with the rest.
Many sank, riddled like sieves, in the Northern Ocean;
others fell away to leeward and were wrecked on the rocky
coasts of Northern and Western Ireland.[3] If the soldiers
and sailors on board them were fortunate enough to escape
death in the waves, they were most of them robbed and

[1] Fernández Duro, ii, p. 396.
[2] Corbett, ii, p. 300.
[3] Cf. W. S. Green, "The Wrecks of the

Spanish Armada on the Coast of Ireland," *Geographical Journal*, xxvii
(1906), pp. 429–451.

murdered by the wild Irish, or else shot in cold blood by the English garrisons; the narrative of Captain Francisco de Cuéllar, who was one of the very few to escape, gives a vivid picture of the conditions in Ulster and Connaught at the time.[1] Medina Sidonia, in compliance with the royal command, sent off letters to Philip as often as he could, to report the state of affairs. At least two of them, written respectively on August 21 and September 3, apparently reached the king's hands, and gave him a terribly vivid picture of the miseries of his fleet.[2] A week after the battle of Gravelines, Philip had believed that the Armada had been triumphant. On August 18 he had written to Medina Sidonia a letter of congratulation on the victory which he had learned from "the reports of an eyewitness" had been won.[3] At the end of the month he knew that the Armada had been beaten, but he had not yet given up hope that it might return to the narrows of the Channel, unite with Parma, and get its revenge.[4] Four weeks later, however, he had to face the whole of the horrid truth. On September 22 Medina Sidonia crawled into Santander; on the 23d he sent in the last and most tragic of all his reports to the king.[5] He had had sixty or more ships with him when last he had written to Philip, but most of these had since been scattered by the fury of the waves, and he had only brought eleven of them with him into port. Fifty-five others, in all a little more than half of the fleet that had left Corunna in July, managed, one by one, to fight their way back, but they brought home with them

---

[1] In the form of a letter to Philip, written from Antwerp, October 4, 1589. The original is printed in Fernández Duro, *Armada Invencible*, ii, pp. 337–370; and there are English translations by H. D. Sedgwick, Jr. (New York, 1895), and by Robert Crawford (London, 1897); pages 70 to 79 of Froude's *Spanish Story of the Armada* are based on it.

[2] Fernández Duro, *Armada Invencible*, ii, pp. 225–228, 252 f.

[3] *Archivo Histórico Español*, ii, pp. 272 f.

[4] *Archivo Historico Español*, ii, p. 273; Forneron, iii, pp. 350 f., and references here.

[5] Fernández Duro, ii, pp. 296–300; *Archivo Histórico Español*, ii, pp. 287 f., 297–300.

scarcely a third of the 29,000 men who had bravely gone
forth to fight the battle of the Lord. Hopes still ran high
that more would return. In November word came from
Venice that Alonso de Leyva, the darling of the fleet, had
saved twenty-six ships, and raised a revolt in Ireland ;[1] but
by Christmas time it was learned that de Leyva had been
drowned. Most of the rest of the best officers had also perished. Recalde and Oquendo both died within a few days of
their return.[2] Diego Flores Valdés, who got home with
Medina Sidonia, was punished with a term of imprisonment
in the castle of Burgos, for a scapegoat had clearly to be
found, and he was the obvious one. The Duke was
"permitted to retire" to his estates in Andalusia, and was
not even deprived of his command. The mass of the
Spaniards detested him, and held him chiefly responsible for
the disaster, but Philip stood loyally by him, and it is on
the whole to his credit that he did so.[3] Had the king perhaps
some inkling that he himself was the person really to blame?
Or did he still believe that everything was to be attributed
to the inscrutable will of the Lord? From his famous dictum
that he had sent the fleet "against men and not against the
wind and the seas,"[4] it would look as if the latter were the
more probable, but it was certainly an awkward problem to
explain why the Almighty had been so unkind to an expedition which had been sent out expressly to do His work.

The defeat of the Spanish Armada was unquestionably the
supreme disaster of Philip's reign. It proved that Spain's
navy could be beaten, and that she could be deprived of
the sovereignty of the seas. It presaged the independence

[1] Forneron, iii, p. 352, and reference
there.
[2] Froude, Spanish Story of the Armada, pp. 80 f.
[3] Fernández Duro, Armada Invencible,
i, pp. 132–144; Froude, Spanish Story
of the Armada, pp. 85–89.
[4] On the authorities for this remark
see Forneron, iii, p. 348, note 3; Fernández Duro, i, pp. 127 ff.

of the Low Countries and the break-down of the monopoly of Spain in the New World; indeed, it is usually regarded as the death-knell of the Spanish Empire. One would gather, moreover, from a perusal of the pages devoted by the older English historians to the last fifteen years of the reign of Elizabeth that all these tremendous results were immediately evident, that the English sea-rovers sacked Spanish cities and plundered Spanish colonial ports and treasure fleets at will, and that the Spaniards were powerless to prevent them. More recently a high authority on naval affairs has challenged this classical interpretation of the period, and maintained that the Spaniards, for years after the Armada, remained far more formidable than is popularly supposed.[1] It is probable that he, in turn, somewhat overstates his case, but there is certainly something to be said for the view that he advances. As regarded from the Spanish standpoint, the history of the war with England during the years 1588–98, which alone concern us here, falls into three distinct periods, each with well marked characteristics of its own, and sharply differentiated from one another. We will now proceed to consider them in order.

The first is comprised in the year 1589, and the central event of it is the English expedition against Lisbon. In view of the fury of Drake and his associates at being robbed of their prey when forbidden to pursue the Armada to the northward, it was inevitable that they should ask leave to make reprisals in the following year; the nation virtually demanded it and Elizabeth dared not refuse.[2] In Spain all this had been foreseen, for Philip still had his spies in England, who kept him informed of the enemy's plans; moreover, it had been correctly surmised that the chief objective

---

[1] J. S. Corbett, *The Successors of Drake*, p. vi.

[2] Corbett, *Drake and the Tudor Navy*, ii, pp. 307–318.

would be Lisbon, for the pretender Antonio had the ear of the English government and had promised that the Portuguese would rise in his favor to a man.   With the aid of his Portuguese minister, Cristóbal de Moura, and Pedro Enríquez de Acevedo, Count of Fuentes, Philip accordingly did everything possible to prepare resistance.[1]   In April, 1589, the blow fell, but not at first at the expected point.   A fleet of some 130 sail, carrying upwards of 15,000 men, under Drake and Sir John Norris, suddenly appeared before Corunna.[2] They promptly landed 7000 troops, attacked and captured the lower town, killed 500 Spaniards, and took prisoner the commander of the place; but then they scattered to pillage, and finding large casks of Spanish wines in the cellars of some warehouses, a large proportion of them soon became helplessly drunk.   Prudence, under the circumstances, would have dictated a prompt withdrawal, with such booty as they had managed to collect, but Norris insisted on remaining to lay siege to the upper town, which by this time had had a chance to prepare.   Prodigies of valor were performed by both sides, but the Spaniards were inspired by the heroic example and leadership of some of the women of the town, which apparently produced *mugeres varoniles* of the old Castilian sort, and the English were forced to retire with the loss of 1200 men.   After consoling themselves by cutting to pieces a Spanish reënforcement sent on from Puente de Burgos, and laying waste the surrounding country, they finally withdrew to their fleet.[3]   From Corunna they passed south to Peniche on the Portuguese coast, some thirty-five miles north of Lisbon.   There Norris landed, with 6000 men,

[1] C. de C., iii, pp. 336–338; Forneron, iii, pp. 355–359.

[2] Corbett, *Drake and the Tudor Navy*, ii, pp. 330–334, and references there.

[3] C. de C., iii, pp. 338 ff.; Corbett, *op. cit.*, ii, pp. 334–342; M. A. S. Hume, *The Year after the Armada* (London, 1896), pp. 31–39; Forneron, iii, pp. 359–362.

and easily captured the place; he then started overland for
the Portuguese capital, while Drake sailed around to the
mouth of the Tagus to support him with an attack from the
river. Both parts of the expedition signally failed to accomplish their purpose. The winds were so unfavorable that
Drake could not enter the river, and in the meantime the
army of Norris had been dogged by misfortune. Fuentes
had retreated before him, and denuded the country of
supplies; Norris did not venture to pillage for fear of alien-
ating the sympathy of the Portuguese, from which so much
had been hoped. The heat was terrific, and when the
invaders reached the suburbs of Lisbon and found that the
fleet had not got there, they lost all heart; in fact, they felt
themselves fortunate in being permitted a little later to
reëmbark, virtually unmolested, at Cascaes. Sickness had
decimated their ranks, but their provisions were replenished
by the fortunate capture of a convoy of sixty Hanseatic
ships with cargoes of corn for Portugal. On the way home
they revenged themselves by entering the harbor of Vigo,
burning the town and the ships at anchor there, and devastating the country for miles around; but when the last
scattered remnants of the expedition got back to Plymouth,
it was found that some thirty of the ships were missing, and
that over 9000 men had died or been killed. Practically no
booty had been brought back; the queen was ill pleased, and,
despite the verdict of contemporaries like Camden, it is
evident that the whole affair was regarded in England as a
disastrous failure. On the other hand, it seems equally clear
that Spain was dissatisfied that the invaders had got off so
cheaply. She had merely got rid of them, but they had not
been decisively defeated. Both sides, in other words, felt
that little was to be gained, for the time being, in continuing
the struggle, at least in European waters; and that feeling

must have been intensified, in Philip's case, by the fact that the assassination of Henry III (August 2, 1589) necessarily turned his attention once more in the direction of France.[1]

The result was that the next phase of the war, which lasted till 1595, assumed a complexion totally different from that of its predecessor. Philip made no serious effort against England. Elizabeth did not attempt to invade Spain, but permitted her sea-rovers to harry the Spanish colonies, and lie in wait for the Spanish treasure fleets. From her point of view, it was obviously the proper course. It cost almost nothing; it might conceivably prove very lucrative, and it only semi-officially committed her to the continuance of a war which she never really wished to wage. In the summer of 1589 the Earl of Cumberland sailed with thirteen ships for the Azores and captured Fayal, where he maintained himself till October. He seized the vessels which were lying in the port, and intercepted others homeward bound from the New World and laden with treasure.[2] In the following year both Hawkins and Frobisher returned empty-handed to England, after similar attempts,[3] and 1591 was the year of the last fight of the *Revenge*. If the gallantry of Grenville remains one of the most precious traditions of the British navy, it is but fair to add that his Spanish opponent, Alonso de Bazán, the brother of the Marquis of Santa Cruz, paid him all the honor and courtesy which his heroism so richly deserved.[4] In 1593 the principal scene of interest is transferred to the Indies. The Earl of Cumberland resumed his activities there,

[1] C. de C., iii, pp. 343 ff.; Corbett, *Drake and the Tudor Navy*, ii, pp. 356–358; Fernández Duro, *Armada Española*, iii, pp. 48–51; E. P. Cheyney, *History of England*, i, pp. 153–189. The death of Walsingham (April 16, 1590) and the relegation of Drake to private life after the return of the expedition from Lisbon caused the English end of the war to languish.

[2] Fernández Duro, *Armada Española*, iii, pp. 52 f.; Cheyney, *op. cit.*, i, pp. 519–527.

[3] Fernández Duro, *Armada Española*, iii, pp. 78 f.

[4] Corbett, ii, pp. 383–389, and references there; Cheyney, i, pp. 534 f.

and ravaged Havana and the shores of Trinidad. In that same year Sir Richard Hawkins, the son of Drake's old companion in arms, set sail with a roving commission to harry the Spaniards, and passed through the Strait of Magellan into the Pacific. After plundering Valparaiso and capturing several prizes, he was forced to surrender, grievously wounded, to Don Beltran de Castro in the bay of San Mateo (July 2, 1594), and was sent back a prisoner to Spain.[1] It was partly on the pretext of avenging him that his father and Drake got permission from the queen to sail, in August, 1595, on what proved to be their last voyage. On this occasion they made first for the Canaries, only to be repulsed before Las Palmas; indeed, the chief result of their appearance there was to give the Spaniards a chance to send out warnings to the colonies and treasure fleets in the New World. When the Englishmen reached the Antilles, everything was in readiness for them. After being driven off from Porto Rico by the Spanish artillery, they passed on and seized Nombre de Dios. But when the troops they brought with them tried to cross the Isthmus of Panama on foot, they were stricken with dysentery and had to return. They were also utterly demoralized by the loss of their two great leaders. Hawkins had sickened on the voyage across the Atlantic, and died, off Porto Rico, on November 22, 1595; Drake fell a victim to the yellow fever of the Isthmus on February 7, 1596, and was buried at sea off Porto Bello.[2] Needless to add, the news was received throughout the Spanish Empire with transports of joy, and Lope de Vega, who had had some personal experience of the ways of 'El Draque' and 'Achines' when he

---

[1] *The Hawkins' Voyages*, ed. C. R. Markham (London, 1878), pp. xxiv–xxvii, 83–349.

[2] C. de C., iv, pp. 151–157; Fernández Duro, *Armada Española*, iii, pp. 96–112; Corbett, *Drake and the Tudor Navy*, ii, pp. 413–430; Benson, *Sir Francis Drake*, pp. 293–305; Cheyney, i, pp. 543–549.

served in the Armada, wrote a poem of triumphant gratitude for the removal of the scourge of the church.

The only Spanish reply to the ravages of the *corsarios
Ingleses* was a raid on the Cornish coast in the summer of
1595; it did a certain amount of damage, and caused fear
and irritation in England, but nothing of permanent importance was accomplished.[1] But the same statement holds
true, *mutatis mutandis,* of the much more dramatic exploits
of the English buccaneers in the Antilles; indeed, the chief
result of them had been, as Sir William Monson expressed it,
"to waken rather than to weaken" the Spaniards. In the
first place, Philip's naval men had made good use of the
respite from attack that had been accorded, in these years,
to the Spanish ports themselves, and had constructed a whole
new fleet of fighting ships. One high authority speaks of the
period as actually witnessing "the birth of the Spanish
navy."[2] In the second, the English sea-rovers had signally
failed to accomplish their chief objective, that is, to capture
the Spanish treasure fleets, and get command of the trade
routes. Isolated ships and even smaller squadrons had indeed
been cut off, but the 'Flota' and the 'Galleons' continued
to sail as before; the fact, already noticed elsewhere, that
the sums the Spanish crown derived from the Indies in the
last decade of the reign were nearly four times as large as
those which it got from them in the sixties, speaks volumes
in this connection. Might it not be possible for Philip, who,
as the years rolled by, became increasingly anxious to concentrate all his forces against Henry IV of France, to persuade
Elizabeth that the efforts of her corsairs were practically
fruitless, and terminate the war which neither of them was
really anxious to continue? The older historians used to

[1] Fernández Duro, *Armada Española,*   iii, p. 79; Corbett, *The Successors of*
iii, pp. 92 f.; Cheyney, i, pp. 544 f.   *Drake,* p. vi.
[2] Fernández Duro, *Armada Española,*

believe that Philip attempted in 1594 to get Elizabeth poisoned, and bribed her Portuguese physician, Dr. Rodrigo López, to accomplish it for him. More recently this view has been attacked, and it has been demonstrated that López was never really proved guilty of the crime for which he was executed. Is it not even possible that Philip was really trying to utilize him simply to approach the queen with an offer of peace? In view of the state of feeling in the England of the time, it would have been essential for him to have a very secret agent to accomplish this, and the use of physicians for diplomatic purposes was by no means unfamiliar in the sixteenth century.[1]

If Philip actually made an offer of peace, it never had a chance of success. The queen, as we have remarked, might have been willing to entertain it, but she dared not fly in the face of the wishes of England, and England longed to avenge the death of Drake. The war party, too, was once more dominant in the Royal Council, and was vigorously led by Elizabeth's youthful favorite, the Earl of Essex, whom she was at all costs anxious to please. Since buccaneering had not accomplished what had been expected of it during the last five years, it was decided to revert to the tactics of 1589, and make a great thrust at the heart of Spain. Cadiz was selected as the point of attack; on June 30, 1596, a fleet of sixty ships, commanded by Howard, of Armada fame, and carrying 10,000 English soldiers under Essex, and 5000 Dutch under Louis of Nassau, suddenly appeared at the mouth of the harbor. Practically no preparations had been made to

---

[1] Arthur Dimock in *English Historical Review*, ix (1894), pp. 440–472; Martin A. S. Hume, *The Year after the Armada* (London, 1896), p. 17, note 2; idem, "Conspiración del Dr. Ruy López contra Isabel de Inglaterra y supuesta complicidad de Felipe II," in his *Españoles é Ingleses en el Siglo XVI* (Madrid, 1903), pp. 205–233; idem, "The So-Called Conspiracy of Dr. Ruy Lopez," in *Jewish Historical Society of England, Transactions*, vi, pp. 32–55 (1908); Forneron, iv, pp. 266–268.

receive them, and the Duke of Medina Sidonia, who as
governor of Andalusia was summoned to protect Cadiz,
showed himself even more incompetent than he had been in
1588; he did practically nothing save to report to Philip
almost hour by hour the rapid progress of the enemy, which
he was totally unable to impede. His indecision prevented
the few Spanish warships in the harbor from giving as good
an account of themselves as they otherwise might. Several
of them were sunk by the cannon of the foe; some of
the rest escaped up the Guadalquivir; all the merchant
vessels were burnt by the Spaniards themselves in order to
save them from capture. Meantime the enemy's troops had
been landed, and entered Cadiz practically without resistance. The inhabitants promptly fled inland, and the English were left to plunder the place at their good pleasure. For
sixteen days the process continued, and then, after Cadiz had
been completely emptied, it was set on fire, and a large portion of it, including the old cathedral, reduced to ashes. Raids
into the interior would have yielded a rich harvest and were seriously contemplated by the invaders, but the English did not
realize the extent of Spain's unpreparedness; they also feared
for the personal safety of the favorite of the queen, and so they
finally decided to make for home. Faro on the south shore of
Portugal was plundered on the way, and there was even talk
of an attack on the Azores; but the members of the expedition had been so demoralized by the booty that they had
taken that they were in no condition to attempt anything
further. They reached England safely on the 8th of August.[1]

---

[1] On the Cadiz expedition see *D. I. E.*,
xxxvi, pp. 205–435; Herrera, *Historia
General del Mundo*, iii, pp. 632–643;
C. de C., iv, pp. 204–211; Pedro de
Abreu, *Historia del Saqueo de Cadiz
por los Ingleses en 1596*, ed. Adolfo de
Castro y Rossi (Cadiz, 1866); Great
Britain, Historical Manuscripts Commission, *Calendar of Manuscripts Preserved at Hatfield House*, vi, pp. 379–
383; Fernández Duro, *Armada Española*, iii, pp. 117–133; Corbett,
Successors of Drake, pp. 56–133; Cheyney, ii, pp. 43–91.

The expedition to Cadiz had the merit of proving to Philip that his dreams of a peaceful settlement with England were illusory ; during the two remaining years of his life he burned for revenge.[1] In some respects he was now better situated than he had ever been before for a direct attack on England. He was in close touch with the Catholics of Ireland, who longed to strike a blow for their faith, and promised him a base there if he would support them.[2] The Spaniards, too, as we shall subsequently see, had captured Calais in April, 1596,[3] and were thus possessed of the Channel port whose lack had been so fatal to them in 1588. And so orders were sent out for the assembling of a new armada at Lisbon and San Lucar. Medina Sidonia had proved so useless at Cadiz that the command of it was given to Martín de Padilla y Manrique, the *adelantado mayor* of Castile. But despite the change of commanders there were the usual interminable delays. Philip did his utmost to hurry things, but the tradition of tardiness and inefficiency had been too firmly planted to be uprooted in a day ; the fleet was but half-ready by the middle of October, when the king had absolutely insisted that, ready or not, it should set sail. No sooner had it put to sea than it was struck by a southwest gale and scattered ; a third of the ships that composed it were wrecked, and over 2000 men were lost. "Truly," wrote Herrera in his *Historia General del Mundo*, "an admiral, like a doctor, must have fortune on his side."[4]

[1] Agostino Nani, the Venetian ambassador to Spain, wrote to the Doge and Senate in midsummer, 1596, that, in talking with the papal nuncio, the king "seized a candelabra, and with energy declared that he would pawn even that in order to be avenged on the queen, and that he was resolved to accomplish this. These are words which, in the mouth of a king who has never shown any passion in fortune, good or evil, prove that his mind is fully set upon undertaking that war again." *C. S. P.*, *Venetian*, 1592–1603, no. 473.

[2] *C. S. P.*, *Spanish*, 1587–1603, nos. 634–666, *passim*.

[3] Cf. *infra*, p. 657.

[4] *Historia*, iii, p. 643; Fernández Duro, *Armada Española*, iii, pp. 129 f. ;

Still Philip did not despair. A new though unsuccessful attempt of England to invade Spain in July, 1597,[1] still further infuriated him; and later in the same year, when Essex, with the best of the English fleet, was off on the 'Islands Voyage' at the Azores,[2] where he hoped to intercept the Flota from the Indies, the king sent the last of his armadas against England. It was a most imposing fleet, almost as large, in fact, as that of 1588. A detachment of the Spanish soldiers in Brittany was to coöperate with it. Its commanders had had experience of English naval tactics, and its destination, the port of Falmouth, had been kept profoundly secret.[3] But the munitions and supplies were of poor quality and insufficient; worst of all, the departure of the expedition was so long delayed that it had no chance to reach the Channel and establish a base there, as had been originally planned, before the return of Essex from the Azores. Instead, the two fleets, in complete ignorance of each other's positions, sailed simultaneously, on converging courses, for the mouth of the English Channel, from Corunna and from the Azores; but before contact between them could be established, the inevitable northeaster blew up and dispersed the Armada, while the English found refuge in their own ports.[4] The king was deeply cast down when he got the news, and the renewal of the exploits of the *corsarios Ingleses* in the Indies, particularly the capture of Porto Rico by the ubiquitous Earl of Cumberland in the summer of 1598, must have further enhanced the agonies of the last weeks of his life. Yet no one could possibly maintain that he had tamely surrendered or abandoned the fight without a struggle; moreover, the

Corbett, *Successors of Drake*, pp. 134–151.

[1] Cheyney, ii, pp. 424–430.

[2] *Ibid.*, pp. 430–440.

[3] C. de C., iv, pp. 266 f.; Corbett, *Successors of Drake*, pp. 212–217.

[4] Fernández Duro, *Armada Española*, iii, pp. 166 f.; Corbett, *Successors of Drake*, pp. 217–227.

example that he had set was followed in the next reign, and
England did not cease to be worried over 'invisible armadas'
and Spanish invasions of Ireland until the peace of 1604.[1]
The great issue between Spain and England had indeed been
settled in 1588, but neither side was aware of it at the time,
and it was primarily owing to the Spaniards' heroic, if mis-
guided, continuance of the struggle during the next sixteen
years that the real facts of the situation remained so long
concealed, not only from the two contestants, but also from
the rest of Europe as well.   The Spanish Empire of the early
seventeenth century was a ghost of its former self, but the
world at large did not realize it until after the peace of the
Pyrenees in 1659.   The legend of its invincibility was kept
alive, by a masterly game of bluff, long after it had ceased to
be in any way formidable, and James I often grovelled at the
feet of the Spanish ambassador in London, the Count of
Gondomar.

[1] Corbett, *Successors of Drake*, pp. 253 ff.; Cheyney, ii, pp. 496–499.

BIBLIOGRAPHICAL NOTE

See note at the end of Chapter XXXIV, and add :

Sources. — The *Archives ou Correspondance inédite de la Maison d'Orange-Nassau*, première série, ed. Willem Groen van Prinsterer (Leyden, 1835–47, 8 vols. and supplement), is valuable for the period to 1584, as are also the *Actes des États Généraux des Pays-Bas, 1576–1585*, ed. L. P. Gachard (Brussels, 1861–66, 2 vols.). The one small volume of the *Correspondance d'Alexandre Farnèse avec Philippe II pour les années 1578, 1579*, ed. L. P. Gachard (Brussels, 1853), is drawn from the Belgian archives at Brussels ; Gachard did not complete his work by printing the letters for 1580–81 preserved in the same collection. From the archives of Simancas A. Rodríguez Villa edited the correspondence of Farnese and Philip, in Spanish, of the years 1577–78, in *R. A.*, 1883, pp. 60–66, 131–135, 160–163, 246–250, 305–312, 348–352, 381–384, 437–440. Captain Alonso Vázquez, *Los Sucesos de Flandes y Francia del tiempo de Alejandro Farnese*, in vols. lxxii–lxxiv of the *D. I. E.*, is the standard Spanish contemporary account of the military operations of that period. The originals of Bernardino de Mendoza's letters to Philip from London are printed in vols. xci–xcii of the same collection. The note on the authorities for the Armada campaign on pp. 442–451 of vol. ii of J. S. Corbett's *Drake and the Tudor Navy* renders it unnecessary for me to add anything in regard to the English end, save perhaps to mention the following publications of the Navy Records Society : the *Naval Tracts* of Sir William Monson, edited by Michael Oppenheim (1902–14, 5 vols.) ; and the *State Papers Relating to the Defeat of the Spanish Armada*, ed. J. K. Laughton (1894, 2 vols.). For the Spanish side of the story, C. Fernández Duro's *La Armada Invencible* (Madrid, 1884–85, 2 vols.) still holds its place as the primary collection of contemporary letters and *relaciones*, and also gives a useful bibliography (ii, pp. 503–513). It needs, however, to be supplemented by the documents from the archives of the house of Medina Sidonia in *D. I. E.*, xxviii, pp. 364–424, the Armada letter of Pedro Estrade in Monson's *Naval Tracts*, ii, pp. 299–308, and still more by the *Documentos procedientes del Archivo General de Simancas*, selected by Enrique Herrera Oria, transcribed by Miguel Bordonau and Ángel de la Plaza, and published in the *Archivo Histórico Español*, ii (Valladolid, 1929). This last-named work contains numerous letters between Philip and the Duke of Medina Sidonia which have never been published before. *Papers Relating to the Navy during the Spanish War, 1585–1587*, ed. J. S. Corbett (1898), is a publication of the Navy Records Society. Sir William Monson's account of the Cadiz voyage of 1596 is in his *Naval Tracts*, ed. M. Oppenheim, i, pp. 344–395; ii, pp. 1–20.

Later Works. — The standard authorities for the Low Countries and for France in this period remain pretty much what they were in the preceding one, save that J. L. Motley's *History of the United Netherlands* (New York, 1861–68, 4 vols.) replaces his *Rise of the Dutch Republic* after the murder of Orange in 1584. Pietro Fea's *Alessandro Farnese, Duca di Parma* (Rome, 1886) has long been the standard biography. It is now being superseded by Léon van der Essen's brilliant biography, of which, unfortunately, only the first volume (to 1578) has yet appeared (Brussels, 1933). Francisco Barado y Font, *Sitio de Amberes, 1584–1585* (Madrid, 1891), is very useful. For the Armada campaign and the ensuing events, J. S. Corbett's *Drake and the Tudor Navy* (London, 1898, 2 vols.) and his *Successors of Drake* (London, 1900) are still in my opinion the most valuable authorities, if taken in conjunction with Fernández Duro; they may be supplemented, on the technical side, by W. F. Tilton's painstaking *Katastrophe der spanischen Armada* (Freiburg i. B., 1894) and by Gervasio de Artíñano y de Galdácano's *La Arquitectura Naval Española* (Madrid, 1920), already cited. The most recent life of Drake is that of E. F. Benson (London, 1927); that of Hawkins is by J. A. Williamson (London, 1927). Professor E. P. Cheyney's *History of England from the Defeat of the Armada to the Death of Elizabeth* (New York, 1914–26, 2 vols.) gives an excellent account of Anglo-Spanish relations during the last years of Philip II, and a great deal more besides.

CHAPTER XXXVIII

ANTONIO PÉREZ AND THE LIBERTIES OF ARAGON

THE foregoing chapter will have made it clear that the defeat of the Spanish Armada in 1588 marks the turning point in the history of Spain's struggles with England and with the Netherlands. The dispersal of Philip's great fleet saved the former; it made it probable that the latter would ultimately go free. The crucial years of Spain's conflict with France were to come, as we shall subsequently see, somewhat later. Not till Henry IV renounced his Protestantism in 1593 — perhaps not, indeed, until five years afterwards, when the Edict of Nantes was issued and the peace of Vervins signed — was it evident that Philip's projects in that quarter were also destined to fail. Between these two great sets of disasters in the field of foreign affairs, there occurred a most extraordinary contest on the soil of Spain itself, a contest which reveals perhaps more clearly than any other episode in Philip's whole reign the nature of the king's methods and viewpoint, and the measure of his impotence in coping with the new foes which were springing up all around him. The accumulated weight of long centuries of tradition enabled him, indeed, to emerge officially victorious from this contest at home; but the way that the story of it was circulated in foreign lands increased the bitterness of the hatred of his fellow sovereigns, and encouraged some of them to believe that they could safely give vent to it. The legend of Spain's invincibility, though it was not broken till the middle of the seventeenth century, received rude shocks during the two closing decades of the reign of the Prudent King.

We have had many occasions to remark that the process of Castilianization of the Spanish Empire, initiated really under the Catholic Kings and advancing rapidly under the Emperor, had reached its climax in the reign of Philip II. The fact that the Prudent King fixed his capital at Madrid in 1561[1] was the outward and visible symbol of it, and his refusal, during the twenty-six years after his return to Spain in 1559, to pay more than one visit[2] to the realms of the crown of Aragon made a most painful impression on his subjects in these kingdoms.[3]   Their pride was wounded by the fact that he ignored them for so long, save for the viceroys and governors who represented him in his absence;[4] in this respect, as in others, his reign stood out in marked and disagreeable contrast to that of his father, whose long and patient sojournings among his East Spanish subjects went far to atone, in their eyes, for his numerous absences from the peninsula.[5] Their resolution to maintain all the forms and emblems of their ancient liberties and privileges — inanimate, almost, though they had now become — was vastly enhanced by the policy of the Prudent King.   Material began rapidly to accumulate, from the very beginning of the reign, for the conflagration which finally burst forth in 1591.

Of all the defenders of the ancient autonomies of the eastern realms, the most ardent, and perhaps also the most unreasonable, were the nobles of the kingdom of Aragon. It will be remembered that they inherited from mediaeval

[1] Cf. ante, p. 42.

[2] This was in 1563–64. Danvila, ii, pp. 291–304; Coroleu and Pella, Las Córtes Catalanas, pp. 361–366.

[3] After the establishment of Philip's capital at Madrid, the realms of the crown of Aragon, and also Navarre, came to be called virreinatos.

[4] Pidal, Philippe II, Antonio Perez, et le royaume d'Aragon, i, p. 36.

[5] Cf. ante, Vol. III, p. 158.

times a position almost unique among the aristocracies of
Europe; that they formed two of the four *brazos* into which
the Aragonese Cortes were divided; and that they had given
evidence on countless occasions of their uncompromising
obstinacy and lack of cosmopolitanism.[1]   They were zealous
indeed for the maintenance intact of all the national liberties
of the kingdom of Aragon, but they were more zealous still
for the preservation of their own special privileges within
that kingdom, and of their position as a caste within the body
politic.   Certainly some of these privileges were such as had
no place in the civilization of Western Europe in the latter
part of the sixteenth century.   We may cite as an instance
that which gave some of them the unquestioned right to
strangle their vassals without hearing what they had to say
in their own defence, a right of which Don Diego de Heredia,
of whom we shall shortly hear much, was afterwards not
ashamed to boast that he had twice availed himself.[2]   Small
wonder if Philip ardently longed to break down such a
position and such pretensions as these.   Not only were the
traditional rights of the Aragonese aristocracy a flagrant
contradiction to the principles of the strong monarchy which
he and his predecessors had established; they were also, from
a purely humanitarian point of view, atrocious, and we must
not forget that Philip was a humanitarian in his own way.
Certainly this group, at least, of the Prudent King's subjects
was far more mediaeval than he.   But Philip was too much
attached to Castile, and too busy with other affairs, to be
able for a long time to take effective measures to remedy
these things.   Like almost every other problem with which
he was confronted, he preferred to deal with it from afar off,
by instructing his representatives in Aragon to support the
attempts of the rural population to transfer themselves from

---

[1] Cf. *ante*, Vol. I, pp. 431 ff., 460 ff.   [2] Pidal, *op. cit.*, i, pp. 34 f.

seigniorial to royal jurisdiction, and by using his efforts in favor of marriages in Castile of the heads of the more prominent Aragonese families, in the hope of breaking down the barriers between the two kingdoms and of making his East Spanish subjects enter more sympathetically into his own point of view.[1] A single instance will suffice to show what measure of success this policy attained.

The great and ancient county of Ribagorza, extending north from the neighborhood of Monzon to the Pyrenees near Bagnères-de-Luchon, and including seventeen towns and 200 villages, with some 4000 vassals,[2] was held, at the accession of the Prudent King, by John of Aragon, Count of Ribagorza, who was descended, though illegitimately, from Alfonso of Aragon, the bastard brother of Ferdinand the Catholic. In 1564 he married Luisa, of the Castilian house of Pacheco, and went to live with her in Toledo; but shortly afterwards, on the ground that his wife was unfaithful to him, the Count caused her to be brutally murdered.[3] It was the beginning of a terrible blood feud. The sister of the murdered Countess was the Countess of Chinchón,[4] who spurred her husband on to vengeance. The Count of Ribagorza was forced to flee from Spain, was finally captured in Milan, brought back to Madrid, and publicly garroted, like a common criminal, in 1572. Needless to say, the news of these events was hailed with delight by the vassals of Ribagorza, who had suffered cruelly under the harsh rule of the Count, and now eagerly seized the opportunity to

---

[1] Pidal, i, pp. 53 ff., *passim.*

[2] *Ibid.,* i, pp. 78–81.

[3] *Ibid.,* i, pp. 55–57: "l'on suppose généralement qu'elle périt par les mains du Comte lui-même et de ses serviteurs"; Forneron, iii, p. 258, states definitely that the Count killed her with his own hand.

[4] Mother of the Count of Chinchón viceroy of Peru (1629–39), whose wife was cured of an attack of fever in 1638 by the use of Peruvian bark. On her return to Europe she brought with her a supply of this invaluable remedy, which took from her the name of chinchona or cinchona bark (i.e., quinine).

demand that they be attached to the royal domain. They were, of course, vigorously supported by Philip, who asked nothing better than an opportunity to increase his own power and lands in Aragon at the expense of the most unruly of his subjects. At one stage of the proceedings he is said to have tried, though vainly, to get the Inquisition to exhume traces of Jewish blood in the family of the Count of Ribagorza; if such had been found, he would have insisted that the territories in question must not be allowed to remain in the hands of any of its descendants, especially since Ribagorza lay so perilously close to the heretical viscounty of Béarn.[1] But the Justicia decreed that the Ribagorza lands went lawfully to the Duke of Villahermosa, the brother of the executed count,[2] and the Justicia's verdict was law; the Council of Aragon supported him, and so, much as Philip disliked it, did two of his own most trusted Castilian advisers, Idiáquez and de Moura. Legality, if not expediency, was clearly against the crown, and the Prudent King saw that he must submit. But the vassals of Ribagorza, having come so close to the attainment of their ends, were far less respectful than their monarch to the sentence of the Justicia. They rose in revolt, organized their forces, elected leaders, and virtually took the control of the county into their own hands. A situation, in fact, not remote from civil war had begun to exist, and the necessity of dealing with it, together with that of getting the recognition of the future Philip III by the representatives of the eastern kingdoms, was the principal cause of the resolution of the king to summon and personally attend a meeting of the General Cortes at Monzon in the summer of 1585. The pleasure of accompanying his daughter

[1] So Forneron, iii, p. 259.

[2] A third brother, the Count of Luna, wrote Comentarios de los Sucesos de Aragon en los Años 1591 y 1592, mentioned in the bibliographical note, p. 605, below.

Catharine, who had just married Charles Emanuel of Savoy, as far as Barcelona on her wedding journey, was an added inducement to the Prudent King to depart from his beloved Castile.[1]

An account of that journey has been left us by Henry Cock,[2] of Gorcum in Holland, notary apostolic and archer of the royal guard; but as it concerns itself chiefly with brilliant ceremonies and descriptions of the places through which the court passed, it has little of interest for us here. Certainly most of the solid business that was transacted at Monzon passed wholly over Cock's head. Philip was forced, much against his will, formally to recognize the rights of the Duke of Villahermosa to the Ribagorza lands, but he made no efforts whatever to put down the revolutionists. Indeed, he tacitly encouraged their worst outrages, and gladly seized the opportunity to incorporate into the crown domain other territories, such as Teruel and Albarracín, where the seigniorial rights were less clear.[3] Needless to add, under these circumstances, the revolts in Ribagorza continued with unabated violence after Philip's return to Castile, and they were rendered more horrible still by risings of local Moriscos, who were massacred with relentless cruelty by the mountaineers.[4] The decision taken at Monzon had not improved matters; it had really made them worse, and Philip, whose chief adviser for Aragonese affairs was now Villahermosa's mortal enemy, the Count of Chinchón, was convinced that he would have no peace until the Duke was induced to abandon his lands. Much plotting ensued, for the purpose of inducing the Duke's friends to desert him, and finally Villahermosa

---

[1] Philip's absence was ultimately prolonged for over a year. Cf. Forneron, iii, p. 255, note 4, for details.

[2] Cf. edition published in 1876 by A. Rodríguez Villa and A. Morel-Fatio.

[3] Pidal, i, pp. 59–102, *passim*.

[4] Argensola, *Informacion de los Sucesos del Reino de Aragon*, pp. 61–65; Pidal, i, pp. 122–127.

was obliged to give way. He unwillingly surrendered his territories in return for a few high-sounding titles and a generous money indemnity, and Ribagorza was at last incorporated into the royal domain.[1] But others of his countrymen were even less content with this solution than he. The risings in Ribagorza were indeed soon suppressed, but Philip's policy had entailed too much going and coming of Castilians to suit the mass of the Aragonese. The municipal authorities of Saragossa, the Cortes, and, most of all, the Justicia were firmly convinced that the national *fueros* were in danger; and their anger reached its climax when, at the beginning of 1588,[2] the king sent to Aragon the Marquis of Almenara, of the great Castilian house of Mendoza,[3] to oust the existing viceroy and bring order out of chaos. This was certainly a practical, if not a technical violation of the law which provided that all the king's officers in Aragon should be Aragonese;[4] and this was promptly brought home to Philip by the way in which Almenara was treated on his arrival. The court of the Justicia, always a stickler for the letter of the law, was inclined indeed to be favorable to his pretensions; but he was regarded with contempt by almost every one else. The aristocracy refused for the most part to accept his invitations, while the populace characterized as 'Soup Knights' those who did;[5] before long he retired to Castile, to report to the king, leaving behind him what had started as a mere local disturbance in Ribagorza already half transformed into something like a national uprising. But Philip was not to be denied. Shortly after Almenara's return to Madrid, the Count of Sástago, who had filled the office of

---

[1] Pidal, i, pp. 142 f.
[2] C. de C., iii, p. 526.
[3] He was also first cousin of the Count of Chinchón. Cf. Mignet, *Antonio Perez et Philippe II*, p. 209.

[4] Argensola, *op. cit.*, pp. 53–57; Pidal, i, p. 159.
[5] *Ibid.*, i, pp. 160 f.

viceroy of Aragon for the past twelve years, was removed;
his successor, Andrés Ximeno, the bishop of Teruel, was the
son of a plain citizen of Saragossa, and obviously only
intended as a stop-gap; and when Almenara came back, in
the spring of 1590, with increased emoluments and powers,
it was evident to all men that it was the king's plan that he
should have all the authority, and the viceregal title [1] also,
provided he could extract from the Justicia's court a definite
verdict favorable to his pretensions. With all his irritation
Philip was not yet quite prepared openly to defy the existing
law; that was to be reserved till later.

With things thus balanced, as they were, on the point of a
needle, a new and dramatic personality was brought upon the
scene by the arrival in Saragossa of Antonio Pérez, the dis-
graced minister of the Prudent King, escaped from his
gloomy prison in the dungeons of Madrid.

Antonio Pérez had led a most unhappy existence since his
sudden arrest and fall from power, on the night of July 28,
1579.[2] At first the king did not seem disposed to be severe.
He gave no immediate orders to institute any process against
his late minister, and sent the Cardinal Quiroga to assure
Pérez's wife, the devoted Juana Coello, who had stood loyally
by him through all his divagations, that her husband had been
only temporarily removed because of the hatred of Rodrigo
Vázquez de Arce,[3] the new royal favorite. Pérez himself
was visited by the royal confessor, and even permitted to see

---

[1] This, however, he never actually
got; cf. Argensola, p. 57: "en este
lugar es bien que se entienda que el
marques de Almenara no era virei,
ni exercitaba en Aragon ningun magis-
trado público."

[2] Cf. *ante*, p. 328.

[3] Not to be confused with Mateo
Vázquez de Leca, the informer, who
was also an enemy of Pérez, and sub-

sequently became secretary of the
Junta de Noche; they were not even
related. Vázquez de Arce was just
coming into prominence at the time
of Pérez's fall. He became president
of the Council of Castile in 1591, and
continued to hold the office until the
reign of Philip III. Cf. Forneron,
iii, pp. 62 f., 78, note, 263; iv, pp. 163 f.

his children. When, in spite of these encouraging signs, he fell ill, he was allowed to remove to his own house; and after eight months' seclusion there, he was given leave to go out to mass, and to receive visitors. Shortly afterwards the king departed for Portugal, and Pérez, taking advantage of his absence, began to lay plans for the recovery of his influence and position.[1]

But Philip was only dissembling. He cherished a mortal grudge against Pérez, and, as usual, was only waiting to feed it fat. The king had every reason to be cautious. Pérez was in possession of important state secrets and numerous documents; above all, if he were driven to extremities, he would infallibly reveal damning evidence that the king had formally authorized the murder of Escovedo. But the reports that he played for high stakes with his friends in his house gave his enemies the opening which they desired; and when the facts were reported to Philip, he ordered Vázquez de Arce to start a secret inquiry into the honesty of Pérez's career as a minister. His venality, needless to add, was only too easy to prove; it was found that, although his father had left him nothing, he had amassed an enormous fortune and lived in regal luxury.[2] But the king, after his return from Portugal at the beginning of 1583, was still in no hurry to act; not until fresh rumors began to circulate in regard to the responsibility for the murder of Escovedo did Philip decide to strike again. On January 23, 1585, merely on the ground of his peculations, Pérez was sentenced to two years or more of imprisonment in a fortress, according to the king's pleasure, to perpetual banishment from the court, and to the payment of an enormous fine.[3] But when the royal *alcaldes* arrived to arrest him, they found him, to put it mildly, a

[1] Mignet, *Antonio Perez et Philippe II*, pp. 139–144.
[2] Cf. *Fragmentos del Archivo Particular de Antonio Pérez*, ed. A. González Palencia, pp. 11–47.
[3] Mignet, *op. cit.*, pp. 157–160.

troublesome prisoner. While they were ransacking his house for documents, he escaped to sanctuary in a neighboring church, and when the king's officers made bold to arrest him there, a quarrel was started between the secular and ecclesiastical authorities of Madrid which did not terminate till four years later. The documents, moreover, which were found in Pérez's house were not at all what Philip wanted. Two more large boxes of them were indeed subsequently delivered up by Juana Coello, on receipt of a written order to do so from her husband, who feared for her safety if she refused; but even then, the wily Pérez contrived to retain the most important of them all, and particularly a number of notes signed in the king's hand. He was destined at a later date to make good use of them for his own advantage.[1]

After the papers had been delivered up, in the summer of 1585, orders were given for another brief intermission in the rigor of Pérez's captivity, most probably for the purpose of putting him off his guard. He was brought back to Madrid, installed in a sort of semi-confinement in one of the best houses of the town, and permitted to receive visitors from the court. But the king, at this juncture, was absent in Aragon, and the implacable Vázquez, who accompanied him thither, seized the opportunity to interrogate a native of Saragossa, who had confessed himself implicated in the killing of Escovedo. The son of the murdered man was on hand in Madrid to feed the flames. A formal though secret investigation of the crime was decreed, and Pérez was once more placed in strict confinement. For more than four years the miserable affair dragged on. There were countless phases and ramifications of it, into which it is not worth while to enter. From first to last Pérez took the line that he had nothing whatever to do with the crime, and in September,

[1] *Infra*, p. 581; Forneron, iv, pp. 133 f.

1589, by a marvellously clever series of secret missives and insinuations, he persuaded young Escovedo to abandon his case and request that his enemy be set at liberty.[1] But the rancorous Vázquez had by this time so poisoned Philip's ear against his former minister that the government pursued the matter on its own account more relentlessly than ever. Not only was the imprisonment of Pérez continued and its rigor increased; he was actually placed in irons. Finally, as all other efforts to make him confess anything had failed, the king, on January 4, 1590, sent to tell him that he admitted having ordered him to murder Escovedo, but that,. for his own satisfaction and that of his conscience, he must know whether or not the causes which had been given him for this action were adequate; he therefore ordered Pérez to state these causes in detail and give proof. In this way he hoped to lure the latter into a confession of the crime, while he trusted that, having secured the incriminating evidence in the documents that he had obtained from his former minister, he could clear himself in the eyes of the world from all complicity therein.[2] But Pérez refused to fall into the trap. He persisted in denying all knowledge of, or participation in, the crime, until Vázquez and his minions, despairing of eliciting a voluntary confession, determined to extort it from him by force. On February 21, 1590, Pérez was chained to the wall of his prison. The following day he was once more put to the question, and when he continued to remain obdurate, he was handed over to the executioner to be tortured. The rack was brought in, and after he had suffered eight turns of the rope, he finally confessed, in great detail, the part that he himself had played in the murder of Escovedo.[3] When, however, he was told to explain the reasons that had moved him to persuade the king to order the crime to be committed, his

---

[1] Mignet, p. 180.   [2] Ibid., pp. 180–186.   [3] Ibid., pp. 430–433.

replies were less satisfactory. The information, he protested, would be found in the documents which had been taken from him; the murder, too, had taken place twelve years ago, and most of those who could bear witness to the truth of what he said were no longer to be found. And so the proceedings were again left unfinished. The king had got only half of what he wanted; moreover, despite all the secrecy of the inquisitors, enough leaked out of Philip's complicity in the whole affair to evoke strong protests at the court. Men asked what manner of crime it could be, in which the king and his fallen minister had collaborated, but for which, nevertheless, one ordered the other to be put to the torture, and sympathy for Pérez was aroused on every side.

But the end was close at hand, though not in the way which Philip had expected. Pérez was keen enough to perceive that after the king had got everything out of him that he could, there was no reasonable doubt that he would be given over to the executioner, and he determined to make one final effort to save himself by flight. There was only one place where he could possibly find a safe retreat. Philip had been willing to violate a sanctuary in Castile in order to recapture him, but the soil of the kingdom of Aragon and the authority of its mighty Justicia offered Pérez a far surer refuge. He was accurately informed of all that had recently occurred there. Five years earlier he had had a project of escaping thither, and the situation there now was far more favorable to him than it had been then.[1] As ever, his devoted wife was at hand to aid and abet him.[2] She was far advanced in pregnancy at the time — indeed, the record of her confinements and miscarriages through all this harrowing period is

---

[1] Mignet, pp. 163, 170 f.
[2] Cf. their correspondence in *Frag-* *mentos del Archivo Particular de Antonio Pérez*, pp. 76–82.

by no means the least remarkable feature of this extraordinary tale —, but she finally contrived to obtain access to him in his prison, on the plea that his sufferings on the rack made his death an immediate probability, and the two laid their heads together with excellent results.   About nine o'clock on the evening of April 20, 1590, Pérez passed through his guards and out of his prison, disguised in his wife's cloak. Just outside one of his friends awaited him ; farther on was another with horses.   On the way from the one to the other the local constabulary was encountered, but Pérez played the sulky servant, and remained behind in discreet silence while his companion engaged the officers in talk.   But when he reached the horses he hesitated no longer.   The pains of the torture did not prevent him from making thirty good Spanish leagues to the eastward without stopping, until he had crossed the frontiers of the kingdom of Aragon.[1]

The battle between Philip and Antonio Pérez had been fought thus far under most unequal conditions.   In Castile the king held all the cards, and the wellnigh universal sympathy which the cause of the fallen minister had evoked bore eloquent testimony to that love of fair play which happily characterizes the mass of mankind.   But the moment that Pérez reached the kingdom of Aragon the whole situation changed.   He found himself under the protection of a constitution which gloried in defending the rights of the individual against any and every sort of tyranny, and in the midst of a people whose sensitiveness to its own dignities and privileges had just been stirred to the depths by the events recounted in the early pages of this chapter; he could not possibly have arrived at a more propitious moment. No essential feature of the government of Aragon had been

[1] Mignet, pp. 195 f.

abolished, or even seriously modified by the Emperor or the Catholic Kings. They had simply followed the plan of concentrating their efforts on the increase of the royal power in Castile, and of leaving Aragon as far as possible alone, in the hope that what they deemed it imprudent to subvert by force might ultimately perish from inanition. Thus far, for more than a century past, this policy had, on the whole, worked well. But now the Aragonese were suddenly thrust forward into the limelight again. They became all at once a centre of interest. Stirring memories were inevitably aroused. They had a cause to fight for once more, and proposed to show that they were capable of defending it. A battle royal was obviously imminent, and most of the rest of Spain proposed to sit by and enjoy it. Even Philip's favorite court fool ventured to twit him about the situation in open court.[1]

Naturally the king could not endure the thought of being openly defied in his own dominions. At all costs Pérez must be recaptured and brought back. Philip's first act was to vent his anger on the only victims who were for the moment within his reach. On Holy Thursday, the day after Pérez's escape, his wife and children were seized and cast into the public prison in Madrid.[2] Pérez, on his part, had not yet reached the stage of bidding his former master defiance. On April 24, from his place of refuge in Calatayud, he had written the king a most humble and respectful letter, offering peace and abandonment of all attempts to rehabilitate himself, provided he were only permitted to withdraw, with his family, into obscurity ; and he was deeply incensed when he learned what Philip had done.[3] Meantime the king lost no time in the pursuit. Ten hours after the fugitive reached

---

[1] Pidal, *Philippe II, Antonio Perez, et le royaume d'Aragon*, i, pp. 225–227 ; Mignet, pp. 200 f.

[2] *Ibid.*, p. 201.

[3] *Ibid.*, pp. 198–203.

Calatayud, there arrived a royal order to seize him, dead or alive, before he passed the Ebro.[1] But Pérez had already taken his precautions. Though right of asylum had not availed him in Castile, he still had some faith in its efficacy in Aragon; and when the king's representatives arrived to arrest him, they found that he had sought refuge in a Dominican convent. Even this step, however, might only serve as a stop-gap, with Almenara and his officers rallying to the royal cause; the only permanent hope of safety lay in a *manifestación* and the protection of the Justicia of Aragon.[2] Gil de Mesa, Pérez's devoted friend, who had accompanied him on his flight from Madrid, was accordingly despatched in hot haste to Saragossa to obtain it, and with the happiest results. Juan de Luna, one of the deputies of the realm, appeared at Calatayud with fifty arquebusiers, to claim for Pérez the ancient privileges of Aragon, just at the moment that Philip's emissaries were about to seize him in the convent and deport him to Madrid. The people of the town rose for the defence of their liberties, and Pérez was carried off in triumph to Saragossa, where the whole populace turned out to bid him welcome; he was lodged at once in the *cárcel de los manifestados*. Philip had been decisively beaten in the first round of the fight; but, legal minded as ever, he was not yet prepared to infringe the established constitution. He accordingly entered a formal plea against Pérez before the Justicia's court, on the grounds of his having compassed the murder of Escovedo on false pretences, of his having altered despatches and divulged state secrets, and, finally, of having escaped from prison.[3]

The conflict now entered upon a prolonged judicial phase. Pérez had the good sense not to be rendered over-confident

---

[1] Mignet, p. 204.
[2] Cf. *ante*, Vol. I, pp. 469–471.
[3] Mignet, p. 206; Pidal, i, pp. 241–245.

by the evidences of popular favor which greeted him on every hand. Once more he wrote to the king and to the royal confessor from his refuge in the *cárcel de los manifestados*, offering peace if Philip would only leave him alone, but hinting, in unmistakable terms, that if the king continued to persecute him, he had ample means of defending himself.[1] But Philip would not listen; he was determined to fight to a finish. On July 1, 1590, he ordered Pérez to be condemned to the death of a common criminal by the tribunals of Madrid, and sent word to the Marquis of Almenara to push the case vigorously in Saragossa.[2] Pérez was prompt with his reply. He now confessed before the Justicia that he had ordered the murder of Escovedo, but only at the king's own command; moreover he produced a number of documents which he had secreted about his person, many of them written by Philip himself, in proof of the truth of his assertions. The effect of these revelations was tremendous. The people of Saragossa took delight in them and circulated them broadcast. Philip and his worst methods were exposed to the gaze of Spain, and also to the rest of Western Europe, for the case had by this time begun to attract universal attention; it was a terrible blow to the king's prestige.[3] Obviously nothing was to be gained by continuing the royal suit before the Justicia's court, and an attempt of the Marquis of Almenara to subject Pérez to an *enquesta*, on the ground that he had been unfaithful in his services as crown minister, was also speedily disposed of; the Justicia issued a *firma*, and the process was stayed.[4] At several junctures during these trying months the king had plans of using force, as is proved by his orders to the Castilian grandees dwelling

[1] Forneron, iv, p. 132; Pidal, i, pp. 245 f., 428–433.
[2] Forneron, iv, p. 133; Pidal, i, p. 249.
[3] *D. I. E.*, xii, pp. 22–24; Forneron, iv, p. 134.
[4] *D. I. E.*, xv, p. 480; Pidal, i, pp. 261–265.

on the confines of Aragon to muster their vassals and be ready for war;[1] but Philip could not bear actually to appeal to arms until the uttermost resources of his various jurisdictions had been exhausted. There still remained one tribunal in Spain against which the *fueros* of Aragon and the authority of its mighty Justicia were of no avail, the tribunal of the Supreme and Holy Inquisition; and into its clutches Philip now planned to deliver Pérez. The necessary preparations were made with devilish ingenuity. The king and his confessor, Almenara, and Chinchón collaborated to furnish evidence to show that Pérez, during his imprisonment and torture, had uttered words implying doubts of the existence of God, that he had planned to flee to the heretics of France and Béarn, where his knowledge of weighty affairs of state and important papers could have done much harm, and that the fact that he had succeeded in winning such devotion from the people gave reason to suppose that he possessed diabolical powers.[2] The evidence was despatched to the tribunal of the Suprema at Saragossa. Precautions were taken to make certain that the worst possible interpretation was placed upon it.[3] The local inquisitors in haughty terms demanded of the Justicia's court that Pérez be given up; and the Justicia, Juan de Lanuza, who, though zealous for the maintenance of the authority of his office against all secular jurisdictions, belonged to a generally royalist family, and was in mortal terror of the church, soon decided, with the

[1] *D. I. E.*, li, pp. 226 f.; Forneron. iv, p. 132.

[2] *D. I. E.*, xii, p. 129; Pidal, i, pp. 276–283. Forneron, iv, pp. 135–137, supposes that one charge against Pérez before the Inquisition was that he had fled from prison on a horse, which he might have taken with him to Béarn, thereby furnishing heretics with the material of war. It is true that the Inquisition was charged with the prevention of the export of horses to Béarn and other heretical lands (*supra*, pp. 82 f.; Lea, *History of the Inquisition of Spain*, iv, pp. 278–281); but the passage which Forneron cites (*D. I. E.*, xv, p. 482) relates not directly to Pérez but to his friend Diego de Heredia. On Heredia's case see also Lea, *History of the Inquisition of Spain*, iv, p. 282.

[3] Forneron, iv, pp. 136 f.

unanimous approval of his lieutenants, to do what was required of him. On the morning of May 24, 1591, Pérez was transferred from the *cárcel de los manifestados* to the secret prison of the Inquisition in the palace of the Aljafería.[1]

The people of Saragossa were less overawed than the Justicia by the authority of the Holy Office. The Inquisition had never been really popular in Aragon, where its essentially Castilian origin caused it to appear, in the present tense state of popular excitement, almost in the light of an importation from abroad; certainly it was far less national and less ancient than the *fueros* which all men were now sternly resolved to defend. Rapid though the Inquisition had planned that its prisoner's removal to the Aljafería should be, Pérez had been able to notify his friends; and on the way he was met by a group of them, including some of the most eminent men of the city.[2] Efforts to make the Justicia interfere proving fruitless, the tocsin was sounded, and the populace called out; a vast crowd, nobles, clergy, and commons, shouting *Contra fuero! Viva la libertad!* rushed to the palace of the Marquis of Almenara, who was popularly held responsible for what had occurred. The Justicia, hooted in the streets as he passed, had already taken refuge there; realizing the seriousness of the crisis, he begged the Marquis to flee. But the scion of the Mendozas knew no fear.[3] He had, moreover, a Castilian's contempt for a rabble horde, and was confident that he could assert his own authority. His sole reply was to send an order to the inquisitors forbidding them to deliver up Pérez. Meantime the rioters had broken down his door; and the Justicia, as a last resort, mounted to the balcony above, and called out to ask them whether, if he would consent to take the Marquis and his adherents to

[1] Mignet, pp. 231 f.   [2] Mignet, pp. 232–238.
[3] *D. I. E.*, xii, pp. 161–166.

prison, they would engage, on their word as gentlemen and cavaliers, to do no violence to him on the way. The promise was given by the leaders of the crowd below, but the rage of the mass of the rioters had by this time mounted so high that it proved impossible to make them keep it. When the Justicia and the Marquis issued from the palace, they were suffered indeed to proceed a few paces in safety, but soon the Justicia, jostled by the crowd, fell and was trampled under foot; and when he was lost to view, the mob became uncontrollable. In front of the ancient Iglesia de la Seu, the rioters hurled themselves on Almenara, beat and stabbed him; they would have killed him on the spot, had not a few of the nobles interfered; his servants, too, were treated as cruelly as he. Obviously there was no chance of getting him, alive, as far as the *cárcel de los manifestados*. He was therefore deposited, bruised and bleeding, in the old town prison, which was on the way, and there two weeks later he died.[1] In the meantime another band of rioters had rushed to the prison of the Inquisition at the Aljafería. They demanded that the inquisitors deliver Pérez into their hands, and threatened, in case of refusal, to fire the building, in order that the inquisitors might themselves experience the same suffering to which they sentenced others.[2] For a time the inquisitors hesitated; but at last the bishop of Teruel, who was still officially viceroy, the *zalmedina*[3] of Saragossa, and two representatives of the archbishop succeeded in persuading them that only by yielding could they hope to end the revolt. And so, finally, about five o'clock in the afternoon of the day that the insurrection had broken out, the Holy Office surrendered its prisoner, with the stipulation that he should be guarded with special care, and treated in all respects as if he

---

[1] Luna, *Comentarios*, pp. 46–48, 464–467; Argensola, pp. 83–89.

[2] *D. I. E.*, xii, p. 319; Mignet, p. 243.
[3] Cf. *ante*, Vol. I, p. 463.

were still in its clutches.[1] Pérez was driven back to the *cárcel de los manifestados* in a coach. His progress thither was like a triumphal procession, and as he disappeared behind the walls of the *cárcel*, he was adjured to show himself thrice a day at the window, in order that all men might know that their *fueros* were not infringed. In one day he had made himself the emblem of the maintenance of the liberties of Aragon.

Philip was in bed, at nine o'clock in the morning, when he was told by the Count of Chinchón of the death of Almenara. Stroking his beard thrice, he rose, dressed himself, and issued orders which resulted, in a few weeks, in the concentration of large forces of infantry and cavalry at the town of Agreda on the confines of Aragon.[2] Evidently it was his first idea that the rebellion must be put down by force. But, as ever, he was slow to take vigorous action ; and while his troops were assembling, a number of considerations began to present themselves, all of which strengthened his unwillingness to appeal to arms. If he invaded Aragon in force, he would be virtually proclaiming to the world that Spain was in a state of civil war, and this, in the existing condition of his foreign relations, he was extremely reluctant to do. The English were harrying his Atlantic coasts. The war in the Low Countries was not going well. He was already deeply involved with the League in France. Antonio of Crato threatened to make trouble on the Portuguese frontier, and Catalonia, to put it mildly, was restive. Better, far better, dispose of this Aragonese trouble quietly, if possible, than reveal his internal weakness to his numerous foreign foes. As usual, he made every effort to demonstrate that legality was on his side. He got most of the cities of Aragon, with

---

[1] " . . . y asi cesó la tormenta, como se dice de Jonas quando fue echado en el mar." Argensola, p. 93.

[2] Pidal, i, pp. 305 f.; C. de C., iii, p. 554.

the exception of Saragossa, to pronounce against the revolt. Some, even, of the more conservative of the Saragossans obviously felt that the easiest way out of the situation would be to return Pérez to the custody of the Holy Office, and the officials of the Inquisition aided these sentiments by publishing the bull *Motu proprio* of Pius V against all those who hindered its activities. Even the *Diputación Permanente del Reyno*, after consulting with the most learned men in the kingdom, was persuaded to fall into line, with a somewhat equivocal resolve that, though the inquisitors had no authority to annul the right of *manifestación*, they might lawfully suspend it, and that if they again demanded the custody of their prisoner in such language as respected this distinction, the Justicia would have no excuse for refusing to deliver him up.[1]

But all these favorable factors were more than counterbalanced by the extraordinary activity of Pérez and his friends. There were plenty of old-fashioned radicals still left in Saragossa, and he speedily succeeded in binding every one of them to his cause. The events of May 24 had proved to him, if he still needed proof, that he had a real genius for moving the masses. He produced inflammatory pamphlets by the score, and they were smuggled out of his prison and circulated among the crowd.[2] His pretensions, moreover, had by this time become stronger than they had been at the time of his arrival in Aragon; he now spoke openly of forcing Philip to restore the 200,000 ducats he had unlawfully taken from him. There is even reason to believe that he was

[1] Mignet, pp. 256 f. Cf. also the *consulta* of the Council of Aragon to Philip (June 4) on the general situation in Aragon, and the way to remedy it, in Pidal, i, pp. 390–405.

[2] Mignet, pp. 258–261. The most famous of these pamphlets, the so-called *Pasquin del Infierno*, popularly attributed to Pérez (cf. Argensola, p. 94), is a dialogue of the dead between Vázquez de Arce, Almenara, the chronicler Blancas, and others on the events of May 24. It is printed in Pidal, i, pp. 410–429; cf. also ii, pp. 332–361.

already in correspondence with Henry IV of France. His physical activity, too, fully matched his intellectual. In three nights he sawed through the grating of his window in the *cárcel de los manifestados*, and had it not been for the treachery of one of his friends, he would certainly have escaped. The news of this attempt made the king more desirous than ever to finish matters up; and despite the advice of his counsellors in Madrid, who did not believe the thing could be done without the aid of Castilian troops,[1] he sent word to his officials and to the inquisitors in Saragossa that Pérez was to be brought back to the prison of the Holy Office. Orders were despatched that the transfer was to be effected on September 24; but just two days before, Philip's projects suffered a heavy blow in the death of Juan de Lanuza, the Aragonese Justicia, whose complaisance and moderation during the past five months had been infinitely helpful to the royal cause.[2] His son, also named Juan, who succeeded him at the age of twenty-seven, was far less respectful to the authority of the crown, and wholly lacking in experience.[3] He complied, indeed, with the legal formalities which were necessary before his prisoner could be given up — in loyalty to the memory of his father he could scarcely do less; but when September 24 came, he found himself powerless to see to it that the king's orders were carried out. Pérez and his friends had been too active; among the crowd which assembled at the time of the transfer, they were fully as numerous and far more desperate than the supporters of the constituted authorities. Another scene of violence ensued, more terrible in some respects than that of four months before. After a

---

[1] Philip created a special *Junta de Estado para los negocios de Aragon* in the summer of 1591; the names of its ten members are given in Pidal, ii, pp. 2 f.; and the *consulta* it sent the king on August 29 in Pidal, ii, pp. 320–331.

[2] Luna, *Comentarios*, p. 109; Pidal, ii, p. 32.

[3] Mignet, pp. 267 f.

brief resistance, the royal guards took flight, and Pérez, delivered from the *cárcel de los manifestados*, was borne off in triumph to the house of his best friend, Diego de Heredia.[1] There he mounted a horse and fled north toward the mountains, at first with the intention of escaping to France. On hearing, however, that the royal troops were pursuing him, he lay hidden for a few days; and then, dare-devil that he was, returned in disguise on October 2 to Saragossa, where his faithful adherents took care that he was kept well concealed. He now had plans of heading a real revolution against Philip, and he was loyal, for the time being at least, to those who had helped him in distress, and who now desperately needed his leadership to save them from the vengeance of the king.[2]

But Philip still dissembled. The news of the insurrection of September 24 doubtless convinced him that force would ultimately have to be used. His advisers at Madrid were convinced of it, and their views were confirmed by the letters that poured in from Saragossa, where the rebels, led by Diego de Heredia, had made themselves masters of everything. The royal forces at Agreda had by this time increased to upwards of 12,000 men, most of them raw levies, but with a nucleus of 800 veterans. The command of them was now given to an Estremaduran officer, Alonso de Vargas, who had served in the Netherlands;[3] he was doubtless selected principally because he came from the West of Spain, and could therefore have no real sympathy or affiliation with the Aragonese. But it was not till the very end of October that Vargas was permitted to cross the frontier. Most of the intervening weeks were occupied with correspondence between the king and the rebel leaders. Both sides were

---

[1] Argensola, pp. 101–105.

[2] Luna, *Comentarios*, pp. 136 f., 381–383; Mignet, pp. 270–276; Pidal, ii, pp. 41 f., 46–51.

[3] Pidal, ii, pp. 30, 54–57; Mignet, p. 280; Forneron, iv, p. 145.

anxious, if possible, to avoid bloodshed, but each was determined to assert what it regarded as its inalienable rights. The rebels, who had always maintained in their most violent moments that they were acting solely in defence of the ancient liberties of the realm, stoutly asserted that the entrance of a Castilian army on Aragonese soil would constitute a breach of their *fueros*. They persuaded the *Diputación del Reyno*, and also the youthful Justicia, to give them formal support in this contention; they notified the king of the position they had taken and of their intention to organize armed resistance if he ignored it; they even sent word to Vargas to inform him that he was condemned to a traitor's death in case he should invade the realm.[1] The king, on the other hand, took the line that, *fuero* or no *fuero*, order must be restored and the royal authority maintained. He was encouraged by the fact that most of the Aragonese cities, except Saragossa, had declared themselves favorable to his cause, and he was vastly relieved by the news that the rebels had been unsuccessful in their efforts to get help from the sister county of Catalonia and the kingdom of Valencia. The Valencians refused to have anything to do with them at all. The *Diputación* of Catalonia and the councillors of Barcelona were more sympathetic, and wrote to Philip to beg him not to invade Aragon; on the other hand, they were quite unwilling to lend armed support to the revolt, and it was chiefly because of their refusal actively to participate therein, that their own lands were later left untouched by the royal vengeance.[2] Meantime in Saragossa the rebel forces became divided among themselves. Diego de Heredia was too much of a firebrand to suit the views of those whose chief aim was to preserve intact the letter of the ancient laws. He circulated a rumor that the Justicia and the chief nobles who

[1] Pidal, ii, pp. 57–78, *passim*. [2] Pidal, ii, pp. 92–97, 364–371.

had stood by him had sold themselves to the crown. A riot
ensued, in which the youthful Juan de Lanuza was violently
handled, while the Duke of Villahermosa and the Count of
Aranda took refuge in flight. On the following day calmer
counsels prevailed. The Justicia was persuaded once more
to accept the official responsibility of defending the liberties
of the realm. On November 8 he issued forth from the town,
with all pomp and ceremony, holding aloft the banner of
San Jorge at the head of a company of some 400 men, to stop
the army of Vargas, now advancing to the bridge of Alagón.[1]
But this demonstration was no better than a solemn farce.
Vargas and his forces had been generally well received in the
cities of the realm through which they had already passed,
and their power was plainly irresistible. After a futile
attempt to negotiate with him, in the hope of inducing him
not to enter Saragossa, the Justicia and his adherents fled
north to Epila. On receiving this news, the rebels in
Saragossa dispersed. Pérez, who, whether because he did
not venture to issue from his hiding place, or because he had
temporarily lost his genius for moving men, had failed to
accomplish anything since his return, took flight for the last
time on November 11, and found safety in Béarn. On the
following day Vargas and his army made their entrance
unresisted into the ancient capital of Aragon.[2]

Although the rebellion now seemed utterly crushed, the
slow-moving king determined to make assurance doubly sure
before he enjoyed his vengeance. Well informed, as always,
on the situation as it developed day by day, he learned that
the Justicia, Villahermosa, and Aranda were now planning to
create a new centre of resistance at Epila, that they had high
hopes of aid from the Catalonians, incensed by the presence

[1] Pidal, ii, pp. 101 f.; Forneron, iv, [2] Argensola, p. 125; Mignet, p. 288.
pp. 146 f.

of a Castilian army on the soil of Aragon, and that Pérez was striving for intervention from France; if possible, these new perils must be averted without the use of force.[1] Vargas played his part to perfection. Whether owing to the royal commands, or to his own admiration of the sturdy patriotism of the Aragonese, he showed the utmost courtesy and kindliness in his dealings with every one with whom he came in contact. In a few weeks he so succeeded in convincing all men that Philip's sole desire was a peaceful solution of the existing difficulties, that the 'Junta of Epila' broke up, and the Justicia and his adherents returned to Saragossa.[2] Prolonged correspondence with the king ensued, in which Vargas and his advisers unanimously advocated lenient treatment; but the majority of the royal counsellors in Madrid took the other view, and insisted that an example be made of the rebel chiefs. For some time Philip hesitated; but the Castilian element in him was too predominant for the issue to remain long in doubt. He had everything now under his hand; at last it was safe to strike. On the morning of December 12 a secret messenger was despatched with a note to Vargas, who, when he opened it, is said to have burst into tears. "On the receipt of this paper," so it ran, "you will seize the person of Juan de Lanuza, Justicia of Aragon, and — let me hear of his death at the same moment that I learn of his arrest. You will have his head cut off."[3] The order was obeyed. The youthful Justicia was seized, cast into prison, and given one night to prepare for death. His protest, perfectly valid under the *fueros*, that he could not legally be condemned "save by the full Cortes, the king, and the kingdom," availed him nothing; and at ten o'clock on the following morning, December 20, the last of the independent Jus-

[1] Pidal, ii, pp. 116–121.
[2] *Ibid.*, pp. 121–124.
[3] Mignet, pp. 291–293; Forneron, iv, pp. 149 f.; cf. the comment of Motley, *History of the United Netherlands*, iii, p. 534.

ticias of the kingdom of Aragon was beheaded in the public market-place of Saragossa. The soldiers of Vargas, under arms, were the sole witnesses of the scene. The Saragossans were a prey to terror and dismay, and dared not issue from their houses.[1]

Obviously there were other victims to follow. The ancient *fueros* were for the moment in abeyance; men wondered where the next blow would fall. On January 17, 1592, Philip issued a general amnesty and pardon; but twenty-two persons were specifically excepted therefrom, in addition to those actually in prison at the time, a category which included the Duke of Villahermosa and the Count of Aranda, who had been carried off to Castile. The king, moreover, was at great pains to state that the Holy Office had full liberty to demand satisfaction for the indignities to which it had been subjected.[2] Before effect could be given to these orders, the attention of all parties concerned was diverted once more by the necessity of repelling an invasion from the north which Pérez and his friends had organized in Béarn. This, in itself, was a very trifling affair. The invaders, a mere handful, got no farther than Sallen and Biescas, and Vargas and his forces soon drove them back across the mountains.[3] Perhaps the most notable thing about the whole matter was the success with which the government used the war cry of 'Navarrese heresy' to stimulate the ardor of the Spaniards against the new danger, and the loyalty with which the mass of the Aragonese supported Vargas. Much though they feared the loss of their *fueros*, they dreaded still more the prospect of invasion from a foreign country under the rule of a Protestant king; and Pérez, who, while he had dwelt among them, had been a popular idol, was now branded as a

[1] Luna, *Comentarios*, pp. 251–255; Pidal, ii, pp. 150–158.

[2] Pidal, ii, pp. 165–168, 388–407.
[3] Pidal, ii, pp. 168–184.

traitor to his native land.[1] These events occupied the greater part of February, and Philip was highly gratified at the evidences of returning loyalty which had been afforded him; the original leaders of the insurrection, however, he could not bring himself to forgive.[2] The spring, summer, and autumn of 1592 witnessed a tragic series of executions and torturings, the chief object of the latter being to obtain evidence from the leaders of the revolt in Aragon which would enable Philip to proceed legally against Villahermosa and Aranda in Castile. Both of these noblemen, however, died mysteriously in prison, Aranda probably on August 4, and Villahermosa on November 6, "before it was even known that he was ill"; but the process against them continued into the reign of Philip III, and ended, significantly, with an acquittal.[3] The final vengeance of the Inquisition took the form of an unusually imposing auto-da-fé at Saragossa, on October 20, in which six of the condemned were burnt alive, and over seventy others sentenced to different forms of lesser punishments.[4] Since Pérez, the arch-fiend in the eyes of the Holy Office, was now beyond its reach, there was nothing left save to burn him in effigy, in *coroza* and *sanbenito*, with all possible attendant maledictions and vilifications, which was done. His children and his descendants in the male line were declared incapable forever of holding secular or ecclesiastical office, and were forbidden "to wear gold, silver, pearls, precious stones, coral, silk, camlet, or fine cloth, to ride on horseback, or carry arms, or do anything else that is forbidden by the laws of the realm and the regulations of the Holy Office to those under similar disabilities."[5]

The insurrection was thus put down, its ringleaders

---

[1] Forneron, iv, pp. 152 f.
[2] Pidal, ii, p. 185.
[3] Forneron, iv, pp. 155 f.; Pidal, ii, pp. 228–230.

[4] Pidal, ii, p. 223.
[5] Mignet, pp. 302 f., and references there.

punished, and peace restored; there now remained the further problem of how to prevent its recurrence. That the situation demanded radical modifications of the existing *fueros* was clear. However admirable the spirit of independence in which they had been originally conceived, they certainly had no place in an absolute monarchy such as Philip and his predecessors had set up.[1] The real question at issue was whether it was safe to stop at that, or whether advantage should not be taken of the excuse which the rebellion had offered to abolish entirely the constitution of the kingdom of Aragon, as was ultimately to be done by Philip V in 1707.

That the Prudent King finally decided not to go so far as this has often provoked surprise. Certainly he had all the power in his hands, and the pretext which his great-grandmother, Isabella the Catholic, had so often desired for 'conquering Aragon'[2] had been amply afforded him. But there were a number of considerations which inclined him to the more lenient course. In the first place, he had always declared that he proposed to respect the *fueros*, and he did not wish to go back on his word. In the second, he desired to show his gratitude for the loyalty with which the mass of the Aragonese had rallied to his side, when it was a question of repelling the invasion from Béarn. Thirdly, the situation in Catalonia and Valencia doubtless counted for much. The former had perhaps sympathized with, but nevertheless had abstained from any active interference in the rebellion in Aragon, while the latter had held wholly aloof. The king, therefore, had no possible excuse for proceeding against them, and unless their separate governments were abolished, as well as that of Aragon, he could not have a constitutionally united Spain; if their autonomy, in other words, not to

---

[1] Pérez in his *Epistolarum Centuria*, no. lxxvi, discusses from abundant experience the nature of monarchical power and the dangers arising from its excess.

[2] Cf. *ante*, Vol. II, p. 85.

speak of that of Portugal on the other side of the peninsula, must necessarily continue, there was not much point in putting an end to the *fueros* of Aragon. And, lastly, there was Philip's innate reluctance to violate the traditions of his native land. Even more than his father before him, he was reverent of the past. Separatism, of wellnigh every sort, was, as we have repeatedly pointed out, the most ancient and dominant inheritance of Spain; being Spanish, it must necessarily, in Philip's eyes, be right. Aragon must be brought into line with Castile, but her autonomy was to remain intact.

Negotiations were therefore begun between the victorious king and the representatives of his rebel realm. Of these the foremost was Martín Bautista de Lanuza, a kinsman and lieutenant of the executed Justicia, who, however, was a royalist at heart, and had carefully refrained from any active participation in the recent insurrection. In pursuance of the policy which the king had decided to adopt, the Cortes of the kingdom of Aragon were summoned to Tarazona, in order that the changes which were contemplated should have the sanction of the representatives of the realm; but the agenda for their deliberations were drawn up by a *junta* specially constituted for the purpose and carefully instructed by the crown. Of this *junta* the most important members were Andrés de Cabrera y Bobadilla, archbishop of Saragossa, who was then at the court, and the Count of Chinchón. Moreover, the first of these two was delegated by Philip formally to open the assembly in his name, for the king cherished bitter memories of his experiences at Monzon in 1585, and did not propose to appear until all the real business of the session had been done.[1] The meeting, originally fixed for May 9, 1592, did not finally take place until June 15.[2] The

---

[1] Pidal, ii, pp. 241–246; C. de C., iii, pp. 596–599. [2] Pidal, ii, pp. 244–247.

brazos, needless to add, made difficulties over the royal absence, which they regarded as derogatory to their dignity. There was also much trouble over getting them to accept the king's demand for the abolition of the ancient *fuero* requiring absolute unanimity of the votes of each estate, and the substitution of majority rule; but authority, if not tradition, was now on the royal side, and in the end they submitted.[1] In the course of these events, the archbishop of Saragossa died, and Philip appointed Doctor Juan Campi, the regent of the Council of Aragon, to take his place as the royal representative; but the news that daily poured in from Tarazona made it increasingly evident that everything was ultimately bound to turn out in accordance with the royal desires, and in mid-November the king, with Prince Philip, arrived in Aragon. They were welcomed at least with outward cordiality.[2] There was a solemn *solio* of the four *brazos* in the archiepiscopal palace at Tarazona on December 2,[3] at which the Prince of Asturias swore to observe the *fueros* of the realm. The king solemnly sanctioned all the changes in the constitution which the Cortes had made, and formally

---

[1] Pidal, ii, pp. 245–253, and references there; and cf. also pp. 412–415, a "Papel sobre que la mayor parte de cada brazo haga brazo, presentado á las Córtes de Tarazona por el Arzobispo de Zaragoza," which concludes with the following curious paragraph:

"La election del Emperador es legítima si es hecha con parescer de la mayor parte de los electores, y hasta el mismo Reyno de Aragon, cuando en él faltó Rey, se cometió la election á nueve personas, y lo que la mayor parte de ellos determinó fué sentencia y bastó para dar el Reyno de Aragon; y agora no quieren que baste para hacer y determinar en las Córtes, lo que á la mayor parte parezca que conviene, siendo así que la vida y la muerte, la hacienda y la honra, el imperio, y el mundo, hasta la conciencia están sujetos al juicio de la mayor

parte; de lo cual se ve quan escrupulossa cossa es no atender á remediar una singularidad tan grande como es querer en las Córtes conformidad sin discrepacion; y los que se han hallado en algunas anteriores tienen mas obligacion de advertirlo y mas escrúpulo en facilitarlo; por todo lo cual paresce á Su Majestad que al bien de este Reyno conviene, que luego se haga fuero para que la mayor parte de brazo haga brazo y la mayor parte de Córte haga Corte."

[2] Over the gate by which they entered Tarazona appeared the following verses:

"A dos Felipes espero,
En quien hoy espera el mundo:
El segundo es sin primero,
Y el tercero es sin segundo."

Cf. Pidal, ii, p. 259.

[3] A list of those present is given by Pidal, ii, pp. 416–419.

declared the session closed. On the following day he granted a general amnesty to all who were still prisoners in the realm. On December 5 he left Tarazona. On the 30th he was back at Madrid.[1]

The constitutional changes which had been voted by the Cortes of Tarazona were simple but effective. Dictated, as they virtually had been, at the fiat of the monarchy, they put an end to the real independence, if not to the formal autonomy of the kingdom of Aragon. Nothing was absolutely suppressed, but all power to resist the crown was removed. The king was given the right, at least until the next meeting of the Cortes, to nominate a foreign viceroy; Aragon alone, of all his different realms, had hitherto succeeded in reserving this office for natives, and she was now brought into alignment with Valencia, Granada, and Navarre.[2] In the Cortes, the abolition of the *fuero* requiring unanimity was the most important change; the right to vote also, though not to attend, was taken away from those members of the two *brazos* of the aristocracy who had not attained the age of twenty years; the *Diputación Permanente*, too, was deprived of a large measure of its control over the use of the national funds and over the national guard, and of its right to call together the representatives of the cities of the kingdom. The Justicia became for the first time removable at the pleasure of the king, and the chief guarantee of his independence was thus annulled. The nomination of his five lieutenants and of the seventeen legists who advised him was also rearranged in such fashion as to put their selection much more largely in the royal hands; indeed, it was the changes in matters judicial that were the most important of all.[3] A

[1] Luna, *Comentarios*, pp. 330–335; Pidal, ii, pp. 260–269. Cf. also Luna, pp. 372 ff., and Mignet, pp. 377 f., on the reception of Philip III at Saragossa in 1599.
[2] Pidal, ii, pp. 270 f.
[3] Pidal, ii, pp. 271–274.

number of other constitutional anachronisms were either
radically modified or else done away with. Notable among
these was the so-called *fuero* of the *via privilegiada*, which
enabled a prisoner to regain his liberty, temporarily at least,
in case of any illegality in the form of his arrest; its
operation was now greatly restricted by the enumeration of
some thirty important crimes for which it was no longer to be
valid.[1] All in all, it is impossible to deny that most of these
modifications, save perhaps that which provided that the
Justicia should cease to be irremovable, brought real
improvement; for conditions had so altered since the
ancient Aragonese constitution had first come into being,
that it was no longer possible that it should be practically
enforced. The tragedy lay in the fact that the changes had
not been evolved as a result of the constitutional development of the kingdom itself, but imposed, instead, at the command of a monarch who was so incorrigibly Castilian in his
viewpoint that the Aragonese really regarded him almost in
the light of a foreigner.

A few minor difficulties still remained to be settled after the
dissolution of the Cortes of Tarazona. Of these the most
important was the withdrawal of the Castilian army, which
the Cortes had demanded, and the whole realm ardently
desired. It was not effected, however, until December,
1593, and Philip insisted, as a price of it, on the construction
of a fort and the establishment of a royal garrison in the
Aljafería, on the plea that the safety of the Inquisition must
be insured.[2] He followed this up, in the next two months,
with a general disarmament of all the Moriscos in the realm.
Their outbreaks during the preceding troublous years furnished a pretext for it. The measure was in fact a foreshadowing of the edict of general expulsion which was to be

[1] Pidal, ii, pp. 275–277.   [2] Pidal, ii, pp. 418–421.

put forth for all Spain in 1609.[1]   All in all, there was no question that the king had issued victorious from his struggle with
the rebel Aragonese; in Spain, at least, he had triumphantly
asserted the absolute supremacy of the crown.   On the other
hand, his most powerful enemy had escaped, and was already
revealing the most closely guarded secrets of his ancient
master at the courts of France and England, and moving
heaven and earth to induce them to combine against him.
The 'troubles of Aragon' were not merely a *cosa de España*.
They also had an international significance; and in order to
appreciate what that significance was, we must follow the
fortunes of Antonio Pérez after his flight across the Pyrenees
to Béarn.

The fugitive burned for revenge on the Prudent King; as
long as Philip occupied the throne, his life's ambition was to
humiliate him.[2] His resentment, moreover, was greatly
enhanced by the king's attempts against him after his escape.
He was relentlessly pursued until he got across the frontier.
When he was in Béarn Philip sought to lure him back to
Spain on false pretences, and finally, when all else had failed,
did his utmost to get him assassinated.[3] Three Spaniards
tried to kill him while he was still in Navarre, without

[1] Pidal, ii, pp. 279–288; cf. also the
frontispiece to this volume.

[2] There can be no doubt that the
words and writings of Pérez went far
towards creating that hostile conception of Philip II which continued to
prevail north of the Pyrenees till the
middle of the nineteenth century (cf.
Bratli, *Philippe II*, pp. 19 f.). His
influence on the development of French
literature during the succeeding decades
is also incontestable; for everybody
read him. Cf. "Antonio Perez," by
Philarète Chasles, in the *Revue des deux
mondes*, quatrième série, xxii, pp. 701–
716 (1840), which contains the following sentences (pp. 703, 714): "L'élo-

quent exilé avait donné l'impulsion
castillane à cet esprit français que le
moindre souffle fait vibrer, et qui se
laisse entraîner avec tant de facilité
et de force vers des régions inconnues.
Alors l'Espagnole Anne d'Autriche
épouse Louis XIII; tout devient
espagnol en France. . . . Le bannisse-
ment d'Antonio a donc été l'*accident
nécessaire* qui devait greffer le génie
de l'Espagne sur celui de la France."
On the questions of loyalty involved
in Pérez's conduct, cf. the remarks of
A. Morel-Fatio, *L'Espagne au XVIe et
au XVIIe siècle*, p. 263.

[3] Mignet, pp. 314–317.

success. A beautiful harlot, bribed to make the same
attempt, was so fascinated by her intended victim that she
ended by offering him protection and support. Two Irish-
men, at the behest of Philip's representative in the Netherlands, sought to compass his death when he was in England
in 1594, but were promptly seized and executed; and the
same was the fate of the Baron de Pinilla, who was paid
600 ducats to shoot him in Paris in 1595.[1] Small wonder if Pérez vowed vengeance on the author of these
dastardly attempts, and there was no question where he
could most effectively seek it. Henry IV did not officially
declare war on Spain till January 17, 1595; but Philip since
1584 had been ardently supporting the League, which continued to hold Paris till 1594, and thus prevented the union
of France under Henry's sceptre. The French king could
make excellent use of a man with the genius and disposition
of Pérez. Henry therefore wrote to his sister Catharine at
Béarn, who had befriended the fugitive minister ever since he
had crossed the Pyrenees, to send him northward at once;
and the two men met at Tours in the spring of 1593.[2]

One of Henry's chief desires at this time was to gain for
himself the alliance of the cautious Elizabeth of England
for the defence of his northeastern frontier in the war against
Philip, which, though not yet declared, he foresaw was inevitable; and he promptly despatched Pérez to London, with a
letter to the queen, to obtain it. But there were grave difficulties in the way. Lord Burleigh and the majority of the
Council were averse to participating in a Continental war.
Elizabeth, as ever, was loath to spend money, and Pérez was
driven to seek the support of the Earl of Essex, who led the
small group which advocated a bolder policy. While in
London Pérez really lived at his expense, and on the proceeds

[1] Mignet, pp. 317–336, *passim*.   [2] Mignet, p. 321.

of a beggarly pension which Essex obtained for him from the queen; through Essex he became friendly with Francis Bacon, much to the alarm of the latter's Puritanical mother, who could not endure to see her son in the company of such "a proud, profane, costly fellow." [1] But to attain the real object of his mission, and induce England to join France against Spain, proved for the time being to be quite impossible. [2] All of political consequence that Pérez achieved during his first visit there was to inform the English government of the state of Spain and to circulate exaggerated stories of the infamies of her king; it was at London in the summer of 1594 that he first published his famous *Relaciones*, under the significant pseudonym of Raphael Peregrino. [3]

A year later he was back in France, where war, in the meantime, had been declared on Spain, and operations had begun on the northeastern frontier. Henry was now more than ever in need of English aid, and after begging for it in vain during the autumn and winter, he sent Pérez back to London once more on a last desperate effort to secure it in the spring of 1596. [4] At the time of his arrival the Spaniards were besieging Calais, and shortly afterwards (April 25) captured it. Elizabeth consequently changed her tactics, and began once more to flirt with the French alliance which she had hitherto opposed; all this was of course highly favorable to the success of Pérez's mission. But, unfortunately, when he reached London he found that the Earl of Essex, on whose ardent support he had counted, had gone off to Plymouth to

[1] Mignet, p. 330, note. See also "Antonio Pérez en Inglaterra y Francia" by C. Fernández Duro, in his *Estudios Históricos del Reinado de Felipe II*, pp. 247–380, especially pp. 249–256 and 379 f., and "Lettres d'Antonio Perez écrites pendant son séjour en Angleterre et en France," ed. A. Morel-Fatio on pp. 257–314 of his *L'Espagne au XVIᵉ et au XVIIᵉ siècle*.

[2] Despite all the correspondence and plottings described on pp. 93–97 of Mr. Lytton Strachey's *Elizabeth and Essex*.

[3] Mignet, pp. 328–330.

[4] Mignet, pp. 344–350, 434–437.

prepare for the great expedition against Cadiz. Nothing would induce the queen's favorite to return and run the risk of seeing the dramatic stroke on which he had staked his reputation diverted to a tamer purpose in the English Channel, and Pérez recognized with bitterness that he had become merely the sport of factions and the plaything of political chance.[1] He bore no real part in the settlement of the Anglo-French treaty, which was signed on May 24 and ratified later in the year;[2] and when he at last returned to France, he was disheartened and worn out. He was encouraged once more in January, 1597, by being taken over, on generous terms, into the service of the French monarch; for Henry recognized his great abilities, and as long as the war with Spain should last, he was confident that he could make good use of him. For some months thereafter Pérez devoted his best energies to maintaining intact the Anglo-French alliance, but this ultimately proved to be a task beyond his powers. Henry's recapture of Amiens, on September 24, convinced Philip that he could no longer profitably continue the war, and he soon afterwards offered the French king terms which induced him to abandon the ally who had so often disappointed him in the past, and sign a separate treaty with Spain at Vervins on May 2, 1598. When Pérez saw that the peace which he had labored to prevent was inevitable, he made a strong effort to get himself included in it, with provision for the liberation of his wife and children and the restoration of his property; but he hopelessly failed. The new turn of events made him a liability, not an asset, at the court of Henry IV. Moreover, his numerous reverses and rebuffs in the course of the past six years had converted into bitterness and insolence that rare personal charm which had

---

[1] Mignet, p. 353; Strachey, *op. cit.*, pp. 99–102.

[2] Mariéjol in Lavisse, vi, 1, p. 409;

Cheyney, ii, pp. 146–148; *C. S. P., Venetian*, ix, nos. 449, 455, 468, 474, 486.

hitherto been his most powerful asset ; every one now turned him the cold shoulder. The sole consolation brought him by the year 1598 was the news of the death of Philip, on September 13.[1]

Pérez survived his ancient master for more than thirteen years, but the last part of his life saw no betterment of his fortunes. He was encouraged, indeed, in 1599, by the events that signalized the initiation of the rule of Philip III : the rumor that Philip II had advised his son to get reconciled to his exiled minister, the fall from grace of his 'arch-executioner,' Vázquez de Arce, the liberation of Juana Coello and her children, and the general atmosphere of hedonism and forgiveness which characterized the reign of the 'Picture King';[2] more than ever did he hope to be allowed to return to Spain. With the idea of gaining favor with the new monarch, he tried to make himself useful in connection with the Anglo-Spanish peace negotiations of 1604, and so confident was he of success that he rashly resigned his pension at the French court; the attempt, however, was a miserable fiasco, for the French government had warned the British that Pérez's aims were purely selfish, and James I was furious when he learned that he had been even permitted to land in his realm.[3] Returned to France, Pérez was hard put to it to find a living. He was obliged to move from one lodging to another, each meaner than the one before. His petitions to the different Spanish ambassadors at Paris to intercede for him at Madrid were fruitless. A final hope that he could make capital for himself out of the negotiations for a

---

[1] Mignet, pp. 351–370; Pidal, ii, pp. 313 f.

[2] Mignet, pp. 371–378 ; also *Harleian Miscellany*, ii (1809), pp. 395–397, "A Declaration of the last Wordes and Death of Philip the Second." On p. 397, the king, speaking to the prince, says, "Let the wife of Antonio Perez also be set at libertie, so that from hencefoorth shee live in a monasterie, and let her daughters inherite the patrimonie which she brought."

[3] Mignet, pp. 384–389.

double marriage between the courts of France and Spain in the spring of 1611 was cruelly disappointed, and on November 3 of that year he died, and was buried in the church of the Célestines at Paris.[1]

In Spain Juana Coello continued to labor for the repeal of the harsh sentence which the Inquisition had pronounced against Pérez and his descendants in 1592, and in June, 1615, she was finally successful.[2] It would appear to have been stipulated, however, that this act of leniency should be kept secret, or, at least, unheralded; for when Gonzalo, one of the sons of Pérez, ventured to make it public too ostentatiously, he was promptly cast into prison, and his mother, on learning of his arrest, died of grief shortly afterwards in the arms of her daughter Luisa.[3] The rancors that had been engendered by her husband's extraordinary career were not to be allayed in his own generation.

[1] Mignet, pp. 389–403, *passim.*
[2] Cf. C. de C., iv, pp. 292 f.
[3] Mignet, p. 404; *D. I. E.*, xii, pp. 573 f.; Forneron, iv, p. 162, note 2.

BIBLIOGRAPHICAL NOTE

See note at the end of Chapter XXXV, and add:

Sources and Contemporary Authorities. — The whole of volume xii of the *D. I. E.* and pp. 397–553 of volume xv are filled with original documents in regard to Pérez. Ángel González Palencia published some *Fragmentos del Archivo Particular de Antonio Pérez* in the *R. A.*, 1918–21, and also separately, in 1922; my references are to the separate edition. Eugenio de Ochoa edited Pérez's letters from 1591 onward in the *B. A. E.*, Epistolario Español, i (1850), pp. 463–570, and A. Morel-Fatio added some more on pp. 257–314 of his *L'Espagne au XVIᵉ et au XVIIᵉ siècle*; and numerous other manuscripts bearing on the case are published in the works of Mignet and Pidal, described below. Pidal also gives a full list of the works of Pérez and the various editions of them on pp. xxxiv-xxxvi of volume i and pp. 316–319 of volume ii of his great book; it is worth noting that though the *Relaciones* and *Obras* were published four times in Paris and twice in Geneva before the end of the seventeenth century, they were not printed in Spain till 1849. Cf. also *Enciclopedia Universal Ilustrada*, xliii, p. 647, on the question of the authorship of the *Norte de Príncipes* and the *Arte de Gobernar*; the latter work was first published at Paris in 1867, in Spanish and French, edited by J. M. Guardia. The "capítulo adicional" on pp. 520–612 of vol. iii of C. de C. gives an excellent account of the 'troubles' in Aragon and Pérez's part therein from the Castilian point of view. The two standard contemporary histories of the same events by Aragonese are the *Informacion de los Sucesos del Reino de Aragon en los Años de 1590 y 1591*, written in 1604 by Lupercio Leonardo de Argensola, "cronista mayor del rei . . . en la corona de Aragon, a instancia de los diputados del reino," but not published till 1808 at Madrid; and the *Comentarios de los Sucesos de Aragón en los Años 1591 y 1592*, by Francisco de Gurrea y Aragón, Conde de Luna, who lived from 1551 to 1622 and was deeply involved in the affairs of the county of Ribagorza; this last work, which contains copies of a number of contemporary letters, was first published at Madrid by Marcelino de Aragón y Azlor, Duque de Villahermosa, in 1888.

Later Works. — The most valuable modern book on the Aragonese end of the story this chapter has to tell is still the *Historia de las Alteraciones de Aragon en el Reinado de Felipe II*, by Pedro José, Marquis de Pidal: it was first published in three volumes at Madrid in 1862–63, but it was subsequently translated into French by J. G. Magnabal, and published in two volumes at Paris in 1867, under the title of *Philippe II, Antonio Perez, et le Royaume d'Aragon*; my references are to this edition. It scarcely seems worth while to enumerate all the monographs, plays, and essays which have been written in regard to the personal character and career of Pérez. The most important are F. A. Mignet, *Antonio Perez et Philippe II* (Paris, 1845; my references are to the fifth edition of 1881); Gaspar Muro, *Vida de la Princesa de Éboli* (Madrid, 1877); J. A. Froude, "Antonio Perez: An Unsolved Historical Riddle," in the *Nineteenth Century* for April and May, 1883; subsequently printed on pp. 90–154 of his *Spanish Story of the Armada* (New York, 1892); C. Fernández Duro, "Antonio Pérez en Inglaterra y Francia," on pp. 247–460 of his *Estudios Históricos del Reinado de Felipe II* (Madrid, 1890); M. A. S. Hume, "El Enigma de Antonio Pérez," on pp. 167–203 of his *Españoles é Ingleses en el Siglo XVI* (Madrid and London, 1903); Andrew Lang, "The Murder of Escovedo," on pp. 32–54 of his *Historical Mysteries* (London, 1904); José Fernández Montaña, *De Cómo Felipe II no mandó matar á Escobedo* (Madrid, 1910); and Louis Bertrand, *Philippe II, une ténébreuse affaire* (Paris, 1929). Those desiring a fuller list will find it on pp. vii–x of Julia Fitzmaurice-Kelly, *Antonio Perez* (Oxford, 1922); cf. also Pidal, *op. cit.*, i, p. xxxvi.

CHAPTER XXXIX

SPAIN, FRANCE, AND THE NETHERLANDS, 1584-98

THE dramatic interest of the story of the defeat of the Spanish Armada and of the subsequent naval struggle with England must not make us forget that the period during which they took place was also of critical importance in the history of Spain's relations with France. To the history of those relations we now return, and therewith, at the same time, to the history of the revolt in the Netherlands, which, as the years rolled on, became more and more closely involved with them.

Down to the death of the Duke of Anjou in June, 1584, the policy of the Prudent King with regard to France can fairly be summarized as one of 'watchful waiting.' The last Valois were so fully occupied at home in their struggle to maintain themselves against the Guises on the one hand, and the Huguenots on the other, that it was out of the question for them to wage a foreign war in any such fashion as their predecessors had done in the Emperor's day. The most they could do, when they wished to make trouble for Philip, was to lend aid, directly or indirectly, to the rebels in the Low Countries. Philip, in turn, sought to parry these thrusts, and also to make additional capital for himself out of the situation in France, by secretly intriguing, through his ambassadors and other agents, with the various malcontents there. He might have minor grievances, indeed ; but, in general, the status quo — a France internally disrupted but still officially Catholic

— was highly satisfactory to him.   Certainly he had nothing to gain by provoking war, and if any of his representatives at the Valois court threatened to become too belligerent, he promptly recalled him.[1]

The continuance of this policy became impossible after 1584.   The death of Anjou was the first of a series of events destined to force Philip into vigorous intervention in France. The Duke was the last, save one, of the sons of Henry II and Catharine de' Medici; his death meant that when his elder brother, the childless reigning sovereign, Henry III, should follow him to the grave, the legal heir of the crown of France would be the Protestant Henry of Bourbon, who in 1572 had inherited from his mother, Jeanne d'Albret, the French fragment of the kingdom of Navarre.   The succession of a heretic, and of a heretic with a tradition of bitter hostility to Spain, was now an imminent peril.   Something must be done, and done at once, to avert such a catastrophe; and the obvious move under the circumstances was for Philip to draw near to the ultra-Catholic party in France, then headed by the three sons of François de Lorraine, second Duke of Guise.   Hitherto the Spanish monarch had been generally opposed to the projects of this family,[2] whose interests, though intensely Catholic, were politically opposed to his own, but now there seemed no alternative to an alliance with them.   Henry III had been officially recognized as their sovereign by the rebels in the Low Countries in the previous April, and since his brother's death in June, he had been suspiciously friendly to Henry of Navarre; clearly, for the moment, there was nothing to be expected from him.[3]   So, on December 31, 1584, Philip's ambassador in France, Juan

---

[1] Cf. C. Pérez Bustamante, "Las Instrucciones de Felipe II a Juan Bautista de Tassis," in *Revista de Historia*, xvi (1927–28), pp. 177–196.

[2] Forneron, i, pp. 123, 225, 278, and references there.

[3] Mariéjol in Lavisse, vi, 1, p. 239.

Bautista de Tassis, and the representatives of the Guises signed a treaty at Joinville which reanimated the League of 1576 by bringing it the support of the monarchy of Spain.[1] The high contracting parties made a perpetual offensive and defensive alliance for the preservation of the Roman Catholic faith, for the extirpation of heresy in France and in the Low Countries, and for the exclusion of the Bourbons from the French throne. Philip was not yet ready to send his *tercios* to the aid of his new allies, but he promised subsidies to the amount of 50,000 crowns a month, and even agreed to pay in six months the total amount that he had pledged for the year. He was not wont to make such promises as this. The crisis must indeed have seemed to him grave.

The year 1585 saw several fresh developments of the situation. In April the masterful Bernardino de Mendoza, who had recently been ordered out of England, supplanted Tassis as Spanish ambassador to France.[2] He immediately established contact with Henri, third Duke of Guise, and soon became, in fact, rather Philip's representative with the League than at the Valois court to which he was officially accredited. At the same time it is evident that his confident and imperious bearing made a profound impression on the vacillating Henry III. The French king desired above all things to detach the king of Spain from the League, and even offered Philip his alliance against England as the price of it ;[3] but Mendoza was not to be tempted by any such proposal as this, and the final result was that in midsummer Henry weakly capitulated to the Guises. By the treaty of Nemours (July 7) he came to agreement with the forces of the League

[1] Text in Dumont, *Corps universel diplomatique*, v, 1, pp. 441–443.
[2] G. Baguenault de Puchesse, in *Revue des questions historiques*, xxv (1879), pp. 30–33 ; Forneron, iii, p. 233, note 4.
[3] Forneron, iii, p. 232.

on terms which made it perfectly clear that the Guises and
not the Valois were the master.[1] A furious edict against
heresy was put forth, giving the Huguenots the naked
alternative of confession or exile.   All sorts of powers and
favors were accorded to the Guises; the monarchy virtually
placed itself under their tutelage in the conduct of the now
inevitable war against the followers of Henry of Navarre.
But since the Guises, in turn, took their orders from
Mendoza, the treaty of Nemours meant not merely the
extirpation of French Protestants; it signified that France's
political destinies were being delivered over to the king of
Spain, and that Spanish preponderance, already intolerable,
was to be still further enhanced in a new and unexpected
direction.   But this the new pontiff, Sixtus V, who had been
elected in the preceding April, was resolved, if possible, to
prevent.   The saving of French Catholicism was in his eyes
of paramount importance, but he wished it accomplished
without the interference of the Spanish king; for the maintenance of a powerful united monarchy in France was essential to the preservation from Spanish dictation of the independence of the Holy See.[2]   Accordingly, when the Guises
asked for his alliance, he refused to commit himself.   Against
heresy, indeed, he took a definite stand by launching a bull
of excommunication against Henry of Navarre,[3] but he
was unwilling to make common cause with the dominant
faction in France for fear of indirectly increasing the power
of Spain.   He wished the Valois to fight their own battles
against Protestantism and civil war and reap the full rewards
of victory.   Philip knew from that moment that the political
jealousy and distrust of the Holy See, of which he had so

---

[1] Mariéjol in Lavisse, vi, 1, p. 248.
Text of the treaty in Dumont, *Corps
universel diplomatique*, v, 1, pp. 453 f.
[2] Pastor, xxi, pp. 262 ff., 274 ff.

[3] Though not, be it observed, until
after he had learned of the treaty of
Nemours. Pastor, xxi, p. 285.

often complained in preceding years, were certain to be continued, if not intensified, as long as Sixtus remained Pope.

During the next three years Philip's attention was centred on the expedition against England, so that the story of his relations to France falls somewhat into the background; but Bernardino de Mendoza was incessantly active there in his efforts to promote the interests of his master. The course of the 'War of the Three Henrys' that broke out in 1585 proved that the king of Navarre was a formidable opponent in the field,[1] and the inconstancy of the Valois monarch caused the scene to shift almost every day; but in general it may be said that the efforts of the Spanish ambassador were directed rather towards the preservation and extension of Spain's political influence in France than to the extirpation of heresy there. Henry III, as was to be expected, at once became terribly restless under the control of the Guises. Before the end of the year 1586 there was talk of his seeking reconciliation with the king of Navarre. This Philip, of course, was determined to prevent, and notified the Pope that he would never consent to it. On the other hand, in France, Mendoza put forth every effort to widen the breach between the Guises and the king, [2] for he wished the factions there to multiply and exhaust themselves in civil strife, and to make sure that the control of the League should remain in the hands of Spain. The success that he attained in this difficult task is a wonderful tribute to the power of his personality; he seemed to tower like a giant above the weaklings who surrounded him. Guise was constantly running to him for Spanish aid, for funds from Madrid, and for soldiers from Alexander of Parma; he took delight in his smile, and trem-

---

[1] Mariéjol in Lavisse, vi, 1, pp. 259 f.   *Valois, et Philippe II* (Paris, 1866,
[2] Joseph de Croze, *Les Guises, les*   2 vols.), ii, pp. 324 ff.

bled at his frown.[1]   Mendoza also found time to intervene
in the affairs of England. He strove to bring about a
Scottish Catholic rising in 1587, and organized fresh conspiracies for the murder of Queen Elizabeth.[2]   When it came
time for the Armada to set sail, he saw to it that the French
monarch was impotent to give effect to the threats he had
made that he would go to the assistance of England; nay
more, when in May, 1588, the Day of the Barricades had
forced Henry to abandon his own capital and take refuge at
Chartres, Mendoza actually had the effrontery to present
himself before him and demand an assurance of his support
in the enterprise on which his master was about to embark.
He virtually insisted that the Most Christian King give
him a definite guarantee that no Frenchman would ever put
let or hindrance in the way of the projects of Philip of
Spain.[3]

The news of the defeat of the Armada was a great shock to
Mendoza, but as soon as he had recovered from it, he
redoubled his own activities; for if England was to be lost to
Spain, there was all the more reason why Spain should maintain her influence in France. Ever since the beginning of the
year the Guises had resolved to force Henry to cast in his lot
again with the League, and on such terms as would reduce
him to impotence; they demanded the capitulation of the
king to a faction admittedly controlled from abroad. All
their actions had been directed to the attainment of this end.
Mendoza ardently supported them, and on July 21, by the
so-called Edict of Union, they had apparently accomplished
their purpose. The king submitted on all points, and
pardoned those responsible for the Day of the Barricades.[4]

[1] Baguenault de Puchesse, *loc. cit.*,
pp. 35 f.; Forneron, iii, p. 248.
[2] *Relations politiques de la France et*
de l'Espagne avec l'Écosse au XVI
siècle, ed. A. Teulet, v, pp. 369–515.
[3] Baguenault de Puchesse, pp. 38 f.
[4] Mariéjol in Lavisse, vi, 1, p. 277.

But the permanence of these arrangements remained to be
tested, and the test was to come at the meeting of the States-
General, which had been summoned to Blois in the autumn.
The Guises did their utmost to secure the return of members
favorable to themselves, and with excellent success. When
the assembly met it was found that they had practically all
the clergy, a majority of the nobles, and nearly three-quarters
of the Third Estate; they were certain that permanent
victory was at last within their grasp.[1] But the wily
Mendoza was less sanguine than they, for he realized, as
they did not, the utter untrustworthiness of the king. In
September, without a word either to his aged mother or to
the Duke of Guise, Henry suddenly dismissed his chancellor
and two secretaries of state, and replaced them with men who
would take their orders from him. In October, when he first
addressed the Estates, he made it evident that he did not
intend to abide by his promises of three months before.[2] The
Guises were furious, and were supported by the assembly.
So confident were they in the assurance of popular support
that they felt sure that in the end the king would be forced
to yield; only Mendoza had any suspicions of foul play, and
even he believed that he would be able to forestall it. For
nine long weeks the struggle continued, but when Henry
became finally convinced that he could not win over the
Estates, he determined to have recourse to murder. On
December 23, the Duke of Guise was summoned to the
royal council chamber, and was slain as he entered by the
royal guard; the next day his brother, the cardinal of Lorraine, suffered a similar fate. On January 5, 1589, the aged
queen-mother died in the castle of Blois, and the last
wretched scion of the house of Valois was left quite alone to

---

[1] Mariéjol in Lavisse, vi, 1, p. 280.　　[2] Baguenault de Puchesse, pp. 40 f.;
Forneron, iii, p. 250.

wrestle with the herculean task of unifying and enfranchising his native land.[1]

Mendoza was utterly cast down when he learned of the murder of Guise. Four days later he wrote to Philip, assuring him of the many warnings that he had given the Duke, and bewailing the fact that all the hopes which he and his master had built upon the League had now "gone up in smoke."[2] Philip, too, was deeply disheartened by the news, and is reported to have declared that he counted it an even worse misfortune than the loss of the Armada.[3] Yet both the king and his ambassador underestimated the intensity of the anti-royalist feeling in France that had been aroused by the murder. The central committee of the League in Paris, popularly known as the Seize,[4] not only raised the standard of revolt at the capital, but sent messages to all the chief cities of the realm, urging them to do the same. Guise's sole surviving brother, Charles, Duke of Mayenne, was made "lieutenant-general of the state and of the crown of France." The material was ready to hand which would have enabled Philip, had he utilized it promptly and effectively, to keep France under Spanish control for many years to come. But just at the very moment when he should have acted boldly, the Prudent King elected to play safe. He liked to have the French monarchy in leading strings, but he could not quite bring himself to countenance open rebellion. He instructed Mendoza to keep close to Henry III at all costs, to refrain from asking him to explain what he had done, and to strive in all possible ways to rekindle the courage of the Catholics;[5] instead of stimulating the activities of the League, the ambas-

---

[1] Forneron, *Les Ducs de Guise*, ii, pp. 382–390.

[2] Baguenault de Puchesse, p. 42.

[3] Froude, xii, p. 529.

[4] So called because composed of the heads of the local councils of the sixteen districts into which Paris was divided.

[5] Forneron, iv, p. 3; Baguenault de Puchesse, p. 43.

sador was given the impossible task of preventing an understanding between the Valois and the king of Navarre. In
the meantime Mendoza's courage had come back. He saw
the chance to play the bolder game, and finally, in defiance
of Philip's commands, he betook himself to Paris; but he
was not able to accomplish much after he arrived there, and
his departure from the court gave Henry an excuse for sending a special messenger to Madrid to demand that he be
recalled.[1]

Again Philip hesitated, but this time hesitation was wise.
Even before Mendoza had left the court, it was perfectly
obvious what the king of France would do. The successes
of the League and the ebullitions of anti-royalist sentiment
which it had evoked left him no alternative save an alliance
with Henry of Navarre. He made one last effort, indeed, to
draw close to Mayenne, but it was evident from the first that
it was certain to fail; and while he was awaiting the inevitable refusal, the king of Navarre put forth his famous appeal
to the French nation (March 4) which proved that even
though he might be a heretic, he was a patriot first of all,
who would tolerate no interference by foreigners within the
realm. On April 3 the two Henrys agreed to the terms of an
alliance. On the 30th they met at Plessis-les-Tours. In the
succeeding weeks they advanced together on Paris, their
forces rapidly increasing every day. By the end of July they
were prepared to lay siege to the capital.[2] Within the walls
there was terror and confusion. It was bitter indeed for the
Leaguers to lose, after victory had seemed so near; and finally
a fanatic Dominican persuaded himself that the only way to
save the cause was to do unto Henry of Valois as he had done
unto Henry of Guise. On the last night of July Jacques

---

[1] Baguenault de Puchesse, p. 44.   [2] Mariéjol in Lavisse, vi, 1, pp. 296–
298.

Clément stole out of the capital. On the morrow, by dint of
forged papers, he obtained access to the king at St. Cloud,
and plunged a dagger into his breast. The assassin was slain
on the spot; that same evening the last of the Valois died.[1]

Mendoza reported to his master on the following day how
"it has pleased our Lord to deliver us by an event so happy
that it cannot but be attributed to His all-powerful hand;
indeed it gives us reason to hope that we are finished with the
heretics."[2] But Philip, when he got the news, was much
less enthusiastic. For the moment he seemed far less
interested in the vast possibilities which the assassination
opened up for him than horrified at the murder, by a monk
of his favorite order, of a legitimate, if unworthy, sovereign.
His servants and counsellors, taking their cue from the king's
mood, though they persisted in speaking of the event as "a
marvellous judgment of God," took pains also to state their
conviction that Philip should make every effort "to care for
the safety and well-being of his own royal person."[3]

Before we can carry further the story of the Spanish monarch's dealings with the situation in France, it is essential that
the state of affairs in the Netherlands be brought up to date.
We left them, it will be remembered, at the time of Parma's
capture of Antwerp on August 17, 1585.

That capture, as we have remarked, was a notable triumph
for Parma, for Philip, and for Spain; it completed the reconquest of the Catholic Southwest, save for Ostend, Sluys, and
a few other places, and isolated the republic and the
Reformation in Utrecht, Holland, and Zealand.[4] But that

---

[1] Mariéjol in Lavisse, vi, 1, pp. 298–
301; L'Épinois, *La Ligue et les Papes*,
pp. 336–338; Pastor, xxi, p. 320, note 3,
gives some account of Clément and the
controversies that have arisen concerning him.

[2] Baguenault de Puchesse, p. 45.
[3] Forneron, iv, p. 6.
[4] In the military plans of the modern
Netherlands government, this region

final stronghold was destined to prove the hardest problem of all; indeed, it was before its walls that Philip's great war machine was ultimately to wear itself out. The three provinces were virtually surrounded by water — on the west by the North Sea, on the north and east by the Zuyder Zee, and on the southeast and south by the Yssel, the Waal, and the Meuse — and could not be taken by assault; obviously a siege would be required, and a siege, not of an isolated town or fort, but of a whole district. That district, moreover, could count on ample supplies. Its defenders had ships in plenty, and the Spaniards almost none. Their many friends could send them, almost at will, provisions, munitions, and men. Though Orange and Anjou were gone, there was no lack of leaders to fill their places. Maurice of Nassau, seventeen years old, son of William the Silent, was promptly elected to fill his father's office. His youth made it necessary that he should be guided for some time by a council; but in a few months he gave evidence of military talent which was subsequently to prove a thorn in the sides of the Spaniards. Though the death of Anjou, and the state of affairs in France, showed that no further help could be expected from that quarter in the immediately succeeding years, that very fact was enough to convince Queen Elizabeth that she must henceforth bestir herself more actively in the rebels' behalf. In the autumn of 1585 she agreed to take them under her protection and send them 5000 troops; in December her favorite, the Earl of Leicester, arrived at Flushing.[1]

has been termed since 1874 the 'Holland Fortress,' and has formed the backbone of all schemes of defence.

The rebels also held part or all of the northeastern provinces of Friesland, Drenthe, Overyssel, Gelderland, and Groningen. These from their geographical position were difficult to conquer while the central stronghold of Holland, Zealand, and Utrecht still held out; on the other hand, had that once fallen, they could have made no effective resistance.

[1] Motley, *History of the United Netherlands*, i, pp. 285–364, *passim*.

Leicester speedily made it evident that he had neither the ability nor the tact to carry out the exceedingly difficult task with which he had been intrusted.   His squabbles with the States-General and with his mistress at home soon reduced him to impotence, and convinced Parma that for the time he could be safely ignored.   And so it came about that the year 1586 saw Philip's representative in the Low Countries principally occupied with the task of separating the United Provinces from another set of allies whom they had recently discovered within the Empire.   In the year 1582 Gebhard Truchsess, the archbishop of Cologne, had gone over to the Reformed religion, thus menacing the integrity of the Rhenish 'priest street,' and offering the Dutch rebels the chance of obtaining valuable support in a position of the highest strategic importance.   The war which broke out in Cologne in 1583, after Truchsess's conversion became known, was thus closely linked from its earliest inception with the course of the revolt in the Netherlands.   Orange had sent troops to help Truchsess; it was his hope to get the whole of the Lower Rhine into Protestant hands and isolate in Friesland the northeastern detachment of the Spanish army under Verdugo.[1]   Parma, on the other hand, did everything he could for Ernest of Bavaria, the bishop of Liège, whom the Catholic members of the chapter of Cologne had elected in place of Truchsess.   He had quartered some of his best regiments on the confines of Gelderland.   There had been a series of inconclusive engagements between the rival forces.   And now, in 1586, Parma determined to concentrate on this problem and solve it.   On June 7, in spite of all the efforts of Leicester and his allies to prevent him, he took Grave, thus opening to the royal armies the passage of the Meuse; three

[1] Cf. F. Verdugo, *Commentario de la Guerra de Frisa*, ed. H. Lonchay (Brussels, 1899).

weeks later Venloo surrendered. Thence Parma advanced rapidly into the electorate, captured Neuss, and massacred its garrison; to complete the task that he had set himself to perform it only remained to capture Rheinberg. But this he was unable to accomplish. His foes had by this time discovered the way to thwart his plans, not indeed by meeting him at the point of attack, but by diversions, for which their command of rapid river transport rendered them particularly apt; no sooner had Parma begun the siege of Rheinberg than he was obliged to go to the rescue of Zutphen. During the remainder of the year, and also in 1587, he continued, indeed, to win a majority of victories in the field; but save for the capture of Sluys (August 5, 1587) [1] they brought him little advantage. The centre of the rebellion continued successfully to defy him.[2]

Parma's capture of Sluys was an evidence to all men that the expedition against England, so often mooted and postponed, was now to be carried through to the exclusion of everything else. The duke had always maintained that a port on the coast of the Netherlands was essential to success, and he wished to be permitted to follow up the taking of Sluys with that of Flushing; but Philip would not hear of it.[3] Though Parma had been almost the first person whom the king had consulted when the plan of the expedition had been originally broached, matters had developed in such fashion in the intervening years as to make effective coöperation between them no longer possible. The root of the difficulty was, as usual, Philip's perennial jealousy of distant and too efficient subordinates, a jealousy of which Parma, since the

---

[1] Cf. "Documents inédits sur la prise de l'Écluse," ed. Ernest van Bruyssel, in Belgium, Commission Royale d'Histoire, Compte rendu des séances, troisième série, iv (1863), pp. 173–182.

[2] Vázquez in D. I. E., lxxiii, pp. 139 ff.; Pirenne, iv, pp. 195–197; Fea, Alessandro Farnese, pp. 256–276; Motley, History of the United Netherlands, ii, pp. 260–281.

[3] Pirenne, iv, p. 198.

capture of Antwerp, had become the principal object; it was largely that jealousy which had caused the king to concentrate the control of the expedition in Spain and thereby get it out of the duke's hands.[1] The delays and postponements were another source of friction. Parma had counted from the first on the effects of a surprise, but that was now impossible; the English knew more of the state of Philip's preparations than Philip knew himself. Add to all this the fact that the king kept his nephew terribly short of funds, and it is no wonder that Parma was gradually becoming lukewarm with regard to the whole enterprise against England; indeed, in letters to Philip of January 31 and March 20, 1588, he frankly foretold its failure.[2] His misgivings had also manifested themselves in another form at a much earlier date. In the first months of the year 1586 he had made overtures for peace to the government of Queen Elizabeth.[3] Philip had consented, not indeed with any idea that the negotiations could possibly be successful, but rather in the hope of lulling the English into a feeling of security and thereby gaining time. The queen was anxious at all costs to avoid war, and though her counsellors had little faith in the sincerity of the Spanish offers, there was apparently some hope that Parma could be induced to betray his uncle in return for a promise of independent sovereignty in the Low Countries.[4] The negotiations dragged lamely on for over two years. In March, 1588, Parma was so certain that the Armada must fail that he advised Philip to abandon pretence and seek an accommodation in earnest before it was too late,[5] but the king refused. The negotiations continued,

---

[1] Cf. ante, p. 527; Gossart, Domination espagnole, p. 160.

[2] C. S. P., Spanish, 1587–1603, nos. 209, 241, 242.

[3] Gossart, op. cit., p. 166, note 1.

[4] At least so Bernardino de Mendoza reported to Philip; cf. C. S. P., Spanish, 1587–1603, no. 143. It is, however, fair to note that Mendoza was a bitter enemy of Parma. Ibid., p. xlvii.

[5] C. S. P., Spanish, 1587–1603, no. 241.

and finally culminated in conferences held at Bourbourg in June, 1588,[1] needless to add, without success. Each side knew by this time that the invasion of England was inevitable, and merely sought to feint and spar for time. The only real significance of the whole affair is the light it incidentally sheds on the relations of Parma and the king. There is no reliable evidence that the duke actually intended to play his master false. On the other hand, he was disgusted at the delays and inefficiency of Philip's plan of campaign, and unenthusiastic, to say the least, about coöperating with it.[2]

The king was fully aware of his nephew's state of mind, but under the circumstances he could neither replace nor dispense with him. On September 4, 1587, he wrote him a most intimate letter[3] to tell him how completely he depended on him, and how essential it was that he should be ready to do his part when the crucial moment should arrive. And so, with a heavy heart, since his own wiser plans had been rejected, Parma prepared to conform to the king's, which he knew were certain to fail;[4] he must adhere to the strict letter of his instructions, in order to avoid any share in the responsibility for the inevitable defeat. In the early part of 1588 his headquarters were for the most part at Ghent; but in May he moved over to Bruges, where his flatboats were assembled in the canals,[5] and whence he had arranged to have them towed to Nieuport and Dunkirk when the Armada should have reached Calais Roads. The expeditionary force was quartered in the adjacent villages, and on July 18 he wrote to the king that everything was at last in readiness.[6] Thereafter he began to receive constant, increasingly plaintive, and

[1] C. S. P., Spanish, 1587–1603, nos. 239, 308.

[2] Ibid., nos. 209, 210, 223, 241, 242, 264, 265, 308, 309, 319.

[3] Ibid., no. 141.

[4] Ibid., p. xxxv.

[5] Gossart, op. cit., p. 165.

[6] C. S. P., Spanish, 1587–1603, no. 348.

self-contradictory letters from Medina Sidonia, informing him of the Armada's condition and whereabouts; the last three of these, written on August 6 and 7 from Calais Roads, beg him to "hasten his coming out," and "bear aid in resisting the enemy's fleet." [1] All this Parma had foreseen; and he would not, because he knew he could not, comply. In two letters to Philip (August 8 from Bruges and August 10 from Dunkirk) [2] he indignantly reiterated that it was the Armada's duty to protect *his* passage and clear the sea of enemies, and that he would not stir until it was in a condition to do so. And so the duke bore silent witness, in an impotence that was probably not altogether ungrateful to him, to the tragedy of the next three days, the battle of Gravelines and the dispersal of his master's great fleet. If Philip had trusted him, he would have done his utmost to bring him victory. If his original advice had been followed, it is even possible that the Armada might have accomplished its object; but in view of the way in which the king had listened to the slanders of his rivals and enemies, it is small wonder that when the critical moment arrived he refused to do more than the part that had been assigned to him. "What adds more than I can here express to my grief at this disaster," so he wrote to Philip from Dunkirk on August 10, "is that it was humanly impossible to remedy it, or aid in any way." [3]

Parma came in for more than his share of the taunts and invectives with which Spain resounded when the shattered remnants of the Armada got back to port; he was blamed, indeed, quite as much as the Duke of Medina Sidonia. He was accused of unwillingness to perform the part that had been assigned to him, and of treachery to his master. The

[1] *Supra*, p. 544, and *C. S. P., Spanish,* 1587–1603, nos. 355, 364, 368, 371, 372.

[2] *Ibid.,* nos. 374, 380.
[3] *Ibid.,* no. 380 (p. 371).

old report that he was aiming to obtain a separate sovereignty for himself in the Low Countries was circulated once more. It would even appear that Elizabeth, taking advantage of the resentment which she knew these cavils would inevitably arouse in him, consented to have it suggested to him that he assume the crown of the Netherlands as the ally of England — a proposal which Parma indignantly rejected.[1] Philip for the time being refused to listen to these calumnies of his traducers; possibly he began to realize how much wiser it would have been to have placed more reliance on Parma from the outset. In letters of October 10 and 17, 1588,[2] he assured his nephew of his complete satisfaction, and directed him to draw up plans for a new expedition. For the moment, however, it was obvious that nothing more could be accomplished against England; and Parma, his courage restored by the renewal of the royal confidence, returned in the end of 1588 to the problems of the rebels in the Netherlands and of the Protestants in Cologne. He sent troops to the aid of Ernest of Bavaria; and though he himself was unsuccessful in an attempt to take Bergen-op-Zoom, his lieutenant, Peter Ernest of Mansfeld, seized Wachterdonk, and thus extended his power in Gelderland. In 1589-90 he gained greater victories still. In Cologne Ernest of Bavaria decisively defeated the adherents of Truchsess, so that Parma was relieved of all anxiety in that direction.[3] Rheinberg, which had defied him in 1586, finally surrendered to Mansfeld in January, 1590, and nine months earlier Parma himself had got possession of Gertruydenberg. Holland and Zealand were isolated at last as they had never been before; and Farnese, whose achievements had been the more remarkable in view of the wretched state of his own

---

[1] Gossart, *op. cit.*, p. 180; Fea, pp. 311–319.

[2] Gossart, p. 180.

[3] Pirenne, iv, pp. 198 f.

health and the mutinies of his discontented soldiery, was confident that the last embers of the rebellion could be speedily stamped out.[1]

But once more it was the duke's hard fate to be called off from the task which he had originally been given, and was on the way to accomplish, to attack another, which in the estimation of his master was of even greater importance. The assassination of Henry of Valois on August 1, 1589, convinced the king that everything must be sacrificed to the opportunities thus opened for him in France, and Parma was ordered to bear aid to the forces of the League. To serve a master with as many irons in the fire as Philip was almost more hopeless than the serving of two.

Never had the Spanish monarch shown himself more 'prudent' than when he received word of the murder of Henry III. He had been profoundly shocked, as we have already seen, and at first a little terrified by the news ; then, when he began to realize the opportunities that it offered him, he elected, instead of acting promptly, to lay plans for the remoter future. As son-in-law of Henry II, he could himself lay claim to the vacant throne, if the Salic Law were ignored,[2] and some of the French, in their first enthusiasm at getting rid of Henry III, declared for the "election of the king of Spain, and the placing of everything in his hands."[3] But Philip at first seemed in no way desirous to grasp the prize. Quite the contrary, he instructed his representatives at Paris to favor the candidacy of the aged cardinal of Bourbon, who had been proclaimed king by Mayenne under the title of Charles X.[4] Having made excellent use of a moribund

---

[1] Vázquez in *D. I. E.*, lxxiii, pp. 379 ff.;   Forneron, iv, pp. 40–51; Fea, pp. 323–331.

[2] Mariéjol in Lavisse, vi, 1, p. 306.

[3] Nicolas de Neufville, Seigneur de Villeroy, *Memoires d'Estat*, ed. Du Mesnil Basire (Sedan, 1622), p. 150.

[4] Baguenault de Puchesse, p. 46. A plan of Mendoza that Philip should

cardinal as a stop-gap once before under similar circumstances, at the time of the annexation of Portugal, he was
happy to repeat the experiment. It would serve to
embarrass the king of Navarre and give cohesion to the forces
opposed to him; on the other hand, it could not place any
permanent obstacle in the way of Philip's own ultimate plans,
for the cardinal had been a prisoner of the French crown ever
since the assassination of the Guises, and the League was
never able to liberate him.[1] At the same time Philip
despatched his former ambassador Juan Bautista de Tassis
and a certain Commander Moreo to collaborate at Paris with
Mendoza, who had displaced Tassis there. Apparently
the principal objects of their mission were merely to keep the
king informed of everything that occurred and to distribute
bribes; in any case, when their money ran out, in June, 1590,
they both of them returned to Madrid.[2] One thing, however, they accomplished during their brief stay in France,
which was very encouraging to the king of Spain; and that
was the establishment of cordial relations with the papal
legate, Cardinal Errico Caetani, whom Sixtus had despatched
to Paris when he learned of the murder of Henry III.[3] That
event had dealt a rude blow to the pontiff's hopes of reërecting
the supremacy of the Catholic church in France without
the aid of Spain. Unless the king of Navarre would turn
Catholic, which at that moment seemed improbable, the
Pope would have to make common cause with Philip in
order to keep France within the Roman fold; and in
December, 1589, he actually offered to conclude an alliance

assume the title of 'Protector of the
realm of France' was wrecked by the
opposition of Mayenne and the papal
legate, Caetani, who insisted that his
Holiness "did not regard it as fitting
that any one save himself should be
declared Protector of the Catholic
religion in France." Cf. Villeroy,
op. cit., pp. 165–167; Mariéjol in
Lavisse, vi, 1, pp. 329 f.; Pastor, xxi,
pp. 321 ff., passim.

[1] Pastor, xxi, pp. 325, 363. The
cardinal died on May 9, 1590.

[2] Baguenault de Puchesse, pp. 45 f.

[3] Pastor, xxi, p. 327.

with the Prudent King in order to effect this end. Before Philip had had time to accept, representatives of the Catholic adherents of Henry of Navarre arrived in Rome, and revived the pontiff's hopes that he might do without Spanish aid. When Philip's ambassador, the Count of Olivares, tried to bully him, he became furious, and even threatened to excommunicate the Spanish king; in fact, down to the day of his death, which occurred on August 27, 1590, he avoided definitely committing himself to the Spanish cause in France. But in the meantime the legate Caetani, in spite of the Pope's complaints, did everything possible to favor the designs of Philip; moreover, the Prudent King rightly foresaw that, when Sixtus should die, the worst of his troubles with the papacy would be over, for it was inconceivable that another Pope should be as violent in his opposition to him.[1] As long as the king of Navarre remained a heretic, it now seemed almost inevitable that Spain should have the support of Rome.[2]

While Philip planned and plotted, his rivals and enemies were far more active. The king of Spain was not the only foreigner who aspired to control, or if that were impossible, to dismember France. His son-in-law Charles Emanuel 'the Great' of Savoy, who as grandson of Francis I had a claim to the French throne,[3] saw a chance in the prevailing confusion to fulfil a long-cherished dream of reconstituting for himself the ancient kingdom of Arles, and launched an

[1] During the brief pontificate of Gregory XIV (1590–91), the Spanish embassy at Rome "urgently importuned" the Pope (1) that the whole house of Bourbon be declared incapable of reigning in France, because of its support of heretics; (2) that all the Catholic nobility of Navarre's party be excommunicated; (3) that the Pope pay 50,000 crowns a month to maintain the war in France, "in order that the Catholic faith may not perish in that kingdom." Letter of Cardinal Dal Monte to the grand duke of Tuscany, January 4, 1591, in Société de l'Histoire du Protestantisme Français, *Bulletin*, lxxxi (1932), p. 36.

[2] Pastor, xxi, pp. 340–374, *passim*, and xxii, p. 356; also L'Épinois, *La Ligue et les Papes*, p. 660.

[3] Villeroy, *op. cit.*, p. 150.

army against Provence in the autumn of 1589. A little later
the duke of Lorraine, who was a son-in-law of Henry II, made
a similar attempt against Champagne.[1] But these efforts
and others like them encountered vigorous opposition. The
Savoyards soon became "rather the besieged than the
besiegers in Provence," and Charles Emanuel betook himself to Madrid to ask for Spanish help. The principal Lor-
rainers, too, after their initial repulses, tended to gravitate
in the same direction. By the end of the year 1591, it
became evident that the king of Spain was the only
foreign pretender whose ambitions need be taken seriously;
the battle, in other words, was to be fought by him and those
in France whom he could induce to support him, against the
patriotic though heretical king of Navarre. The latter had
lost no time after the assassination of Henry III. On August
4, 1589, he had put forth his famous declaration promising
the maintenance of the Catholic faith within the realm, in the
hope of rallying all true Frenchmen to his cause; but it did
not produce the effect he had anticipated. Too many of the
recognitions it elicited were but provisional, and there were
many defections. Some even of his Protestant friends
deserted him because he had promised too much; his army
soon dwindled to half its original size. But he speedily
demonstrated that he could make good use of his shrunken
forces in the field. Realizing that it would be madness, for
the present, to attack Paris, he retired into Normandy, pursued by Mayenne with a much larger army; and so sure were
the Parisians that their champion would return victorious
that they hired windows in the Rue St. Antoine to witness
the spectacle of the king of Navarre brought back in chains.
But Mayenne was fatally hesitant when the critical moment
arrived. He had all the worst of that series of skirmishes dur-

[1] Mariéjol in Lavisse, vi, 1, pp. 331–334.

ing the last ten days of September, which are collectively designated as the battle of Arques; finally, in October, he retreated to Paris, pursued by the rival whom he had been expected to capture. Henry even ventured to attack the suburbs, but, realizing that he was not yet strong enough to take the capital, he soon retired westward, and established the seat of his government for the winter at Tours.[1]

Against such an active adversary a policy of mere bribery and plotting could not avail; every day it became increasingly evident that Philip must send military aid to the forces of the League. But the question was where to find the money and the men. The defeat of the Armada had been a terrible blow both to his treasury and to his *tercios*; and he was more than ever in need of military and financial resources in Spain, to repel the counter-attacks of the English and to stifle potential rebellions.[2] Under all the circumstances, then, it seemed to Philip that the wisest course was to send the duke of Parma from the Low Countries against Henry of Navarre. His ability as a soldier was well known. He was nearer the scene of action than any other of the king's commanders. Possibly Philip was influenced by the old fear that, if left with nothing else to do but suppress the rebellion in the Netherlands, Parma might possibly prove too successful, and set up an independent sovereignty there. As far back as 1586 he had commanded him to keep his eye on the situation in France. On September 7, 1589, after he had learned of the murder of Henry III, he wrote him to rest on the defensive in the Low Countries in order to save money to be distributed to his French friends, and even spoke of the possibility of armed intervention; in November, after he had

---

[1] Mariéjol in Lavisse, vi, 1, pp. 307–310; Forneron, iv, pp. 18–22; L'Épinois, *La Ligue et les Papes*, pp. 339–350.

[2] It will be remembered that Pérez had escaped to Aragon in April, 1590; cf. *ante*, p. 578.

received news of Arques, he evidently regarded such intervention as ultimately inevitable, and sent Juan Moreo to the Netherlands to bear aid in organizing it.[1] To Parma, as will be readily imagined, all this was unwelcome in the highest degree. He was very ill; he longed to finish his task in the Netherlands; he knew that, at the best, he had barely enough money and men to accomplish that. He could not believe that an expedition into France would have any hope of success, and in letters to Philip of March 24 and July 22, 1590,[2] he plainly told him so; at the same time Moreo aroused Philip's suspicions of Parma once more by writing back from Flanders, on June 22, that the duke's ill-will would be the ruin of all his plans.[3] But meantime the king of Navarre was again advancing on Paris. Unless something were speedily done, there was every probability that he would take it; and so Parma, not yet ready to move himself, sent the Count of Egmont from Flanders with 500 arquebusiers and 1200 Walloon lancers to the rescue of Mayenne. With the army of the League they met the king of Navarre at Ivry (March 14). Henry won the most brilliant of his victories. Egmont was killed, and his forces took flight. The Bourbon continued his triumphant march on Paris.[4]

Unless Philip was prepared to lose all hold on France, it was evident, after Ivry, that he must have done with half measures. Nothing short of Parma himself, with all his available forces, could possibly save the situation, and the king sent Tassis to Flanders to hasten the departure of the duke.[5] Parma's misgivings were unabated, but it was not his reluctance that was the chief cause of the delay; it was the

---

[1] Gossart, *Domination espagnole*, pp. 263 f.; Fea, pp. 332–341.

[2] Gossart, pp. 273–278, 281–284.

[3] *Ibid.*, pp. 278–280. Moreo died suddenly at Meaux, August 30, 1590, not without suspicion of poison. Coloma, *Guerras*, p. 85.

[4] Mariéjol in Lavisse, vi, 1, pp. 312–316; Forneron, iv, pp. 23–27.

[5] Baguenault de Puchesse, p. 47.

lack of funds to pay his troops, and the incipient mutinies among his soldiers which followed as the inevitable result. By midsummer, however, the money had at last arrived, and in the early days of August he crossed the frontier.[1]   Henry had invested Paris on April 25.   Within the next two months the food had run out.   Mendoza won golden opinions by his liberal giving and by his organization of relief.   At this crisis he played the part of the Roman Catholic fanatic, declaring that his master had no political ambitions in France, but cared only for the preservation of the ancient faith ; he was even credited with a plan for making bread out of dead men's bones.[2]   But by early August things had reached a point which flesh and blood could no longer endure ; 13,000 people had already died of starvation, and negotiations preliminary to a surrender had begun, when suddenly news came, on the 30th, that Parma had united with Mayenne at Meaux and was rapidly advancing to the rescue.   Henry, anxious to prove his valor against the most celebrated soldier in Europe, raised the siege of Paris and advanced to meet the foe. Parma, whose object it was to save the capital without the decisive battle which the king of Navarre desired, intrenched himself between the Marne and a swamp, and awaited the enemy's attack.   So strong was the position that Henry did not venture to assault it ; then at last, after seven days of waiting, the duke, under cover of a sally, got two of his regiments across the Marne on a bridge of boats, and took Lagny. With both banks of the river in his control, he soon was able to revictual Paris, but the reception accorded him within the walls did not measure up to his expectations.   The inhabitants seemed less grateful to him for their deliverance than suspicious of the Spanish domination which his arrival

[1] Forneron, iv, pp. 50 f.
[2] Baguenault de Puchesse, pp. 47 f.,   and references there to the *Satire Ménippée.*

portended; and Parma, after writing frankly to the king of the unpopularity of the Spanish army in France, and the dangers of attempting to dominate the country, retired in November to the Low Countries. He had brilliantly accomplished the almost impossible task which his master had given him to perform, but he had the gravest forebodings for the future.[1]

The achievements of Parma should certainly have convinced Philip that his representative in the Low Countries was by far the most efficient of his servants; had he sent him at once all his available troops and supplies, the duke, though he might not have been able to make his master king of France, would almost certainly have succeeded in putting an end to the revolt in the Netherlands. But just at the very moment when he should have concentrated his resources, Philip elected to dissipate them; never before, in his entire reign, had the disastrous results of the multiplicity of his plans and of his jealousy of overcompetent subordinates been so painfully apparent. If he could not gain control of the whole of France, the next best thing, from his point of view, would be to dismember her. At the very moment that he was utilizing Parma in an attempt to effect the one, he despatched two other armies in the hope of accomplishing the other. The first of these was a comparatively small force which he sent into Languedoc in the spring of 1591, at the invitation of the Maréchal of Joyeuse, the chief representative of the League in that province; he had hopes of regaining at least a part of the great domain north of the Pyrenees which had formed part of the county of Catalonia in the Middle Ages. But the whole affair was half-heartedly conducted. Philip desired to have his army ready in the neighborhood of

---

[1] Vázquez in *D. I. E.*, lxxiii, pp. 489 ff.; Carlos Coloma, *Guerras de los* *Estados Baxos*, pp. 75-97; Fea, pp. 332-370.

the realms of the crown of Aragon to deal with any insurrection which the activities of Antonio Pérez might stir up
there; he also wished to keep an eye on the progress of the
duke of Savoy farther eastward; and these and other dis-
tractions were fatal to the success of the invasion of
Languedoc. A certain number of small towns and petty
fortresses were taken, but there were many desertions.
The French Leaguers did not coöperate effectively; and all
Spain's hopes of gaining territory in that quarter were blasted
by a decisive defeat at Villemur (September 10, 1592);
their commander was drowned in the ensuing flight.[1]

In Brittany, on the other hand, whither Philip despatched
3500 men by sea from Corunna in September, 1590, there was
a different tale to tell. In the eyes of the legist, that province
had never become fully part of the realm of France, but was
still the property of the ancient ducal line; on that theory
Philip could plausibly lay claim to it on behalf of his daughter
Isabella Clara Eugenia, the great-granddaughter of Claude,
the wife of Francis I. At that moment Brittany was
occupied by the brother-in-law of Henry III, Philippe
Emmanuel de Lorraine, Duke of Mercoeur, whose wife,
Marie of Luxemburg, was a descendant of the ancient ducal
house. Mercoeur had declared for the League, and Philip
probably thought he could utilize him for his own purposes
and get rid of him afterwards; while Mercoeur, who had
solicited the intervention of Spain, doubtless counted on
reversing the process. In November, 1590, the allies began
to besiege Hennebont; but their military achievements were
far less notable than the scandalous bribery which the Spaniards employed to win the Bretons to their cause, and keep
them from being too friendly to Mercoeur; the natives were
too poor to refuse, but they lost all respect for the Spaniards.

[1] Forneron, iv, pp. 78–80; Mariéjol in Lavisse, vi, 1, pp. 331, 352 f.

Philip's army, however, remained in Brittany, and was to be heard from again in the ensuing years.[1]

But the centre of interest still remained at Paris. Since his general had rescued it, Philip felt that some recognition of the services of Spain was due him. Until the death of Charles of Bourbon, he had desired to have the title of Protector of the realm, on conditions so generous that "no one believed he would observe half of them." [2] Now he openly put forward the claims of his daughter Isabella Clara Eugenia to the throne; [3] and Mayenne sent Pierre Jeannin, the president of the Parlement of Dijon, to Madrid to discuss the validity of the Salic Law with the chief jurisconsults of Spain.[4] Mendoza in Paris was the king-pin of these negotiations. He also succeeded, in February, 1591, in bringing into the capital a small permanent garrison of Spaniards, Neapolitans, and Walloons from across the frontier of the Netherlands — an even more visible proof that his master meant business. It was the last important service which the great ambassador was to render to the Prudent King. He had suffered cruelly during the siege of Paris; since 1586 he had had a painful cataract of the left eye and was nearly blind.[5] Worst of all, though his policies had been loyally supported by the Seize, he was now completely at odds with Mayenne, who was profoundly jealous of the intervention of Spain, and tolerated it solely because for the moment he

[1] Forneron, iv, pp. 81–86, and references there; Mariéjol in Lavisse, vi, 1, p. 335. The correspondence of Mercoeur and the Leaguers in Britanny with Philip was edited, with a learned introduction by Gaston de Carné, in *Archives de Bretagne*, xii (Nantes, 1899).

[2] Mariéjol in Lavisse, vi, 1, p. 329.

[3] A memorandum on the French succession drawn up by Philip in January, 1592, is translated into French by Gachard in *Lettres de Philippe II*

à ses filles, pp. 74–80. In it he insists that Isabella Clara Eugenia was the lawful heiress, though obviously with little hope that the French would accept his point of view.

There are two recent biographies of the Infanta, one by Miss L. Klingenstein (London, 1910) and the other by Félix de Llanos y Torriglia (Madrid, 1928–   ).

[4] Forneron, iv, pp. 115, 201.

[5] Forneron, iv, p. 99, note 1.

realized that he was not strong enough to get on without it.[1]
For months past he had been begging Philip to release him,
but the king had insisted that he remain at his post.[2]
Whether or not he had been given formal leave to depart at
the time he quitted the capital (late January, 1591), does not
appear; but it would seem that he left for the Netherlands
with an escort of 200 Germans, and met the oncoming Spanish garrison which he had procured for Paris on the way.
The garrison brought with it as his successor the ubiquitous
Tassis who had preceded him, and a certain Diego de Ibarra,
"a vile and haughty fellow"; and their ineptitude soon
drove the Seize to such excesses that they lost their authority,
undermined the prestige of Spain, and strengthened the
hands of Mayenne.[3]   The loss of Mendoza was irreparable,
though he continued to correspond with Philip and advise
him for many months to come.   One gathers from his letters
that, like almost all the rest of the ablest and most faithful
servants of the Prudent King, he had been traduced at the
last by jealous rivals, and that their accusations had not
fallen on unwilling ears.   To the day of his death Philip
could never learn to give his whole confidence to a really
able man.[4]

By the autumn of 1591 the situation in France had become
somewhat clarified, but the position of Philip was not on the
whole so strong as it had been earlier in the year. The
troubles in Aragon were beginning to embarrass him at home.
The power of the fanatics in Paris, whom Mendoza had
manipulated to such good effect, was by this time broken;
the more definite statement of the Spanish claims had

[1] Baguenault de Puchesse, p. 50;
Mariéjol in Lavisse, vi, 1, pp. 328–330,
336–339.
[2] C. S. P., Spanish, 1587–1603, no.
590 (p. 579).
[3] Forneron, iv, pp. 99–103; Baguenault de Puchesse, pp. 50 f.; Mariéjol
in Lavisse, vi, 1, pp. 336–347.
[4] Cf. A. Morel-Fatio, "D. Bernardino
de Mendoza," in B. H., viii (1906),
pp. 20–70, 129–147.

aroused the patriotic opposition of all good Frenchmen.
Henry of Navarre had not again ventured to besiege Paris,
but he still maintained a partial blockade of it. Elizabeth of
England and the Protestant states of the Empire were sending him reëenforcements. Clearly Mayenne and the League
could not hope, unaided, to defeat him in the field.[1]
Mayenne was more hostile than ever to Philip's designs on
the throne, which he coveted for himself. On the other hand,
unless he were willing to make terms with the king of Navarre
— and this, despite tentative negotiations, he was not yet
prepared to do —, he could not afford to dispense with Spanish aid; he longed, in other words, for a fresh intervention by
Alexander Farnese. Parma was even more reluctant to
invade France now than he had been in 1590. The Netherlanders, as we shall later see, had profited by his first absence
to strengthen their forces, and Parma desired to be left alone
to deal with them. Philip, however, was convinced that he
must make another demonstration of his military superiority
in France, and in August, 1591, Parma received orders to
cross the frontier again. His main object on this occasion
was to relieve Rouen, which Henry of Navarre with English
auxiliaries began to besiege in December, and this he
brilliantly accomplished in April, 1592. Another splendid
demonstration of the power of Spanish arms was given in the
following May, when Mercoeur and the Spaniards in
Brittany joined forces to defeat the Prince of Conti before
Craon.[2] Naturally Philip did not propose to render such aid
as this without recompense. From the time that Parma
entered France, the king's representatives never ceased to

[1] Mariéjol in Lavisse, vi, 1, pp. 323, 348–354.
[2] Coloma, *Guerras*, pp. 140–177; Fea, pp. 415–424; L'Épinois, *op. cit.*, p. 551; Mariéjol in Lavisse, vi, 1, p. 352. Cf. also R. B. Wernham, "Queen Elizabeth and the Siege of Rouen, 1591," in Royal Historical Society, *Transactions*, fourth series, xv, pp. 163–179.

demand of the chiefs of the League that they recognize the
rights of his daughter to the French throne, and that the
Estates-General be forthwith convoked to ratify this action
and select a husband for the princess.[1]   The Leaguers, under
the circumstances, dared not definitely refuse; but they
replied with counter-demands for concessions from the Spanish king, and above all for subsidies in such quantity as Philip
was unwilling to grant.   Until the delivery of Rouen the
Spaniards had, ostensibly at least, the best of the bargaining;
after that service had been rendered, the backs of the
Leaguers stiffened.   Mayenne showed no disposition to proceed with the summoning of the Estates; he even had hopes
that after they had assembled, they might be brought to do
his will rather than that of the king of Spain.   In the meantime Parma had been grievously wounded in attacking the
little town of Caudebec (April 25), and soon afterwards drew
off his forces to a place of safety at Château-Thierry; he
himself was carried back in a litter to the Netherlands, and
spent most of the summer at Spa in a vain effort to regain his
health.   Without the inspiration of his leadership, the Spanish forces were comparatively valueless, and Philip was at
his wits' end to find other equally effective means to bring
pressure on Mayenne and the League to do his bidding.[2]

After the summer of 1592 there was a lull in the military
operations in France.   Parma had received orders to undertake a third campaign there in the autumn, but death overtook him in December, before anything could be accomplished. Though his successor, the Count of Mansfeld,
advanced in the following spring and captured Noyon
(March 30, 1593), it would seem that the chief object of this
final invasion of France from the Low Countries was not so

[1] Baguenault de Puchesse, p. 51.   Fea, pp. 424–441; Forneron, iv, pp.
[2] Mariéjol in Lavisse, vi, 1, pp. 354 f.;   123–126.

much to wage war as to bring pressure on the Estates-
General, which Mayenne, in fulfilment of his promises, had
summoned in the previous June; on them all eyes were now
focussed, for it was by them that the great decision must be
made.[1] Rheims had been chosen as their meeting place.
Since it was to be their duty to elect a king, there was
historical justification for this, but the real reason for the
choice was pressure from Spain; for Philip wished to have
the business done in proximity to Parma's army, and
Mayenne dared not refuse. But Parma's death (December
2-3, 1592)[2] removed the only one of Philip's representatives
whom Mayenne really feared or respected; and as soon as he
learned of it, he promptly transferred the meeting of the
Estates to Paris, where he felt that he would be free from
Spanish tutelage and able to play his own game. He was
further encouraged by the support of the new Pope Clement
VIII, who took a vigorous stand against the claims of the
king of Navarre;[3] and though Henry declared against the
Estates, and forbade all the parts of the realm which he controlled to send deputies, he did not succeed in discrediting
them. At the time of the opening session, which took place
on January 26, 1593, at the Louvre, the deputies had some
justification in feeling that they really represented France.[4]

Well informed, as always, of the march of events, Philip
recognized the importance of the approaching crisis, and in
October, 1592, he despatched a special ambassador, Lorenzo
Suárez de Figueroa, Duke of Feria,[5] to represent him at the
Estates. Feria was instructed to do his utmost to have the
Infanta Isabella Clara Eugenia either declared or elected

---

[1] Mariéjol in Lavisse, vi, 1, pp. 365 f.
[2] Cf. *infra*, p. 650.
[3] Pastor, xxiii, pp. 61-64.
[4] Mariéjol in Lavisse, vi, 1, pp. 368 f.
[5] Baguenault de Puchesse (p. 52) is

wrong in identifying this man with
Philip's representative in England
in 1558. That Duke of Feria had died
in 1571; this man was his son.

queen, or, failing that, to have the choice of the new monarch
left in Philip's hands. Failing that, again, he was to urge
the election of Albert or Ernest, the archducal brothers of the
Emperor Rudolf. If he could not compass this, he was to
support, as a last resort, the claims of the Duke of Guise or
of the cardinal of Lorraine; and he was commanded to do
his utmost to prevent the dissolution of the assembly until
one of these candidates had been chosen.[1] Feria, travelling
by way of Genoa and the Netherlands, joined the Spanish
army in February, 1593, at Landrecies; a few days later
Mayenne came out to meet him at Soissons. The latter did
not yet feel strong enough to dispense with Spanish aid. If
Parma's death meant the loss of an effective army, he was
still more than ever in need of funds; and so he drew up a
sort of treaty with Feria, in which he promised to recognize
Isabella Clara Eugenia as *his* queen, provided the Estates
accepted her, and to use all his influence to persuade them so
to do. Feria, in return, pledged himself to furnish large subsidies.[2] On the second of the following April, the Spanish
ambassador was received with impressive ceremonies by the
Estates. On this first occasion he made no mention of the
claims of the Infanta, but contented himself with enumerat-
ing the vast services rendered by his master to the Catholic
cause in France since the days of Henry II. It was not altogether tactfully done; and Cardinal de Pellevé, who replied
for the Estates, did not omit to point out that France had
also done many favors to Spain in the past, from the time

---

[1] These instructions are contained
in a paper, dated January 25, 1592,
and entitled "El intento que tiene
su Magestad en las cosas de Francia
. . ."; a French translation is printed
in *Lettres de Philippe II à ses filles*,
ed. L. P. Gachard (Paris, 1884), pp.
74–80 (cf. also pp. 43 f.). The whole
document is a curious commentary on
the psychology of Philip II; every
possible contingency seems to have
been foreseen and provided for, and
yet one is oppressed, from first to
last, with a conviction that the king
did not really believe that any of his
alternatives could possibly succeed.

[2] Mariéjol in Lavisse, vi, 1, p. 376;
Baguenault de Puchesse, p. 53.

when the Catholic Franks chastised the heretic Visigoths of Spain and forced them to renounce the Arian faith, to that when Bertrand du Guesclin overthrew Pedro the Cruel.[1] Nevertheless, the impression of Philip's power and prestige which Feria had succeeded in producing was undeniable. If no other outside influence were brought to bear on the Estates, it seemed that he might win his game.

But the very prospect that Philip would attain his ends roused the royalist Catholics in France to make a last desperate effort to keep the crown out of foreign hands. They demanded a conference with the chiefs of the League. The Estates accepted, and when their delegates left Paris to meet the royalists at Suresnes, the acclamations of the populace convinced them that they had made no mistake.[2] When they met the representatives of the other side, they embraced each other; the first thing that they did was to arrange a truce; clearly their dominant feeling was the desire to unite all Frenchmen and rid the realm of strangers. But when the first effusions of patriotic ardor were over, it became evident that the heresy of the king of Navarre would prove a stumblingblock to complete accord; the most that the deputies of the Estates would do was to recognize the priority of his rights to the French throne, but they stoutly maintained that they were nullified by his Protestantism. There was but one way out of the *impasse*, and Henry had the wisdom to see it. On May 17 the archbishop of Bourges announced to the conference at Suresnes that the king had declared his intention to be converted. On the 25th of the following July, in the ancient cathedral of St. Denis, he received him into the communion of the church of Rome. It

[1] *Procès-Verbaux des États-Généraux de 1593*, ed. A. Bertrand, pp. 113–115, 132–142; Mariéjol in Lavisse, vi, 1, pp. 370 f.

[2] Mariéjol in Lavisse, vi, 1, pp. 371–375; J. Nouaillac, *Villeroy*, pp. 227–240.

was indeed "the marriage ceremony of the king and the kingdom of France." [1]

The Spanish representatives at Paris, when they first got word of the king's intention to be converted, did their utmost to prevent the step from having any effect. It probably did not greatly surprise them or their master, for who could put faith in a heretic? They justifiably doubted its genuineness, or at least were convinced, and with good reason, that Henry had abandoned his Protestantism as a means to a political end. But it had come at a most awkward moment for them. Their attention had been wholly concentrated on Mayenne and the Estates, and the problem of the Infanta's recognition there. They had counted on getting that settled first, and on dealing with the heretic pretender afterwards, and now the news of the intended abjuration had thrown everything into the melting pot again. But they did not despair. They opened their purses and distributed bribes. Over 24,000 crowns were handed out to the Estates, and lesser sums to the captains and magistrates of Paris, and more was promised in the near future. Meantime, in the end of May, the candidacy of the Infanta was definitely put forward. When the Estates demurred on account of the Salic Law, it was announced that Philip would be entirely satisfied if they would elect as king the Archduke Ernest of Austria, whom the Spanish monarch had selected to be the husband of his daughter. Then, when the Estates insisted on having a Frenchman for their king, the Spaniards assured them that Philip would not object, provided that he could have the choosing of him, that he should marry the Infanta, and that the crown of France should be held conjointly (*in solidum*) by them both. The Spanish representatives even proposed, as a last resort, in the middle of July, that the Infanta

[1] Mariéjol in Lavisse, vi, 1, pp. 380 f.

be married, under the same conditions, to Charles, the young Duke of Guise, whom all the Parisians adored.[1] But these rapidly mounting concessions merely proved how completely the ground had been cut from beneath the Spaniards' feet by the action of the king of Navarre. The real scene of interest had been shifted elsewhere. In early August the Estates were prorogued, having signally failed to accomplish what had been expected of them, though in different ways, both by Philip and by Mayenne. They had not succeeded in providing France with a king.

In the meantime the Spanish monarch, with a truer sense of where his best chance lay, had been moving heaven and earth to prevent the acceptance of Henry's conversion by the see of Rome. The personalities had shifted there since Philip's last great issue with the papacy in 1589. The place of the fiery Sixtus V was now occupied by the gentler but perhaps even more conscientious and hard-working enthusiast Clement VIII, while that of the Count of Olivares had been taken by the Duke of Sessa; and the latter was commanded to do everything in his power to turn the new Pope against the king of Navarre. At first this did not seem an impossible task.[2] Clement was full of scruples and fears. For him religion was the only thing that mattered, and he fully realized that Henry's action had been dictated by *raison d'état*. He was also indignant that the Gallican church should have taken the initiative in the matter of the absolution, to the prejudice of his own sovereign pontifical rights. By showing tact and sympathy with the hard position in which the Pope was placed, Sessa could have effected much; but instead he took the bullying tone, and threatened to retire to Naples if Clement permitted the envoy of the king of Navarre

---

[1] Mariéjol in Lavisse, vi, 1, pp. 376–382; Baguenault de Puchesse, pp. 55–58.

[2] Pastor, xxiii, pp. 77–85.

to remain in Rome.[1] Such menaces simply served to turn the Pope against the Spanish cause. In November, 1593, he consented to give an audience to Henry's ambassador, the Duke of Nevers, though he still firmly refused to grant the absolution for which he prayed.[2] For nearly two years more the matter hung fire. Sessa surrounded the French envoys at the Vatican with spies in the hope that they might discover something that he could use to good effect. He was encouraged, in the end of 1594, by the expulsion of the Jesuits from France, as the result of two attempts to assassinate Henry which were traceable to their influence, and by the anger the measure evoked at Rome.[3] As a last resort he protested not against the absolution, but against the recognition of Henry as king of Navarre and duke of Brittany, on the ground that this was an infringement of the rights of the king of Spain.[4] But this shift from considerations religious to political spelt the final ruin of the Spanish cause. Clement had come to his decision before Sessa made his protest, and it only served to strengthen his conviction that he had decided right. On the very next day (September 17, 1595), the representatives of Henry received the papal pardon and recognition for their master, and the Bourbon was at last formally reconciled with the see of Rome.[5]

Long before the papal absolution had been obtained, the situation in France had completely altered to the prejudice of the League and the Spaniards and to the advantage of the king of Navarre; in fact, the latter, though fully realizing that reconciliation with Rome was indispensable to him, had elected to act as if it were ultimately inevitable. All sorts of gratifying evidences reached him, in the last part of the year

[1] Pastor, xxiii, p. 87.
[2] Ibid., xxiii, pp. 88–99.
[3] Mariéjol in Lavisse, vi, 1, pp. 396 f.
[4] Pastor, xxiii, p. 134.

[5] The whole story is told, from the French side, with a wealth of detail, in L'Épinois, La Ligue et les Papes, pp. 581–634.

1593, of the growing strength of his cause. On the 27th of the following February, at Chartres, he was formally crowned and anointed king of France.[1] Everything now depended on Paris, for until he was master of the capital of his realm he was sovereign only in name; and in spite of their recent reverses, the Spanish army and diplomats in Paris were by no means negligible. There was even talk of sending the Spanish forces in the Netherlands to its rescue again, and on March 6 Mayenne left the city to go and consult with Mansfeld.[2] His place at the capital was taken by a violent Catholic named Brissac, who was apparently on the best of terms with Feria and the Spaniards. All in all it looked as though Paris might be able to withstand the attack which Henry was obviously planning to deliver.[3] But the king wished to avoid further bloodshed. He coveted popularity at all costs, and knew that his subjects were weary of civil war. If he could bribe Brissac to turn traitor and open the city's gates, he was only too glad, and Brissac rose to the bait. It speaks volumes for the extent to which Feria and his Spaniards had lost their hold there, that they had not the wit to forestall his treachery. They had received warning of his intentions on March 21, and Feria had made him go the rounds on the following night, in a pouring rain, accompanied by some Spanish captains, who had orders to kill him at the slightest sign of trouble; but Brissac survived the test, and a few hours later opened three of the gates of Paris to the soldiers of the king.[4] So accurately had the affair been timed that the Spanish troops were completely surrounded before they realized what had happened, and could offer no

---

[1] Mariéjol in Lavisse, vi, 1, p. 385.

[2] *Ibid.*, pp. 386 f.; Forneron, iv, pp. 214–216.

[3] Forneron, iv, p. 217. Ibarra referred to Brissac as a "cavallero muy católico," under whom "paresce que Paris quedava muy assegurada."

[4] Pierre de L'Estoile, *Mémoires-Journaux* (Paris, 1875–96, 12 vols.), vi, pp. 179 f., 258–261; Baguenault de Puchesse, pp. 60 f.; Forneron, iv, pp. 218–220.

resistance. Henry could have captured or killed them all, had he so desired ; but he preferred to pose as the purveyor of universal happiness, and notified Feria that if the Spaniards would leave Paris that day and swear never again to bear arms against him, he would gladly grant them their liberty and their lives. And so at three in the afternoon the Spanish garrison evacuated the capital of France, which they had occupied since 1591, and turned their faces toward the Low Countries. "We left," reported Ibarra to Philip, "with our flags flying and our drums beating, and without giving the semblance of despairing of our cause." But the dignity of the Spanish retirement made a far less permanent impression than the conduct of the French monarch as the *tercios* filed past. Men never forgot, to their dying day, how Henry, from a window in the Porte St. Denis, saluted his departing enemies, and called after them, "Commend me to your master, but never come back again." The haughtiness of the Spaniard was no proof against such tactics as these.[1]

There were touches of comedy, too, of which Henry made the most, in the story of the relations of Spain and France in the months which succeeded the evacuation of Paris. It was the heyday of the intercepting of letters. During the final weeks of the Spaniards at the capital a last desperate plea for help had been despatched to Philip. Henry had caught the bearer of it on the way, and then, simply for the fun of seeing how the Spanish king would reply, sent it on to Madrid by a henchman of his own, one Fouquet de La Varenne, an old cook of Margaret of Valois, with instructions to play the part of messenger of the League. So well did this man perform the role that had been assigned to him that he was twice called before the king's *consulta*, and sent back with a packet of letters, which, needless to add, he delivered to the king of

[1] Baguenault de Puchesse, pp. 61 f. ; Forneron, iv, pp. 221–223.

France. After the Spaniards had evacuated Paris, Henry made use of Varenne a second time. Rumors of the king's intention to divorce his first wife on account of her sterility had already reached the Spanish court, and it occurred to Philip that since it was now obviously impossible to keep the Bourbon off the French throne, he might save something from the wreckage of his plans by offering him the Infanta in marriage; he therefore sent a messenger with such a proposal to Paris. Henry's counsellors did not wish their master even to receive him, but the king insisted on doing so; and shortly afterwards he once more despatched Varenne to Madrid, with instructions to get in touch with Bernardino de Mendoza, who was living in retirement near by, and see what could be made of the situation. It is difficult to believe that Henry took the matter seriously, and Varenne's efforts at Madrid merely resulted in imperilling his master's reputation with Elizabeth of England and the Protestant princes of the Empire; but both of the envoy's missions seem to indicate that, for the time being at least, the French king believed that the wisest way to deal with Philip was to try to make a fool of him.[1]

The mass of Frenchmen had not the same sense of humor as their king. Mayenne, who appeared with a safe-conduct at Brussels, was loaded with reproaches by Feria and Ibarra, who accused him of ruining their master's cause in France, and wished to have him arrested. A letter of Feria to Philip on the matter was intercepted by Henry and sent back to Mayenne, who was furious when he read its contents, and solemnly demanded leave to vindicate his honor by a duel with his principal accuser.[2] The resentment of Mayenne against Spain and the Spaniards was shared, though for very

---

[1] Baguenault de Puchesse, pp. 62 f., and references there. [2] Baguenault de Puchesse, p. 62.

different reasons, by most of the rest of France.   There was
a feeling that Spanish influence had not yet been wholly
eliminated.   Though Philip's soldiers had by this time been
cleaned out of Picardy, except La Fère,[1] they still hung on in
Brittany, and threatened on the southern and eastern frontiers.   It was rightly feared that the Spanish monarch, defeated in his hopes of gaining control of all the realm, would
revert to plans for its dismemberment.[2]   Under the circumstances there was no alternative save to transform what
had hitherto been a civil strife into a national one, and bring
it to a conclusive end.   On January 17, 1595, Henry formally
declared war by land and sea against the king of Spain.[3]

In order to be able to follow the course of the ensuing conflict, we must once more revert to the story of the parallel
struggle in the Netherlands.

The calling off of Alexander of Parma to relieve Paris in
the autumn of 1590 had given the rebels in the Low Countries
an admirable opportunity to resume the offensive, and under
the lead of Maurice of Nassau they prepared to take advantage of it.   Hitherto their foreign alliances had availed them
little.   Anjou had been a flat failure, Leicester a disappointment, and the Protestants in Cologne had been crushed ; but
the king of Navarre promised better things.   His interests
were now almost identical with those of the Netherlanders,
and geographical proximity virtually compelled them to work
in unison.   The alliance between France and the United
Provinces, which Orange had sought in vain to inaugurate,
was now practically established by the march of events, and
was destined to endure, to the undoing of Spain, down to the
age of Louis XIV.[4]

---

[1] Mariéjol in Lavisse, vi, 1, p. 390.   [3] Mariéjol in Lavisse, vi, 1, pp. 398 f.
[2] Forneron, iv, p. 227.   [4] Pirenne, iv, pp. 199 f.

Parma, on his departure for France, had intrusted the government of the Low Countries to Peter Ernest of Mansfeld, and the command of such troops as were left there to his son Charles; the small detachment under Verdugo in Friesland had been almost cut off from communication both with Brussels and Madrid since 1587, and was to remain so till 1594.[1] The Mansfelds, moreover, proved quite unable to discharge the duties that had been laid upon them. The younger resigned, almost immediately after his appointment, in a huff, and thereafter succeeded in so poisoning his father's ear against Parma that the old man began to write letters, traducing the duke, to Madrid.[2] All this furnished a golden opportunity for young Maurice. Encouraged both by Elizabeth and Henry, he soon seized the offensive. He used the period of Parma's first absence in France to make his preparations. In the spring of 1591, when Parma had got back, with his attention divided and his forces diminished, Maurice was ready to strike. The campaign of that year was disastrous to the Spanish cause. In May and June, Maurice took Zutphen and Deventer, and thereby gained control of the course of the Yssel, which, while in Spanish hands, had cut off Drenthe, Overyssel, and most of Gelderland from communication with the heart of the republic. The next three months were largely spent in a struggle to get command of the Waal, so as to render the provinces of Holland and Utrecht safe from Spanish attacks on the south. The most important fortress on this river, Nimwegen, on the left bank, was still occupied by Philip's troops; but their position there was made uncomfortable by the garrison of a hostile fort on the opposite side, which Parma besieged in July but was unable to take. Soon after he had drawn off his forces, the

[1] Verdugo, *Commentario*, ed. Lonchay, pp. 83 ff.

[2] Motley, *History of the United Netherlands*, iii, pp. 76, 216.

counter-stroke came. On October 21 Maurice captured
Nimwegen. He had not only solidified the defences of Holland, Zealand, and Utrecht; he had prepared points of attack
against the territory of the Spaniards. Parma was already
on his way to the relief of Rouen when he learned the news.
It was a crowning demonstration of the wisdom of his counsels to Philip to concentrate, not to dissipate, his energies.[1]

But Parma, though he was spared the pain of ever knowing
it, was being dealt, at that moment, a blow far more cruel
than assignment to an impossible task; the master whom he
had served so loyally and so long had at last made up his
mind to betray him. It was the old, old story, in its final and
most aggravated form, of royal suspicion of a distant and too
competent representative. Ever since the tragedy of the
Armada and the days when there had been rumors of Parma's
ambition to set himself up as an independent sovereign in the
Low Countries, Philip had been on the watch for accusations
against the duke. It was no wonder that they were
furnished him. The atmosphere of his court and his methods
of government lent themselves readily to just that sort of
thing; and the jealousy of the Spaniards was easily aroused
by the brilliant successes of one whom they never ceased to
regard as an Italian and a foreigner. One of his principal
detractors was the Duke of Medina Sidonia, whose calumnies
were passed on to Philip by his friends. Old Verdugo, who
was convinced that it was Parma's fault that he was isolated
in Friesland, was another; the commander Juan Moreo,
vilest of intriguers, was a third. Parma had had some
inkling of these accusations at the time of his first campaign
in France, and wrote vigorously to the king to complain of
them and to assure him of his loyalty and devotion. He also

[1] Pirenne, iv, p. 200; Blok, *History of the People of the Netherlands*, iii, pp. 248 f.; Geyl, *Revolt of the Netherlands*, pp. 220–222.

took pains to remind him that he had several times requested, in the course of the last few years, to be relieved of his post in the Netherlands. He was in failing health, and his views of his duties and responsibilities were so diverse from the instructions which were sent him from Madrid that he was utterly discouraged. All Philip needed to do, if he wished to get rid of his nephew, was to accept these requests at their face value and give him permission to retire. But the king and his most intimate advisers did not dare to do this; they were afraid of what Parma might do if he were at large. They determined that somehow or other Alexander Farnese must be got back to Spain.[1]

So in February, 1592, Philip sent the Marquis of Cerralvo to the Netherlands, the bearer of a letter to Parma, requesting him to report to Madrid; but as Cerralvo died before he could accomplish his task, it was intrusted in the following June to Pedro Enríquez de Acevedo, Count of Fuentes, who had come into some prominence three years before in defending Lisbon against the English.[2] He was sent on the pretext that his presence was necessary in order to retrieve the military situation, but he carried a commission as governor and lieutenant-general, and subsequently received a confidential letter which implied in almost every paragraph that Parma was to be got rid of and sent back to Spain. But Philip did not propose that his nephew should have any suspicion of the fate that was awaiting him until the blow was ready to fall. Four days after signing his instructions to Fuentes, the king wrote to Parma to congratulate him on the delivery of Rouen and urge him to take care of his health. In several subsequent letters he spoke indeed of his desire to consult with the duke in Spain, but assured him that he

[1] Gossart, *Domination espagnole*, pp. 187–192, and references there; Fea, pp. 440–453.

[2] Cf. on the details of this man's life, and the different authorities thereon, Forneron, iv, pp. 337 f.

would receive the warmest welcome there, that he enjoyed the full confidence of the king, and that no calumnies against him would be heard.   On December 6, he even wrote a final letter of instructions to his nephew in regard to the conduct of his third campaign in France; but Parma was already beyond its reach.   After an inspiring exhibition of physical courage before his troops, holding himself bolt upright on horseback when he was in no condition to leave his bed, he had died, at the age of forty-seven, at Arras, on the night of December 2–3, 1592.[1]

Parma was the last of the really great servants of Philip II ; after his death, the Prudent King was reduced, in Europe at least, to valiant captains and obsequious secretaries.   Philip was not the first Spanish sovereign to treat his ablest representatives as he had Parma.   He had inherited the practice from his forbears, though he may have carried it to greater extremes than they.   It was after the same fashion that the Emperor had rewarded Ximenes and Cortés, and Ferdinand the Catholic the Great Captain.   And the inevitable reflection which occurs in connection with all these tragedies — in the case of Parma it is particularly true — is that, judged by modern standards at least, it was the servant who was always right, and the master who was invariably wrong. The worst of all Philip's faults was his intolerance, political as well as religious, his inability to see that any conception of state or church save his own could have any virtue in it whatsoever.   His worst error in his dealings with the Netherlanders had been his contempt for them, his refusal to believe that they were even to be regarded as honorable foes. Parma made neither of these mistakes.   In matters religious he was always in favor of concessions ; he was, in fact, an advocate of liberty of conscience before its time.   He always

---

[1] Vázquez in *D. I. E.*, lxxiv, pp. 351 f.; Fea, pp. 453–460.

made a point of treating the rebels in the Low Countries like
gentlemen; even in the moments of his most notable
triumphs, he invariably accorded them the courtesies due to
a valiant, if defeated foe.   Had he been given a perfectly free
hand in the great task that had been laid upon him, at the
focal point of international politics during the age in which he
lived, the whole course of European history might well have
been changed.

The years 1593 and 1594 were almost as disastrous to the
progress of the Spanish arms in the Low Countries as they
were to Philip's hopes of gaining control of the kingdom of
France.   As Parma's successor in the government of the
Netherlands, the king had designated his own nephew, the
Archduke Ernest of Austria, the brother of the Emperor
Rudolf, who had spent most of his youth at Madrid, and was
familiar with his uncle's ideas; but as he was not able to
arrive in the Low Countries until nearly twelve months after
his appointment, all authority remained concentrated in the
hands of the Count of Fuentes during the year 1593.
Fuentes was a competent soldier, but also a Spaniard of
Spaniards, a brother-in-law of the Duke of Alva, and his term
of office gave the king a chance to return to his old policy of
complete Hispanicization of the government of the loyal
provinces, in a way which Parma would never have allowed,
and which violated the terms of the peace of Arras.   All
Parma's Belgian and Italian advisers were dismissed, and their
places taken by Spaniards.   Exchanges of prisoners with
the rebels were henceforth definitely forbidden; any soldiers
of the enemy who were captured were promptly sentenced
to the gallows.   Small wonder if the change infuriated the
Netherlanders.   They had feared, but also respected the
duke of Parma; but now this reversion to the methods of Alva,

under a leader whom they believed to be less able, inspired them to efforts of desperation. They had made good progress under Maurice of Nassau in 1591–92. They now had high hopes that they could rid their country of the Spaniards.[1]

Fuentes was in no position to meet such determined foes. Since Philip kept him even shorter of funds than his predecessors, there were many mutinies among his troops, with the usual results. Furthermore his attention was divided, quite as much as Parma's had ever been, between his difficulties in the Low Countries and the necessity of interfering in France. At the time of his appointment, the king's interest was chiefly there. One of the main reasons why Philip had sent his nephew Ernest to the Netherlands was that he might be close at hand if the États-Généraux could be persuaded to elect him king of France; and Fuentes received constant orders to have his army in readiness on the French frontier, or, if possible, across it, so as to bring pressure on the assembly at Paris when the decisive moment should arrive. His efforts in this direction, however, were quite sterile, save for Mansfeld's rather futile capture of Noyon;[2] moreover they prevented him from offering any effective opposition to Maurice. On June 24, 1593, the latter recaptured Gertruydenberg, thus closing one of the last breaches which had been opened by the Spaniards in the defences of Holland; thence he turned northward against Friesland and Groningen. The key to the control of these regions was the strong fortress of Koeworden in Drenthe, which commanded

---

[1] Pirenne, iv, pp. 203 f., and references there. Even in the States-General of the 'obedient' Netherlands at Brussels it was openly declared that the salvation of the country required a change of sovereignty. "Vemos perder la Religion cathólica, nuestras haziendas y vidas: Al Rey viejo, tardo, y sin resolución; . . . me paresçe mas que tiempo que . . . busquemos otro amo, porque ya paresçe que La casa de Austria ha llegado á la cumbre donde puede llegar." Brussels, September 3, 1593: Boletin Histórico, i (1880), p. 157.

[2] Cf. ante, p. 636.

the chief access to them across the morasses, and old Verdugo had attempted intermittently, for the previous six months, to wrest it from the hands of the rebels; but in May, 1594, Maurice appeared before the place and drove him off.[1] The siege of the city of Groningen followed; it surrendered on July 24,[2] and its fall was the signal for the elimination of the last vestiges of Spanish control in the northern provinces. Verdugo's long term of isolation was at an end, and he was permitted to retire to Luxemburg, where he continued to fight valiantly until his death in the following year. In January, 1595, the rebels were still further encouraged by the news that Henry IV had formally declared war on Spain and was anxious to act in concert with them against their common foe; and the death of the Archduke Ernest in February seemed at first sight to deal another blow to the authority of Philip in Northern Europe.[3]

But the death of the archduke was to prove rather an aid to Spain than the reverse. It was a full year before his successor could be appointed and reach his post. During the interval all authority was once more concentrated in the hands of Fuentes, and, under his able and energetic leadership, the Spanish infantry were to give one more splendid demonstration that they were still the finest soldiers in Europe. The cause for which they strove was ruined, indeed, by the intolerance and ineptitude of the monarch whom they served; but they valiantly fought on to the bitter end. Henry's schemes for the coöperation of the French and Dutch armies were effectively checkmated. His general, the Duke of Bouillon, was speedily driven out of Luxemburg by Verdugo. The nonagenarian Colonel Mondragon had all the best of a series of ensuing skirmishes

---

[1] Verdugo, *Commentario*, pp. 134–148.   *History of the United Netherlands*, iii,
[2] *Ibid.*, pp. 182 f.   pp. 317–320.
[3] Pirenne, iv, p. 206; Motley,

with Maurice of Nassau and his cousin Philip.[1]   In the meantime Fuentes had led another army across the French frontier to rescue the few places that still held out against Henry in the region of the Somme and the Oise.   He arrived too late to save Ham.   The town was captured and its Spanish garrison massacred on June 21; but three days later he occupied Le Catelet, and on July 24 he won a splendid victory over the combined forces of the Duke of Bouillon and the Count of St. Pol outside Doullens.   A week afterwards he entered Doullens itself, one of the "bulwarks of the frontier," and slew its garrison as the French had slain that of Ham.   Finally, on October 7, he took Cambray.[2]

In other parts of France the course of the struggle was less favorable to the Spanish cause.   A threat of Henry against Franche Comté had brought Juan Fernández de Velasco, the governor of Milan, across the Alps to its rescue, with an army of over 15,000 men.   Mayenne had joined forces with him, and they finally encountered the French at Fontaine-Française outside Dijon, in a battle which had been virtually won by the Spaniards when a last desperate charge by the French monarch, an act of foolhardy courage of the sort which Henry loved, turned victory into defeat.   Mayenne was so much discouraged at the issue that he shortly afterwards made his submission to the king, and many of the other old chiefs of the League followed his example in the ensuing months.[3]   In Brittany Mercoeur held out till 1598, but three years earlier his opposition had ceased to be serious. He was now completely at odds with the Spanish detachment there.   They fought against each other quite as often as in alliance; the whole province was turned over to brigandage;

---

[1] On Mondragon see Ángel Salcedo y Ruiz, "El Coronel Cristóbal de Mondragon," in *Ciudad de Dios*, lxvi, lxvii (1905).

[2] Coloma, *Guerras*, pp. 300–350; Villalobos y Benavides, *Comentarios*, pp. 49–93; Forneron, iv, pp. 246–251.

[3] Forneron, iv, pp. 240–245.

it was a "forest of robbers." [1]   Clearly Henry could not call himself master of his kingdom while Brittany was in such a state.   On the other hand, it was perfectly obvious that he could take his time in reducing it ; as long as he was content to leave it alone, it would certainly do the same by him.   His only important problem, and the sole remaining hope of the Spaniards, lay on the northeastern frontier.

Fuentes was not given the opportunity to win further military victories in 1596.   In February a new governor-general arrived in the Low Countries, and Fuentes soon afterward departed to Spain.[2]   The man to whom Philip had now decided to confide the administration of the Netherlands was another of his archducal nephews, Albert, the younger brother of Ernest, who had died in the preceding year ; like him, he had been sent at an early age to be brought up at the court of the Prudent King.   He had absorbed far more of Spanish ways than Ernest.   He spoke Spanish in preference to any other tongue.   In his aspect, his temperament, his methodical laboriousness, and his fervent piety, he closely resembled his royal uncle ; there was complete confidence and intimacy between them.   In 1577, at the age of eighteen, he had been appointed a cardinal by Gregory XIII ; but his uncle had more need of him in the state than in the church, and in 1583 he had been sent as viceroy to Portugal.   So successfully, in Philip's eyes at least, did he fulfil his duties there, that when the governorship of the Netherlands became vacant on the death of Ernest the king soon selected him as his successor.[3]   Philip had previously cherished plans, as we have already seen, of solving his problem in France by getting the Archduke Ernest made king there and marrying him to

[1] Mariéjol in Lavisse, vi, 1, p. 405.
[2] Coloma, *Guerras*, pp. 365–367.
[3] Pirenne, iv, pp. 211–213. He had been considered for the place before, both in 1576 and in 1586. *Correspondance de Philippe II*, iii, p. 432, and ii, p. lxxix.

the Infanta. By this time it had become probable that
France would escape him; but might it not be possible that,
if things continued to go wrong there, he might still find both a
satisfactory solution of his difficulties in the Netherlands and
the peace for which his whole soul longed, by marrying Isabella Clara Eugenia to Albert, and establishing them as joint
sovereigns of the Low Countries? Certainly dispensations
from vows of clerical celibacy were not difficult to procure.

At the time, however, that the cardinal-archduke arrived
in the Netherlands, there was no open evidence of such
ulterior designs. Albert was sent there at the outset to carry
on the campaign which Fuentes had begun; he was furnished
with fresh troops and, what was even more important, with
money. There is no reason to think that he knew anything
of military affairs, but there were officers left in the Spanish
army who did. The morale of the troops had been restored by
the fact that at last they had got their pay; they burned to
capture more towns and booty in France, and Albert was only
too glad to be carried along with them, officially as their chief,
but really little more than a figurehead. Since the close of
the last campaign the French king had been besieging La
Fère, which was still held by a Spanish garrison, and which
commanded the most direct route from the Low Countries
to Paris, and the most obvious thing for the invading army
to do was to relieve it. But that was not the plan of the
Spanish captains who were managing the cardinal-archduke's
campaign for him; they showed an originality, an unexpect-
edness, which reminds one of the Great Captain. La Fère,
surrounded by swamps, proved even more difficult to relieve
than to invest, and the invaders left it to its fate; it was
starved out on May 22.[1] Instead, the Spaniards diverted

---

[1] Villalobos y Benavides, *Comentarios*, pp. 127–131; Forneron, iv, pp. 252–256;
Mariéjol in Lavisse, vi, 1, p. 406.

their attack to the north, and in early April they suddenly
appeared before Calais.   The place was utterly unprepared.
Its garrison was inadequate and its fortifications almost in
ruins; there was no resistance worthy of the name.   On
April 17, 1596, the Spaniards entered the city without striking a blow.   A week later they captured the citadel and massacred its few defenders; on May 23 they also took Ardres
without firing a shot.[1] Both places yielded them an
enormous booty.   Guisnes and Le Catelet surrendered
shortly afterwards, and the commander at Ham was bribed
to follow their example.[2]   All and more than the old 'Calais
Pale' of the days of the English occupation was now in Spanish hands; moreover its capture had at last given Philip the
Channel port whose lack had been so fatal to him in 1588;
another Armada might use it to excellent advantage.   Yet it
is worth noting that when Henry sent over a hurried message
to Elizabeth to beg for her aid, after the siege was begun, the
queen at first refused to help him, save on the condition that
Calais be restored to England.   Rather than see it in French,
she preferred that it should remain in Spanish hands; for
the moment she seemed far more alarmed by the prospects
of the recovery of France than by this temporary recrudescence of the power of the Spanish arms.[3]   The progress of
the Spaniards in the next four weeks convinced her, it is true,
that it would not do to hold off too long.   On May 24 she
finally signed a treaty by which she granted Henry a force of
2000 men and a loan of 20,000 crowns, in return for his
promise not to make peace with Philip without her consent.[4]
But it was at best a half-hearted step, and Elizabeth deeply
repented it two years later when Henry broke his word and

[1] Herrera, *Historia General del Mundo,*
iii, pp. 607–616.
[2] Forneron, iv, p. 256.
[3] Mariéjol in Lavisse, vi, 1, p. 408;
Cheyney, *History of England*, ii, pp.
131–142.
[4] Mariéjol in Lavisse, vi, 1, p. 409;
Cheyney, ii, pp. 148–152.

deserted her. She always sought to envisage the future, while Philip scrutinized the past, and she rightly foresaw that a united France would prove a far more formidable enemy of England in the years to come than the tottering empire of the Prudent King. Had she lived on into the succeeding age she would not have been misled, as was her successor, into thinking that Spain was still "the greatest of all the kingdoms of the earth."

The capture of Calais was the last great military achievement of Philip's reign; from that time onward the tide turned steadily against the Spaniards. In August, 1596, the cardinal-archduke felt obliged, despite the desire of his captains to pursue their advantage in France, to return again to the Low Countries to deal with Maurice of Nassau; like Parma and Fuentes before him, he was distracted by the impossible task of being in two places at once. In August he recaptured the town of Hulst from the rebels; but this triumph was rendered nugatory by the great victory of Maurice at Turnhout in the following January, and during the rest of the year 1597 one important town after another fell back into the hands of the Netherlanders.[1] One more attack in France, led by Hernán Tello Portocarrero, the Spanish commander at Doullens, succeeded, indeed, in taking Amiens by surprise on March 11, 1597; but the Marshal de Biron hurried across from Rouen to recapture it, and was successful in the following September, despite all that the cardinal-archduke could do for its relief.[2] Worse than all these defeats in the field was the shortage of money. The year 1596 had seen Philip repudiate his financial obligations, and without money it was impossible to continue to fight. And

---

[1] Coloma, *Guerras*, pp. 395 ff.; Motley, *History of the United Netherlands*, iii, pp. 422–434, 455–458; Pirenne, iv, p. 213.

[2] Villalobos y Benavides, *Comentarios*, pp. 202 ff.; Mariéjol in Lavisse, vi, 1, p. 410.

there were various other considerations which made for a general movement towards peace. The French king was also in great straits for funds, and anxious to spare his kingdom from a prolongation of the wars which had devastated it for so long; the merchant classes in the Netherlands were weary of fighting. Pope Clement VIII, too, had been laboring, ever since his absolution of Henry IV, to bring about a reconciliation between Spain and France; he rightly feared that it would be the Protestant states of Europe that would reap the sole benefit of the continuance of the strife between the two chief Catholic powers.[1] Perhaps most important of all was the ardent desire of the Prudent King himself to end his days in peace. He had never really liked war, and had often gone to great lengths to avoid it. Since 1595 he had known that he could not live much longer;[2] he desired reconciliation with his enemies on earth, in order to have opportunity to become reconciled to his Maker. After the French had recaptured Amiens, in September, 1597, there was no longer any doubt of the speedy end of the war. Negotiations for peace between Spain and France, already begun in Paris through the instrumentality of the papal legate and the general of the Franciscans, were formally opened at Vervins in the following spring.[3] The course of the proceedings there was closely followed by the cardinal-archduke, who had been given full powers to treat in the name of Spain. He had his own interests, as we shall see in a moment, in having them reach a successful termination.

Elizabeth of England did her best to prevent an accord. She had counted on Henry IV to bear his share on land in the war against Philip which she was to continue to wage on sea;

---

[1] Pastor, xxiii, pp. 134–146; Mariéjol in Lavisse, vi, 1, p. 411.

[2] C. S. P., Venetian, ix, no. 348.

[3] Mariéjol in Lavisse, vi, 1, p. 411;

cf. also Louis Calendini, "Notes sur le Traité de Vervins," in Revue Henri IV, i, pp. 86–88 (1905).

and she complained with justice that the French king had promised her two years before that he would not conclude a separate peace. The news of the 'perpetual and irrevocable' Edict of Nantes (April 30, 1598),[1] by which Henry granted a measure of toleration to the French Huguenots, may well have given Philip pause. There seems to be no record of what he said or did when he learned of it, though we know that his representatives at Rome did their utmost to make use of it to poison the Pope's ear against the French king;[2] it was a harbinger of modernity, of a totally different world, which Philip could not comprehend, and in which he felt he had no place; very possibly it may have strengthened his desire to be gone. In any case the peace conference at Vervins was not interrupted, and on May 2, 1598, a treaty was signed there, which was characterized by a contemporary as "the most advantageous that France had concluded for five hundred years."[3] The Spanish king gave up Calais, and all the other places that he still held in Picardy and Brittany. His claims to the duchy of Burgundy were recognized in theory, but as he promised to seek to vindicate them solely "by the friendly way of justice and not by appealing to arms" the recognition was tantamount to a renunciation.[4] For forty years past he had alternately aspired to influence, to control, and to dismember France; now, in order to have peace with her before he died, he had been obliged to recognize her integrity and independence under the rule of a king who had been a heretic born, and had recently announced his intention

[1] On this date, see the very convincing article of P. E. Vigneaux, "La véritable date de l'Édit de Nantes," in *Revue des études historiques*, 1909, pp. 144–187.

[2] Pastor, xxiii, p. 160.

[3] Such was the verdict of Pompone de Bellièvre, one of the negotiators of the peace, afterwards chancellor of France. Pirenne, iv, p. 214, and reference there. Text of the treaty in Dumont, *Corps universel diplomatique*, v, 1, pp. 561–564.

[4] Cf. the comment of Coloma, *Guerras*, p. 497, on this provision: "como si los Reynos, ò Señorios tan grandes, estuviesen sujetos à las leyes del derecho, y no à las que dan las armas, y el valor."

to be tolerant of heretics.   Finally, after all his concessions, he failed actually to obtain one of the principal advantages which the treaty ostensibly accorded him.   One of the chief reasons why he had been in such haste to obtain peace with France was that he might be free, before he died, to settle the question of the Netherlands; and he had every right to expect that, after the treaty of Vervins had been signed, the French king would cease to support his enemies in Holland.   But Henry, in this matter, did not live up to his word. He heartened the United Provinces with promises of his continued support.   Though he had ceased to wage war openly against the king of Spain, he continued it covertly by aiding the rebels in the Low Countries, and the latter were encouraged to persist in their struggle until they won formal recognition of their independence at the peace of Westphalia.[1]

We turn finally, then, to the settlement in the Netherlands; for if Henry was not altogether loyal in his observance of the treaty of Vervins, Philip was not quite free from duplicity in the arrangements which he sanctioned in the Low Countries.   If he had been really wise, if he could have had a glimpse into the future, he would have gone the whole way in his quest for reconciliation, and granted the Netherlanders their freedom in return for the peace for which his whole soul longed.   They had been a liability throughout his reign, a 'plague spot,' a 'running sore'; it was largely through the ramifications of his difficulties with them that he had become involved in his disastrous struggles with France and England. Spain and the Spanish Empire would have been vastly better off if he could have got rid of them.   But Philip could not possibly bring himself to see this.   As we have often remarked, he looked backward, not forward.   The decision

[1] Pirenne, iv, p. 215; Nouaillac, *Villeroy*, pp. 362–378. Villeroy was spoken of as "un des pères de la paix d'Espagne."

of his father that the Low Countries should go to Spain — the worst mistake the Emperor ever made —, and his precepts to Philip to cherish and retain them, counted for far more in the king's eyes than the problems inherent in the future. The fact that half of the Netherlands were now in full revolt against him, and were trying to set up, in defiance of his authority, a system of government and religion which he abhorred, made him all the more certain that it was his bounden duty to get them back into Spanish control. On the other hand, he had the wit to see that for the present it was utterly impossible for him to accomplish this. His treasury was empty, his army in poor shape. He probably already realized that his son, so shortly to succeed him, was little more than a pleasure-seeker, who could not be trusted to expend the energy and labor which were essential to the continuance of the Netherland campaigns. Everything pointed, under the circumstances, to the necessity of devising a stopgap — some arrangement by which Spain could be given an opportunity to rest and recuperate, so as to be able to carry on the struggle successfully in later years, and by which, in the meantime, the Low Countries should not be permitted to pass out of her hands.

Philip, as we have seen, had contemplated such a solution of his difficulties at the time that he had sent the Cardinal-Archduke Albert to the Netherlands in 1595–96. To marry Albert to his cousin, the Infanta Isabella Clara Eugenia, and set them up as joint sovereigns of the Low Countries under Spanish suzerainty seemed now to be the only way out. The Spanish king was strengthened in his determination to adopt this expedient by the fact that there was ample historical precedent for what he proposed to do. Clear back in 1539, his father had had a scheme of detaching the Netherlands from the rest of his possessions by giving them as a dowry to one of his daughters and marrying her to the Duke of Orleans.[1] A similar plan had been considered for one of the Infantas in 1573 ; Requesens had advocated it in 1574, and Juan de Zúñiga in 1586.[2] On all these occasions the solution had been refused. In those happier days it had seemed unnecessary, for it looked as though Spain could keep the Netherlands without adopting it ; but now the situation had completely changed. And so, on May 6, 1598, four days after the conclusion of the treaty of Vervins, Philip put his signature to the act by which the Low Countries were handed over to the cardinal-archduke and the Infanta, who were to be married as soon as possible,[3] to be ruled by them as 'sovereign princes' ; the seven rebel provinces of the Union of Utrecht were of course theoretically included in the arrangement, as well as the loyal ones of the Union of Arras.[4] But the phrase 'sovereign princes' must not be interpreted to mean that the 'archdukes' were in any sense really emancipated from the tutelage of Spain. In the first place, it was provided that whenever either Albert or the Infanta should die, the Low Countries should revert to Spain, unless there were issue of their marriage ; and Philip had good reason for believing that their union would prove, as it ultimately did, to be sterile.[5] In the unlikely case of their producing offspring, it was stipulated that the child, if a boy, should not

[1] E. Gossart, "Notes pour servir à l'histoire du règne de Charles-Quint," pp. 68 ff., in Académie Royale de Belgique, Mémoires couronnés et autres mémoires, collection in octavo, lv (1897) ; idem, "Projects d'érection des Pays-Bas en royaume sous Philippe II," in Académie Royale de Belgique, Bulletin, classe des lettres, 1900, pp. 558–578.

[2] Pirenne, iv, p. 216, and references there.

[3] The proxy marriage took place at Ferrara on November 15, 1598, and the wedding ceremonies at Valencia

on April 18, 1599. Pirenne, iv, p. 222.

[4] Ibid., pp. 220 f. For a detailed account of the negotiations preceding the marriage, see Gustav Turba, "Beiträge zur Geschichte der Habsburger : Aus den letzten Jahren des spanischen Königs Philipp II.," in Archiv für österreichische Geschichte, lxxxvi (1909), pp. 309–452.

[5] Cf. H. Lonchay, "Philippe II et le mariage des archiducs Albert et Isabelle," in Académie Royale de Belgique, Bulletins, classe des lettres, 1910, pp. 364–388.

marry without the consent of the Spanish crown, and if a girl, should be wedded either to the Spanish king or to his son. The archdukes, furthermore, were obliged to give assurances that they would maintain the Roman Catholic faith and do their utmost to extirpate heresy; if the Pope should accuse them of being contaminated by it, they promised to renounce all their rights.[1] It is worth noting also that they were rigorously excluded from commerce with the Indies; though hedged about with all kinds of Spanish restrictions, they were denied the privileges of Spaniards in the New World. And there were other secret clauses besides, by which the archdukes were still further bound. Altogether the arrangement was such as made them little more independent than the various royal representatives in the Low Countries from the days of Margaret of Parma to those of her son. Under their rule all the traditions of the Spanish régime were maintained, and on the death of the cardinal-archduke in 1621, the Netherlands reverted once more to the Spanish crown, in accordance with the plans that had been laid by the Prudent King.[2]

Certainly Philip had earned his rest. He may have taken the wrong turn with disastrous persistency, but no one could deny that he had labored, valiantly and unremittingly, to the very last, to do his duty as he conceived it to be. And, in addition to the political reverses and economic disasters of the last few years, he had been tortured all the time by the steadily increasing ravages of a terribly painful disease.

Rumors that he was not well had reached Rome and even Constantinople as early as 1593,[3] but it was not until two years later that his condition began to give cause for real

[1] Pirenne, iv, p. 218.
[2] *Ibid.*, p. 247.
[3] *C. S. P., Venetian,* ix, nos. 150, 218.

alarm. On May 13, 1595, the Venetian ambassador reported that the doctors said that the king's body 'was so withered and feeble that it was almost impossible that a human being in such a state should live for long.' [1] Philip's original ailment was the gout; but in the later stages he also suffered intermittently from a "double tertian [fever] with irregular spasms," and painful sores and ulcers broke out all over his body.[2] A crisis was feared on Good Friday, 1596, chiefly, it would appear, because there was an eclipse, and Philip "recalled how his father, his mother, and others of his house had died at a similar conjuncture"; [3] but on that very day an improvement took place, possibly because he had been bled, "though the blood flowed with difficulty and two-thirds of it was watery humor." There were also other occasions, in December of that same year, and in September, 1597, when it was believed that he was likely to die,[4] but Philip survived them all, and in May, 1598, when there was a great festival, "the King, though in bed, gave his orders and directed the ball with as quick and lively spirit as if he had been at the head of his army." [5] On the last day of the following June he insisted on being carried in a litter from Madrid to the Escorial, against the advice of his doctors, who dreaded the effects of the journey.[6] Their apprehensions were more than justified by the event. For a week after his arrival at San Lorenzo Philip had another violent attack of fever; in July there was a temporary improvement, but in early August all his different afflictions came back upon him at once, with redoubled violence, and continued unabated to the end.[7]

[1] C. S. P., Venetian, ix, no. 348.
[2] Ibid., no. 418.
[3] Ibid., nos. 418, 422.
[4] Ibid., nos. 528, 610.
[5] Ibid., no. 690.

[6] Ibid., no. 707, and Cervera in C. de C., iv, p. 298.
[7] C. S. P., Venetian, ix, nos. 707, 709, 714, 715, 717–722.

It is useless to follow the harrowing details of the progress of the king's malady during those last dreadful weeks. He was in constant agony. His bed linen was impregnated by the suppuration from his abscesses, but it was apparently impossible to change it, for he could not bear to be moved; the odor was frightful, and vermin began to appear.[1] He seemed literally to be rotting away, a microcosm of the vast empire which had begun to disintegrate under his rule. But neither Philip nor those who watched by his bedside gave their principal attention to these terrible things. The king transacted such business of state as he could, but his thoughts were chiefly fixed on the next world. His patience in suffering was the wonder of all who beheld it; they compared it to the patience of Job.[2] He constantly harped on the sins of which he had been guilty, and humbly expressed his hope that they would be forgiven. He took comfort in confession, in the prayers of the priests at his bedside, and in gazing on the sacred relics of the Escorial which were brought to be contemplated by him for the last time;[3] the church was more than ever his principal interest now, for it opened for him the way to eternal life. The Infante was frequently called in to see his father, and on August 28 he was given two sealed packets, "with instructions to open them only after his Majesty's death."[4] What had been placed in those packets does not appear, but we are fully informed of the contents of a paper which, two days before he died, the king handed to his confessor with orders to read it to his son the moment that he had gone.[5] That paper was not filled with the sort of advice which the Emperor had so often given Philip, with full and specific comments and facts concerning

---

[1] *C. S. P., Venetian*, ix, no. 731; C. de C., iv, pp. 298 f.; Forneron, iv, p. 290, note.

[2] *C. S. P., Venetian*, ix, no. 727; C. de C., iv, pp. 300 ff.

[3] C. de C., iv, pp. 300–317.

[4] *C. S. P., Venetian*, ix, no. 727.

[5] C. de C., iv, pp. 317–319.

the state of his realms, and the character of his ministers. Philip had not even written it himself. It was an excerpt from the life of St. Louis IX of France, by his contemporary, the Sieur de Joinville,[1] which had been translated into Spanish and published in 1577; it contained the advice which that monarch had given to the son who was to succeed him, and who, like the Infante, was to bear the title of Philip III. It is filled with exhortations to love God and live righteously; to reverence the church and avoid war; to administer justice fairly; not to be cast down by adversity nor puffed up with pride by success.[2] Certainly it contained nothing to which any one could take exception; but it was no more apposite to the needs of the Spain of 1598 than it is to those of any country or any age, and it speaks volumes for the extent to which Philip at the last had managed to forget the rivalries of this world, that he preferred it, written as it was by a monarch of the realm which had been the traditional enemy of his house, to anything that he could have invented himself.

In the early days of September it was evident that the end could not be long delayed. Philip's courage never deserted him, and his love of minutiae exhibited itself to the very last. "He has made himself most familiar," wrote the Venetian ambassador, Soranzo, "not only with the thought of death, but with the details and the discussion thereof, and with all that should be done after he is gone. He has arranged every detail of his funeral, and has ordered the purchase of a large quantity of black cloth to drape the church of the Escurial. He has caused them to bring into his room and to his bedside a shirt of lead, in which he is to be wrapped after he has breathed his last, and a leaden coffin for his corpse when his hour is come. He examined both and caused

---

[1] Antonio Cervera de la Torre gives the name as 'Lonvilla.' C. de C., iv, p. 317.

[2] C. de C., iv, pp. 317–319, 390–392.

himself to be measured, and gave orders for the necessary alterations." [1] At daybreak on the morning of September 13, he died, in a little room twelve feet square, whence he could look out on the altar of the great monastic church whose construction had been one of the deepest satisfactions of his life. It would have been impossible to find a more fitting spot for the termination of his arduous labors.

Just two weeks later Soranzo reported that he had "heard the Adelantado of Castile declare that they would see what the Spanish were worth now that they have a free hand, and are no longer subject to a single brain that thought it knew all that could be known, and treated everyone else as a blockhead." [2] But this was only the view of a discontented grandee, who rejoiced in the relief from the tension to which Philip's rule had subjected him and others of his kind; he doubtless foresaw for himself both financial favors and political preferments in the reign of a king who delegated everything to subordinates and was immersed in the pursuit of pleasure. A far truer picture of the feeling of the Spanish people when the news of Philip's death was first known is given by a brief paragraph in a letter from the same Venetian ambassador, which was written on the day that the king expired. "Although change is usually popular," so he reported, "yet nobles and people, rich and poor, universally show great grief." [3] Despite all the misfortunes which his reign had brought them, the Spaniards loved their Prudent King.

[1] C. S. P., Venetian, ix, no. 727.
[2] Ibid., no. 744. The adelantado was Martín de Padilla y Manrique, sub-sequently prominent in plans for the invasion of Ireland.
[3] C. S. P., Venetian, ix, no. 737.

BIBLIOGRAPHICAL NOTE

See notes at the end of Chapters XXXIV and XXXVII, and add:
Sources and Contemporary Authorities. — In addition to the standard sources and chronicles of this time, such as the *Procès-Verbaux des États Généraux de 1593*, ed. Auguste Bernard (Paris, 1842), and Enrico Caterino Davila's *Historia delle Guerre Civili di Francia*, which it does not seem worth while to enumerate here, there are three notable contemporary accounts of the course of the war in the Netherlands during this period, all by men who participated therein. These are the *Commentario de la Guerra de Frisa* by Francisco Verdugo, edited, with an admirable introduction and the text of a number of letters from Verdugo, by Henri Lonchay for the Commission Royale d'Histoire (Brussels, 1899); *Las Guerras de los Estados Baxos desde el año de M. D. LXXXVIII. hasta el de M. D. XCIX.*, by Carlos Coloma (Antwerp, 1625; my references are to this edition; also in *B. A. E.*, Historiadores de Sucesos Particulares, ii, pp. 1–203); and the *Comentarios de las Cosas Sucedidas en los Paises Baxos desde 1594 hasta 1598*, by Diego de Villalobos y Benavides, ed. Alejandro Llorente (Madrid, 1876) in the *Libros de Antaño*. None of them, save possibly Coloma, who was subsequently to attain eminence as an ambassador, makes any pretension to historical insight or perspective; but their narratives are full of color and vividness; and Coloma's work has been characterized as "el mas precioso arsenal de noticias que poseemos referentes al periodo de 1588 a 1600." The two standard contemporary accounts of Philip's last illness, by Antonio Cervera de la Torre and Christóval Pérez de Herrera, are to be found on pp. 297–402 of vol. iv of C. de C.

Later Works. — As a detailed narrative of events, J. L. Motley's *History of the United Netherlands* (New York, 1861–68, 4 vols.) is still useful, though its point of view is so unfriendly to the Spaniards that it is difficult to place much reliance on its judgments. An article by Gustave Baguenault de Puchesse on "La Politique de Philippe II dans les affaires de la France, 1559–1598," in the *Revue des questiones historiques*, xxv (1879), pp. 5–66, contains much that is still valuable; and Henri Forneron, *Les Ducs de Guise et leur époque* (Paris, 1877, 2 vols.), and Henri, Comte de L'Épinois, *La Ligue et les Papes* (Paris, 1886), throw much light on the policy of the Prudent King in France. Joseph Nouaillac's *Villeroy* (Paris, 1908) is a model of what such a monograph should be; and his "Règne de Henri IV, sources, travaux, et questions à traiter," in *Revue d'histoire moderne et contemporaine*, ix (1907–08), pp. 104–123, 348–363, give precious indications for those who wish to pursue the story further from the French point of view. The forty-seventh volume of the *Ciudad de Dios*, published on September 13, 1898, to commemorate the tercentenary of the death of Philip II, contains a number of interesting estimates of the king, and accounts of his different achievements. The names of numerous other books and articles, of too special a nature to be inserted here, will be found in the appropriate places in the footnotes.

CHAPTER XL

FINAL REFLECTIONS

AT the close of so long a book, the author may be permitted, if not expected, to moralize. And the question on which his opinions, if they be worth anything, will naturally be desired, is that of the fundamental reasons which combine to explain why the Spanish Empire, so overwhelmingly preponderant in the middle decades of the sixteenth century, should have disintegrated with such tragic rapidity in the succeeding age. Like every other similar phenomenon in the history of the human race, its fall was the product of a complex of different causes; and we are still quite as far from having discovered them all, and from having reached any general agreement as to the relative importance of those that have been already assigned, as we are in the case of those that have been given for the fall of Rome. Yet it is only by constant statement and restatement of the views of successive generations of historical students that there is any hope of ultimately obtaining the truth. Even if opinions be expressed which are subsequently proved wrong, there is always a chance that they may render a real service; for it is not seldom through the very process of subverting them that fresh light is incidentally revealed.

The first, and, in some respects, the most far reaching of the considerations that must be borne in mind by those who seek to know the causes of its fall, is that the Spanish Empire was rather the result of a series of accidental and artificial agglomerations than of a normal and natural growth. It exhibits, indeed, a certain magnificent continuity, the product of the crusading ideals which animated and inspired it from the cave of Covadonga to the death of Philip II; but those crusading ideals were shared in very unequal proportions by the different realms in the Iberian peninsula. They furnish, it is true, a chief impetus to Castile, in completing the great work of the Reconquest; but we must not forget that down to the days of the Catholic kings, and the discovery of the New World, Castile played a relatively small part in the upbuilding of the Spanish Empire. Save for the Canaries, to which Spain's title was not definitely established till the time of Ferdinand and Isabella, all the various mediaeval conquests of Spain beyond the seas were the result of the activities of the realms of the crown of Aragon, and the origins of those activities were rather hostile than friendly to the church. Two really divergent currents were united by the marriage of the Catholic Kings. The events of the succeeding period, particularly the discovery of America, served to place Castile, which had had far less imperial experience than the Eastern Kingdoms, permanently in the forefront of the picture, and the Spanish Empire became progressively Castilianized. Small wonder, considering her fresh responsibilities and opportunities across the Atlantic, that Castile was reluctant to assume the duty of maintaining the Italian and Mediterranean possessions which had been foisted on her by the union with Aragon. And then, on top of all this, came the Hapsburg inheritance and all that it implied, particularly the baleful responsibility of the Netherlands, an even more heavy and unnatural burden for a nation, which for eight centuries had been almost exclusively occupied at home, to be called upon to bear. After long ages of comparative isolation, Spain was summoned to assume, under the leadership of her most uncosmopolitan part, the stupendous task of governing a world empire composed of a large number of widely scattered and heterogeneous units accidentally drawn together as a result of two fateful marriages.

There can be no doubt that all the difficulties arising from the conditions described in the preceding paragraph were perpetuated and intensified by that tendency toward separatism and diversification which, as we have often remarked, is a distinguishing characteristic of the Iberian peoples. It rendered it impossible for Ferdinand and Isabella and their Hapsburg successors to unify the administration of the various territories over which they held sway. It was a chief barrier to the efficiency that ought to have been the finest fruit of the system of royal absolutism which, in full accord with the prevailing political theories of that day and generation, they established and attempted to maintain. The variety of the problems with which they were inevitably confronted was so bewildering that no monarch could possibly deal with them all, particularly if, like Philip the Prudent, he was unwilling to delegate anything to subordinates. No doubt the Catholic Kings and their successors were fully conscious of this difficulty, and Philip, in abolishing some of the most cherished of the 'liberties of Aragon,' took a step toward remedying it; but he was far too good a Spaniard to go the whole way, and put an end to the separate constitutions of the Eastern Kingdoms. Their corpses — for all the vitality had long since gone — were suffered to remain unburied, until the advent of the Bourbons in the eighteenth century changed the government of Spain from a decentralized to a centralized despotism on the model of that of Louis XIV. The Hapsburgs' maintenance of the constitutional emblems of Spanish separatism is one of the most striking, if unfortunate, proofs of the fact that they became in some respects far more thoroughly Hispanicized than their successors from across the Pyrenees.

It is but a platitude to remark that the Spanish Empire of the sixteenth century was vastly over-extended, that Spain was called upon to shoulder a burden which it was beyond her capacity to bear. But if the process of over-extension had been more gradual, the effect of it might well have been less unfortunate; it was the appalling suddenness with which world empire was thrust upon her that accounts in large measure for Spain's failure to maintain it. We have already remarked that the only portions of the Iberian peninsula which had had any practice worthy of the name in the management of overseas possessions, down to the reign of Ferdinand and Isabella, were the realms of the crown of Aragon. When, under the Catholic Kings and the Emperor, the really great advances came, things so fell out that the leadership of the Spanish Empire was shifted to Castile, which was totally unprepared to assume it; the Eastern Kingdoms gradually faded from the picture, and their imperial experience was thus largely thrown away. Of course the non-Spanish responsibilities of the Emperor made the situation even more difficult still. Charles saw it all, plainly enough, in the closing years of his life. His division of his inheritance, and his advice to Philip to forbear to attempt any further increase of his territories or power, show that he realized that fate had suddenly saddled Spain with a burden beyond her power to bear. For the first twenty-five years of his reign the Prudent King followed his father's counsels. Though champion of the forces of militant Catholicism, he rested, politically speaking, on the defensive. Then Destiny once more intervened and another great empire fell into his lap. From Philip's own standpoint, his annexation of Portugal and its dominions was not an act of aggres-

sion, but merely the gathering in of an inheritance indubitably his own; but it is easy to see why the rest of Europe
refused to regard it as such, and was appalled at the incred-
ible rapidity of Spain's rise, in little more than a century,
from a position of comparative insignificance to the leadership of the most extensive empire that the world has ever
seen. And not only did the suddenness of the trans-
formation put the rest of Europe up in arms, in a way which
in all probability a more gradual growth would not have
done; it was also fatal to Spain's hope of a successful defence.
Such widely scattered and highly diversified territories could
not possibly be welded together, under an efficient imperial
organization, in such a comparatively short space of time.

Without the Indies, and the revenues they yielded, the
picture would of course have been totally different; and a
paragraph may well be devoted at this point to the consideration of the dictum of a recent writer that "America, in
Spanish history, was a white elephant." [1] If one thinks
solely of the role of Spain in Western Europe, this verdict is
unquestionably sound. Had it not been for the monopoly
which she claimed in the New World she would not have
gained the position in the Old, which drew down on her the
jealousy and hatred of her neighbors; she might well have
devoted herself, with their full approval and support, to the
conquest of a more permanent domain in North Africa. But
the subject of this book is not so much Spain as the Spanish
Empire, and if we envisage the question of the American
lands from the standpoint of empire, we are likely to be led to
a very different conclusion. They were, after all, a *sine qua
non* of its existence, and a fundamental cause of Spain's greatness while it lasted; without them she could scarcely have
attained imperial power at all, at least in the sixteenth

[1] S. de Madariaga, *Spain*, p. 351.

century. And though, three hundred years later, the American colonies declared and won their political independence, the language and culture which they had inherited from their mother country remain as their permanent possession. If empire be measured by standards other than the political and economic, the Latin American lands are still a part of the picture, and the glory of having settled and civilized them belongs forever to Spain.

Another consideration, of tremendous significance in the problem of the causes of the fall of the Spanish Empire, is the fact that the main principles and ideals which underlay it had become antiquated by the end of the sixteenth century. Its most ancient tradition, namely, that of crusading, lost its hold on men's minds after the battle of Lepanto, and the kindred idea that it was the duty of all true Christians to extirpate heresy collided with the nascent conception of religious toleration. Politically, too, the tale was much the same. The overwhelming preponderance which the Hapsburg inheritance and the discovery of America had given to Spain was a flagrant contradiction of the principle of national individuality, and of the modern idea of the balance of power, which was being gradually evolved as the most obvious method of maintaining it. Certainly it was rather Spain's misfortune than her fault, the result of her inheritance rather than of her own choice, that she found herself committed to these antiquated ideals; but it was none the less inevitable that when the crisis came, she found that practically all the more modern states of Europe were arrayed against her. Her failure to grasp any of the principles of sound economics, which were just beginning to emerge in the end of the sixteenth century, and were subsequently to become one of the chief controlling forces of the modern world, is but another chapter of the same story; the phrase of Sigüenza, "those good old centuries when there was so much faith and so little money," is deeply significant in this connection. Spain longed for the return of them, because she was out of place in the modern world. *Laudator temporis acti* was the role that appealed to her most; she hated to look forward; she loved to look back. And perhaps the hardest part of it all was the suddenness with which Spain was brought into collision with all these unsympathetic forces of modernity during the last two decades of the reign of Philip II. Until the annexation of Portugal he had made a strong effort to maintain the good old ways. In obedience to his father's counsels he had rested, politically speaking, on the defensive; the Counter-Reformation had given him a welcome opportunity to champion the ancient faith. Then, in a trice, the scene had shifted, and the Prudent King had assumed the offensive, only to be confronted with new foes who used weapons which he could neither compete with nor comprehend. The suddenness of the rise of the Spanish Empire has already been noted. If it partially explains, it was certainly exceeded by the suddenness of its fall.

The breed of empire builders, who had been responsible for Spain's greatest triumphs under Ferdinand and Isabella and Charles V, had begun to die out before the accession of Philip II, and nothing worthy to be compared with them was produced during his reign. His best soldiers and sailors, such as Alva and Santa Cruz, were inheritances from his father. In politics and diplomacy the decline was perhaps not quite so marked, but the fact that he had been obliged to call on a Burgundian — Cardinal Granvelle — to aid him in the gathering in of the Portuguese inheritance, was certainly ominous for the future. But the further question still remains: What were the reasons for the disappearance of this race of empire builders? Was it that Spain had been so exhausted by what she had accomplished in the preceding period that she was no longer capable of producing them? Or was it the result of the transference of so much of her best talent to the New World? Was it due to the unconscious growth of a conviction that her empire was already so great that it could not, with safety, be further enlarged? Of the spirit of defensiveness that Charles had commended to Philip? Of Philip's well known aversion to war? Of a progressive paralysis of initiative by a system of monarchical surveillance and *residencias*? Or was it just the inevitable ebb which sooner or later succeeds the flood of the "tide in the affairs of men"? None of these questions is susceptible of definite answer; none of the alternative explanations which have been offered is wholly satisfactory; yet there is probably a measure of truth in every one of them. Perhaps, after all, it would be fairer to regard the phenomenon which we have just been considering, not as a process of decline and decay, but rather as a transference of the energy and genius that had hitherto manifested themselves in conquest and in war, to the gentler realms of literature and art. Certainly the Spain of the seventeenth century — the dreariest of all periods in her political annals — produced writers and painters whose names will remain immortal.

The considerations which we have thus far put forward as possible causes of the decline of the Spanish Empire are all, of course, of the most general nature; to complete the picture it is essential to bear in mind that there were also a large number of more immediate and specific ones. Of these, Charles's utilization of Spanish resources for non-Spanish purposes, his bestowal of his Burgundian inheritance on Philip instead of on Ferdinand, the Prudent King's meticulous paternalism, and still more his ruinous economic impolicy, are among the most important; but as these matters have been fully set forth in the last two volumes of this work, it scarcely seems worth while to enlarge upon them here.   One of the principal objects of this concluding chapter has been to remind the reader of a fact which we attempted to emphasize in the opening paragraphs of our first volume, namely, that though nine-tenths of the history of the Spanish Empire is concentrated between the accession of Ferdinand and Isabella and the death of Philip II, the origins of it reach back to the early Middle Ages and beyond, and that its development, during the century of its greatness and decay, cannot possibly be understood without some knowledge of what had gone before.   Its story, from first to last, is full of amazing contradictions, and the comparison with the British Empire, with which this book began, may well be recalled at its close.   The Spanish Empire had a continuity, a background, which the British Empire lacked. Spain's expansion under the Catholic Kings in North Africa and in the New World was but the logical sequel of the Reconquest.   The wars with France which occupied the latter part of their reign, and were bequeathed by them to their successor, followed inevitably as the result of the mediaeval achievements of the Catalans and the Aragonese in Italy and in the western basin of the Mediterranean.   England, on the other hand, had been practically driven off the continent of Europe, and had virtually renounced all thought of further conquest there, by the time that the exploits of the Tudor sea-dogs opened visions to her gaze of an empire beyond the seas.   She had got out of the Old World before she started to win the New.   By breaking with her mediaeval traditions and turning her back upon the past, she was enabled to concentrate her attention on the future, and to develop, normally and gradually, in the now fields to which she had elected to devote herself.   But Spain could not bring herself to relinquish her inherited responsibilities in Europe at the time that she was presented with an empire across the Atlantic. Her reverence for the past and the accidents of fate combined to overwhelm her with a load of responsibilities, all over the world, so tremendous that she could not carry it for long. Paradoxical as it may seem, it was the very continuity of her imperial tradition that furnishes the chief explanation of the suddenness of her rise and of her fall. For her it was all or nothing; and her loyalty to the great task which Destiny had given her brought her into fatal conflict with the principles that rule the modern world.

THE HOUSE OF HAPSBURG IN THE SIXTEENTH CENTURY

Names of Emperors are printed in capitals. Names of kings of Castile are printed in heavy-faced type.

MAXIMILIAN I, = Mary of Burgundy
1493–1519,

Philip I, = Joanna la Loca, dau. of Ferdinand and Isabella,
1504–06, ob. 1555.

Eleanor, (1) = (3) Emmanuel of Portugal.
ob. 1558, (2) = (2) Francis I of France.

CHARLES V, = Isabella, dau. of
1519–56, Emmanuel of
ob. 1558. Portugal, ob. 1539.

Isabella, = Christian II
ob. 1525, of Denmark.

Margaret, (1) = Alessandro de' Medici.
ob. 1586, (2) = Ottavio Farnese,
duke of Parma.

Philip II, (1) = Maria, dau. of John III of Portugal.
1556–98, (2) = Mary, queen of England.
(3) = Elizabeth, dau. of Henry II of France.
(4) = Anne, dau. of Emp. Maximilian II.

Maria, = Emp. Maximilian II.
ob. 1603,

Joanna, = John, son of
ob. 1578, John III of
Portugal.

Don John
of Austria,
ob. 1578;

(1) Alexander = Maria
of Portugal.

(2) Don Carlos,
ob. s. p.
1568.

(3) Isabella Clara Eugenia, = Albert of Austria.
ob. s. p. 1633,

Catharine, = Charles Emanuel
ob. 1597, of Savoy.

(4) Philip III,
1598–1621.

FERDINAND I, = Anne, dau. of Ladislas of
1556–64, Hungary and Bohemia.

Mary, = Louis II of Hungary
ob. 1558. and Bohemia.

Catharine, = John III of Portugal.
ob. 1571,

MAXIMILIAN II, = Maria, dau. of
1564–76, Emp. Charles V.

Anne = Albert III
of Bavaria.

Ferdinand,
C. of Tyrol.

Charles,
D. of Styria.

Maria = William,
duke of Cleves.

Joanna = Francis of Tuscany.

Anne = (4) Philip II
of Spain.

RUDOLF II,
1576–1612,
ob. s. p.

Ernest,
ob. s. p.
1595.

Elizabeth = Charles IX
of France.

MATTHIAS,
1612–19,
ob. s. p.

Maximilian,
ob. s. p. 1620.

Albert, = Isabella Clara Eugenia,
ob. s. p. 1621. dau. of Philip II of
Spain.

Wenceslas,
ob. s. p.
1578.

GENERAL INDEX

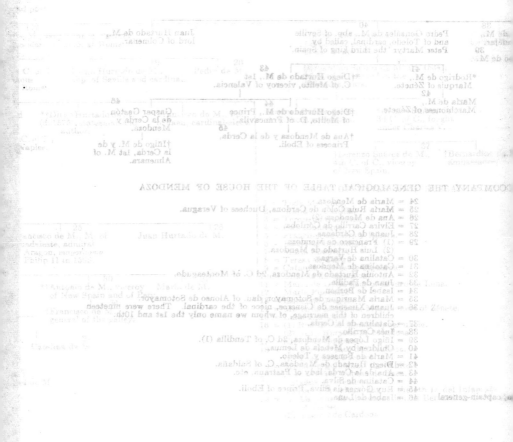

1
Juan Furtado de Mendoza, called Longbeard (13th century).

Gonzalo Ibáñez de M.
2
Juan Hurtado de M.,
mayordomo of Henry III.
3
Diego Hurtado de M.,
defended Jaen against the Moors.
4
Juan Hurtado de M. (d. 1490),
favorite of the Catholic Kings.
5
Honorato de M. (d. before 1490).
6
Diego Hurtado de M., 1st M.
of Cañete, viceroy of Navarre
(d. 1542).
7
*†Andrés Hurtado de M., 2d M.
of C., viceroy of Peru.

Diego Hurtado de M.,
3d M. of C., accompanied
Philip II to England.

*†García Hurtado de M.,
4th M. of C., gov-
ernor of Chile, vice-
roy of Peru.

Diego Furtado de M.
9
‡Iñigo López de M. (d. 1458), 1s
Marquis of Santillana, celebrat

10
Diego Hurtado de M., 2d M. of S., 1st Duke
del Infantado, fought at Toro and Zamora.

Iñigo López d
famous comm

11
Iñigo Hurtado de M.,
2d D. del I.
12
*Diego Hurtado de M.,
3d D. del I.
13
Iñigo Hurtado de M.,
4th D. del I.
14
8
Diego Hurtado de M.,
C. of Saldaña.
Iñigo de M.,
5th D. del I.
16
Ana de Mendoza,
Duchess del Infan-
tado.

18
*Iñigo López de M., 2d
1st M. of Mondéjar, fam
commander and amb. at

21
*†Luis Hurtado de M., 3
C. of T., 2d M. of M.
22
†Iñigo López de M., 4th
3d M. of M., viceroy of

23
Luis Hurtado de M., 5th C. of T.,
4th M. of M.

24
Iñigo López de M., amb.
to Venice.

Bernardino de M., cleric.

F
G
o
o

27
*†Bernardino de M.,
captain-general of
the sea (d. 1557).

28
†Juan de M.,
general of the galleys

33
*María Pacheco.   Isab

GENERAL INDEX

References are to volumes and pages, Roman numerals indicating the former, Arabic the latter. In a compound item, each volume reference carries until it is superseded by another.

The abbreviations 'f.' and 'ff.' indicate that the reference is to the page designated and, respectively, to that next following or to the two next following. (In the footnotes to the text, on the other hand, 'ff.' is not restricted to the two pages following, but may include a larger number.)

Abancay, battle of the (1537), iii, 573 f.

Abbadie, Jean Pierre de, French secret agent, iv, 361.

Abbassides, Mohammedan dynasty, i, 17 ff.

Abd al-Mumin, Almohade leader, i, 23.

Abd al-Wahid, Almohade ruler, i, 81.

Abd ar-Rahman, first Omayyad ruler of Spain, i, 18.

Abd ar-Rahman III (an-Nasir), Omayyad caliph of Cordova (912–961), i, 18, 19 f., 21, 25, 65 ff., 69, 77.

Abd ar-Rahman al-Ghafeki, Mohammedan viceroy in Spain, i, 30; death of, 31.

Abd-el-Aziz, Hafside prince, ii, 255, 256.

Abd-el-Malek, claimant to the throne of Morocco, iv, 342, 344.

Aben Aboo, Morisco leader, iv, 94.

Abencerrages, massacre of the, ii, 64.

Aben Humeya, Morisco leader, iv, 89, 91, 94.

Abogado del fisco, i, 507, n. 1.

Abou-Abd-Allah Mohammed, claimant to the throne of Morocco, iv, 342 f., 345.

Absolutism, royal, i, 448, 449; ii, 79, 84, 149, 166 f.; the Castilian

sovereigns of the fourteenth and fifteenth centuries not absolute, even in theory, i, 207.

Abu Bekr, governor of Constantine, i, 324, 325.

Abu-el-Abbas, claimant to the throne of Morocco, iv, 342, 345.

Abul Hassan, king of Granada (1462–82, 1483–85), ii, 62, 63, 64, 65.

Abu Mohammed Abdallah II, king of Tlemcen (1528–40), iii, 320.

Abu Yahya, king of Majorca, i, 312 ff.

Abu Zeid, king of Valencia, i, 293 f.

Abyla, i, 6.

Abyssinia, iv, 337.

Acachinanco, iii, 500.

Academic titles, iii, 214, n. 4.

Acapulco, iii, 512; iv, 229.

Acciajuoli, Florentine family, i, 378–381.

Acentejo, Spanish defeat at, ii, 182.

Achaia, principality, i, 364, 374, 379, 381, n. 1.

'Achines' (Hawkins), iv, 557.

Acropolis, the, in Athens, i, 379, 380.

Actium, naval battle of (31 B.C.), iii, 324.

Act of Resumption, the (1480), i, 255; ii, 106, 108, 131.

Acuerdos, iii, 646 f.

683